THE
ILLUSTRATED
ENCYCLOPEDIA
OF
CROSSWORD
WORDS

THE
ILLUSTRATED
ENCYCLOPEDIA
OF
CROSSWORD
WORDS

MICHAEL
DONNER
&
NORTON J.
BRAMESCO

Additional material:
Maura B. Jacobson

WORKMAN PUBLISHING
NEW YORK

Library of Congress Cataloging in Publication Data

Donner, Michael.
The illustrated encyclopedia of crossword words.

1. Crossword puzzles—Glossaries, vocabularies, etc.
2. Encyclopedias and dictionaries. I. Bramesco,
Norton J., 1924-   II. Title.
GV1507.C7D63   1982   793.73′.03   82-60067
ISBN   0-89480-222-4
ISBN   0-89480-221-6 (pbk.)

Cover design: Paul Hanson
Book design: Wendy Palitz

Workman Publishing Company, Inc.
1 West 39 Street
New York, New York 10018

Manufactured in the United States of America
First printing November 1982
10 9 8 7 6 5 4 3 2 1

DEDICATIONS

To Hannah Donner,
who does not yet suspect her father's love
of palindromes.
M.D.

With much affection,
to Erica Bramesco Stull
and to Clint Bramesco who share
their father's love of words.
N.J.B.

ACKNOWLEDGMENTS

We wish to thank Ronnie Bramesco for her unstinting help. In preparing the manuscript, contributing ideas, and lending support, she made a truly valuable contribution to this book. Crossword canonization also is warranted for the following individuals who worked long and hard to gather up, assemble and produce this book: Suzanne Rafer, who provided excellent editorial guidance with unfailing good spirits, and Maura B. Jacobson, whose insights and suggestions lent a measure of authority to our book. Helen Witty and Alexandra Halsey ably fact-checked and coordinated the entries. Rona Beame directed the enormous picture research with more than a little help from Audrey Labaton and Danny Peary. The design by Wendy Palitz was faithfully executed by Julienne McNeer and Gabrielle Maubrie with the assistance of Richard Rew, Larry Burns, Ludvik Tomazic, Kathy Herlihy, and Rocco Alberico. Thanks also go to Lynn Strong for developing the special boxed material, Jim Harrison for his editorial input, and Marjorie Coven and Margie Malczycki for keeping all the pieces filed in the right places. We wish to also thank John Boswell who went far beyond his role as literary agent in helping us. And for their aid and counsel, our thanks go to Patty Brown, Murry S. Koenig, and Lester B. Shimberg.

CONTENTS

INTERSECTION

Cruciverbalists* owe their thanks to Arthur Wynne, who, in 1913, put words that could cross together in a puzzle that appeared in the *New York World*. Since then, thousands upon thousands of these wordy mind-stretchers have been created, with a dizzying array of themes, content, and format.

There are many possible levels of sophistication in a crossword puzzle, and a good puzzle will incorporate several. The clues should be apt and concise—neither too difficult or obscure, nor too easy and obvious; neither too clever nor too bland—and never pejorative in any way. A typically challenging puzzle will have a number of strategically placed phrases, names, titles, or elaborate wordplays that run across or down the full length or breadth of the grid (collectively referred to as the theme words of the puzzle), surrounded by a neatly woven net of mostly interesting and novel words—all legitimate, of course. These words are the meat and potatoes of every puzzle, and they fall into a number of categories:

1. Familiar words such as "boy," "girl," "cat," "dog." The more familiar (and shorter) they are, the more regrettable, but they are acceptable in small numbers. After all, they *are* words, and sometimes essential for the puzzle constructor who's in a tight spot.

2. Any word of seven letters or more. These are entitled to more than an ordinary amount of respect.

3. Abbreviations, prefixes, suffixes, and other word fragments. Inelegant, but, again, sometimes necessary. Puzzles with lots of these produce yawns.

4. Foreign words. Apart from a certain tolerance for selections from first-year Latin,** French, German, Spanish, and Italian (also the solitary Russian word *nyet*), crossword editors wisely reject foreign words out of concern for those among us who are not at home in Tlingit and Maori.

5. Arcana. Roman numerals, symbols from flour sacks, and chemical formulas are acceptable only up to a point.

6. And last, but by no means least, the pushy words, also known as crossword clichés, repeaters, regulars, zombies, and exotics. These words are pushy because they tend to crop up all the time; certainly a lot more often than their place and value in everyday life would lead us to expect. They are zombies because they necessitate a large store of trivial and not so trivial knowledge on the part of the puzzle doer—historical, literary, biological, and more. They are the stuff of which this volume is almost exclusively comprised.

This special class of words consists predominately of three-, four-, and five-letter words, like "moa," "esne," "liana," but a few two- and six-letter examples, like "aa" and "essene," have also made their way into crossword currency on the strength of the rude persistence of their unique letter combinations. They are neither fragments nor foreign (though often of foreign origin), and are almost never anything but real—albeit obscure—people, places, and things. Taken all together they are the lore, mythology, drollery, and legerdemain of crossword puzzles.

Inveterate crossword doers have encountered these words time and again, and inserted them into grids with glee and abandon, but often without any idea of their deeper meanings, lineage, or romance—nothing, in fact, beyond the meager, sterile clues supplied by the constructor: "Hawaiian goose"; "oriental nurse"; "Celebes ox"; "three-toed sloth"; "minced oath"; and so on. We have come to love these words and are convinced

---

*A word coined by the Rev. Edward J. O'Brien and derived from the Latin words *crux* and *verbium*, meaning, respectively, cross and word.

**For those who did not make it through first year Latin, the abbreviation *q.v.*, often found in parentheses in the text, stands for *quod vide*, Latin for "which see" and it means, in this book at least, that related material will be found by looking up the term immediately preceding the interruption.

that we are not alone. Out of that conviction grew the idea for this book. Nowhere could we find a reference work that was devoted only to crossword zombies, thoroughly researched and set down in encyclopedic style.

The words you'll find in *The Illustrated Encyclopedia of Crossword Words* are accessible to everyone. But you would have to hunt though an entire reference library of encyclopedias, gazetteers, Baedekers, texts on botany, zoology, taxonomy, astronomy, medicine, and the like to find them. And in none of these weighty tomes would you be likely to find background information on FDR's Scottish terrier or the names of the crew aboard the starship *Enterprise*.

We have plowed through the appropriate sources, prized out the desired terms, expanded them, and present them in this one volume for the convenience and edification of fellow cruciverbalists. Solvers will, it is hoped, think of the book as a fireside companion, something to browse and mull over when all the campaigns of a hard day's puzzling have already been fought and it remains only to wait for the solutions in the next day's paper.

aa *(AH-ah)* A rough, cinderlike, and generally dark form of volcanic lava resembling slag (refuse from the smelting of ores and metals). Aa is produced by the expansion of trapped gases in volcanic sediment and thus has a bubbly look. In Hawaiian the word is distinguished from its opposite, *pahoehoe*, a non-crossword lava that has congealed in smooth and ropy forms.

aalii *(ah-LEE-ee)* A small tree or bushy shrub of subtropical and tropical regions, having unusually sticky foliage; it is prized for its hard, dark wood. Its name is of Hawaiian origin, as are many words whose vowels so greatly outnumber their consonants. The Latin scientific name, *Dodonaea viscosa*, means "Zeus's sticky one."

aam *(awm; ahm)* An old Dutch and German liquid measure. The word originally meant "water bucket," but the large, roughhewn containers called by this name varied so much in size that an aam could hold anywhere from 36 to 42 U.S. gallons. Think of an aam as two-thirds to three-quarters of a standard oil drum.

Aar *(ahr)* or **Aare** *(AHR-uh)* The longest (183 miles) and most important river entirely in Switzerland. It rises high in the Alps and after passing through Interlaken and Bern joins the Rhine at the German border. The Aar is a frequent crossword repeater, and is often clued as "Bern's River." When Aare has the *e* in puzzles, so does Berne (usually).

The Aar snakes its way through the city of Bern.

Ab *(ahb)* or **Av** *(ahv)* The eleventh month of the Hebrew calendar, corresponding to late July/early August. The ninth day of Ab, or Tishab B'Ab, is sacred to Jews because it was on that day that the Temple of Jerusalem was twice destroyed, the Temple of Solomon in 586 B.C. by the Babylonians and the Second Temple in A.D. 70 by the Romans.

The Western, or "Wailing," Wall is all that remains of the temple of Jerusalem, destroyed the 9th day of Ab.

aba or **abba** *(ah-BAH; AHB-ah)* A loose, sleeveless outer garment worn by Arabs, sometimes made of silk but more often made from a coarse, usually striped, fabric (also called aba) woven from the hair of camels or goats. There's also a song, "The **Aba** Daba Honeymoon," written in 1914 by Arthur Fields and Walter Donovan. It was revived in 1951, and a record of it by Debbie Reynolds and Carleton Carpenter sold over a million copies.

An aba as worn by an Arab.

abaca or **abaka** *(ah-bah-KAH)* The fiber obtained from the leaf bases of a banana plant *(Musa textilis)* native to the Philippines and also called Manila hemp. Abaca is the world's most important raw material for making rope. The pulp left over after the fiber is extracted is used in making Manila, the yellowish-brown paper found in elementary schools, and, formerly, Manila envelopes.

Abaco *(AB-ah-ko)* The name of two islands in the northern Bahamas, Great Abaco and Little Abaco, and the numerous small keys that surround them in a group officially named Abaco and Cays. Great Abaco was settled by British loyalists from New York City just after the American Revolution. Its most famous sight is the Hole in the Wall, a large rock with a hole.

abama *(ah-BAY-mah)* A rhizomatous bog herb of the lily family, represented in the United States by a bog asphodel *(Narthecium americanum)* of New Jersey and points south. The abama was formerly thought to cause lameness in cattle. This is reflected in its name, which in ancient Greek means "no step."

abb *(ab)* Generally low-grade wool, and specifically the poorest part of the skirtings and edgings of a fleece. Among weavers, abb yarn is deemed suitable only for the warp, and is never used for the woof.

Abba *(AB-ah)* A title, meaning "father" in Hebrew, used by Talmudic Jews as a sign of reverence; by Christ and early Christians when referring to the Deity; and by later Christians of the Eastern Church when referring to bishops and patriarchs. **Abba** is often defined in puzzles as the given name of an Israeli statesman, Abba Eban. Also, a popular Swedish rock group who recorded their first American album with no knowledge of English, singing the lyrics phonetically.

Abba Eban.

Abbai *(ah-BIE)* A local name for the Blue Nile. It rises at Lake Tana, in Ethiopia, and joins the White Nile 1,000 miles downstream at Khartoum, in the Sudan. This highly erratic river accounts for 68 percent of the water in the lower Nile at its late summer peak, but only 17 percent at its May low, when many of its own tributaries have dried up entirely.

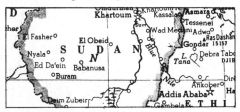

The Blue Nile joins the White Nile at Khartoum.

Abbas *(AB-ahs)* The name of Mohammed's uncle, who at first was opposed to the religious movement, but later converted and was its chief financial supporter. Also, the name of a Persian shah and an Egyptian khedive of the early twentieth century.

abbe *(ah-BAY)* By definition, an ecclesiastical priest. However, abbé is also a title of respect given in France to anyone who wears the garb of a secular ecclesiastic, including many clerics not in holy orders. *The Abbé Constantine,* by Ludovic Halévy (1834–1908), is a novel about the Roman Catholic priest of the title, published in 1882. More recently, **Abbe** has stood (in crosswords) for Abbe Lane the vocalist, one of Xavier Cugat's wives.

abele *(ah-BEEL)* The white poplar tree *(Populus alba)* of Eurasia, now widely cultivated and naturalized in the United States. It has whitish bark and leaves whose lower surface is covered with densely matted, silvery-white hairs.

Abie's *(AY-beez)* The husband referred to in the long-running Anne Nichols play, *Abie's Irish Rose,* which had over 2,300 performances on Broadway. Rose was Rose Murphy, and the play concerns the vicissitudes of a Jewish (Abie)–Catholic (Rose) marriage. **Abies** is also the genus of all true fir trees, evergreens of the pine family. There are about 40 member species. These graceful and usually large trees can be distinguished from spruces by their erect cones and flattened needles. Some species are valued for timber; one, the balsam fir, yields fragrant resin such as Canada balsam, also called balm of Gilead.

Abie hugs Rose (left), in an early production.

Abo *(AB-oh)* An Australian aborigine, for short; the Swedish name, **Abo** *(aw-BOO)* for Turku, Finland; a tribe of the Cameroons *(AH-bo);* and a town in southern Nigeria *(ah-BO).*

aboma *(ah-BO-mah)* This originally African word for a snake of the Congo region now applies also to any of several large South American constrictors, a frightening snakelike fish (guavina) of the Mexican Pacific coast, and a fish (goby, q.v.) of the West Indies.

acara *(ah-kah-RAH)* The name for several Brazilian fishes of the family *Cichlidae* which build nests and guard their young like birds. Like the American sunfish, another nest builder, they live in fresh water and have spiny fins. The name *Cichlidae* comes from a Greek word for "thrush."

acca *(AK-ah)* A medieval fabric of silk and gold, probably made in Syria and taking its name from the Arabic name for the city of Acre (q.v.), located today in northwest Israel.

Accra or **Akkra** *(uh-KRAH; AH-krah)* The capital of Ghana (formerly the British colony of Gold Coast), and today one of the leading cities of West Africa. Accra grew up around three colonial forts which were at times occupied simultaneously and peaceably by British, Dutch, and Danish military forces.

Early European fort at Accra.

Acer *(AH-ser)* A large and widely distributed genus of trees and shrubs that includes the maples and the box elder. This genus is distinguished by its winged seeds and many of its members are valued for their wood. *Acer saccharum* yields maple syrup.

acier *(ah-SYAY)* A yellowish-gray color, from the French word for "steel," which it resembles. It is also called gray drab and Quaker gray.

Acis *(AY-sis)* A youth of Sicily, the son of a river nymph and lover of the sea nymph Galatea. He was slain by the Cyclops Polyphemus, who was jealous of his success with her, and his blood was changed into the river Acis near Mount Etna.

Acoma *(AH-ko-mah)* An Indian of New Mexico occupying a pueblo of the same name. The village, on a precipitous mesa 357 feet high, was established somewhere between A.D. 1100 and 1250 and is considered the oldest continually inhabited community in the U.S. It was visited by Coronado in 1540. It is also widely known for its distinctive pottery.

Acoma Andres Ortis, 1890.

Acre *(AH-ker)* A northern Israeli seaport a few miles up the coast from Haifa; its present name is Akko. Originally a Phoenician city, Acre was ruled at various times by Assyria, Egypt, and Persia. In the thirteenth century, it became an important center of Christianity.

acus *(AH-cuss)* In Roman antiquity, a pin for fastening the hair. It is the base for the word acupuncture.

Ada *(AY-dah)* A town southeast of Oklahoma City. Also, the title of Vladimir Nabokov's complex novel *Ada or Ardor: A Family Chronicle.*

adad *(AH-dahd)* A coarse fiber made from the bristly stems of the pilewort, a Eurasian plant of the buttercup family so named because of its remedial effect on those afflicted with piles. This fiber, also called burbark, is like jute and can be used for sacking, burlap, and twine; it is widely cultivated in the Marshall Islands and throughout Micronesia.

Adana *(ah-da-NAH)* A city of southern Turkey, on the banks of the river Seyhan, founded in 66 B.C. by the Romans. In 1909 Adana was the site of a great massacre during a period of concentrated genocidal activities directed against the Armenians.

Adana can be seen close to the Mediterranean coast.

Adano *(ah-DAH-no)* A fictional Italian town, the setting of John Hersey's Pulitzer Prize–winning novel, *A Bell for Adano,* which depicted life during the Allied occupation of World War II. The hero was Major Joppolo, played by John Hodiak in a 1945 film adaptation, the year the book won the prize.

adda *(AD-ah)* The common Egyptian skink (q.v.), a small scaly lizard with a notched tongue and strong, short legs. This secretive, agile creature, also called the sand-fish, spends most of its time burrowing in the deserts of North Africa, but when it surfaces, North Africans covet it for its supposed power to cure leprosy and other diseases. **Adda** is also an Italian river, a tributary of the Po (q.v.). Napoleon won the battle of Lodi on its shores in 1796.

addax *(ADD-ax)* A large, light-colored antelope found in North Africa, Arabia, and Syria. Because the male addax has four-foot-long twisted horns and white rump, it is believed to be the creature "pygarg" mentioned in the Bible (Deut. 14:5).

The addax has spiral horns that can be as long as three and a half feet.

ade *(ade)* Either a summer cooler of iced, sweetened citrus juices or the surname of American humorist and playwright George **Ade** (1866–1944). A prolific journalist, Ade also wrote parlor comedies which were produced from the turn of the century through the roaring twenties; one of his noted, if not enduring, successes was the exotically titled *The Sultan of Sulu.* A Hoosier by birth, Ade was a contemporary of the better-known American wit Will Rogers.

George Ade.

Aden *(AH-den)* Once a sizable British colony at the southern tip of the Arabian peninsula, Aden today is the capital city and major port of the now-renamed Democratic Republic of Yemen. It is situated on the Gulf of Aden, between the Arabian and Red Seas.

adit *(AD-it)* From the Latin meaning "approach or entrance," this word hasn't made it into popular usage as has its opposite and twin, *exit.* Instead it has stayed underground and is commonly used to refer only to the entrance of a cave or mine. Unlike a shaft, which inclines almost to be vertical, the adit is a tunnellike horizontal entrance or passage used for haulage, drainage, and ventilation.

adlay or **adlai** *(AHD-lie)* The name of certain varieties of Job's-tears, an ornamental Asiatic grass whose white, beadlike seeds are used in barter or strung in necklaces. Adlay has soft-hulled seeds and is cultivated for food and forage in the Philippines, southeastern Asia, and Japan. **Adlai** Ewing Stevenson II (1900–1965), one of our nation's great statesmen, was elected Democratic governor of Illinois in 1949, ran three times for the office of President of the United States (losing twice to Eisenhower and once to Kennedy), and was U.S. Ambassador to the United Nations until his death.

Adler *(AD-ler)*

The commonness of this crossword surname is matched only by the ubiquity of its nonrelated "family" members. Alfred Adler (1870–1937) was the Austrian psychiatrist who broke with his colleague Sigmund Freud after founding his own influential school of "individual" psychology. Felix Adler (1851–1933), on another hand, was the German-born educator who founded, at the age of 25, the Society for Ethical Culture. Stella Adler (1902–1982) was the actress and teacher who founded the famed Group Theatre of the thirties and conducted a long-running debate with the late Lee Strasberg on the meaning of the Stanislavski method of acting. Her younger brother Luther (1903–   ), also an actor, played the title role in *Golden Boy* on Broadway in 1937. (Poppa Jacob played Shylock in 1903.)

adz or adze *(ads)*

A cutting tool used to trim wood surfaces. It differs from its cousin the ax (or axe) in that it has a thin,

curving blade set at right angles to the handle, rather than parallel. The adz varies with the trade, so that a cooper's adz is something quite other than a carpenter's or shipbuilder's adz.

Aedes *(ay-EE-deez)*

A genus of mosquitoes (from a Greek word meaning "not sweet") that includes the feared transmitter of both the frequently fatal yellow fever and the less dangerous dengue fever.

Disease-carrying insects and unwitting host, 1491.

Aegir *(AY-gur; EE-jur)*

Scandinavian god of the sea, a giant and the head of a formidable family. Aegir's wife, Ran, is the death deity and lures sailors to the ocean's depths; their nine daughters rule the surf and turbulent waves.

ASSORTED ADLERS

Felix Adler
Educator
(1851–1933)

Jacob Adler
Actor
(1855–1926)

Stella Adler
Actress
(1902–1982)

Alfred Adler
Psychiatrist
(1870–1937)

Luther Adler
Actor
(1903–   )

aegis *(EE-jiss)* According to Homer, a shield first used by Zeus, the "aegis-bearer," to ensure victory in sport and battle. The Greek poet described it as a shaggy, gold-tassled accouterment, but later, as it became associated with Athena, it appeared as a scaly or hairy breastplate, bordered with serpents and set with the head of a Gorgon. These days, aegis simply denotes the protective shield of patronage or sponsorship.

Aegle *(EE-gluh; EH-gluh)* One of the Hesperides, the nymphs who (with help from a dragon) guarded the grove of golden apples which Hera had received as a wedding gift from the earth goddess Gaea. To procure some of these apples was one of the labors of Hercules. **Aegle** is also the tree itself, any of a thorny, deciduous genus bearing orangelike fruit known as the golden apple, wood apple, or Bengal quince.

aerie or **aery** *(AIR-ee)* The massive, grass and leaf-lined stick nest of hawks and eagles, which these creatures construct on crags and often maintain for several years. Any cliff-dwelling, even a human one, can be regarded as an aerie, as may its inhabitants such as, most notably, the members of a royal or noble family.

Aesir *(AYE-ser)* Once one of two factions of gods, the Aesir finally defeated and absorbed the Vanir (q.v.), and came to mean the entire assemblage, or pantheon, in German and Norse mythology. Members included: Odin, Freya, Thor, Frey, Tyr and Loki (all of whom, q.v.). Aesir is the plural of *ass,* which is Old Norse for "god."

Aesop *(EE-sop)* The somewhat legendary deformed Greek slave (c.620–560 B.C.) of Samos who supposedly wrote his way out of servitude by amusing his master with wise and witty stories in which the antics of animals provided insight into human nature. Aesop's name has become synonymous with fables, but some of his "original" works have been found on Egyptian papyri predating him by a millennium. (See *edile.*)

Aga or **Agha** *(AH-gah)* A leader who bears this title of respect, as in the Ottoman empire and certain Muslim lands. The most familiar representative was Aga Khan III, leader of the far-flung Ismaili Muslims from the age of eight until his death in 1957, at the age of 82. A wealthy and outspoken man, he represented India in the League of Nations and raised thoroughbreds that won the English Derby five times. He was succeeded by his grandson, Prince Karim, son of Aly Khan, who later married the actress Rita Hayworth. Karim is Aga Khan IV.

Aga Khan III.

Agave *(ah-GAY-vuh; ah-GAH-vay)* A large genus of tropical plants with long, often toothed or spine-tipped leaves, abundant in the American Southwest and downward to South America. Agaves include the century plant (or American aloe [q.v.] or maguey), the source of the beverage pulque and the potent distilled liquors tequila and mescal. Mescal is not to be confused with the drug mescaline, obtained from peyote, a cactus. Some Agave species, the amoles, yield soap and some supply sisal hemp (see *hemp*) and other useful fibers.

Agee *(AY-jee)* James Agee (1909–1955), American writer who collaborated with photographer Walker Evans on *Let Us Now*

Praise Famous Men, the classic Depression study of Southern tenant farmers (1941). Agee's film criticism is highly regarded. His novel *A Death in the Family,* published posthumously in 1957, won the 1958 Pulitzer Prize for fiction. In 1961 Tad Mosel based a play, *All the Way Home,* on *A Death in the Family;* it won the Pulitzer for drama that year. There is also a baseball outfielder named Tommy Agee, who was the American League Rookie of the Year in 1966, when he played for the Cleveland Indians.

James Agee, circa 1940.

aggie *(AG-ee)* Any person attending an agricultural college or school; by one reckoning the opposite of a preppy. The school itself may properly be called an aggie as well. **Aggie** is also the familiar name for a playing marble which resembles agate or is made from agate. An immie is imitation agate.

Agib *(AY-gib)* A wandering dervish of the Arabian Nights who tarries for a year in the palace of the forty princesses, and as punishment for overwhelming curiosity about these lovely ladies, ends up losing his eye.

Agni *(AHG-nee)* The god of fire and most important of the Vedic divinities. Agni represents the trinity of lightning, sun, and earthly fire, and as the god of the altar fire mediates between man and the gods. He is represented as red, two-faced, and forked of tongue. The **Agni** are also a people of West Africa, kin of the Ashanti.

Agni has both a malevolent face and a benevolent one.

agora *(AG-or-ah)* In ancient Greece, the marketplace and place of assembly, like our village green plus business district. The daily, mundane side of life was played out in the agora, and it was also here that men of letters and state addressed the issues of the day. A curious offspring of the agora is the word allegory ("other than agora"), which was coined to indicate the metaphysical realities beyond the world of the senses, and which soon became a powerful medium of satire and discourse.

Agra *(AG-ra)* City in India, established in the 1560s by the Mogul emperor Akbar as his capital; the site of several fine examples of Mogul architecture including Akbar's fort and tomb and the Pearl and Great mosques. The most renowned building in Agra, however, and one of the most renowned in the world is the Taj Mahal, Shah Jahan's memorial to his favorite wife, Mumtaz Mahal, who is interred there.

The beautiful temple of love: the Taj Mahal at Agra.

ague *(AY-gyoo)* A fit of recurring shivering. The word derives from the Medieval Latin *acuta,* short for *febris acuta,* meaning "sharp fever." To a doctor, ague is a specific malaria-like fever characterized by regular paroxysms, each attended by chills, fever, and sweating, often in that order.

Ahab *(AY-hab)* A king of Israel in the ninth century B.C. whose wife, the notorious Jezebel, a Phoenician princess, persecuted the prophets and introduced the worship of Baal (q.v.) into Israel. Also, the crippled but courageous and inhumanly tenacious captain of the whaleship Pequod in Herman

Melville's *Moby Dick*. Ahab's obsessive pursuit of Moby Dick, the white whale, led to tragedy for himself and his crew.

ai *(AH-ee)* The three-toed sloth of South and Central America, most commonly found suspended upside down from trees in the tropical forests. The three-toed feet of this sloth appear only on the front legs; there are five toes on the hind feet. Though very slow-moving, ais are difficult to spot amidst the mosses and foliage due to their grayish-green fur, which camouflages them well. Subsisting entirely on the leaves, shoots, and fruits they can grab from their favorite position, and even traveling in the pendant mode, they are a prosperous, if lazy, breed, running roughly the size of a pet cat.

Aiken *(AY-kin)* Conrad Aiken (1889–1973), the American poet, critic, and novelist whose *Selected Poems* won a Pulitzer Prize in 1930 and who himself won the National Medal for Literature in 1969. He has probably had more influence on successive generations of poets than some of his more famous, better-publicized peers such as Robert Frost and Archibald MacLeish, and today enjoys high regard among poets and scholars.

Ailey *(AY-lee)* Alvin Ailey (1931–   ), the American dancer and choreographer whose predominantly black repertory company, the Alvin Ailey American Dance Theater, founded in 1958, has enjoyed great success performing innovative, contemporary ballet for audiences the world over.

Alvin Ailey.

Ainu *(EYE-noo)* A member of an indigenous race of Japan, once living throughout the archipelago but now to be found mainly on the northernmost islands of Japan, as well as on the Kurils and Sakhalin (U.S.S.R.). The Ainu are short and robust, with light skin, European features, and a fairly hirsute face and body.

Aipi *(EYE-pee)* The cassava, the root of the manioc plant native to Brazil but cultivated throughout South America. A starchy vegetable not unlike the sweet potato, aipi is a staple of the South American diet; it also yields tapioca and cassava flour.

The aipi, or cassava.

Aire *(air)* River in northern England, a tributary of the Ouse. In its valley, called Airedale, the popular breed of terrier of that name originated.

Aisne *(ain)* French river, 175 miles long, which flows north and west from the Argonne forest to the Oise. Its banks, near the town of Craonne, were the site of heavy trench warfare during the First World War. **Aisne** also appears in crossword puzzles as a French department, the capital of which is Laon. Like the river, it is near Belgium.

Aix *(aix)* A genus of freshwater ducks noted for the beauty of their plumage. Counted among its members are the Asiatic mandarin duck and the North American wood duck. Otherwise, **Aix**—Aix-en-Provence, in full—is the capital city of Provence, home of the painter Paul Cézanne, about 15 miles north of the port of Marseilles.

The North American wood duck.

Akita *(AH-kee-tah)* Japanese city, on Honshu, on the Sea of Japan. Site of an ancient fort (built A.D. 733) and a university, Akita is at the center of the largest oil fields and copper mines in Japan. **Akita** *(ah-KEE-ta)* is also the name of a breed of hunting dog developed in Japan.

Akko See *Acre.*

ako *(AH-koh)* Hungarian liquid measure equivalent to 14.34 U.S. gallons or nearly 12 imperial gallons. **Ako** is also a Japanese industrial city.

alala *(ah-lah-LAH)* An ancient Greek war cry, as distinct from the admiring French exclamation *"Oo-la-la."*

alb *(alb)* The long white linen robe with tapered sleeves worn by Roman Catholic and some Anglican priests when celebrating the Mass. The garb was taken up by minor clergy and, at times, by the newly baptized and by penitents.

alba *(AHL-bah)* A medieval lyric poem, often accompanied by music and sometimes of a religious bent. In its primary form the alba tells of lovers parting at dawn; its refrain always ends in *alba,* the old Provençal word for "dawn." *Alba* also means "white" (feminine form) in Latin and Italian, and is the white matter of the brain and spinal cord. In crosswords, **Alba** often refers to the Duchess of Alba, the "naked Maja" of Goya's painting (see *Goya*), and it appears in **Alba** Longa, the mother city of Rome, founded by Ascanius, son of Aeneas.

Albi *(ahl-BEE)* Town in southern France, on the river Tarn (q.v.); the old city is called *ville rouge,* or "red town," because of its medieval red-brick buildings. The birthplace of artist Toulouse-Lautrec, Albi houses a museum displaying his works. The **Albi** *(AL-bie)* were alb-clad (see *alb*) fourteenth-century flagellants. Flagellantism, the extreme penitent lashing of oneself and fellow believers, reached its heyday during the Black Death of this period.

The Palais de la Berbie, a 13th–15th-century fortress in Albi, houses many of Toulouse-Lautrec's works.

Alcor See *Mizar.*

Alden *(AWL-din)* John Alden (1599–1687), a signer of the Mayflower Compact, a deputy governor of the Plymouth Colony, and popularly believed to have been the first Pilgrim to set foot on Plymouth Rock. His romantic pursuit of Priscilla Mullens, with whom he settled down in Duxbury, Massachusetts in 1627, and who eventually bore him eleven children, was immortalized by Longfellow in *The Courtship of Miles Standish,* wherein the most famous words ever said to Alden were "Speak for yourself, John," Priscilla's advice when he called on her posing as a romantic emissary from Standish.

aleph or **alef** *(AH-lehf)* The first letter of the Hebrew alphabet, corresponding to the Greek *alpha,* the Arabic *alif,* and our own letter *A.* In Hebrew *aleph* means "ox," a resemblance to which creature can still be seen in the shape of a capital *A*. Aleph-beth, root of "alphabet," originally meant "ox-house."

Aleut *(el-OOT; AL-yoot)* A member of either of two tribes, the Atka and the Unalaska, who inhabit the 1,100-mile arc of volcanic islands known as the Aleutians, stretching westward from Alaska toward the U.S.S.R. between the Bering Sea and the North Pacific. The Aleuts are a peaceful people of medium stature and high cheekbones, but with a darker complexion than other Eskimos. Many are members of the Russian Orthodox Church, reflecting Russia's former ownership of the region.

alga *(AL-gah),* A vast and varied group of lower plants (plural: algae *[AL-jee]*), mostly aquatic, lacking true roots, stems, and leaves, although some have leaflike and stemlike parts. Algae include almost all seaweeds (rockweed, sea moss, sea lettuce, etc.) and many freshwater weeds as well, among them pond scums, stoneworts, and fallen stars, and range in size from microscopic cells to giant 600-foot kelp. They are variously green, brown, or red. A major food for fish and a minor one for humans, algae are being investigated as a possible solution to food needs arising from overpopulation.

Laminaria.

allee *(al-AY)* A formal avenue or mall bordered by trees, or a garden aisle passing among trees and shrubs twice as high as its width. From the French, meaning a "walk" or "passage"; the considerably less pictur-

esque word "alley" evolved from the same source. It is also a German word, meaning exactly the same thing as the French, e.g. Stalin-**Allee** in East Berlin (now renamed).

Alma *(AHL-mah)* A feminine proper name which connotes a cherishing or nourishing nature, as in the term *alma mater,* "foster mother." In Italian, *alma* means the "soul" or "spirit," and is related to alms, charity. These meanings are united in Edmund Spenser's epic poem *The Faerie Queene,* in which the character **Alma** represents the personified soul. **Alma** is often clued as an Egyptian dancing girl in crossword puzzles. Other crossword clues: _____ Tadema (English painter, 1836–1912); _____-Ata (Siberian city); _____ Gluck (American soprano, 1884–1938); and the heroine of Tennessee Williams's *Summer and Smoke.*

Aloe *(ay-LOH-we; AH-loe)* A large and important genus of succulent plants whose common name is also aloe (the second pronunciation), native to arid regions of Africa but also widely cultivated. The juices of some species yield a drug used as a purgative, a tonic, to promote menstrual flow, and to relieve pain from burns. Aloe leaves also yield fiber. Aloe is a member of the lily family and is often clued in crosswords as "lily plant" or "lily's kin." The plant called American aloe is an agave (q.v.).

Altai or **Altay** *(AHL-tie)* Mountain system in central Asia, mainly in the U.S.S.R. but also in Mongolia and China. Belukha, at around 15,000 feet, is its highest peak. Altaic *(ahl-TAY-ik)* is the name of the language family believed to have originated in this region. It is spoken by some 80 million people in Turkey, Iran, the Soviet Union, and parts of Mongolia and China. It has no grammatical gender.

alula *(AL-yoo-lah)*   The sparsely quilled bastard wing of a bird, corresponding to the human thumb; out of delicacy it is usually defined in crosswords as an "extra joint" of the wing. The squama, or scalelike structure at the base of the wing of certain double-winged flies, is also called the **alula.**

amah *(AH-mah)*   An Oriental nanny or wet-nurse, often employed by Europeans in India and east Asia. Believed to derive from the Portuguese *ama,* meaning "governess," amahs were probably first used—in speech and in the home—by early Portuguese settlers and explorers who were among the earliest visitors to the Far East.

Amana *(ah-MAN-ah)*   Religious community in Iowa, comprising of seven villages whose members belong to a communal craft guild specializing in woolen and wood handicrafts. The community is incorporated as and called the Amana Church Society, and is an offshoot of the Pietist movement in Germany; its founders came here in 1842 to escape persecution. The Amana Refrigerator Company, which is located here, is not owned by the society, but takes its name from it. **Amana** is also the start of a once-popular palindrome about Goethals, who supervised the construction of the Panama Canal: "A man, a plan, a canal, Panama."

Amati *(ah-MAH-tee)*   Family name of Andrea Amati (c. 1520–1578), progenitor of the Cremona school of violin makers and designer of the modern instrument. Andrea's descendants followed in his footsteps. A grandson, Niccolo Amati (1596–1684), became the teacher of Antonio Stradivari (see *Strad*) and Andrea Guarneri, who also made it big in the fiddle-making business.

amber *(AM-ber)*   A translucent fossil resin, usually yellowish to brownish, which can take a fine polish. It is used for small objects both ornamental and functional, and in high-quality varnishes. When rubbed, it acquires a strong electrical charge. For-

merly, amber, or gray amber, was a name for ambergris, a valuable waxlike substance occasionally found in tropical waters, where it floats to the surface after being expelled from the digestive system of sperm whales. It contains the sterol ambrein, important as a fixative in the manufacture of perfumes.

ambry *(AM-bree)*   A repository or niche in the wall of a church reserved for the storage of sacramental vessels, vestments, and holy books. In ancient times, the ambry was always a closed cupboard, like the ark that houses the Torahs in Jewish synagogues, but today it is simply a storage area, and may even be just an open shelf or cupboard.

An ornamental ambry.

ame *(ahm)*   "Soul," in French. Among archaeologists **âme** is used in a derivative sense to refer to any core or form, usually of wood, upon which hollow metal objects were wrought by an ancient technique.

ameba or **amoeba** *(ah-MEE-bah)*   A microscopic one-celled protozoan and one of the simplest forms of animal life. Amebas (or amebae) have a nucleus but no cell wall, and may slink in any direction they wish by extruding a part of their body (pseudopod) and moving toward the extrusion. They dwell in stagnant ponds, and multiply by dividing.

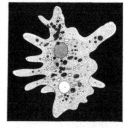

Ames *(aims)*   City in Iowa on the Skunk River, 28 miles north of Des Moines; site of the National Animal Disease Laboratory and an Iowa State University campus. Also the name of the **Ames** Brothers, a popular singing group.

Amiens *(ahm-YEHN)* French city on the Somme River, north of Paris; home of a thirteenth-century Gothic cathedral which is the largest in France. The Treaty of Amiens was signed here in 1802, marking the end of the French Revolutionary Wars; it succeeded, however, in delaying new hostilities between France, under Napoleon, and Britain for only about a year. Amiens is also famous for its velvet.

The cathedral at Amiens.

Amin *(ah-MEEN)* The Ugandan despot Idi Amin (c. 1925–   ) who forcibly overthrew Milton Obote in 1971. In the following years, as president and until his displacement in 1979, at which time he was driven into exile, Amin initiated various genocidal and political purges and generated much controversy over his unpredictable policies.

Idi Amin.

amir or **ameer** *(ah-MEER)* Generally the title of a Muslim noble, and more specifically of the Afghan princes be-lieved to be direct descendants of Mohammed through his daughter, Fatima (see *emir*). The word **Amir** also appears in the verses of a popular song, author unknown, called "Abdul Abulbul Amir."

Three amirs in Kabul.

Amman *(ah-MAHN)* Capital of Jordan, 50 miles northeast of Jerusalem. Known in biblical times as Rabbath-Ammon, it was the capital of the Ammonite tribe, which was absorbed by the Arabs in the eighth century B.C. Known as Philadelphia during Roman and Byzantine times, it was renamed Amman in 635 B.C. after the Arab conquest, and declined to the point of being only a small village at the time it was chosen as capital for Trans-Jordan in 1921.

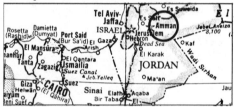

Amman, shown circled, in relation to Tel Aviv in Israel and Cairo in Egypt.

amok or **amuck** *(ah-MUK)* A Malaysian malady of the nervous system in which the unfortunate victim runs wild ("amok") in a murderous frenzy, attacking all who cross his path.

Amoy *(ah-MOY)* Seaport city of southeastern China, on the Formosa Strait opposite Taiwan. On an island connected to the mainland by railroad, it was one of the earliest seats of European commerce to China, and was a port of emigration.

Amur *(uh-MOOR)* A river in northeastern Asia forming a 1,000-mile border between Manchuria and the Soviet Union, and thence flowing through the far eastern regions of the U.S.S.R. into the Pacific Ocean. It is about 1,800 miles long.

ana *(AY-nuh; AH-nah)* Originally a collection of the wit and wisdom of a particular person, such as Boswell's *Johnson,* ana has come to be used to describe any collection of unusual bits of information on a particular subject of interest. Most frequently it occurs in suffix form, as in Americana or cruciverbiana. **Ana** is also the missing half of Santa _____ .

ani *(AH-nee)* Any of three species of black-feathered birds of the cuckoo family, native to South and Central America. The common ani and its groove-billed cousin have been known to fly as far north as the southern United States. Anis have the peculiar habit of laying their eggs communally in a large nest. In this they are unlike the parasitical Old World cuckoos, which deposit their eggs in the nests of smaller birds; the foster parents rear the voracious young cuckoos at the expense of their own fledglings.

anil *(AN-il)* A West Indian plant which is one of the natural sources of the deep-blue dye indigo. Today most indigo is synthetically produced, but true indigo may be obtained only by soaking the dye plants and extracting a colorless compound, and then oxidizing the solution.

Indigofera macrostachya.

anima *(AN-im-ah)* The soul, the life, the vital element in a being. Originally a Latin word, anima has been appropriated by theologians and philosophers, and most recently by psychiatrist Carl Jung (see *Jung*), for whom it represented the true but latent self. Jung further distinguished anima (the feminine nature in a man) from animus (the male nature in a woman). Anima is the root of such words as animal and animosity.

Anjou *(AHN-zhoo)* A former province of western France, Anjou is an agricultural region watered by the Loire and other rivers, renowned for its Vouvray and Saumur wines. Certain Angevin (Fr., ''of Anjou'') rulers were forebears of the Plantagenet kings of England.

A vintner of Anjou.

Annam or **Anam** *(ah-NAHM)* A former kingdom on the east coast of Indochina, Annam occupied the region of what is now central Vietnam. Its capital was Hué, site of the famed 1968 Tet (''New Year's'') offensive of the Vietcong.

anoa *(ah-NO-ah)* A small wild ox native to the island of Celebes, east of Borneo. The anoa is related to the buffalo but can be distinguished by its straight horns. In light of all the above, anoa is almost invariably clued as ''a Celebes ox'' or ''a pygmy buffalo.''

anomie or **anomy** *(AN-oh-mee)* Rootlessness or lack of purpose, identity, or ethical values in a person or a society. In individuals it is often characterized by anxiety and isolation.

Anous *(AN-oo-us)* The tropical noddy (q.v.), a particularly stupid and tame genus of tern. Short-tailed and sooty brown in color, it is common to the southern Atlantic and the Gulf Coast of the U.S. Taking its name from the Greek meaning ''silly'' or ''mindless,'' the anous would seem to be kin of the now-extinct dodo (q.v.), to which it is otherwise unrelated.

ansu *(AHN-zoo)* A variety of apricot, native to Korea but also cultivated in Japan. This oval, smooth-skinned orange fruit has a slightly bitter taste, and resembles a cross between a peach and a plum.

Anu *(AY-noo)* In ancient Babylonian lore, the god of the skies and supreme deity of the trinity that included Enlil, god of the earth, and Ea, god of water. Another **Anu** in an old Hindu myth refused to shoulder a curse placed on his father, earned the enmity of the gods, and was promptly placed under another curse.

Anzio *(AHN-see-oh)* Italian town on the Tyrrhenian Sea, about 30 miles from Rome. A popular resort since antiquity, when it was called Antium, Anzio was the birthplace of Caligula and Nero (q.v.). Anzio was also the landing site of the Allied troops in 1944.

aoudad *(AY-oh-dad)* A wild sheep of North Africa, often called Barbary sheep, with curved horns and a long, shaggy beard. It is believed to be the "chamois" mentioned in the Old Testament (Deut. 14:5).

Apis *(AY-pis)* A sacred bull of ancient Egypt, thought to be the incarnate of Ptah, chief god of Memphis, and to have been engendered by a moonbeam. Upon the death of an Apis, a new one was born. **Apis** is also a genus of bees, including the common honeybee, prized for its wax and honey. Though widely "kept," certain species, including the hardy but bad-tempered German bee and the yellow and gray Italian bee, have escaped and established themselves in colonies throughout North America. In Latin, *apis* means any bee and it is the base of such bee words as apiary.

apnea *(ap-NEE-ah)* The state of being temporarily without respiration, either intentionally through holding one's breath, or more often, involuntarily because of a lack of oxygen. Four minutes without respiration is usually enough to do irreparable damage to the brain.

apod *(AY-pod)* Any of a number of footless animals such as leeches. The bird of paradise was once assumed to be apodal on the basis of some unfortunate specimens brought back from the East Indies. In crosswords **apod** sometimes appears as two words in a clue, e.g., "as alike as two peas in _____ ."

apse *(aps)* The usually semicircular and domed part of a church, projecting always from the east end. In early Christian basilicas, the apse held the bishop's throne. Often referred to in crosswords as "altar site or locale."

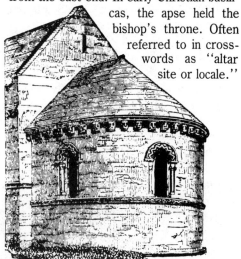

Apsu *(AHP-soo)* In the Babylonian creation epic, Apsu and Mummu, the primordial waters situated above and below the earth, together representing chaos and confusion, were overthrown by Ea, the supplanting god of the watery elements.

Aqaba or **Akaba** *(AH-kah-ba)* Gulf of the Red Sea, between the Sinai Peninsula of Egypt and Saudi Arabia, accessible via the Strait of Tiran. Of strategic importance in Arab-Israeli conflicts, the gulf was blockaded by the Arabs from 1949 to 1956, and again in 1967. The city of Aqaba, at the head of the gulf, is a Jordanian port, the only one on the Red Sea. Elath (q.v.) is an Israeli resort and port close to Aqaba. Both are popular with winter vacationers. The absence of the letter *u* after *q* in many Arabic words is often a help to crossword constructors in a tight corner.

Ara *(AY-ruh)* A constellation of eight stars in the southern skies. Latin for "altar," it apparently resembled such a structure to early astronomers. Ara lies just north of the constellation Scorpius, and is barely visible, except on very clear nights. **Ara** is also a parrot genus, which includes the macaw; and the given name of former Notre Dame football coach **Ara** Parsighian.

araba *(AH-ruh-bah)* A horse-drawn coach formerly used in southern Russia and the Near East; otherwise, the South American howling monkey.

Aral *(AH-rahl; AR-uhl)* A sea in central Asian U.S.S.R., the fourth largest inland body of water in the world, after the Caspian Sea, Lake Superior, and Lake Victoria. With a rough area of 26,000 square miles, it has no outlet, many small islands, and a generally shallow bed that permits only limited navigation.

Aram *(AHR-am)* Ancient country of southwestern Asia extending from the Lebanon Mountains to beyond the Euphrates, more or less equivalent to modern Syria. Aram was the birthplace of Aramaic, the Semitic language in which much of the Old Testament was originally written. **Aram** is also the composer Khachaturian's first name, and the last name of Eugene Aram, an eighteenth-century linguist and murderer who was the subject of Thomas Hood's poem, *The Dream of Eugene Aram*. There is also a William Saroyan play called *My Name Is Aram*.

Aran *(AHR-an)* An island group at the entrance to Galway Bay, in northwestern Ireland. Desolate, rocky, and sparsely populated by people whose speech is Gaelic, the Arans are the setting for J. M. Synge's classic play of Irish country life, *Riders to the Sea*. Life on the Aran Islands was depicted in a memorable film made in 1937,

An engraving of the Arden forest in a scene from Shakespeare's As You Like It.

Robert Flaherty's *Man of Aran*. There is also a rocky, wild island called **Aran** in the Firth of Clyde, Scotland.

arar *(AHR-ahr)* The Moroccan sandarac tree, whose hard and fragrant wood has been used through the ages in building. Its brittle resin, also called sandarac, is used in making incense and varnish.

arbor *(AHR-bur)* A shaded walkway or garden shelter, or bower of vine-covered latticework; or a tree, botanically and genealogically speaking, as distinguished from a shrub. Arbor Day is celebrated in the United States in the spring, usually by schoolchildren planting trees. **Arbor** is also found in crosswords clued as Ann _____, seat of the University of Michigan.

arca *(AHR-kah)* In early Roman Catholicism, a chest or box used to store alms or the holy wafer, and upon whose lid the Eucharistic elements are consecrated. The word arcane (meaning "hidden" or "secret") derives from *arca,* as does ark.

ardeb *(AHR-deb)* A measure of volume in many Islamic countries, problematic because it varies so widely from place to place. In Egypt, for example, an ardeb equals less than six bushels; in Ethiopia, however, it represents only four quarts, or one-eighth bushel.

Arden *(AHR-den)* A forest in Warwickshire, England, once believed to have covered most of the Midlands and extended to the eastern coast. The forest is the setting for Shakespeare's *As You Like It.* **Arden** is also the name of a city in the redwood district of northern California.

are *(air)* One hundred square meters; a basic unit of metric measurement. It is often used as the plural present tense of the verb "to be," as **are** *(ar),* clued in crosswords with quotations, e.g., "Where _____ the snows of yesteryear?"

areca *(AR-ee-kah; ar-EE-kah)* The betel palm, native to tropical Asia. Arecas have a slender, ringed trunk, pinlike leaves, and a thick-rinded orange fruit containing seeds called areca nuts or betel nuts (see *betel*). The nut is the equivalent of chewing gum to East Indians. It has an astringent taste and stains the teeth black.

arena *(ah-REE-nuh)* The center of an amphitheater, in which gladiatorial battles and other spectacles occurred, in Roman antiquity. It means "sandy place," and indeed, the sand was there to absorb blood. Most famed, of course, is Rome's Coliseum. Today, the word has spilled over to signify any place of public contest or, sometimes, a sphere of activity.

A Roman arena at Arles, France.

arend *(AH-rend)* The European bearded vulture, also called the *lammergeier.* About three and a half feet long, with a ten-foot wingspread, it sports a bristly, beardlike tuft below its beak and resembles a cross between an eagle and a vulture.

The formidable arend appears to be perched in thought.

Ares *(AY-reez; AH-reez)* The Greek god of war, son of almighty Zeus and Hera, and unlikely if ardent lover of Aphrodite, goddess of love. He is usually depicted in full armor, bearing a spear and torch, and is virtually identical to the Roman god Mars.

Ares, Aphrodite, and their son Eros, from the School of Fontainebleau.

argali *(AHR-gah-lee)* A large wild sheep, remarkable for its huge (close to four feet in length) spiral horns, found in the mountains of northeastern Asia and in the United States, where it is better known as the bighorn. If bearded, an argali is called an aoudad (q.v.).

Argo *(AHR-go)* The ship that carried Jason (q.v.) and the fifty or so Argonauts from Thessaly to Colchis, where Jason, aided by Medea (q.v.), retrieved the Golden Fleece from the sacred grove where it lay guarded by a sleepless dragon. Consequently, **Argo** is also a southern constellation comprising parts called Carina

The Argo and its sailors, by Parentino.

(the Keel), Malus (the Mast), Puppis (the Stern), Vela (the Sails), and Pyxis (the Mariner's Compass).

Argos *(AHR-gohs)* Odysseus's dog. Faithful Argos recognized his master upon his return home after an absence of twenty years, then died on the spot. **Argos** was

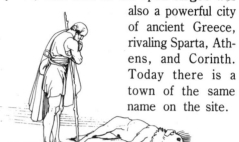

also a powerful city of ancient Greece, rivaling Sparta, Athens, and Corinth. Today there is a town of the same name on the site.

argot *(AHR-go)* To lexicographers, the private, arcane jargon or slang used among hoods, tramps, and the like, or within a particular economic or professional class. The users of argot just call it "talking."

Argus *(AHR-guss)* The humanoid monster with 100 eyes, in Greek mythology. Hermes put all the eyes to sleep one by one in order to rescue Io (q.v.), whom Argus was assigned to guard. After Argus's death at the hands of Hermes, Hera used the eyes to decorate the peacock's tail. The Argus butterfly is so named for the numerous eyelike spots on its wings.

Arhat *(ER-hot)* Any Buddhist monk or saint who has reached Nirvana, the state of enlightenment.

Arias *(AHR-ee-ahs)* Arnulfo Arias (1901–), the three-time (and thrice-ousted) president of Panama. His most recent term of office was in 1968 and lasted ten days.

Arica *(ah-REE-kuh)* A seaport in northernmost Chile that was a bone of contention between Chile and Peru in the 1920s. Its earlier loss by Bolivia in one of the frequent squabbles among the three nations doomed Bolivia to landlocked ignominy; Chile and Peru today share the use of the port's facilities.

Ariel *(AHR-ee-ehl)* A volatile spirit of the air in Shakespeare's *The Tempest*. **Ariel** is also the name of the innermost satellite of Uranus and of the Australian flying squirrel.

Ariel, painted by Robert Fowler.

Aries *(AIR-eez)* Name of a constellation and first of the twelve signs of the Zodiac (March 21–April 19), represented as a ram. In Roman warfare, **aries** referred to the battering ram used for knocking down the walls of besieged towns, the end of which was often shaped like a ram's head.

aril *(AH-ril)* A specialized seed covering which develops only after a seed has been fertilized. The scarlet coating of the bittersweet's seed capsule is a true aril.

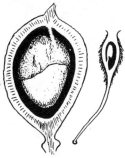

Arion *(ah-RIE-uhn)* A Greek poet of the seventh century B.C. who, robbed by pirates and forced to jump into the sea, was rescued by a dolphin upon whose back he rode to shore. According to Herodotus, the dolphin was charmed by the poet's music, presumably issuing from a waterproof instrument.

arista See *awn*.

Arkie See *Oakie*.

Arles *(ahrl)* Southern French city on the banks of the Rhone. Artist Vincent Van Gogh spent some of his most productive years here, producing such masterpieces as *L'Arlesienne* and *View of Arles with Irises*. Arles (then Arelas) was the capital of Roman Gaul, and there remain many Roman ruins such as a second-century amphitheater, which today is used for bullfights.

St. Trophime at Arles.

armet *(AR-met)* A medieval helmet constructed of many lightweight sections held closely around the head by contoured and hinged chin and neck pieces.

arna *(AR-nah)* The water buffalo of India, once wild but now domesticated and used as a draft animal throughout Asia. Larger and less docile than the common ox, the arna is fond of rivers and marshy places. Its skin is used in sandals, wallets, handbags, and many other Indian leather goods.

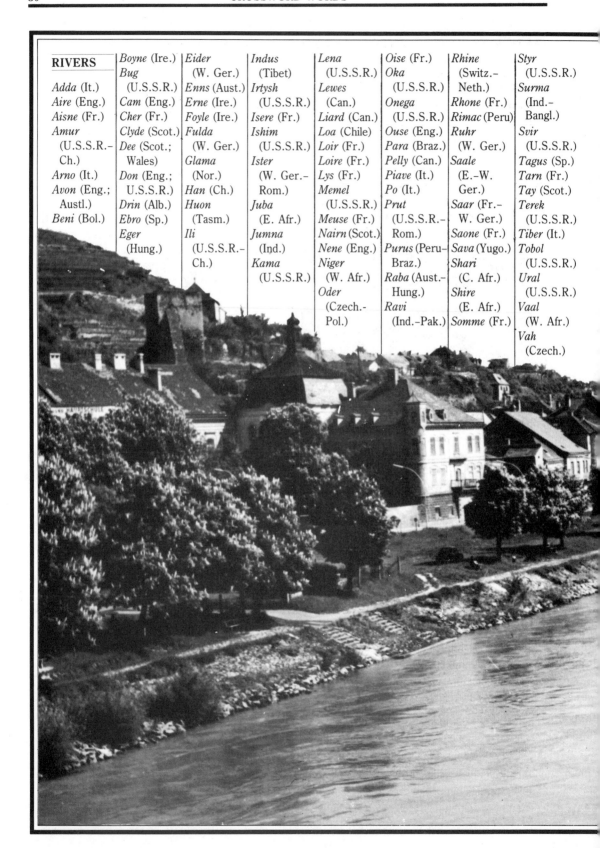

RIVERS

Adda (It.)	Boyne (Ire.)	Eider (W. Ger.)	Indus (Tibet)	Lena (U.S.S.R.)	Oise (Fr.)	Rhine (Switz.-Neth.)	Styr (U.S.S.R.)
Aire (Eng.)	Bug (U.S.S.R.)	Enns (Aust.)	Irtysh (U.S.S.R.)	Lewes (Can.)	Oka (U.S.S.R.)	Rhone (Fr.)	Surma (Ind.-Bangl.)
Aisne (Fr.)	Cam (Eng.)	Erne (Ire.)	Isere (Fr.)	Liard (Can.)	Onega (U.S.S.R.)	Rimac (Peru)	Svir (U.S.S.R.)
Amur (U.S.S.R.-Ch.)	Cher (Fr.)	Foyle (Ire.)	Ishim (U.S.S.R.)	Loa (Chile)	Ouse (Eng.)	Ruhr (W. Ger.)	Tagus (Sp.)
Arno (It.)	Clyde (Scot.)	Fulda (W. Ger.)	Ister (W. Ger.-Rom.)	Loir (Fr.)	Para (Braz.)	Saale (E.-W. Ger.)	Tarn (Fr.)
Avon (Eng.; Austl.)	Dee (Scot.; Wales)	Glama (Nor.)	Juba (E. Afr.)	Loire (Fr.)	Pelly (Can.)	Saar (Fr.-W. Ger.)	Tay (Scot.)
Beni (Bol.)	Don (Eng.; U.S.S.R.)	Han (Ch.)	Jumna (Ind.)	Lys (Fr.)	Piave (It.)	Saone (Fr.)	Terek (U.S.S.R.)
	Drin (Alb.)	Huon (Tasm.)	Kama (U.S.S.R.)	Memel (U.S.S.R.)	Po (It.)	Sava (Yugo.)	Tiber (It.)
	Ebro (Sp.)	Ili (U.S.S.R.-Ch.)		Meuse (Fr.)	Prut (U.S.S.R.-Rom.)	Shari (C. Afr.)	Tobol (U.S.S.R.)
	Eger (Hung.)			Nairn (Scot.)	Purus (Peru-Braz.)	Shire (E. Afr.)	Ural (U.S.S.R.)
				Nene (Eng.)	Raba (Aust.-Hung.)	Somme (Fr.)	Vaal (W. Afr.)
				Niger (W. Afr.)	Ravi (Ind.-Pak.)		Vah (Czech.)
				Oder (Czech.-Pol.)			

Volga (U.S.S.R.)	Gatun (Pan.)	Taupo (N.Z.)	**BAYS**	Baku (U.S.S.R.)	Haifa (Isr.)	Oban (Scot.)	Sete (Fr.)
Volta (W. Afr.)	Iznik (Turk.)	Tay (Scot.)	Fundy (Can.)	Bari (It.)	Hanko (Fin.)	Parnu (Est.)	Sfax (Tun.)
Vaal (W. Ger.-Neth.)	Lanao (Phil.)	Volta (W. Afr.)	Gaspe (Can.)	Basra (Iraq)	Havre (Fr.)	Pinsk (U.S.S.R.)	Sudak (U.S.S.R.)
Varta (Pol.)	Moro (Phil.)		Ise (Jap.)	Batum (U.S.S.R.)	Icel (Turk.)	Pisco (Peru)	Surat (Ind.)
Veser (W. Ger.)	Ness (Scot.)	**SEAS**	Pylos (Gr.)	Brest (Fr.; U.S.S.R.)	Izmir (Turk.)	Ponce (P.R.)	Susak (Yugo.)
Xingu (Port.)	Nyasa (S.E. Afr.)	Aral (U.S.S.R.)	**PORTS OF CALL**	Cadiz (Sp.)	Jaffa (Isr.)	Poti (U.S.S.R.)	Suva (Fiji)
Yser (Belg.)	Onega (U.S.S.R.)	Azov (U.S.S.R.)	Acre (Isr.)	Caen (Fr.)	Jedda (Saudi Arabia)	Pula (Yugo.)	Tunja (Col.)
	Poopo (Bol.)	Banda (Indonesia)	Aden (Yemen)	Cebu (Phil.)	Jolo (Phil.)	Pusan (S. Kor.)	Turku (Fin.)
LAKES	Shiel (Scot.)	Black (Eur.-Asia)	Amoy (Ch.)	La Ceiba (Hond.)	Juba (Sudan)	Pye (Burma)	Vaasa (Fin.)
Chad (N. Afr.)	Taal (Phil.)	Java (Java)	Aqaba (Jor.)	Dakar (Senegal)	Kobe (Jap.)	Rauma (Fin.)	Vardo (Nor.)
Como (It.)		Sulu (Phil.)	Arica (Chile)	Elath (Isr.)	Lagos (Nig.)	Reisa (E. Ger.)	Varna (Bulg.)
Eyre (Austl.)			Azov (U.S.S.R.)	Emden (W. Ger.)	Lome (Togo)	Riga (U.S.S.R.)	Vidin (Bulg.)
			Bahia (Braz.)	Fiume (Yugo.)	Macao (Port.)	Rouen (Fr.)	Vigo (Sp.)
			Balboa (Pan.)	Galle (Sri Lanka)	Memel (Lith.)		Visby (Swed.)
					Natal (Braz.)		Warri (Nig.)
							Wuhan (Ch.)

CROSSWORD CRUISE

THE WORLD'S WATERWAYS FOR
THE ARMCHAIR TRAVELER.

The Arno River in picturesque Florence.

Arno *(AHR-noh)*   An Italian river about 150 miles long, flowing from the northern Apennines through Arezzo, Florence, and Pisa to the Ligurian Sea. Extensive flood-control works, some devised by Leonardo da Vinci, failed to prevent the river from flooding Florence in 1966 and destroying many of the city's art treasures.

Arp *(arp)*   Jean (or Hans) Arp (1887–1966), French artist whose free-form sculptures, such as the early-1930s *Head with Three Annoying Objects,* exemplified his desire to create nonrepresentational, organic art. A founder of the Dada movement (see *Dada*), Arp was a major force in the avant-garde art of the early twentieth century.

Arras *(AR-ahs; ah-RAHSS)*   Northern French city on the Scarpe River near Lille. It was settled during Roman times and became prosperous in the Middle Ages as a banking and weaving center. Its tapestries were known and admired throughout the world; the English word arras is synonymous with "tapestry." Now, its main industries are metalworking and brewing. Be-

ing near the Belgian border, Arras has a Flemish flavor, and traces of Spanish influences also remain.

arrau *(AHR-ow)*   A large turtle of the Amazon whose eggs are used for food and as a source of oil. Also, Claudio **Arrau** *(ahr-RAHW),* the Chilean classical pianist.

arrie *(AHR-ee)*   The murre (q.v.) or razor-billed auk (q.v.), native to Alaska and the North Atlantic. About 16 inches long, it has a black back and a white breast; its sharp bill is black with a white cross-band.

ars *(ahrs)*   From Latin, the genius, or "art," of any craft, seen in such titles as Horace's *Ars Poetica* (The Art of Poetry) or *Ars Artium* (The Art of Arts, i.e., logic). *Ars Amatoria* (The Art of Love) is a poem by Ovid; *Ars Gratia Artis* (Art for the Sake of Art) is the motto of MGM.

artel *(ar-TELL)* A labor collective or co-operative craft guild, common in the Soviet Union. In the guild, individual artists work collectively on a project, and then divide the profits. Sometimes formed to accomplish a single job, it can also function on a permanent basis, like a medieval craft guild.

artha *(ER-tuh)* In Hinduism, one of the four parts of *purushartha,* or the aims of man, which encompass the four things you can do in this life: artha, the quest for worldly success; dharma, the performance of duty; kama (q.v.), the pursuit of love and pleasure; and moksha, the pursuit of salvation, considered by some to be the highest aim and actually on another plane. Each of the four comes with at least one how-to manual or traditional treatise, the most famous of which is the *Kama Sutra.*

Aruba *(ah-ROO-bah)* A popular Caribbean resort island in the Netherland Antilles. Visited by Christopher Columbus in the fifteenth century and captured by the Dutch in 1634, the island today has some heavy industries, including oil refining, and exports sea salts and phosphates.

arui See *aoudad.*

arx *(arx)* A citadel or strong fortress from which a city was controlled and protected in Roman antiquity.

An arx was a fortified structure used to protect an ancient city. Shown here is Rome's Appian Gate.

arzun *(AHR-zun)* Italian millet, cultivated in Europe, Asia, and America as a cereal grain and for animal feed.

asak, asok *(ASS-ahk),* or **asoka** *(ass-OH-kuh)* A showy tree of tropical Asia, with orange-scarlet flowers. Its blossoms are used to decorate temples. It is a source of cork, and its sap is used as a remedy for colic.

asana *(ah-SAH-nah)* Posture as an element in the practice of yoga, designed to calm the body. Sometimes, the cross-legged manner of sitting depicted in seated figures of Buddha.

Asch *(ash)* Sholem Asch (1880–1957), Yiddish novelist and playwright who came to the United States from Poland in 1909 and did much to popularize and secularize Yiddish literature with such works as the

play *The God of Vengeance* (1910) and the trilogy *The Nazarene, The Apostle,* and *Mary,* which appeared between 1939 and 1949. Asch sought to illustrate in his works the common spiritual heritage of Judaism and Christianity.

Sholem Asch.

ascian *(ASH-ee-an)* One who has no shadow. Often applied to inhabitants of equatorial regions where the sun is vertical, and thus casts no shadow, at noon for several days each year.

ascon *(ASS-kahn)* A type of simple sponge whose canals, through which nourishment is taken from the sea, run directly into its paragaster, or inner digestive cavity. Ascon comes from a Greek word meaning "wineskin."

Ashur, Assur, or Asur *(AH-shoor)*   The principal Assyrian deity, after whom Assyria itself was named. Ashur was god of military might and empire, and was symbolized by a winged sun disk with a bow in its center.

Asin *(AH-sin)*   The sixth (or seventh, in some reckonings) month in the Hindu lunisolar calendar, corresponding to a period in September/October. (The Hindu year begins in March or April, variously). More often, **asin** appears as a two-word phrase in crosswords, e.g., "It's _____ to Tell a Lie," or "B _____ Baker," or "Softly, _____ a Morning Sunrise."

Askr *(ASS-ker)*
According to Norse myth, Askr was the first man, created from the ash tree by the combined efforts of Odin, Lothur, and Hoenir, who at the same time created Embla, the first woman, from the alder.

Embla and Askr.

asor *(ASS-or)*   An ancient Hebrew musical instrument having ten strings, played with a thin plectrum of ivory or wood, or a quill.

asp *(asp)*   A small venomous snake of Egypt, either a viper or an African cobra, whose major claim to fame is that it was the

instrument of suicide for Cleopatra, who held it to her breast. The uraeus, or sacred asp, appears in stylized form on the headdress of ancient Egyptian rulers as a symbol of sovereignty.

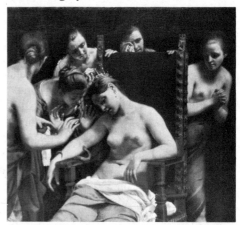

Cleopatra's death, painted by Cagnacci (1601–1681).

aspic *(ASS-pik)*   A savory jelly used as a garnish or in the preparation of a meat, fish, or vegetable mold. Also, the European spike lavender, which yields fragrant oil used in perfumery. Also an old name for the asp (q.v.).

assai *(ASS-ah-ay)*   A slender-trunked feather palm of Brazil and Guyana which bears dark purple fruits. Also, a highly nutritious and popular Brazilian beverage made from a sweetened infusion of the assai fruit. **Assai** is also a common term in music meaning "very" or "quite."

Assam *(ah-SAHM)*   State in northeastern India, bordered by Bangladesh, Nepal, Bhutan, China, and Burma. Because of its almost complete separation from the Indian heartland, it became a self-governing province in 1937. Since then it has provided asylum for Hindu refugees from Muslim East Pakistan, now Bangladesh. A silkworm native to Assam, the eri or eria, is a frequent crossword filler.

asse *(ahs)*   A South African fox sometimes called the caama (or cama) fox; or the unrelated caama, an African antelope.

assi *(ASS-ee)* A holly native to the American South; also called yaupon. Its smooth,

elliptical leaves are dried and brewed for tea, and were formerly used in the preparation of a medicinal and ceremonial Indian beverage called "black drink."

Astor *(ASS-ter)* Nancy Witcher Langhorne Astor (1879–1964), the first woman to serve in the British House of Commons, although she was American-born. A proponent of women's and children's rights, temperance, and school reform, Lady Astor also, with her husband, the Second Viscount Astor, supported what was seen as appeasement of the Nazis before World War II. Their country home, Cliveden, was a gathering place for prominent persons in the arts and politics.

Lady Astor, 1924.

Astur *(ASS-ter)* The genus of goshawks, long-tailed, short-winged hunting hawks noted for powerful flight and great courage. There are European, American, Mexican, and Australian asturs, the last being remarkable for their pure white plumage.

Aswan *(ahs-WAN)* Egyptian city on the east bank of the Nile, called Syene, meaning "marketplace," by the ancients because of its importance as a trading center. Now it is the site of 12,565-foot-long, 364-foot-high Aswan High Dam, for which the temples and figures hewn from the rocks of Abu Simbel were moved piece by piece to higher ground. Lake Nasser, created by the dam, has benefited both Egypt and Sudan by reclaiming land for agriculture, but has otherwise proved ecologically catastrophic.

The Aswan Dam.

Ata *(AH-tah)* A primitive tribesman of Mindanao, dwelling in the region east and north of Mt. Apo, the highest peak in the Philippines (9,690 feet). The Ata are not related to the Ati (q.v.), who inhabit the islands of Negros and Panay (q.v.). More often **ata** appears in crosswords as the phrase "at a," e.g., "_____ standstill" or "_____ glance."

atap or **attap** *(AT-ahp)* The versatile nipa (or nypa) palm of Malaysia, India, and the Pacific Islands. Its leaves serve for thatch, its seeds are edible, and its sap provides nipa sugar and the alcoholic beverages nipa (from fermented sap) and beno (from fermented and distilled sap).

ates *(AH-tess),* **atis** *(AH-tis),* or **atta** *(AH-tah)* Name in the Philippines for the sweetsop, a green, scaly-rinded tropical fruit with glossy black seeds.

Athol *(AH-thuhl)* A town in central Massachusetts and butt of numerous crude jokes by neighboring townspeople. Also, **Athol** Fugard, South African playwright who writes frequently on apartheid themes and is the author of such recent works as *A Lesson from Aloes* and *Master Harold . . . and the Boys.*

Athos *(ATH-ohss)* One of the famous Three Musketeers created by French novelist and dramatist Alexandre Dumas (1802–1870); the other two were Porthos and Aramis. **Athos** is also a peak in northeastern Greece, about 6,670 feet high, inhabited since the tenth century by the monks of St. Basil. Athos, long independent, was deemed a theocratic republic in 1927, and was placed under Greek jurisdiction. It is renowned for its collection of rare Byzantine manuscripts, which no woman has ever seen, since they are not allowed in the community. The chief town is Karyai.

The monastery atop Mt. Athos houses Byzantine manuscripts.

Ati *(AH-tee)* A member of the Negritoid Ati tribe of Panay and Negros, in the Philippine Islands. They are of small stature and are thought to be aboriginal to the region.

atis *(ah-TEES)* A monkshood (aconitum) native to the Himalayas; it is a poisonous plant with delicate, plum-colored flowers. **Atis** can also be ates (q.v.), a tropical fruit.

Atka *(AHT-kah)* The Atka mackerel (or Atka fish, actually a greenling), named for Atka Island in the Aleutians. It is a valuable commercial fish, especially popular in Japan. Also a tribe of people in the Aleutians (see *Aleut*).

atle, atlee *(AT-leh)*, or **athel** *(ATH-ahl)* A small tamarisk evergreen tree or large shrub native to arid North Africa and the eastern Mediterranean, now cultivated in many hot, dry regions, such as the American Southwest and Australia. Its delicate, heathlike appearance lends it some ornamental value, but the atle is chiefly prized as a windbreak or shelter-belt tree.

Atli *(AHT-lay)* A legendary king in Germanic mythology who wooed a woman named Gudrun, invited her two sons to court, and then slew them. Gudrun avenged her sons' deaths by killing the king's sons and finally Atli himself. See *Etzel*.

Atman *(AHT-mun)* In Hinduism the inner self of man, especially in relation to, and ultimate identity with, the universal reality of being, or Brahman.

atoll *(AH-tahl)* A doughnut-shaped tropical island or chain of islands, actually a coral reef surrounding a lagoon. Theories of atoll creation differ; early sailors thought they were divine handiwork placed there as safe havens at sea. Many islands of the South Pacific are atolls; some have lagoons scores of miles in diameter.

atrio *(AH-tree-oh)* Not a safe place to visit: the depression between twin cones of certain volcanos.

attar *(AT-er)* A strongly fragrant oil distilled from flowers, especially roses (attar of roses or rose oil). Also Farid ad-Din **Attar,** celebrated thirteenth-century Persian mystic poet.

Attis *(AT-iss)* or **Atys** *(AY-tiss)* A Phrygian nature god identified with the death and rebirth of plants. Attis was loved to distraction by the earth goddess Cybele, who, in a fit of jealousy, drove him mad: he castrated himself and upon dying was transformed by her into a sacred pine. His flowing blood turned into bunches of violets. His death and resurrection were celebrated at spring festivals in honor of Cybele. In some legends Attis corresponds to Adonis.

Attu *(AH-too)* The westernmost of the Aleutian Islands and end of the chain that extends 1,200 miles westward, between the Pacific and the Bering Sea, from the tip of the Alaskan mainland. Attu and neighboring islands were occupied briefly by the Japanese during World War II and are the only portion of the fifty states of the union located outside the Western Hemisphere.

Atua *(ah-TOO-ah)* A Polynesian spirit or being, sometimes good, sometimes evil, sometimes just plain spooky.

Auau *(ow-ow)* Channel separating the Hawaiian Islands of Lanai and Maui.

Auca *(ow-kah)* A semiprimitive Indian of central Chile and nearby parts of Argentina. Aucas are classed between the relatively civilized Incas and the quite primitive Patagonians. Several thousand survive in uneasy coexistence with European settlers.

Auden *(AW-den)* W.H. (Wystan Hugh) Auden (1907–1973), the English playwright and essayist, and one of the twentieth century's most influential poets. He was part of the circle of young British writers (including Christopher Isherwood, Stephen Spender, and Louis MacNeice) who came of literary age in the 1930s. He went to the United States in 1939 and became a citizen a few years later. In 1967, he won the National Medal for Literature.

auger *(AW-ger)* A carpenter's tool for boring holes larger than those that can be made using the smaller but similar gimlet; it consists of a drill bit with a handle, affixed crosswise, to be turned with both hands. A geologist's auger is used to bore into soil or rock for sampling purposes. The familiar kitchen meat grinder uses an augerlike screw to force the food between the cutting blade and the die, or face plate, which determines the fineness of grind.

augur *(AW-ger)* The highest ranking of ancient Rome's official diviners, whose sole function was to interpret signs and omens. The main mode of augury was the observation of the flight patterns of birds, also known as auspice. This was done from a rectangular spot called the templum, informally chosen by the augur. Generally speaking, birds crossing in front of you from left to right signify good luck. Today *augur* is used as a verb meaning "to predict."

auk *(awk)* A short, stocky seabird of the Arctic somewhat similar to the Antarctic penguin, except for the fact that it can fly. The razor-billed auk, or arrie (q.v.), nests in colonies, dives for food, and lays solitary eggs on barren coastal cliffs. The  flightless great auk, which grew to 31 inches in height, became extinct in the nineteenth century. **Auk** is also the name of an Alaskan people of Tlingit stock residing south

The now-extinct great auk. of Juneau.

aulos *(AW-loss)* A twin-reeded wind instrument of Asian origin, very popular in ancient Greece. Depicted in concert with the lyre on many amphorae, the aulos produces a haunting, high-pitched tone similar to that of a shrill oboe.

aune *(own)* An old French measure chiefly used for cloth and corresponding to the English ell (q.v.). Varying in length at different times throughout France, Belgium, and Switzerland, the aune is still used today by Swiss textile merchants and tailors, and is equivalent to about four feet.

aurum *(AW-rum)* Gold, in Latin and in chemistry (in which its symbol is Au). Aurum mosaicum is gold or bronze dust used in gilding, and aurum potabile, a cordial or medicine in days of yore, was made of a volatile oil to which tiny particles of gold were added. **Aurum** is also the name of a modern Italian gold-colored liqueur.

aute *(OW-tay)* The paper mulberry tree, or tapa-cloth tree native to New Zealand, also grown as a shade tree in Europe and America. In the Pacific Islands its inner bark is beaten to make cloth (see *tapa*).

avahi *(AH-vah-hee)* A woolly, long-tailed lemur (q.v.) of Madagascar. A nocturnal mammal, the avahi resembles a monkey, but has small pointed ears, a sharp foxlike muzzle, and soft fur.

avatar *(ah-vah-TAR)* The descent of a Hindu deity to earth and its incarnation in human or other living form. Used with reference to the god Vishnu (q.v.).

Vishnu, sculpted in the 10th century.

ave *(AH-vay)* Hail, as a salutation, from the Latin, especially as used in the Roman Catholic church in a prayer to the Virgin Mother: *Ave, Maria, gratia plena...*, which translates, "Hail, Mary, full of grace..." **Ave** also appears in crosswords as the nickname of Averill Harriman (1891–), statesman and public official; and of course, as the abbreviation for avenue.

Avila *(AH-vee-lah)* Spanish town noted for its medieval architecture, especially an eleventh-century wall. Avila was the birthplace of the great Christian mystic St. Théresa of Avila, who later lived in a convent there.

A wall surrounding Avila.

avis *(AY-viss)*   Bird, in Latin. Thus, *rara avis,* "a rare bird." In French, opinion, sentiment, or the mind itself. The phrase *a mon avis (ah-VEE),* "to my mind," is generally followed by a statement of opinion or feeling rather than fact. In the U.S., **Avis** is famous as the second-largest car rental agency, self-obliged to "try harder."

Avon *(AY-vohn)*   The name of three rivers in England. The Upper Avon, called The Shakespeare River, flows through Stratford-on-Avon and into the Severn near Tewkesbury. The Lower (or Bristol) Avon carves an arc from Tetbury to Bath and thence to Bristol and the mouth of the Severn, at Avonmouth. The Avon (or East Avon) of southern England flows south past Salisbury to the English Channel. The upper course of Australia's Swan River is also called the Avon.

The Royal Shakespeare Theatre at Stratford-on-Avon.

awa *(AH-wah)*   The Hawaiian milkfish, a large, silvery, swift-swimming, and toothless creature. **Awa** can also be kava, a shrubby species of Australasian pepper from whose root an intoxicating drink is made. See *kava.*

awabi *(ah-WAH-bee)*   A Japanese abalone. Living in a large ear-shaped shell, it clings to a rock by means of a strong, muscular "foot," which is the edible portion. The mother-of-pearl lining of the shell is used to make ornamental objects.

aweto *(ah-WAY-toe)*   A New Zealand oddity known as the vegetable caterpillar, consisting of the mummified body of a caterpillar and the fruiting body of the parasitic fungus that killed it. When burned, dried awetos make a fine black pigment.

awl *(awl)*   A fine-pointed hand tool for starting and punching holes in wood, leather, and other materials. Every shoemaker, woodworker, and saddler has one.

awn *(awn)*   A bristle in the beard on a head of wheat, barley, or oats. In crosswords, awns of grain are often clued as "arista." **Awns** are also the barbed protuberances one may see on reptilian hemipenises (of which there are two per male creature).

Awns sprouting from a head of wheat.

axis *(AX-iss)*   A white-spotted deer of India and southern Asia possessing antlers which are single-tined at the base and forked at the tip. During World War II, Germany, Italy, and Japan made up the Fascist triumvirate known as the **Axis**. An **axis** is also the imaginary spindle, terminating at each pole, around which the earth rotates.

ayah *(AH-yah)*   A nurse or maid of India, corresponding to an amah (q.v.). In India, **ayah** is also a chapter of the Koran (see *sura*).

aye-aye *(EYE-eye)*   A nocturnal lemur of Madagascar, related to the avahi (q.v.). The aye-aye has rodentlike teeth, sharp nails on its long fingers, and is named and famed for its shrill cry, which resembles a nautical affirmation.

ayin or **ain** *(AH-een)*   Name of the sixteenth letter of the Hebrew alphabet; it is often unpronounced, but sometimes is a faint, guttural sound.

aylet *(AY-let)*   A black crow of glossy plumage, with a red bill and legs. Also called the Cornish chough, it is found in mountainous regions of Europe and northern Africa but is now rare in Britain.

ayllu *(EYE-ehl-yoo)*   The basic family unit among the Inca. The ayllu consisted of an extended family, or sib (q.v.), all of whose members were related to the ayllu's leader. Today ayllus are administrative units of extended Peruvian families with common landholdings.

ayu *(AH-yoo)*   The sweetfish, a small salmonlike fish of Japan. Unlike the salmon, it lives in fresh water but goes to sea to spawn.

ayuyu *(ah-YOO-yoo)*   The purse crab of Guam, Sri Lanka, and other islands in the Pacific and Indian oceans. This large land crab, related to the hermit crab, lives in a burrow, feeds on coconuts, and can weigh up to twenty pounds.

Azam *(AH-zahm)*   A respectful Persian form of address, meaning "greater," which is used as we use "Mister" or "Sir."

azan *(ah-ZAHN)*   The Moslem call to prayer, intoned five times a day from the minaret, or tower, of a mosque. The man who does the calling is called a muezzin. In many modern Moslem countries the azan is recorded.

azoth *(AHZ-awth)*   Mercury or quicksilver, once believed to be the first principle of all metals and extractable from them. Mercury was also the universal remedy of the sixteenth-century Swiss physician Paracelsus, who advocated the use of alchemy and chemistry for curing diseases rather than producing gold.

Azov *(AH-zoff)*   The Sea of Azov, in the U.S.S.R. between the Ukraine and the Crimean peninsula, is an arm of the Black Sea, via the Kerch Strait. Shallow and only

Azov, circled, in the center of the above map.

slightly salty, it is roughly 14,500 square miles in area, or the size of Vermont and Connecticut combined. **Azov** is also a Russian port city on the Don near Rostov. See *Pruth.*

Azrael *(AZ-rah-ell)*   The angel of death, figuring originally in Judaism and borrowed by Islam; Azrael watches over the dying and separates the soul from the body.

azure *(AZH-er; AH-zhoor)*   A clear skyblue; sometimes the richer blue of the semiprecious stone lapis lazuli (see *lapis*). In heraldry, azure was represented in engraving by horizontal parallel lines. Variations of the word are found in Cote d'Azur (French) meaning "Blue Coast" and Grotto Azzurro (Italian) for "Blue Grotto," near Capri (q.v.).

azyme or **azym** *(AH-zim)*   Unleavened bread, such as the matzoh Jews eat at the feast of Passover, or the wafer consecrated by Christians and used in the sacrament of the Eucharist.

Baking azyme for a Passover feast.

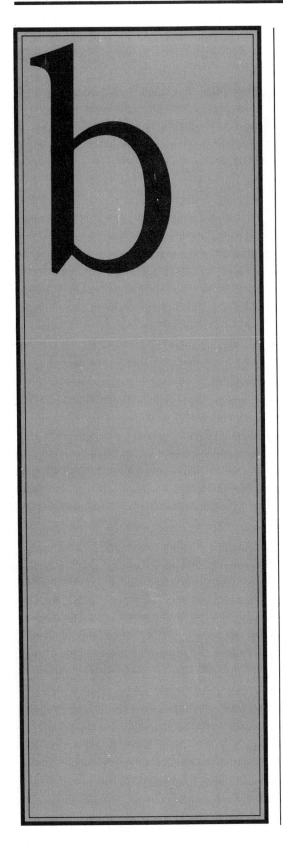

Baade *(BAH-deh)* Walter Baade (1893–1960), a German-born American astronomer who discovered the asteroid Hidalgo, but devoted most of his research at California's Mt. Wilson Observatory to extragalactic systems and cepheid variable stars, the "twinkling" stars whose regular pulsations help determine intergalactic and interstellar distances.

Baal *(BAH-ull)* The Phoenician (or Canaanite) supreme god and god of fertility, among other things, who met Mot, the god of sterility, in battle once every seven years. The outcome determined whether the next seven years would be lean or fat. There were actually numerous Semitic gods named Baal, among them Baalzebub, "lord of the flies," whose indulgence was sought with offerings of fruit and livestock. The use of this name, or Beelzebub, to mean Satan in the Old Testament, indicates the ancient Israelites' detestation of the practices associated with Baal, such as holy prostitution and child sacrifice. Baal's name had other forms (such as the Babylonian Bel) and a plural, Baalim; Baalat was Baal's feminine counterpart.

An ancient stone figure of Baal.

Bab *(bahb)* Short for Bab-ud-Din ("Gate of the Faith"), the name taken by Sayyid Ali Mohammed, who founded the Persian Muslim movement called Babism in 1844. The Babists believe in an imminent messiah. In 1848 they seceded from mainstream Islam. The ensuing revolt was stamped out and the Bab put to death by the shah, but in 1863 the remaining Babists were removed to Constantinople, and in 1868, after dissent splintered the sect, Bahaiism (see *Bahai*) took root there.

baba *(BAH-bah)*   Either a Slavic midwife or granny; or a Near Eastern title of respect bestowed on patriarchal types; or a Malaysian-born Chinese; or, in India, a baby. When preceding "au rhum," **baba** is a sweet, rum-soaked cake for dessert.

Two babas in attendance.

Baboo or **Babu** *(BAH-boo)*   "Mister," in Hindi. This form of address also refers, usually in a cutting way, to native Indians who have been well schooled in the ways and language of the English in order to become clerks in the colonial bureaucracy.

badam *(bah-DAHM)*   The so-called bitter almond of Persia, used as legal tender in parts of India. It is called Indian almond and is exported also as a substitute for tragacanth, which is widely used in medicine and in the patterning of woven goods.

Badb *(bahv; bahb)* or **Bodb** *(bohv)*   The legendary Irish goddess of carnage, in the form of a demonic crow that fed upon human carrion.

Baer *(behr)*   Maximillian Adelbert "Max" Baer (1909–1959), a boxer from Omaha, Nebraska, who attained the world heavyweight title in 1934 by defeating Primo Carnera, "The Ambling Alp." He lost the title to John J. Braddock the following year.

Max Baer, 1934.

baff *(baf)*   A golf stroke named for the slightly awesome sound it makes as the club strikes the earth and sends the ball aloft. This shot is often used to gain distance or to overcome obstacles such as sand pits or groves of trees.

baft *(baft)*   A coarse woven cloth, usually of cotton, made in India and used for rugs and handbags. A less dense, machine-woven imitation of baft is made for export.

bago *(bah-GOE)*   An Asiatic evergreen whose seeds and young leaves are edible, and whose bark yields a fine fiber (see *bast*) used in making rope and mats.

bagre *(bah-GREH)*   Either of two large catfish of the Nile River; or the gaff-topsail catfish of the Atlantic and Gulf coastal waters of North America, so named (in both regions) because of its enormous dorsal fin.

bagwyn *(BAG-win)*   A mythical heraldic beast resembling an antelope, but with goat's horns and the tail of a horse. It appears on shields and medieval armor.

Bahai *(bah-HAH-ee)* or **Bahaist** *(bah-HAH-ee-ist)*   An adherent to a religion that sprang in the late nineteenth century from Babism (see *Bab*). Bahaism advocates the spiritual unity of mankind, universal peace, and the practice of a strikingly ethical and tolerant mysticism. Founded by Baha Ullah, the faith was promulgated by his son, Sir Abdul Baha Bahai.

bahan *(bah-HAHN)*   A poplar tree native to Asia Minor, believed to be the Babylonian willow mentioned in Psalm 137: "By

Bahans bear the instruments of grieving Jews.

the waters of Babylon, there we sat down and wept, when we remembered Zion./On the willows there, we hung up our lyres.''

bahar *(bah-HAHR)* A variable East Indian unit of weight used to measure such goods as sugar and iron. One bahar is roughly equivalent to 20 maunds, or 500 pounds, in Ceylon and Rangoon, but closer to 560 pounds in Bombay and Madras.

Bahia *(bah-EE-uh)* An eastern Brazilian state whose capital is the seaport of Salvador, also called Bahia. A lush agricultural area that exports minerals, cacao, sugar, oil, lumber, and tobacco, Bahia is the setting for Jorge Amado's novel *Doña Flor* and the movie *Doña Flor and Her Two Husbands*, based on the book, filmed there in 1976.

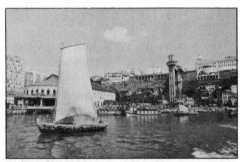

Bahia's capital, Salvador.

bahr *(BAH-hur)* A sea, lake, or large river in Arabic place names, such as Bahr el-Azrak, the Blue Nile. Egyptians call the whole of the Nile River simply El Bahr.

baht or **bhat** *(baht)* A silver coin of Thailand and its chief monetary unit, roughly equivalent to five cents. It is also called the tical (q.v.) or tikal, a word which originally denoted the worth of a coin in weight.

bahur *(BOO-khur)* In Hebrew, a young, unmarried Talmudic scholar or Yeshiva (religious school) student. Once clued: ''A real catch, as a yenta might put it.'' The Yiddish version of bahur is *bocher;* a common descriptive term is ''yeshiva bocher.''

Baiae *(BAY-ee)* or **Baia** *(BAY-ah)* Ancient city on the Bay of Naples in Italy, now called only Baia. Thermal springs and a pleasant climate made Baiae a popular spa in Roman antiquity. Both Julius Caesar and Nero (q.v.) built summer villas there. An outbreak of malaria in the Middle Ages caused its abandonment as a resort. Ruins of ancient baths remain in the present-day village.

Baja *(BAH-hah)* for Baja California, ''Lower California.'' A peninsula extending almost 800 miles south between the Pacific and the Gulf of California in extreme northwestern Mexico; it is divided into the Mexican States of Baja California and Baja California Sur. It was once an unspoiled area, but the recent upgrading of a highway running the full length of the rugged peninsula has brought Baja tourists, pollution, and the highest standard of living between the Paseo de la Reforma and San Diego. The waters of the Gulf (the ''Sea of Cortez'') are famous for sport fishing, and gray whales annually come here to calve.

Bajau *(bah-JOO)* A population of Bornean sailors who at one time were rather well known locally as pirates and gypsies; now, a general term for natives of Borneo.

Baker *(BA-ker)* Josephine Baker (1906–1975), a cabaret singer and dancer born in St. Louis, who came to fame in Paris as a music-hall entertainer. Known as the ''Dark Star'' of the Folies-Bergère, Miss Baker made quite a sensation with her costume: a G-string adorned with

Josephine Baker in 1936.

bananas. Sherlock Holmes lived on **Baker** Street at No. 221 B; **baker** is also the middle man of the nursery rhyme discussing "butcher, _____ , candlestick maker."

Baku *(bah-KOO)* Soviet capital city of the Azerbaijan Republic and an important oil-shipping port on Baku Bay of the Caspian Sea. A trade and craft center in earlier times, Baku houses many medieval mosques and fortresses, but it is best known today as the site of the Soviet Academy of Sciences and of numerous oil refineries. Interestingly, as early as the sixth century B.C., constantly burning fires fed by oil and gas emerging from the ground here were shrines for worship. **Baku** *(BAH-koo)* is also a lightweight fiber (buri straw) obtained from the buri palm, or a hat made of it. It is also the name of a tropical African tree valuable for its hardwood timber, and a fine Caucasian rug distinguished by its angular designs, which often depict animals fighting.

A medieval mosque (left) on Neftyaniki Avenue in Baku.

balao *(bah-LAU)* A Philippine timber tree; or, a fish of the halfbeak variety, small but elongated, with a "beak" consisting of a very lengthy lower and a very short upper jaw. The balao prefers to swim in warmer waters, and it is capable, like the flying fish, of traveling through the air as well.

balboa *(bal-BOH-ah)* The silver Panamanian coin and monetary unit, equal to the American dollar. Panamanian and American coinage is interchangeable locally; U.S. paper dollars are also called balboas. The city of **Balboa** is the port for Panama City and is the largest town in the Canal Zone. Both

Balboas may have been named for Spanish conquistador Vasco Nuñez de **Balboa** (c. 1475–1519), who overthrew Martín Fernández de Enciso on a journey to Panama, befriended the Indians there, and crossed the isthmus to discover the Pacific Ocean.

Balder or **Baldr** *(BALL-der)* The Norse god of light, peace, eloquence, and goodness, and the son of Frigg and Odin (q.v.). He was murdered by the wily Loki (q.v.) and the blind Hodur, who slipped him a mistletoe dart. His mother had made all things in nature promise not to harm him, but had neglected the mistletoe, making it the one substance harmful to him.

Bali *(BAH-lee)* A demon of Hindu mythology who encountered the god Vishnu (q.v.) in his dwarf avatar (q.v.) and foolishly promised him as much land as he could cover in three steps. Vishnu's three steps covered earth, air, and heaven. **Bali** is also an island province of Indonesia, just east of Java, between the Indian Ocean and the Java Sea. Noted for its natural beauty and Hindu culture, it is a popular and exotic tourist resort.

baloo, balu, or **bhalu** *(BAH-loo; bah-LOO)* The sloth bear of India and Sri Lanka. The baloo has long black hair, very large claws, a brownish muzzle, and a white, V-shaped insignia on its breast. It differs from other bears in having small and few teeth but has a very agile tongue and lips with which it feeds on insects, fruit, and honey. (See also *sloth*.) **Baloo** the bear is a character in Kipling's *Jungle Book*.

A strolling baloo.

Balor *(BAH-lor)* A giant and king of the Fomorians (or Fomors), a legendary Celtic race of pirate-gods who ruled Ireland from the sea. Balor possessed an evil eye that blighted all upon whom it gazed.

balu *(BAH-loo)* The striped wildcat of Sumatra, a short-tailed, vicious creature inhabiting the tropical rain forest and preying on rodents and other small mammals.

Bana *(BAH-nah)* A thousand-armed giant of Hindu myth, whose daughter Usha fell in love with and magically enchanted Krishna's grandson Aniruddha. When Krishna learned of this, he conquered Bana and thus freed his grandson from Usha and her charms.

Banda *(BAN-dah)* A sea of the Pacific Ocean in the Indonesian region, southeast of Borneo and west of New Guinea; 600 miles long and 300 miles wide. Buru and Ceram islands are to the north, Kai and Aru to the east, the Tanimbar and Timor to the south, and Celebes to the northwest. The ten volcanic Banda Islands, south of Ceram, export nutmeg and mace. Also Dr. Hastings Kamuzu **Banda,** who became the first president of Malawi in 1966 and has since been made president for life.

banga *(BANG-ah)* In the Philippines, a large, round ceramic water jug. In Australia, a squashlike vegetable whose seeds are baked and eaten.

Banks *(banks)* Ernie "The Cub" Banks had a superb 19-year career with the Chicago Cubs, playing shortstop for the first nine (1953–1961), and first baseman the next ten. He was elected to the Baseball Hall of Fame in 1977.

Cub shortstop Ernie Banks.

Bantu *(BAN-too)* A member of the great ethnic and linguistic family of tribes living south of the Congo in equatorial and southern Africa. Classified as Bantu by their languages rather than physical types, they include speakers of about 100 tongues, including Zulu, Swahili, Xhosa, Ganda, Kongo, and Kikuyu. The term Bantu is used indiscriminately in South Africa to refer to the native population under apartheid.

baobab *(BAY-oh-bab)* A tropical tree native to Africa, Madagascar, and northern Australia. Its stout bottle-shaped trunk often attains a diameter of 30 feet, and its gourdlike fruit, called monkey bread, contains a tart, edible pulp from which a beverage is made. The leaves and bark of the baobab are used medicinally; its bark is also used in the manufacture of paper and cloth.

Bara See *vamp.*

Bari *(BAH-ree)* A southern Italian port on the Adriatic, capital of the Apulia region. Bari was an ancient colony of Greece, then of Rome, and was later ruled by Goths, Saracens, Byzantines, Normans, and Germans. Its archaeological museum and a Norman castle house relics of its past.

The Norman Castel del Monte in Bari.

barm *(barm)* The yeast formed during fermentation of alcoholic beverages, such as beer, evident as a white foam.

Barre *(BAR-ee)* A central Vermont city, just south of the capital, Montpelier. Settled in 1788, Barre is well endowed with ski slopes and granite quarries; its most distinguished longtime guest was the Scottish poet Robert Burns, whose statue stands in the town square. Also, a handrail *(bahr)* along the wall in a dance studio used to maintain balance while doing ballet exercises.

Dancers warming up at the barre in a scene from the 1948 film The Red Shoes.

Barth *(barth)* John Barth (1930–   ), an American author whose difficult but highly imaginative works include *The End of the Road* (1958) and *The Sot-Weed Factor* (1967), both novels; *Chimera* (1972), a trilogy of novellas for which he won the National Book Award in fiction; and *Letters* (1979), an epistolary novel. Also, Karl Barth (1886–1968), the Swiss theologian and leader of twentieth-century Protestantism, whose philosophy emphasized the revelation of God through Jesus Christ. Barth's system of thought, known as "theology of the word," is put forth in his four-volume *Church Dogmatics,* which took him 30 years (1932–1962) to complete.

John Barth.

barwal *(bar-WALL)* The unicorn sheep of northern India, whose backward-sweeping horns are seared with a hot iron as soon as they begin to grow in, causing them to grow closely together. This modification makes barwals good fighters.

Bashon See *Pasha.*

Basra *(BAHSS-ruh)* Iraq's only port, on the Shatt al-Arab, some 75 miles from its mouth on the Persian Gulf. Second in importance only to Baghdad during the early Middle Ages, Basra was destroyed by Mongols in the thirteenth century and was not fully rebuilt until after World War I. It figured prominently in the recent Iran-Iraq war. Its main exports now are oil from its important refineries, grain, and dates.

Bast *(bast)* Egyptian goddess whose center of worship was Bubastis; represented either as a lion- or cat-headed woman. When cat-headed her name is Pasht and she is the goddess of fertility. As lion-headed Bast, she personifies the life-giving sun. On a more mundane level, **bast** is a type of fiber obtained from the inner bark layer of the linden and other trees, and is used in the making of rope, cord, matting, and fabric.

Bast.

Batum *(bah-TOOM)* A Soviet port and industrial city on the Black Sea near Turkey. Anciently the Greek colony of Batis, Batum is today a terminal of the Soviet oil pipeline, and a major naval base.

Baugh *(baw)* Samuel Adrian "Slinging Sammy" Baugh (1914–   ), an American football player born in Temple, Texas. Known for his passing and punting, he was an All-American at Texas Christian University; then, as quarterback, he led the Washington Redskins to two NFL championships (1937, 1942), and then coached the New York Titans and the Houston Oilers. He is a charter member of the National Professional Football Hall of Fame.

bavin *(BAV-in)* A bundle of light wood or brush used for kindling, in low fencing, and in primitive drainage systems.

A youth gathers up a bavin in an engraving by Gustave Doré.

baya *(BAY-ah)* The finchlike Indian weaverbird, often kept as a pet in a cage. Those that are at liberty construct elaborate nests of grass which are entered from the side or bottom and often house numerous winged couples.

Bean *(been)* Roy Bean (1825–1903), a frontier judge of the American West, who after a checkered career on both sides of the border had himself appointed Justice of the Peace in Langtry, a Texas railroad camp he renamed and there conducted trials from his saloon, the Jersey Lily, with the aid of his six-guns. Bean dubbed himself "The Law West of the Pecos" (see *Pecos*).

Judge Bean.

Bearn *(bey-AHRN)* A region of southwestern France in the Pyrenees and bordering on Spain. Once a part of Roman Aquitania, Béarn became a county of Gascony in the ninth century, later passed to other rulers, and was not united with France until 1620. A rugged area, its main industries are cattlebreeding and winter sports, and its capital is Pau. Béarnaise sauce, a tarragon-flavored emulsion similar to Hollandaise, takes its name from Béarn.

Beck *(bek)* Jozef Beck (1894–1944) was a Polish statesman and active anti-Hitlerite who drafted and cosigned the treaty bringing Britain into World War II. Martin Beck (1868–1940) was an American theatrical producer, the inventor of the booking system that kept the vaudeville circuit in motion, and the builder of several "legitimate" theaters, including the one that bears his name on West 45th Street in New York. Dave Beck (1894–   ) was a president (1952–1957) of the American Teamsters' Union, succeeded by James R. Hoffa in 1957.

Jozef Beck, 1936.

Bede *(beed; BEE-duh)*   A British monk and scholar who lived from A.D. 673 to 735. The Venerable Bede, as he is known, spent much of his life in the Benedictine monastery of Jarrow, near Newcastle-upon-Tyne. A prolific writer in the fields of science, grammar, history, and theology, he is best known for his *Ecclesiastical History of the English Nation*, which encompasses the period from Caesar's conquest to A.D. 731. Bede was officially recognized as a saint in 1899. *Adam Bede*, a novel by George Eliot, published in 1859, is often used for Bede in crosswords, e.g., "George Eliot's Adam."

begum *(BEE-gum)*   In India, a Muslim woman of royal or high rank, and in England, a title applied to heiresses of Anglo-Indian stock.

beisa *(BAY-sah)*   The East African oryx (q.v.), an antelope whose long, cone-shaped horns grow straight back on a plane with the forehead. Usually tan to brown with black markings and weighing up to 450 pounds or more, they live in large herds and have been known to kill lions.

Beja *(BEY-jah)*   A peaceful tribe of eastern Hamitic nomads who roam the regions between the Nile and the Red Sea. They are related to many other groups, including the Somali and Egyptians.

bema *(BEE-mah)*   A platform for public speaking in ancient Greece and particularly the stone-cut platform of the Pnyx in Athens. In later usage it came to signify the portion of a temple or church containing the altar.

Oration from a bema.

bena *(BEN-ah)*   A tall East Indian grass, also called veviter or khus-khus, cultivated in the tropics and now in Louisiana as well. Its fragrant roots are used for making mats and screens, and its essential oil in perfumery. **Bena** are also a Bantu (q.v.) people living north of Lake Nyasa in Africa.

bene *(BEN-eh)*   The wild hog of New Guinea, resembling the European wild boar; also, the adverb and interjection "well" in Italian, and in Latin before that. The Italian and New Guinean usages are unrelated. More often in crosswords: "nota _____." **Bene** is also a prefix meaning "well" or "good," in such words as benefactor, benefit, and benediction. As such it is the opposite of *mal* (evil).

Benes *(BEH-nesh)*   Eduard Beneš (1884–1948), a twentieth-century George Washington who was the first prime minister of modern Czechoslovakia and twice its president. Elected in 1935, Beneš resigned in 1938 in protest to Hitler's occupation of the Sudetenland; reelected in 1946, he resigned again in 1948 after the Communist takeover.

Beni *(BEH-nee)*   A river rising in central Bolivia that flows over 1,000 miles north to unite with the Mamore and form Brazil's Madeira River.

Benin *(beh-NEEN)*   An ancient kingdom of West Africa, now a part of Nigeria, which was a great center of African civilization and Portuguese slave trade from 1400 to 1897. Modern Benin, situated between Togo and Nigeria on the Bight of Benin (part of the Gulf of Guinea), is an independent nation, formerly Dahomey, whose 3.5 million people earn an average annual income of $122 per capita (1980 estimate), and whose major exports are peanuts, cotton, and palm oil.

benne *(BEH-nee)* The sesame, an East Indian herb, whose flavorful seeds yield an oil used widely in Oriental cuisines. Sesame (or benne) seeds are also used in cooking, baking, and confectionery.

The benne herb, with its seed and flower shown at right.

benu *(BEN-oo)* A heronlike bird sacred to Osiris, Egyptian god of the underworld. Benu was deified and worshiped as an aspect of Osiris and is the prototype of the Greek phoenix.

ber *(ber)* The jujube, a dark red, fleshy fruit of trees of the Ziziphus genus, native to the Old World and America. The jujube is often called the Chinese date because of the shape of the fruit and its sweet, crisp flesh. Perhaps more familiarly, a jujube can be a fruit-flavored candy lozenge.

Bern See *Aar.*

Bes *(bes)* Ancient Egyptian god of pleasure and sanctuary, represented as a bearded dwarf bearing a sword and shield, and clad in a panther skin.

beta *(BEY-tah)* The second letter of the Greek alphabet, corresponding to our *B* and similar to it in orthography. It is used to connote second in position or value: in astronomy, beta denotes the second brightest star in a constellation; and in psychology it designates the secondary, intellectually passive "wave" that brains produce (beta waves). Closer to the ground, **Beta** is a small genus of Old World herbs of the goosefoot family, grown for their fleshy edible roots and/or foliage; the most famous members include the common beet, the sugar beet, and Swiss chard.

betel *(BEE-tul)* An Asiatic palm, the areca (q.v.), whose nutlike seeds, called betel or areca nuts, wrapped with lime paste in a betel leaf, are a popular stimulating East Indian masticatory or "chewing gum." Also, the betel pepper, a climbing plant yielding the betel leaf.

Beti *(BEH-tee)* Monto Beti (1932–   ), the pen name of African novelist Alexandre Biyidi, a native of Cameroon who writes satirically on modern African life and the effects of colonialism on black Africans. His works include *The Poor Christ of Bomba, Mission to Kala,* and *King Lazarus.*

Bevan *(BEH-van)* Aneurin Bevan (1897–1960), British Labour Party leader and editor of the *Tribune.* As minister of health following World War II, he established the National Health Service, through which the British government today absorbs much of the cost of health care in the United Kingdom.

Aneurin Bevan.

Beyle *(behl)* Marie Henri Beyle (1783–1842), who, after spending much of his youth with Napoleon's armies in Italy and Russia, returned in 1814 to Milan to write, under the pseudonym

Stendahl, on subjects ranging from aesthetics to autobiography, and in moods ranging from romanticism to the affecting realism of his best-known novels: *The Red and the Black* (1831) and *The Charterhouse of Parma* (1839).

M. H. Beyle, a.k.a. Stendhal.

bezel *(BEZ-ul)* In jewelry, either the upper facets sloping down from the table (or top) of a cut gem, or that part of the gem's setting from which the stone protrudes.

bhang or **bang** *(bang)* Cannabis, the Indian hemp plant, whose dun-colored dried leaves contain a narcotic that can be chewed, smoked, or infused in water; marijuana, to many. Bhang is also the source of hashish and an ingredient of the more intoxicating majoon, a hashish-like mixture that includes henbane, poppy and datura seeds, honey, and ghee (q.v.).

Bibi *(BEE-bee)* An Indian title of respect usually applied to European women, but at times to Hindu ladies as well. Also **Bibi** Andersson, the Swedish actress who has appeared in many popular Ingmar Bergman films such as *Wild Strawberries, The Seventh Seal,* and *Smiles of a Summer Night.*

bice *(bice)* A color, specifically that of the copper ores azurite (bice blue) and malachite (bice green).

bidar *(BIE-dar)* A large, skin-covered canoe made and used by the Aleuts (q.v.).

biga *(BEE-gah)* In ancient Rome and Greece, a chariot pulled by a pair of horses, similar to the one driven by Charlton Heston in the movie *Ben-Hur.* **Biga** is also used when referring to Aqueduct Race Track (New York), but is pronounced *big-AY* and is two words in that context.

bija *(BEE-jah)* The East Indian kino tree (see *kino*). Its sap, a tanning agent, also finds use as an astringent and hemostatic (blood clotter).

bikh *(bik)* A deadly poison extracted from certain plants of the Monkshood genus, innocent-looking and even ornamental members, often with purple, hood-like flowers, of the buttercup family. (Monkshoods are also called aconite and wolfsbane and have medical uses.)

bilbi or **bilby** *(BIL-bee)* The rat kangaroo of Australia, a burrower in the night. Also, the name for another marsupial, the rabbit bandicoot.

bilbo *(BIL-boh)* An old and finely tempered sword named after Bilbao, the Spanish city made famous in song by Bertolt Brecht and Kurt Weill. Theodore Gilmore **Bilbo** (1877–1947), a well-known white supremacist politician, twice governor of Mississippi and U.S. senator for 12 years, is no relation. A **bilbo** is also a bar of iron with sliding shackles, used to confine prisoners' feet. Also, the hobbit **Bilbo** Baggins, a main character in J.R.R. Tolkien's fantasy trilogy *Lord of the Rings*.

Bilin *(bih-LEEN)* The language of the Bogos, a peaceful Muslim tribe of the Ethiopian highlands west of the Red Sea.

bine *(bine)* Short for woodbine, the common honeysuckle, a fragrant, flowering vine usually found entwined about trees. Similarly, the twining system of the hop or any like vine.

Binet *(bee-NEY)*

The earliest viable intelligence test for children and adolescents, the Binet (or Binet-Simon) test was named after two French psychologists of the early twentieth century. *Alfred Binet.*

Bioko See *Muni.*

birn *(bern)* The socket in clarinets and similar woodwinds (from the German word for it) into which the mouthpiece fits; also the heather stubble on Scotch or Irish moors that have been scarred by fire.

bise *(beez)* A cold northerly wind which blows across parts of western Europe, and generally any dry, icy wind.

bixa *(BIK-sah)* The annatto tree, bearing attractive flowers and seeds, and yielding a tasteless red-yellow dye used in many foods. Also known as the orellin tree (be-

cause it flourishes on the Amazon, the river first explored by Francisco de Orellana) and achiote.

Black *(blak)* The Black Sea, an inland body of water of tremendous strategic importance, lies between Europe and Asia; it is connected to the Sea of Marmara by the Bosporus, and thence to the Aegean by the Dardanelles. Framed by Turkey, Bulgaria, Romania, and the Soviet Union, it is ice-free and has major fisheries. The Black Sea is the Soviet Union's only access to other warm seas. Its main tributaries are the Dneiper and the Danube; a major port is Odessa, a crossword repeater often defined as "Black Sea port."

blair *(blare)* A Scottish marsh or battleground. This word is used in many place names in conjunction with descriptive modifiers, e.g., Blair Atholl, in Perthshire.

Blanda *(BLAN-dah)* George F. Blanda (1927–   ), the "ageless wonder" of football, who began his professional career at the age of 22 and remained active into his fifties. He scored a record 2,002 lifetime points as a quarterback and kicker and held a number of other records in the NFL, including the one for career longevity.

The ageless George Blanda.

blay *(bley)* The bleak, a small European fish with silvery scales that are used in the manufacture of pearl essence (for fake pearls and lacquers). **Blay** is also the Irish word for unbleached linen.

bleo *(BLEY-oh)* An American cactus which makes for good hedges and bears an edible fruit also called bleo.

blite *(blite)* The common name of certain edible potherbs, including the sea blite, the strawberry blite, and Good-King-Henry, often called goosefoot blite or fathen. Do not confuse with the homonym blight, whose meaning is quite different.

Good-King-Henry.

Blois *(blwah)* A central French town, in the Loire valley southwest of Orléans. In the tenth century, the counts of Blois began

the rise that made them the most powerful lords in feudal France, and the town was a favorite royal residence after the fifteenth century. Chateaux still remain, as well as the rich soil and vineyards supporting a large trade in wine and brandy.

The chateau at Blois.

bluet *(BLOO-eht)* Bluets include the perennial farkleberry, related to blueberries, and species of Houstonia (after William Houston, the eighteenth-century Scottish botanist), beloved for their small blue flowers, and often called innocence and Quaker-ladies.

bo *(boh)* A Japanese Buddhist monk; a Burmese military rank equal to captain; slang for hobo; and the tree under which the Buddha received enlightenment (see *Bodhi*).

A lacquered wood bo, from the Muromachi Period (A.D. 1392–1573).

boa *(BOW-uh)* General name for a large family of nonpoisonous snakes which strike with their teeth, quickly coil about their victims, and squeeze them to death. The largest snake in the world, the anaconda of South America, is a boa, and may reach a length of 25 feet. Because it wraps snakelike around the neck, the long feathery scarf worn by women is known as a **boa**.

Boann *(BOH-ann)* The mother of Aengus, Irish god of love, youth, and beauty. The Boyne (q.v.) River takes its name from Boann.

Boas *(BOH-ass)* Franz Boas (1858–1942), was an American anthropologist noted for his study of the languages and cultures of American Indians. His works, on that subject and others, include: *Primitive Art* (1927), *The Mind of Primitive Man* (1911; rev. ed. 1938), and a posthumous collection of essays, *Race and Democratic Society* (1945).

Franz Boas.

bobac *(BOH-bak)* Eastern European and Asian marmot, in a family whose members include the groundhog or woodchuck, the chipmunk, and the prairie dog. Burrowers all, they hibernate in winter.

A bright-eyed bobac.

bobo *(BOH-boh)* The Central American mullet, a river fish; or the owala of tropical Africa, a tree related to the mimosas whose seed oil is used as a lubricant. More often, **Bobo** in crosswords is clued as "a popular name for a clown"; or it may refer to boxer Olson or a Rockefeller spouse.

boce *(bohss)* A European fish (*Box vulgaris*) notable for its gaudy coloring, and a cousin of the American grunt and porgy.

Boche *(bohsh)* A disparaging World War I nickname for the Germans, from the French *caboche,* colloquially meaning "thick-headed" or "square-headed," which comes from the same root word as "cabbage."

Bock *(bahk)* Hieronymus Bock (1480–1554), a founder of modern botany, who devised a system of plant classification based on physical characteristics. His pioneering work on German plants, *Neu Kreutterbuch,* served to assist modern botanists, including Linnaeus, who is generally credited as the father of classification. **Bock** is also a leather made from sheepskin, used in bookbinding; and a variety of dark beer usually brewed in the spring.

Bodhi *(BOH-dee; BOHD-hee)* The Great Enlightenment which Gautama, the Buddha, is said to have received under the sacred bo (q.v.), or pipal, tree at Buddh Gaya in Bihar, India, and available to any Buddhist who has practiced the Eightfold Path. There is alive today in Anuradhapura, Sri Lanka, a bo tree planted from a cutting of the original tree, which became the sacred Bodhi Tree (Tree of Enlightenment).

Buddha beneath the bo tree.

Bod-Pa *(BOHD-pah)* The Tibetan (native Lhasan) name for the true indigenous Tibetans inhabiting what is now south-central Tibet.

boga *(BOH-gah)* A fish swimming in West Indian waters, very like the North American bass.

bohea *(boh-HEE)* The best Chinese black tea was once called bohea, after the Wu-i or Bu-i hills where it was grown; bohea now denotes tea of inferior quality.

bohor *(BOH-hor)* A reedbuck, a small brown antelope of Africa. The bohor is cousin to the reitbok and the nahor. Only the male is horned.

Bohr *(bohr)* Niels Bohr (1885–1962), Danish physicist renowned for his discoveries in quantum theory and the structure of the atom. Bohr was awarded a Nobel Prize in 1922 for his work on atomic structure, and he later helped develop the first American atom bomb. He spent his later years in Copenhagen, campaigning for international peace. Both his names are crossword repeaters, Bohr being one of the rare words with an *–hr* combination (Bert Lahr is another), and Niels being a rare word in English with an *–iels* combination.

Niels Bohr, 1945.

Boii *(BOY-ee; BOH-ee-ee)* A tribe of Celts, who eventually settled in northern Italy and along the Danube in present-day Bohemia, which takes its name from them.

Born *(bawrn)* Max Born (1882–1970), a British physicist who was born in Breslau, Germany, but who left the country in 1933 first for Cambridge, then the University of Edinburgh, where he continued his studies in quantum mechanics. He shared a 1954 Nobel Prize in physics for his research.

Bose *(bohz)* Sir Jagadis Chandra Bose (1858–1937), an Indian physicist and plant physiologist who developed a highly sensitive recorder to detect and demonstrate "feeling" in plants, by monitoring their movements and responses to external stimuli. He founded the Bose Research Institute in Calcutta. Subhas Chandra Bose (1897–1945), an Indian nationalist, advocated militancy to obtain independence and collaborated with the Axis powers during World War II.

Bowie *(BOO-ee)*   Surname of James Bowie (c. 1796–1836), Kentucky-born frontiersman and hero who died in defense of the Alamo. He is usually given credit for having invented the long, single-edged bowie knife. The name has also been made famous by David Bowie (BOW-ee), an English rock music star, who has two notable dramatic performances to his credit as well: as the mysterious alien in the film *The Man Who Fell to Earth,* and as the deformed protagonist in the Broadway play *The Elephant Man.*

Boyne *(boin)*   Irish river rising in the Bog of Allen in County Kildare and flowing 70 miles northeast through County Meath to the Irish Sea; its banks were the site of the Battle of the Boyne (1690), the first major engagement in the 300-year conflict between Catholics and Protestants still being fought today in Northern Ireland.

The Boyne River flowing past Slane Castle in County Meath.

Bragg *(brag)*   Braxton Bragg (1817–1876), a Confederate general and commander of the Army of Tennessee. After he was forced to retreat in 1863 he served as adviser to Confederate President Jefferson Davis for the remainder of the Civil War. Fort Bragg, North Carolina, is named for him. Also, Sir William Henry Bragg (1862–1942) and Sir William Lawrence

SETTLING THE SCORE

FIGHTING WORDS

flail	*flout*	*fusee*
flak	*foray*	*fuze*
flare	*fray*	
flite	*fret*	

THE ARSENAL

aries	*fleam*	*Minie*
bilbo	*foil*	*pome*
bowie	*fusil*	*quirt*
Colt	*gat*	*riata*
cosh	*jerid*	*Sten*
dirk	*kris*	*ulu*
epee	*lasso*	

WHEN ALL ELSE FAILS . . .

atis	*ombu*	*tabun*
bikh	*ricin*	*toxin*
curare	*sumac*	*upas*
ipecac		

Bragg (1890–1971), a father-and-son team of British physicists, pioneers in the field of X-rays, who were jointly awarded a Nobel Prize in 1915.

Braxton Bragg.

Brahe *(bra; BRA-eh)* Tycho Brahe (1546–1601), a Danish astronomer who studied law in Copenhagen and Leipzig, but returned to his observatory on the island of Ven to become the most accurate astronomer of his time. He discovered a nova (since named for him) in 1572, and laid much of the groundwork for the great discoveries that were made with the aid of a telescope in the seventeenth century. A crossword repeater because of his unusual first-and-last-name letter combinations.

Brant *(brant)* Joseph Brant (1742–1807), a Mohawk Indian chief who became an Anglican convert and missionary. Brant served as a British army captain during the American Revolution, and after the war he retired to Ontario, where he had obtained

"Renaissance" man Joseph Brant.

land for his tribe. There he translated the Anglican Book of Common Prayer, and the Gospel of Mark into Mohawk. His Indian name was Thayendanegea. A **brant** is also a name given to a number of birds, especially geese and shorebirds.

Brest *(brest)* French seaport on the Atlantic coast with an unusually deep natural harbor; during World War II, Germans maintained a huge submarine base there. Today Brest is the home port of much of the French navy. **Brest** is also a

The French seaport of Brest.

Soviet city and river port, formerly Brest-Litovsk, situated at the confluence of the Western Bug and Mukhavets rivers; variously controlled through the ages by East Slavs, Mongols, Lithuanians, Swedes, Russians, and Poles, until 1939, when Brest was repatriated to the U.S.S.R. along with all of Latvia, Lithuania, Estonia, etc. The Treaty of Brest-Litovsk was signed here in 1918.

Briand *(bree-AHN)* Aristide Briand (1862–1932), a French statesman who helped draft the law separating church and state in France. A pacifist and advocate of international cooperation, he shared the Nobel Peace Prize in 1926, and later drafted the controversial Kellogg-Briand Pact (1928), a U.S.-French agreement renouncing war as a solution to disputes.

Brice *(brice)* Fanny Brice (1891–1951), an American singer and comedienne who began her career in Florenz Ziegfeld's *Follies* and gained fame with her radio character, the spoiled brat Baby Snooks. The 1964 musical *Funny Girl* was based on her life and career.

Fanny Brice.

Brie *(bree)* Historical region of northern France, watered by the Marne River, which is renowned for its vineyards and the mild, white-rinded cheese that bears its name.

Brno *(BEHR-no)* or **Brunn** *(broon)*
Industrial city in central Czechoslovakia, southeast of Prague; site of a thirteenth-century castle and the Gothic cathedral of St. Paul, and setting for an annual international trade fair.

Gothic cathedral of St. Paul, Brno.

Broun *(broon)*   Matthew Heywood Campbell Broun (1888–1939), a Brooklyn-born American journalist and critic who wrote the syndicated column "It Seems to Me" during the 1920s and '30s; he also helped to found the American Newspaper Guild, the first successful union for editorial workers, and served as its president. His son, Heywood Hale Broun, also became a writer.

Bruce *(broose)*   Blanche Kelso Bruce (1841–1898), a Mississippi native who was the first black senator to serve a full term. He championed the rights of blacks, American Indians, and Asians in this country, and held posts in the Treasury. Bruce was also the name of a Scottish royal family founded  by a Norman duke after the conquest; it included most famously the Bruce who ruled Scotland as Robert I. Many Bruces are entertainers: Virginia and Nigel in motion pictures, singer Carol, and the late Lenny, *Senator Blanche K. Bruce.* noted comedian.

Buber *(BOO-buhr)*   Martin Buber (1878–1965), Jewish philosopher, theologian, and Zionist, and editor of *Die Welt* and *Der Jude,* two Zionist intellectual journals. Buber settled in Palestine in 1938, where he taught at Hebrew University and wrote *I and Thou* (1923), which elaborates his conception of the man-God relationship, among many other important books.

Bug *(boog)*   Two unconnected rivers in Eastern Europe, each about 500 miles long. The Southern Bug rises in the Ukraine, flows southeast to the Black Sea (see *Black*), and is navigable for about 100 miles above its mouth. The Western Bug also rises in the Ukraine, but flows northwest to the vicinity of Brest (q.v.), forming part of the Soviet-Polish border, and thence toward Warsaw, where it joins the Vistula en route to the Baltic Sea.

Bunin *(BOO-nyen)*   Ivan Alekseyevich Bunin (1870–1953), a Russian writer who migrated to France after the 1917 revolution. His works, influenced by Turgenev, lament the loss of Russia's past grandeur; they include a novel, *The Village* (1910); a noted short story, "The Gentlemen from San Francisco"; and the autobiographical novel *The Well of Days* (1930). Bunin won a Nobel Prize for literature in 1933.

Butte *(byoot)*   Southwestern Montana city, named for the **butte,** or table-like plateau, on which it is situated, in the northern Rockies. Headquarters of Deer Lodge National Forest, the Montana College of Mineral Science and Technology, and the Anaconda Company, Butte thrives on silver, copper, and magnesium mining.

Buttes, land forms for which the city was named.

cabal *(kah-BAL)* A cabal, from the Hebrew meaning "mysterious doctrine," is a small circle of individuals involved in intrigue. One such cabal was made up of advisers to Charles II whose initials coincidentally form the word cabal: Clifford, Ashley, Buckingham, Arlington, and Lauderdale. During the American Revolution, the so-called Conway Cabal was believed to have been organized to unseat Washington in favor of General Horatio Gates.

caber *(KAY-buhr)* A heavy pole, usually a young tree trunk, used for throwing in Gaelic games as a test of muscular strength. The pole is grasped at the base, held upright, and flipped upward and forward. Bare chest and kilt is the prescribed uniform for throwing the caber at present-day Scottish games.

Cabot *(KAB-uht)* Surname of John Cabot, originally Giovanni Caboti, Italian explorer who sailed for Henry VII of England and discovered the North American coast in 1497. His son, Sebastian Cabot (c.1483–1557), explored for both England and Spain. On a voyage in 1509, he probably reached Hudson Bay.

Sebastian Cabot.

cache *(kash)* From the French *cacher,* "to conceal," a place to store or hide such things as provisions or supplies. Advancing armies would frequently leave such stores hidden in conquered territory in case the tide of battle should turn and the materials be needed for retreating purposes.

Caddo *(KAD-oh)* An American Indian belonging to the Caddoan linguistic group and also to a federation of tribes that inhabited lands in Louisiana, Arkansas, Kansas, and eastern Texas. Among the tribes of the Caddo confederacy were the Arikara, the

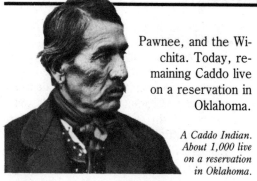

Pawnee, and the Wichita. Today, remaining Caddo live on a reservation in Oklahoma.

A Caddo Indian. About 1,000 live on a reservation in Oklahoma.

cade *(kade)* A European juniper tree. The dark, tarry fluid—oil of cade—distilled from its wood is used to treat skin disorders. Also the surname of Jack **Cade,** possibly an Irishman, who in 1450 led 20,000 men from Kent in an uprising against political and social conditions and captured London. A **cade** is also a barrel for herrings, or a suffix meaning "procession" in such words as aquacade, motorcade.

cadge See *kedge.*

cadi, qadi, or **kadi** *(KAH-dee)* In Muslim lands, a town magistrate or judge charged with the interpretation as well as the administration of the religious law.

Cadiz *(KAH-deez; KAH-deeth)* An Andalusian seaport city on the southwest coast of Spain. Founded by the Phoenicians as Gadir in the twelfth century B.C., the city was held variously by Carthaginians, Romans (who called it Gades), and Moors before being retaken by the king of Castile in 1262. Columbus sailed from Cádiz in 1495 on his second voyage. The composer Manuel de Falla (1876–1946) is buried there. Nearby is Rota (q.v.), U.S. naval base site.

A view of the lovely Spanish port city of Cádiz.

cadre *(KAD-ray)* From the French for "frame," a cadre is a personal framework (or core group) around which an organization can be built. The word is used widely in the military, where groups of staff officers and noncommissioned officers commonly serve as nuclei for units to be commissioned or for units being formed for training purposes. In prerevolutionary Russia, a cadre was a group of indoctrinated leaders prepared to promote the interests of their (usually) revolutionary party.

Caen *(kahn)* Northern French city and seaport located on the Orne River, in Normandy. Caen's historical importance began with William the Conqueror, who lived and is buried there. Caen was also home to Charlotte Corday, the revolutionary patriot who stabbed the terrorist Jean Paul Marat to death in his bath. Much of Caen was destroyed during the Normandy campaign of World War II, but several fine eleventh-century structures survived. Caen is the center of the Calvados region, whence comes the drink of that name.

Charlotte Corday in a Caen courtyard.

cairn *(kairn)* A conical heap of stones piled in a special place, as either a landmark or a memorial. In ancient times, the Scots built cairns to mark graves. A small, shaggy dog of Scotland, the **cairn** terrier is bred to sniff out fur-bearing animals from the rocky cliffs of its native habitat, the Isle of Skye.

calla *(KAL-ah)* A plant of the large and varied arum family, which includes, among others, monsteras, philodendrons, and skunk cabbages. Calla lilies (or arum lilies) are thus

not true lilies. They have blooms in the form of large, usually white modified leaves (spathes), petal-like in appearance, that enclose a central spike closely set with the actual tiny flowers. They were popularized by Katharine Hepburn, who declared, "The calla lilies are in bloom again," in the film *Morning Glory.*

calx *(kalks)* The powdery residue that remains after a metal or mineral has been calcined, or roasted without burning, to bring about one of several physical or chemical changes.

calyx *(KAY-lix)* The outer ring of leaves (the sepals, q.v.) at the base of a flower. These are usually but not always green, and sometimes match the petals in color.

cam *(kam)* In machinery, a rotating or sliding part which engages other parts in a way that causes them to move precisely in a desired pattern or patterns. With a capital *C*, it's the river that flows through Cambridge, England, where "punting on the **Cam**" is a favored recreation.

camas or **camass** *(KAM-uss)* An attractive flowering plant of the lily family, thriving in damp soil in the western U.S. The camas has sweetish, edible bulbs, formerly a basic food of the Indians but now chiefly eaten by the **camas** rat. This large, dark gopher is capable of distinguishing the esculent camas from the death camas, a distantly related plant that can poison grazing livestock.

Campi *(KAM-pee)* Family name of four Italian brothers whose forte was art. Giulio Campi (c. 1500–1572) founded a painting school at Cremona which was attended by Antonio Campi (c. 1535–1591), who was also an architect and a historian; Vincenzo Campi (1532–1591); and Bernardino Campi

(1522–c. 1590). Bernardino is famous for his biblical frescoes in the cupola of San Sigismondo, Cremona, and Giulio's frescoes are to be seen in the church of Santa Margherita in the same city.

Camus *(kah-MOO)* Albert Camus (1913–1960), Algerian-born Frenchman, editor of a French underground newspaper during World War II, and a major literary figure of the twentieth century. He is possibly best known for his novels, *The Stranger* (1946), *The Plague* (1948), and *The Fall* (1957). In 1957 he was awarded the Nobel Prize for Literature.

Albert Camus, important modern writer.

Canby *(KAN-bee)* Henry Seidel Canby (1878–1961), editor, critic, writer, and Yale professor. Canby co-founded the *Saturday Review of Literature* and edited it from 1924 to 1936. Another Canby was Edward Richard Sprigg Canby (1817–1873), Union general who captured Mobile in 1865 and received the surrender of the last Confederate armies.

E.R.S. Canby.

canis *(KAN-iss)* Latin for "dog" (and thus root of "canine"), canis appears in the names of two constellations—Canis Major, or large dog; and Canis Minor, small dog, or puppy. Canis Major, near Orion, contains Sirius, the Dog Star, the brightest star in the heavens. The Little Dog, long identified as one of Orion's hunting dogs, contains the bright star Procyon.

The constellation Canis Minor.

canna *(KAH-ah)* Tropical and subtropical plant with large leaves and flamboyant red or yellow flowers in torchlike heads;  widely grown as an ornamental. Some canna species are grown in the tropics for the starch (a type of arrowroot) yielded by their roots. The canna is only distantly related to its coincidental rhyme, the banana.

canon *(KAN-uhn)* In religion, a decree, a body of church laws (canon law), the books of the Bible accepted as authentic, the central portion of the Mass, a list of saints, or the title of certain clergymen. In printing, a large type size. In music, a round, such as "Row, Row, Row (Your Boat Gently Down the Stream)," or a type of counterpoint.

cant *(kant)* Any type of insincere, meaningless argot (q.v.), or a whining, singsong speaking pattern ascribed to mendicants and thieves. Also, the corner of a building, a bevel, or a sudden movement that causes something to tilt.

Capek *(CHOP-ek)* Karel Čapek (1890–1938), Czech playwright, novelist, and essayist. His best-known play, *R.U.R. (Rossum's Universal Robots)* introduced the word "robot" to the language in 1921. Čapek also wrote *The Makropoulos Secret* (1923).

Rossum's robots in a scene from R.U.R.

Capri *(kap-REE)* A small island celebrated in song and story, off the tip of the Sorrento peninsula near Naples, Italy; there are two towns, Capri and Anacapri. Major tourist attractions are the famous Blue Grotto (see *azure*), a cave, partly underwater, that can only be entered at low tide, and the ruins of villas built there by the emperors Augustus and Tiberius.

A statue overlooks the harbor on idyllic Capri.

carafe *(kah-RAF)* From the Arabic *gharafa,* "to draw water": a pitcher or bottle for serving wine.

Carib *(KAR-ib)* A member of the warlike tribe of aboriginal Indians who sailed out to greet Columbus on his arrival in the Lesser Antilles. Remnants of the Caribs survive on islands in the Caribbean (which was named for them) and in Central America.

cark *(kark)* This word, both a noun and a verb denoting solicitude or sympathetic feeling, has fallen from common usage.

However, it is very useful for crossword buffs, who are among the few who know that cark is not simply a typographical error for the word care, whose meaning it closely resembles.

Carl or Karl *(karl)*
A popular given name, unrelated to the lower-case **carl** or carle, with its less than complimentary connotations: originally carls—like churls (q.v.), from the same root—were common fellows, even, as in Scotland, where they could be either sturdy chaps or misers.

carny or carney

(KAR-nee) A carnival or a person who works in one.

A carny often features animals.

carob *(KAH-rub)*
An evergreen tree indigenous to the Mediterranean region. The

carob's edible seed pods, whole or ground to powder, are found in health-food stores as a substitute for chocolate, and carob candy is popular. The pods are also called St.-John's-bread in the belief that they were the "locusts" eaten by the saint in the wilderness.

A branch of the carob tree.

carom *(KAH-rum)*
A striking and rebounding of one object off another; a ricochet. In billiards, a carom occurs when the white (or cue) ball hits two other balls, in no particular order. The term is also used in such sports as basketball, curling, and shuffleboard.

carp *(karp)*
Any one of a number of edible fishes inhabiting temperate-zone lakes and ponds. Related to the goldfish, the minnow, and the dace (q.v.), carp is a

staple in the smoked-fish departments of fancy delicatessens, and unsmoked is starred in many Central European recipes.

carte *(kart)*
A menu, as in "à la carte"; a playing card or card game; a position in fencing; or, followed by "blanche," unlimited discretion to act. With an upper-case *C,* the surname of Richard D'Oyly **Carte** (1844–1901), famed impresario of Gilbert and Sullivan operettas and founder of the theatrical company that bore his name.

Richard D'Oyly Carte.

Cary *(KA-ree)*
Surname of, among others, Joyce Cary (1888–1957), English novelist whose works convey a sense of the change in English mores; and the sister poets Alice (1820–1871) and Phoebe Cary (1824–1871). Also, the given name taken by actor Archibald Leach, a.k.a. Cary Grant.

Joyce Cary.

Casa *(KAH-sah)*
The surname of Giovanni della Casa (1503–1556), Italian cleric and poet. Also, the Spanish word for "house," and **Casa** Grande, the main structure of prehistoric Indian ruins in Casa Grande Ruins National Monument in southern Arizona.

caste *(kast)*
In India, a hereditary social class, traditionally with rigid limitations on occupation and social activity, within the Hindu population. The four main castes are Brahmins, priests; Kshatriyas, the military; Vaisyas, farmers and tradesmen; and Sudras, laborers. Persons lower in the social

A high caste Indian family.

order were considered outside the caste system and hence were called "untouchables." Mahatma Gandhi preached against the caste system, and untouchability was declared illegal in 1949, but old habits die hard, and the caste system still does exist in India.

caul *(kahl)* The membrane enveloping a baby at birth. Occasionally, a section of this membrane covers the head of the newborn infant. A child thus "born with a caul" is believed to be destined for rare good fortune, or the possessor of second sight. Caul fat, used in cookery, is the web of lacy fat taken from a pig's abdominal cavity.

Cavan *(KAH-vahn)* Either a county in northern Republic of Ireland, or a Philippine unit of dry measure for grain or fruit equal to 2.13 bushels, a little over 17 gallons, or about 8½ pecks.

cavil *(KAV-uhl)* A frivolous, unnecessary objection, trivial finding of fault, or quibble.

cavy *(KAY-vee)* Any of several species of South American nocturnal rodents that includes the familiar guinea pig. Small, brown, and tailless wild cavies live in heavy undergrowth and forage for food at night. Largest member of the family is the 2½-foot-long, rabbitlike Patagonian cavy, also known as the mara.

caw *(kaw)* The loud and lugubrious cry uttered by birds of the family that includes magpies, jays, and crows. "Caw" is an approximation of the actual sound and is specific to the black bird that traditionally flies the shortest distance between two points.

The "voice" of a raven can be characterized as a caw.

cay *(kee; kay)* From the Spanish word that evolved into the alternate term "key," both meaning a small, low islet or above-water coral reef or sandbar, in the West Indies and southern Florida. Also (from the Guarani word for "bashful") the Capuchin monkey, known for its habit of hiding its face in its hands.

Cebu *(say-BOO)* One of the Visayan Islands of the Philippines, lying between Leyte (q.v.) and Negros. A wooden cross planted here by Magellan in 1521 remains the major tourist attraction. The seaport city of Cebu, second only in size and importance to Manila, was a major Japanese base in World War II.

cecum *(SEEK-um)* A pouchlike anatomical structure that makes up the first part of the large intestine, which is linked to the small intestine by the ileum. Into the cecum opens the wormlike blind pouch called the vermiform appendix.

The cecum is the leaflike segment of the intestine in the lower left-hand corner of this drawing.

Ceiba *(SAY-ee-bah)* A genus of tropical American trees with attractive, bell-shaped blossoms. The major species is very tall, with a massive trunk, and bears seed pods containing the commercially important silky, cottonlike fiber kapok (q.v.). The ceiba is also called the God tree, kapok tree, and silk-cotton tree. La **Ceiba** is a port in Honduras on the Caribbean.

Celt *(selt; kelt)*

Any of an ancient western European people, surviving among the Irish, Scotch, Bretons, Cornish, and Welsh; or, in antiquity, any of the Celtic speakers spread across Europe to Asia Minor. The surviving Celtic languages are related to ancient Gaulish and include Goidelic (Scottish Gaelic, Irish Gaelic, or Erse [q.v.], and Manx) and Brythonic (Breton, Cornish, and Welsh). A Celt is often defined as a Gael, and a Celtic is a member of Boston's professional basketball team.

A Celtic cross.

Cenci *(CHAIN-chee)*

Surname of Beatrice Cenci (1577–1599), an Italian noblewoman known as the Beautiful Patricide. To avenge herself on her cruel father, she plotted with her stepmother, brothers, and lover to have him murdered and was executed following a sensational trial. These events were chronicled in *The Cenci* (1819), a tragedy by Shelley, and other works, including an opera.

Cenis *(seh-NEE)*

Mont Cenis, an Alpine pass almost 7,000 feet above sea level, on the border between France and Italy. An eight-mile-long railroad tunnel that connects Turin with Chambéry, and a road that dates back to 1810, have updated this historical invasion route to Italy. In Italian the pass is Montcenisio.

cento *(SEN-toe)*

From the Latin word meaning "patchwork," a literary or musical composition stitched together from other works. This may have been the music referred to by Nanki Poo, hero of *The Mikado,* in his "Wand'ring Minstrel" number.

cere *(seer)*

From the Latin word for "wax," the soft, fleshy patch found at the base of the upper beak in certain birds. The nostrils open through this mass, which is bare in birds of prey like the eagle, and may be feathered in some other birds.

Ceres *(SEER-eez)*

An early if not original earth mother. In Roman belief, Ceres was the goddess of grain, particularly of harvests. At her chief temple on the Aventine Hill, especially during the festival of Cerealia, she was worshiped through fertility rites and rites for the dead. She is also identified in Greek legends with Demeter. The English word cereal derives from her name, which was also given to the first asteroid to be discovered (1801).

Ceres's main festival, the Cerealia, is celebrated on April 19.

cess *(sess)*

An onerous tax in money or provisions, formerly levied for the support of the household staff and soldiers of the lord lieutenant of Ireland. The term survives in the phrase "bad cess," which is what an Irishman might wish his enemies.

Chad *(chad)*

A landlocked republic in north-central Africa whose capital is N'Djaména (Fort Lamy); about half of its territory lies within the Sahara. Formerly a part of French Equatorial Africa, Chad was given

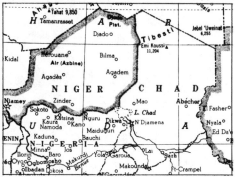

Chad, in north-central Africa.

republic status within the French Community in 1958, and achieved independence in 1960. Also, the name of a large (but variable) lake bordered by Chad and Nigeria; the local name of the lake is also N'Djaména.

chaff *(chaff)*   The husks and broken bits that remain when grain has been threshed and winnowed, or hay or straw chopped for use as fodder. Figuratively, light chatter, banter, or any discourse worth as little as chaff.

cham *(kam)*   In the Middle Ages, a khan (q.v.) or ruler, in Tartary—the vast region of Siberia and southern Russia where dwelt the Mongolian and Turkic tribes who overran eastern Europe under such chams as the infamous Genghis (1167–1227). **Cham** is also a people, and their language, of Annam.

Chaos *(KAY-ohss)*   In Greek mythology, the god of confusion who presided over a disorganized mass of earth, fire, water, and air before these elements were forged into the ordered universe. This occurred when the daughter of Chaos, the so-called egg of Nox (q.v.), was hatched.

chape *(chape)*   On a scabbard or dagger sheath, the metal plate at the tip that protects the point of the weapon, or the metal fitting at the top of the sheath, with a device for fastening it to the belt. Also, the metal fastener that attaches a strap to a buckle.

chard *(chard)*   Edible leaf stalk of the cardoon and the related artichoke, when used as a potherb. Also Swiss chard, with edible white (or red) stalks and large succulent leaves, which is unrelated.

chay *(chay)*   A tropical plant of the huge madder family, which includes those that

provide coffee, quinine, and ipecac. The roots of chay yield a red dye called turkey red. Madder-dyed cloth has been found in the sarcophagi of Egyptian mummies.

Che *(chay)*   Nickname of Ernesto Guevara (1928–1967), Argentine-born revolutionary who studied medicine, worked in a leper colony, agitated against Juan Perón, and became the right-hand man of Fidel Castro after his landing in Cuba in 1956. While involved in revolutionary activity in Bolivia, he was captured and executed.

Ernesto "Che" Guevara.

chela *(KEE-lah; CHAY-lah)*   The first pronunciation refers to the business end of a scorpion, crab, or lobster claw with its pincerlike structure. Pronounced the second way, **chela** comes from a Sanskrit word meaning a follower or disciple of an Indian guru or philosophy.

The pincers are called chelas.

Cheops See *Khufu.*

cher *(share)*   The word preceding your name in a letter from France, meaning "dear" (it can also mean "expensive"); the department in central France whose capital is Bourges; a 200-mile-long river that flows northwest across France and joins the Loire below Tours; or a popular monomial songstress, formerly part of the team of Sonny and **Cher.**

chert *(churt)*   A mineral often found as an impurity in limestone or similar rocks composed of hydrated silica, a salt of the element silicon. Chert is a dull-colored quartz with the properties of flint.

chi *(kie)* The twenty-second letter of the Greek alphabet. The pronunciation of chi is unique to Greek, but it closely resembles that of the English letter *K*. **Chi** (pronounced *shy*) is also a popular nickname for America's "second city," Chicago.

chiao *(tyow)* A unit of currency. On the Chinese mainland, one chiao is worth 100 fen, or 1/10 of a yuan (q.v.).

chic *(sheek)* One of those delicious Gallic words that convey much more than they say. Generally understood to mean smartness, elegance, or stylishness in dress, it refers usually to women, despite being a masculine noun in French. Also **Chic** *(chik)* Young, cartoonist who originated Dagwood and Blondie.

chiel *(CHEE-ul)* From the same Middle English word that developed into "child," a chiefly Scottish colloquialism for any young fellow, youth, or lad.

chine *(chine)* The spine, and therefore the section of the backbone in certain cuts of meat. Physical resemblance also gives chine the picturesque meaning of "a

"The Needles" on the Isle of Wight.

ridge"; the term is thus used on the Hampshire coast of England and on the Isle of Wight. **Chine** (pronounced *sheen*) is also the French word for China, and thus of a silk fabric, *crêpe de chine*.

chino *(CHEE-no)* Either a strong cotton twill material, usually pale tan in color, used for sportwear or uniforms; or as a plural (chinos), trousers of such material. Chino is also a city in San Bernardino County, southern California, the home of a state prison and a state game-bird farm.

chirm *(cherm)* A rare, somewhat onomatopoeic word that conveys the humming (or sometimes louder or more confused) sound you might expect to hear from a swarm of insects or birds, or even a crowd of humans.

chit *(chit)* Either a pert, saucy child (usually a girl) or a kind of signed voucher or IOU to acknowledge trifling sums of money owed for food, drink, or lodging. Also, in Britain, a short note such as might be left for the milkman. (See also *scrip*.)

Chloe *(KLOW-ee)* A shepherdess, the sweetheart of Daphnis, a goatherd, a son of Hermes in the Greek pastoral *Daphnis and Chloe* by the sophist Longus. Chloe was also Uncle Tom's wife in Harriet Beecher Stowe's *Uncle Tom's Cabin* and, in an old popular song, the name of a character whose beloved called her to no avail through the black of night.

chott or **shott** *(shot)* A topographical feature of the arid lands of North Africa, a chott is either a shallow lake of salt water or the dried bed of such a lake, which glistens as if covered with snow when seen from the air. In the Atlas Mountains, the Plateau of the Chotts is named for its many salt lakes and salt flats.

Chou *(joe)* The famed Chinese Communist leader Chou En-lai (1898–1976), who lived in England, studied in Germany, helped found the Chinese Communist party, and worked with Sun Yat-Sen. When the People's Republic of China was formed in 1949, Chou became premier and foreign minister; he was premier until his death. **Chou** was an ancient Chinese dynasty; in French, it means "cabbage."

Chou En-lai, 1973.

chow *(chow)* or **chow-chow** A breed of dog whose origins trace back to prehistoric China. The powerful animal weighs about 60 pounds, sports a dense, shaggy coat, often red, and is the only breed with a black tongue. **Chow** is often defined in crosswords as a meal, especially a military meal.

chroma *(KROE -mah)* An index of color intensity. Also, the purity of a color based on how much white or gray it contains. Thus, red would be much richer in chroma than pink, assuming the same brightness.

chub *(chub; kub)* A fish of the minnow family, which includes such other freshwater denizens as the carp and the squawfish. Other members of the family are called shiners, breams, roaches, and bleaks. With the second pronunciation, **Chub** is an African land mentioned in the Bible (Ezekiel 30:5).

chuff *(chuff)* A rude, crude, or insensitive person. For variety, verbalists substitute this word for the more familiar boor (q.v.) or churl (q.v.).

chukka or **chukker** *(CHUK-uh)* What an inning is to baseball, a chukka is to polo (q.v.). This period of play,

equal to 7½ minutes, is predicated more on the man's endurance than the horse's. **Chukka** also refers to an ankle-high boot similar to the type sported by polo players.

chum *(chum)* Derived from "chamber mate," one's chum was originally his roommate, especially if one was an Englishman or Rover Boy, but now is any close personal friend. The word also refers to chopped-up oily fish scattered on the water as a lure for other piscine creatures.

churl *(churl)* From the Old English word meaning "man," or "husband," a freeman ranking just above serfs. Today, the term denotes a rude, ill-bred individual.

Churlish behavior as seen by Honoré Daumier.

churn *(chern)* A container in which milk or cream is beaten, rocked, or otherwise agitated to unite the fat globules to produce butter. The milk of goats, sheep, and mares, as well as cows, can be churned, although horse butter is not generally regarded as a delicacy. As an intransitive verb, **churn** means to be in violent mental or physical activity.

chute *(shoot)* Either an inclined channel used for transferring such items as coal or laundry from one location to a lower one via gravity; a waterfall or narrow cascade; or a parachute, to those who use them often enough for familiarity.

chyle *(kile)* From the Greek word for "juice," a milky-appearing lymph, containing emulsified fats, that is taken up by the intestinal lymphatics from digested food and thus passes into the blood and tissues.

chyme *(kime)* Alphabetically, chyme comes after chyle, but physiologically it precedes it. Chyme is the thick, semisolid gruel of partly digested food that proceeds from the stomach into the duodenum (first section of the small intestine), and is then transformed into chyle.

Ciano *(CHAN-oe)* Galeazzo Ciano (1903–1944), Count of Cortelazzo and husband of Mussolini's daughter Edda (q.v.). While foreign minister of Italy, he helped engineer his father-in-law's downfall in 1943, was arrested by the Germans, and executed by Fascists in northern Italy.

Ciano and Edda Mussolini on their wedding day, 1930.

Cid *(sid)* From the Arabic *sayyid,* a lord, the Spanish national hero and warrior Roderigo (or Ruy) Diaz de Vivar (c. 1040–1099). El Cid served Castilian kings, was later emir (q.v.) of Moorish-held Saragossa,

Diaz de Vivar—El Cid.

and conquered Valencia in 1094 astride his horse, Babieca. His deeds were celebrated in the twelfth-century epic *Song of the Cid* and have been dramatized by the French playwright Corneille *(Le Cid,* 1637*)* and the producers of the movie starring Charlton Heston (1961).

cilia *(SIL-ee-ah)* Tiny, hairlike processes on the free surface of single-celled organisms that vibrate or sweep rhythmically to provide a means of locomotion. In higher organisms, including humans, cilia in certain structures beat constantly to set up a current in a bodily fluid. Technically, an eyelash is a cilium.

cimex *(SIE-mex)* Latin word for "bug" and name of a genus of insects including those not known for retiring habits, despite their designation as bedbugs. Cimices include such nuisances as *Cimex boveti,* the tropical bedbug of West Africa, and *pilosellus,* an American bedbug that lives on bats and thus manages to sleep during the day.

cine *(SIN-ay)* Short for cinema, the fancy word for a motion picture theater in the U.S., but the usual word in Spain and Italy. In France, ciné is the short version of *cinematographe,* or motion picture.

Circe *(SIR-see)* In Greek legend, the infamous enchantress, daughter of Helios, who shipwrecked Odysseus for slaughtering his sacred cattle. As a further gesture of disapproval, Circe changed all of Odysseus's crew into swine. It wasn't until Odysseus forced her to break the spell that the odyssey got moving again.

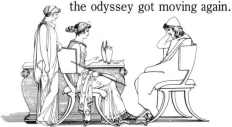

Circe receives Ulysses at her table.

cisco *(SIS-koe)* Any of several white-fishes that make up an important food source in the Great Lakes region. Also, the famed **Cisco** Kid—the "Robin Hood of the West"—based on a character in "The Caballero's Way" by O. Henry. Cisco was played on TV by Duncan Rinaldo; Leo Carillo played his partner, Pancho.

civet *(SIV-uht)* Any of several members of the civet family, especially the nocturnal carnivores, related to the cat, found in Africa, India, and Asia. **Civet** is also the name given to the thick, yellowish, fatty secretion from scent glands in the animal's anal pouch.

A Malay palm civet.

clan *(klan)* A social group based on descent from a common ancestor and bearing the same name, as in clans of the Scottish Highlands. Several clans may be combined into a larger group called a phratry. If a tribe includes two clans or two phratries, each is called a moiety. Clan (from the Gaelic) is often clued as "Highland group" or, referring to the tartan plaid kilt worn by each clan, as "kiltie's group."

Clare *(klare)* A county in western Ireland between Galway Bay and the river Shannon. Also a feminine given name, and the surname of John **Clare** (1793–1864), English nature poet eventually confined to an insane asylum; Ada Clare, John Jarndyce's ward in Dickens's *Bleak House;* and Angel Clare, a character in Hardy's *Tess of the D'Urbervilles.*

claro *(KLAH-roh)* From the Spanish word for "clear," a type of cigar noted for its light color and mildness. Other types of cigars include colorados, maduros, panatelas, and perfectos. Despite the estimable qualities of the claro, its smoke still contains nicotine, carbon dioxide, carbon monoxide, ammonia, and various tarry compounds.

clary *(KLAIR-ee)* An aromatic herb belonging to the sage genus, clary is native from the Mediterranean region to Iran, has bluish or pinkish blossoms, and yields a useful oil. An infusion of clary was once used to clear the eyes, and a drink called **clary** (no relation), made of wine, honey, and spices, did the reverse.

cleat *(kleet)* On the bottom of an athlete's shoe, one of several projections of metal or hard rubber that give secure footing on turf or dirt. On board ship, a **cleat** is a metal fitting around which a rope can be fastened.

cleek *(kleek)* From the Scottish word meaning "to clutch" or "snatch," a large hook. In golf, the cleek at one time was an iron with a moderately sloped narrow face. Today it is a small, wooden-headed club, also called a number 4 wood, that gives more loft than a spoon.

clef *(kleff)* A musical symbol that communicates the pitch of notes on a particular staff. There are three types of clefs: the G clef, looking like a flowery ampersand, for treble; the F, a top-heavy comma, for bass; and the C, which looks like it was adapted from the Russian alphabet, for tenor or alto.

cleft *(kleft)* A natural split or one accomplished by a cleaving device. Clefts may appear in the earth's surface as crevices, or fissures; in wood, as cracks made by ax blows; or as dimples in the chins of leading men like Kirk Douglas and Cary Grant.

Kirk Douglas, famous for his cleft.

clew *(kloo)* A ball of yarn such as that used by Theseus to find his way out of the labyrinth in Crete (q.v.). Also, the lower corners of square sails or the lower after-corner of the fore-and-aft sail. Clew lines connect the **clew** to the yard and are used in raising or lowering square sails. **Clew** is also an alternate spelling for clue, and is the preferred spelling in some dictionaries.

cline *(kline)* In biology, a graded series of changes in size or function exhibited by related organisms with changes in environment. For example, in birds and mammals, a cline is usually seen in body size: smaller members of the group are found in warmer climates, while larger ones tend to inhabit colder climates.

Clio *(KLIE-oh)* One of the nine Muses of classic myth, Clio was the Muse of History. In ancient art, she is usually shown with an open scroll or a chest of books. The English essayist Joseph Addison (1672–1719) used **Clio** as a pseudonym; rather than a classical reference, this was probably an acronym for *C*helsea, *L*ondon, *I*slington *O*ffice.

Clyde *(klide)* A 106-mile-long river of southwestern Scotland. The Clyde empties into the Firth of Clyde, and is crossed at Glasgow by a ten-lane bridge opened in 1970. Also, the nickname of Walt Frazier, former star of the New York Knicks professional basketball team, and half of the outlaw team completed by Bonnie.

coati *(koe-AH-tee)* A small Central and South American omnivore related to the raccoon, but with a long snout and long, bushy tail, also called a coati-mundi. Females and their young live together. Males,

however, are loners and join the group only during the mating season.

In Mexico, people often keep coatis as pets.

cob *(kahb)* A useful crossword word conveying several meanings, including: a chunk of something such as coal; the part of an ear of corn that carries the kernels and is sometimes made into pipes; a short, husky horse; an early coin of Spanish America; and a male swan.

cobb *(kahb)* As an ordinary noun, a type of sea gull. As a proper noun, the surname of Irvin S. **Cobb** (1876–1944), American humorist and writer; Ty Cobb (1886–1961), the famed "Georgia Peach" who played centerfield for the Detroit Tigers and was the first player elected to baseball's Hall of Fame; and actor Lee J. Cobb (1911–1976).  *Irvin Shrewsbury Cobb.*

cobia *(KOE-bee-ah)* A large saltwater game fish that swims in tropical waters and is valued as food.

coble *(KOE-bul)* A small fishing boat equipped with a lug sail, a four-cornered sail having no lower yard. In the waters off northeast England, this craft is also used for piloting, In Scotland, the coble is nothing more than a stubby, flat-bottomed rowboat.

cobra *(KOE-bra)* A highly poisonous snake of Africa and Asia, distantly related to the American coral snake. The cobra's most unusual feature, an inflatable neck hood it spreads when excited, is a warning  device. Contrary to popular belief, cobras are not charmed by music. Deaf, they simply follow the snake charmer's movements. Cleopatra's asp (q.v.) was probably an Egyptian cobra.

coca *(KOE-kah)* A family and genus of shrubs and trees mostly native to South America. The leaves of the shrubby species widely grown in Bolivia and Peru resemble tea leaves when dried, and are habitually chewed by natives of the Andes foothills to give them "strength." This is not surprising, since the leaves are rich in the alkaloid drug cocaine, which is also produced commercially from this source. **Coca** is also the surname of comedienne Imogene, and is part of the name of several soft drinks in which an extract (drug-free) of coca is used.

cod *(kahd)* Usually the Atlantic cod, a large North Atlantic food fish weighing up to 25 pounds. The cod fishery is important in Massachusetts, long celebrated as the "Land of the Cod" because of the rich offshore fishing banks. Cape **Cod** is the hook-shaped peninsula jutting from the Massachusetts coast.

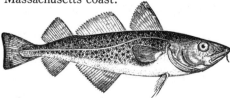

coda *(KOE-dah)* In music, that section of a composition that brings it to a logical, definite conclusion, except in certain symphonies of Beethoven, which always draw applause before they are completed. In Italian, *coda* is "tail."

codex *(KOE-deks)* The Latin word, and old-fashioned name, for a code or collection of written laws. Also, an important volume, such as the Bible. In the Catholic Church, for example, the main body of church laws is known as the *Codex Juris Canonici*, or Code of Canon Law. **Codex** is also a collection of drug formulas, the basis of pharmacology.

Cody *(KOE-dee)* William Frederick Cody (1846–1917), the American plainsman, army scout, and impresario of Wild West shows, celebrated in song and story as Buffalo Bill. Also, the town founded by and named after him; **Cody** sits on the Shoshone River in northwestern Wyoming, and features an historical center containing Buffalo Bill memorabilia and a gallery of Western art.

"Buffalo Bill" Cody.

cog *(kog)* An important element in machinery. Cogs are the teeth in the rims of wheels that engage the teeth of other cogwheels, and thus transmit motion produced in one part of the machine to another. Also, someone who contributes specifically to the operation of a business; or a name given over the centuries to several types of small boats.

Charlie Chaplin enmeshed in the cogs of progress in the film Modern Times.

cogon *(koh-GONE)* Several species of tall, coarse grass native to the Philippines and other islands of the southwest Pacific. Cogon is harvested by machete and used as thatching for roofs. The ubiquitous plant is also known as alang-alang.

coif *(koif)* A type of headgear now found, except for nuns' coifs, only in museums and crossword puzzles. The coif, which took many forms, fit the head tightly, and was worn by both men and women. Men in armor wore sturdy coifs to protect them from the abrasion of helmets. Also, a white cap formerly worn in England by barristers and sergeants-at-arms. As a modern verb, to **coif** is to arrange the hair.

coir *(koir)* A stiff fiber obtained from the husks of coconuts, used in Sri Lanka and the islands of Indonesia for making rope. The word derives from the Tamil *kahiru*, meaning "rope."

col *(kahl)* In physical geography, a pass across mountains, generally spanning a watershed or a depression in the crest of a ridge. In meteorology, an area of low pressure between two high-pressure systems.

cola *(KOE-lah)* Anglicized name of the African kola tree, part of a large genus bearing capsulelike fruits containing large seeds (cola nuts) about the size of chestnuts. The nuts contain caffeine and are chewed as a stimulant. Also, cola drinks, a collective name for soft drinks made with cola nut extract, the best known being Coca-Cola, or "Coke," which also contains an extract of coca (q.v.)

cole *(kole)* Any of several plants (the coleworts) of the mustard genus, including cabbage, kohlrabi, kale (q.v.), and rape, as well as the mustards. Also, the given name of **Cole** Porter (1893–1964), the inimitable composer of witty, sophisticated songs; the famous nursery rhyme monarch with a hankering for fiddle music; and Nat (King) Cole (1919–1965), beloved popular singer;

Cole Porter was an elegant, debonair man despite a crippling riding accident.

his daughter Natalie, also a popular singer; and drummer Cozy Cole.

colic *(KAH-lik)* General medical term for intense abdominal pain or cramping. Among the most common colics are those caused by spasm and contraction of the stomach or colon. Colic is particularly prevalent in very young infants with indigestion, or those who have not been properly burped.

Colin *(KOH-lin)* The patron saint of Cornwall; the bobwhite or any bird of its family, which also includes pheasants and partridges. These birds are known to sleep in a circle, tails to the center, so that if alarmed they can take off in all directions, ensuring the survival of the majority.

colon *(KOE-lon; koe-LON)* With the first syllable accented, the section of the large intestine just ahead of the rectum; or a punctuation mark (:). With the second syllable stressed, it is the Spanish form of the name Columbus. **Colón** is also the name of a city in Cuba and one in Panama, at the Caribbean end of the Panama Canal.

colt *(kolt)* A young horse, donkey, or zebra, usually male; or a rope with a knotted end, formerly used for flogging aboard ship. Also, the surname of Samuel **Colt** (1814–1862), the Hartford, Connecticut, inventor who gave the world the revolving-breech pistol named for him; Colt is now virtually a synonym for revolver. In professional football, a **Colt** is a member of the Baltimore team.

A young colt with his mother.

Coly *(KOE-lee)*　Any of a genus of small, long-tailed crested birds commonly found in the brush of sub-Saharan Africa. Colies are also known as mousebirds because of their gray, furlike feathers and scurrying motions. They usually travel in large flocks, and both parents tend the nest.

coma *(KOE-mah)*　Profound unconsciousness, associated with an injury or disease, from which the patient cannot be roused. Also, from the Greek word for "hair," the glowing, fuzzy area resembling hair around the head of a comet. **Coma** Berenices is a constellation of seven stars—supposedly the hair sacrificed by Berenice, the wife of Ptolemy III—near the tail of Leo.

combe or **coomb** *(koom; kome)*　In Britain, a deep ravine or a steep-sided valley in the side of a hill; often part of a place name (Ilfracombe, for example). Also the surname of William **Combe** (1741–1823), the English satirist who created "Dr. Syntax"; the henpecked but erudite cleric-hero of three volumes of doggerel verse with humorous illustrations.

combo *(KOM-boe)*

The colloquial term meaning a combination, usually a small group of musicians who play piano, bass, guitar, or drums, and whose forte is jazz. Also, in less than ele-gant restaurants, a sandwich combining two or more fillings: e.g., a ham-and-Swiss **combo.**

comet *(KOM-et)*　An astronomical body consisting mainly of glowing gases, with a bright head and a luminous tail as long as 100 million miles. The most famous is Halley's Comet, which appears about every 76 years, and is due again in 1986. **Comet** is also the name of a Santa Clausian reindeer.

Como *(KOE-moe)*　A city and province in northern Italy, near the Swiss border and at the southwest end of beautiful Lake Como, which lies like a jewel in the Alpine foothills and attracts tourists from everywhere. **Como** is also the surname of Perry, the ever-popular pop singer.

Lake Como.

Comus *(KOE-mus)*　The god of merry-making, according to late Roman mythology. He was a follower of Dionysus (who as Bacchus was sometimes credited with his parentage) and is usually represented in his cups. He is the main character in Milton's masque *Comus* (1634), and is traditionally represented at New Orleans's Mardi Gras celebration.

conch *(konk)*　Common name of various ocean-dwelling mollusks with heavy, whorled shells. Of these, the largest is the horse conch, a two-footer that inhabits

This photograph clearly reveals the coma on the head of a comet.

warm Atlantic coastal waters. Conch shells are used in jewelry, and the meat is used as a food, notably in the famous chowder of the Florida Keys.

coney or **cony** *(KOE-nee)* Another name for the rabbit, or its fur. The name also often refers to the pika (q.v.). Also, the island that is actually a peninsula, **Coney Island**, famous amusement park for New Yorkers, and home of Nathan's, the dean of the American hot dog.

conga *(KONG-gah)* The Latin-American dance craze of the 1940s, in which the participants formed an undulating line. Music for the conga was in 4/4 time, with a syncopated beat and a heavy accent on the fourth beat of each measure. Conga dancers often chanted, "One-two-three-*kick*" as they performed the basic step.

Roz Russell and Janet Blair, leading a conga line in the film My Sister Eileen.

congé *(KOHN-zhay)* Anything from a formal permission for departure to a curt dismissal—i.e., "You may go," or "Beat it." By extension, the word also describes the stiff little bow sometimes made by leave-takers. In architecture, **congé** is a type of concave, quarter-round molding.

congou *(KON-goo)* A type of black tea native to China. The name is an approximation of a Chinese dialect word for "effort," and refers to the work required to produce the tea. This is the same word that has become familiar in another spelling and context—the martial art of kung-fu.

Conon *(KOE-nun)* Athenian naval commander who was defeated in the Peloponnesian War. Later, as commander of a Persian-Greek fleet, restored with the help of Pharnabazus, he soundly trounced the Spartans off Cnidus. **Conon** was also the Greek astronomer who discovered the constellation Coma Berenices. (See *coma*).

conte *(kohnt)* A French word that has passed into English and is related to account, as in "story." Contes are short tales of derring-do or adventure. Among the better known are the *Contes Drôlatiques* by Honoré de Balzac and *Contes de la Mère l'Oye,* the Mother Goose stories.

Cooke *(kuuk)* Surname of several famous people, including Jay Cooke (1821–1905), the American financier; Rose Terry Cooke (1827–1892), American poet and writer of stories about New England; Josiah Parsons Cooke (1827–1894), the American chemist; Mordecai Cubitt Cooke (1825–1912), the English botanist; and Alistair Cooke, British-born author and commentator, often on television.

Josiah Parsons Cooke.

coon *(koon)* A familiar name for the raccoon, a small, nocturnal, tree-climbing, stripe-tailed omnivorous mammal of the New World, related to the kinkajou and panda. Also, the surname of Carleton Stevens **Coon** (1904–   ), controversial

A raccoon—commonly called a coon.

anthropologist who suggested that various races have advanced at differing rates due to inherent disparities of intellect and ability.

coot *(koot)* A marsh bird of Europe and America. The coot counts the gallinule and the rail as its cousins, and lives on a diet of aquatic plants. The American coot is also called the mud hen and is known for its slow, awkward take-offs. Scoter ducks are also called **coots.**

A coot swimming past two other shore birds.

copal *(KOE-puhl)* A resin obtained mainly from certain tropical and subtropical trees, but sometimes found in fossil form. Copal was once used in the manufacture of hard-surface lacquers and varnishes, but for economic reasons, synthetic materials are now used almost exclusively.

cope *(kope)* A large and long capelike garment worn by clerics at certain ceremonies, and by extension, anything that serves as a covering, such as a canopy. As a verb, to **cope** means to hold someone or something at bay; or, more specifically, to contend successfully. Also the surname of Edward Drinker **Cope** (1840–1897), a celebrated American naturalist.

copra *(KOE-pra)* The dried meat of the coconut from which coconut oil is extracted. The oil content of copra may range as high as 70 percent, and it is used in margarine, cooking fats, and soap. Copra without the oil is called coco cake and is an excellent food for livestock.

Copt *(kopt)* A native Egyptian Christian, usually a member of the Coptic Church. The church holds its services partly in a dead language called Coptic.

corbel *(KOR-buhl)* In architecture, a kind of bracket made of masonry, stone, or wood. The corbel projects from a wall to help support a cornice, the spring of an arch, a balustrade, or any other architectural structure in need of support.

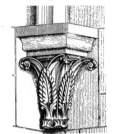

corf *(korf)* A corf was originally a small wicker basket used by British housewives for shopping at their greengrocers, or gathering flowers. This is a far cry from the present-day corves, used to transport coal in mines.

Corfu *(KOR-foo)* Also known as Kérkira, this is an island off the western coast of Greece, the second largest of the Ionian group. The ancient Corcym, it has been identified with Scheria, the island of the Phaeacians in Homer's *Odyssey,* and has been held at various times in history by Corinthians, Romans, Normans, Venetians, Britons, and Greeks.

corm *(korm)* In botany, the short, fleshy, often bulblike underground stem of certain plants, serving to store food and in vegetative reproduction. Corms grow upright and produce buds from the upper nodes and roots from the lower surface.

cornu *(KOR-noo)* Anything shaped like a horn. The word appears as part of cornucopia, literally "horn of plenty," traditionally represented in art as overflowing with bounty, usually fruit, heads of grain, flowers, and nuts. In Greek legend, the

cornucopia would fill itself with whatever provender its owner asked for.

corona *(koh-ROE-nah)* The Latin word for "crown," and meaning just that or anything shaped like a crown. This includes the halo around the sun during an eclipse, the  cuplike central portion of certain flowers, or the top projection of a cornice. An uncrowned **corona,** however, is the long, untapered cigar favored by businessmen.

Corot *(koh-ROE)* Surname of Jean-Baptiste Camille Corot (1796–1875), a French painter sometimes misidentified as one of the Barbizon school of landscape artists. Corot's landscapes include sunlit scenes in France or Italy, and misty, romanticized forests. He is also known for his paintings of women, mainly indoors.

A self-portrait of Jean-Baptiste Corot.

corse *(korse)* Either the archaic word for "cadaver," or, with a capital *C,* the French name for the rugged island of Corsica. The birthplace of Napoleon, Corsica lies in the Mediterranean southeast of France. It was long known for its blood vendettas and banditry, and has been held at times by Romans, Vandals, Byzantines, Arabs, and Pisans. Today it is a department of France.

corso *(KOR-so)* The Italian word for a course, a promenade, or walkway for leisurely strolling. One of the main streets in Rome is called the Via del Corso. It runs from the Piazza Venezia to the Piazza di Popolo, and is lined with boutiques and sidewalk cafés that invite the casual stroller.

cos *(koss)* A variety of lettuce with long, spoonlike leaves, wide, crisp midribs, and a cylindrical or loaflike shape. Cos lettuce, also called romaine, looks undressed to some without anchovies, garlic, croutons, and other trappings of a Caesar salad. **Cos** (or Kos) is also the second largest of the Dodecanese Islands of Greece; Hippocratus founded a school of medicine there in the fifth century B.C.

cosh *(kosh)* From the Romany word for "stick," a short weapon weighted at the end and designed to be brought down sharply against an enemy's or victim's head. Coshes are carried by British bad guys. In America, where speech is more picturesque, the weapon is called a blackjack.

Cosmos *(KOZ-mos)* From the Greek word for "order" or "harmony," the universe as an orderly system, in contrast to Chaos (q.v.). Also, a group of annual garden plants with feathery leaves and daisylike blooms of crimson, pink, orange, or white. **Cosmos** is also the name of a New York professional soccer team.

Costa *(KOH-stah)* Isaäc da Costa (1798–1860), the Dutch poet and historian, born to a Sephardic Jewish family, who became a distinguished Protestant theologian. Also, Artur de Costa e Silva (1902–1969), army general who became president of Brazil in 1967 by military coup. Lower-case **costa,** from the Latin, is a rib or riblike part, as of a leaf, insect wing, or shell. As **costa** also means "coast" in Spanish, it appears in such names as _____ Rica; _____ del Sol; _____ Brava.

cote *(kote)*   A rough shelter or outbuilding for livestock, especially sheep, or for doves; and by extension, any small dwelling. **Côte** is also the French word for "coast," and appears in such glamorous place names as _____ d'Azur, the Blue Coast of southeastern France (see *azure*).

The city of Nice on France's Cote d'Azur.

Cotes *(kotes)*   Roger Cotes (1682–1716), English historian, philosopher, and professor of astronomy at Cambridge. Cotes wrote the preface to the second edition of Sir Isaac Newton's *Principia*.

cotta *(KOT-ah)*   A white waist-length ecclesiastical garment with short sleeves, worn in church by choir members, altar boys, and acolytes. The cotta is the shorter brother of the surplice, which has large, open sleeves, extends to the knees, and is worn by various clerics in Catholic and Anglican churches. A crossword favorite is terra _____, "baked earth," or earthenware.

Coty *(koe-TEE)*   René Coty (1882–1962), the French jurist who rose to become second president of the Fourth Republic in 1954. He was a staunch follower of Charles de Gaulle, and left office in 1959 when the Fifth Republic was created.

Coue *(koo-AY)*   French psychotherapist Emile Coué (1857–1926), who made self-improvement an international pastime. In the early years of this century, Coué emerged as a cult figure, whose followers ritually repeated his positive formula: "Day by day, in every way, I am getting better and better."

Emile Coué (with beard).

coulee *(KOO-lee)*   From the French word meaning "to flow," either a deep ravine in which water races during rainy seasons, or a stream of volcanic lava, molten or solidified. One of the world's largest concrete structures is Grand **Coulee** Dam, built between 1933 and 1942 on the Columbia River in north-central Washington.

The coulee of the volcano threatens to engulf the town.

coup *(koo)*   The French word for "blow," therefore any precipitate action that produces a desired result. Among better-known coups are the _____ d'état, a sudden takeover of a government involving actual or threatened use of force, and the _____ de grace, or "stroke of mercy"—a shot that finishes the work of an inept firing squad.

coupe *(koop)* A small two-doored automobile whose seating capacity is limited to two people. With the last syllable accented *(koo-PAY)*, it is either the same automobile owned by a European motorist, or a half-compartment at the end of a European railway coach, with seats on just one side. Also with the accent, a special footed glass dish and the dessert served in it, usually involving ice cream and fruit.

coven *(KUH-ven)* A specific collective noun. Just as ''school'' denotes a group of fish and ''exaltation'' does the same for larks, coven is used when referring to a band of witches, usually 13 in number.

covert *(KUV-ert)* From the old French word that means ''to cover,'' a place in the underbrush or woodland where game can hide from hunters. Also, a small feather that conceals the base of larger feathers in a bird's wing or tail. As an adjective, the opposite of overt.

covey *(KUV-ee)* What coven (q.v.) is to witches, covey is to quail or partridges, give or take a few birds.

Cowes See *Wight*.

cowl *(kowl)* A hood worn by a monk, or any object shaped like a hood. This includes the device installed at the top of a chimney to improve the draft, or the section of the front of an automobile that holds the windshield and dashboard. Also, the surname of Jane **Cowl** (1890–1950), the American actress, playwright, and producer.

cox *(koks)* Another name for a coxswain, the person in a ship's boat or a racing shell responsible for steering. Also, the surname of Jacob Dolson **Cox** (1828–1900), Canadian-born Union general in the Civil War, and of James Middleton Cox (1870–1957), Democratic candidate in 1920 for the Presidency of the United States. Also the married name of Tricia Nixon (Mrs. Edward Cox).

coypu *(KOY-poo)* A large South American aquatic rodent, also known as the swamp beaver because of its superficial resemblance to that industrious fellow. The coypu may be up to two feet long and weigh as much as 14 pounds. It is bred in captivity for its fur. Both the animal and the fur itself are also called nutria.

crag *(krag)* A large, steep rocky mass or cliff that extends from a rock base. Also, in the dialect of northern England and Scotland, a **crag** is one's throat, neck, or craw. Rock crags are featured in the big ''Ride of the Valkyries'' scene from Wagner's opera *Die Walküre*.

crake *(krake)* A bird related to the rails, but with a shorter bill. The corncrake, or land rail, is hunted for the table in Europe. It is an endangered species, proving you can't have your crake and eat it too.

crane *(krane)* Either a piece of heavy equipment for moving great weights on construction sites and in factory yards; or a large wading bird with a long neck, legs, and bill. Also, the surname of Hart **Crane** (1899–1932), and Stephen **Crane** (1871–1900), author of *The Red Badge of Courage*, a novel, and many short stories.

A crane family member.

craw *(kraw)* The saclike, muscular-walled expansion of a bird's gullet where food is predigested. This organ is also known as a crop. By extension, a craw is the gullet of any animal, including man, in whose craw unpleasant things often stick.

creche *(kresh)* A small diorama representing the Nativity, with figures of the infant Jesus in the manger, Mary, Joseph, the Magi, shepherds, and animals. Crèches have traditionally been displayed between Christmas Eve and January 6, ever since St. Francis of Assisi initiated the custom in 1223.

credo *(KREE-doe)* A creed or faith, or the statement of its doctrines. *Credo* is Latin for "I believe," and is the first word of several creeds. Important Christian creeds include the Nicene Creed of the fourth century; the Apostle's Creed, dating from some centuries later in its present form; and the Augsburg Confession (1530).

Cree *(kree)* North American Indians of Algonquian stock, who inhabited a region roughly from the southern end of Hudson Bay to Northern Alberta. One branch of the Cree became the Plains Cree. The Woodland Cree did business with the Hudson's Bay Company until decimated by smallpox in the late 1800s.

In traditional tribal dress.

creel *(kreel)* A wicker basket with a slotted top, in which anglers keep their catch. Creels are usually carried on the hip, so as not to interfere with the business of landing a fish. Spinners of thread will also recognize the **creel** as a frame for storing bobbins.

creme *(krem)* Cream with a lifted pinkie. The word crème (literally, "cream") from the French, is generally used to indicate something smooth or especially pleasing to the taste. Crème-de-menthe and the dessert crème brûlée are two such examples. The crème-de-la-crème in any category is the ultimate, the best.

Creole *(KREE-ohl)* A descendant of the French and Spanish settlers of old Louisiana, in the southern United States. The term is still used widely there to differentiate between these individuals and the Cajuns—descendants of the Acadians who came as refugees from the area now known as Nova Scotia.

Creon *(KREE-on)* In Greek myth, the name of various monarchs, including the brother of Jocasta who became the king of Thebes following the death of the sons of Oedipus; the king of Corinth murdered by Medea in the play by Euripides; and an earlier king of Thebes in the works of Apollodorus.

crepe *(krape)* From the Latin word for "crisp," a thin, delicate crinkled fabric, originally silk. Hard-finished crêpe was usually dyed black and used as a sign of mourning; thinner crêpes include crêpe de chine (see *chine*). Also, a very thin pancake. For **crêpes** suzette, the pancakes are folded and flambéed in a sauce of sugar, butter, orange zest, and liqueur.

Crete *(kreet)* Largest of the Greek islands, located in the Mediterranean about 60 miles south of mainland Greece. The

The Minoan Palace of Knossos on Crete.

capital is Iraklion. Crete was home to the Minoan civilization, one of mankind's earliest, and it was in Crete that Theseus slew the Minotaur in the palace of King Minos (see *Minos*), then escaped with Ariadne, one of the king's daughters. Over the centuries Crete has been ruled by Greeks, Romans, Byzantines, Venetians, Turks, and, finally and again, Greece. During World War II, Crete was held by the Germans. Many ruins, including the partly restored palace of Gnossos (or Knossos), are here, as is Mt. Ida, more than 8,000 feet high.

crick *(krik)* As a Western pronunciation, a crick is a creek. It also means a painful muscular spasm, usually in the back or neck. Also, the surname of Francis Harry Compton **Crick** (1916–   ), the English scientist who in 1962 was one of the winners of the Nobel Prize in medicine and physiology for his work on DNA.

crimp *(krimp)* In material, a narrow fold or pleat. In hair, a wave or curl. In British fish cookery, a gash that causes muscular contraction and hence firmer flesh after a cold soak and cooking. Also, a person who recruited men for military or naval service through deceit, and trickery, thus putting a distinct **crimp** in their future plans.

Dancer Mary Eaton with crimped hair.

croak *(kroke)* A husky, deep sound usually made in the back of the throat, often by frogs on a moonlit night. A croaker is any of several fish (also called drums) that croak, or a member of the family immortalized in Goldsmith's *Good-Natured Man* (1768). Mr. Croaker's greatest pleasure was attending funerals; these may or may not have come about through inept medical treatment (by a "croaker") having caused the patient to "**croak**."

Croat *(krote)* A native of Croatia, the federated Yugoslavian republic whose capital is Zagreb. Demands for increased autonomy and even secession have kept Croatia in the news over the past decade. The most famous Croat was Josip Broz, also known as Tito (q.v.), Marshal of Yugoslavia.

crock *(krok)* A pot or jar usually made of baked clay. In recent years, the word has taken on the pejorative connotation of a  falsehood or unacceptable account—probably a truncated version of the expression "That's a crock of nonsense," or words to that effect. A **crock** can also be a broken-down person; "**crocked**" is a synonym for intoxicated.

croft *(kroft)* In the British Isles, a small tenant-worked farm; a small enclosed field; or a small piece of land leased for farming. From this usage comes the word crofter, meaning a tenant farmer, often with the hereditary right to work (but not own) the land.

crone *(krone)* From the Old Dutch word *kronje,* conveying the sense of an old ewe, any old woman, but especially a wrinkled or unattractive one. Among the famous crones of literature were the witch in *Hansel and Gretel;* Stheno, one of the Gorgons of Greek mythology; Sycorax, the foul hag in Shakespeare's *Tempest;* and the three witches in his *Macbeth.*

crony *(KROE-nee)* Originally a close friend or companion, now something less savory. The distinction is simple: if they are your friends, they are colleagues; if they are your enemies' friends, they're cronies.

croon *(kroon)* Originally defined as to bellow, later to moan, and now modified to mean to sing or hum gently. New shades of meaning were imparted by such popular singers as Bing Crosby, who made crooning a romantic, sexy type of singing which reached its zenith with Frank Sinatra and his legions of swooning bobby-soxers.

Bing Crosby accompanying himself on a squeezebox as he croons to Grace Kelly in the film High Society.

crore *(kror)* From the Hindu word for "highest money," the word means mega-bucks in India. A crore is equivalent to 10 million rupees (q.v.), or 100 lakhs (q.v.) of rupees.

croup *(kroop)* Either a medical disorder of children in which inflamed respiratory passages cause coughing, difficult breathing, and hoarseness; or a horse's rump.

croze *(kroze)* An example of the cooper's art. The croze is the groove on the inside of either end of the staves of a barrel or cask into which the heads of the barrel are fitted and secured.

cruet *(KROO-et)* A small bottle or jar used to hold a liquid condiment such as oil or vinegar for table service. Cruets are also the vessels holding water or wine on altars.

Table cruets.

crump *(krump)* An onomatopoeic reproduction of the sound made by an exploding shell or bomb—an unpopular popular word in Great Britain during the Blitz of World War II. Also, the surname of Edward Hull **Crump** (1876–1954), the Democratic politico who dominated Tennessee politics as "Boss" Crump.

crus *(krus)* A loose designation of that part of the human leg or animal's hind leg between the ankle and the knee. Also, any other anatomical structure that resembles legs or roots, such as the crura (pl.) of the stapes in the human ear.

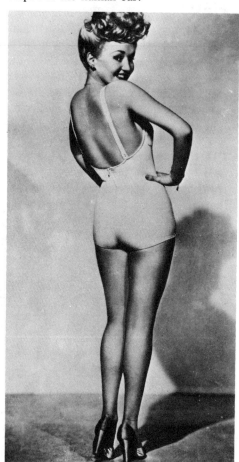

Betty Grable displays a nice pair of crura in this famous pin-up photo of World War II.

cruse *(krooz)* In ancient times, a small jar used for holding honey, water, or oil. The best-known cruse was the miraculous container of oil that burned for eight days in the Temple of Jerusalem, now recalled by candles burned in the Chanukah festival.

crux *(kruks)* Literally, "cross"; figuratively, a crucial point where different sets of circumstances or considerations meet like arms of a cross. **Crux** is also a brilliant constellation whose four brightest stars form the famous Southern Cross. The long arm points to the south celestial pole, and the constellation includes the Coalsack, a famous dark nebula.

crwth or cruth

(krooth) In Wales, an ancient stringed instrument. The crwth usually had six strings, four played with a bow, violin-style, and the other two plucked by the thumb.

Musical antiquarian Arnold Dolmetsch plucks a crwth.

crypt *(kript)* From the Greek for "hidden," an underground chamber or vault, usually used as a burial place beneath the floor of a church. Crypts probably developed from the catacombs used by early Christians for secret worship and burial of the faithful. At Canterbury Cathedral in England, the twelfth-century crypt makes up a complete church in itself. The root of crypt is evident in cryptic and cryptogram.

The crypt of Canterbury Cathedral in England.

cubby *(KUH-bee)* Any narrow, enclosed space, such as a cramped room or a small storage niche or cabinet; a cubbyhole. A cubby pen is a small enclosure made of upright sticks, with bait inside to trap small game. And in British automobiles, the cubby locker is nothing more than the glove compartment.

cubeb *(KYEW-beb)* Cubeb pepper, the berry of a climbing shrub of the pepper family found in the East and West Indies. The crushed unripe berry and its oil have been used medicinally. Dried, the pungent berry is a seasoning. It was also incorporated into a cigarette for treating catarrh.

cubit *(KYEW-bit)* Name of several ancient measures of length, somewhere in the range of 18 to 22 inches. This, like the ell (q.v.), is based on the length of a man's arm from the end of his middle finger to his elbow. The cubit is employed in the Bible to specify the dimensions of Noah's Ark (Gen. 6:15), among many other things.

cud *(kud)* A mass of food being chewed a second time. This is done by cattle and other ruminants, who regurgitate previously swallowed food from their first stomach and rework it over slowly in their mouths before swallowing again. That it tastes better the second time around is a moot point.

cuddy *(KUH-dee)* Either a small shipboard cabin, like the cook's galley; a donkey of Scotland; or one of several fish called coalfish. Also known as the pollack, this coalfish is a member of the cod (q.v.) family and is caught in the northern Atlantic.

cue *(kyew)* On the stage, a signal to an actor, usually a line delivered by another actor, that tells him it's his turn to speak; or any signal to begin an activity. Also, the long, leather-tipped stick used to hit the white **cue** ball in billiards or pool. Professional cues can be dismantled for easy carrying by pool sharks.

culch or **cultch** *(kulch)* Material on the bottom of a body of water where oysters breed, either natural (shells, etc.) or provided by oyster farmers (tiles). This is a foundation for the attachment of spats, the free-swimming baby oysters. Culch may consist of debris, which is probably why it is a colloquial term for rubbish in New England.

culet *(KYEW-let)* The flat bottom facet of a diamond whose face is cut as a brilliant, that is, with many facets to increase its brilliance. The "bottom" sense of culet is a reflection of the Latin word from which it is derived: *culus,* meaning "buttock."

culex *(KYEW-leks)* Any of a large genus of mosquitoes that includes the species that cause encephalitis and filariasis, a worm infection that can lead to elephantiasis. All mosquito species pierce the skin and suck blood from mammalian hosts, but only the females feed this way; male mosquitoes live happily on plant secretions alone.

cull *(kull)* Something that has been sorted out of a lot and rejected because it does not measure up to standards. A classic cull, and also a tremendous bargain, is the one-clawed lobster—just as tasty as his brethren with the normal complement of appendages, but providing less meat. To **cull** is to select or choose either the best or worst in a batch of anything.

culm *(kulm)* Either coal dust or small chunks of anthracite; or, in botany, the jointed, usually hollow stem of certain grasses.

cult *(kult)* A complex of rituals and practices devoted to worshiping a religious figure; or the extravagant following of any person, idea, or fad. For example, some modern authors who were thought to write obscurely—like Cummings, Eliot, Joyce, Stein, and Sitwell—were once character-ized as the Cult of Unintelligibility in a celebrated essay by the critic Max Eastman. Many modern "fringe" religious movements are considered to be cults.

The 1982 wedding of 2,075 couples, all members of the cultlike Unification Church.

Cumae *(KYEW-mee)* Ancient Italian city, on the Bay of Naples, that was the earliest Greek colony in Italy. It was captured by the Samnites in the fifth century B.C. and then came under Roman rule. The city declined and disappeared in the thirteenth century A.D. Cumae was the home of the famous Sybil (q.v.), priestess of Apollo.

cumin or **cummin** *(KUM-in)* A small annual herb that produces diminutive white or pink blossoms, followed by seed pods. Cumin is native to Mediterranean countries, and be-  longs to the carrot family. Its piquant seeds are used to flavor many foods, and its aromatic oil gives certain liqueurs their flavor and bouquet.

Cupid *(KYEW-pid)* The Roman god of love, also known as Amor, corresponding to the Greek Eros (q.v.). The name Cupid comes from the Latin meaning desire, longing, or passion. According to legend, Cupid, the son of Venus, loved Psyche, but forbade her to look upon him. When she did so anyway, he departed. She was united with him forever after long and dangerous searching, proving that love conquers all. Cupid is most often represented in art as a winged child.

CROSSWORD CUPIDS

Venus and Cupid
Paris Bordone

Venus and Adonis
Simon Vouet, 1635–40

Cupid and Psyche
François Gérard
1798

Mars with Venus and Cupid
School of Fontainebleau

The Education of Cupid
Correggio
1523-25

Adonis Discovers Venus
Annibale Carracci
1590

cur *(kur)* From a Middle English word for "growl," a dog of indeterminate breed, or

a mongrel. Because of the putative personality of alley dogs, any person with a mean, contemptible, or cowardly streak is also called a cur. This is a favorite put-down of villains by fair maidens.

curare *(kyew-RAH-ray)* Complex poisons extracted from the root of the wourali plant, among other curare sources, and used as an arrow poison by Indians of the Amazon jungle. Curare causes motor paralysis. It has therefore found use in medicine as a muscle relaxant in tetanus, spastic paralysis, and similar conditions.

curch *(kurch)* The sound of this word indicates both its origin and its meaning—in Scotland, a scarf (kerchief) worn on the head by a woman or girl. In Russia, this item of attire is known as a babushka, from the Russian word for "grandmother."

Harpo Marx in a curch.

curd *(kerd)* When milk turns sour and clabbers, or curdles, the part that coagulates is the curd. This is the portion from which cheeses are made. According to the popular nursery rhyme, it formed a staple of the diet, along with whey, of the tuffet-sitting Ms. Muffet.

Curie *(kyew-REE)* Family name of Pierre Curie (1859–1906) and his wife, Marie Sklodowska Curie (1867–1934), who together achieved fame and the 1903 Nobel Prize in physics for their work on radioactivity. Marie Curie won the 1911 Nobel Prize in chemistry, and became the first person to be awarded two Nobels. One of

Pierre and Marie Curie near their home outside of Paris.

their daughters, Irene (1897–1956), was also a scientist. She and her husband, Frederic Goliot-Curie (1900–1958), continued her parents' work and shared the 1935 Nobel Prize in chemistry. The **curie** is a unit of radioactivity and roughly equals the decay rate of one gram of pure radium.

curn *(kern)* A Scotch variation of kernel, meaning a single grain of corn. Since this is obviously a minute quantity, the meaning has been broadened to denote a small number. The Scotch use the word in lieu of "few."

Cush *(kush)* According to the Bible (Gen. 10:6-8), the eldest son of Ham; he is traditionally the settler of northeastern Africa and sire of the Hamites. The "land of Cush" is probably Ethiopia. With a lower-case *c*, **cush** is also a Southern U.S. dish made of cornmeal dough, either fried, baked, or cooked in pot liquor. Its name probably comes from the Arabic by way of Africa, where couscous was a staple food of many natives who came to America as slaves.

cusp *(kusp)* A general term designating points formed by the meeting of two curves, as on the edge of a tooth; in an archway; or on either tip of a crescent moon. In astrology, the **cusp** is the point where one zodiacal sign changes to another.

Cuzco *(KOOZ-koe)* Renowned southern Peruvian city, once capital of the Inca empire, founded by Manco Capac, son of the sun god. Cuzco boasted the fabulous gold-encrusted Temple of the Sun, plundered with the entire city by Pizarro during the Spanish conquest. In 1950, an earthquake destroyed much of Cuzco, which had been rebuilt by the conquerors on the Inca ruins, but many buildings have been restored.

Cuzco as it might have looked in the 17th century.

cycad *(SIE-kad)* Any plant belonging to the major order of plants called Cycadales, all tropical and subtropical evergreens. Cycads, which bear cones and mostly resemble palms (some are 30 feet high), appeared during the Permian period and are among the most primitive plants on earth. Many cycads are cultivated as ornamentals, and some yield a type of sage or edible nutlike fruit.

cygnet *(SIG-net)* A young swan. The word derives from Cygnus, mythical Ligurian monarch who was transformed into a swan and placed in the heavens as a constellation. The Swan can be seen in the northern skies and is sometimes called the Northern Cross, because its five brightest stars, including Deneb (q.v.), a crossword favorite, are in that configuration.

cylix *(SIE-liks)* or **kylix** *(KIE-liks)* An ancient Greek drinking vessel with a strong, stubby stem, a shallow bowl,

and a handle on each side. It was obviously the cup preferred by two-fisted drinkers.

cyma *(SIE-mah)* In architecture, a type of molding used with cornices. The cyma is partially concave and partially convex, thus presenting an undulating profile.

cyme *(sime)* Botanical term denoting certain plants' mode of bloom. The flower (or flower cluster) at the top of the main stem opens first; others follow, emerging as lateral blooms. **Cyme** is also an ancient Greek city on the Ionian Sea in Asia Minor, the largest of the 12 cities of Aeolis.

Cynic *(SIN-ik)* Member of an ancient Greek school of philosophy founded around 440 B.C. by Antisthenes. The Cynics held virtue to be paramount in all things, and were critical of materialism and pleasure. The word has been slightly twisted into its current meaning—one who thinks people are motivated only by self-interest.

W. C. Fields was one of film's great cynics.

Cyrus *(SIE-rus)* Either of two ancient, regal Persians—the Great, and the Younger. Cyrus the Great founded the Persian empire in the sixth century B.C., conquered much of the Mideast, and put the Jews in power in Palestine, thus rehabilitating Israel (2 Chron. and Ezra). The Younger, a prince and ruler of satrapies, lived about 100 years later. His friendship with Lysander helped Sparta win the Peloponnesian War.

dab *(dab)*   A small dollop of something moist and soft, like butter; often defined "smidgen." Or colloquially, the British equivalent of a maven or expert. **Dab** is also the name given to certain small flounders. Perhaps the most glamorous dab is the prized lemon sole; the sand dab is a California favorite.

The asymmetrical dab.

Dacca *(DAK-ah)*   The capital city of Bangladesh. The Bara Katra palace, built in 1644, and the Lal Bagh, fort built in 1678, are leftovers from Dacca's halcyon days in the seventeenth century, when it held sway as the Mogul capital of Bengal.

dace *(dace)*   Another small fish, this one belonging to the same family as carps, tenches, and minnows. Strictly a fresh-water species, dace (or daces) are found in both Europe and North America.

dacha *(DAH-shah)*   In old Russia and the present U.S.S.R., a small country house or bungalow to which city dwellers repair for weekends or vacations. A dacha was the setting for both *The Sea Gull* and *Uncle Vanya*, by Chekhov.

Dacia *(DAY-shah)*   The ancient name for an area of eastern Europe that roughly corresponds to what is now known as Dracula country—the Transylvanian region of Romania. In A.D. 102, Trajan invaded Dacia and established it as a Roman province. The Romanian language is based on the Latin spoken at the time.

Dada *(DAH-dah)*   A European movement begun in 1916 by artists and writers in reaction to the madness of World War I. Dada attacked conventionality in art and behavior, and stressed absurdity. Among noted Dadaists were the painters Jean Arp (q.v.) and Marcel Duchamp. Dadaism eventually became the basis of Surrealism.

dado *(DAY-doe)* Either that section of a pedestal between the top and the base; or the lower part of the wall of a room, if paneling or a molding ornament separates it from the upper portion.

daeva *(DEE-vah)* In Persian mythology, one of a group of evil demons distinguished by long horns, staring eyes, great fangs, ugly paws, and a generally unkempt look.

dag *(dag)* Either a portion of a serrated edge, or an appliqué ornamenting a medieval garment; or the given name of **Dag** Hjalmar Agne Carl Hammarskjöld (1905–1961), Secretary General of the United Nations from 1953 until his death. He died in a plane crash while on a peace mission. The Nobel Peace Prize was awarded to him posthumously.

Dag Hammarskjöld.

Dagda *(DAHG-dah)* The principal god of the pagan Irish pantheon, who vanquished the Tuatha de Danann (the rest of the pantheon). A kind of Jupiter of the Gaels (q.v.), his name means "good god."

Dagon *(DAY-gon)* The fertility god of the Philistines and later the Phoenicians, who is represented as half man and half fish (the lower half, according to Milton in *Paradise Lost*).

Dagon the merman god.

Dahak *(DAY-hak)* In Persian myth, the devil and serpent king destined to wreak the most frightful havoc on humankind as a prelude to the benign reign of Ormuzd, chief god in Zoroastrianism.

dais *(DAY-us)* A platform raised above the floor and located prominently in a hall or dining room. Traditionally, a place for guests of honor, including toastmasters, celebrities, dignitaries, high government officials, and bar mitzvah youths.

Speaking from the dais to a packed house.

Dakar *(dah-KAR)* Seaport, largest city, and capital of Senegal on the Cape Verde peninsula, westernmost point of Africa. Dakar was the former capital of French West Africa (1902–1958) and the short-lived Mali Federation (1959–1960). During World War II, Free French forces under General Charles de Gaulle fought a losing battle to liberate Dakar from Vichy control.

dale *(dale)* A small valley, especially a stream valley in Britain. Also, half of the vaudeville team of Smith and **Dale,** on whom the play *The Sunshine Boys* was based. In their most famous sketch, Joe Smith played Dr. Cronkheit to Charlie Dale's Frankly Dubious. **Dale** is also "actress Evans."

Joe Smith and Charles Dale (right).

Dali *(DAH-lee)* The Spanish Surrealist painter Salvador Dali (1904–). His works are characterized by such incongruous objects as melting clocks in the foreground, and ex-

Dali with his mustache.

quisite backgrounds executed with the precision of a draftsman. Dali has collaborated on the scenarios of two surrealistic films.

daman *(DAM-un)*   A rodentlike animal about the size of a marmot found in parts of the Near East and Africa. It is also called Syrian hyrax. Curiously, a daman's molars are, except for their size, exactly like those of a rhinoceros. The daman is referred to in the Bible (Psalms 104:18 and Prov. 30:26) as a coney (q.v.).

Damon *(DAY-mun)*   So inseparable was he from his bosom friend Pythias that the two Syracusans are considered the symbols of true friendship. When Pythias was condemned to death, Damon offered himself as hostage so that Pythias could leave to set his affairs in order. When Pythias actually returned, the tyrant Dionysius I was so moved that he set both the lads free.

Dana *(DAY-nah)*   Surname of several famous men, including Charles Anderson Dana (1819–1897), one of America's most celebrated editors and journalists; Richard Henry Dana (1815–1882), the American lawyer and author who wrote *Two Years Before the Mast* (1840); and James Dwight Dana (1813–1895), geologist, South Seas explorer, and academician.

Danae *(DAN-ay-ee)*   The daughter of Acrisius, King of Argos, who locked her in a tower when told that she would bear a son who would kill him. Zeus, who loved Danaë, managed access by changing himself into a shower of sunbeams that bathed her body, according to Renaissance paintings. The result was a son, Perseus. Thus, despite Acrisius's best efforts, the prophecy was fulfilled.

Danaë by Flemish artist Jan de Mabuse.

Dante *(DAHN-tay)*   First name of the great Italian poet Alighieri (1265–1321), who, according to Carlyle, "gave a voice to ten silent centuries." Dante's masterpiece was *The Divine Comedy,* consisting of 100 cantos (q.v.) in *terza rima.* This work encompassed the entire spectrum of human and divine knowledge.

A nineteenth-century painting of Dante.

Danube See *Ister.*

darb *(darb)*   In schoolboy slang, something or someone superlative, as in "That's a darb!"

Dard *(dard)*   An Indo-Aryan people of the upper Indus valley, or a group of languages (also called Dardic) spoken by the Dard (or Dards), and including Shina, Khowar, Kafiri, and Kashmiri.

data *(DAY-tah)*   Factual information used as a basis for discussion or decision-making. Data is actually a plural of the word datum, but as information can be both singular and plural, so can data. Often clued nowadays as "computer input" or "computer bank."

dato or **datto** *(DAH-toe)*   A local headman in Muslim communities in Malaysia and in the southern Philippines, where members of many groups are known as Moro (q.v.) or Moros.

Davao *(DAH-vow)*   A place where you might find a dato (q.v.). Davao is the principal city on the southern Philippine island of Mindanao. Its major industry is the production of hemp (q.v.).

davit *(DAV-it)*

Aboard ship, one of a pair of outward-curving uprights from which a boat is slung for launching at sea. Also, a crane or boom for hoisting cargo. The word davit evolves from the biblical David, who used a sling to lower the boom on Goliath.

Using a davit to lower a cannon.

Davos *(dah-VOSE)*

A small Swiss town located in the eastern canton of Grisons, near Davos Lake. Like many areas of Switzerland, it is a mecca for winter-sports enthusiasts. Formerly, because of its pure air, it was a health resort for people with tuberculosis.

Davy *(DAY-vee)*

Sir Humphrey Davy (1778–1829), the English scientist whose work in electrochemistry led to the isolation of potassium and sodium, among other elements. He also invented a safety lamp for miners. **Davy** is also Davy Jones, a personification of the sea, whose "locker" is the traditional resting place for the drowned.

Humphrey Davy.

daw *(daw)*

Also called a jackdaw or belfry crow, this black bird with gray neck feathers is found throughout Europe and in parts of Asia. The daw is related to the common crow but is smaller. He is common, often lives in cities, and has a reputation for thievery.

Dawes *(dawz)*

Surname of several famous Americans, including Charles Gates Dawes (1865–1951), who shared the Nobel Peace Prize in 1925 and was Vice-President of the U.S. under Coolidge; Henry Laurens Dawes (1816–1903), the senator responsible for the establishment of the Dawes Commission and Dawes Act to deal with Indian affairs; and William Dawes (1745–1799), who, on April 18, 1775, warned of the British advance on a famous ride from Boston to Lexington (where he was joined by Paul Revere).

Charles Gates Dawes.

Dax *(daks)*

A small town on the Adour River in southwestern France. In Roman times, the town was known as the Aquae Augustae ("consecrated waters") and is still famous for its hot mineral springs.

Dayak or Dyak *(DIE-ak)*

In Borneo, a member of any of a number of indigenous peoples. Dayak is also the language spoken by these people.

Debs *(debz)*

Eugene V. Debs (1855–1926), the locomotive fireman who became a Socialist leader and a five-time candidate for President of the U.S. Convicted of violating the Espionage Act in 1918, Debs, a pacifist, was pardoned by President Harding in 1921, and ever since has been revered by his admirers as a martyr to principle.

Socialist Eugene Victor Debs.

decoy *(DEE-koy)*

Derived from the Dutch word meaning "cage," a decoy was originally a place, such as a net-enveloped area of a lake, into which game birds were lured for capture. More often, the term applies to an artificial bird, set out by

hunters to lure real birds, especially water-fowl, within shotgun range. A **decoy** is also a person used as a lure, as a policeman whose behavior or appearance induces a suspect to commit a crime, or a swindler's aide.

Dee *(dee)*   Three rivers in the United Kingdom bear this name, yet there seems to be no confusion among the 50-mile-long Dee flowing through southwestern Scotland to the Irish Sea; the 90-mile-long Dee, famous for salmon, that flows to the North Sea through northeastern Scotland, including an artificial channel at Aberdeen; and the 70-mile-long Dee that takes a roundabout but generally northerly course through northwestern Wales to the Irish Sea. Other **Dees** are actresses Ruby and Sandra, and a word in the title of the song "Zip-a-_____-Doo-Dah."

Defoe *(deh-FOE)*   The English writer Daniel Defoe (1659–1731), best known for such works as *Robinson Crusoe* (1719) and *Moll Flanders* (1722). In *An Essay upon Projects* (1698) he advocated education for women.

Degas *(deh-GAH)*   French Impressionist painter Hilaire Germain Edgar Degas (1834–1917). The son of a banker, he studied law but abandoned that field to render his favorite subjects—ballet dancers, race-track scenes, and women at their ablutions—in oils and pastels. He was also a sculptor. He ranks among France's greatest artists.

Edgar Degas with an unidentified child.

CROSSWORD CLASSICS

THE GODDESSES

Greek		Roman
Aphrodite	(love; beauty)	Venus
Artemis; Selene	(moon)	Diana; Luna
Athena; Pallas	(wisdom)	Minerva
Demeter	(fertility)	Ceres
Elpis	(hope)	Spes
Eos	(dawn)	Aurora
Gaea	(earth)	Tellus
Hera	(queen of gods)	Juno
Hestia	(hearth)	Vesta
Hygeia	(health)	Salus
Irene	(peace)	Pax
Nyx	(night)	Nox
Rhea	(harvest)	Ops
Tyche	(fortune)	Fortuna

THE GODS

Greek		Roman
Ares	(war)	Mars
Cronus	(agriculture)	Saturn
Dionysus	(wine & revelry) Bacchus	Comus
Hades; Erebus	(lower world) Pluto	Orcus; Dis
Helios	(sun) Apollo	Sol
Hermes	(messenger of gods)	Mercury
Hephaestus	(fire)	Vulcan
Pan	(nature)	Faunus
Poseidon	(sea)	Neptune

Deil *(deel)* In Scotland, the designation for Beelzebub, Mephistopheles, Satan, Mr. Scratch, Old Ned, or, simply, the Devil.

Ezio Pinza sings the title role in Boito's Mefistofele.

deism *(DEE-izm)* The belief that nature demonstrates the existence of God, but that the deity (q.v.) exercises no control over the lives of men. In the seventeenth and eighteenth centuries, formal religion was rejected as superstition by deists, or "freethinkers," who included Voltaire, Rousseau, George Washington, Benjamin Franklin, and Thomas Jefferson.

deity *(DEE-ih-tee)* From the Latin *deus,* or "god," the generic term for any god (or goddess) of any religious belief. In addition to the Judeo-Christian God, deities include Allah, supreme being of Islam; Brahma, Vishnu (q.v.), and Shiva (q.v.), the three supreme gods of Hinduism; and the many divinities of ancient civilizations, notably Greece and Rome.

dele *(DEE-lee)* This pure Latin word is the imperative singular form of *delere,* "to delete." In printing, it is a direction to the typesetter to remove a word or words. The dele is a mark used by editors to convey this instruction, and is obviously a bane of writers.

delft *(delft)* Glazed ceramic ware, now usually blue in color but originally brown, named for its place of manufacture, the city of Delft in the western Netherlands. An important commercial center until the seventeenth century, Delft was the home of Jan Vermeer, whose famous painting *View of Delft* reveals that the city has scarcely changed since his time.

Delhi *(DELL-ee)* A small territory and city in north-central India. Old Delhi was the capital of the Mogul empire until 1739, when the city was sacked and the Peacock Throne removed to Persia. The English took Old Delhi in 1803, and it was the interim capital of India between 1912 and 1931. Among its points of interest are the Red Fort of Shah Jahan, who also built the Jama Masjid (Great Mosque). Adjoining the old city is New Delhi, capital of India since 1931.

The Red Fort, one of the sights of Delhi, India.

Delos *(DEE-los)* Smallest of the Cyclades Islands. According to Greek legend, it was made fast to the bottom of the sea by Poseidon and was the birthplace of Artemis and Apollo. An important center of culture and commerce in antiquity and a chief center of Apollo's worship, it was abandoned in the first century B.C. and is virtually uninhabited today.

delta *(DELL-tah)* Fourth letter of the Greek alphabet, corresponding to the Roman *D* but shaped like a triangle. Also, because it often takes the same shape, an alluvial plain formed at the mouths of certain rivers, usually large, and traversed by branches of the stream. Among rivers that boast **deltas** are the Mississippi, Nile, Rhine, Rhone, Ganges, and Niger.

deme *(deem)* From the Greek word for "populace," any one of the 100 districts into which ancient Attica was divided. In biology, the word is used to denote a population of closely related organisms.

demon *(DEE-muhn)* Originally, a good or evil supernatural spirit of lesser stature and power than gods. Today, demons are generally considered to be fiendish servants of the Devil. Among major demons listed by a demonologist named Binsfield in 1589 (the heyday of study of such beings) were Lucifer, Asmodeus, Mammon, and Leviathan, each with its own particular realm of evil.

Persian White Demon.

demos *(DEE-mose)* Again from the Greek word for "populace," the people of an ancient Greek community as a political unit. From demos comes the word demography—the statistical study of human populations; and demagogue—a person who in ancient times championed the people's interest, today often one who seeks power through the exploitation of prejudices.

demy *(deh-MEE)* A term referring to a sheet of paper for writing or printing. A demy is generally 16 by 21 inches in size, but can vary slightly in either dimension.

Demy also refers to a foundation scholar at Magdalen College, who formally receives an allowance half as large as that of a fellow.

dene *(deen; DAY-nay)* Without any accent marks, a word the British use to denote low sandhill country by the sea, with roots like those of dune (q.v.). Also, with accents over each *e,* an Athabaskan people who live in northwestern Canada and the interior of Alaska. The **Déné** (or Dénés) speak a language also called **Déné.**

Deneb *(DEHN-eb)* A first-magnitude star in the constellation of Cygnus, the Swan (see *cygnet*). One of the 20 brightest stars in the heavens, Deneb shines with about 60,000 times the light of the sun and is 1,600 light-years distant. Deneb is Arabic for "hen's tail," which precisely positions it in the constellation.

denim *(DEN-um)* A strong twilled cotton fabric, originally used for overalls and work clothes. Today denim jeans usually sport an *haute couture* designer's name on the back pocket and a commensurate price tag. The word "denim" comes from the French *serge de Nîmes,* indicating the town where the fabric was first made.

deodar *(DEE-oh-dahr)* A species of large, handsome cedar tree indigenous to the Himalayas. The wood of the deodar is light red, sturdy, and obviously highly prized, since its name is derived from the Sanskrit for "timber of the gods."

depot *(DEE-poe)* A storehouse or warehouse, especially for military supplies. Also, a military station where troops are received

and assigned as replacements. In its transport-station function, a **depot** is a place where trains stop. With reductions in railroad service, many depots across small-town America have become restaurants.

derby *(DER-bee; DAHR-bee)*   A stiff felt hat with a domed crown and up-curved brim, now out of fashion except in Britain, where it is termed a bowler, and in Peru, where it is worn by women. The hat is named after the county seat of Derbyshire, England. An early Earl of **Derby,** of that country, gave his name to various horse races called derbies (see *Epsom).*

derma *(DER-mah)*   Another name for the dermis or cutis, an inner layer of skin tissue just below the epidermis. Retaining its skin connotation, derma is also the casing used in stuffed **derma,** a roasted sausagelike Jewish delicacy consisting of chicken fat, flour, onion, and seasonings.

Devon *(DEHV-uhn)*   Either an island between Baffin and Ellesmere islands, in part of Canada's Northwest Territories; a county in southwestern England from whose principal port, Plymouth, the Pilgrims set sail; or a breed of cattle, red in color, brought to America by colonists as early as 1623.

dewan or **diwan**   *(deh-WAHN)* Title of a government functionary in India, especially the prime minister of a state. The word comes from the Persian word for "account book," an item apparently of some interest to the average dewan.

Dewar *(DOO-uhr)*   The Scottish chemist and physicist Sir James Dewar (1842–1923). One of the inventors of the smokeless explosive cordite, Dewar is perhaps best known for his invention of the Dewar flask, which evolved into that familiar lunch-box item, the thermos bottle.

A derby was one of the trademarks of Charles Chaplin, here seen with Paulette Goddard in Modern Times.

Dewey *(DOO-ee; DYOO-ee)* Surname of several famous Americans: George Dewey (1837–1917), admiral and hero of the Battle of Manila Bay during the Spanish-American War; John Dewey (1859–1952), the philosopher and champion of progressive education; Melville Dewey (1851–1931), deviser of the decimal system widely used to clas-

Admiral George Dewey.

sify library books; and Thomas E. Dewey (1902–1971), three-term governor of New York, best known for snatching defeat from the jaws of victory in the presidential election held in 1948 and won by Harry S. Truman.

dey *(day)* From the Turkish word for an uncle on the maternal side, dey was originally a title for friendly older folks. It subsequently designated the sixteenth-century Ottoman rulers of Tunis and Tripoli; and it stood as the title of the governor of Algiers before that territory was taken over by France in 1830.

dhole *(dole)* A fierce wild dog of India that hunts in packs and will attack animals much larger than itself. The dhole is related to the Siberian wild dog and resembles a shaggy Alsatian but with more teeth and numerous teats.

dhoti *(DOE-tee)* The long loincloth worn by Hindu men, sometimes as a sole garment in the tropical heat of India, or as a kind of shorty pajama.

dhow *(dow)* A small vessel in which Arabs and lascars ply the Red Sea and Indian Ocean. Dhows feature high poop decks, sharp prows, and open waists. The craft has one or more triangular lateen sails, each rigged on a long yard suspended obliquely from a short mast. Two of Columbus's ships, *Niña* and *Pinta,* were lateen-rigged.

The distinctive silhouette of the dhow has been seen in the Red Sea and the Indian Ocean for centuries.

Diana *(die-AN-ah)* In Roman mythology, the goddess of the moon and of the hunt, protectress of maidenhood and goddess of nature. Also known as Artemis, Selene, and Hecate, among other names in other places, she was the twin sister of Apollo. The Temple of Diana, built in her honor at Ephesus, was one of the Seven Wonders of the World. The best-known bearer of the name today is Princess Diana of Wales, Britain's next queen.

dibs *(dibs)* Short for dibstones, or jacks, the familiar, six-pointed children's playthings, and the game played with them. The word designates insignificant amounts of money, and has been used as slang by generations of children to indicate a claim on something, as "I've got **dibs** on his frog."

dice *(dice)* Small cubes with from one to six spots on each face, used in games of chance. Dice (singular: die) have been found in the ruins of Babylon and in ancient Egyptian tombs, apparently used by the pharaohs with no greater success at making 10 the hard way than today's Las Vegas crapshooters. Roman familiarity with dice is reflected in Julius Caesar's comment, "The die is cast" when he had made a crucial decision and crossed the Rubicon.

dickey *(DIH-kee)* A detachable shirt front, once a standard item of apparel for burlesque comedians. Also, James **Dickey** (1923–), American poet whose only novel, *Deliverance,* was made into a major motion picture; also Bill Dickey, catcher now in the baseball Hall of Fame.

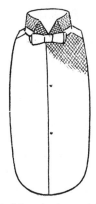

A dickey also lessened the need for clean shirts.

dicot *(DIE-kot)* In botany, an abbreviated reference to a dicotyledon, or plant with two seed leaves called the cotyledons. Non-botanists will be pleased to learn that there is nothing unusual in all this, since dicots outnumber monocots four to one.

dicta *(DIK-tah)* The plural of dictum, which was Latin and is now English for something spoken, and refers to a formal or authoritative statement or rule you'd better abide by.

Dido *(DIE-doe)* According to Vergil's *Aeneid,* a princess of Tyre who, to escape her treacherous brother, fled to Africa, founded Carthage, and became its queen. Aeneas met Dido after being shipwrecked after the fall of Troy, and when he abandoned her, she committed suicide by immolation. Nowadays a **dido** means a caper or prank, usually absurd; "to cut a _____ " is a common clue.

Diem *(dyem)* Ngo Dinh Diem (1901–1963), prime minister of South Vietnam from 1954 until his death. His preferential treatment of Roman Catholics over

Ngo Dinh Diem.

Buddhists, plus reverses suffered in the Vietnam War, proved his undoing. In 1963, dissident generals staged a coup, and Diem was assassinated in the process.

digit *(DIDGE-it)* A finger or toe. Also, any number from 1 to 9, an obvious link to the practice of early mathematicians who counted on their fingers. In astronomy, a digit is one-twelfth the diameter of the sun or moon, and in England it is three-fourths of an inch—or, roughly, a finger's breadth.

dill *(dill)* An herb of the carrot family. The pungent, aromatic dill seeds and leaves are used as a food seasoning and in pickling; dried, the leaves are called dill weed. Dill, in fact, has become a special modifier for pickle lovers everywhere—a far cry from its early use in charms and amulets to protect against witchcraft. An old name for dill was anet, often clued in crosswords as "dill, old style."

dinar *(dih-NAHR)* A coin of gold, minted originally in the seventh century A.D. and long a monetary unit in many Muslim countries. In Iraq, the dinar is equal to five riyals, 20 dirhams, or 1,000 fils (q.v.).

d'Indy *(dahn-DEE)* Vincent d'Indy (1851–1931), the French composer known for his *Symphony on a French Mountain Air* (1886).

dinghy *(DING-ee)* From the Hindi word for "small boat," dinghies were originally rowboats, later sailboats, used on the rivers and coastal waters of India. Over the years, dinghy has come to refer to several craft, including small boats carried aboard ships or yachts as tenders, and, especially in Britain, several classes of racing sailboats.

dingo *(DING-goe)*   The yellowish-red, carnivorous wild dog of Australia, believed to have been brought to the continent in prehistoric times as a pet. Today, dingoes are anything but man's best friend because their predations on sheep and other livestock have caused significant financial loss.

dinky or **dinkey** *(DINK-ee)*   From the adjective meaning "tiny" or of "no consequence," the dinky (or dinkey) is a small locomotive used in railroad yards to

shunt cars from track to track. It thus could have inspired the children's story about the little engine that could.

The railroad dinky.

diode *(DIE-ode)*   A two-terminal vacuum tube with low resistance to the flow of electricity in one direction and high resistance in the other. This property makes the diode useful for converting alternating current into direct current.

dirge *(dirj)*   Derived from Psalm 5:8, via the prayer for the burial of the dead— *"Dirige, Domine"* ("Direct, O Lord")— dirge has come to mean a funeral hymn or song of sadness and grief.

dirk *(derk)*   In Scotland, a long dagger with a straight blade.

Dis *(diss)*   Another name for Pluto (q.v.), ruler of the lower world in ancient Greek religion. By extension, Dis has also come to denote Hades, his dark realm. Milton mentions Dis in his *Paradise Lost:* "Proserpine gathering flowers...by gloomy Dis was gathered."

ditty *(DIH-tee)*   From the Latin *dictare,* "to dictate" or "to compose"—a simple, short poem intended to be sung. The unmusical term **ditty** bag refers to a small sack used to carry sewing gear, toilet articles, and so on, usually by soldiers and sailors.

diva *(DEE-vah)*   In grand opera, the leading woman singer; also called prima donna. She is expected to sing like a goddess (the word derives from the Latin *divum*—"divine").

Geraldine Farrar, one of the leading divas of her day.

divan *(DIE-van* or *dih-VAN)*   With the former pronunciation, from the same root that gave us dewan (q.v.), a collection of poems, especially in Arabic, or any book of many leaves, such as an account or record book; or the room, council, chamber or smoking room in which accounts or other written material is discussed. With the latter, a low, backless and armless sofa found in the former.

dives *(dives; DIE-vez)*   Pronounced as one syllable, the word usually refers to watery plunges, disreputable bars, or faked knockouts in the boxing ring. As two syllables, **Dives** is the name usually given to the rich man in Christ's parable of the rich man and Lazarus (Luke 16:19-31).

divot *(DIH-vut)* In Scotland, a thin section of sod used as a roofing material. On golf courses everywhere, the chunk of turf excavated by the overly zealous stroke of an inept golfer, often defined as "evidence of a golfing goof."

Dix *(diks)* Preceded by Dorothy, the pseudonym of Elizabeth Meriwether Gilmer (1870-1951), premier adviser to the lovelorn in a widely syndicated column which first appeared in the New Orleans *Picayune* in 1896; preceded by a variant of Dorothy, the name of Dorothea Lynde Dix (1802-1887), a famous social reformer. Occasionally, tricky crossword constructors will clue this word as the number 10 in France, in which case it's pronounced *dees*. As a military installation in New Jersey, it's Fort **Dix.**

Dorothy Dix.

Dixie *(DIKS-ee)* Affectionate name for the American South, as in the song "Dixie," written by D.D. Emmett in 1859. The word probably derives from the ten-dollar note that was used in Louisiana before the Civil War—so-called from the large "Dix" (10—see *dix*) printed on one side.

dodo *(DOE-doe)* An extinct bird that lived on Mauritius Island, the dodo was related to the pigeon but was heavier than a turkey and unable to fly. By extension, the word has come to mean an individual who falls hopelessly behind the times.

Alice meets the Dodo in Tenniel's illustration from Alice's Adventures in Wonderland.

doe *(doe)* Female counterpart of any male animal called a buck. This includes deer, antelopes, and rabbits. **Doe** is also John Doe, masculine counterpart of Jane, both frequent parties to legal proceedings, as a stand-in for a person whose name isn't known. Hence, often in crosswords, "anonymous John" or "anonymous Jane."

doge *(dozhe)* The Italian equivalent of duke, the chief magistrate of the former republics of Venice and Genoa. The pink marble Doge's Palace in Venice is an outstanding attraction for tourists.

The Palace of the Doges, Venice.

dogie *(DOE-gee)* On the cattle ranges of the West, a stray or motherless calf, particularly one disinclined to "git along" despite the urgings of generations of cowpokes.

dole *(dole)* A welfare payment by a government to needy or unemployed persons. Also, the surname of Sanford Ballard **Dole** (1844-1926), first president of Hawaii after the overthrow of Queen Liliuokalanai in 1893 and first governor after the islands were annexed by the U.S. in 1898. Also Robert J. Dole, U.S. senator from Kansas, who was Gerald Ford's Republican running mate in the 1976 presidential election.

dolor *(DOE-lor)* A poetic word for sorrow, anguish, or grief, directly from the Latin. Part of the name of the Via Dolorosa in Jerusalem, the route Jesus took on his way to Golgotha (Mat. 27:33). In the brand of dolor referred to by poetic Britons, the letter *u* precedes the *r*.

dolt *(dolt)* Epithet for a person who is too slow, dull-witted, or stupid to be insulted when he is called a dolt.

Dom *(dahm)* The highest Alpine peak located entirely within Switzerland. Almost 15,000 feet high, it is part of the Mischalbelhörner group in the southern canton of Valais. Dom is a title of respect in the Roman Catholic Church, and is the Portuguese for Don (q.v.). In several languages, including Polish, **dom** is a church.

Don *(dahn)* From the Latin *dominus,* "lord" or "master," a title of respect used with the given names of Spanish men; or with a lower-case *d,* the term denoting an academician at Oxford or Cambridge. Also, a name for rivers, including the 1,100-mile-long Russian **Don,** which flows quietly to the Sea of Azov; and the 70-mile-long Don in Yorkshire, canalized to allow shipping to reach Sheffield.

Donar *(DOE-nahr)* The god of thunder in Germanic mythology, known in Norse legend as Thor (q.v.). Donar was the patron protective of warriors and peasants, not necessarily in that order, and had functions in domestic affairs. He was also wont to throw a hammer which returned to him, boomerang style.

Donna *(DOHN-uh)* Reflecting its origin in the Latin word *domina*—"mistress"— Donna is a title of respect used with the given name of Italian women. The word is also Italian for "lady," as in prima donna, a first lady or diva (q.v.) of opera, and in the famous aria from Verdi's *Rigoletto, "La donna è mobile"*—"the lady is fickle."

Donne *(dunn)* John Donne (1573– 1631), English clergyman and metaphysical

John Donne.

poet. Largely forgotten, he came to the attention of a readership beyond academics when a quotation from one of his sermons became the title of Ernest Hemingway's best seller: *For Whom the Bell Tolls.*

Doone *(doon)* Surname of the heroine of R.D. Blackmore's historical novel, *Lorna Doone,* in which the young hero, John Ridd, is saved by Lorna from the robber Doones, a gang of highborn Devonshire outlaws. Ridd and Lorna eventually marry. Today Lorna Doone is the name of a cookie.

Dore *(doh-RAY)* Gustave Doré (1832– 1883), French illustrator, engraver, painter, and sculptor. He specialized in eerie, supernatural scenes of fantasy etched in fine lines, and is perhaps best

Gustave Doré.

known for his illustrations for Coleridge's *Rime of the Ancient Mariner* and *The Divine Comedy* of Dante (q.v.). **Dore** (*DOH-ray*) is also film producer Dore Schary, and the first two notes of the musical scale (do/re/mi, etc.).

Doric *(DOH-rik)* A word that refers to the institutions and culture of the ancient Greek Dorians. In architecture, the Doric order is characterized by columns without bases and with a simple capital. **Doric** was also the dialect spoken in, among other places, Peloponnesus, Corinth, and Crete. Today it can refer to any northern, especially Scottish, dialect considered uncouth by genteel speakers of Standard English.

The Parthenon is a Doric temple.

dorp *(dorp)* A small town, village, or hamlet, particularly in the Netherlands. The word is now mostly poetic, but with its

Dutch origin, it is still used to designate a small settlement in South Africa. A dorp is mentioned in John Dryden's *The Hind and the Panther* (1685).

dorsa *(DOR-sah)* Plural of dorsum, the back, or any part of an animal that corresponds to the back in a human. Also, the back of any smaller bodily structure, such as the dorsum manus—the back of the hand.

dory *(DOR-ee)* From a Central American Indian word for "dugout," a small flat-bottomed boat with high, flared sides, used for fishing. But not necessarily to catch the oddly named John **Dory** (sometimes just "dory"), a highly edible, golden-yellow saltwater fish.

Doseh *(DOE-seh)* A ritual held in Cairo until its abolition in 1884. During the festival of the Prophet's birth, the sheikh of the Sa'di dervishes would mount his horse and gallop wildly over the bodies of his followers. While spiritually beneficial, this practice was not reported to improve physical well-being among the dervishes.

Dover *(DOE-vuhr)* Several American cities bear this name, including the capital of Delaware, on the St. Jones River south of Wilmington. The best-known Dover, however, is the port city on the Strait of Dover,

The famed white cliffs of Dover face the English Channel.

in Kent, England. Its famous chalk cliffs are riddled with subterranean caves, once used by smugglers, that became shelters from German bombardment in World War II. Dover sole, the most esteemed of flatfish, takes its name from this place.

dowel *(DOW-el)* A cylindrical peg made of wood, used to join two pieces of wood closely together with the peg fitting into two mating holes. Glue is used to guarantee the union only by insecure woodworkers.

dower *(DOW-er)* The portion of a man's real property that his widow inherits to use during her lifetime to support her family; often related to dowry. Dower rights have been abolished in many states and replaced with other provisions. A widower's use of his deceased wife's property when they have had children is known as curtesy.

doxy *(DOK-see)* Originally, a beggar's sweetheart; today, an uncomplimentary reference to a wench or mistress. In a completely unrelated sense, **doxy** is also a suffix indicating that the term refers to a belief system, or creed, as in such words as orthodoxy and heterodoxy.

doyen *(DWA-yen)* A word used instead of dean by francophiles, to whom a female dean is a doyenne. The word comes across from the Latin *decanus* ("leader of ten individuals"), and signifies a presiding church leader, an academic VIP, or the senior member of a particular group, e.g., a diplomatic corps or a literary conclave.

Doyle *(doil)* Sir Arthur Conan Doyle (1859–1930), the Scottish-born English physician who gave up his medical practice to write full-time about the exploits of his creation, the brilliant de-

Besides his Sherlock Holmes classics, Doyle also wrote historical romances.

tective Sherlock Holmes. Holmes classics include *A Study in Scarlet, The Hound of the Baskervilles,* and *The Sign of the Four.*

Draco *(DRAY-koe)* or Dracon *(DRAY-kon)*

In the seventh century B.C., an Athenian statesman, politician, and codifier of laws whose harshness has made the word Draconian synonymous with cruelty and severity. **Draco** is also the Dragon, a constellation of the northern skies. The tip of the Dragon's tail lies directly between the North Star and the Big Dipper.

Drake *(drake)*

Sir Francis Drake (c.1540–1596), the English admiral who was the first of his nation to circumnavigate the globe, and who also preyed on Spanish treasure ships and colonies in the Americas, enriching the coffers of Queen Elizabeth in the process. His ship was the *Golden Hind.* With the first letter in lower case, the **drake** is a male of any duck species.

Sir Francis Drake.

dram *(dram)*

A unit of liquid measure. To your pharmacist, a dram is equal to 60 grams, or ⅛ of an ounce; a fluid dram contains about 60 drops, delivered from a standard dropper. The word dram is also used loosely to designate a small serving of liquor, especially in Scotland, or a small quantity of any liquid.

Drew *(drew)*

Surname of a famous acting family that included John Drew (1853–1927) and his sister, Georgiana Drew Barrymore (1856–1893), mother of the noted character actor Lionel Barrymore (1878–1954); his sister, Ethel Barrymore (1879–1959); and the tempestuous

Georgiana Drew.

matinee idol John Barrymore (1882–1942). All three Barrymores appeared in the 1932 film *Rasputin and the Empress.*

Drin *(dreen)*

Largest river in Albania. About 175 miles in length, it is formed by the White Drin and the Black Drin, which rise in Yugoslavia and join in northeast Albania. The Drin flows through deep gorges in a generally southwest direction, into the Adriatic Sea.

droit *(droit; drwah)*

French for "right," as in right hand, a droit is also a right or equity, as to, or in, property. The word appears in the motto of the arms of England (*Dieu et mon droit:* "God and my right"), and was first used by Richard I to taunt his French foes.

dross *(dross)*

The scum that forms on the surface of molten metal as it cools. This residue, made up of impurities in the metal, is scooped off during the smelting process. The word **dross** has therefore come to mean anything of little or no value.

druid *(DROO-id)*

A priest of an ancient Celtic religion. Druids worshiped nature deities and held the oak, and its parasitic mistletoe, sacred. Their badge was an egg, believed to have been hatched by serpents and kept afloat by their hissing. Anyone who caught the egg and escaped the serpents would become invincible.

drupe *(droop)*

A simple fruit with a soft, fleshy pericarp surrounding an endocarp that has hardened into a pit or stone enclosing the seed. Nonbotanists will immediately recognize such drupes as the peach, plum, cherry, and olive. Strawberries and raspberries are aggregate drupes called drupelets.

Druse or **Druze** *(drooz)* Member of an ancient and secretive sect in Syria, Lebanon, Israel, and Jordan. Its beliefs are thought to contain elements of both Islam and Christianity. Druses believe the eleventh-century Fatimite caliph Hakim to be God. Traditionally, Druses have resisted assimilation, but in Lebanon, Druses held high political office during the 1960s and 1970s.

dryad *(DRIE-ad)* According to Greek mythology, any wood nymph who lived in a tree and whose life span matched that of the tree was a dryad (or hamadryad).

ducat *(DUK-at)* The name for a number of silver or gold coins used in various regions of Europe, some in this century. The first ducat is believed to have been struck in silver in A.D. 1140 by Roger II of Sicily. **Ducat** is also slang for a ticket of admission to a sporting event.

duce *(DOO-chay)* Italian for "leader," from the Latin *ducere*, "to lead," usually preceded by the article *il* ("the"), as in Il Duce. This was the title taken by Benito Mussolini, Fascist head of government in Italy from 1922 to 1943 and thereafter head of a German-backed puppet government. He was summarily court-martialed and executed, together with his mistress, when the Germans collapsed in 1945.

*Benito Mussolini—
"Il Duce".*

duchy *(DUTCH-ee)* The territory ruled over by a duke or duchess.

duct *(duct)* From the past tense *(ductus)* of the same Latin word that became the Italian *duce* (q.v.), a channel through which something is conveyed from one place to another. Ducts may be pipes containing electric wires, metal channels used in air conditioning, or tubes for the passage of bodily fluids, like the bile duct. Duct is often clued as "conduit."

Ducts being used to transport oil above the snowfall.

dulse *(dulse)* Name of several coarse seaweeds with large, usually red, fronds. Dulse is generally found in northern waters, and is used in many areas as a food or condiment.

Duma *(DOO-mah)* The former Russian parliament set up by an edict of Tzar Nicholas II in 1905 and abolished by the Revolution of 1917. The word Duma is of Germanic origin, and is related to the English "doom," as in judgment.

dune *(doon)* A rounded ridge or mound formed in sandy deserts or along seashores by sand blown against obstacles, such as rocks. If they are not held down by vegetation, dunes tend to move with the wind.

The dunes of a desert in Saudi Arabia.

Specimens 500 feet high can be seen in the Great Sand Dunes National Monument in Colorado.

Dunne *(dun)*   Irene Dunne (1904–), film actress of the 1930s and 1940s. Among her most memorable films were *Theodora Goes Wild* and *The Awful Truth*. She played Queen Victoria in *The Mudlark*. The name was also made famous by Finley Peter Dunne (1867–1936), American humorist and creator of Mr. Dooley.

Irene Dunne athwart the handlebars of Cary Grant's motorbike in The Awful Truth.

duroc *(DUE-rok)*   A large, solid-red breed of hogs developed in the northeastern United States during the 1880s, and today one of the most common swine. Females can produce up to three litters a year, each numbering up to 20 piglets. If continuously bred for ten years, a sow can have seven million descendants.

durra *(DOOR-ah)*   A species of grain sorghum common to warm, arid regions. In addition to durra, grain sorghums include feterita, kaffir corn, milo, kaoliang, and shallu. The grain is mainly used as livestock feed, but it is also eaten by humans in some poorer lands.

Duse *(DOO-za)*   Surname of the Italian actress, Eleonora Duse (1859–1924). With her portrayals of Juliet (at age 14) and Dumas's *La Dame aux Camélias*, she became the only rival of the incomparable Sarah Bernhardt. A leading exponent of Ibsen, she made her farewell appearance in his *Lady from the Sea* in 1923.

Eleonora Duse.

Duval *(due-VAL)*   Claude Duval (1643–1670), legendary English highwayman of Norman extraction. Captured while drunk, he was hanged at Tyburn and promptly became the subject of numerous romantic ballads. His epitaph in the Covent Garden Church warns men to watch their purses and women to watch their hearts.

dyad or **diad** *(DIE-ad)*   Generally, any two things considered to be one; in other words, a fancy word for "pair." In biology, a double chromosome representing half of a tetrad, a fancy word for "foursome."

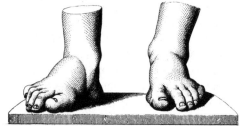

One of the many dyads of the human body.

dyne *(dine)*   A unit of force, denoting the force that causes a mass weighing one gram to increase its speed by one centimeter per second for each second the force is applied. The amount of work this small push achieves is called an erg (q.v.).

Ebal *(EH-bal)*   A mountain in the Holy Land, in present Jordan. It was here that the curse for disobeying the Law was delivered. Ebal lies on the north edge of the valley where Schechem (now Nablus) is located.

ebbet *(EB-eht)*   A common green newt (q.v.) found along the edges of ponds and lakes in the eastern United States and Canada. This amphibious creature is related to other salamanders, but not to the **Ebbets** baseball family who gave their already plural name to the former home field of the Dodgers in Brooklyn.

Ebert *(AY-behrt)*   Friedrich Ebert (1871–1925), a saddlemaker and innkeeper who rose from such humble beginnings to become first president (1919) of the German Republic following World War I. During his presidency, Germany accepted the Treaty of Versailles.

Friedrich Ebert.

Eboli *(EB-oh-lee)*   A small town in Campania, southern Italy, known for its medieval castle which overlooks the modern central city. Tourists traditionally visit the nearby ruins of ancient Eburum, a Greek colony which came under Roman domination and was sacked by the Visigoths in the fifth century. Carlo Levi's 1947 novel *Christ Stopped at Eboli* told of his exile for anti-Fascist activities.

ebon *(EB-uhn)*   A generally poetic word meaning "like ebony," the highly prized dark wood, almost black, obtained from trees of the persimmon family (the genus *Diospyros*), in Asia and Africa. Eb-

One of the trees that provides ebony is the European date plum.

ony is hard and weighty and takes a high polish, making it ideal for ornamental trimmings and piano keys. Mentions of ebony appear in the works of Herodotus, Theophrastus, and Vergil as well as in the Bible (Ezek. 27:15). Often clued as "poetic black."

Ebro *(EE-broe; AY-broe)*   Measuring only 575 miles from its source in the Cantabrian Mountains to its mouth on the Mediterranean, this is the longest river completely within Spain. It flows in a southeasterly direction between the Pyrenees and Iberian mountains, and supplies much of the country's hydroelectric power. In the Spanish Civil War, a major battle, won by the Franco forces, was fought along the Ebro from late summer to November 1938.

ecce *(EH-kay)*   Part of the Latin expression *ecce homo*, "behold the man." These were the words uttered by Pilate when he presented Christ to the populace (John 19:5).

eclat *(ay-KLAH)*   A dazzling effect or display of brilliance, derived from the French word for "burst." Éclat is a word favored by music critics who wish to convey the bravura performance of a virtuoso and appear erudite in the process. It is often clued as "star quality" or "charisma."

ecole *(ay-KOLE)*   In France, a school or place of learning. Perhaps the most famous of such institutions is the École des Beaux-Arts, the French national school of fine arts, founded in 1648 and located on the Quai Malaquais in Paris. The word école was also used in the titles of two plays by Molière, *L'École des Maris (The School for Husbands)* and *L'École des Femmes (The School for Wives)*.

ecru *(ay-CROO)*   The color of natural, undyed wool fiber, a nondescript beige or light tan, often clued as "stocking shade." Ecru comes from the Latin *ex* (out of) and *crudus* (raw).

ecu *(ay-KOO)*   An old French coin. Its name was derived from the Latin *scutum*, meaning "shield," as the coin included a shield in its design. Gold écus, issued from

the fourteenth century until 1640, would bring three livres in change. Later, écus were minted from gold and silver, and varied widely in value.

Edam *(EE-dam)*   A city on the Ijsselmeer in North Holland province of the Netherlands. Edam is best known for its cheese, which is seen as pressed, red-wax-covered balls in most dairy cases.

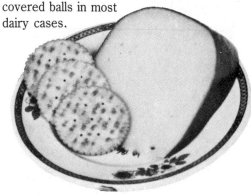

Edda *(ED-dah)*   Two collections of Scandinavian mythological and heroic verse, made in the thirteenth century, both preserved in Old Icelandic. The *Prose Edda*, probably written by Snorri Sturluson and also called the *Younger Edda*, is concerned with Icelandic skaldic poetry; the *Elder*, or *Poetic, Edda* is a collection of Old Norse texts. Another **Edda** was the daughter of Mussolini and wife of Ciano (q.v.).

eddo *(ED-oh)*   Starchy edible root, also called tora (q.v.), of the elephant's ear and several other plants belonging to the Colo-

casia genus. Eddo and other taros are widely grown for food in the world's tropics, including Hawaii, where poi (q.v.) is made from them.

eddy *(ED-ee)* Either a current of water moving counter to the direction of the main current, or the surname of the woman who founded the Church of Christ, Scientist, Mary Morse Baker **Eddy** (1821–1910). Influenced by Dr. Phineas Parkhurst Quimby, she disseminated his teachings and practiced a system of healing without drugs which led, after 1866, to the founding of the church. In 1898 Mrs. Eddy founded the Christian Science Publishing Society, which has published *The Christian Science Monitor* since 1908. Eddy is also singer Nelson Eddy (1901–1967), famous for his films with Jeanette MacDonald.

Mary Baker Eddy.

edema *(eh-DEE-mah)* Directly translated from the Greek, this word means "swelling" or "tumor." Doctors use the word to indicate a condition also called dropsy, in which an abnormal accumulation of fluid occurs in tissues or certain cavities of the body and produces swelling.

Eden *(EED-uhn)* The biblical Paradise. The country and garden of the same name where God established Adam and later created Eve (Gen. 2:8–25). While the word means a place of pleasure or delight, Charles Dickens used it as the name of a dismal backwoods community in his novel *Martin Chuzzlewit*. **Eden** is also the English statesman, Sir Anthony Eden (1897–1977), who served as prime minister from 1955–1957.

Sir Anthony Eden giving an address at the U.N.

Edfu or **Idfu** *(ED-foo)* A city on the Nile, in south-central Egypt. The center of a predynastic kingdom that flourished around 3400 B.C., Edfu is the site of a well-preserved and architecturally remarkable temple of Horus, built by the Ptolemys. Also discovered there were a field of mastabas (structures marking burial chambers) and a Roman cemetery.

edh or **eth** *(eth)* A letter used in the Old English, the Icelandic, and sometimes in phonetic alphabets, to represent an interdental fricative. If it's any help, a voiced interdental fricative sounds like the *th* in *than* rather than the *th* in *thane* (where it is called unvoiced).

edile or **aedile** *(EE-duhl)* From the Latin meaning "belonging to the temples." Title of the Roman magistrates who not only had charge of temples, but controlled food markets, set up public games, regulated the grain supply, and kept law and order. In the first century B.C., Augustus changed the ediles' job description, and they were eventually phased out of existence. Many Latin and Greek words starting with *ae* have *e* as their variant form in English. It's the reason many of these words have the abbreviation *var.* after their clues; e.g., "Fabulist: Var." is Esop, instead of Aesop (q.v.); similarly, Egean instead of Aegean; and eon is sometimes spelled aeon.

Edo *(EH-doe)* Former name of the city of Tokyo. In crosswords, it is often clued "ancient Tokyo."

Edom *(EE-dum)* The mountainous biblical land where Esau (q.v.) and his descendants lived. Edom stretched from the Dead Sea to Elath (q.v.) on the Gulf of Aqaba (q.v.), along the eastern border of the Arabah valley. The Edomites were anything but peaceful, constantly warring with the Jews, Assyrians, and Syrians. Edom was finally vanquished by the Maccabees and came under control of the Jews.

Edsel *(ED-suhl)*   Given name of Henry Ford's son, Edsel Bryant Ford (1895–1943). The name gave new meaning to the word "lemon" when it was appended to the highly promoted but spectacularly unsuccessful Edsel automobile produced between 1957 and 1959. Edsel models included the Ranger, Pacer, Citation, and Corsair.

An Edsel without the famous "horse collar" grille.

eft *(eft)*   A newt (q.v.) or a semiamphibious, long-tailed, lizardlike salamander. The common spotted newt is known as the red eft in its land phase, when it sports a brick-red or orange skin with black-ringed vermilion spots. When mature, it turns olive green with a yellowish underbelly, and takes up residence in lakes and ponds.

egad *(ee-GAD)*   Undoubtedly a euphemism for "Oh, God" and/or "Ye, gads!" It is now used exclusively as a mild oath by constructors of crossword puzzles when other four-letter words don't fit. Major Hoople of the comics often used this expression, and a common crossword clue is "Major Hoople's expletive."

Eger *(EE-ger)*   A city in northeastern Hungary on the Eger River, in a wine-growing region producing Hungary's famous "bull's blood." In 1552 its fortress, under the command of one Stephen Dobo,

The basilica in the Hungarian city of Eger.

stood off a siege by the Turks, whose plans for annexing Hungary were thus derailed for decades. Through treachery, the city eventually did fall to the Turks, who held it for nearly 150 years. Because of its many churches, Eger is known as the Rome of Hungary. A city of the same name appears on the map of Czechoslovakia, in northwest Bohemia near the German border. The Czech **Eger** (pronounced *EH-ger*), is also known as Cheb.

egger or **eggar** *(EG-er)*   Literally, one who lays eggs; specifically, any of a wide variety of moths who as caterpillars eat the leaves of trees.

ego *(EE-go)*   Latin (and Greek) for "I," the first person singular, ego is now used to denote the self. Freud popularized the word when he divided the human personality into the id, ego, and superego. The ego was considered to be a part of the id modified by contact with the world at large. It comprises most of what we think of as consciousness.

egress *(EE-gress)*   An exit or way of leaving, from the Latin term meaning "to go out." An egress is often mistakenly thought to be the female of an animal species, presumably the egret (q.v.). According to an apocryphal story, the shrewd showman P.T. Barnum posted a sign in his circus saying "This way to the egress," to induce gullible customers to leave the premises so that others might be admitted.

egret *(ee-GREHT)*   Several birds, actually species of heron (q.v.), known for the long, white plumes (aigrettes) they bear during the breeding season. In search of these lush, silklike feathers for the millinery trade, hunters nearly exterminated the egrets. These birds are now protected by law.

Eider *(EYE-der)* Either a North German river about 120 miles long which separates Holstein on the south from Schleswig on the north, and is part of the Kiel Canal; or, with a lower-case *e*, a large northern sea duck whose fine, soft down, used to line its nest, is collected as a highly prized stuffing for pillows, coats, etc.

ein *(ein)* or **eine** *(EIN-uh)* In German, the indefinite articles, "a" and "an;" or the number "one." Unlike English, German is a highly sexed language in which every noun has a gender. Moreover, associated words must reflect this sexual orientation. Thus, *ein* as an article is masculine, as in Strauss's tone poem *Ein Heldenleben* ("A Hero's Life"), and the article *eine* is feminine, as in Mozart's delightful *Eine Kleine Nâchtmusik* ("A Little Night Music"). As a numeral adjective, *ein* means "one" and "the same."

Eire *(AIR-uh)* Eire is nothing more than the Irish, and official, name for the Republic of Ireland. Also known by such picturesque names as Erin, Hibernia, Emerald Isle, and the Auld Sod, and second largest of the British Isles, it is famous for its linen, tenors, potatoes, and poets.

Thatched cottages in County Donegal, Republic of Ireland—more poetically known as Eire.

Elam *(EE-lam)* An ancient Mesopotamian land, north of the Persian Gulf and east of the Tigris in what is now Khuzistan,

Iran. The Elamites led raids into southern Mesopotamia and overthrew Babylonia in the eighteenth century B.C. In crosswords it is frequently defined as "where Susa was capital."

elan *(eh-LANH)* Ardor, enthusiasm, impetuosity, or vigor. Élan comes from the French word meaning to "dart" or "hurl." The philosopher Bergson used the term *élan vital* to denote the original life force in the evolution of all organisms.

eland *(EE-land)* Dutch for "elk," eland is the name of the two largest species of African antelopes. Males may stand as high as six feet at the shoulder and weigh up to 2,000 pounds. The beast's straight-up, twisted horns, up to four feet long, and its hide make it a great prize for hunters. For this reason, the eland has become an endangered species.

Elath *(EE-lahth)* An ancient port on the Gulf of Aqaba (q.v.) and modern Israel's only outlet to the Red Sea. Elath, in the land of Edom (q.v.), was noted for its verdure, and its name is the Hebrew word for "grove." The town was built by King Uzziah (or Azariah) of Judah, and lost by King Ahaz in the eighth century B.C. (Deut. 2:8; 2 Kings 14:22, 16:6; 1 Kings 9:26; 2 Chron. 8:17). Today, as Elat or Eilat, it is both a seaport and a resort.

Taking to the waters off the city of Elath.

Elba *(EL-bah)* A mountainous island in the Tyrrhenian Sea, six miles off the coast of central Italy. Elba is known for its iron mines, which date back to Etruscan and Roman times. The island is also famous as the place of Napoleon's first exile (1814–1815), and for the use of its name in a classic palindrome attributed to Napoleon: "Able was I ere I saw Elba."

Napoleon arriving on Elba, welcomed by the locals.

eld *(eld)* An archaic word meaning "ancient times," "antiquity," or "days of yore." Contained in the word elder, eld also denotes old age, a term which has given way to senior citizenship.

elemi *(EL-eh-mee)* A fragrant resin obtained from various tropical trees. Gum elemi has been incorporated into varnishes, and was once used by apothecaries to compound medicinal ointments. The word is almost exactly transliterated from the Arabic *al lami*. Elemi is also the name of any incense resin related to the biblical myrrh (q.v.), one of the gifts of the Magi (q.v.).

Elgon *(EL-gahn)* A mountain peak over 14,000 feet high located in central Africa, astride the Kenya (q.v.)-Uganda border. It is an extinct volcano.

Eli *(EE-lie)* In the Bible, a high priest and judge of Israel. Eli tutored the boy Samuel, who eventually became a great leader and popular figure of Jewish legend (1 Sam. 1:4). On the cross, Christ said, "*Eli, Eli lama sabachtani?*", Aramaic for "Lord, Lord, why hast thou forsaken

John Singleton Copley's painting Samuel and Eli.

me?" A Yale student, as well as the university itself, is frequently nicknamed **Eli,** after Elihu Yale, founder of the university.

Elia *(EEL-ya)* Pen name of the English essayist, poet, and critic Charles Lamb (1775–1834). Lamb's best-known work, the *Essays of Elia,* presented thoughtful opinion on a wide variety of subjects with universal appeal. Elia is also stage and film director Kazan (1909–   ).

Charles Lamb from a watercolor by G. F. Joseph.

Eliot *(EL-ee-ut)* The surname of a number of famous persons, including a former president of Harvard, a landscape architect, an American scientist, an English statesman, and a missionary. The two best-known Eliots are: George Eliot (1819–1880), the English novelist whose real name was Mary Ann Evans. Her best-known novels are *Adam Bede* (1859), *The Mill on the Floss* (1860), and *Silas Marner* (1861). T.S. (Thomas Stearns) Eliot (1888–1965) was the American poet who became a British subject. Among his most

George Eliot, a.k.a. Mary Ann Evans.

famous works are the poems *The Waste Land* (1922) and *Ash Wednesday* (1930), and the verse play *Murder in the Cathedral* (1935). In 1948, T.S. Eliot was awarded the Nobel Prize for Literature.

Elis *(EE-lus)* A region of ancient Greece in the western Peloponnesus. Elis was most notable for the Olympic Games held at Olympia. The Elians were allied with Sparta until a falling out in 420 B.C., which resulted in loss of territory to their western neighbor, Arcadia. Elis declined rapidly after the Olympic Games were suppressed in the fourth century A.D.

ell *(el)* The twelfth letter of the English alphabet or anything shaped like that letter; e.g., an extension to a building at right angles to the main structure. The **ell** was also a measure of length used for cloth, and derived from the length of a man's arm (L-shaped when the elbow is bent). In the Low Countries an ell was 27 inches; in England, where arms are longer, it was 45 inches. Today, the ell (equal now to a meter) survives in the Netherlands.

Elli *(EL-ee)* In Norse mythology, the nurse who attended Loki (q.v.). Although a toothless crone, only Elli could best Thor (q.v.) in wrestling because she was the personification of Old Age, conquerer of all men.

Ellis *(EL-iss)* An island of about 27 acres in upper New York Bay, southwest of Manhattan. From 1892 until 1943, it served as an immigration station—gateway to the New World for hundreds of thousands. Also, the surname of (Henry) Havelock **Ellis** (1859–1939), English psychologist, author, and physician. The first volume of his landmark *Studies in the Psychology of Sex* (1897–1928) was banned as obscene.

A room at the immigration station on Ellis Island.

Elman *(EL-man)* The noted Russian-born American violinist Mischa Elman (1891–1967). He was best known for his rendition of the Tchaikovsky violin concerto.

Mischa Elman.

Elul or **Ellul** *(ehl-OOL)* The twelfth month of the Jewish calendar. Twenty-nine days in length, Elul corresponds roughly to September, as the new Hebrew year starts in late September or early October with the Rosh Hoshana holiday. The source of the word is the Hebrew *alal,* "to reap" or "to harvest."

elver *(EL-ver)* A young eel, particularly of the species that are born at sea and ascend streams as larvae. Considered a delicacy along the European shores of the Mediterranean, eels are also plentiful along the Baltic coast and the Atlantic coast of North America.

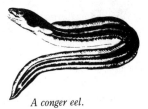

A conger eel.

em *(em)* M, the thirteenth letter of the English alphabet. In typesetting, **em** is the term for the square (□) of any size of type, used as a unit of measure; an **em** dash is a long dash, as opposed to, for example, a hyphen. Often in crosswords, "_____ cee" is clued as "master of ceremonies."

Emden *(EM-den)* A German seaport in the province of Lower Saxony in northwest Germany. Emden, at the mouth of the Ems River, is the terminus of major canals and is known for its shipyards, industries, and herring fisheries.

eme *(eem)* In Scotland, a parent's brother, or an older friend who enjoys uncle status. This avuncular type appears when the need for a three-letter word makes puzzle constructors cry "eme."

emery *(EM-eh-ree)* A dark, very hard mineral used as an abrasive material for polishing or grinding. Emery is a common form of corundum consisting mainly of aluminum oxide, with impurities of magnetite and hematite. Less common forms of corundum include the ruby and sapphire.

emir or **emeer** (*eh-MEER*) Translating this word from the Arabic tells all—a

"commander," "ruler," or "prince"; an amir (q.v.). Emir is the title usually borne by the leaders of Muslim states, particularly the United Arab Emirates.

Emma (*EM-ah*) A name made famous in fiction by Jane Austen and Gustave Flaubert. The novel *Emma*, published by Jane Austen in 1816, tells the story of Emma Woodhouse, a wealthy woman who does nothing but take care of her invalid father and meddle in other people's affairs. The second Emma is the heroine of Flaubert's *Madame Bovary*, a tale of disillusionment and unhappy extramarital love affairs that ends in suicide. *Madame Bovary* was published in 1856, one of the first novels of the realistic school. A well-known Emma in real life was Emma Lazarus (1849–1887), a poet who wrote a sonnet, "The New Colossus," engraved as the inscription on the Statue of Liberty.

emmer (*EM-er*) A hard red wheat of inferior quality, an ancient species still grown in the U.S.S.R., Germany, and the U.S. as feed for stock. What distinguishes this grain is its spikelets containing two kernels which, after threshing, remain in the glumes, or husk (see *glume*).

Emmet (*EM-et*) Either the Irish nationalist Robert Emmet (1778–1803) who, aided by the French, led an unsuccessful uprising in Ireland in 1803 and was hanged; or, with the initial letter in lower case, a derivative of the early English word *emete*, the lowly red or black ant.

emu or **emeu** (*EE-moo*) A large, flightless bird of Australia. Like its larger relative the ostrich, the five- to six-foot-tall emu is a very fast runner. It lays about half a dozen dark green eggs which are sat on by the father over a two-month period. The bird is almost extinct.

en (*en*) N, the fourteenth letter of the English alphabet. Also, in typesetting, a space half the width of an em (q.v.).

Enns (*enz*) One of the oldest towns in Austria, situated on the Enns River, near its mouth on the Danube. Enns dates back to the tenth century, when a fortress was built on the site. Lorch, a town incorporated into Enns in 1938, was the site of a Roman camp established by Marcus Aurelius.

The St. Laurence church in Lorch, Enns.

ennui (*ahn-WEE*) A feeling of worldweariness and general dissatisfaction brought on by inactivity or a dearth of events that sustain interest. Ennui (from the French) is the word people use when they are bored with saying "bored."

enol (*EE-nole*) A class of organic chemical compounds related to phenol.

eolith (*EE-eh-lith*) Derived from two Greek words meaning "dawn" and "stone," eolith is the word used by paleontologists to designate any of the crude stone tools and axes used by Flintstone types early in the Stone Age.

Eos *(EE-ose)* A Greek goddess, the personification of the dawn. Eos was the daughter of Hyperion and Theia. She was married to Astraeus and her children were the winds and the stars. Homer's adjective for her was "rosy-fingered," and the Romans called her Aurora.

Eos, the dawn, with Cephalus, the dawn wind.

eosin *(EE-eh-sin)* A rose-colored dye extracted from coal tar, this material is used in cosmetics as a toner, and in chemistry to differentiate between acid and alkaline solutions.

epact *(EE-pakt)* A period of about 11 days. This is the length of time by which the solar year of 364¼ days exceeds the lunar year of 12 months, each about 29½ days long, for a total of 354⅓ days. When an epact is added to this, the total approximates the solar year. It is often clued as "solar year excess."

epee *(eh-PAY)* A sword, usually thin and pointed, but without a cutting edge. The épée is used in fencing and differs from a foil (q.v.) in its greater weight and rigidity. Also Charles Michel, Abbé de l'**Epée** (1712–1789), a teacher who developed a one-handed sign alphabet for deaf-mutes and founded an academy for their instruction.

ephah or **ephi** *(EE-fah)* An ancient Hebrew measure for dry substances equal to about ¹/₁₀ of a homer. A homer is approximately 11 bushels or 100 gallons. That makes the ephah equal to about 37 quarts.

ephod *(EE-fahd; EH-fahd)* In ancient times, an elaborately embroidered sacred garment worn by the high priest of Israel (Ex. 28:4). Prescribed to be worn with the ephod was a breastplate containing the Urim and Thummin, two objects believed to be sacred, used to divine the will of God (Exodus 28:30).

ephor *(EH-fur)* An overseer among the ancient Spartans. The ephors were a legislative/executive/judicial board of five citizens, elected annually. One of their prime responsibilities was to check and balance the power of Sparta's dual kings; another was the education of youth. Election was by the drawing of lots.

epoch *(EH-pok)* This is a Greek word meaning "pause" or "hold in check," which, by extension, has come to mean "point in time." An epoch signifies a period dating from a landmark event that leaves its imprint on subsequent times. Thus, the glacial epoch refers to a time during the Pleistocene period when much of the northern hemisphere lay covered with ice.

epode *(EH-pode)* A type of lyric poem, invented by the Greek satirist Archilochus, and usually associated with the poet Horace. In epodes, shorter verses follow longer ones. Another way to recognize an epode is by its location: it is that part of an ode sung after the strophe and antistrophe.

epopt *(EH-popt)* A person initiated into the highest grade of the Eleusinian mysteries, the religious rites of ancient Attica held at Eleusis. With initiation, epopts (or epoptae) gained an appreciation of how the legends of Demeter, Persephone, and Dionysus related to the immortality of the soul and to the annual growing cycle of plants.

epos *(EH-pose)* A short word for long poetry, especially the epic kind that predates writing and has therefore been passed down by word of mouth. Eposes are usually concerned with heroic themes and often embody the tradition of a people, as does the Finnish *Kalevala*.

Epsom *(EP-sum)* Either the English town that gives its name to Epsom Downs, setting for such horse races as the Derby (q.v.) run annually there, or the white crystalline salt, magnesium sulfate, a legendary but real and powerful cathartic. The salts take their name from the town, famous for its mineral waters.

The British royal family view the horses at Epsom Downs.

Erato *(ER-a-toe)* One of the nine Muses, Greek goddesses of the arts and sciences. Erato presided over the poetry of love. In fact, her name is related to that of the love-god, Eros (q.v.). Erato is pictured with a lyre (q.v.) to accompany her poetry reading.

Erebus *(EH-ree-bus)* In Greek mythology, the son of Chaos (q.v.) and the personification of darkness, also used for Hades (q.v.), the underground region of darkness through which the dead pass on their way to reward (the Elysian Fields) or punishment (Tartarus).

erg *(uhrg)* From the Greek word *ergon* meaning "work," an erg is a unit by which work is measured. Using enough force (a dyne—q.v.) to move a one-gram weight one centimeter per second may not be particularly tiring, but it counts as one erg of work, equal to 0.00001 newtons.

ergot *(ER-got)* A fungus growth which affects cereal grains, particularly rye. One chemical derivative of ergot causes muscle contractions and is used to help the uterus contract in labor, or to arrest hemorrhaging. Another derivative is lysergic acid diethylamide, a hallucinatory drug better known as LSD-25. Ingestion of bread made with ergot-contaminated rye can cause gangrene or convulsions, but fortunately cases of so-called ergotism are rare nowadays. Medieval outbreaks of ergotism were dubbed St. Anthony's fire.

eri See *Assam*.

Erica *(EH-rik-ah)* The name of a large genus of plants belonging to the heath family, consisting mainly of low, heavily branched evergreen shrubs, many of them ornamental. Many Ericas bear "heath" as a common name. Ericas are related to, but distinct from, heathers. In the same family with both are rhododendrons and azaleas.

Erie *(EE-ree)* The name of one of the Great Lakes, a canal in New York State, cities in Colorado, Illinois, Kansas, and Pennsylvania, and an Iroquoian Indian tribe after which all these are named. After a devastating war with the Iroquois, the surviving Eries were enslaved.

An Erie tribesman.

Eris *(EE-rihs)* Greek goddess of discord, and sister of Ares (q.v.). Piqued at not receiving an invitation to a wedding, this troublemaker threw into the gathering an apple inscribed: "To the Fairest." When such beauties as Hera, Aphrodite, and Athena laid claim to the apple, the resulting brouhaha precipitated the Trojan War.

One of the original troublemakers, Eris throws herself once more into the fray.

Erle *(erl)*

Given name of Erle Stanley Gardner (1889–1970), the mystery writer who is best known for creating Perry Mason. Thanks to their name spelling Gardner's parents ensured him crossword immortality.

Erle Stanley Gardner.

erne or ern *(ern)*

A large white-tailed sea eagle that preys on both marine and terrestrial life; it is powerful enough to fly off with a lamb. The **Erne** is also a 72-mile-long river rising in County Longford, Republic of Ireland, and flowing northwest through County Cavan into Northern Ireland, and back again into the Republic, reaching the sea at Donegal Bay.

Eros *(ER-os)*

The Greek god of love, intense longing, amorous dalliance, and desire. The son of Aphrodite and Ares (q.v.), he is usually pictured as a winged youth armed with bow and arrows. As the Roman Cupid (q.v.), he is often represented as a child playfully shooting arrows of love into the hearts of passersby. In Roman

legend, he was the spouse of Psyche.

Ers See *vetch*.

Erse *(erse)*

In the Goidelic branch of Celtic languages, Erse is synonymous with Irish, and frequently refers as well to Scottish Gaelic, which is spoken primarily in the Highlands of Scotland.

Esau *(EE-saw)*

The hairy, redheaded son of Isaac and Rebecca who in the Old Testament (Gen. 25:30–34) was persuaded to sell his birthright to his twin brother Jacob for a mess of pottage. This loss prompted Esau, now called Edom (q.v.), to seek his fortune elsewhere, and he became the ancestor of Israel's enemies the Edomites. The first settlement of Elath (q.v.) lay in ancient Edom (or Idumea).

Jacob receives the blessing that should have gone to Esau.

esker or eskar *(ES-kuhr)*

A long, narrow ridge of sand, gravel, and rocks, deposited by a stream running under the ice of a glacier.

esne *(EZ-nee)*

From the Old High German, *asni,* or "day worker," this was the name by which the Anglo-Saxons referred to laborers or men of the lower classes. The neat combination of four commonly occurring letters make this word virtually indispensable to crossword constructors who usually clue it as "old-time domestic slave."

Essen *(EH-son)* A German city near the Ruhr River, about 20 miles from Dusseldorf. Situated in the center of the vast Ruhr coal-mining area, Essen is the site of the Krupp steelworks, after 1933 a major supplier of weapons for Germany's rearmament and, in World War II, for Hitler's armies. Allied raids destroyed three-quarters of the city during World War II. In German, **essen** also means ''to eat,'' and, as a noun, ''meal.''

Essene *(EH-seen)* Member of a monastic Jewish sect existing from the second century B.C. to the second century A.D. The Essenes were vegetarians and teetotalers, always dressed in white to symbolize purity, and practiced voluntary poverty, sharing of goods, and celibacy. The belief of some that Christ was an Essene has been hotly debated.

Essex *(EH-seks)* A county of southeastern England, to the north of the Thames estuary. Essex was once part of the East Saxon kingdom from which its name evolved, and both Roman and Saxon ruins remain. Essex was also the ancestral earldom of the Devereux family. Robert, the second earl, was often linked romantically with the first Queen Elizabeth, until she had him executed for treason.

Este *(EH-stay)* An ancient and noble Italian family which ruled over Ferrara from 1240 to 1597, and over Modena from 1288 to 1796. Known as patrons of the arts during the Renaissance, the family originated in the northeastern town of **Este,** in Venetia. As Ateste, it was an ancient center of civilization from the tenth century to the second century B.C. In crosswords, *este* is

BEST OF
THE D'ESTES

Isabella
(1474–1539)

Beatrice
(1475–1497)

Alfonso
(1476–1534)

Leonello
(1407–1450)

often clued as Spanish for "east," as in Punta del ____ , or as Tivoli's Villa d' ____ .

ester *(EH-ster)* In chemistry, any of a group of organic compounds comparable to an inorganic salt. An ester consists of a metal ion such as sodium, and the radical of an organic acid such as benzoic acid. Where sodium chloride would be a salt, sodium benzoate is an ester.

eta *(AY-tah)* The seventh letter of the Greek alphabet, usually written in upper case as *H,* and in lower case as *n*. But eta corresponds in English not to *h* or *n* but to a long *a,* as in *fade.* Often in crosswords, **E.T.A.** (estimated time of arrival) is clued as "incoming flight abbr."

etape *(ay-TAHP)* A public warehouse and also a place where troops pitch their tents after a day's march. It is also the length of a day's march.

Soldiers taking their ease at an etape.

ethos *(EETH-os)* From the Greek word meaning "character," the customary, distinguishing attitudes and guiding beliefs of a national, political, racial, or occupational group. Ethos also refers to intellectual elements of art, as opposed to the emotional elements, which are called pathos.

Eton *(EE-tun)* In Buckinghamshire, England, Eton College, a famous school for boys founded in 1440 by Henry VI. It was on Eton's playing fields, according to the Duke of Wellington, that the Battle of Waterloo was won. **Eton** also refers to the short jacket and broad linen collar worn at the school.

These Etonians have outgrown the school's eponymous uniform; they wear tails and long pants.

etude *(EH-tood)* From the French word meaning "study," études are usually musical pieces composed for a single instrument as exercises in technique. Some études, however, particularly those for the piano composed by Frédéric Chopin, are performed in concert for their artistic merit.

etui or **etwee** *(EH-twee)* A small case used to hold the items—articles and sewing equipment—that a sailor or soldier might keep in a ditty (q.v.) bag. Not exactly a standard household item, but indispensable to crosswords.

This etui is made of chased steel

Etzel *(EHT-sul)* In Germanic heroic legend, the name given to Attila the Hun. Etzel appears briefly in the *Nibelungenlied,* where he ineffectually watches his family being destroyed, and later marries Kriemhild, the widow of Siegfried. In the *Völsungasaga,* the Scandinavian form of the epic, Etzel goes under the name Atli (q.v.).

Eurus *(YEW-rus)* In classical mythology, the god of the southeast or east wind, usually shown on ancient maps as a dour man pouring water from a vase. This was in keeping with his role as the bringer of rainy weather.

eusol *(YEW-sole)* A chemical solution used as an antiseptic, made with chlorinated lime, boric acid, and hypochlorous acid. In recognition of its origins, the word is an acronym made up of the first letters of Edinburgh University and the first syllable of solution.

evoe or **evhoe** *(EE-voe; EE-voe-ee)* Transliteration from the Greek, *eu hoi,* an interjection which participants at orgies in honor of the god Bacchus were wont to shout during moments of extreme exuberance. Evoe is roughly equivalent in both definition and usage to the modern ''Whoopee!''

ewer *(YEW-ehr)* A large, vase-shaped water pitcher or jug. Before the advent of modern plumbing, wide-mouthed ewers standing in basins were standard washstand items.

exeat *(EK-say-aht)* A word derived from a Latin expression that provides an exact definition (''let him go out''). Thus, an exeat permits temporary absence from a British college. In the United States, exeat goes under the less glamorous designation, leave of absence.

Exuma *(ek-SOO-mah)* The name given to two out islands—Great and Little Exuma—in the central Bahamas, in a group officially known as Exuma and Cays. The original inhabitants, the Lucayo Indians, were enslaved and exterminated within a few years of Columbus's discovery of nearby San Salvador in 1492.

exurb *(EK-serb)* A term coined in 1955 by the writer A.C. Spectorsky to denote a semirural area beyond the suburbs where reside the upper middle class who may or may not commute to the city. Many exurbanites are also ex-urbanites.

eyas *(EYE-ahs)* A young hawk or falcon taken from its nest before it has flown, to be trained in the hunting sport of falconry (or hawking); if taken after it learns to fly, the bird would be termed a haggard. American falcons include the pigeon hawk, the sparrow hawk, the kestrel, and the merlin.

Eyre *(air)* A shallow and frequently dry salt lake, largest lake in the country, 39 feet below sea level in southern Australia. Also the surname of Charlotte Brontë's heroine, Jane **Eyre,** who triumphs over adversity to marry her employer, the passionate and self-willed Mr. Rochester.

eyrie See *aerie.*

eyrir *(AY-reer)* In Iceland, a unit of money not worth much or used much. The plural of eyrir is aurar, and 100 aurar equal one krona. At last report it took about 50 aurar to equal a mill, or 50,000 aurar to the U.S. dollar.

Ezra *(EZ-rah)* A Hebrew scribe, prophet, and priest who lived in Babylon in the fifth century B.C. Ezra gave his name to a book of the Old Testament and is credited with much restoring, correcting, and editing of Scripture. In the Apocrypha, he is called Esdros. Another Ezra is poet Ezra Pound (1885–1972), whose chief works gave new life to the term canto (q.v.).

Ezra Loomis Pound.

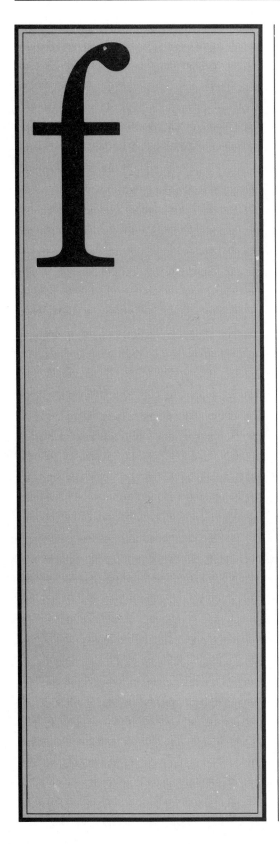

facet *(FAS-et)* Literally, "small face." The word is used to designate the plane surfaces of a cut gemstone; any smooth surface of a bone; or a minute plane in the compound eye of an insect. Also, aspects of an individual's or a subject's disposition, as in "I know that facet of his personality."

fado *(FAH-thoo)* In Portugal, a sad, plaintive song, usually sung lugubriously to the accompaniment of a guitar. Most often, fados are tales of unrequited love. For this reason, they have been compared to the blues songs of America.

Fagin *(FAY-gin)* A Dickens character, the villain of *Oliver Twist*. Fagin presided over a band of thieves, mostly boys whom he trained as pickpockets and petty thieves. In *Oliver*, the musical version of the story, Fagin is given a lovable side, which he definitely does not deserve.

Fagin in prison, as seen by nineteenth-century caricaturist Edward Cruikshank.

fakir *(fah-KEER)* In Muslim lands, an itinerant religious beggar who may claim supernatural powers. Fakirs, also sometimes known as dervishes, can be recognized by red handkerchiefs often worn over their black turbans. They frequently hold menial jobs, like cleaning mosques.

Fako *(FAY-koe)* An active volcano, the highest point in West Africa. Towering 13,354 feet in the Cameroon Highlands, it is also known as Cameroon Mountain. The western side is one of the rainiest spots on earth, receiving over 400 inches annually. Fako was first climbed in 1861 by Sir Richard Burton, the noted English explorer.

Fala *(FAH-la)* Perhaps the most famous Scottish terrier in history. Fala and Medworth were two dogs owned by President Franklin D. Roosevelt, but Fala was by far his favorite, appearing with him on public occasions and in many photographs. When Roosevelt was attacked by Republicans who mentioned his dog, F.D.R. defended Fala (and himself) in a famous line in a Teamster's dinner speech in Washington: "These Republican leaders have not been content with attacks on me, on my wife, or on my sons. No, not content with that, they now include my little dog, Fala. Well, of course, I don't resent attacks . . . but Fala *does* resent them . . . I think I have a right to resent, to object to libelous statements about my dog." It can now be told that Fala's real name was Murray of Falahill.

Falla *(FAH-yah)* Manuel de Falla (1876–1946), Spanish composer. His work reflects the influence of Ravel (q.v.) and other impressionists, but retains a strong Spanish character. Among his compositions is the celebrated ballet *The Three-Cornered Hat.*

Manuel de Falla.

fanon *(FAN-un)* A band of material hanging from the left arm of priests during Mass, or a capelike garment, worn by the Pope, that is also called an orale. Pronounced *fan-OHN*, it is the surname of Frantz Omar **Fanon** (1925–1961), the French West Indian psychiatrist who became leader of the Algerian National Front and champion of the Third World.

farad *(FAH-rad)* A unit of electrical capacitance. The farad is named for Michael Faraday (1791–1867), the English bookbinder's apprentice who educated himself and went on to become one of the greatest chemists and physicists in scientific history. Faraday developed the first dynamo and discovered electromagnetic induction.

Fargo *(FAR-goe)* William George Fargo (1818–1881), the resident agent for a Buffalo, New York, express company who joined with Henry Wells to found a stagecoach and banking empire. Formed from their dealings were the American Express Company (1850) and Wells, Fargo & Company (1852). The largest city in North Dakota was named for him.

William George Fargo.

faro *(FAH-row)* A card game whose name derives from "pharaoh," an old card design. Faro is played with a full deck, and participants bet on which of the 13 spade cards will win. The dealer draws three cards from the dealing box: the first is discarded, the second loses, and the third card indicates the winner. **Faro** is also the southernmost town in Portugal.

fasti *(FAST-ee)* In ancient Roman practice, days on which public business could be transacted without offending the gods. The word was eventually applied to calendars or almanacs which contained information on holy days, festivals, and other noteworthy occasions.

faun *(fawn)* A mischievous, satyrlike creature represented as half man and half goat, an attendant of Faunus, a Roman woodland deity. The festivals of Faunus, the Faunalia, were celebrated on December 5 and February 13. Stéphane Mallarmé evoked the faun in his celebrated poem *The Afternoon of a Faun,* which was set to music by Debussy; the ballet caused a scandal when first danced by Nijinsky, in 1912.

Fauna *(FAWN-ah)* In Roman religion, a fertility goddess, Faunus's female counterpart, variously believed to be his daughter, sister, or wife. Also known as Bona Dea, she was worshiped only by women. With a lower-case *f,* **fauna** represents the animal equivalent of flora (q.v.). Fauna now refers to the animal life of a particular region.

Faure *(fawhr)* Surname of some notable Frenchmen, including Félix Faure (1841–1899), the president of the Republic who refused Alfred Dreyfus a new trial in the celebrated Dreyfus Affair; Élie Faure (1873–1937), the physician and art historian who wrote the five-volume *History of Art;* and with the *e* accented, Gabriel Urbain Fauré *(fawhr-AY)* (1845–1924), the French composer and student of Saint-Saëns, whose own pupils included Ravel (q.v.) and Enesco. He is best known for his songs, including "Clair de Lune," and his *Requiem.*

Gabriel Fauré.

Faust *(fowst)* That figure of medieval legend, Dr. Johann Faust, sometimes called Faustus, who lived in Germany in the sixteenth century. The good doctor supposedly sold his soul to the Devil in exchange for youth and power, according to poet-dramatist Christopher Marlowe (in *Dr. Faustus,* 1593); or in exchange for knowledge, according to Goethe (1808), who saw him as a heroic striver. The Goethe version inspired further literary examination and notable music by Gounod and Berlioz, among others.

fava *(FAH-va)* A legume also called the broad bean; the "bean" of the ancients, unrelated to the New World "true" beans. The fava bean is the large, edible seed of an Old World upright vetch, a plant also used as animal fodder. Human sensitivity to the fava bean produces a condition known medically as favism—or acute hemolytic anemia—common in Sicily and Sardinia.

A broad bean—or fava—plant.

fay *(fay)* Either a fairy; an archaic term for faith, as in the expression "My fay preserve us"; or the surname of Charles Ernest **Fay** (1846–1931), called the dean of American mountain climbing. Mt. Fay in the Canadian Rockies is named after him. Fay is also actor Frank Fay, who was Elwood P. Dowd in the original Broadway cast of *Harvey.*

Fayal or **Faial** *(fah-YAHL)* One of the Portuguese islands in the Atlantic that make up the Azores. Its chief town is Harta. Fayal has a population of about 20,000. Its closest neighbors are the islands of Pico to the southeast and São Jorge to the northeast. The Azores were first mapped in 1351 and were colonized by Portugal in 1445.

"BOZ" AND THE BARD

Barnaby Rudge
Rudge

Our Mutual Friend
Silas Wegg

David Copperfield
Uriah Heep

Oliver Twist
Bill Sikes

Oliver Twist
Fagin

Old Curiosity Shop
Daniel Quilp

Martin Chuzzlewit
"Sairey" Gamp

Nicholas Nickleby
Smike

Othello
Iago

Timon of Athens
Timon

As You Like It
Phebe

Twelfth Night
Viola

Henry IV
Poins

Henry V
Nym

King Lear
Regan

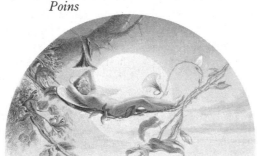

The Tempest
Ariel

Merchant of Venice
Tubal

felid *(FEE-lid)* The general name for any member of the *Felidae*—a family of carnivorous animals with soft and often patterned fur, short limbs, sharp, retractable claws, and eyes designed for seeing in dim light. The family includes lions, tigers, panthers, leopards, cheetahs, and their city cousin, the house cat. Felid is from the Latin *feles*.

Two felids—commonly called cats—in an urban setting.

felly or **felloe** *(FELL-lee)* On a wheel, the exterior rim, or section of the rim that is supported by a spoke.

Some medieval fellies are visible in this woodcut.

felon *(FELL-un)* The perpetrator of a serious crime, as opposed to a misdemeanor. Felons are those guilty of murder, rape, arson, and other deeds that carry sentences longer than a year in prison.

feme *(fem)* or **femme** *(fahm)* From the Latin *femina*, "woman"; what a wife is called in legal documents—a married woman is a *feme covert*, and *feme sole* refers to a single woman or a married woman acting for herself (without reference to her marital status). In French, *femme* can mean both "woman" and "wife."

femur *(FEE-mer)* The thighbone and the largest bone in the human body. The upper end of the femur forms a ball-and-socket joint with the hipbone. Its lower end joins with the upper end of the tibia to form the knee joint. The femur is also the third segment of an insect's leg.

fen *(fen)* A low-lying marshland. In eastern England, the **Fens** district is a rich agricultural lowland about 70 miles long by 35 miles wide southwest of The Wash. Once the largest swamp in England, it was formed by the silting up of a North Sea bay and is crisscrossed by many streams, dikes, and channels.

feod See *fief*.

fere *(feer)* In archaic terms, a close associate, equal, or companion. Also, a husband or wife. The word derives from an Anglo-Saxon term meaning "together."

feria *(FER-ee-ah)* Any day of the Roman Catholic or Anglican Church calendar which is not designated as a holiday, but falls within a special period like Lent. In Spain, the feria is a market festival (or fair), often lasting several days, celebrating a local religious holiday and often including bullfights. The annual spring feria at Seville is world-famous.

In Spanish towns, feria often include corridas—bullfights.

Fermi *(FAIR-mee)* Enrico Fermi (1901–1954), Italian-born American physicist who won the 1938 Nobel Prize in physics for his studies of radioactivity. Fermi's research helped produce the atomic bomb, and he headed a group responsible for the first self-regulating nuclear chain reaction at the University of Chicago in 1942.

fess *(fess)* In heraldry, part of a coat of arms. The fess runs horizontally across an escutcheon, making up the middle third of the shield-shaped surface. **Fess** as a proper noun belongs to Fess Parker, an actor responsible for crowning Davy Crockett king of the wild frontier on television.

fete *(feht)*   From the French word for "feast," a festival, usually of a gala nature, and customarily held outdoors; in short, what in Spain would be called a feria (q.v.), but shorter in duration and without the bullfights. *Fêtes* is one of three famous nocturnes for orchestra by the French composer Claude Debussy.

fetor *(FEE-ter)*   A strong, offensive odor. The word is included in such medical terms as *fetor ex ore* (halitosis).

fetus or **foetus** *(FEE-tus)*   The unborn or unhatched young of any vertebrate animal that gives birth to live offspring. In order for the unborn to qualify as a fetus, a certain amount of development must have taken place in major structures. This point is generally reached in humans about three months after fertilization. Earlier, the future offspring is called an embryo.

feu or **few** *(few)*   In Scottish law, a holding of land in exchange for cash or grain, rather than in exchange for military service, as was usual under feudalism. **Feu** *(fuh)* is also French for "fire." *Le Feu (Under Fire)*, a famous novel by Henri Barbusse, depicted French army life during the horror of World War I. Pot-au-feu is a French stew.

Fez *(fez)*   A city in north-central Morocco that dates back to 808 B.C. and is noted for its Muslim art and its handicrafts. Fez gave its name to a brimless red felt hat, shaped

Casablanca's *Sydney Greenstreet, in fez, listens to Paul Henreid and Ingrid Bergman.*

like a truncated cone with a long black tassel. Its wearer is usually a man of the Muslim faith, or a member of the Shriners at a convention.

fiat *(FEE-at)*   From the Latin "let there be," a decree or binding order issued by legal authority. Fiat money, for example, is not backed by a gold or silver standard, but constitutes legal tender by decree of a government. As a proper noun, **Fiat** is the name of a popular Italian automobile.

A 1982 Fiat X1/9.

fichu *(FISH-oo)*   A kerchief worn shawl-fashion over the shoulders. The fichu (from the French *ficher*, "to stick" or "to pin") is triangular, so that one point occupies the middle of the back while the other two fasten across or below the bosom. Fichus are often worn by women who have had second thoughts about the lowness of their necklines.

A fichu-covered neckline.

fid *(fid)*   Nautical term for a tapered pin used for separating the strands of a rope before splicing; a cousin of the marlinspike. A **fid** is also a square bar that helps to support a topmast.

Fidia *(FID-ee-ah)*   A genus of small beetles belonging to the large *Chrysomelidae* family, or any beetle of this species. These insects have shiny carapaces and come in a variety of bright colors. They include the leaf beetle, the cucumber beetle, the Colorado potato beetle, and others named to reflect their dietary preferences.

Leaf beetle.

Fido *(FIE-doe)* An acronym for Fog Investigation Dispersal Operations. This system, installed along airport runways, causes fog to be evaporated by heat from burning liquid fuel, thus permitting planes to take off and land in bad weather. **Fido** is also (along with Rover, Rags, and Spot) the prototypical name for a dog. The dog name Fido comes from the same word in Latin meaning "I trust," which is a good way to describe owners' feelings for their pets.

fief *(fife)* The term for the estate of a feudal baron (formerly called a feod). The feudal system embraced the economic, political, and social life of medieval Europe. It provided for the disposition of lands by lords (often kings) to vassals (often lords), and in turn these made disposition to tenants. Certain tenets of feudalism survive in English and American real-estate law.

Fife *(fife)* An eastern Scottish county, between the Firth of Forth and the Firth of Tay (see *firth*), where the famed St. Andrews Golf Course and ancient St. Andrews University are situated. Also, with a lower-case *f*, a small transverse flute with a shrill, insistent tone. The combination of **fife** and drum is sufficiently stirring to set even the wounded marching, viz. *The Spirit of '76.* Nowadays, the piccolo has largely replaced the fife.

Edoard Manet's painting The Fife Player.

Fiji *(FEE-jee)* A native of the Fiji Islands (also called the Viti Islands) or their Melanesian tongue. Composed of more than 300 islands, only about 100 of them inhabited (the largest is Viti Levu), the Fiji Islands, now a dominion, were Great Britain's most important Pacific colony. The capital is Suva. They were discovered by the Dutch explorer Abel Tasman in 1643, and were visited by Captain James Cook in 1774. Not until the missionaries arrived in 1835 did the natives stop the practice of cannibalism.

filly *(FILL-ee)* A female horse, usually under four years of age. Also, among the Damon Runyon Broadway set, the term is used (like broad, skirt, chick, and babe) to indicate a girl or young woman.

fils *(fills)* In Iraq and Jordan, a unit of currency equal to $^1/_{1000}$ of a dinar (q.v.). In France (pronounced *feece*) it means "son" and is employed like "junior," as in *Dumas fils.* The French word for daughter, or girl, is *fille* (pronounced *FEE-ya*).

filum *(FIE-lum)* An anatomical structure resembling a thread or filament, from the Latin for "thread." The word is pluralized as fila. Thus, doctors can bandy terms like *fila radicularia nervorum spinalium* about when they want to refer to threadlike filaments that attach the dorsal and ventral roots of each spinal nerve to the spinal cord.

finis *(FIH-nis)* With or without the terminal *h*, this word still means the end, just as in the original Latin. It is often used affectedly by filmmakers and writers who feel that what they have created requires something special to signal its conclusion.

fink *(fink)* Originally the name of an infamous American strikebreaker, and now the generic term for a professional scab, or for an informer in a penal institution. A rat fink is the worst fink. Also Mike **Fink** (c. 1770–1823), American frontiersman whose exploits as marksman, keelboatsman, fighter, and teller of tall stories have made him a legend.

Finn *(fin)* A native of Finland. Also, the indefatigable title hero in Mark Twain's novel *Huckleberry Finn;* and the mythical

Irish hero of the Fenian ballads named **Finn** MacCool, of whom the protagonist in James Joyce's *Finnegans Wake* is something of a literary reincarnation. The name change is coined in a Joycean pun: "Mister Finn, you're going to be Mister Finn again." Finnegan represents mankind.

A drawing by E. W. Kemble for the original edition of The Adventures of Huckleberry Finn.

firkin *(FER-kin)* A small wooden tub of indeterminate size designed to hold butter or lard. **Firkin** also refers to certain British volume units and is usually equal to ¼ barrel or nine imperial gallons. In this system, one firkin equals 56 pounds of butter, or eight ale gallons.

firn *(fern)* The loose granular, rather than compacted, snow (firn snow) found at the upper ends of glaciers. Also, a field of such granular snow. The development of firn, or névé (q.v.), is called firnification and is a topic of lively interest whenever alpinists gather around the fireside to talk shop.

firth *(ferth)* In Scotland, a narrow estuary or arm of the sea. To firth experts, a classic example is the Firth of Clyde in

The Forth Railway Bridge across the Firth of Forth.

southwestern Scotland, where the Clyde River debouches into a 64-mile-long inlet ringed with resorts that cater to estivating Glaswegians.

fisc *(fisk)* A rare word meaning a royal or state treasury; an exchequer. Fisc comes from the Latin word *fiscus,* "money basket," hence treasury, from which derives the word fiscal, meaning "relating to financial matters." Thus, a fiscal year is the 12 months between financial accountings. In the U.S., the government's fiscal year starts on July 1.

Fiske *(fisk)* Surname of several famous Americans, including Bradley Allen Fiske (1854–1942), the naval officer who invented, among other shipboard instruments, the electric range finder; and Minnie Maddern Fiske (1865–1932), Louisiana-born actress and director, best known for her portrayal of Becky Sharp.

fitch *(fitch)* Another name for the fitchew, or Old World polecat—a two-foot-long carnivorous, weasellike animal, valued for its pelt. Also, the surname of (William) Clyde **Fitch** (1865–1909), American dramatist; John Fitch (1743–1798), inventor of the first American steamboat; and Thomas Fitch (c. 1700–1774), colonial governor of Connecticut.

Fiume *(FEW-me)* Yugoslavia's largest seaport, also called Rijeka, on the Adriatic. After centuries of Croatian rule, it passed to the Hapsburgs in 1466, and became a Hungarian city in 1779. It came under partial Italian and partial Yugoslav control after World War I, and was transferred to Yugoslavia in 1947 under the Allied peace treaty with Italy. (See also *Susak.*)

fjeld *(fyeld)* In Scandinavia, a treeless plateau. The word derives from the Old Norse *fjall,* or "mountain," which also evolved into the English word fell, meaning a barren hill or moor.

fjord or **fiord** *(fee-YORD)* A narrow inlet of the sea rimmed by high, steep cliffs or mountain slopes. Fjords were probably scooped out along the courses of valleys by Ice Age glaciers, and were flooded by the sea when the land later subsided. Fjords are found on the coasts of Norway, Scotland, Greenland, Alaska, British Columbia, southern Chile, New Zealand, and Antarctica. The most spectacular are in Norway, especially the 4,000-foot-deep and 100-mile-long Sognafjord.

The majestic Sognafjord in Norway is the longest fjord in the world.

Flagg *(flag)* James Montgomery Flagg (1877–1960), the American artist and illustrator. His work was seen extensively in popular magazines until his death, but he is perhaps best known for his World War I posters, including the famous recruiting poster on which a grim Uncle Sam tells the reader, "I Want You."

flail *(flail)* From the Middle English word for "whip," an implement used for manual threshing of grain. Flails consist of wooden handles with shorter, heavier lengths of wood suspended from them to swing freely. Related to the flail is the morning star, a medieval weapon sporting a lethal, free-swinging, spiked ball.

flak *(flak)* Antiaircraft fire, the most feared defensive measure against World War II bombing attacks, because the bursting shells spread deadly shrapnel over so large an area. Flak is an onomatopoeic acronym from the German word for antiaircraft gun, *FLiegerAbwehrKanone.*

flan *(flan)* Several dessert specialties. In Hispanic cuisine, a flan is custard baked into a layer of caramel, then unmolded. A flan is also a dessert tart filled with custard or fruit. In numismatics, a **flan** is a blank coin—a disc of metal ready to be made into a coin by a stamp of the proper die.

flare *(flare)* A brilliant, unsteady blaze of light, often of short duration. Flares are usually used as nighttime signals, for example, to warn oncoming motorists of trouble on the road ahead; or for temporary illumination of aircraft landing strips. Also, an outward curve such as occurs at the bottom of a sailor's trousers.

flax *(flaks)* Common name for a family of annual herbs. Typical flax plants bear delicate blue or white flowers. Their stem fibers are spun into linen thread, or used to make such byproducts as insulating material and writing and cigarette paper. Flaxseed is crushed to obtain linseed oil and is used medicinally in several preparations.

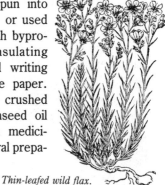

Thin-leafed wild flax.

fleam *(fleem)* Passé term for a small, pointed surgical knife or lancet, used in medicine to open a vein for bloodletting—a former "cure" for certain disorders. This practice is known as phlebotomy, from two Greek words meaning "vein" and "cut"; it explains why fleams are also called phlebotomes.

flews *(flooz)* Anyone who has ever owned an old hound dog will be delighted to learn that the loose sections of a dog's upper lip that overhang his lower jaw are his flews. There is no such thing as one flew, except in the title of a popular film, ending with "Cuckoo's Nest."

flit *(flit)* A rapid, darting movement, such as that made by an insect. Also, with a capital letter, a commercial insecticide of the pre-D.D.T. and aerosol-bomb era. **Flit** was used in a "gun" consisting of a reservoir and cylindrical plunger. Its advertising slogan—"Quick, Henry, the Flit"—became a national catch phrase of the 1930s.

flite *(flite)* Aside from being a deliberate misspelling of flight in trademarks of products that "fly," such as golf balls, flite is an archaic English verb meaning "to quarrel" or "to contend." In the Dickens novel *Bleak House,* Miss **Flite** was the little old lady driven to distraction by the delay of her suit in chancery.

A flite scene from a medieval manuscript.

Flora *(FLOR-ah)* The Roman goddess of flowers, and therefore of all plant life of a specific region. Her festival, the Floralia, was celebrated in late April. Flora is to plants what fauna (q.v.) is to animals. The Latin word for "flower" is *flos, floris* (all Latin nouns have two forms in Latin dictionaries). It is the base for the English words flower, floral, florid, etc., and the Spanish *florida* (full of flowers). When the word came into modern Italian, the *l* changed to an *i*. *Fiore* is the Italian word for "flower," from which came Fiorello ("little flower") Laguardia, New York's famed mayor.

Flora.

flout *(flowt)* Any word or deed used to convey contempt or scorn. Also, an insult. Thus, a master of the flout would be the popular comedian Don Rickles. Flout should not be confused with its distant cousin flaunt—which means to show off.

flue *(floo)* Either a barbed point, as of an anchor, harpoon (see *fluke*), or feather (see *harl*); a loose, fluffy mass, as of lint; a type of fishing net; or a hollow shaft, often within a chimney, through which smoke or hot air escapes. Also, the surname of Nicholas von der **Flüe** (1417–1487), leader of Swiss forces against Austria and counselor to the Duke of Saxony.

fluff *(fluff)* A soft, loose clump of hair, fur, dust, down, or similar material, or a food into which air has been beaten for lightness. Also, in radio, the theater, live TV, or when speaking before an audience, a misreading of lines, often with hilarious results. A classic **fluff** was a newscaster's introduction on the air of a President named Hoobert Heever.

fluke *(fluke)* Either a flatfish, often called summer flounder; any of several parasitic worms whose favorite habitat is a sheep's liver; or one of the barbs of an anchor or arrow (see *flue*). Also, an unusual, accidental stroke of good luck, such as a good stroke at billiards, from poolroom slang for an easily duped person (an easily caught fish, or fluke).

flume *(floom)* A trough, or manmade channel, usually on a mountainside. Flumes are used to transport water or logs to a desired location by gravity. Also, a narrow natural gorge with water running through it. Flumes form the basis of such popular amusement park rides as Shoot the Chute.

flux *(fluks)* From the Latin for "flow," a streaming, such as tidal flux, and by extension, any continuous movement, as in the expression "Things are in a state of flux." In soldering, **flux** is a third substance that helps fuse two metals together. And magnetic **flux** quantifies magnetism in a specific area.

foal *(fole)* A young horse or other equine animal, such as the donkey or zebra. The male foal is called a colt (q.v.), while the young female is known as a filly (q.v.). It takes mares of the various equine groups from 11 to 13 months to produce a foal.

fob *(fahb)* Either a small pocket under the waistline on a man's trousers, or a watch ornament that hangs from that pocket when it holds a watch. With periods after each letter, **F.O.B.** stands for "free on board," and is used to quote the price of an article, exclusive of shipping charges.

Foch *(fosh)* Ferdinand Foch (1851–1929), marshal of France during World War I. He, along with Joffre and Gallieni, was responsible for halting the German advance at the Marne in 1914. In 1918, Foch was appointed supreme commander of the British, French, and American armies.

foehn *(fane)* Any warm, dry wind that blows down the leeward side of a mountain ridge. The original foehn (or *föhn*) winds

MEN OF THE CLOTH

abbe
Arhat
bo
cadi
druid
druse
epopt
fra
friar

hafiz
imam
lama
Mahdi
rabbi
Sufi
swami
vicar

occurred in the Alps. Other foehns include the Chinook of the Rockies, and the *aspre* in France. The Chinook can raise temperatures as much as 20°F. in 15 minutes.

foil *(foil)* One of those words with a variety of unrelated meanings, including: a thin sheet of metal such as silver foil; the scent or spoor of an animal; a thin, blunt-pointed fencing sword, somewhat resembling an épée (q.v.); or what in show business would be called a straight man.

Foix *(fwa)* A town in the department of Ariège in southern France that grew up around an oratory founded by Charlemagne. Also, the surname of Gaston de **Foix** (1489–1512), nephew of Louis XII, commander of the French army in Italy, and so-called Thunderbolt of Italy. His sister was the Queen of Aragon and Naples.

font *(font)* A stone basin that holds water for symbolic cleansing when entering a church, or for baptismal purposes. Also, in printing, a complete set of any style of type in a particular size. When used poetically, **font** means, as in the original Latin, "source of origin," or fountain.

Fonz *(fahns)* The cool high-school dropout played by Henry Winkler in the TV series *Happy Days*. The Fonz (full name, Arthur Fonzarelli) proved irresistible, because his tough exterior and basically decent-guy interior had universal appeal. The part, originally a small one, was beefed up when the Fonz became an overnight sensation.

fop *(fop)* From the Middle English word *foppe*, meaning "fool." Since men inordinately concerned with their clothing were considered fools by most Britons, the word came to denote a vain, affected man so

preoccupied. Beau Brummell (1778–1840) was a famous fop. His real name was George Bryan Brummell, and his name today would be used as a crossword clue for fop. Only a fop would stick a feather in his cap and call it macaroni, a term that then meant fop or dandy and now means a form of pasta.

George Bryan Brummell, well-known fop.

foray *(foh-RAY)* This word evolved from the Old French *forrer*, or "to forage," into a more bellicose type of foraging. Today it is a sudden raid for the purpose of plundering or pillaging. Also, by extension, any such action that produces a prize, like forays in the baseball free-agent market.

forge *(forj)* As a noun, a place, including a furnace, where metal is heated before it is wrought into the required shapes, village smithy-wise. As a verb, to hammer out hot metal or, figuratively, something false, as a signature; or to **forge** ahead or make progress.

forint *(FOR-ent)* Formerly a pengo (q.v.), this is the monetary unit of Hungary, as established following World War II. A forint is worth 100 fillers.

forte *(fort)* An individual's strong point, or what he's particularly good at. Also, the strongest section of a sword blade—between the middle and the hilt—as opposed to the weakest point, or foible, between the middle and the tip. As a musical adjective *(fore-TAY)*, it means "loud" as opposed to *piano*, which means "soft." The musical symbol for *forte* is F. *Fortissimo* is FF or FFF. For *piano*, it's P, and *pianissimo* is PP or PPP.

fosse *(foss)* From the Latin word for "cavity" or "trench," this indicates a trench or moat dug as a fortification. Pronounced *FOS-see*, it's the surname of Bob **Fosse**, redoubtable Broadway director/ choreographer who created such hits as *All That Jazz* and *Dancin'*.

Director/choreographer Bob Fosse.

fovea *(FOE-vee-ah)* A small pit in the surface of an anatomical structure. A very small pit is called a foveola. In the eye, the area of the retina called *fovea centralis* is a small depression where vision is most acute.

foy *(foy)* A party or feast given by a farmer to his hands after the harvest; or a similar send-off to someone departing on a journey. Also, the surname of a famous vaudeville family, including Eddie **Foy,** Jr., one of the "seven little Foys."

Eddie Foy, Jr.

foyer *(FOY-uhr)* Pronounced *fwa-YAY* in France, where it originally meant "hearthside," and *foy-YAY* by sophisticated Americans who preferred the word to hallway, foyer now refers to an entrance area in a theater or apartment building. Most people, however, call it a lobby; when it is within an apartment, a foyer is often called a vestibule.

Foyle *(foil)* A river formed by the junction of the Mourne and Finn Rivers at Strobane in County Tyrone, Northern Ireland. It flows through the city of Londonderry to Lough Foyle, an inlet of the Atlantic. Also, the heroine's surname in Christopher Morley's novel about working women, *Kitty Foyle* (1940).

Fra *(frah)* The Italian word for "brother," and therefore the title of a monk or friar. Among famous Fras are Fra Angelico (c. 1400–1455), the Florentine painter of religious subjects, a.k.a. Giovanni da Fiesole; and Fra Filippo Lippi (c. 1406–1469), one of the most celebrated Italian painters and the teacher of Botticelli; he was also called Lippo Lippi. His son, Filippino Lippi (c. 1457–1504), also became a painter of lasting fame.

The Annunciation, a fresco painted by Fra Angelico.

Fraka *(FRAY-kah)* The name of the trained falcon that delivered messages for the comic-strip character, the Phantom. Conceived by Lee Falk and Ray Moore, the masked avenger known as Kit Walker was the twenty-first in a line of phantoms who ruled the African Bandari jungle. Fraka, however, came from North America.

frat *(frat)* College slang for fraternity—a men's organization or brotherhood—from the Latin *frater* (brother), bound together by common interests and identified by Greek letters, such as Sigma Chi for the frat with a sweetheart. A similar organization for women is called a sorority, but is never referred to as a sor.

Chico Marx (right), here with Groucho Marx in Horsefeathers, *makes an unlikely frat brother.*

Frau *(frow)* German for wife, also used as the title for a married woman, much the same as Mrs. in America or Mme. in France. The plural is Frauen. The equivalent for unmarried women is Fräulein, a title frequently applied to German governesses.

fray *(fray)* As a verb, it means to become ragged or worn due to hard wear. As a noun, it describes altercations ranging from noisy quarrels to actual conflicts. Fray is a popular synonym for an athletic contest in school fight songs, perhaps because it is easier to rhyme with than "confrontation."

Clifton Webb and Gene Tierney watch as Dana Andrews delivers a right to Vincent Price in Laura.

Freki *(FREK-ee)* According to Norse mythology, one of two pet wolves belonging to Odin (q.v.). Freki could always be found at Odin's feet when the god occupied the throne.

Freon *(FREE-on)* Trademark name for any of several chemical compounds used as refrigerants and aerosol propellants. As a gas, Freon is colorless, nontoxic, noncorrosive, nonflammable, and chemically inert. The most common Freon is dichlorodifluoromethane.

fresco *(FRES-koe)* From the Italian word for "fresh," the art of painting on damp, fresh lime plaster so that the pigments will combine with chemicals in the plaster as it dries. If the painting is done on dry plaster, it is fresco secco, or just secco.

Alfresco is Italian for outdoors, where the air is presumably fresh, and usually describes a picnic setting.

The Mourning of Christ, *a fresco by the great Giotto.*

fret *(fret)* Either an ornamental network of interlacing lines, such as certain borders in Greek art; certain designs with interlacing in heraldry; or a ridge in the series on the fingerboard of a stringed instrument against which the musician presses a string to finger a specific note. As a verb, to **fret** is to fuss and fume, to be peevish.

Frey *(fray)* In Germanic mythology, a Vanir (q.v.) who joined the Aesir (q.v.) following a war between the two sets of gods. Frey was a Norse god associated with the lifegiving powers of sun and rain, and was widely worshiped in Scandinavia. His wife was Gerda (q.v.), and among his prized possessions was Skithblathnir, a magic ship that folded into a tent.

Freya or **Freyja** *(FRAY-ah)* Sister of Frey (q.v.), wife of Odin (q.v.), and Norse goddess of beauty, love, marriage, and fertility. She and Odin were also deities of the dead, dividing between them all the warriors slain in battle. Freya got around in a chariot drawn by cats, and gave her name to the day after Thursday.

friar *(FRY-uhr)* A member of certain Roman Catholic religious orders such as the

Dominicans, Carmelites, Augustinians, and Franciscans, who are vowed to poverty and thus live as mendicant ministers. Famous friars include Robin Hood's Friar Tuck and Romeo and Juliet's Friar Lawrence, who married them. In printer's slang, a **friar** is a section of paper improperly inked; and the Australian **friar** bird enjoys that name because his unfeathered head resembles a friar's tonsure.

Frick *(frik)*

Ford Christopher Frick (1894–   ), the former sportswriter who became commissioner of major-league baseball in 1951. He was elected to the Baseball Hall of Fame in 1970. Also, Henry Clay Frick (1849–1919), the American industrialist and art connoisseur who endowed and willed to the public the Frick Collection, housed in his former mansion in New York City.

Ford Christopher Frick.

Friml *(FRIM-ul)*

Charles Rudolf Friml (1879–1972), the Bohemian-born American composer of 33 romantic operettas featuring strong heroes, lovely heroines, and fairy-tale plots. Among Friml favorites are *Rose Marie* (1924), *The Vagabond King* (1925), and *The Firefly* (1912), which gave the world the lovely "Donkey Serenade."

Rudolf Friml (left) photographed with Jeanette MacDonald and Arthur Hammerstein.

Frio *(FREE-oh)*

The name of two points of land that face each other across the South Atlantic: Cape Frio in southeastern Brazil, to the east of Rio de Janeiro; and Cape Frio on the coast of Namibia, in southern Africa.

frise *(free-ZAY)*

From the French word meaning "to curl," frisé is a type of upholstery fabric, sometimes called frieze, roughly considered to have curls. It has a thick pile composed of uncut loops. In certain types of frisé material, some of the loops are cut to form a design.

frit *(frit)*

In the manufacture of glass or vitreous china, frit is the partly fused mixture of sand and fluxes that is then vitrified to make the finished product. Also, a small, two-winged fly (of the genus *Oscinis*) that destroys grain in European countries.

friz or frizz *(friz)*

Related to the word frisé (q.v.), friz is hair curled into tight ringlets, à la the style made famous by Little Orphan Annie, or hair tangled in whorls. Advertising copywriters use it pejoratively when extolling the virtues of hair products intended to fight friz.

Frankenstein (Boris Karloff) gets a frizzy-haired mate (Elsa Lanchester) in The Bride of Frankenstein *(1935).*

froe or frou *(frow)*

A tool used for splitting wood from a block. Unlike a cleaver, whose handle is in line with the blade, a froe has a handle at right angles to the blade. **Froe** also means a wedge for splitting logs.

frond *(frond)*

Name given to certain distinctively shaped leaves, especially of palms and ferns. Certain fern fronds resemble leaves but carry reproductive cells on their lower surfaces. The most familiar fronds are the palm leaves distributed in churches on the Sunday before Easter, recalling those strewn in Jesus' path upon his entry into Jerusalem.

frosh *(frosh)* A turn-of-the-century German university slang expression for first-year students. The word has now passed into American slang to designate a freshman at any institution of learning, or a person in his first year of some particular activity—a freshman (or frosh) senator, for example.

froth *(frawth)* A foam, such as the head on a glass of beer or the saliva at the mouth of a hard-ridden horse. Froth, by extension, is also anything with the substance of foam, therefore unimportant, like light banter. Certain minerals, particularly sulfides and phosphates, are concentrated by floating them out of solution on a froth.

The water passing through this rock formation is whipped into a froth.

frump *(frump)* In current usage, a dowdyish or ill-dressed woman, often one with an unpleasant disposition. Well-known frumps in comic strips include Mrs. Katzenjammer and Mrs. Andy Capp.

fucus *(FEW-kus)* Marine plants of the genus *Fucus*, brown or dark-green algae with flat, leathery fronds and bladderlike buds. The plants are a source of commercial algin. Also, red or purple pigment used in antiquity as face paint.

Fuji *(FOO-jee)* The Japanese sacred mountain also called Fuji-yama or, often, Fuji-san. Mount Fuji, in central Honshu, is a stunningly symmetrical snow-capped volcano, inactive since 1707. The highest (12,389 feet) mountain in Japan, it was created, according to legend, by an earthquake in 286 B.C.

Japan's famous geologic feature, Mt. Fuji, seen here from Shizuoka Prefecture.

Fulah or **Fula** *(FOO-lah)* Muslim people of West Africa, now residing principally in Sudan, and their language. Also called Fulani, they are of mixed Berber and Black African origin.

Fulda *(FUL-dah)* A West German city that developed on the banks of the Fulda River around the Benedictine abbey founded by a follower of St. Boniface in A.D. 744. Christianity spread throughout Germany from Fulda, and Catholic bishops still attend an annual conference there. **Fulda** is also the surname of Ludwig Fulda (1862–1939), a playwright who translated Shakespeare and Ibsen into German.

The Dom in Fulda designed by Johannes von Dientzenhofer was completed in 1712.

Fundy *(FUN-dee)*   A large bay indenting the Atlantic coast between New Brunswick and southwestern Nova Scotia; it is about 170 miles long and up to 50 miles wide. The bay is famous for its unusually high tides, reaching to 50 feet at the upper end. The ebb and flow of the tides creates the "reversing falls" of the St. John River.

fungi *(FUN-gee)*   A division of very simple plants without true roots, stems, or leaves, and also lacking flowers and chlorophyll. They therefore live as saprophytes or parasites. Included among the fungi (the singular form is fungus) are mushrooms, yeasts, mildews, and such molds as the blue and green strains yielding the antibiotic penicillin and those that ripen Roquefort and other "blue-mold" cheeses.

fungo *(FUNG-oh)*   A baseball drill in which a batter tosses a ball in the air and hits it as it descends. A good fungo hitter can hit the ball just about anywhere he wishes.

furan *(FYOO-ran)*   A colorless liquid chemical compound found in wood tar and used as a solvent and to tan leather. Derivatives of furan include furfural, used in the manufacture of pesticides and tetrahydrofuran, which is important in the production of nylon.

furfur *(FIR-fir)*   To dermatologists, it's a branny desquamation of the epidermis. To shampoo manufacturers and white-speckled wearers of dark clothing, it's dandruff.

Furth *(feert)*   A city in Bavaria, at the junction of the Rednitz and Pegnitz rivers near Nuremburg. Founded in A.D. 793, reputedly by Charlemagne, Fürth became noteworthy in the fourteenth century when the Jews who had been denied admittance into Nuremburg settled there. Fürth and Nuremburg were termini of the first German railroad, completed in 1835.

furze *(firz)*   A low, dense shrub of the pulse family, with spiny leaves (or no leaves at all) and fragrant yellow flowers. Also called gorse (q.v.) and whin (q.v.), it was originally native to Europe.

Needle furze.

Fusan   See *Pusan.*

fuse or **fuze** *(fews)*   Spelled with a *z,* this is a device filled with combustible material, such as wicks that burn or percussion caps that explode on contact, used for detonating an explosion. Spelled with an *s,* it is a wire or strip of metal inserted in an electrical circuit, designed to melt when the current gets too strong, thus interrupting the flow of electricity.

fusee or **fuzee** *(few-ZAY)*   Either a special type of match that won't blow out easily, even in a high wind; a red flare (q.v.) used to warn oncoming motorists or train engineers of a stalled vehicle or train; part of the spring mechanism of an old-fashioned clock; or a bony growth on a horse's leg.

fusil or **fuzil** *(FEW-zuhl)*   From a French word meaning "to strike sparks," an obsolete, light flintlock musket in which the powder is ignited by a spark created when a flint in the hammer strikes against a metal plate.

fyke *(fike)*   A long sack kept open by hoops. Also, therefore, a particular type of fish net (fyke net) in the shape of a long bag.

Fyn *(fun)*   Second largest of the Danish islands, located between Jutland and the island of Sjaelland. Largely a fertile lowland, its chief products are cereals, milk, and cheese. Major cities of Fyn include Odense (birthplace of Hans Christian Andersen), Nyborg, and Svendborg.

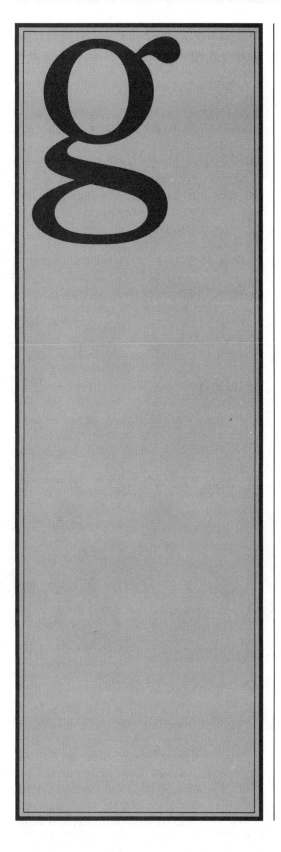

Gabes *(GOB-us)* or **Qabis** *(KAIB-us)* A city on the Gulf of Gabès in east-central Tunisia. Founded by the Romans, Gabès is at the center of an oasis of date palms.

Gabon *(gah-BONE)* Since 1960, a republic on the Gulf of Guinea in what formerly was French Equatorial Africa. Beginning in the fifteenth century, this region was long a hub of the slave trade, which was officially abolished in 1815 by the Congress of Vienna. The capital, Libreville, was founded by the French in 1849 as a settlement for freed slaves. Dr. Albert Schweitzer established his famous hospital at Lambaréné in 1913.

gad *(gad)* In mining, a spike- or chisel-ended iron bar used to break up ore. As a proper noun, the seventh son of Jacob, and therefore the name of the biblical land where his descendants, the Gadites, settled (see *Levi*). As a verb, to roam about in search of diversion. A person partial to this pursuit is known as a gadabout.

gadid *(GAY-did)* Any fish belonging to the cod family, the *Gadidae*. The best known of these are the Atlantic cod, the whiting, the haddock, and the pollack or green cod. That palate-pleaser of Boston's seafood restaurants, the scrod, is actually a young gadid—a baby codfish, sometimes a haddock, filleted for cooking.

Gael *(gale)* A Celt (q.v.) of Scotland, Ireland, or the Isle of Man. Many Gaels live in the Scottish Highlands. Their language is Gaelic, or Goidelic, one of the Indo-European family of languages still spoken, but less than formerly. Scottish and Irish Gaelic became separated as languages only in the seventeenth century and much literature has survived. A Scottish Gaelic culture hero is Rob Roy (Gaelic for "Red Rob"), who flourished in the eighteenth century. An Irish Celtic hero is Finn (q.v.) MacCool, a third-century warrior.

Famous Gaels include actor Sean Connery, shown here with Tippi Hedren in a scene from Hitchcock's Marnie.

gaff *(gaff)* A stout barbed hook mounted on a pole, used by fishermen to bring the fish on their lines into a boat. Also, a sharp spur fastened to the leg of a fighting cock; a spar from which a fore- and aft-sail hangs; or in English slang, a dance hall of questionable credentials. **Gaff** can also be abusive talk or ridicule, hence the refusal to "stand someone's gaff."

gaffe *(gaff)* A word that comes directly from the French and means a social or political blunder, or, as we say, putting one's foot in one's mouth.

gage *(gaje)* Either the shortened name of the greengage, a type of plum; an item held to ensure the keeping of a promise; or in days of knight-errantry, an item (such as a glove) cast before an opponent as a pledge to meet in combat. Also, the surname of Thomas **Gage** (1721–1787), English general and governor of colonial Massachusetts, who ordered the arrest of Samuel Adams and John Hancock. His later orders to seize military stores at Concord precipitated the American Revolution.

Gagra *(GAH-grah)* or **Gagry** *(GAH-gree)* A city located in Georgia (the Soviet Socialist Republic, not the Peach State) on the shores of the Black Sea. Nestled at the foot of the Greater Caucasus, it is particularly picturesque and is popular, at least in Georgia, as a subtropical health resort.

Galax *(GAY-laks)* From the Greek word for "galaxy," a genus of low evergreen plants with white flowers, native to the mountains of the southeastern United States. The glossy heart-shaped leaves, which turn bronze in the autumn, make *Galax* popular for wreaths.

Galba *(GAL-bah)* Servius Sulpicius Galba (3 B.C.–A.D. 69), proclaimed Emperor of Rome following Nero's suicide in A.D. 68. Galba's reign came to an untimely conclusion when he was killed in a rebellion led by Otho, who succeeded him. **Galba** is also a genus of freshwater snails that includes major Old World hosts of the liver fluke.

Galen *(GAY-len)* The illustrious Claudius Galenius (c. 139–200), a Greek physician who eventually relocated his practice to Rome and became physician to Emperor Marcus Aurelius. Galen systematized medical knowledge and wrote extensively on medical subjects. His teleology, "Nature does nothing in vain," was a guiding principle of medicine until the Renaissance. Up to that time, his writings were considered the ultimate authority; as a result, progress in medicine was slow.

Galen teaching.

gall *(gawl)* A tumor of plant tissue, such as those seen on oak trees, caused by physical damage or by irritants released by fungi, bacteria, nematodes, or insects. Some galls have commercial value and are used in manufacturing and tanning. **Gall** is also a synonym for bile, the bitter, greenish fluid secreted by the liver and stored in the gall bladder; or temerity, usually unmitigated. Also, the Sioux war chief **Gall** (c. 1840–1894) who, with Sitting Bull, made General Custer's stand at the Little Bighorn his last.

Galla (GAL-*ah*)   A Hamitic tribesman of western and southern Ethiopia or parts of Kenya, or the language spoken by the Gallas. **Galla** Placidia (c. A.D. 388–450) was a Roman empress of the West. After being captured and held hostage by the Visigoths under Alaric I, she eventually married Alaric's successor, and later on the Roman General Constantius, who became coemperor in 421. Following his death in 425, Galla served as regent for her son Valentinian III.

Galle (*gahl*)   The southernmost large city in Sri Lanka. An important Indian Ocean port for Chinese and Arab trade since 100 B.C., it was a Portuguese colony for almost 600 years. **Galle** (GAH-*leh*) is also the surname of Johann Gottfried Galle (1812–1910), the German astronomer who discovered the planet Neptune.

gam (*gam*)   A collective noun, as in a gam of whales, which is also known as a pod (q.v.); or a social visit by the crews of whaling vessels on the open seas. **Gam** is also slang for a woman's leg (derived perhaps from the French word *jambe*—"leg"), as in "Check the gams on that chick."

gamma (GAM-*ah*)   The third letter of the Greek alphabet, corresponding to the sixth (*G*) of the English alphabet. Gamma is the third of any series in mathematics, physics, etc.; for example, a gamma is the third brightest star in a constellation. It appears in the name of many scientific entities, such as gamma globulin, gamma acid, and the formidable gamma ray of the futuristic weapons of early comic-book heroes and villains.

gamp (*gamp*)   A large, usually poorly furled cotton umbrella named for its comical

bearer—Sarah ("Sairey") **Gamp,** the nurse in Dickens's *Martin Chuzzlewit.* The word gamp has also become a slang synonym for any woman with a share of Sairey's zestfulness and a similar taste for strong tea and other stimulating beverages.

gamut (GAM-*ut*)   Originally a musical term denoting the lowest note in the medieval scale in the system of Guido d'Arezzo. Later it meant Guido's complete scale, and still later the entire range of notes recognized in modern music. Guido's highest note was ELA, a frequent repeater in crosswords. The word gamut has broadened to mean the entire range of anything.

gandy (GAN-*dee*)   Railroad slang and part of the term gandy dancer, meaning a section-gang laborer. This man's rhythmic motions as he drove spikes into the ties to secure lengths of track suggested a kind of stately dance. As for his tools, they came from the Gandy Manufacturing Company of Chicago, Illinois.

ganja (GAN-*jah*)   In India, a preparation of *Cannabis sativa,* a.k.a. hemp (q.v.), source of marijuana. A tea is brewed from the mature female plant tops, and the dried material can also be smoked or eaten. When incorporated into sweetmeats, it is known as majoon. The smoking of ganja is a ritual practice of the Rastafarian religious cult of Jamaica.

gar (*gar*)   Any of a family of predatory freshwater fishes found in the warmer lakes and rivers of the southern U.S. as well as Central America, Mexico, and the West Indies. Gar have long, cylindrical bodies, hard, diamond-shaped scales, and sharp teeth used to kill other fish. They are sometimes up to nine feet long. The saltwater garfish, usually clued as "needlefish" in crossword puzzles, resembles the true gar but is not closely related.

Garbo (GAR-boe) The legendary American movie actress born Greta Gustafson (1905–   ) in Stockholm. Garbo was first cast in sexy roles and then as tragic heroines. She retired and has lived largely in seclusion since 1941. It may be only coincidence, but **garbo** means "elegance" in Italian.

Greta Garbo.

Gard (gahr) A department of southern France, located where the Rhone River flows to the Mediterranean Sea. The capital of Gard is Nîmes. Also, part of the surname of Roger Martin du **Gard** (1881–1958), the French novelist best known for his eight-part work *The World of the Thibaults,* translated into English in 1939–1941. In 1937, Martin du Gard won the Nobel Prize in literature.

Garm (garm) Part of "Garm: A Hostage," the title of a Rudyard Kipling story. In Norse mythology, **Garm** was the demon watchdog of Hel (q.v.), goddess of the land of the dead. At Ragnarok, Garm slew and was slain by the god Tiw (q.v.).

Garmo (GAR-moe) Former name of the highest mountain in the Soviet Union at 24,590 feet. This peak is situated in the Tadzhik Republic in the central Asian Pamirs. The shifting sands of Soviet history are evident in the other names for this mountain that succeeded Garmo: it was Stalin Peak, and is now Mt. Communism.

garth (garth) An archaic term for an enclosed garden or yard. Also, a fish weir; the name of **Garth,** a major character in Maxwell Anderson's *Winterset;* and Sir Samuel Garth (1661–1719), the English poet-physician who in *The Dispensary* (1699) advocated free clinics for treating the poor.

Gaspe (gas-PAY) Various place names in eastern Quebec, including the rugged Gaspé Peninsula, 159 miles long and up to 90 miles wide, bounded by the St. Lawrence and Chaleur Bay and jutting into the Gulf of St. Lawrence; Gaspé Bay, a deep inlet at the eastern end of the peninsula; Cape Gaspé, which extends into Gaspé Bay; and the city of Gaspé, the landing place on Gaspé Bay of Cartier in 1534.

gat (gat) A narrow navigable channel in northern European waters. The word is part of Kattegat, name of a strait about 140 miles long and from 40 to 100 miles wide, separating Denmark from Sweden. It is linked to the North Sea by the Skagerrak. **Gat** is also passé gangster slang for a pistol.

A gat being used on a priest in the 1947 semi-documentary style film, Boomerang.

Gath (gath) In the Bible, a Philistine city located on the borders of Judah, southernmost of the two Hebrew kingdoms (the northern being Israel). Gath's most famous

David does in Gath's famous citizen, Goliath.

citizen was Goliath, who called it his home town. David sought refuge there as a fugitive (2 Sam. 21:10–15).

Gatun *(ga-TOON)*

A town, a dam, and a lake in Panama. Gatún Lake was formed during the excavation of the Canal, when the Chagres River was impounded by the 1½-mile-long Gatún Dam. The lake forms part of the canal route; its level is controlled by the dam.

gaud *(gawd)*

From the Middle English word for "jewel" or "ornament," any cheap, ostentatious trinket which has little value except to proclaim the tastelessness of the wearer. In the plural, gauds are flamboyant gaieties or ceremonies.

Carmen Miranda was one of Hollywood's leading ladies of gaud.

Gaul *(gawl)*

In antiquity, a part of the Roman Empire eventually comprising what is now France (Gaul proper), Belgium, and sections of Italy, the Netherlands, Switzerland, and Germany. Gaul fell to Julius Caesar, who described the campaign in his *Commentarii de Bello Gallico*—a book destined to plague second-year Latin students millennia later. Today, both the word and its derivative "Gallic" refer to France.

Gaur *(gawr)*

Former Hindu capital of Bengal, also known as Lakhnauti, in the West Bengal state of India. Gaur was captured by the Muslims around 1200, and remained a center of their culture until its abandonment in the late sixteenth century after siege and destruction by the Afghans. The Kadam Rasul Mosque built in 1530 was supposedly built over relics of Mohammed. A **gaur** is also a large wild ox of southeast Asia, more than six feet high at the shoulder. It is related to the slightly smaller gayal of Burma.

gauss *(gowss)*

A unit for measuring magnetic field intensity until 1932, and magnetic induction thereafter. One gauss equals one line of magnetic force per square centimeter. The unit is named for Karl Friedrich **Gauss** (1777–1855), the German mathematician-astronomer who first explained electricity and magnetism according to mathematical theory.

Karl Friedrich Gauss.

gavotte *or* gavot *(gah-VAHT)*

Originally, a circle dance performed by the Gavots—inhabitants of the Hautes Alpes region of France—and later popular in the court of Louis XIV. A dance in 4/4 time, the gavotte is similar to the minuet but more spirited. Music for gavottes was composed by Lully, Couperin, and Bach.

The gavotte gained "respectability" at the French court.

gayal See *Gaur.*

Gaza *(GAH-za)* An ancient Philistine city on the plain between the Mediterranean Sea and Israel, the nearest settlement to Egypt. It was here that Samson pulled down the temple and Alexander the Great laid siege. Today Gaza, whose name means "the strong," is the center of the disputed Gaza Strip.

Geb *(geb)* In ancient Egyptian religion, the god of the earth, father of Osiris. Geb is usually represented as having a human figure and the head of a goose.

gecko *(GEK-oh)* There are more than 300 species of this small-to-medium-size, nonpoisonous lizard found throughout the warmer regions of the world. Geckos are the only lizards that can make sounds, and their uniquely constructed foot pads enable them to run upside down on ceilings.

gee *(jee)* Command to a horse, mule, ox, or whatever animal pulls your wagon, to turn to the right, or to move ahead. See *haw.* **Gee** is also an exclamation, usually to express surprise; it is a euphemistic contraction of "Jesus."

geest *(geest)* From the German, a term used in geology to denote loose alluvial deposits of considerable age, laid down by flowing water in what are now dry riverbeds. Geest is also a loose earth created by the decay of rocks.

geld *(geld)* From the Old English word for "tax" or "tribute," a tax paid by landholders to the Anglo-Saxon and Norman kings, also spelled gelt. As a verb, to **geld** is to castrate a male animal, often a horse, which presumably modifies his temperament and allows him to concentrate on winning races. Gelding is the noun for such an animal.

gemel *(JEM-al)* Related to the Latin word for "twin," a gemel is either of two closely spaced bars that traverse a shield in heraldic design (usually called bars gemels). In mechanics, it is either of two parts that form a single unit—like a hinge.

gemma *(JEM-ah)* In biology, a bud or budlike body composed of one or many cells. Gemmae (pl.) are the means by which certain organisms like yeasts reproduce asexually. The gemmae become detached and grow into new organisms.

genet *(JEN-et)* Any of a group of small, spotted, skunklike animals belonging to the civet family, found in Spain, southern France, and Africa. They have retractile claws and prey on small mammals and birds. As a proper noun and pronounced *zhe-NAY,* the surname of Jean **Genet** (1910–   ), the French dramatist whose plays exemplify the theater of the absurd.

genie or **jinni** *(JEE-nee)* A demon or spirit of Arabian myth created from fire 2,000 years before Adam. These spirits (jinn) live on the mountain of Kaf, can assume any shape or size, or even become invisible. The best-known genie is probably the one Aladdin found in an old lamp.

genro *(gen-ROE)* Literally the "elder statesmen" who ruled Japan in a collective leadership until the mid-1800s and then served as an advisory cabinet to emperors until the early 1930s.

gens *(jenz)* Any ancient Roman clan comprising families descended through the male line from a common ancestor. All members of the gens would therefore have the same name and jointly worship their common progenitor. A political subdivision made up of several gens was a curia (q.v.).

genu *(JEE-noo)* A word taken directly from the Latin, meaning the "knee," or any anatomical structure that bends like the knee. The word is part of such medical terms as genu valgum and genu extrorsum, which describe knock-knees and bowlegs, respectively. Genu is the root of genuflect, "to bend the knee (or to kneel) in worship."

One way to bend a genu.

genus *(JEE-nus)* In taxonomy, or classifying organisms into categories, genus, meaning "birth" or "origin" in Latin, is more specific than family, but more general than species. This is like relating the category of family to your country; genus to your state; and species to your city. The plural is genera. Scientific names of organisms are composed of genus and species, in that order. Thus, *Rosa gallica,* the French rose, is of the genus *Rosa* and the species *gallica.* Additional words sometimes indicate the name given a subspecies, a race, or a variety.

geode *(JEE-ode)* From the Greek word for "earthlike," a stone whose center is hollow and lined with gem crystals. These stones are often cut in half and displayed in mineral collections. Also, any body structure resembling a geode, such as a dilated lymph space.

gerah *(JEE-ra)* In biblical times, a Hebrew unit of weight, equal to 11 grains, or a coin equal to 1/20 of a shekel. The shekel contained about half an ounce of silver, but the gerah's actual worth may have been no more than a bean. That's what the word gerah means in Hebrew.

Gerda *(GUR-dah)* According to Scandinavian mythology, a young giantess whose father was Gymer, the giant of frost, and whose husband was Frey (q.v.), god of fruitfulness. Gerda's beauty was such that her arms lit up the air and sea. Her story is told in the *Skirnismal.*

gesso *(JESS-oh)* A special type of gypsum or plaster of Paris, from the Italian, Latin, and Greek words meaning "chalk," "gypsum," or "plaster." Gesso is applied by artists to canvas or wood to prepare a surface for painting. It is also used in making bas-reliefs.

gest or **geste** *(jest)* An exciting exploit or a romantic tale, often in verse, relating the daring adventures of a valorous hero. Just such a hero was the man who took the name **Geste** in Percival Wren's novel about the French Foreign Legion, *Beau Geste.*

Gary Cooper in Beau Geste, *1939.*

Ghana *(GAH-na)* The West African republic named for a medieval African empire. Ghana, made independent in 1957, encompasses the former British colony of the Gold Coast and the mandated territory of British Togoland; its capital is Accra (q.v.). The republic, dating from 1960, was originally ruled by Kwame Nkrumah, a dictator who was overthrown in 1966.

ghat *(gawt)* From the Hindi for "steps," a flight of steps leading down to a river, used for ceremonial bathing or, as a burning ghat, for cremation. Because they resemble steps, two mountain ranges of south India are called the **Ghats.** Pronounced *gaht,* the name of a walled town in southwestern Libya, and scene of heavy World War II fighting in 1943.

The ghats of Varanasi (formerly Benares), India, lead to the Ganges river.

Ghazi or **Gazi** *(GAH-zee)*   A title of honor derived from the Arabic word for "warrior." In many Muslim countries, it is ceremoniously accorded to heroes, particularly those who make war against infidels.

ghee *(gee)*   A dairy product of India. When buffalo-milk or cow's-milk butter is melted, boiled, and strained, the oily fluid that remains is ghee. Used widely in cookery, ghee keeps well in hot climates and is often bottled with aromatic essences.

Ghent *(gent)*   Capital of East Flanders province, Belgium, dating back to the seventh century. Its strategic location has involved Ghent in conflicts ranging from the medieval Hundred Years War to World War II. The Treaty of Ghent, signed there in 1814, ended the War of 1812 between Great Britain and the United States. The city is a major port and industrial center and has notable ancient buildings. The poet and dramatist Maurice Maeterlinck *(The Blue Bird)* was born in Ghent.

gib *(gib)*   In various machines, a plate of metal or wood inserted to keep moving parts from moving where they shouldn't. Also, the hooked appendage that appears on the underjaw of a male salmon in spawning season.

Gibil *(GIB-uhl)*   In the Assyro-Babylonian pantheon, the god of fire, also known as Girru *(GIR-oo).* If you suspected that an enemy was engaged in bringing misfortune down upon you through the invocation of sorcery or magic, Gibil was the god you beseeched to save you.

gibus *(JIE-bus)*   That indispensable item of attire for stage-door Johnnies and magicians, the opera hat. Named for its nineteenth-century inventor, this tall topper consists of a silky fabric stretched over a collapsible frame. It is the only hat you can sit on with impunity.

gid *(gid)*   In veterinary medicine, a brain disease most often seen in sheep, but occasionally in cattle. Caused by the larva of a tapeworm *(Multiceps multiceps),* it induces jerky, circling, and rolling movements that suggest drunkenness.

Gide *(zheed)*   Surname of André Gide (1869–1951), the unconventional French novelist, essayist, and playwright whose works include the semiautobiographical *The Immoralist* (1902). His *Travels in the Congo* (1927) helped change France's colonial policies. Always controversial because of his Communist sympathies (later changed) and defense of homosexuality, Gide won the Nobel Prize for literature in 1947.

André Gide.

gig *(gig)*   Either a two-wheeled, one-horse open carriage; the long, light ship's boat reserved for the use of commanding officers of naval vessels; a machine for raising a nap on cloth; an official report for some minor transgression, like an unbuttoned button in the army; or, in musicians' slang, a playing date.

gigot *(JIG-uht)* From the old French word for "fiddle," because of its supposed resemblance to that instrument, a leg of mutton or lamb, especially in Britain and France, where it is pronounced *zhee-GOH*. Also, the leg-of-mutton sleeve that's tight in the forearm and widely puffed at the shoulder.

Gila *(HEE-lah)* A 630-mile-long river rising in New Mexico, flowing west across Arizona, and joining the Colorado River near Yuma. Also, the monster of the same name—a poisonous, 18-inch-long lizard of the deserts of the southwestern United States and Mexico. **Gila** monsters are distinguished by their loud orange, pink, yellow, white, and brown coloration.

gilly, gillie, or **ghillie** *(GILL-ee)* The male attendant or personal servant of a well-born Scottish Highlander; or a guide to fishing or shooting on the moors. The **gilly**flower, whose name derives from medieval French for "clove," is any of several garden plants with flowers redolent of cloves, such as the clove pink, the common stock, and the European wallflower. A **gillie** is also a woman's low-cut walking shoe with decorative laces.

gimel *(GIM-ul)* The third letter of the Hebrew alphabet, corresponding in sound to the letter *g* in the English alphabet and to the Greek letter gamma (q.v.).

gimp *(gimp)* Either American pejorative slang for a limp or one who limps, or a narrow trimming, usually made of braided cotton and sometimes stiffened with wire, used on certain garments. Gimp comes from the French word *guimpe,* for "wimple"—the head covering worn by medieval ladies which has been retained by certain orders of nuns.

Ginza *(GIN-zah)* In Tokyo, a major shopping and entertainment district. The Ginza has been said to combine the various features of such famous streets as Broadway, the Champs Élysées and the Via Veneto.

The Ginza, Tokyo's commercial and nightlife district, blazes with neon.

Gipp *(gip)* George Gipp (1895–1920), football player for Notre Dame. Gipp died of pneumonia at 25 and thereby inspired the famous speech by coach Knute Rockne in which the team was exhorted to "Win this one for the Gipper." In the movie about Rockne's life, Gipp was played by the future fortieth President of the United States.

Giza or **Gizeh** *(GEE-zah)* Also known as Al Jizah, a suburb of Cairo, Egypt. Near Giza are the Sphinx, the Great Pyramid of Cheops, and the tombs of his mother and daughter. Giza has grown into a thriving tourist and resort area, and because of its film industry, it's also known as the Hollywood of Egypt.

The famous Sphinx at Giza.

DOWN UNDER

dingo

kiwi

bilbi

kakapo

emu

NOT APPEARING HERE

BIRDS

astur	lory
friar bird	mako
kagu	moa
kaki	pitta
koel	weka

FLORA

atle	kauri
aute	kava
awa	kiwi
banga	mako
baobab	miro

ANIMALS

ariel	jerboa
bene	koala

FISH

mako

glair *(glare)* From the Latin word *clarus*, meaning "clear," the clear part of the egg, or egg white. This albuminous material is water-soluble, can be coagulated by heat, and is composed of hydrogen, oxygen, nitrogen, and carbon. Outside the kitchen it is applied as a sizing before gilding book edges.

Glama or Glomma *(GLOW-mah)*

The longest river in Norway (about 365 miles), flowing south past Sarpsborg into the Skagerrak at Fredrikstad. The Glåma's many hydroelectric stations produce energy for the urban areas of southern Norway, and most of the timber cut in the north is floated down the Glåma.

Hydroelectric plants along the Glåma River.

glebe *(gleeb)* From the Latin word *gleba*, meaning "clump of earth," a parcel of land belonging to a parish church and assigned to a vicar, rector, or other incumbent of a benefice to assist in his support. **Glebe** is also used poetically to denote the soil or a field.

glede *(gleed)* A species of kite native to Europe. This bird of prey is known for stealing food from falcons and ospreys. Gledes feed on mice, reptiles, and insects, but are generally scavengers, even lining their nests with rags, newspapers, and other byproducts of human habitation.

Glenn *(glen)*

John Herschel Glenn, Jr. (1921–   ), the first American astronaut to be rocketed into orbital flight. Glenn circled the earth three times on February 20, 1962, on a flight lasting just under five hours. After leaving the space program, he was elected to the Senate (D-Ohio) in 1974.

Gluck *(glook)*

Famous musical name belonging to Alma Gluck (1884–1938), the legendary Romanian-born American operatic soprano whose real name was Reba Fiersohn; and Christoph Willibald von Gluck (1714–1787), the operatic composer who revolutionized opera by his introduction of lyrical tragedy, as in *Orfeo et Euridice* (1762) and *Iphigénie en Aulide* (1774).

glume *(gloom)* In botany the dry, rough external covering, husk, or chafflike bract of grasses, including certain cereal grains. Glumes grow at the base of the spikelets in the seed head. See *emmer*.

glyph *(gliff)* From the Greek for a "carving," a symbolic figure or character carved in relief or cut into stone. Examples include Egyptian hieroglyphs, pictures or symbols representing words, syllables, and sounds. In architecture, a **glyph** is a vertical groove or channel.

Hieroglyphs describe the carved reliefs.

gnome *(nome)*

The word comes from the Latin term *gnomus*, meaning "earth dweller," and is supposed to have been invented by Paracelsus. Gnomes are small, misshapen creatures who live underground and guard mines and precious metals.

gnu *(noo)* Generations of puzzle constructors owe an eternal debt to the Bushmen who named this large African antelope. Gnus have a beard, a short mane, one humped shoulder, downward-and-outward curved horns, and a long tail. They graze in herds of up to thousands of animals, sometimes in company with zebras. In Afrikaans, gnus are known as wildebeests.

Goa *(GOE-ah)* A former Portuguese colony on the Malabar Coast of India. Goa was conquered by Muslims in 1312, became part of the Hindu Vijayanagar kingdom in 1370, was recaptured by the Muslims a hundred years later, annexed in 1510 by Portuguese commander Alfonso de Albuquerque, and seized by India in 1961. It is now a union territory of three non-contiguous former Portuguese colonies and is known as Goa, Daman, and Diu. Its capital is Panjim, in Goa.

Gobi *(GOE-bee)* The half-million-square-mile desert of China and Mongolia, also known, in Chinese, as the Sha-moh. This wasteland, averaging about 4,000 feet in elevation, has few living inhabitants except the handful of Mongols who graze their animals on its sparse grasslands.

gobo *(GOH-boe)* In Japan, a species of burdock cultivated as a vegetable. In any television or motion-picture studio, a black cloth screen that shields the camera from unwanted light, or a sound-absorbing screen that protects the microphone from unwanted sound. In *Bambi,* Felix Salten's animal story, **Gobo** is Bambi's cousin.

goby *(GOE-bee)* As one word, a small fish with ventral fins modified to form suction discs. These fins permit certain Pacific gobies, like the mudskipper, to leave the water and cavort over sand or mud, and even climb mangrove tree roots (see *aboma*). With a hyphen between syllables, a go-by *(GOE-bie)* is an intentional snub.

Godot *(goh-DOE)* Central character in Samuel Beckett's famous ironic play *Waiting for Godot* (1952) who never appears but who nonetheless exerts enormous influence on the other characters. Godot may be interpreted to represent God.

Godoy *(ga-DOY)* Manuel de Godoy (1767–1851), chief minister of Charles IV of Spain. He favored waging war on France during the Revolution, but nevertheless made peace and was designated Principe de la Paz. Subsequently, his increasing Francophilic tendencies led to his overthrow at the hands of Ferdinand VII in 1808.

Gog *(gahg)* In the Book of Revelation, half the alliance of Gog and Magog, two symbolic nations which, under the leadership of Satan, were destined to wage war on the kingdom of God (Rev. 21:8).

Gogol *(GOE-gul)* Nikolai Vasilyevich Gogol (1809–1852), the Cossack novelist and playwright considered the father of Russian realism. Among his best-known works are *Taras Bulba,* a tale depicting the adventures of a seventeenth-century Cossack; *Dead Souls,* a picaresque novel; and *The Inspector General,* a play satirizing small-time officialdom which found a new audience in a film version starring Danny Kaye.

Nikolai Vasilyevich Gogol.

Gogra *(GOH-grah)* A 640-mile-long river rising in the Himalayas in Tibet and flowing southeast through Nepal (where it is called the Karnali) and into India, where it becomes a major tributary of the Ganges in the state of Bihar. Also known as the Ghaghara *(GAH-grah)*, it has shipping on its lower reaches.

golem *(GOE-lem)* In medieval Jewish legend, a creature fashioned of clay and brought to life by a charm. One such golem was supposedly created in the sixteenth century by a Rabbi Low of Prague. When the creature ran amok (q.v.), it had to be destroyed.

Goon *(goon)* Originally Alice the Goon, a comic character created, together with Popeye, Olive Oyl, Wimpy, et al., by car-

toonist E. C. Segar for his "Thimble Theatre." It is now slang for an awkward, stupid, or otherwise undesirable person. Somewhere in its evolution the term **goon** was adopted by trade unionists to designate unsavory ruffians hired by management to terrorize strikers.

Alice the Goon.

goral *(GOE-ral)* A goat antelope native to the Himalayas, western China, and Korea. Gorals are closely related to the Rocky Mountain goat. Both sexes have horns.

Gorky *(GOR-kee)* Maxim Gorky (Russian for "Maxim the Bitter") is the pen name of Aleksei Maximovitch Pyeshkov (1868–1936), born in Nizhny Novgorod, since renamed Gorky in his honor. Considered the father of Soviet literature, Gorky was a Communist folk hero. Many think his death was actually an assassination carried out by anti-Soviet hit men.

A. M. Pyeshkov.

gorse *(gorse)* Another name for the common furze (q.v.), a member of the pulse family (the *Legumino-sae*) that has roughly 550 genera and 13,000 species, including peas, beans, lentils, peanuts, and soybeans. Gorse is sometimes called whin (q.v.).

Gotha *(GOE-tha)* A city in East Germany dating from the late twelfth century. Gotha has long been known as a publishing center and is the home of the publisher of the famous *Almanach de Gotha*, the definitive source of information on the royal houses and nobility of Europe.

Gouda *(GOW-dah; GOO-dah)* A western Netherlands city located at the juncture of the Gouwe and Hollandsche Ijssel rivers. Chartered in 1272, Gouda was a medieval textile center. Erasmus studied in Gouda in the late fifteenth century. Today its main product is a famous mild-tasting yellow cheese with a bright red wax coat.

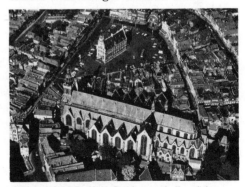
Aerial view of Gouda's Gothic town hall and the Groote Kerk.

gout *(gowt)* A painful type of arthritis in which an excess of uric acid in the body is a factor. In time, gout can cause the deposition in the joints of uric acid crystals, causing deformity. Most common is gout of the big toe, a condition often treated lightly by comic-strip cartoonists. Most gout sufferers are men. The French word from which our word derives is *goutte.* **Goût** *(goo),* from the Latin *gustus,* means "taste" in French, and appears in the common phrase *chacun à son goût* ("each to his own taste").

Goya *(GOI-yah)* The celebrated Spanish painter whose full name was Francisco José de Goya y Lucientes (1746–1828). Goya

designed famous cartoons for tapestries, and became court painter in 1786, creating memorable portraits. He is best known for his later, savagely satirical works concerned with Spanish life and with

Goya, from a self-portrait. the horrors of war.

Graf *(grahf)* In Germany, Austria, or Sweden, a title of nobility corresponding to the English earl or French count. Some famous German *Grafen* were immortalized in the names of air and sea craft: the dirigible *Graf Zeppelin* was named for Ferdinand, Graf von Zeppelin (1838–1917); the battleship *Graf Spee* took its name from Maximilian Graf von Spee (1861 – 1914; see *Spee*).

Graz *(grahtz)* The second largest city in Austria and capital of Styria. Located on the Mur River, Graz has both important industries and many medieval buildings. The German astronomer Johannes Kepler (1571–1630) taught at the University of Graz during its early years of existence.

The Mur runs through the Austrian city of Graz.

grebe *(greeb)* A widely distributed group of aquatic birds related to the loon (q.v.). The grebe is a good swimmer and adept at surface dives (it is often called "hell-diver"), but is a poor walker; it secures its nest to floating vegetation.

Greco *(GREK-oh)* With El, meaning "the Greek," the name used by the great Greek artist Domenicos Theotocopoulos (1541–1614). Born in Crete, El Greco studied under Titian in Venice and settled in Toledo, Spain, where he painted an enormous number of masterpieces, including *View of Toledo.* His works can be seen in Toledo and at the Prado (q.v.) Museum in Madrid. Greco is also the surname of José Greco, a Spanish-American dancer and choreographer.

El Greco.

grego *(GREE-goe)* A short, warm, hooded jacket made of a rough material, once worn by seamen. The garment from which Herman Melville's novel *White-Jacket* takes its title was, wrote Melville, in lieu of "a grego, or sailor's surtout."

Grieg *(greeg)* Edvard Grieg (1843–1907), Norwegian composer who made extensive use of folk themes in his work. Grieg's most successful opus was the *Concerto in A-Minor for Piano,* but his *Peer*

Gynt suite is popular in music-appreciation classes. This suite supplies crossword constructors with the names of Peer himself, Ase, and Anitra—other characters who both have songs named for them.

Grimm *(grim)* Jakob Grimm (1785–1863), German philologist and folklorist, and his brother, Wilhelm Grimm (1786–1859). The two did much lasting scholarly work but are best remembered for collecting German folk tales and publishing them as *Grimm's Fairy Tales* (1812–1815).

The brothers Grimm.

grith *(grith)* From the Middle English, Anglo-Saxon, and Old Norman words for "home," grith means sanctuary, security, or defense. In Old English law, it was the security given or guaranteed by means of associations with places, institutions, or people.

groat *(grote)* Related to the German *groschen* (penny), at first a coin of little value circulating in the Low Countries; then an obsolete English coin worth fourpence; and finally any insignificant sum. When pluralized as groats, it's the same as grits, except that the grain is usually buckwheat or oats instead of corn. Buckwheat groats are best known as kasha.

Austrian 5-groschen piece.

grog *(grahg)* A drink of rum cut with water, served to British sailors. Grog came from the nickname of the officer who ordered the daily rum ration diluted—Admiral Edward Vernon, known as Old **Grog** because he wore a cloak made of the coarse fabric called grogram, an English version of grosgrain. Grog, by extension, now means any alcoholic drink.

Grosz *(grose)* George Grosz (1893–1959), German-born painter and caricaturist. His savage, nightmarish depictions of post–World War I Germany led to his arrest for blasphemy and corrupting public morals. Grosz became a U.S. citizen in 1938. His later works dealt with the horrors of World War II.

George Grosz.

grout *(growt)* From the same roots that generated grits and groats (see *groat*), a coarse meal, or, when pluralized, oats. **Grout** is also a Britishism for grounds, dregs, or sediment. Everywhere else, **grout** is a plaster used for setting tiles.

grub *(grub)* From the Anglo-Saxon verb meaning "to dig," a slang word for food (presumably, that which is dug for). **Grub** is also the fat, wormlike larva of various beetles and also a drudge. As a proper noun, the name of a former London thoroughfare, **Grub** Street was once described by Dr. Samuel Johnson as "much inhabited by writers of small histories, dictionaries, and temporary poems" and has come to be synonymous with any community of literary hacks (q.v.).

gruel *(GROO-uhl)* That staple of invalid diets, a thin porridge prepared by cooking meal in water or milk. As an obsolete verb in Britain, **gruel** means to exhaust by punishment, hence its survival in the phrase "grueling punishment."

grume *(groom)* From the Latin word *grumus,* meaning "heap," a grume is a clot, usually of blood. The word is rarely seen anywhere but in medical dictionaries and crossword puzzles.

Grus *(gruss)* A Southern Hemisphere constellation. The word, from Latin, means "crane," and to the ancients this configura-

tion of stars, including the first-magnitude Al Na'ir, probably suggested that long-legged bird. Adjacent to Grus is the first-magnitude star Fomalhaut, in the constellation of Picis Austrinus, the Southern Fish.

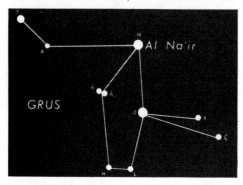

Grutli See *Rütli*.

guaco *(GWAH-koe)* Two plants, one each of the *Mikania* and *Aristolochia* genera of South America. These aromatic plants were once used extensively in folk medicine of the region as cures for gout (q.v.), worm infestation, syphilis, and snakebite. The bitter resin gaucin, obtained from guaco, was used to stimulate vomiting and sweating.

Guam *(gwahm)* The largest and southernmost of the Marianas Islands in the western Pacific. The capital is Agana. An unincorporated territory of the U.S.,

Guam, the Pearl of the Pacific, is the site of a large naval base at Apra Harbor. The island was discovered by Ferdinand Magellan in 1521 and belonged to Spain until the Spanish-American War in 1898.

guan *(gwahn)* The Carib Indian name for large roosting birds, the curassows, of the southern U.S., and Central and South America, belonging to the order of pigeon-toed fowls. Curassows also include the rufous-bellied chachalaca. Their meat is considered a delicacy, and certain species, attracted by fire, are lured and captured by igniting branches.

guar *(gwahr)* The originally Hindi word for a leguminous plant native to India and now grown in the United States as forage for cattle. Guar seeds yield a gum used as a food additive.

guava *(GWAH-vah)* A small evergreen tree of the myrtle family. The small, sweet fruits have red, pink, or white flesh, depending on variety, and a sweet flavor that can resemble strawberries, pineapples, or other fruits. Native to South and Central America, guavas are now grown commercially in Florida and Texas and used in jellies, sweet preserves, and beverages. The fruit is rich in vitamins A and C.

Government House in Agana on Guam. About a quarter of Guam's population consists of U.S. military personnel.

Gula *(GOO-lah)* The Assyro-Babylonian goddess of healing who thus had the power of life or death over her supplicants. Gula was the consort of Ninurta, a sun god whose specific job description included presiding over wars, farming, and the chase. In anatomy, the **gula** (from the Latin word meaning "throat") is the part of the throat next to the chin; a plate that forms the lower surface of insects' heads; or a molding or moldings, in architecture, with a large hollow.

gules *(goolz)* One of those heraldic terms that make life a little easier for crossword puzzle constructors. This word simply means the color red. Before the advent of color printing, reproducing a shield with gules was tricky, until it was decided to represent red by parallel vertical lines.

gumbo *(GUM-boe)* The name by which okra is sometimes known in Creole cuisine. Also, the name for Creole dishes such as seafood or chicken gumbo, thickened with pods of okra or by powdered dried sassafras leaves (file). Because it becomes soggy when wet, a rich, black, silty soil of the western U.S. is called **gumbo.**

Guyon *(GIE-ahn)* In Spenser's *Faërie Queene*, a knight who is a paragon of self-control and who resists all base impulses. All of which indicates why, in the story, he felt impelled to destroy the witch Acrasia and her home, the Bower of Bliss, a hotbed of lust in which men became like animals.

Gwyn or **Gwynn** *(gwinn)* Eleanor (Nell) Gwyn (1650–1687), the one-time orange-seller at London's Theatre Royal who became a comedy actress widely known for her beauty. Her qualifications also proved to be ideal for the job as mistress of Charles II. She bore him two

Nell Gwyn (perhaps).

sons, one of whom was later made a duke. The play *Sweet Nell of the Old Drury* was written about her by Paul Kester.

Gyes *(guys)* In Greek mythology, one of a race of good giants, distinguished from other giants by their friendliness toward the gods. What further made these giants unique was the 100 hands possessed by each of them. Despite such obvious assets, Gyes and his brothers, Briareus and Cottus, were killed by Hercules.

Thetis summons the giant Briareus to assist Jupiter.

Gyges *(GIE-jeez)* A Lydian king of the seventh century B.C. According to Plato, Gyges discovered a hollow bronze horse containing a corpse with a gold ring on one finger. The ring was supposed to make the wearer invisible.

Gynt See *Grieg.*

gyve *(jive)* From the Middle English word meaning "thong" or "band," an archaic term, both noun and verb, for fetter or shackle.

Prisoners find themselves in gyves in the 1932 movie I Am a Fugitive from a Chain Gang.

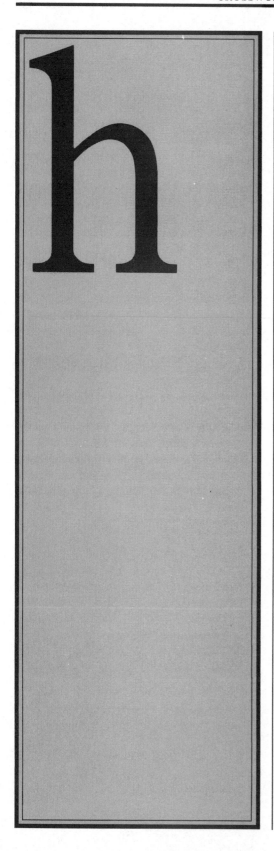

haaf *(hahf)* From the Old Norse word for "high seas" or "ocean," a term for the deep fishing waters in the North Sea and Atlantic Ocean off the Shetland and Orkney archipelagos north of Scotland. The haaf was also used for maneuvers by British naval vessels based at nearby Scapa Flow.

Haber *(HAH-ber)* Fritz Haber (1868–1934), the German chemist who directed his country's chemical warfare activities in World War I. In 1918, he won the Nobel Prize in chemistry for discovering a process for synthesizing ammonia. When Hitler came to power, Haber went into exile in England.

habit *(HAB-it)* Either an act repeated so frequently that it becomes automatic; an addiction, such as a smoking habit; or a particular type of attire. The latter is usually designated by activity (e.g., a riding habit) or by wearer (e.g., a monk's habit).

A riding habit.

hack *(hak)* A word of many definitions, including: a cutting tool, or the gash it makes; a taxicab; a dry, harsh cough; a skin bruise in rugby football; or, from the word hackney, "a horse for hire," a writer of marginal talent who works like a horse.

hade *(hade)* A geological term referring to faults, veins, or lodes within the earth. A hade is the angle between a fault plane (or a vein of ore) and the vertical. In mining and prospecting, knowledge of the hade can be critical, since it can indicate the direction to dig to obtain the maximum yield.

Hades *(HAY-deez)* In Greek mythology, the underground world of the dead, presided over by Pluto (q.v.), sometimes called **Hades,** and Persephone. Hades was separated from the land of the living by the river Styx (q.v.) across which souls were ferried by Charon. Charon's pay was the coin left in the mouth of the dead upon burial.

hadji or **hajji** *(HAJ-ee)* A Muslim who has made his obligatory pilgrimage, or hadj (also spelled hajj), to Mecca. The word is also used as a title of respect. Thus, a character in a Karl May story is called Hadji Halef Omar ben (son of) Hadji Abbul Abbas ibn (grandson of) Hadji David al Gossarah.

Hafiz *(hah-FIZ)* Pen name of the renowned fourteenth-century Persian poet Shams ad-Din Muhammad. His sonnets, in the form called the *ghazel,* deal with love, life, and Allah. **Hafiz** is also a title accorded to Muslims who memorize the Koran (q.v.).

haft *(haft)* From the Old English word for "handle," that part of a sword or dagger which is held in the hand while wielding it, as opposed to the blade. The haft is also called the hilt, giving rise to the expression "to the hilt," meaning totally.

Hagar *(HAY-gar)* In the Bible, a servant of Abraham's wife Sarah, and his concubine, who bore him his first son, Ishmael. The mother and child were cast out into the desert by Sarah in a fit of jealousy. But an angel visited Hagar in the wilderness and led her to water (Gen. 16:1-3; Gen. 21:9-12). In the comics, "Hagar the Horrible" is a strip about a family of Vikings and their adventures, drawn by Dik Browne.

Hagen *(HAH-gen)* In the *Nibelungenlied,* and in Wagner's *Die Götterdämmerung,* the treacherous son of a mortal and a sea goblin who murders Siegfried and steals the Nibelung hoard of gold. Also, Johannes Georg **Hagen** (1847-1930), the American astronomer known for his research on variable stars; Walter Hagen (1892-1969), the great golfer; and Uta Hagen, the actress.

haggis *(HAG-iss)* From the Middle English word meaning "to chop," a Scottish meat pudding dish made from the lungs, heart, and liver of a sheep, cooked, chopped up with suet, oatmeal, seasonings, and sometimes onions, and boiled in the sheep's stomach, which serves as pudding bag. It is considered epicurean by Scotsmen, who take a dram (q.v.) of whiskey with the dish.

Hague *(haig)* English spelling of 's Gravenhage or Den Haag, seat of government of the Netherlands, one of the few major cities whose names take a definite article. The Hague dates back to the Middle Ages, and since the first Hague conference in 1899, has been a center for the advancement of international accord. All major organs of government have their headquarters here, although the nation's capital is Amsterdam.

An aerial view of The Hague.

ha-ha *(HAH-hah)* From the French interjection expressing surprise, a type of barrier, also known as a sunk fence. It consists of a ditch or moat with a fence running its length, thus dividing different areas without obscuring the view. Ha-has are used in zoos to keep animals within prescribed areas.

Haida *(HIE-dah)*

A tribe of North American Indians native to the Queen Charlotte Islands off the coast of British Columbia. The Haida are related to the Tlingit and Tsimshian tribes; their language is probably an Athabascan tongue, and their customs include the potlatch—a feast where gifts are heaped on guests as conspicuous displays of wealth. The guests are expected to reciprocate eventually with even larger gifts.  *Haida chieftain.*

Haifa *(HIE-fah)*

A bustling Mediterranean seaport at the foot of Mount Carmel in northwestern Israel. Haifa dates back to at least the third century A.D., but the place did not achieve importance until the Crusades. It was destroyed by Saladin in the twelfth century and languished for 600 years. Port development has augmented its growth during this century. Haifa is the world center of the Bahai (q.v.) faith.

The port city of Haifa was known as Caiffa in medieval times.

haik or haick *(hike)*

From the Arabic, a sheetlike piece of cloth, usually white, worn as an outer garment by Arabs. The haik differs from its cousin, the aba (q.v.), in that it is not usually made from goat or camel hair.

haiku *(HIE-koo)*

A short unrhymed Japanese poem of strict construction and restricted subject matter, dealing with nature and human nature. A haiku in Japanese consists of 17 *jion* or symbol-sounds; when the form is borrowed for English, 17 syllables are employed. A haiku has three lines, five, seven, and five syllables respectively.

Haiti *(HAY-tee)*

A French-speaking West Indian republic on the island of Hispaniola, which it shares with the Dominican Republic. Its capital is Port-au-Prince. Discovered by Columbus, Haiti was ceded to France by Spain in 1697 and, after a series of struggles, achieved independence in 1804. Since then, political instability and oppression have been the lot of 95 percent of its population, among whom voodoo rites are widely practiced. François "Papa Doc" Duvalier ruled as a dictator from his election as president in 1957 until his death in 1971. His son, Jean-Claude "Baby Doc," succeeded him as "President for Life."

hake *(hake)*

Any of several genera of food fishes belonging to the cod (q.v.) family, found in the oceans of the world. The name is loosely given to some fish (such as white hakes, growing up to four feet long) that are not true hakes. Silver hakes average three pounds in weight. Hakes are also called codlings.

hakim *(hā-KEEM)*

In Muslim countries, a magistrate, governor, or revered physician. In the play *Oklahoma!*, Ali **Hakim** *(HAK-um)* is the sweet-talking "peddler" who wins the hand of Ado Annie.

Halle *(HAH-leh)*

An East German city near Leipzig. Halle can trace its roots back to the ninth century, when it became the seat of the archbishops of Magdeburg. In 1694, the University of Halle was founded, and in 1695, philanthropist A.H. Francke selected Halle as the site of his famous school for paupers, the first of the institutes bearing his name. Composer George Frederick Handel was born in Halle.

halm or haulm *(hawm)*

To the British, the stalks and stems of certain cereal grains and other crops, left after the harvest, or an individual plant stem. To **haulm,** as a verb, is to prepare straw for use as thatching.

Hals *(hahls)*

Frans Hals (c. 1580–1666), the celebrated Dutch portrait and landscape painter. Of his 250 known works, about one-third are in American museums. Hals's most famous canvases include *Governors of St. Elizabeth Hospital,* at the Frans Hals Museum in Haarlem, the Netherlands; and *The Merry Drinker,* at Amsterdam's Rijksmuseum. As a given name, **Hals** include Messrs. March, Linden, and Prince. Preceded by Prince, it is Shakespeare's Hal, later Henry V of England.

Hals's Laughing Cavalier.

Hama or Hamah *(HAM-ah)*

A city in west-central Syria, located on the Orontes River. Hama, dating back to the Bronze Age, has a long and colorful history. It has been controlled by Hittites, Assyrians, Persians, Romans, Turks, Arabs, Crusaders, and Egyptian Mamelukes. Hama is thought to be the Hamath-Zobah taken by Solomon (2 Chron. 8:3).

Hamad *(hah-MAHD)* or El Hamad

The southwestern region of the Syrian Desert that makes up the eastern part of the country. Hamad lies on a high plateau, elsewhere bisected by the range of the Anti-Lebanon and Jabal ad Duruz mountains.

hamal or hammal *(hah-MAHL)*

From the Arabic word meaning the same thing, a porter in the eastern Mediterranean regions. At one time, in certain remote areas, commerce largely depended on hamal-power.

Haman *(HAY-man)*

In the Old Testament, chief minister of Ahasuerus, King of Persia. Haman decreed that all Jews should be massacred. But Esther interceded with the king, who not only reversed Haman's edict, but ordered the tyrant hanged (Esther 3–7). These events are commemorated by the Jewish holiday Purim (q.v.), during which *hamantaschen,* three-cornered cakes filled with poppyseeds or prunes, are eaten.

hame *(hame)*

Used in hooking up a draft horse to a wagon, hames are the curved, rigid wooden or metal projections to which the traces are fastened on either side of the animal's collar.

Hamm *(hahm)*

The name of two European cities: one in the Ruhr district of West Germany, an iron and steel center heavily damaged in World War II; and a village in the Grand Duchy of Luxembourg which is the site of a large U.S. military cemetery, where General George S. Patton is buried.

Han *(hahn)*

A Chinese dynasty dating from 202 B.C. to about A.D. 220. Under the Han emperors, culture and education flourished and Buddhism was introduced from India. Two Chinese rivers also bear the name: the 700-mile-long **Han** that joins the Yangtze at Wu-han (q.v.); and the southern Han, about 200 miles long, emptying into the South China Sea. Author **Han** Suyin wrote the famous novel *Love Is a Many-Splendored Thing.*

Hanko or Hango *(HAHNG-koe)*

A Baltic seaport and summer resort in Uusimaa province, southwest Finland. Hanko is also Finland's most important winter port, and was leased to the Soviet Union as a naval base after the Finnish-Russian War of 1939–1940. It was exchanged for a lease on Porkkala in 1944.

Orthodox church in Hanko.

Hansa or **Hanse** *(HAN-suh)* From the Old High German word *hansa*, meaning "group of men," any guild of German medieval merchants, or the tax it exacted from nonmembers. **Hansa** also refers to the famous Hanseatic League, whose members included Lübeck, Bremen, and Hamburg.

Hari *(HAH-ree)* With Mata, the name used by the Dutch dancer and World War I German spy named Margaretha Geertruida Zelle. Mata Hari had danced in Paris and intimately knew many high Allied officers who confided military secrets to her. She was arrested and executed by the French in 1917.

harl *(harl)* or **herl** *(herl)* From the Middle English, either a wispy strand of hemp (q.v.) or flax or the barb on a feather used for fishing flies (second spelling). With the demise of home spinning, the word has fallen into disuse and is now simply a lexicographic curiosity.

harpy *(HAR-pee)* A foul creature of Greek mythology, usually represented as having the head and breasts of a hideous woman and the tail, legs, and claws of a bird of prey. Harpies were instruments of divine vengeance who stole food from tables and generally tormented the designated victims. Thus, ugly, grasping women are now referred to as harpies.

Harpies attacking the daughters of Pandarus.

hart *(hart)* A mature male deer with antlers fully grown. Also, the surname of three entertainment-world figures: Lorenz

Milton **Hart** (1895–1943), the lyricist associated with Richard Rodgers; Moss Hart (1904–1961), the playwright associated with George S. Kaufman; and William S. Hart (1870–1946), the cowboy film actor associated with his horse, Paint. It is the first name of **Hart** Crane (1899–1932), the influential poet.

Harte *(hart)* Francis Brett Harte (1836–1902), the American author of short stories and humorous verse. Among his best-known works are *The Luck of Roaring Camp* and *The Outcasts of Poker Flat*. Between 1878 and 1885, Harte served as a United States consul in Germany and Scotland.

Bret Harte.

Harum *(HAH-rum)* Surname of David Harum, the shrewd country philosopher, banker, horse-trader, and hero of E.N. Westcott's 1898 novel. In the Bible, **Harum** (pronounced *HAY-rum*) was a descendant of Judah (1 Chron. 4:8). Make the *h* lower case, add a hyphen plus the word scarum, and you get an adjective meaning "reckless."

Kent Taylor, Will Rogers, and Evelyn Venable in the 1934 film, David Harum.

Harz *(harts)* A mountain range on the border between East and West Germany, lying between the Elbe and Leine rivers. The region is rich in mineral deposits, and after World War II ended, it was the scene of extensive prospecting for uranium ore.

hasp *(hasp)* A piece of hardware used to lock a door or gate. The base of the hasp, which is hinged, is fastened to the door frame. Its free end is slotted to fit over a staple or loop on a plate affixed to the door. A padlock through the hook secures the door.

Havre *(HAH-vur)* or **Le Havre** *(luh HAH-vruh)* A French seaport in Normandy, located at the mouth of the Seine on the English Channel. It was founded in 1517 by Francis I as Le-Havre-de-Grace. During World War I, the city was heavily bombed by the French to prevent the Germans from using it as a base for the invasion of England.

haw *(haw)* Fruit of the hawthorn, a plant of the rose family. Haws resemble tiny apples, varying in color with the species. Also, as opposed to gee (q.v.), a command to a horse or other draft animal to turn left. During World War II, the American-born British traitor William Joyce broadcast Nazi propaganda as Lord **Haw**-Haw. To bray, a donkey prefaces **haw** with "hee." Speaking hesitantly, a person may hem and **haw.**

hawse *(hawz)* A term familiar to sailors. Either the section of a ship's bow perforated by openings (hawsholes) through which anchor cables are run; the space between the bow and the paid-out anchor; or the arrangement of cables when the ship is moored by anchors on both the port and starboard sides.

Hearn *(hern)* Lafcadio Hearn (1850–1904), the partially blind American author of Greek-Irish descent who is famous for his macabre tales and unfettered imagination. In 1890 he was sent to Japan to write a series of articles. He married a Japanese woman, became a Japanese citizen, changing his name to Yakumo Koizumi, and taught in Japanese universities while writing some of his most memorable works.

heath *(heeth)* In the British Isles, open land or moorland with little vegetation except heather and other plants of the heath family. In botany, the heaths include, besides plants of the *Erica* genus, rhododendrons, azaleas, mountain laurels, as well as blueberries and cranberries. In literature, Egdon **Heath** figures in Thomas Hardy's *Return of the Native.* Edward Heath was prime minister of England, 1970–1974.

Common heath.

Hebe *(HEE-bee)* In Greek mythology, Hebe was the goddess of youth, with the power to make the aged young again. She was also cupbearer to the gods until the job went to Ganymede, a handsome Trojan youth who rode to Olympus on an eagle.

Heep *(heep)* Uriah Heep, an odious character who served as Mr. Wickfield's clerk in Charles Dickens's *David Copperfield.* Given to protestations of humility, which he couched as being " 'umble," he was really a venal hypocrite and toady whose double-dealing was finally exposed by the immortal ne'er-do-well Micawber.

Hegel *(HAY-gul)* Georg Wilhelm Friedrich Hegel (1770–1831), the influential German philosopher whose system of metaphysics maintained that every thesis evokes its opposite, or antithesis, leading to a unified whole or synthesis. His theories formed the basis of the unification of Germany.

Hegira or **Hejira** *(heh-JIE-rah)* In September of A.D. 622, Mohammed's flight from Mecca (q.v.) to Medina to escape the wrath of Meccans unhappy with his preaching of monotheism. The Muslim calendar begins with the first day of the lunar year in which this occurred, and the abbreviation A.H. is used to denote years after the Hegira, just as A.D. designates a year subsequent to the birth of Christ.

Heidi *(HIE-dee)* The children's story about life in the Alps, by Johanna Spyri. A scheduled TV showing of the film *Heidi* created a stir when it preempted the final minutes of a crucial New York–Oakland football game in 1968. Oakland scored twice to win what is known as the Heidi game.

Heine *(HIE-nah)* Heinrich Heine (1797–1856), a German lyric poet born of Jewish parents, but baptized a Christian in 1825. His poetry has been set to music by Schumann, Schubert, Mendelssohn, and Liszt, among others. More than 3,000 compositions have incorporated Heine's lyrics, including Franz Silcher's ever-popular "Die Lorelei."

Heinrich Heine.

Hejaz *(heh-JAZZ)* A region on the Red Sea and Gulf of Aqaba (q.v.), now part of Saudi Arabia, into which Muslims pour each year on pilgrimage (see *hadji*) to the holy cities of Mecca (q.v.) and Medina. The Hejaz has been ruled by Egyptians, Hashemites, and Turks since the thirteenth-century fall of the Caliphate of Baghdad. The World War I campaigns of T.E. Lawrence (Lawrence of Arabia) ended Turkish authority. Ibn Saud, founder of Saudi Arabia, annexed the Hejaz in 1932.

Hel *(hell)* or **Hela** *(HELL-ah)* In Norse mythology, the goddess of the dead, a hideous crone who ruled in Niflheim (or Hel), the land of eternal snow and darkness. She received all souls except those of heroes, who went directly to Valhalla. In Christian times, Hel became Hell, a place of eternal damnation.

helix *(HEE-liks)* From the Greek word for "spiral," any spiral shape such as a spring, a coil, or the thread of a screw. The spiral staircase is a perfect example of a helical construction, as is the structure of DNA, the substance that carries genetic information to succeeding generations. **Helix** is also the generic name of a group of land snails that includes the *escargots* of French cuisine.

helm *(helm)* The device, such as a wheel or tiller, by which a ship is steered by controlling the rudder. By extension, the position of control or leadership of any organization. As a proper noun, **Helm** is the surname of Matt Helm, the private eye played by actor Dean Martin in a series of films in the 1970s.

Manning the helm.

Helot *(HELL-uht)* Originally a native of Helos, a town in ancient Laconia whose people were enslaved by the Spartans; subsequently, a member of the lowest class, actually serfs, in the ancient Spartan pecking order. Today a **helot** is anyone who might be considered a slave or serf because of his status or working conditions.

helve *(helv)* From the Old English word *hielfe,* the handle of a tool, especially an ax or hatchet. It is also the business end of a helve hammer—a driving device in which a heavy weight is lifted by a lever and allowed to drop of its own weight.

hemin *(HEE-min)* A chloride of heme, the nonprotein part of the hemoglobin molecule. Hemin is formed when hemoglobin is treated with an acid and salt, appearing as reddish-brown crystals called Teichmann's crystals. The reaction is used to test for blood in fluids or stains. The formula for hemin is $C_{34}H_{32}H_4O_4FeCl$.

hemp *(hemp)* Common name for a tall annual herb *(Cannabis sativa)* of the nettle family. Native to Asia and widely grown elsewhere, hemp yields a tough bast (q.v.) fiber used in making rope, paper, and cloth. Various preparations of hemp also yield the drugs marijuana, hashish, bhang (q.v.), and ganja (q.v.). Hemp refers as well to other fibers, such as sisal.

hent *(hent)* An obsolete word from the Middle English *henten* (hand), it originally meant something that could be grasped in the hand. The word evolved to mean ''hunt'' or ''comprehend.''

Hera *(HEER-ah)* In classical mythology, the queen of the gods. Hera (called Juno by the Romans) was the daughter of Cronus and Rhea, mother of Ares (q.v.) and Hephaestus, and both sister and wife of Zeus (q.v.). She protected all women and was associated with the symbol of marriage and fecundity, the pomegranate.

Hera was famous for her jealousy.

herm *(herm)* or **herma** *(HER-mah)* In sixth-century Greek art, a pillar capped with a masculine bust, at first of Hermes, messenger of the gods, often with a phallus below. Later herms had portrait busts. Herms were placed at street corners in Athens, and also served as milestones outside the city.

Herod *(HEH-rud)* A dynasty ruling Palestine at the time of Christ. Its members included Herod the Great, a bloodthirsty tyrant who ordered the massacre of all baby boys in Bethlehem at the time of Christ's birth (Matt. 2:16); and his son Herod Antipas, who gave his stepdaughter, Salome, the head of John the Baptist (Mark 6: 20–28).

heron *(HEH-ruhn)* A large wading bird belonging to a family that includes the bitterns and egrets (q.v.). Some heron species lead solitary lives; others become gregarious during the mating season; and most roost in large colonies called heronries.

A purple heron.

herse *(herse)* Either a framework on which to spread and dry animal skins; or a portcullis, like the medieval castle appurtenance constructed as a grating of heavy, spiked, iron bars that could be lowered to close off a gateway or hinder an enemy's advance.

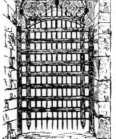

Hertz *(herts)* Heinrich Rudolph Hertz (1857–1894), German physicist who first produced radio waves. A unit of frequency called the **hertz** (equal to 1 cycle per second) is named for him.

Herzl *(HERT-suhl)* Theodor Herzl (1860–1904), the Hungarian-Jewish newspaper reporter who founded modern Zionism. The idea of a Jewish state occurred to Herzl while he was in Paris covering the infamous Dreyfus Affair, with its overtones of rampant anti-Semitism. In 1949, after his death, Herzl's body was buried in Jerusalem with great honors. A city in Israel, Herzliya, is named after him.

Hess *(hess)* Several well-known European figures, including Dame Myra Hess (1890–1965), the English piano virtuosa; Victor Francis Hess (1883–1964), the American physicist of Austrian origins, who discovered cosmic rays and shared the 1936 Nobel Prize for physics; Walter Rudolf

Hess (1881–1973), the Swiss physiologist whose work on brain function garnered a shared Nobel Prize for physiology and medicine in 1949; and Rudolf Hess (1894–), Hitler's henchman who fled to Scotland during World War II and was sentenced to life imprisonment in 1946 at the Nuremberg war-crimes trial.

Dame Myra Hess.

Hesse *(hess)* Formerly, a kingdom and duchy, and now a state in West Germany. The capital is Wiesbaden. Hesse was the home of mercenaries, called Hessians, who fought for England during the American Revolution. Also, the surname of Hermann **Hesse** (1877–1962), the German novelist and poet, known for his pacifism, whose best-known work is perhaps *Steppenwolf* (1927). In 1946, he was awarded the Nobel Prize for literature.

het or **chet** See *kheth.*

hex *(heks)* A witch's spell, or a person who practices witchcraft. These practitioners are thought capable of controlling the powers of nature, curing sickness, and confounding one's enemies through magic. The colorful hex signs seen on Pennsylvania Dutch barns are reputed to protect animals from the evil eye, one kind of hex.

Hilo *(HEE-lo)* A major city on Hilo Bay of Hawaii Island, the second largest island in the state of Hawaii. This important tourist area's main attractions include the volcanoes Mauna Kea and Mauna Loa, which serve as a backdrop to the city.

Rainbow Falls, near Hilo.

hilum *(HIE-lum)* From the Latin meaning "little thing," the anatomical term for the part of an organ through which blood vessels, nerves, or ducts pass. In botany, hila (plural) are the marks left on seeds showing the place of attachment to the seed vessel.

hind *(hinde)* A skilled farm laborer, in northern England and Scotland. Also, the female red deer, as opposed to the hart (q.v.). A **hind** is mentioned in Dryden's allegorical poem "The Hind and the Panther," in which the hind represents Roman Catholicism, and the panther, the Anglican Church. **Hind** as an adjective means "situated at the rear," as in hind legs.

Hindi *(HIN-dee)* A language of the Indic group of the Indo-European family of languages. Spoken by the Hindus, it is written in the Devanagari alphabet used for Sanskrit, and breaks down into two dialectical groups called Western and Eastern Hindi. Understood by more than 133 million Indians, Hindi is India's official language.

Hindu *(HIN-doo)* An adherent of Hinduism, the religious beliefs held by most of the people of India. Hinduism is closely interwoven with many cultural and social practices. Hindus worship no central founding figure, but relate to caste (q.v.) and conduct. Embodied in this system is karma, or destiny; nirvana, or ultimate salvation; dharma, or duty; and respect for a religious teacher, or guru. See *artha.*

hinny *(HIN-ee)* A hybrid that differs from a mule in the sexes of its parents. Whereas a mule is the offspring of a male donkey and a female horse, a hinny is born from the union of a female donkey and a stallion.

hoar *(hore)* From an Old English word meaning "old," or "gray," often referring to frost, or to hair in old age. Also, the surname of Ebenezer Rockwood **Hoar** (1816–1895), who served as attorney gen-

Ebenezer Rockwood Hoar.

eral under President U.S. Grant; and George Frisbie Hoar (1826–1904), member of the U.S. congressional electoral commission that decided in 1876 for Rutherford B. Hayes.

hoax *(hokes)* A deceitful trick, often meant as a practical joke. The word is probably derived from a contraction of hocus-pocus, the mock-Latin formula used by magicians or charlatans when bamboozling an audience.

hod *(hahd)* A coal scuttle, or a device used by construction laborers to transport bricks or mortar. A hod usually consists of a V-shaped trough with one end closed, mounted on a pole so that it can be carried on one shoulder.

Hodur *(HOE-der)* In Norse mythology, the blind deity of darkness and night, who unwittingly killed his brother Balder (q.v.), god of light, with an arrow of mistletoe given to him by the mischievous Loki (q.v.). When the gods discovered the cruel trick, they restored Balder to life.

Hoffa See *Beck.*

hogan *(HOE-gan)* Directly from the Navaho word meaning "house," a Navaho

A hogan, typical Navaho dwelling.

dwelling with earth walls supported by timber beams. As a proper noun, the surname of Ben **Hogan** (1912–   ), legendary American golfer who in 1953 won the three major golf titles—the U.S. Open, the Masters, and the British Open.

Hogg *(hog)* James Hogg (1770–1835), Scottish poet known as the Ettrick Shepherd, whose career was helped by Sir Walter Scott; James Stephen Hogg (1851–1906), a governor of Texas; and Thomas Jefferson Hogg (1792–1862), friend of Percy Bysshe Shelley, whose life he grossly misrepresented in a biography that precipitated a literary scandal.

hokum *(HOE-kum)* Derived from the same root as hoax (q.v.), a slang word used to describe crude comedy, such as that featured in burlesque, or overly sentimental melodrama designed to elicit an on-the-spot, profuse emotional response. By extension, hokum has come to mean nonsense, trash, or showy rodomontade.

holm *(holme)* From an Anglo-Saxon term closely related to Scandinavian counterparts, a small island in a lake or river, or just off the mainland. Holm frequently appears in names, like Stockholm, of places encompassing islands. As a proper noun, surname of Eleanor **Holm,** the Olympic swimmer who married showman Billy Rose; and of actress Celeste Holm.

Stockholm's Old Town is in the foreground; the modern section on the mainland in rear.

Holst *(holst)* Gustav Holst (1874–1934), English composer, best known for his innovative work *The Planets,* composed between 1914 and 1916. Also, the surname of Hermann Eduard von Holst (1841–1904), Russian-born American historian, who published the seven-volume *Constitutional and Political History of the United States* in the years 1876–1892.

holt *(holt)*   Related to the German word *holz,* for "wood," the archaic term for a wooded hill, or grove. Also, the surname of Henry **Holt** (1840–1926), American

author and publisher, founder of a still extant publishing house; Joseph Holt (1807–1894), controversial judge advocate general of the army during President Lincoln's administration; and Tim Holt, the actor.

Joseph Holt was a well-known 19th-century public figure.

Homs *(hawms)* or **Hims** *(hims)*   A region and city in west-central Syria, on the Orontes River. In the third century A.D., Homs, then called Emesa, was the home of a priest in the temple of Baal (q.v.) who became Emperor of Rome as Heliogabalus. Emesa was taken by the Arabs in the seventh century and renamed. Homs was part of the Ottoman Empire until after World War I, when it became a French mandate.

Honan *(HOE-nan)*   A province of northeastern China encompassing about 65,000 square miles. Periodic flooding of Honan was corrected by the San Men Dam on the Yellow River and by the People's Victory Canal. An important agricultural region, Honan has been a center of culture since at least 2000 B.C., and Stone Age artifacts have been discovered there.

hone *(hone)*   A fine-textured whetstone for sharpening cutting implements, such as razors. The usual procedure is to finish off by stropping the razor on leather to remove any metallic burrs on the edge. As a verb,

to **hone** is to sharpen. **Hone** is also the surname of Philip Hone (1780–1851), American businessman and politician whose diary provided valuable information on the development of the Whig Party.

Honing a blade.

hong *(hawng)* From the Chinese word *hong,* meaning "mercantile firm," a commercial establishment or warehouse in China. From this, it is easy to deduce how the city of **Hong** Kong was named.

Hooch *(hoke)*   Pieter de Hooch (1629–1677), Dutch painter of interior scenes. Pronounced *hooch,* it's a slang term

for liquor, especially if inferior and/or of the type bootlegged during Prohibition. It's thought to be a contraction of the Tlingit Indian word for an alcoholic drink, *hoochinoo.*

Pieter de Hooch.

hooka or **hookah** *(HOOK-ah)* Transliterated from the Arabic, a hooka is an Eastern smoking pipe fitted with a flexible tube that draws the smoke through water, or sometimes rose water, contained in a bowl or vase. The liquid effectively cools the smoke.

The hooka-smoking Caterpillar, in Alice's Adventures in Wonderland.

Hooke *(hook)*   The English physicist, mathematician, and inventor Robert Hooke (1635–1703). Among his most notable achievements was a postulation of the law of elasticity that still bears his name; a workable method of telegraphy; the spiral spring in watches; and the first calculator.

Hoople See *egad.*

Hopeh *(hoe-PAY)*

Temple of Heaven, Peking.

A province in northeastern China on the Po Hai, an arm of the Yellow Sea. The capital is Shih-Chia-Chuang. Hopeh (or Hopei) is known for its agricultural output and for its production of machinery and textiles, especially in the big cities, which include the autonomous municipalities of Tientsin and Peking, the capital of China.

Hopi *(HOE-pee)* A native American belonging to the Hopi group of the Pueblo Indians of the South-west. About 6,000 Hopis live in northeastern Arizona. The social unit is the clan, each with specific responsibilities to the community. The Badger clan, for example, conducts the kachina (or fertility) ceremony, while the Snake clan performs the famous snake dance at Walpi and other pueblos.

Hopi Indian kachina (spirit doll).

Horeb *(HOE-reb)* A biblical mountain mass with several peaks which is usually identified with Mount Sinai. It was to Horeb that Elijah fled (1 Kings 19:8), and also where the Jews fashioned and worshiped the golden calf while waiting for Moses to come down from the mountain (Psalm 106:19).

Horsa *(HOR-sah)* One of two semilegendary brothers (the other was Hengist) believed to have led the Jutes (q.v.) in their invasion of Britain in the fifth century A.D. The brothers are also credited with founding the kingdom of Kent.

horst *(horst)* In geology, a block of the earth's crust that rises between two faults. Also, the given name of **Horst** Wessel—a German hero of the Nazi Party, whose anthem was the *"Horst Wessel Lied"*—and more recently of actor Horst Buchholz.

Horus *(HOR-us)* In the ancient Egyptian pantheon, deity of the sky, light, and goodness. The son of Isis (q.v.) and Osiris, he avenged the killing of his father by besting Set, god of evil and darkness. Horus is represented as a sun god with a falcon's head.

houri *(HOO-ree)* From the Arabic meaning "black-eyed," a beautiful (and obviously dark-eyed) damsel of a troupe believed by some Muslims to dwell in Paradise. Houris are perpetually young and their virginity is renewable. According to the Koran (q.v.), every true believer (male) in Paradise will have houris to attend him. By extension, houri now means a seductively beautiful woman.

howdah *(HOW-dah)* From the Hindi word for "canopied seat," an ornate, covered chairlike device borne on the back of a camel or elephant. This permits the animal to be ridden with comparative comfort, usually by a rich man or noble.

A howdah is good for attention-getting entrances.

Howe *(how)* Surname of many illustrious figures, including Elias Howe (1819–1867), American inventor of the

sewing machine; Julia Ward Howe (1819–1867), American author active in the antislavery and women's suffrage movements, who wrote *The Battle Hymn of the Republic;* William Howe, the fifth Viscount Howe (1729–1814), English general in the American Revolution; and Gordie Howe (1928–   ), immortal hockey star of the Detroit Red Wings.

Elias Howe.

Julia Ward Howe.

William Howe.

Gordie Howe.

hoy *(hoi)*   A small coasting vessel, usually sloop-rigged, or a type of barge. As a proper noun, second largest of the Orkney Islands, lying along the Scapa Flow anchorage. A landmark for mariners is a high pinnacle known as the Old Man of **Hoy.**

Hoyle *(hoil)*   Fred Hoyle (1915–   ), British astronomer-cosmologist and author of *Galaxies, Nuclei, and Quasars.* Also Edmond Hoyle (1672–1769), the English gamesman who codified the rules of card games and other divertissements. He gave English the phrase "according to Hoyle," meaning straightforward and in line with the rules.

Hrolf See *Rollo.*

hue *(hew)*   Either a specific tint of a color; or, in "hue and cry," any loud uproar or clamor. With a capital *H* and an accent on the *e (hway),* it is a South Vietnamese city, the former capital of Annam, near the South China Sea, which is noted for its tombs of Annamese kings and as the scene of the heaviest fighting in the Têt offensive (January–February 1968) during the Vietnamese War.

huff *(huff)*   Probably onomatopoeic, based on the sound of blowing or puffing, and now also meaning a fit of anger, as in "He left in a huff." Also, the surname of Sam **Huff,** member of the football Hall of Fame and linebacker for the New York Giants in the 1950s and 1960s.

Hugin *(HOO-gin)*   In Norse mythology, one of two pet ravens who sit upon Odin's shoulders. Hugin was required to fly across the earth each dawn and give Odin a report of all he had seen or heard. Thus, Hugin can be considered to have set the pattern for early morning newscasting.

hulk *(hulk)*   From the Greek for "barge," a big, clumsy ship, especially one that no longer can sail. By extension, **hulk** also applies to a big, clumsy person. In the comic strips and on TV, The **Hulk** is an immense, green-skinned hero whose secret identity is Dr. Robert Bruce Banner.

hull *(hull)*   The body of a ship, or the outer covering of a seed. As a proper noun, the surname of Cordell **Hull** (1871–1955), President Franklin D. Roosevelt's first Secretary of State and winner of the 1945 Nobel Peace Prize; Bobby Hull, former left wing star of the Chicago Black Hawks hockey team; and actress Josephine Hull.

huma *(HYOO-mah)*   In East Indian legend, a bird that never alights. Any mortal touched by his shadow is destined to wear a crown. This belief is symbolized by the bird suspended over the throne of Tippoo Sahib at Srirangapatna, once capital of Mysore.

Hume *(hyoom)* David Hume (1711–1776), the Scottish philosopher-historian who was famous for his skepticism and nominalism; and Joseph Hume (1777–1855), English politician and reformer who fought against antilabor laws and for a free press. Also, the name of **Hume** Reservoir, largest water storage area in Australia, and of the actor Hume Cronyn.

Hun *(hun)* One of the savage Asiatic people who ravaged eastern and central Europe in the fourth and fifth centuries A.D. Their infamous leader was the feared Attila or Atli (q.v.). By extension, Huns became a name for any barbaric, destructive people, and the name was applied contemptuously to German soldiers during World War I.

A marauding Hun.

Hunan *(HOO-nahn)* In south-central China, a populous province whose capital is Ch'uang-sha. Hunan is justly known for its large annual rice crop, its mineral production, and, in recent years, its spicy cuisine, which has taken its place with the Cantonese, Shanghai, and Szechuan cuisines in the favor of American aficionados of Chinese food.

Huon *(HYEW-ohn)* A gulf indenting the southeastern coast of New Guinea; and a river in Tasmania. The **huon** pine, a large timber tree of Tasmania, is valued for its aromatic yellow wood, used for shipbuilding and carving.

Hupa or **Hoopa** *(HOO-pah)* A member of a tribe of North American Indians of the Trinity River valley of northwestern California; or the Athabascan language they speak.

The Hupa Indians are culturally associated with the Northwest Coast tribes.

Hur *(her)* The name of several biblical characters, including a supporter of Moses at Rephidim (Ex. 17:10,12; 24:14); a Midianite ruler slain by the Hebrews (Num. 31:8); and the father of Solomon's officer Ben-Hur ("son of Hur") (1 Kings 4:8). Another son of Hur is the hero of Lew Wallace's novel *Ben Hur,* the story of a young Jew converted to Christianity in ancient Rome. Actor Charlton Heston won an Academy Award for his portrayal of Ben Hur in the movie of the same name.

Hurst *(herst)* The American author Fannie Hurst (1889–1968), who was noted for such "women's" novels as *Back Street* and *Imitation of Life;* and John Fletcher Hurst (1834–1903), founder of American University in Washington, D.C. **Hurst** is also an industrial and residential suburb of Fort Worth, Texas, noted for the manufacture of helicopters.

Fannie Hurst giving a speech in the 1940s.

Hyads *(HIE-ads)* or **Hayades** *(HIE-ah-deez)* In Greek mythology, seven nymphs, all daughters of Atlas, who were placed among the stars by Zeus. This is the

V-shaped cluster of stars in the constellation of Taurus. In folklore, when the Hyads rise with the sun, it is a sure sign of rain.

Hydra *(HIE-drah)*　In classical mythology, a serpent with nine heads. If any were cut off, two new heads would be generated in its place. The monster was destroyed by Hercules, using a torch to burn the neck to prevent head regrowth. Also, a constellation of the southern skies, the Serpent; a Greek island in the Aegean; and, with a lower-case *h,* a small, tentacled, freshwater animal.

hyena *(hie-EE-nah)*　From the Greek for "sow," a doglike animal that is more closely related to cats. Nocturnal animals, hyenas hunt in packs, eat carrion, and will even rob graves. Hyenas are considered repulsive because of their stench and their cry, which sounds like maniacal laughter. Hence, to "laugh like a hyena."

hyla *(HIE-lah)*　From the Greek word for "wood," a tree frog. Found throughout the world, tree frogs are expert climbers with gripping discs so effective they can cling to a vertical pane of glass. Despite living in trees, hylas still spawn in the water and the young are tadpoles, just like their aquatic cousins.

Hylas *(HIE-las)*　In Greek myth, a handsome youth and boon companion of Hercules. With the Argonauts, Hylas went ashore on the coast of Mysia to draw water. He was spirited away by amorous water nymphs and never seen again.

Water nymphs drag Hylas into oblivion.

Hymen　*(HIE-men)*

The Greek deity of marriage, usually represented as a handsome youth carrying the nuptial torch. Because of his association with marriage, the name **hymen** was given to the membrane that partly covers the vaginal opening of a female virgin.

Hymen.

Hymir *(HIE-mur)*　According to Norse mythology, a white-bearded demon who personified the forbidding sea. The tale goes that he invited Thor (q.v.) onto his boat to cast for the Midgard serpent, and when the monster was hooked, Hymir cut the line. For this affront, he was flung by his ears into the briny.

hypha *(HIE-fah)*　From the Greek word for "web," one of the threads that make up the mycelium, the spore-producing part of a fungus that is instrumental in reproduction. **Hypha** is also the term for outgrowths on certain large seaweeds.

hypo *(HIE-poe)*　In photographer's slang, the compound sodium thiosulfate, used in solution to fix a photograph to the sensitized paper on which it is printed. The formula for sodium thiosulfate is $Na_2S_2O_35H_2O$. In hospital slang, a **hypo** is either a hypodermic syringe or a hypochondriac.

hyrax *(HIE-raks)*　The small, chunky, and short-legged mammal with molars like a rhinoceros and incisors like a rat, mentioned in the Bible as a coney (q.v.; see also *daman*). Also, a medium with high refractive index, used in mounting semiopaque structures for viewing through a microscope.

hyson *(HIE-sun)*　From the Chinese for flourishing spring, a variety of green tea in which the leaves are twisted and thinly rolled. Lighter leaves that are separated out in winnowing are known as hyson skin.

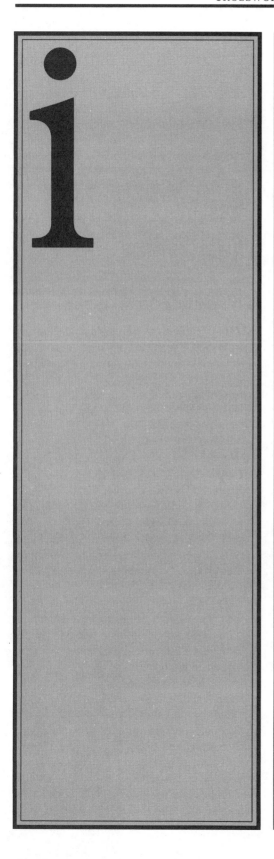

Iago *(ee-YAH-go)* In Shakespeare's tragedy *Othello,* the diabolical villain. Iago, out of envy and hatred of Othello, for whom he works, assembles circumstantial "proof" to convince the Moor that his wife Desde-

mona has been unfaithful. In a fit of jealous rage, Othello slays his innocent wife, making Iago's revenge complete. It's not complete for long, however; Iago's wife finally tells all, and Othello kills Iago, then himself.

Lawrence Tibbett as Iago.

iamb *(EYE-amb)* A poetic foot made up of a short syllable followed by a longer one, as in Hamlet's "... to sleep, perchance to dream," which comprises three iambs. In iambic verse, the meter is designated by number of feet in the line. Thus, iambic pentameter has five iambs, or ten syllables, in a line.

Iasi *(yahsh)* The Romanian name for Jassy, the thriving Moldavian industrial city near the U.S.S.R. border. Throughout its history, Iaşi has been burned and sacked repeatedly by Tartars, Turks, and Russians. During World War II, one of the worst pogroms in history was carried out by the Nazis against Iaşi's Jews.

The Palace of Culture in the Romanian city of Iaşi.

ibex *(EYE-beks)* A wild goat native to the mountainous regions of central Asia, southern Europe, and northeastern Africa. Ibex are known for their surefootedness, agility, and long horns, which in some species curve back and down, and in others, make a semicircle. The ibex is related to the tur.

ibis *(EYE-bis)* Common name for several wading birds related to the heron (q.v.), found in warm-climate regions of the world.

One of the best known is the sacred ibis of ancient Egypt. This black and white bird with the characteristic down-curved bill has, however, left the Nile for greener marshes in other parts of Africa.

A white ibis.

Ibiza *(ee-BEE-zah; eve-EE-thah)* One of the Balearic Islands of Spain, in the western Mediterranean. The capital city, also called Ibiza, is terraced and extremely picturesque, a tremendous draw for artists and tourists. The island has been occupied by Romans, Carthaginians, and Phoenicians, and traces of their cultures can still be seen.

The island of Ibiza.

Ibo *(EE-boe)* A major ethnic group in Nigeria, numbering more than seven million people. Ibo history has been shaped by missionaries, who converted them to Christianity, and the British, who educated many when Nigeria was a crown colony. During political strife in 1966, many Ibo fled eastward to the area where the short-lived Republic of Biafra was established in 1967.

Ica *(EE-kah)* A southwestern Peruvian city on the Pan-American Highway. Also, the name of the ancient Chincha empire of Peru, which fell to the Incas in the fifteenth century. Ica was settled by the Spanish in 1563, and today is a major summer resort. The city has twice been destroyed by earthquakes.

Icel *(EE-chel)* Former name of Mersin, a port city of southwestern Turkey, on the Mediterranean. A busy rail terminus, Içel now exports agricultural products and minerals. Archaeological digs in the 1930s revealed traces of early Neolithic culture dating back to 3600 B.C. **Icel** is also seen in crosswords as an abbreviation for Iceland.

Mersin—formerly Içel.

ichor *(EYE-kor)* A word transliterated from the Greek and used to denote the ethereal fluid coursing through the vascular system of the gods, to distinguish them from flesh-and-blood mortals. Today ichor is employed to designate a thin, watery fluid from a body sore or wound.

Ickes *(IK-ess)* Surname of Harold LeClaire Ickes (1874–1952), American lawyer-writer who served as U.S. Secretary of the Interior from 1933 to 1946 under Franklin D. Roosevelt and Harry S. Truman. A progressive known for his bluntness, Ickes's favorite descriptive term for himself was "curmudgeon."

icon *(EYE-kon)* From the Greek *eikon*, meaning "image," any figure, picture, or other representation of a person. In the Orthodox Eastern religions, icons portray Jesus, Mary, or the saints, and are executed in the slowly evolving styles of Byzantine and Russian art. They are venerated in many churches and used at home for devotions or decoration.

Mary, with the baby Jesus.

ictus *(IK-tus)*   From the Latin past participle of the verb to strike, a rhythmical emphasis or metrical accent in poetry. In medicine, a beat of the pulse; also a stroke (acute apoplectic attack).

Ida *(EYE-da)*   On the island of Crete, an 8,058-foot mountain, also known as Mount Psiloriti. **Ida** was also the name of the titular heroine in Tennyson's poem *The Princess* and in Gilbert and Sullivan's satire based on the poem, which they called *Princess Ida.*

ides *(ides)*   The designation of certain days of the ancient Roman calendar, specifically the 15th of March, May, July, and October, and the 13th day of all the other months. The ides always followed the nones (q.v.) by eight days. In Shakespeare's *Julius Caesar,* a soothsayer warns Caesar to "beware the ides of March."

Idfu see *Edfu.*

Ido *(EE-doe)*   Abbreviated name for Esperandido, the international artificial language that functions as a simplified form of Esperanto; **ido** is also the word for "offspring" in Esperanto. In crosswords, and as two words, **I do** *(eye-DOO)* is most often clued as "marriage vow."

Ifni *(EEF-nee)*   Coastal region of southwestern Morocco, formerly a Spanish colony. Originally Moroccan, Ifni was ceded to Spain in 1860 and the city of Sidi Ifni became the seat of government of Spanish Sahara. The scene of border clashes between Spanish and Moroccan troops in 1957, Ifni was returned to Morocco in 1969.

Igor *(EE-gore)*   Titular hero of Aleksandr Borodin's semihistorical opera *Prince Igor.* The work, unfinished at the composer's death, in 1887, was completed by Rimsky-Korsakov and Glazunov and first performed in St. Petersburg in 1890. Igor was also the name of Dr. Frankenstein's assistant in Mary Shelley's novel. A mad shepherd and hanging-survivor, he was custodian of the monster. Other Igors include baritone Gorin; choreographer Moiseyev; and composer Stravinsky.

ihram *(eye-RAHM)*   From the Arabic word for "prohibition," a simple one-piece garment made of white cotton and worn by Muslims during the pilgrimage to Mecca (q.v.). The wearing of an ihram—the word also means the consecrated state of the hadji (q.v.), or pilgrim—imposes strict rules of conduct.

Ikeda *(ee-KAY-dah)*   Hayato Ikeda (1899–1965), prime minister of Japan from 1960 to 1964, following the resignation of Nobusuke Kishi. **Ikeda** is also a Japanese suburban and industrial city in the prefecture of Osaka.

Hayato Ikeda.

ilex *(EYE-leks)*   Botanical name of the many trees and shrubs of the holly family.

The English holly is the one most often associated with Christmas, but others are similar. An evergreen oak (holm oak) of southern Europe, with hollylike leaves, is commonly called ilex.

Ili *(EE-lee)*   The 590-mile-long river that rises in Sinkiang and flows west through China, across the U.S.S.R. border, through the deserts of Kazakstan, and into Lake Balkhash. The entire Ili valley was occupied by Russia from 1871 to 1881, when the present border was worked out.

ilium *(ILL-ee-um)*   In anatomy, the uppermost, flared section of the pelvis. As a proper noun, **Ilium** (or Ilion) is the ancient name of Troy, a city made immortal by Homer's epic of the Trojan War, *The Iliad* (see *Troad*). The excavations of Heinrich Schliemann established a mound now called Hissarlik, in Asian Turkey near the mouth of the Dardanelles, as the site of Troy.

imago *(im-AH-go)* From the Latin for "image" or "likeness," the word adopted by the naturalist Linnaeus to designate the adult, sexually mature stage in the metamorphosis of an insect. In psychoanalysis, an imago is the romanticized conception of a beloved parent, carried into adulthood and retained in the unconscious mind.

imam *(im-AHM)* The Arabic word for "guide," which in English designates a Muslim who leads prayer in a mosque. Leaders of Muslim lands, wielding both spiritual and secular authority, such as the Ayatollah Khomeini in Iran, are also called Imam. According to popular belief, an imam will return at the end of the world to restore the true caliphate (the rule of Mohammed's successors). He will be called the Mahdi (q.v.).

Imroz *(eem-ROZE)* A Turkish island off the coast of the Gallipoli peninsula in the Aegean Sea. Imroz occupies a strategic location near the entrance to the Dardanelles. Most of the island's population are Greek peasants who call the island by its Greek name, Imbros.

Inca *(INK-ah)* A subject of the Inca empire, a federation of western South Amer-

ica, centering in present-day Peru. The word Inca can refer to the emperor; it derives from the Quechan word, *ynca*, meaning "prince." The empire was founded by Manco Capac around the thirteenth century, and it dominated the

Fragment of Inca textile showing Pachacamac, creator of the world.

Andean region from Quito, Ecuador, to the Rio Maule in Chile in pre-Columbian times. Atahualpa was reigning when the conquistador Francisco Pizarro landed in 1532 and began his swiftly completed conquest of the empire.

incus *(INK-us)* From the Latin word for "anvil," the middle bone in the chain of ossicles, or small bones, located in the middle ear. The other two are the malleus and the stapes. As might be expected, the incus is shaped like an anvil.

The incus is the anvil-shaped section in the middle.

indigo *(IN-dih-goe)* From the Spanish, via Latin for "Indian," a deep blue dye now synthesized chemically or made, as formerly in India, from certain plants. Indigo was also in use in Egypt around 1600 B.C. Mummies of the XVIII dynasty have been found swathed in indigo-dyed material. Indigo is also the name for a shade of blue.

Indra *(IN-dra)* A major god of the Hindu pantheon, warrior lord of lightning, thunder, and rainstorms, and slayer of drought. In later accounts, Indra was downgraded to a secondary deity. He is represented in art astride an elephant. He is sometimes shown as possessor of four arms.

Indra, with all his paraphernalia.

indri *(IN-dree)* A fruit-eating lemur, a monkeylike creature native to the forests of eastern Madagascar. Indris (also called silky lemurs) are nearly three feet in length, have mere stumps for tails, are covered with thick, silky fur with markings that serve as camouflage, and occasionally walk on their two hind legs.

Indus *(IN-dus)* A 1,800-mile-long river that rises in Tibet, flows west across northern India, meanders through the arid Punjab plains of Pakistan, and finally empties into the Arabian Sea near Karachi. The Indus was once considered the western border of India, and the use of its waters has long been an issue with Pakistan. **Indus**, is also a constellation near Sagittarius in the southern hemisphere.

Inge *(inj)* William Inge (1913–1973), the American dramatist whose plays dealt with the hopes and disappointments of unremarkable Americans. His best-known works were *Come Back, Little Sheba; Bus Stop;* and *Picnic,* for which he won the 1953 Pulitzer Prize. His death was recorded as a suicide. Another Inge is William Ralph Inge (1860–1954), noted Anglican prelate known as "the gloomy dean."

William Inge

ingle *(ING-uhl)* From the Gaelic *aingeal,* meaning "fire," a term for the cheery blaze that crackles away on a fireplace, sometimes also called an ingle. The inglenook is a chimney corner in England.

ingot *(ING-uht)* Originally a bar-shaped mold for casting metal into what was considered an easy shape to handle, ingot today refers to the bar of metal itself.

Don Rickles weighing an ingot in the 1970 movie Kelly's Heroes.

inion *(IN-ee-un)* From the Greek, meaning "back of the head," the protuberance of the occipital bone at the rear of the human skull. This is one of the measuring points used in the science of craniometry and in the pseudoscience of phrenology.

inkle *(INK-uhl)* This word of unknown origin, familiar only to weavers, seamstresses, and lexicographers, has come to mean either a braided and colored linen trimming woven on a narrow (inkle) loom, or the thread from which this item is made.

Ino *(EYE-no)* In Greek mythology, the daughter of Cadmus, wife of Athamas, mother of Learchus and Melicertes, and stepmother of Phrixus and Helle. When Ino sought to kill her two stepchildren, their real mother, Nephele, saved them with the help of a winged ram who flew away with them. Helle fell off into a body of water named the Hellespont after her; Phrixus made it to Colchis, where he was taken in by Aeetes, who placed the fleece of the ram in a cave guarded by a dragon. The quest of Jason (q.v.) and the Argonants was for this same fleece. When Athamas later went berserk and slew Learchus, Ino and her remaining son leaped to their deaths in the sea and were changed to deities of the deep.

Inoki *(in-OAK-ee)* Surname of Antonio Inoki, a Japanese wrestler whose name is destined to appear only in crossword puzzles and footnotes to sports history. Inoki "fought" Mohammed Ali to a draw in Tokyo on June 26, 1976. The stunt netted Ali six million dollars.

Inonu *(ee-naw-NOO)* Ismet Inönü (1884–1973), Turkish military man and statesman. Inönü fought in the Balkan Wars and in World War I, as chief of staff to Mustafa Kemal (q.v.), later known as Kemal

Ismet Inonu.

Ataturk, who was instrumental in the establishment of the Turkish republic. Inönü was president of Turkey from 1938 through 1950, and served as premier from 1961 until his government fell in 1965.

intima *(IN-tim-ah)* In anatomy, the innermost of the three linings in the wall of an artery, vein, or lymphatic, from the Latin word *intimus,* meaning "innermost." In entomology, the lining membrane of an insect's trachea.

invar *(in-VAHR)* An alloy of steel with a low coefficient of expansion that makes it ideal for use in precision instruments. Invar steel is actually 36 percent nickel. The name was a trademark taken from the first two syllables of the word "invariable," in recognition of its dimensional stability.

Io *(EE-oh)* According to Greek mythology, the beautiful daughter of Inachus, and beloved of Zeus. To foil his jealous wife Hera (q.v.), Zeus turned Io into a white heifer. But Hera had her watched by the hundred-eyed Argus (q.v.), whom Zeus sent Hermes to slay. Hera then sent a gadfly to torment Io, who swam across a sea to escape it, and that body of water still bears her name—the Ionian Sea. **Io** is also the innermost moon of Jupiter, and a large American moth.

Io (left) and Argus. Io is associated with the Egyptian goddess Isis.

ion *(EYE-on)* An atomic particle that has become electrically charged through the loss or gain of one or more electrons. If it loses electrons, its charge is positive and it is called a cation. A gain of electrons charges an ion negatively, in which case it is known as an anion.

Iona *(eye-OWN-ah)* From the Irish word for "island," one of the Inner Hebrides islands off the northwest coast of Scotland. Known as an early center of Celtic Christianity, it was the home of St. Columba in

the fifth century. Later it was a bishopric. A cathedral, the remains of an ancient monastery, and the graves of a number of kings are here.

An ancient Celtic cross.

Ionia *(eye-OWN-ee-ah)* An ancient region of Asia Minor, corresponding to the west coast of Turkey and the neighboring Aegean Islands of Greece. To escape the rampaging Dorians, Greek colonists established themselves in Ionia before 1000 B.C. Among Ionia's ancient cities were Miletus, Samos, Ephesus, and Phocala. The fortunes of the Ionian cities waxed and waned through the Persian Wars, conquest by Alexander the Great, and other vicissitudes until the widespread destruction by Turkish conquest occurred in the fifteenth century.

iota *(eye-OH-tah)* Ninth letter of the Greek alphabet, corresponding to the English letter *I* and written the same way. Because of the small space the letter occupies when printed, **iota** has also come to mean a tiny quantity; similarly, "jot," its Anglicized variant.

I.O.U. *(eye-owe-YOU)* From the sound of the words "I owe you," a promissory note, usually bearing these letters, and given by a debtor to a creditor to acknowledge a specified debt. It is frequently clued in crosswords as "debtor's chit" (q.v.).

ipecac *(IP-eh-kak)* Drug yielded by the roots of a creeping South American shrub with small, drooping flowers. The active component of ipecac is emetine, a poison which, depending on quantity administered, is an expectorant (to relieve a dry cough) or an emetic, an agent that induces vomiting to rid the system of another poison. Emetine has other medicinal uses as well.

Ipin *(EE-pin)* A Chinese city in the province of Szechuan. Located where the Min River meets the Yangtze, Ipin is the last port for shipping bound upriver, and is known as the gateway to Yunnan province.

Ipsus *(IP-sus)* A small city of antiquity, located in Phrygia, in modern Asia Minor. Antigonus, a general of Alexander the Great and governor of Phrygia, was defeated and killed here during the battle of Ipsus in 301 B.C. This helped bring down the curtain on the Alexandrian empire.

irade *(ir-AH-dee)* From the Turkish word for "will" or "wish," a decree issued by a Mohammedan ruler. The word irade has since come to mean any written order from an authority figure.

Irazu *(EE-rah-zoo)* A volcanic mountain in central Costa Rica. More than 11,000 feet in height, Irazú still emits a plume of vapor. It erupted as recently as 1963, blanketing the city of San José with ash. Visitors to its summit can see the Caribbean Sea, the Pacific Ocean, and Lake Nicaragua.

One of the craters of Irazú, an active volcano.

iris *(EYE-ris)* In ophthalmology, the round, colored portion of the eye that surrounds the pupil and adjusts the pupil's size by muscle contractions; this regulates the amount of light entering the eye. In botany, any of a genus of perennial rhizomatous herbs with brightly colored, scented blossoms, related to the wild flags. In Greek mythology, **Iris** is the rainbow goddess.

Irtysh *(ihr-TISH)* A Siberian river, approximately 2,600 miles long, rising in Sinkiang province, China, and flowing into the Ob. The Irtysh flows past such fabled cities as Semipalatinsk, Omsk, and Tobolsk. Originally peopled by Chinese Kalmuks and Mongols, the river's basin was finally annexed by the Russians in the early nineteenth century.

Irun *(ee-ROON)* In Guipúzcoa, northern Spain, a Basque town on the Bidassoa River near the French border, not too far from the Bay of Biscay, and known for its lead and iron mines.

Irus *(EER-us)* In Greek legend, an indigent Ithacan beggar who ran errands for Penelope's suitors while her husband Ulysses was away on his odyssey. For his troubles, Ulysses broke his jaw.

Reluctant Irus being forced to fight Ulysses.

Ise *(EE-suh)* A city in the prefecture of Mie, on Ise Bay, Honshu, Japan, a major center of the Shinto religion. Ise is the site of three famous sylvan shrines dating back to 4 B.C. The Naigu, or Inner Shrine, still holds the Sacred Mirror, one of three ancient imperial treasures.

Isere *(ee-ZARE)* The name of the Isère department in southeast France, of which Grenoble is the capital. Also, a 150-mile-long river, rising in the Graian Alps on the border of France and Italy, and flowing into the Rhone.

The Isère River flowing past Grenoble.

Ishii *(ish-EE)*　Kikujiro Ishii (1865–1945), the Japanese diplomat who in 1908 involved his country in a "gentleman's agreement" to keep Japanese immigrants out of the United States. He was Japan's foreign minister and ambassador to the United States during World War I.

Ishim *(ee-SHEEM)*　A Siberian river more than 1,000 miles long that rises in Kazakstan, flows past Atbasar and Petropavlovsk, and joins the Irtysh (q.v.) at Ust Ishim. Also, Ishim, a city on the river that was formerly called Korkinsk, known as an agricultural center and whistle stop on the Trans-Siberian Railway.

Ishtar *(ISH-tar)*　The ancient Babylonian and Assyrian fertility deity. She was, however, also the goddess of war and cruelty, and the most widely worshiped goddess in the pantheon. She is identified with a number of earth (or mother) goddesses. According to her legend, Ishtar descended into the underworld to rescue her lover, Tammuz.

Ishtar, goddess of fertility.

Isin *(ISS-in)*　The capital city of an ancient Babylonian kingdom captured by the Elamites and Amorites during the third dynasty of Ur. Archaeological excavations have uncovered the legal code of King Lipit-Ishtar, which predates the famous code of Hammurabi. Crossword clues often lower-case and split the word, e.g., "the fat ＿＿＿ the fire."

Isis *(EYE-sis)*　Originally, the ancient Egyptian nature goddess who, along with her husband Osiris and their son Horus (q.v.), was worshiped throughout the Mediterranean basin as late as the sixth century A.D. The symbol of Isis was a throne.

Islay *(EYE-lay)*　Most southerly of the Inner Hebrides islands off the west coast of Scotland, in Argyllshire. Known for its dairy products, livestock, peat bogs, and Scotch whiskey, Islay is also a popular tourist center. Memorials were constructed here to those who died in the sinking of the *Tuscania* and *Otranto* in 1918.

Isna or **Esna** *(ISS-nuh)*　A city on the Nile in central Egypt. The town contains a temple (dating from the Ptolemaic era and "improved" by the Romans) to the ram-headed god Khnum, and a Coptic Christian monastery from the fourth century A.D.

Issei See *Kibei.*

Issus *(EYE-sus)*　Ancient city of Asia Minor, near the head of the Gulf of Iskenderun in modern Turkey. Here Alexander vanquished the Persians under Darius III in 333 B.C., and the Byzantine Heraclius won the first of a series of battles against the Persians 900 years later.

Ister *(ISS-ter)*　Ancient name of the lower reaches of the legendary Danube River. Rising in the Black Forest of West Germany, the Danube flows through the fabled cities of Ulm, Regensburg, Linz, Vienna, and Budapest, and through Yugoslavia and Romania into its vast delta on the Black Sea. Among the rivers of Europe, only the Volga is longer than the 1,770-mile-long Danube, Donau, Duna, Dunarea, Dunai, or Dunav.

The River Danube winds its way through Austria.

istle or **ixtle** *(IST-luh)* From the Nahautl word *ichtili,* a fiber yielded by certain tropical American plants, including a species of bromeliad, and some plants of the *Agave* (q.v.) genus. The fibers are used in the manufacture of rope, nets, and cordage, as well as the Central American baskets so popular with tourists.

Baskets for sale in a market catering to tourists.

Ithunn or **Ithun** *(EE-thoon)* In Norse mythology, daughter of the dwarf Svald and wife of Bragi. Ithunn's job was guarding the golden apples eaten periodically by the gods to renew their youth. Kidnapped by a giant, she was rescued by Loki (q.v.), who changed himself into a falcon and her into a nut.

Ito *(EE-toe)* Hirobumi Ito (1841–1909), the Japanese statesman responsible for bringing Japan into the twentieth century after the Meiji Restoration. He served as a minister in many governmental departments, and consulted to, founded, and led various ruling councils. He then served as prime minister and Japanese resident general of Korea, which he had made virtually a protectorate of Japan. On that tour of duty, his assassination gave Japan the excuse it wanted to annex Korea.

THE EXOTIC EASTERNERS

Ainu	*Lao*
Ata	*Lolo*
Ati	*Malay*
Bajau	*Mogul*
Bod-Pa	*Moro*
Cham	*Naga*
Dard	*Pygmy*
Dayak	*Shan*
Fiji	*Sulu*
Kurd	*Tamil*
Lai	*Vigur*
Lanao	

Ives *(ives)*   Charles Ives (1874–1954), the onetime insurance broker who became one of America's foremost composers, although he was relatively unknown until he was about 65. Among his works are symphonies, chamber music, and sonatas. His *Third Symphony* was awarded the 1947 Pulitzer Prize. Also James Merritt Ives (1824–1895), partner of Nathaniel Currier in Currier and Ives, lithographers famous for their prints of American life; and Burl Ives (1909–), actor and folk singer, winner of an Academy Award in 1958.

Charles Edward Ives.

Iwo *(EE-woe)*   A city in southwestern Nigeria near the city of Ibadan, in a cacao-growing region. Also, the abbreviated name for **Iwo** Jima, famed Pacific island—one of the Volcano Islands—captured by American forces during World War II. The raising of Old Glory on Mount Suribachi during the heat of battle has been immortalized in a sculpture in Washington, D.C.

ixia *(IK-see-ah)*   Any member of a genus *(Ixia)* of South African flowering plants belonging to the iris family. Ixia blossoms have the appearance of small gladiolus, to which they are related.

Ixion *(IK-see-on)*   The ne'er-do-well king of the Lapithes who, according to Greek legend, thought he had made love to Hera (q.v.), only to discover he had seduced a cloud. The issue of this union were the Centaurs. For his presumption, Ixion was condemned by Zeus and chained to a wheel of fire in Tartarus for eternity.

Iyar or **Iyyar** *(EE-yar)*   The eighth month of the Hebrew calendar, falling between Nisan and Sivan, in the middle to late spring of the year. The Jewish holiday Laq b'Omer, which commemorates the heroism

of two Hebrew martyrs, is celebrated on the eighteenth day of Iyar.

Izmir *(iz-MEER)*   Formerly known as Smyrna, an Aegean coastal city on the Gulf of Izmir, the second largest seaport in Turkey after Istanbul. Izmir traces back to the Bronze Age, although it was almost leveled by earthquakes in 1928 and 1939. Among hometown boys who made good was the poet Homer.

Izmir, Turkey's second largest seaport.

Iznik *(iz-NIK)*   A 14-mile-long lake in northwestern Turkey, and a modern Turkish city built on the site of Bithynia (built fourth century B.C.), which was renamed Nicaea by the Romans. The city was captured by the Turks in 1078, and by the Crusaders in 1097. It finally became a Turkish city in 1330. Nicaea was the site of two great church councils, A.D. 325 and 787.

Sailing on Turkey's Lake Iznik.

Jabez *(JAY-bez)*   In the Bible, the man "more honorable than his brethren" (1 Chron. 4:9, 10). Jabez called upon the Lord to bless him and send him wealth, whereupon he became a very rich man and the patriarch of a family of Judah.

jabot *(zha-BOE)*   From the French for "bird's crop," the frilly decoration on the neck or front of a woman's blouse. Jabots, usually made of lace, once decorated men's shirt fronts, as seen in paintings of George Washington.

Marlene Dietrich wearing a jabot.

jade *(jade)*   From the Spanish meaning "stone of the loin" (because it was thought to cure pain of renal colic), a precious gemstone, usually green in color, composed of various metallic silicates. Jade is usually associated with carved Chinese art objects, but **jade** also refers to a worthless horse, a disreputable woman; to be jaded is to have become fatigued or world-weary.

Jael *(jale)*   In the Bible, the wife of Heber the Kenite. Jael provided refuge for the enemy Canaanite captain, Sisera, after his defeat at Megiddo by Deborah and Barak. Then, while he slept, she dispatched him by driving a stake through his head (Judges 4).

Jael's deed, from an engraving by Doré.

Jaen *(hah-ENN)* A provincial capital in the Andalusian region of southern Spain. Now known for its oil, wine, and the output of its rich lead mines, Jaén was once the center of a small Moorish kingdom conquered by Ferdinand III of Castile in 1246. The Moorish castle in Jaén still remains a tourist attraction.

The Andalusian town of Jaén.

Jaffa *(JAF-ah)* An Israeli city on the Mediterranean Sea. Known as Joppa in the Bible, this was originally a Phoenician seaport. It was also held by the Egyptians, Assyrians, and Philistines before becoming Hebrew territory about the sixth century B.C. More recently, Jaffa was mainly an Arab city, although it changed hands repeatedly in the Crusades. In 1950, it became part of Tel Aviv. Jaffa oranges are an export.

The old town of Jaffa on the Mediterranean.

Jain *(jine)* From the Sanskrit word for "saint," a follower of Jainism, the religious belief of some two million people throughout India. Originally rejecting certain Hindu beliefs, Jainism now recognizes certain gods of the Hindu pantheon. The Jains are known for their good works, including the upkeep of asylums for diseased and decrepit animals. They abjure any activity or occupation that endangers animal life.

jakes *(jakes)* An archaic British term for an outdoor toilet, or privy. Jakes is an Anglicized version of the French Jacques, which in English is John, which, lower-cased, is American slang for a toilet. The word has come full circle.

jalap *(JAL-ap)* A medicinal plant whose dried roots, and a drug derived from them, have been used extensively as a purgative. The name comes from Jalapa de Enríquez, the capital of Veracruz state, Mexico, where the plant was first discovered by the conquistadores under Cortes when Jalapa was conquered in 1519.

Janus *(JAN-us)* In Roman religion, the god of beginnings. He therefore presided over gates and other entrances, as well as temporal aspects of beginnings, such as the first month of the year—January was named for him, and his chief festival was held on the first day of that month. Janus is represented with two faces that enable him to look forward and backward at the same time. Janus is also a satellite of Saturn.

Jason *(JAY-son)* The subject of many Greek legends, Jason was the prince, reared by the centaur Chiron, who went in search of the Golden Fleece of Colchis in order to redeem his father's usurped kingdom. (See *Ino.*) Com-

manding the Argonauts aboard his ship, the Argo (q.v.), and with the aid of Medea (q.v.), he obtained the Golden Fleece despite such deterrents as fire-breathing bulls and dragons.

Jassy See *Iaşi.*

jaunt *(jawnt)* A short trip or outing, usually for pleasure. Today, a short trip in time can be thousands of miles long, so the definition has shifted slightly to mean any pleasure trip.

Java *(JAH-vah)* Large Indonesian island (about 50,000 square miles), separated from Borneo by the Java Sea. It is the cultural, economic, and political center of Indonesia; the nation's capital and largest city, Djakarta, is here. The island is one of the most densely populated regions of the world. Fossil remains of *Pithecanthropus erectus* (now *Homo erectus*), or Java man, among the earliest human fossils known, were found on the island in 1891. **Java** also designates a breed of black and white chicken, and is American slang for coffee.

A cup of java being dispensed.

Jedda or **Jidda** *(JED-ah)* A Saudi Arabian city on the Red Sea, and the port for Mecca, which lies about 45 miles inland. It was ruled by the Turks until 1916, when it became part of the Hejaz (q.v.). In 1925, Jedda was captured by Ibn Saud. The so-called tomb of Eve was located here until its demolition in 1927. Nearby are the seventh century ruins of the old city.

jeep *(jeep)* The tough little four-wheel-drive, four-cylinder military car of World War II, named after the comic-strip character Eugene the Jeep, a cute little animal with great power. The cartoon character

was conceived for his "Thimble Theatre" by E.C. Segar (1894–1938), who also created Alice the Goon (see *Goon*). The original vehicle was devised by the Willys Corporation, which has since gone out of business, but later versions by other makers have carried on.

Eugene the Jeep using his favorite exclamation.

Jehol *(jeh-HAHL)* A former province of northeast China and its former capital, which is now called Ch'eng-te. Known as the gateway to Mongolia, the region, now part of Hopeh (q.v.) province, has been overrun at various times by the Tatars (q.v.), Huns, and Khitan Mongols. In 1933, Jehol was captured by the Japanese during the Sino-Japanese War; it was not returned to China until the end of World War II. There are parks and palaces in the city dating from its centuries as China's summer capital (1644–1911).

Jehu *(JEE-hew)* The biblical king of Israel who exterminated the house of Ahab (q.v.) and the worshipers of Baal (q.v.) in Samaria (2 Kings 9, 10). Jehu was noted as a daring and aggressive character, and was probably the only reckless driver mentioned in the Bible: "The driving is like the driving of Jehu . . . for he driveth furiously" (2 Kings 9:20).

Jena *(YAY-nah)* A central German city located on the Saale River, in what is now East Germany, in Thuringia. In 1806, Napoleon scored one of his most impressive victories here, thoroughly routing the Prussians. Jena's famous university, founded in 1548, was staffed in the late eighteenth and early nineteenth centuries by such faculty members as the poet Schiller and the philosopher Hegel (q.v.). It has long been known for its manufacture of optical and precision instruments.

jerboa *(jer-BOE-ah)* This small Old World rodent of northern Africa and Asia is recognizable by short forelegs, long hind legs on which it walks or hops at a remarkably rapid rate, and a long tail used for support when sitting. The name of this kangaroo-like creature comes from the Arabic *yarbu*, the long hind leg muscle used in jumping. Jerboas are popular pets in Egypt. The Australian jerboa kangaroo is classified as a rat kangaroo.

Jerez *(heh-RETH)* Jerez de la Frontera, southern Spanish city in Andalusia, one of many place names including "de la Frontera," indicating the former line of demarcation from the Moorish lands in present Spain. Captured by Moors in A.D. 711, the city was retaken by Alfonso X of Castile in 1264. Jerez is famous for its horses of mixed Arab, Spanish, and English blood, but more famous for its definitive product, sherry, whose name derives from Jerez. The city also ships brandy.

Palacio del Marques de Bertemati, Jerez.

jerid or **jereed** *(jeh-REED)* This approximates the Arabic word for "shaft" or "spear," and a jerid is just such an implement. It resembles a javelin with a blunted end, and is used in Muslim lands to play war games. The mock battles in which these weapons are used are also called jerids.

jess or **jesse** *(jess)* A common word among falconers, this straplike affair fastens around the leg of a bird and provides a metallic ring on which to secure a leash.

jeu *(zhuh)* Like many other French words, this one has passed into English intact. It means a play or diversion, and appears in such expressions as *jeu de mots*, (pun) and *jeu d'esprit* (play of intellect—such as a clever witticism).

jib *(jib)* Either the extension, or boom, of a crane; or a triangular fore-and-aft sail set before the foremast of a vessel. The phrase "the cut of his jib," originally an appraisal of sailmaking, has come into more general use as, simply, the overall impression one creates. As a verb, to **jib** means to balk.

A sloop with its jib set.

jibe *(jibe)* Related to jib only in that it refers to sails, jibe is the term sailors use to designate a change in direction made, intentionally or otherwise, when the sails shift from one side of the vessel to the other while sailing downwind. In American slang, **jibe** also means to agree or harmonize with.

jihad or **jehad** *(jeh-HAD)* From the Arabic word for "contest," a Muslim holy war, fought against infidels or foes of Islam. Jihad has been expanded in its definition to denote any campaign or crusade waged in the spirit of a holy war.

jingo *(JING-oh)* From the meaningless epithet "by jingo," formerly used to underscore strong emotion. Its use in a popular British music-hall song in the 1870s, supporting British ships sent to Turkish waters to oppose a Russian advance, gave rise to the term jingoism: a bellicose patriotism, or national chauvinism.

Jinja *(JIN-jah)* A Ugandan city on the Victoria Nile near Victoria Nyanza. A center of industry, Jinja is connected by rail to the port city of Mombasa, on the Indian Ocean. It was founded in 1901 as a trading post and developed with the opening of the nearby Owen Falls hydroelectric project.

jinn See *genie*.

jinx See *jynx*.

jive *(jive)* A word of indeterminate origin which started out in the argot (q.v.) of jazz musicians. Jive was used to designate a kind of bantering conversation carried on while playing. Eventually, it came to mean either just jazz or, generically, any jargon. As a verb, **jive** also means to jitterbug; or, as slang, to tease.

Joad *(jode)* Family name of the Okies (q.v.) who trekked across the Southwest in John Steinbeck's memorable Pulitzer Prize-winning novel of dustbowls and Depression, *The Grapes of Wrath* (1939). In the film version, Henry Fonda, who played the part of Tom Joad, established himself as an actor of superstar quality.

Jane Darwell as Ma Joad with Henry Fonda in The Grapes of Wrath.

Jodl *(YO-dul)* Alfred Jodl (1892–1946), the German general who as chief of staff directed Hitler's armies during World War II. Jodl signed the military surrender that ended the war in Europe on May 7, 1945. He was tried as a war criminal and executed in October of the following year.

joist *(joist)* In building construction, one of the parallel timbers, such as two-by-fours, which support the floor, and to which floor boards or ceiling laths are fastened.

Jolo *(ho-LOE)* Important island and city in the Sulu (q.v.) archipelago of the Philippines, between the Celebes and Sulu seas. The capital of Sulu, Jolo is the region's chief port and city. Cattle, lumber, and fish are major products. Jolo was long ruled by Muslim sultans, who resisted Spanish domination until the nineteenth century, and piracy was a widespread occupation. The sultanate passed to United States rule in 1899 and was abolished when, in 1940, the Sulu became a part of the Philippine commonwealth.

Jomo See *Kenya*.

Jonah *(JOE-nah)* The Old Testament minor prophet who decided to defy God's command to go to Nineveh and shipped out to Tarshish instead. The ship was tossed in a great storm and he was thrown overboard by the superstitious sailors, only to be swallowed by a whale. After his deliverance, he took up his mission to reform Nineveh. Today, a Jonah is someone whose presence brings bad luck, or a jinx (see *jynx*).

A Scandinavian representation of Jonah and the whale.

Jor-El *(jow-RELL)*   On the planet Krypton, the husband of Lara and father of Superman. These characters first appeared in 1938 in the newspaper cartoon strip that has become a part of American folklore. In the highly successful film version of Superman, Jor-El was played by Marlon Brando.

jorum *(JOH-rum)*   A drinking vessel that holds a prodigious amount of liquid refreshment. The name probably derives from the biblical Joram who "brought with him vessels of silver . . . gold . . . and . . . brass" (2 Sam. 8:10). Today jorum is also used to mean a large quantity of anything.

joss *(jahss)*   A word that has entered English by way of pidgin English for the Portuguese *deus,* or "god." A joss is therefore a Chinese idol; the temples where such idols are worshiped are called joss houses; and joss sticks are the incense-coated reeds burned in these temples.

Josse *(jahss)*   The self-serving jeweler known as Monsieur Josse in Molière's comedy *L'Amour Médecin.* In the play, Josse suggests to a friend that jewelry would make a fine present for his sweetheart. Because of Josse's subjectivity, the advice is taken with the proverbial grain of salt.

Joule *(jool)*   James Prescott Joule (1818–1889), an English physicist who discovered the first law of thermodynamics. In lower case, a unit of energy named after Joule and equal to 10 million ergs (q.v.). This is the energy expended in one second, at a current of one ampere, at a potential of one volt.

Jove *(jove)*   From the Latin *Jovis,* another name for the god Jupiter (see *Zeus*), often invoked by Englishmen who convey astonishment with the expression "By Jove!" From Jove also comes

Jove listening to Thetis.

jovial; it is believed that people born under the influence of the planet Jupiter display this quality.

jowl *(jowl)*   From the Middle English, jowl usually refers to the lower section of the jaw, especially if fleshy and pendulous, but sometimes the cheek. The expression "cheek by jowl" thus means close together. This word has also been applied to the fatty underhang of the lower jaw of a fat pig, the dewlap of a cow, and the wattle of a turkey.

Juba *(JOO-ba)*   Either a 1,000-mile-long river flowing through Somalia to the Indian Ocean; a city and river port in Sudan on the White Nile; a kind of rhythmic dance accompanied by handclapping, in the American South; or father and son kings of Numidia around the time of Christ. Juba II married the daughter of Antony and Cleopatra.

Jubal *(JOO-bul)*   One of Cain's descendants, the son of Adah and Lamech. Jubal was one of the first biblical musicians, and his name is Hebrew for "blast of trumpets." He is credited with inventing such musical instruments as the harp and organ (Gen. 4:21).

Jubal playing a flute, an instrument he is thought to have invented.

DOWN THE HATCH

CUPS & VESSELS

banga	jorum
carafe	pyxis
crock	tass
cruet	tun
cruse	vial
cylix	zarf
ewer	

REFRESHMENTS

ade	kvass
assai	lager
assi	mead
bock	mocha
bohea	negus
clary	nog
cocoa	pisco
cola	soma
congoo	tansy
creme	teil
grog	
hooch	Evoe!
hyson	
ilex	
julep	
kavakava	

jube (*JOO-bee*) A chancel or rood (q.v.) screen, the partition between the nave (q.v.) and chancel of a church. **Jube** is the imperative form of the Latin *jubere*, meaning "to command," and is the first word of a prayer traditionally delivered from this gallery: *"Jube, Domini, benedicere"* (Deign, O Lord, to bless).

Judas (*JOO-das*) Judas Iscariot, the one of the Twelve Disciples who betrayed Christ with a kiss in exchange for 30 pieces of silver (Matt. 26:14,48). Overcome with remorse after the crucifixion, Judas hanged himself. There is a tree called the rebud, or Judas tree, so named because of the belief that it was from an Old World species of this tree that Judas hanged himself. Dante, in *The Inferno*, describes Judas's place of punishment as the mouth of Satan; and the name Judas has become an epithet for the vilest of traitors.

Christ receives the treacherous kiss of Judas.

Jude (*JOOd*) In the Bible, the other of Christ's disciples named Judas, but known by the English form of his name to distinguish him from the execrated Iscariot. Also called Libbaeus and Thaddeus, Jude was probably the brother of St. James the Less. He was martyred in Persia with St. Simon.

Jude is also the penultimate book of the New Testament; the hero of Thomas Hardy's *Jude the Obscure;* and the individual addressed in the Beatles' song "Hey, Jude."

judo *(JOO-doe)* A Japanese sport based on jujitsu, the weaponless system of self-defense consistent with religious proscription of knives and swords. Judo was developed as a sport by Jigoro Kano in 1882. Participants wear a garment called a gi, and indicate their degree of proficiency by belt colors ranging from beginner's white to expert's black. Karate, an offshoot of judo, employs blows, delivered especially with the side of the hand or with the foot.

Judo practice at the Kodokan Institute in Tokyo.

juju *(JOO-joo)* A West African word, possibly from the French *jou* (a plaything), any charm, fetish, or other device used by witch doctors and shamans to cast spells and confound their enemies. The word also refers to the magic itself, or to various taboos associated with its use.

juke *(juke)* Usually used with "box," the familiar coin-operated record player of restaurants and taverns. Juke comes from a Gullah word meaning "wicked" or "disorderly." As a pluralized proper noun, **Jukes** is the fictitious name given a family in the classic sociological work *The Jukes: A Study in Crime, Pauperism, Disease, and Heredity* (1875), by R.H. Dugdale.

julep *(JOO-lip)* From the Persian for "rose water," a cold beverage usually containing aromatic herbs or syrup, sweetening, and liquor. The best known of these concoctions is mint julep, made with bourbon, sugar, muddled mint leaves, and crushed ice, which is consumed like soda pop at runnings of the Kentucky Derby.

Jumna *(JUM-nah)* or **Yamuna** *(YAH-muh-na)* An 850-mile-long river of northern India. The Jumna rises in the Himalayas, flows generally southeast past Delhi, and joins the Ganges at Allahabad. The confluence is a sacred location to Hindus and a center for pilgrimages. On the Jumna's banks, in Agra (q.v.), can also be found the beautiful Taj Mahal.

The Taj Mahal is reflected in the waters of the Jumna.

junco *(JUNK-oh)* One of the American snowbirds, belonging to the finch family and found as far north as the Arctic regions and as far south as Central America. Juncos are small, with gray- or slate-colored back feathers. They travel in flocks and are particularly partial to weed seeds.

Jung *(yoong)* Carl Gustav Jung (1875–1961), the Swiss psychiatrist and founder of analytical psychology. Jung believed that achieving harmony between the conscious and unconscious could make a person one and whole. Jung and Freud disagreed on such issues, and broke formally after publication of Jung's *Psychology of the Unconscious* (1916). See *anima.*

Carl Gustav Jung.

Juno *(JOO-noe)* In Roman religion, the goddess and protector of women, known to the Greeks as Hera (q.v.). In astronomy, **Juno** was the third asteroid to be discovered (1804). This chunk of rock, 120 miles in diameter, is located between the orbits of Mars and Jupiter, and takes 1,594 days to circle the sun. **Juno** is also Juno Boyle, the heroine of Sean O'Casey's *Juno and the Paycock*. The adjective Junoesque is used to describe a stately and regal woman.

junta *(JUN-tah;* HOON-*tah)* From the Latin meaning "to join," the Spanish word for an assembly, council, or legislative body other than the Cortes, the Spanish (or Portuguese) parliament. Juntas are usually convened to perform some special function. Junta also means a faction of political intriguers, often involved in a coup d'état.

jupon *(JOO-pon)* An essential item of apparel for knights, medieval soldiers, and other wearers of armor, also spelled gipon. The word is derived from the Arabic *jubbah,* a long-sleeved outer garment, and designates the close-fitting, often padded tunic or jacket worn between the armor and the skin or, sometimes, over armor.

Jura *(JOO-ra)* A mountain range and picturesque region of the Alps, astride the border between Switzerland and France, and extending from the Rhine to the Rhone. The area is famous for both watches and cheese. The Jura range, with rounded crests about 5,000 feet in height, is composed of sandstone and limestone, and gives its name to the Jurassic geological period. The region has many resorts.

The picturesque town of St. Ursanne in the Jura region.

jurat *(JOOR-at)* From the same Latin word that gives us juror, a person who is legally sworn to perform a specific function; or the municipal magistrate in certain French towns and the Channel Islands. In law, a **jurat** is a statement added to an affidavit that contains specific details about its legality.

Jurua *(ZHOO-roo-ah)* A 2,400-mile-long river that rises in the Cerros de Canchyuaya of eastern Peru and flows generally northeastward to join the Amazon east of Fonte Boa. The Jurua is one of the Amazon's longest tributaries; it was formerly used to bring crude rubber to market.

jus *(jus)* The law, legal principle, right, or power, from Latin. Among such laws (*jura,* plural) usually designated in Latin are the *jus canonicum* (canon law); *jus divinum* (divine law); and *jus naturae* (natural law). Pronounced *zhoo,* the word is French for the natural juices of meat, as in "roast beef au _____."

jute *(joot)* Either of two Indian plants that grow in the Ganges and Brahmaputra valleys, or their strong, glossy fiber, used to make burlap, rope, and twine. As a proper noun, a **Jute** is a member of an ancient Germanic tribe of Jutland. The Jutes accompanied the Angles and Saxons who invaded England in the fifth century A.D., and thus began the Anglo-Saxon conquest. See *Horsa.*

Jynx *(jinks)* A genus of woodpeckers known as wryneck because of their peculiar habit of twisting the neck. Possibly because the wryneck was once used in witchcraft, **jinx** (lowercased and with an *i*) has come to mean something that foredooms bad luck. A person surrounded by misfortune which rubs off is called a jinx.

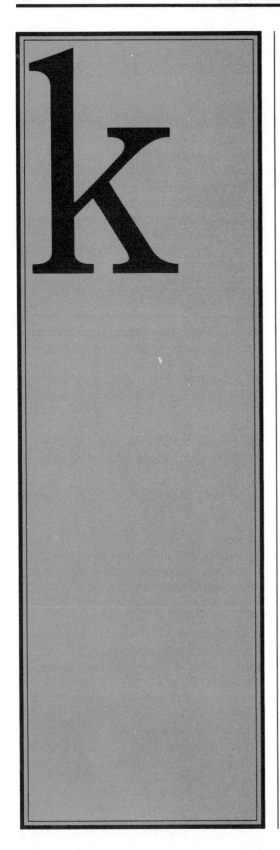

Kaaba *(KAH-ba)* In Mecca (q.v.), a Muslim shrine so sacred that nonbelievers are forbidden to approach it. The Kaaba, a small building in the Great Mosque, is supposed to have been built by Ishmael and Abraham on the spot where Adam worshiped after his expulsion from Eden. Here rests the famous Black Stone, most venerated object in Islam, greatly worn by centuries of kissing by pilgrims. It is toward the Kaaba that all Muslims face when praying.

kabob *(kah-BOB)* A word occurring in Arabic, Persian, Hindi, and Turkish, that has passed directly into English. Kabobs (or kebobs, or kebabs) are seasoned and skewered chunks of meat, roasted over burning charcoal. The skewers are sometimes embellished with sections of onion, green pepper, tomato, or mushroom. The meat used is often lamb, but may be beef, game, liver, fish, or poultry. Shish kabob—kabob prepared with lamb—is a favorite.

Kabul *(KAH-bool)* Largest city, economic center, and capital of Afghanistan. Situated at the northern approaches to the Khyber Pass, Kabul has been occupied by the Soviets, Arabs, Moguls, Persians, and repeatedly by the British, who were almost annihilated in 1842 on their retreat through the Khyber during the Afghan Wars. These events were immortalized in the poem ''Kabul,'' by Rudyard Kipling.

The Hindu Kush mountains rise behind the Afghan capital Kabul.

Kadi See *Cadi.*

kafir or **kaffir** *(KAH-fer)* Arabic for "infidel," the pejorative term by which Muslims refer to those of another faith. Also used by Europeans in southern Africa, first to designate the natives of Kaffraria (later the Transkei), then the Xhosa-speaking peoples, and finally all black Africans. Today, the South African government prefers the term Bantu (q.v.) when referring to the black majority.

Kafka *(KAHF-kah)* Franz Kafka (1883–1924), the German author who supplemented his negligible income from writing by working as a civil servant. Kafka's work is known for its mysticism, symbolism, and portrayals of tragic, pathetic, and humble people. Among Kafka's best-known works are *The Metamorphosis* (1915), *The Castle* (1926), and *The Trial* (1937).

Franz Kafka.

kago *(KAH-goe)* In Japan, that item of luxurious transportation known elsewhere as the palanquin. This is a covered personal litter, suspended on poles and carried on the shoulders of at least two bearers, usually selected for identicality of height.

kagu *(KAH-goo)* A leggy, chicken-size, heronlike flightless bird with gray plumage; white, black, and red markings; and orange-red feet. Once found throughout the islands of the Coral Sea and New Caledonia, the kagu is now virtually extinct, no doubt thanks to the wild dance it does as a prelude to mating.

kakapo *(KAH-kah-po)* This small green parrot with brown and yellow markings is an endangered species of New Zealand. It is also called the owl parrot, night kaka, or ground parrot, because its daytime dwelling-place is a hole in the ground.

kaki *(KAH-kee)* Either the Japanese persimmon, an edible fruit with several cultivated varieties; or a black to dark gray New Zealand bird also called the stilt.

The tall bird here is a kaki. Only flamingos have longer legs.

Kalat *(kuh-LAHT)* A former princely state of Baluchistan, the province of Pakistan bounded by Iran, Afghanistan, and the Arabian Sea. Kalat's population, consisting mostly of pastoral nomads like the Baluchi and Pathans, numbers about 73,000.

kale or **kail** *(kale)* A colewort, a hardy cabbage and a member of the large family of vegetables that includes mustard greens, kohlrabi, and broccoli. Kale plants produce loose, spreading leaves, rather than tight heads. Because of its appearance and green color, **kale** is also slang for folding money. In Scotland, **kail** is a synonym for a meal or for food.

kali *(KAY-lee)* A common name (along with helpwort) for the saltwort, a plant whose ash yields sodium carbonate and was formerly used in glassmaking. In Hinduism, **Kali** is the goddess of death and evil. She has red eyes, four arms, matted hair, and a protruding tongue that drips blood.

OUR FEATHERED FRIENDS

aerie

aix

arend

heron

ibis

jynx

raven

rhea

auk

crake

eider

crane

macaw

petrel

quail

snipe

ruff

tern

wren

Kama *(KAH-ma)* or **Kamadeva**
(kah-mah-DEE-va) Either a 1,200-mile-long river tributary of the Volga in the U.S.S.R.; or, in Hindu mythology, both the god of young love who is husband of Rati, patroness of voluptuousness, and one of the four aims of man according to Hinduism (see *artha*). Kama the god is represented holding a bouquet of flowers and five arrows, and riding a sparrow.

Kama getting a blast of fire from the third eye of Shiva.

kame *(kame)*
A British variation of combe, a deep, narrow valley. Also, in geologic terminology, a **kame** is a hill or short, high ridge of stratified drift deposited by the melting of glacial ice, and somewhat related to an esker (q.v.).

Kandy *(KAN-dee)*
City and mountain resort in central Sri Lanka. Kandy overlooks an artificial lake built in 1806, and houses the famous Temple of the Tooth, where one of Buddha's teeth traditionally rests. This relic was brought here in the fourth century A.D. by a princess who hid it in her hair and is honored by an annual festival.

The Temple of the Tooth in Kandy purportedly houses one of Buddha's teeth.

Kano *(KAH-noe)*
A major northern Nigerian city and a trade, manufacturing, and shipping center. Kano is noted for its leatherwork and especially for its tanned goatskin, known as morocco leather. In former centuries Kano was one of the Hausa city-states, a federation of black African territories inhabited by the Hausa peoples. **Kano** is also the family name of four generations of Japanese painters and of the school named for them, which flourished for roughly 200 years after the mid-fifteenth century.

Kansu *(KAHN-soo)*
A strategic province of northwestern China, with railroad communications into Sinkiang, Mongolia, and the U.S.S.R. The capital is Lan-Chou. This fertile region produces grain, livestock, minerals, and oil. It is populated chiefly by Mandarin Chinese, plus 11 ethnic minorities, the largest of which are Muslims and Mongols.

Kant *(kahnt)*
Immanuel Kant (1724—1804), the Russian-born German philosopher whose major metaphysical concern was determining the limits of human reason. A bachelor, Kant was a creature of habit, and his neighbors reportedly set their watches by his daily routines.

Immanuel Kant.

kaph or **kaf** *(kahf)*
The eleventh letter of the Hebrew alphabet, corresponding to the letter *K* in English. Kaph is written as two symbols, with the one resembling an inverted *L* used when it occurs as the last letter of a word.

kapok *(KAY-pok)*
The tropical silk-cotton tree, or ceiba (q.v.), or the fiber from its ripe pods. This shiny yellowish material is full and resilient, and it resists water and decay. It is therefore ideal for use in life preservers, as a stuffing for bedding and upholstery, and for insulation against heat. Another name for it is Java (q.v.) cotton.

Karma *(KAHR-mah)* In Buddhism and in Hindu (q.v.) and Jain (q.v.) belief, the doctrine that a person's actions in one state of his existence influence his state in his future incarnations.

kasha See *groat.*

Kato *(KAY-toe)* Komei Kato (1860–1926), Japanese statesman and former prime minister; or Tomasaburo Kato (1861–1923), a Japanese admiral during the Russo-Japanese War, and later prime minister; or, in TV, the Green Hornet's valet, played by Bruce Lee, who later went on to fame in martial-arts films.

Bruce Lee (right), as Kato, was the Green Hornet's sidekick.

Kauai *(KAH-oo-WAH-ee)* One of the Hawaiian Islands, 32 miles in diameter and situated northwest of Oahu (q.v.). Lihue is the largest town. Geologically, it is the oldest of the Hawaiian Islands and was formed by its now-extinct volcanic mountains. The northeast slopes of Waialeale peak receive an annual rainfall of 450 inches, making this one of the wettest spots on earth.

The "Fern Grotto" on Kauai.

kauri, kaurie, or **kaury** *(KOW-ree)* A tree belonging to an Australasian genus characterized by juvenile leaves that are larger and different in arrangement from adult foliage. This tall New Zealand timber tree has fine, white, straight-grained wood. Kauri resin, used in the manufacture of linoleum and varnishes, is obtained by tapping live trees.

kava *(KAH-vah)* The Maori word for "bitter," kava is the name given to a plant of the pepper family, native to the Pacific, whose roots are crushed (they were formerly masticated) to make a beverage, kavakava, important in religious ritual and social life. Dried kava roots were once used as a diuretic and genitourinary antiseptic.

kayak or **kaiak** *(KIE-ak)* A transliteration of the Eskimo word for "canoe," a boat used for hunting. A kayak was originally made of sealskins stretched over a whalebone or wooden frame and completely enclosed except for a small opening in which the paddler sat. The craft is usually propelled by a two-ended paddle.

kayo *(kay-OH)* Derived from the first letters of "knock out" and written as K.O., this is boxing terminology for a knockout. The word has been broadened to cover elimination of things or people other than boxing opponents. **Kayo** is also a character in the comic strip "Moon Mullins."

kazoo *(kah-ZOO)* A toy musical instrument whose name is probably an approximate imitation of its sound. Kazoos are whistle-shaped affairs with a membrane-covered top opening that resonates and produces a buzzing sound when one hums or sings into it. Kazoos are also called mirlitons and eunuch flutes.

kedge *(kedj)* Variant form of cadge, meaning "to catch" and used to designate a light anchor that catches on the bottom and is used to warp a ship, usually one that's gone aground. The kedge anchor is carried out by boat and dropped into deeper water, and the ship uses it as a fixed base to pull upon, thus "kedging off."

keef See *cay*.

kef or **kif** *(kaif)*   A transliteration of the Arabic word for "well-being," kef is a drowsy, dreamy state of tranquillity induced by smoking hallucinogenic or narcotic drugs. The name is also applied to the material, such as the derivatives of hemp (q.v.), which produces a state of kef.

kelp *(kelp)*   Any of several large seaweeds, generally coarse in structure and brown in color. Kelp is an excellent source of iodine and potassium. When the seaweed is incinerated, the soluble materials are found in the ashes. In Japan a variety of kelp known as *kombu* is used to season foods.

Kemal *(keh-MAHL)*   Mustafa Kemal (1881–1938), the national leader and founder of modern Turkey, who took the name Kemal Ataturk, meaning "the perfect father of the Turks." He served as president of Turkey from 1923 until his death. In World War I, Kemal's exploits won

Mustafa Kemal.

him the title of Pasha. He was succeeded by Ismet Inönü (q.v.), whose name (as "successor to Kemal" or with "Kemal as predecessor") is often used in clues.

kench *(kench)*   A word of uncertain origin that designates a highly specific object: a box or bin used to hold fish or skins while they are being salted.

Keneh See *Qina*.

keno *(KEY-noe)*   Probably derived from the French *quine*, meaning "five winners," keno is a gambling game which originally produced five winners. The game is similar to lotto and bingo and consists of a caller drawing numbered discs at random, and players converting numbers keyed to the letters K, E, N, O. The first player to produce a covered row wins.

Kenya *(KEEN-yah)*   An East African republic, independent since 1963, formerly a British colony and protectorate on the Indian Ocean. The chief cities are Nairobi and Mombasa, its seaport. Kenya is located right on the Equator, but its highlands are temperate and its national parks, rich in game, attract tourists. Since 1967, it has been a member of the East African Economic Community, with Uganda and Tanzania. Kenya's official languages are Swahili and English. Kenya-related crossword repeaters include Jomo Kenyatta, its first president; and Masai (q.v.), the name of an important tribal group.

kepi *(KEH-pee)*   From the French word for "cap," a military cap, usually round and flat on top and with a stiff visor. This is the headgear so closely identified with the French Foreign Legion that its newspaper was called the *White Kepi*.

Fredrick March in a kepi.

kerf *(kerf)*   Related to the term carve, a slit notch made by a cutting instrument, usually a saw. When a board is cut in two and the pieces are put back together, the reason the board is shorter than it was originally is the kerf—now represented by the sawdust on the floor.

Kerkira See *Corfu*.

kern *(kern)* Either a medieval foot soldier of Scotch or Irish extraction; or the part of a type-cast letter's face that extends beyond its body. As a proper noun, surname of Jerome **Kern** (1885—1945), the renowned American composer who wrote such standards as "Smoke Gets in Your Eyes," from *Roberta*, and "Ol' Man River," from his greatest musical, *Showboat* (1927), with the book by Oscar Hammerstein II.

Jerome Kern.

ketch *(ketch)* A sailing vessel rigged fore and aft, with its tall mizzenmast stepped forward of the steering gear, a placement that distinguishes it from a yawl (q.v.). Also, the surname of Jack **Ketch**, English hangman remembered for his butchery during the Bloody Assizes of 1685. His name, thereafter, was bestowed on all his successors.

kevel *(KEH-vul)* An object universally recognized but rarely identified by its proper name—a cleat or ballard to which are fastened the lines of a vessel tied up to a dock. Ketches are frequently moored to kevels.

Khan *(kahn)* A word of Tartar origin meaning "prince" or "lord" (see *Cham*). It was the title of the Mongol conqueror Genghis Khan (1164–1227), and his descendants, including grandson Kubla Khan (1216–1294), founder of the Mongol dynasty in China. See also *Aga*. The title is now given to various dignitaries and potentates of Arabic lands. A **khan** is also an inn in Turkey and other Eastern countries.

kheth *(kehth)* Eighth letter of the Hebrew alphabet, a variant spelling of *het* or *chet*. It has no equivalent English sound, but comes closest to the Scottish *ch* sound as in loch (q.v.). This sound is called a velar fricative.

Khiva *(KEE-vah)* Former khanate in central Asia, on the Amu Darya River, and the city that was its capital. Founded around 1511, Khiva was capital of the Khorezm kingdom in the next two centuries. It was conquered in turn by the Arabs (seventh century), then the Uzbeks (sixteenth century), whereupon it became a khanate until its conquest by Russia in 1873. After the Russian Revolution, Khiva comprised the Khorem Soviet People's Republic. The region was subsequently divided between the Uzbek S.S.R. and the Turkmen S.S.R.

Khufu *(KOO-foo)* Also known as Cheops, he was a king and the founder of the IV (or Memphite) dynasty of ancient Egypt. Khufu is renowned for having built the largest of the Gizeh (q.v.) pyramids, a monumental task requiring crews of 100,000 men working in three-month relays, and the sale of his daughter to finance the project. Built in 2680 B.C., the pyramid is one of the Seven Wonders of the World—the only one still in existence.

The pyramid of Cheops (Khufu).

kibe *(kibe)* From the Welsh word for "chilblain," exactly that—a crack in the skin and flesh due to cold, marked by itching or burning, sometimes with blisters and ulceration. What makes a kibe distinctive is that it usually appears on the human heel.

Kibei *(kee-BAY)* A native American citizen born to Issei—"first generation" or Japanese immigrants—but sent back to Japan to be educated. If the child were to be educated in America, he would be known as a Nisei (second generation). The American-born child of a Nisei or Kibei is a Sansei.

kier *(keer)* Akin to the Old Norse word *ker*, meaning "bathtub," a large vat used in textile mills to bleach, boil, or dye fibers.

kino *(KEE-no)* An African Mandingo word designating the brownish gum obtained from certain trees and used for tanning leather or as an astringent. Also, the surname of Eusebio Francisco **Kino** (1644–1711), missionary-explorer of the present American Southwest and other parts of New Spain, who voyaged down the Colorado River and proved that California was not an island.

kiosk *(KEE-osk)* From the Persian word for "portico" or "palace," an open

summer house or pavilion in Turkey and Iran. In America, the term is also used to designate a somewhat similar, but much more humble structure, open at one side and used as a newspaper stand or as a covering for the entrance to a subway.

Kirin *(KEER-in)* A province of northeastern China, one of the original Manchurian provinces. It is bounded by the U.S.S.R., North Korea, and Inner Mongolia. The region is a fertile plain and a prosperous agricultural area, also yielding timber and minerals. **Kirin** is also a brand of Japanese beer exported to America.

Kirov *(KEE-rahf)* A city on the Vyatka River in the U.S.S.R., probably best known in the U.S.A. as home of the Kirov Ballet, one of the two major U.S.S.R. ballet companies, the other being the Bolshoi. Founded in 1174, Kirov was annexed to

Moscow by Ivan III in 1489. At one time the city was known as Vyatka and was a refuge for political exiles. It was renamed in 1934 for Sergei Meronovitch Kirov, the revolutionary leader assassinated at Leningrad in 1934.

Kiska *(KISS-kah)* One of the Rat Islands in the Aleutian archipelago curving west from the tip of mainland Alaska. This foggy, rainy region was discovered in 1741 by Vitus Bering, a Dutch explorer sailing for Russia. During World War II, Kiska was occupied by the Japanese.

Vitus Jonassen Bering.

kite See *glide.*

kith *(kith)* From *cuth* (known), the same archaic word that gives us uncouth, one's friends, relatives, neighbors, and drinking partners. Kith usually runs as an entry with kin. The term "kith and kin" is now used almost exclusively to designate only relatives, or kin.

kiva *(KEE-vah)* A Hopi Indian word designating the large, subterranean ceremonial and council room in pueblos. Kivas, entered through a hatchway and down a ladder, have an opening in the floor leading to the lower world. Since women can't enter, the kiva sometimes serves as a kind of corner hangout for the men.

kiwi *(KEE-wee)* A small, nearly extinct, flightless and tailless bird of New Zealand, whose symbol it is. The kiwi has a hunched back, brown hairlike feathers, and an appetite for worms and insects. In ornithologic circles, it's called an apteryx (from the Greek

meaning "without wings"). The more popular name, kiwi, approximates the sound of its call. It is a relative of the ostrich, rhea (q.v.), cassowary and emu (q.v.). These birds are often used in definitions for the kiwi, e.g., "ostrich's kin." It is also related to the extinct moa (q.v.). New Zealanders, especially soldiers, are often called **Kiwis**; and **kiwi** fruit, or "Chinese gooseberry," grown in New Zealand and California, became a ubiquitous garnish in the nouvelle cuisine of the 1970s.

Klee *(klay)*   Paul Klee (1879–1940), the Swiss abstract painter and graphic artist, a giant of modern art renowned for his uninhibited imagination. A member of the Blaue Reiter, a group of expressionist painters that included Kandinsky and Macke, Klee also taught at the famed German art school, the Bauhaus. He is credited with producing more than 9,000 works of art.

Paul Klee.

knurl *(nurl)*   Either a small knot or nodule, or a ridge that's part of a series of ridges on the surface of metal—specifically, those on the edge of certain coins. In Scotland, a **knurl** is a short person of chunky build.

koa *(KOE-ah)*   A native Hawaiian tree of the acacia family with crescent-shaped leaves, small white flowers, and light gray bark that contains chemicals employed in tanning. Especially valued is its fine-grained red wood, used for cabinetmaking.

koala *(koe-AH-lah)*   A marsupial mammal of Australia, also called kangaroo bear, although it is not related to the bears. This furry, defenseless little creature is arboreal and feeds on the leaves of only certain varieties of eucalyptus trees. Like a kanga-

roo, the koala carries its cub in a pouch for the first six months of its life. Resembling a teddy bear, the koala is seen extensively in advertising for an Australian airline.

Kobe *(KOE-bay)*   Seaport on Osaka (q.v.) Bay, on the south coast of Honshu, Japan. A thriving industrial center and rail hub, Kobe is famous for shipbuilding yards, chemical plants, sugar refineries, and steel mills. It was heavily bombed in World War II. The city is also a culture center, with seven colleges and universities doing business within its boundaries. In cuisine, the place has become known for Kobe beef, the best in Japan, from cosseted animals said to be fed (and massaged with) beer.

koel *(KOE-el)*   A tree-dwelling, insectivorous cuckoo of Indonesia and Australia. Koels are social parasites, laying their eggs in the nests of other birds and often removing one of the original eggs so that the total will be the same. Up to five eggs may be laid, each in a different nest. Once hatched, the vigorous young koel shoves its fellow nestlings over the side and is thereafter reared as an only child.

kohl *(kole)*   From the Arabic *al kuhl*, which gives us the word alcohol, a cosmetic preparation, usually containing powdered sulfide of antimony. Kohl is used in Muslim lands such as Egypt and Saudi Arabia by women who apply it as liner to darken the edges of their eyelids. It is one of the most

The piercing eyes of silent film star Theda Bara (here seen as Cleopatra) are rimmed with kohl.

ancient cosmetics, having been used in Cleopatra's time. It doubtless was one of the paints used by Jezebel (2 Kings 9:30) when preparing to greet Jehu (q.v.), who brought about her death.

Koine *(koy-NAY)*   The Greek for "common," designating the common dialect or language used throughout the Greek-speaking world during the Hellenistic and Roman periods. In antiquity, the spoken form was basically colloquial Attic (the Athenian dialect), with various Ionic words thrown in. The New Testament was originally written in the Koine.

koph *(kof)*   The nineteenth letter of the Hebrew alphabet, comparable to the English *K* and the Greek *kappa*.

Koran *(KOR-an)*   The Muslim "Bible," containing the revelations of the prophet Mohammed, as recorded by his secretary, Zain ibn Thabit, over Mohammed's lifetime. The Koran (from the Arabic word *Qur'an*, "to read") is divided into 114 suras (q.v.), or chapters, that are ordered by subject instead of by revelatory chronology, and governs all aspects of Muslim life.

koto *(KOE-toe)*   A stringed musical instrument, structurally similar to the zither, identified almost exclusively with Japanese culture. The koto, which is played by plucking, is basically an oblong body over which are stretched 7–13 strings made of silk for delicacy of tone. Today, the recorded tinkling of a koto serves as background music in many Japanese restaurants.

The koto is played on the floor.

LAW OF THE LAND

THE LONG ARM

amir	ephor	negus
ayllu	genro	nizam
cham	hakim	pasha
dato	jarl	posse
dewan	junta	reeve
dey	jurat	Solon
diet	khan	thane
doge	lan	ulama
Draco	mesne	walla
duce	mufti	witan
Duma	mulla	
edile	nabob	

THE SMALL PRINT

canon	I.O.U.	salvo
cess	jus	taboo
chit	malum	tenet
codex	mete	tithe
debit	mise	ukase
dicta	pone	veto
dower	privy	visa
droit	proxy	writ
feme	rente	
feu		
fiat		
fief		
gage		
geld		

kraal *(krahl)* In southern Africa, Afrikaans version of the Portuguese word *curral* (a pen for cattle), from which the English corral is derived. A kraal can be a fenced enclosure for cattle, but most broadly it means an entire fenced-in village, usually of Bantu (q.v.) or other black Africans, and, by extension, the social unit.

krait *(krite)* Perhaps the most poisonous snake on earth. Native mainly to southeast Asia, kraits are related to the cobras (q.v.), mambas (q.v.), and coral snakes by virtue of fang arrangement. They are unaggressive and will attack only if disturbed. You can recognize a krait by the pattern of colored bands that encircle its body. Kraits feed on other snakes.

kris or **kriss** *(kreess)* A particular type of dagger found mainly on the Malay peninsula and in Indonesia. The kris is particularly nasty-looking because of its wavy cutting edges. It is used as part of a Balinese dance in which the dancer symbolically attempts to stab himself with the weapon. A frequent crossword **Kris** (pronounced *kris*) is singer Kristofferson or gift-giver Kringle.

Kris Kristofferson and Barbra Streisand in the 1976 remake of A Star is Born.

kudos *(KOO-dose)* Despite its ending, kudos is singular, derived from the Greek *kydos*, meaning "glory" or "fame." It is nonetheless frequently treated as if it were a plural, and is used by some for humorous effect when conveying approval, praise, or congratulations for an achievement.

kudu or **koodoo** *(KOO-doo)* Hottentot, and now English, for a large dun-colored, white-striped antelope indigenous to Africa. The kudu, which may be five feet high at the shoulders, is distinguished by his large, ringed, and spirally twisted horns, highly valued as a hunter's trophy. The kudu comes in two sizes: greater and lesser.

kulak *(koo-LAHK)* Russian for "fist," and hence a tightwad, the word used to designate the landed peasantry in Tsarist Russia who made their money off the poorer classes. The kulaks obviously opposed Soviet policies, especially land collectivization, and thus passed into history via confiscation or liquidation.

Kurd *(kerd)* A Muslim of Kurdistan, the mountainous region that includes parts of Turkey, Iraq, Iran, Syria, and the U.S.S.R. Formerly nomadic, the Kurds are mostly seminomadic, or actually settled, today. Their several dialects are related to certain Iranian dialects. Throughout history, the Kurds have exerted a major influence in the area and have been involved in numerous struggles. Perhaps the most famous Kurd was Saladin, nemesis of the Crusaders.

Saladin, a famous Kurd.

kutb See *qutb*.

kvass *(kah-VAHSS)* A kind of homemade near beer favored by Russians despite its somewhat sour taste and low alcohol content. Kvass is made through a fermentation process that begins with soaking rye or barley in water. If these grains aren't available, rye bread does almost as well.

kylix See *cylix*.

laager or **lager** *(LAHG-er)*   The South African equivalent of the defensive wagon-circle deployment commonly seen in Hollywood westerns. However, the Boer carts thus arranged at night during the Great Trek of 1835–1840 looked rather more like milk wagons than prairie schooners. Laager also means a military encampment protected by a ring of heavily armored vehicles.

Laban *(LAY-bun)*   In the Bible, Jacob's father-in-law by two marriages, the second necessitated by Laban's tricky substitution of his eldest daughter (Leah) for her sister (Rachel) at the first. A redoubled dowry, payable by seven extra years of indentured servitude, was then extracted from the hapless groom, who spent a total of 20 years in all earning the lady of his heart.

labis *(LAY-bis)*   The spoon, in Eastern Orthodox Christianity, with which the wine-soaked bread of the Eucharist is administered to the communicant.

lac *(lak)*   Milk, when written on a doctor's prescription. When not, the scarlet resinous substance secreted by a scale insect *(Tachardia lacca)* which hardens around the insect, sheltering it on the twigs of fig, pipal, and jujube trees in the Middle East and India. Lac is an important ingredient in sealing wax and lacquers, and depending on how it is processed it may be called stick lac (natural, just as scraped from twigs), seed or grained lac (crushed and washed), lac resin (melted and stained), shell lac or shellac (in flakes), button lac (discs), caked lac (cakes), and the redundant lac lake (a red dye). What's left is refuse lac. Other crossword **lacs** are the lakh (q.v.) and the American city whose name appears as "Fond du ____ , Wisconsin." (*Lac* means "lake" in French.)

lade *(lade)*   English word that means to load a cargo, to work a soup ladle, or to leak water. Probably reflecting the third sense, Scots call a small watercourse a **lade.**

An English ship being laden at Kobe, Japan.

Ladin *(lah-DEEN)* A Romance (Latin-based) dialect akin to Italian, French, Spanish, Portuguese, and Romanian, spoken in southeastern Switzerland, the upper Tyrol, and northern Italy. It is best known as Romansh.

Lae *(LAH-eh)* An important administrative-commercial center in northeastern New Guinea, on the Huon (q.v.) Gulf about 200 miles straight north of Port Moresby, the capital of Papua New Guinea.

lager *(LAH-ger)* A beer fermented by the German method, which involves storing the beer for several months of slow after-fermentation. It is light in color and well-carbonated. The alternative (British) method of brewing beer is faster but

A couple of frogs enjoying a sip of lager.

can't be said to produce lager.

Lagos *(LAH-gos)* The capital of Nigeria, located partly on the African mainland and partly on offshore islands. Lagos is the major seaport on the Bight of Benin, is home to about a million people, and gives its name to the likes of Lagos ebony and Lagos rubber, which are transshipped there. **Lagos** is also a Portuguese city in the Algarve. The word means "lakes" in Spanish.

Lahr See *Bohr*.

lai *(lay; lie)* This word compounds the confusion between lay and lie. In the first pronunciation it is a medieval tale told in verses with eight-syllable lines and usually treating of King Arthur or his knights. In the second pronunciation, and with a capital *L*, it is a Mongoloid tribesman of the Chin Hills of Burma and also, as is usual with tribesmen, his dialect. Often it is clued in crosswords as "Chou En-_____," the Chinese leader (see *Chou*).

laic *(LAY-ik)* The adjective used to describe the laity and all things secular, as distinct from the clergy and things clerical.

lak *(lak)* The courtship dance of the male capercaillie, during which he struts with drooping wings and fanned-out tail feathers, while crying noisily. A capitalized **Lak** (pronounced *lok*) is a tall Sunnite tribesman of the northern Caucasus who speaks Lak and is sometimes called a Kizi-Kumuk. Also the clue word in Frank Libby Stanton's poem "Mighty _____ a Rose."

lakh or **lac** *(lak)* In India, 100,000 rupees, or 100,000 of anything. A thousand lakhs make a million rupees, or one-tenth of a crore (q.v.). A lakh was worth $11,001.10 when we last checked.

lam *(lam)* Clued almost exclusively by the phrase "on the _____," meaning on the run from an officer of justice, **lam** also is supposed to mean thrash or whack, as well as a lever on certain looms.

Robert Donat on the lam in The Thirty-Nine Steps, *1935.*

lama *(LAH-mah)*   In Tibetan Buddhism, a monk, from the word meaning "superior one." In pre-Communist times, lamas formed a dominant monastic hierarchy, and their chief, the Dalai Lama, was the temporal ruler of the country. He remains the spiritual leader of Tibetan Mahayana Buddhism (sometimes called Lamaism), in many countries of the West. The Panchen Lama was formerly the Tibetan spiritual leader, but was installed in temporal power after the Chinese takeover of Tibet in 1950 was followed by the escape of the Dalai Lama.

At one time more than half the population of Lhasa, the capital of Tibet, were monks.

lamia *(LAY-me-uh)*   A man-eating monster of ancient Greece, with the head and chest of a woman and the lower body of a snake. Later the word was applied with less precision to any vampire, witch, or sorceress. Keats's poem by this title, for example, tells of a bride who reverts to a serpent form.

lan *(lahn)*   A most confusing unit of measure, equal to 1.204 (U.S.) ounces in Russia and Mongolia, 42.67 (U.S.) acres in Czechoslovakia, and 2.24 (U.S.) yards in Rangoon. **Lan** is also a Swedish administrative division which sends members to Parliament on the basis of its population.

Lanai *(lah-NAH-eh; lan-AYE)*   The sixth largest of the Hawaiian Islands, purchased in its entirety by a pineapple company in 1922. The company built Lanai City, the island's major city, with a population of 2,122. Frequently in crosswords, **lanai** is defined as "Hawaiian porch" or "veranda."

Lanao *(lah-NAH-owe; lah-NOW)*   A lake on the island of Mindanao in the southern Philippines, 22 miles long and up to 16 miles wide. The highlands surrounding the lake are inhabited by the Lanao, a leading Muslim (Moro—q.v.) people, after whom the lake is sometimes called Lake Moro.

lant *(lant)*   This word has three extravagantly unrelated meanings. Stale urine, once used by alchemists and cloth manufacturers; a long, thin, bony fish, the sand launce, that hides in the sand at ebb tide; and an early form, lanterloo, of the card game called loo (q.v.).

Lao *(LAH-owe)*   Not, as it might seem, the singular of Laos, but a member of an important branch of the Thai people, dwelling chiefly in Laos and speaking the Lao language, official tongue of Laos. Citizens of Laos, including those who are not Lao, are popularly called Laotians. Lao is a dialect of Siamese.

lapis *(LAP-iss)*   A stone in Latin, and the first word of many phrases denoting various types of minerals, notably lapis lazuli, a rich semiprecious azure (q.v.) stone sometimes confused in antiquity with the sapphire. It was prized by the pharaohs of Egypt, among others.

Lapp *(lap)*   A member of the short, broad-headed people living in Lapland (northern Scandinavia and adjacent U.S.S.R.) and speaking Lapp, a Finno-Ugric tongue. All Lapps used to be nomadic, herding reindeer to seasonal pastures. Lately, their movements have been more restricted.

lares *(LAIR-eez)*   Roman tutelary gods, the deified ancestral spirits associated first with

WHERE THE DEER AND THE ANTELOPE PLAY

DEER

axis
(India; Asia)

red deer
(Europe; Asia)

roe
(Europe; Asia)

ANTELOPES

beisa
(Africa)

gnu
(Africa)

oryx
(Africa)

addax
(Africa; Arabia; Syria)

eland
(Africa)

kudu
(Africa)

NOT APPEARING HERE

asse (Africa) *sasin* (India)
bohor (Africa) *serow* (Tibet)
goral (Asia) *takin* (China)
oribi (Africa) *mohr* (Africa)
puku (Africa)

the fields, and later, as hearth gods, with the home and other specific locations such as crossroads, the sea, public common land, etc. They were often venerated together with the Penates, gods of household possessions. A **lar** is also a gibbon of Malaysia with white hands and feet.

lath *(lath)* A thin, narrow strip of wood that used to be nailed to rafters and joists to form a groundwork for plastering a wall. With the advent of wallboard, lath was relegated to light frame construction such as that seen in rose trellises.

lea *(lee)* or **ley** *(lee; lay)* The words pasture, meadow, and grassland mean the same as lea, but none is as popular with poets and cruciverbalists. In textile manufacturing a **lea** is 300 yards of linen yarn, but only 120 yards if this yarn is made of cotton or silk.

Leah See *Laban.*

Lear See *Regan.*

Lech *(lek)* Until the relatively late arrival of Lech Walesa, popular leader of the Polish "Solidarity" movement against the Communist government in 1980, a **lech** was only a flat prehistoric monumental stone or slab, usually (as at Stonehenge) a capstone resting horizontally above two or more vertical stones. The capstone and uprights together are called a dolmen or cromlech. A circle of these cromlechs is also called a cromlech, or, to avoid confusion, a stone circle. Also, capitalized, **Lech** is a ski resort in Austria.

The slab-like crosspieces here are lechs. The world's most famous lechs can be seen in the megalithic structures at Stonehenge in Wiltshire, England.

Leda *(LEE-dah)* Mother of Helen of Troy, Clytemnestra, Castor, and Pollux—in some variations of the Greek myth by her husband, King Tyndareus of Sparta; in others by Zeus, who assumed the form of a swan in order to seduce her.

Leda and the Swan, *after Michelangelo.*

lek *(lek)* The major unit of currency in Albania, worth, since 1947, 100 quintars. **Lek** is a shortening of the name Aleksandr (the Great), whose likeness the coin bears.

 A **lek** is also a site to which certain birds return for purposes of courtship.

lemur *(LEE-mur)* Two families of soft, woolly or silky, bug-eyed, usually striped-tailed relatives of the monkey that run around in the treetops of Madagascar. Experienced lemur spotters look for the sharp, foxlike muzzle that distinguishes this creature from the monkeys. The indri (q.v.) and the avahi (q.v.) are lemurs.

Flying lemur.

Lena *(LAY-nah)* A major river of the Soviet Union, rising in the mountains west of Lake Baykal and flowing generally northward through the Siberian wilderness into the Laptev Sea, an arm of the Arctic Ocean. After a 2,600-mile journey, it fans out into a delta fully 250 miles wide. It is navigable for almost 1,000 miles below Yakutsk. **Lena** (pronounced *LEE-nah*) is also singer Lena Horne and, prefaced by "Leapin'," a comic-strip creation of Al Capp.

lene *(LEE-neh)* or **lenis** *(LEE-nis)*   In linguistics, any consonant sound that is produced voicelessly (without the activation of the vocal cords) while the exhalation of breath is impeded in the mouth. The sound of the letter *p,* for example, is produced by the closure of the lips; that of the letter *t* by the closure of tongue and teeth; and that of the letter *k* by the closure of the lower tongue and palate.

Lepus *(LEE-pus)*
The genus (within the family *Leporidae,* which also includes rabbits) of most hares, and the name of a Southern Hemisphere constellation commonly known as the Hare.

Albrecht Dürer's drawing of a Lepus.

Ler or **Leir** *(lair)*   The Irish and Celtic god of the sea, equivalent to the Roman Neptune. In British legend Ler appears as a king, and it is upon him that Shakespeare modeled his King Lear. In the original version, Ler's wife turned their children into swans for 900 years.

lerp *(lerp),* **laap** *(lap),* or **laarp** *(larp)*   The sweet secretion left by jumping plant lice (as a protection for their young) on the leaves of certain eucalyptus trees in Australia and Tasmania. For the aborigines, lerp is a delicacy akin to honey.

Lethe *(LEE-thee)*   The river of forgetfulness in Hades, land of the dead, whose water when drunk blots out the past. Although Lethe, used figuratively, simply means oblivion and has no apparent connection to the word lethal (deadly), Shakespeare used Lethe to mean death.

Leto *(LEE-toe)*   Mistress, or possibly first wife, of Zeus, and mother of his children Apollo and Artemis. Hera (q.v.), Zeus's better-known wife, persecuted Leto miserably. Known as Latona to the Romans, she was specially honored by them as an ancestress.

Leto and her children.

Lett *(let)*   A member of a major ethnic group of Latvia, closely related to the neighboring Lithuanians. Not all Latvians are Letts—Russians, Belorussians, Lithuanians, Poles, and others are sizable minorities. Letts speak Lettish (or Latvian), as do Latvians in general. Today Latvians are all captive citizens of the U.S.S.R.

leu *(LEH-oo)* or **ley** *(lay)*   The monetary unit of Romania, equal to about 22 cents when we last checked. For years the Romanian leu was linked to the Bulgarian lev, but the two have recently gone their separate ways, despite the fact that both *leu* and *lev* mean "lion" in their respective tongues.

levee *(LEV-ee)*   A manmade embankment, such as those now lining both banks of the Mississippi River along most of its length, to prevent flooding at times of high water. Also, a social reception, once held by a distinguished person upon getting out of bed in the morning, but now held by a dignitary in honor of another person.

Levi *(LEE-vie; LAY-vee)*   One of the twelve sons of Jacob, and hence the ancestor of the Levites, one of the twelve tribes of Israel. The Levites were entrusted at Jerusalem with the care of the tabernacle, the sacred vessels, and, later, the Temple itself. Leviticus is the biblical book concerned with them. The only other tribes of Israel who make regular appearances in crosswords are Gad (q.v.) and Dan, and, less frequently, Asher and Judah. The other seven tribes have longer names. **Levi** is also Levi Strauss, onetime peddler who struck it rich by making tough work trousers for miners during California's Gold Rush. Called Levi's, his jeans, once cowboy attire, have become high fashion in the U.S. and abroad in recent years.

levir *(LEE-ver; LAY-veer)* In Jewish law, the brother of a deceased husband, who is obliged to marry the widow if she is childless. The first male offspring of the new marriage was considered the legal son and heir of the deceased. Levirate marriage was common among ancient Hebrews. (See *Onan*).

Lewes *(LOO-iss)* A river of the Yukon Territory, northern Canada, about 330 miles long, also called the Pelly, which flows west into the Yukon at a point below Pelly Crossing. Also, the Delaware terminus of the Cape May (N.J.) Ferry across the mouth of Delaware Bay, and a farm market town in East Sussex (England). George Henry **Lewes** (1817–1878) was an English author, perhaps best known for his *Life of Goethe* (1855). He was a close companion of Mary Ann Evans—a.k.a. George Eliot (see *Eliot*).

Leyte *(LAY-tee)* A rich agricultural island in the Visayan group of the Philippines. Leyte has the curious distinction of being separated from its closest neighbor island, Samar, by a channel only 350 yards wide. The capital of Leyte is Tacloban. The island was the place of the first important U.S. landing (October, 1944) in the campaign to recover the Philippines from the Japanese, and Leyte Gulf saw the greatest naval engagement in history, which ended with destruction of the Japanese fleet.

Lhasa, Lasa, or **Lassa** *(LAH-sah)* The capital of Tibet, a city of 175,000 people situated at a dizzying 12,050 feet above sea level. The traditional seat of Lamaism, or Tibetan Buddhism, Lhasa is the site of the Potala, long the palace of the Dalai Lama (see *lama*). The city is often associated with Shangri-La, the imaginary utopia created in James Hilton's *Lost Horizons*. Lhasa also appears in the name of a Tibetan dog breed, the Lhasa apso.

The wondrous former palace of the Dalai Lama in Lhasa, Tibet.

liana *(lee-AN-ah)* or **liane** *(lee-AN)* Technically, any climbing plant that roots in the ground. The lianas of the tropical rain forests are characterized by woody stems, whereas stems of temperate-zone lianas tend to be tender, or herbaceous.

Liard *(LEE-ard)* A river of western Canada, about 750 miles long, rising in the wild Pelly Mountains of the Yukon Territory and flowing southeast into British Columbia before turning northeast into the Northwest Territories, where it joins the Mackenzie River at Fort Simpson. Part of its course is paralleled by the Alaska Highway.

Lido *(LEE-doe)* A famous bathing resort on the northern end of an island in the Adriatic (Lido di Venezia) which separates the Lagoon of Venice from the Gulf of Venice. The Lido's visitors are ferried from Venice by boat.

Aerial view of the Lido in Venice, Italy.

lie See *lai.*

Liege *(lee-EHZH)* With an accent, Liège is a major industrial city of eastern Belgium at the confluence of the Ourthe and Meuse (q.v.) rivers, and also the province of which Liège is the capital. In feudal parlance, a **liege** *(leezh)* may be any lord or superior to whom allegiance and service are due (a liege lord), or the subject who renders such allegiance and service.

The Freedom Fountain in Liège, Belgium.

Lille *(leel)* Formerly Lisle, an old industrial city of northern France, near the Belgian border, former capital of the county of Flanders. Today it is one of Europe's premier industrial and commercial centers, still producing the laces and textiles (including lisle, from Lille's former name) that made it world-famous.

Limbo *(LIM-boe)* The border or edge of Hell, said by Christian theologians to be the resting place of souls who have been barred from Heaven through no fault of their own, as, for example, those of good people who died before the coming of Christ, or infants who were never baptized. In general usage, **limbo** refers to any state of impotent waiting. The **limbo** is also a West Indian acrobatic dance in which the dancer bends backward to pass under a pole.

limma *(LIM-ah)* The Pythagorean semitone (plural: limmata), consisting of the precise difference between a perfect fourth tone and two whole steps.

limn *(lim)* In its technical sense, limn means to illuminate (a page or document) with ornamental letters, borders, etc., usually in gold leaf, and also to decorate, generally in colors, any text. More generally, limn can mean to draw, paint, sketch, or delineate anything at all. More generally still, it can also mean to portray in words, or describe.

Flemish manuscript, c. 1500.

Lind *(lind)* Jenny Lind (1820–1897), the famous nineteenth-century coloratura soprano, promoted as the "Swedish Nightingale" when she toured the United States under the management of P. T. Barnum in 1850–1852. Later, she married Otto Goldschmidt, and lived in Dresden, then London, where she taught at the Royal College of Music.

Jenny Lind.

ling *(ling)* Common name of several saltwater fish. One, *Molva molva,* is of the cod family, swims in northern Atlantic waters, and, like cod, is commonly salted and dried. Another, also called the cobia or cabia, frequents warmer waters and is a game fish. The lingrod of coastal Pacific waters is a greenling, hence neither a ling nor a cod. **Ling** is also a name for the common heather and, in puzzles, part of the phrase "ding-a- _____ ."

lira *(LEE-rah)*   From the Latin *libra*, "balance," hence unit of weight: the name of the monetary unit of both Italy and Turkey (plural: lire *[LEE-ray]* and liras *[LEE-rahz]*). One Turkish lira is usually worth 10 Italian lire. The Syrian pound is sometimes also called a lira. The symbol for the British pound, which resembles the letter *L*, stood for *libra*.

litus *(LIE-tuss)*   A social and legal status in medieval France and Germany intermediate between freedom and slavery.

Livy *(LIV-ee)*   The great Roman historian Titus Livius of Padua (59 B.C.–A.D. 17). His life work was the masterly 142-volume *History of Rome,* 35 whole volumes of which are still extant and studied in classical history and Latin courses.

Livy.

llama *(LAH-mah)*   The humpless South American relative of the camel. Llamas are found mainly in the high Andes both wild and domesticated, have been used for centuries as beasts of burden, and are valued also for their black, brown, and white coat of coarse, shaggy wool.

llano *(YAH-no)*   Not the high, rugged place where llamas live, but the grassy, mostly treeless prairies of northern South America, in Venezuela and Colombia. The llanero is the llano's equivalent of the gaucho of the pampas of Argentina. **Llano** is also the Llano Estacado ("staked plain") of New Mexico and Texas.

A lonely section of the llano in eastern Colombia.

loa *(LOH-ah)*   A slender, threadlike nematode worm of the lower Congo. The adult loa infests the eye of humans and animals (causing filariasis), and the larvae usually develop in those varieties of mosquitoes—aedes (q.v.), culex (q.v.), and anopheles—already well known in other contexts to tropical-disease followers. Capitalized, **Loa** is also the longest river of Chile, and the second half of the name of a Hawaiian volcano usually clued "Mauna _____ " (see *Hilo*).

loach *(lowtch)*   A small freshwater fish found only in the Old World. Like the catfish, to which it is not related, the loach has barbels (whiskerlike structures) around its mouth.

loam *(lome)* Technically, a type of rich soil consisting of a crumbly mixture of clay, sand, and organic matter in varying proportions. Perhaps a bit too casually, it sometimes means any soil at all.

lobo *(LOH-boh)* Out west, the timber wolf or gray wolf *(Canis lupus)*, as distinguished from the prairie wolf, or coyote *(Canis latrans)*, which is smaller. *El lobo* (Spanish for "wolf") varies in color from nearly pure white to pitch black. Thanks to TV, Sheriff **Lobo**, played by Claude Akins, also appears in crosswords.

A gray—or timber—wolf.

loch *(lok)* Meaning "lake" in Scottish, the word is also commonly used to refer to a bay or arm of the sea, especially one that is nearly landlocked, of which Scotland has many. If asked to name a loch other than Lomond (the biggest) and Ness (the scariest), try Loch Lochy (nine miles long).

Locke *(lok)* The English political philosopher John Locke (1632–1704), whose *Essay Concerning Human Understanding*

and other works greatly influenced the fathers of the American Revolution. He is not likely to be confused with American humorist David Ross Locke (1833–1888), who wrote under the name Petroleum V. Nasby.

John Locke.

locus *(LOE-cus)* In geometry, the path made by a point moving according to some law as, by way of illustration, a rock falling under the force of gravity. This path, usually expressed as a line, is called the locus of points (successively arrived at by the moving point). Drop two rocks and you have loci *(LOH-sie*—plural). **Locus** also means place.

Bill Russell interrupts the locus of the ball.

lode *(lode)* Any ore deposit, especially one having definite boundaries separating it from the adjoining rock. The mother lode is the principal vein of a region, such as the Mother Lode on the California side of the Sierra Nevada, or the Comstock Lode on the Nevada side.

Lodi *(LOE-die)* The name of two small towns of about the same size, one each in New Jersey and California. Both probably were settled by Italians from the commune of Lodi, on the Adda (q.v.) River near Milan. This Lodi was the site of an important Napoleonic victory over the Austrians. The formerly larger New Jersey Lodi, a suburb of New York City is now the smaller of the two.

loess *(LOE-ess; looss)* Soil deposited without stratification, composed of particles ranging from clay to fine sand. Loess is the rich soil that covers most of the Mississippi Basin, north-central Europe, Russia, and eastern China. It is usually a buff or yellowish-brown color. Theories of its formation vary; it is most widely believed to have been deposited by the wind.

lof *(lawf)* or **loof** *(lofe)* An old Swedish and later Russian measure of volume equal to 64.72 liters or 1.84 bushels. In the U.S.S.R. today, it takes exactly 592 tchasts to make a lof.

logia *(LOG-gee-ah; LOE-jee-ah)* The collected sayings or maxims (the plural form of logion) of a religious teacher, and especially the sayings of Jesus. Early logia were supposed to have been used by the original evangelists.

Many of the sayings of Jesus have come down to us as logia.

Logos *(LOE-gohss)* The rational principle in the universe. To the early Greeks, it was the moving and regulating principle of the world. In Christian theology, it is the actively expressed, creative, and revelatory thought and will of God, as expressed through Jesus. The Logos is the Word which was "in the beginning" and "was God," according to the Book of John. In crosswords, **logos** are more commonly clued as "advertisers' trademarks."

Loir *(lwahr)* A little river of central France rising south of Chartres and flowing generally southwest into the Sarthe, a tributary of the Loire (q.v.), near Angers. The Loir's 195-mile course runs close by and parallel to the Loire's, and their like-sounding names are often confused by tourists in château country.

Loire *(lwahr)* The longest river of France, flowing from the southern part of the Massif Central generally north, then west to its estuary on the Bay of Biscay near Nantes. Its 625-mile course across much of France takes in Nevers, Orléans, Blois, Tours, and most of the famous châteaux of central France, making it one of the world's most picturesque rivers.

Loki *(LOH-kee)* In Norse mythology, the personification of evil, the god who kills Balder (q.v.), god of goodness and peace, and is overcome by Thor (q.v.), god of strength and thunder. Loki is the eternal contriver of discord and mischief; at the twilight of the gods, he will lead forth the hosts of his daughter, Hel (q.v.), queen of the underworld.

Incised stone slab showing Loki riding on the wolf Fenrir, one of his creations.

Lolo *(LOH-loh)* In China, a people of southern Szechuan and northern Hunan, believed by some to be of Caucasian and by others Tibeto-Burman origin; also called Nosu. The Lolo dialects are distinct from the local Chinese language. **Lolo** is also a mountain pass (elevation 5,187 feet) across the Bitterroot Range of the Rockies, southwest of Missoula, Montana. The pass was on the route taken by the Nez Percé Indians and the pursuing U.S. cavalry during Chief Joseph's ill-fated dash for Canada.

Lome *(loh-MAY)* The capital of the modern republic of Togo (q.v.), a former German and French colony. Lomé, a seaport on the Bight of Benin, is Togo's only real outlet to the sea.

longe or **lunge** *(luhnj)* The long rein used to lead or guide a horse during training, or longeing. **Longe** also refers to an enclosed ring built for this training. When used as a verb, it means to guide or exercise a horse.

loo *(loo)* An old gambling game in the whist and bridge family. In one form, three, and in another, five, cards are dealt to each player. With these hands, players then attempt to win tricks as in whist but must pay the kitty an additional ante, or loo, when they fail to make a trick. The jack of clubs has special properties in five-card loo and is therefore called pam. **Loo** is also a Britishism for a toilet facility, or comfort station.

loon *(loon)* A diving, fish-eating migratory bird of the cooler regions of the northern hemisphere. The common loon, measuring up to three feet long from sharp, pointed bill to webbed feet, has an iridescent black head, white-spotted back and wings, and a soft white belly. Other varieties of loons may be distinguished by special markings (like a red throat or yellow bill) for which they have been named. Loons cannot walk on land and have a distinctive cry, or "laugh;" perhaps because of it **loon** also means a crazy person and is the source of the adjective loony (crazy). A loony bin is an insane asylum.

A member of the loon family.

loris *(LOH-riss)* The name of two terribly slow, small, nocturnal primates of India and beyond. (*Loris* means "simpleton" in Dutch.) The slender loris creeps about in Sri Lanka, and the slow loris inches its way throughout the East Indies. Its shorter, heavier limbs keep it from attaining top speed. African relatives include the potto and the bush baby, or galagos.

A slender loris.

Lorna See *Doone*.

lory *(LOH-ree)* A parrot of Southeast Asia, Australia, and Oceania, whose tongue has brushlike fibers at the tip. An oral examination will also reveal mandibles less toothed than in other parrots. Through this mouth pass substantial quantities of fruit and nectar.

A lory.

lotus *(LOE-tuss)* The name for three totally unrelated kinds of plants: a miscellaneous collection of shrubs and trees, one of which provided the amnesic, narcotic fruit eaten by some of Ulysses's crew in the Odyssey; a flowering water plant related to the common water lily, which is the sacred flower and frequent architectural motif of ancient Egypt, and, in India, the blossom, sacred to Hindus, in which the Buddhists' mystic "jewel" of illumination is also supposed to reside; and a genus of herbs and low shrubs of the pea family, including the bird's-foot trefoil. *Lotus siliquosus.*

Loup *(loop)* The river system that drains the sand-hills country of central Nebraska. The North Loup (longest fork) and the combined Middle Loup and South Loup join at Cushing to form the Loup proper, which empties into the Platte at Columbus. All of this covers about 300 miles.

loupe *(loop)* A magnifying glass used by jewelers, art directors, etc., usually fitted to the outer eye cavity like a monocle but often simply hand-held at close viewing range.

lox *(loks)* Two rich varieties of Jewish smoked salmon; the tamer unsalted version is called Nova for Nova Scotia, and the heavily salted traditional form is called belly lox or just lox. Both may be eaten on a bagel with cream cheese. **Lox** is also a shortened form for liquid oxygen.

luau *(loo-AOW)* An elaborate outdoor feast in the Hawaiian Islands, usually depicted in TV commercials replete with Polynesian drummers and dancers, if not firewalkers, and now held primarily for tourists on package-deal vacations. At a cruciverbal luau, look for poi (q.v.).

Luba *(LOO-bah)* A member of a Negroid people (plural: Baluba) living on the Kasai (Kassai) River along the Congo-Angola border. Also their language, of the Bantu (q.v.) group. The Baluba are sometimes called the Bashilange.

lubra *(LOO-brah)* A girl or woman of the Australian aborigines. When she gets married, she is thenceforth called a gin, a not at all derogatory name which is also a word for a female kangaroo.

luce *(looss)* An old name for a fleur-de-lis; the term for a northern pike (or lucet), whose scientific name is *Esox lucius;* and, as a proper noun, Adriana's serving maid in Shakespeare's *Comedy of Errors.* Famous **Luces** include Henry (1898–1967), founder of *Time* magazine, and his wife, Clare Boothe (1903–   ), playwright and diplomat.

lucre *(LOO-ker)* Profit or riches, today usually in a humorous sense, but originally without negative connotation. The word actually carried with it a shiny image of due reward and just deserts, but now it's usually preceded by "filthy."

Lud *(lud)* The dull-witted Ned Lud, whose name was appropriated by the Luddites (1811–1816), early British radicals who tried to stop the industrial revolution by sabotaging labor-saving machinery. Ned's original ruckus consisted of breaking up some stocking frames, possibly by accident, in 1779.

ludi *(LOO-die)* Plural of the Latin word for "game," these were the games and spectacles seen in Roman arenas, sometimes called the *ludi publici.* They included athletic competitions, horse and chariot races, gladiatorial combats, and the theater. The ludi were customarily dedicated to a god.

luff *(luff)* In sailing, to luff (up) is to turn a vessel toward the wind, whether temporarily—for example, to clear an obstacle—or in the course of coming about, or tacking.

Luffing off the West Indies island of Barbados.

lulab or **lulav** *(LOO-lahv)* The traditional festive palm branch that is carried and waved at the Jewish Feast of Tabernacles (Sukkoth or Succoth). This is the harvest festival, when outdoor booths are built and festooned with the bounty of nature. Meals are taken in the booths during the festival.

Lulabs being displayed during the Jewish feast of Sukkoth.

lumen *(LOO-men)* From the Latin, this word for any light source, such as a candle, is the unit for measuring the luminous power of any light. A uniform source of one candlepower emits four π or 12.5664 lumina (or lumens).

Luna *(LOO-nah)* The moon and, specifically, the goddess of the moon, who seems

never to have been an important figure in Roman mythology. Lunatics are Luna's favorites. Like werewolves, they are most active under a full moon. **Luna** is also a large moth with light green wings.

Luna, the moon goddess.

Lunda *(LOON-dah)* A group of Bantu (q.v.) tribes—likewise any member tribe, any member of a member tribe, and the language they all speak—living in Angola and the southern Congo. Two of the best-known member tribes of the Lunda are the Balunda and the Lobale.

Lundy *(LUN-dee)* A two-square-mile island off the northwest coast of Devon, in England, at the mouth of Bristol Channel. Lundy's ruined castle and its curious postage stamps—bearing images of and denominations in "puffins," the local avifauna and currency—are its two main claims to fame, although it was inhabited in prehistoric times and was more recently a pirate stronghold.

lune *(loon)* From luna (q.v.), anything in the shape of a half-moon. In geometry the idea is extended to include any crescent-shaped figure bounded by two intersecting arcs of circles. This shape became important in 440 B.C. as the first curvilinear figure to have its area determined by a geometer. A **lune** is also a leash for a hawk in the sport of falconry, attached to a jess (q.v.).

Indian moon goddess.

Luo, Luoh *(loo-OH)*, or **Lwo** *(lwoh)* A Negroid people of the White Nile, also called the Jur, living in what used to be the Anglo-Egyptian Sudan, now simply named Sudan.

Lupus *(LOO-pus)* A constellation to the south of Scorpio, shown on pictorial sky charts as a wolf (the Latin meaning of *lupus*) held by the hand of a nearby constellation, the Centaur. Also a disease, systemic **lupus** erythematosis, which involves the body's immune system and has many and varied symptoms.

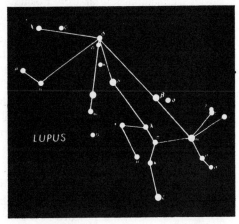

lute *(loot)* A stringed instrument with a large, bulbous body, a long neck with a fretted fingerboard, and a deflected head with screws for tuning. The lute, of Oriental origin, became popular in Europe during the fourteenth century. By the eighteenth century it had few remaining enthusiasts and is today mainly a curiosity. In crosswords, it is often defined as "ancestor of the guitar" or "troubadour's instrument."

The man on the left is playing a lute.

lux *(luks)* An illumination level of one lumen (q.v.) per square meter is the standard for this international unit of direct lighting. Another way of defining it is 0.0929 footcandles. Lux, the originally Latin word for "light," is, however, best known in the expression *fiat lux*, "let there be light." The plural is luxes *(LUHK-sez)* or luces *(LOO-sez)*.

Lvov, Lwow, or Lwiw *(luh-VAWF)*

A city with distinctly Russian, Polish, and Ukrainian names (given in order above) and also a German name, Lemberg, having no cruciverbal significance. At the moment Lvov is the city now situated in the Soviet Ukraine but not far from Poland.

Lycia *(LISH-ee-uh)*

A Persian, then Seleucid, then Roman province occupying the more westerly of the two large promontories that jut into the Mediterranean from the southern coast of Asia Minor. To the northwest lay Caria, to the east Pamphilia and Cilicia, to the north the western parts of Asia Minor.

Lydia *(LID-ee-ah)*

An ancient country in what is today Turkey. Lydia was one of the most important Asiatic powers in the seventh and sixth centuries B.C. and was the first nation to coin money. The wealth of its kings, especially Croesus, who was defeated by Cyrus the Great, is proverbial. Croesus died in 546 B.C. after a reign of about 14 years.

lymph *(limf)*

The nearly colorless, sometimes faintly yellowish, tissue fluid of the body. The lymphatic system is the network of vessels conducting lymph from the tissues into the veins of the blood circulatory system. Among the functions of lymph are transporting nutrients to the cells and removing waste and bacteria. The lymph nodes are collection points for bacteria and other harmful material that is thus kept from entering the bloodstream.

lynx *(links)*

Any of a group of wildcats with relatively long legs, a short, stubby tail, and tufted ears. Lynx fur, black-spotted and ranging from pale grayish buff to tawny, is highly prized. The American lynxes are found throughout Canada, the U.S., and northern Mexico, and include the bobcats.

Lyon or Lyons *(lee-OHN)*

The third largest city in France (the second being Marseilles). Famous for its textiles, Lyon is an industrial center of more than half a million people, situated at the confluence of the Saône (q.v.) and Rhone (q.v.) rivers. The city is famed as a capital of gastronomy. The local talent for cooking with onions has made the designation lyonnaise recognizable throughout the world as meaning "cooked with onions."

lyre *(liehr)*

A stringed harplike instrument, such as those played in ancient Greece to accompany lyric (from lyre) poetry or storytelling. The Greek lyre had a hollow body, two curving arms joined to the body and to a crossbar above it, and gut strings stretched from the crossbar to the bridge. The strings were plucked. In crosswords, often clued as "Orpheus's instrument" or "Erato's instrument"— Erato (q.v.) being the muse of lyric poetry.

Fred Astaire and Gene Kelly strum lyres in Ziegfeld Follies, 1946.

Lys *(leess)* or Leie *(LEE-eh)*

A 120-mile river rising in northern France and flowing northeast, partly along the border with Belgium, to join the Scheldt River at Ghent. Its valley saw heavy fighting in World War I.

Maas See *Meuse.*

Maat *(muh-AHT; MAH-uht)* The ancient Egyptian goddess of truth, justice, and law.

The daughter of Ra, the sun god, she wears a feather in her headband and is often herself symbolized by a feather (appearing in one pan of a weighing scale, with a heart appearing in the other).

A relief-carving of Maat.

Mab *(mab)* Queen Mab, the fairy queen and midwife who delivers men of their dreams. She has been immortalized both by Shakespeare's famous description of her in *Romeo and Juliet* (I:4) and by Shelley in his poem named for her.

Maba *(MAH-bah)* A mixed Negroid people of Chad (q.v.) who established the powerful sultanate of Wadai (q.v.) in the sixteenth century.

Macao or **Macau** *(mah-KAH-owe; muh-COW)* A minuscule (six-square-mile) Portuguese overseas province, on a peninsula and small island near Hong Kong, on the Canton (Pearl) River estuary. It is a free port. **Macao** is also the gutsy version of blackjack they play there: each player is dealt one card, and the target number is 9 instead of 21.

macaw *(mah-KAW)* Any of the numerous brilliantly plumed but harsh-sounding parrots of South and Central America chiefly belonging to the genus *Ara* (q.v.). Macaws are among the largest of all parrots. They have very long tails and strong, hooked bills for cracking hard nuts. Usual color combinations are blue-and-yellow, red-and-blue, and red-and-green.

A blue and yellow macaw.

Madoc *(MAD-ohk)* or **Madog** *(MAH-dog)* The legendary Welsh prince who was said (by people aware of Columbus's later voyages but unaware of Leif Ericson's earlier one in the year 1000) to have discovered America in the twelfth century. There is no evidence to prove this contention, other than tales of those who claimed to have found Welsh-speaking Indians.

Magi *(MAH-jie)* The Magi, or "three kings of Orient," or Wise Men of the East, who visited the infant Jesus in the manger. They were actually members of the Persian priestly caste, practicing a religion believed to be very similar to Zoroastrianism but including belief in the advent of a savior. Their names were Caspar (or Gaspar), Melchior, and Balthazar, and their gifts were gold, frankincense, and myrrh (q.v.). The singular of magi is magus *(MAY-gus)*, the old word for "magician."

"And, lo, the star, which they saw in the east . . . "

magma *(MAG-mah)* The molten rock material, mixed with gases, within the earth. Magma erupts as lava from a volcano and forms igneous rock when it cools off. It can also be any thin, pasty mixture of mineral or organic matter that resembles molten rock, or, in pharmacy, a suspension of precipitated matter in a watery substance.

Mahdi *(MAH-dee)* Among Muslims, the Mahdi (Arabic for "divinely guided") is the last imam (q.v.), or leader of the faithful to salvation. The two great divisions of Islam (Sunnite and Shiite) differ over whether he has or is yet to come. The title has been taken by certain leaders of Muslim sects who have taken a messianic role, notably Mohammed Ahmed, who captured Khartoum in 1885.

Mahri *(MAH-ree)* An inhabitant of the region of Mahra *(MAH-rah)* in southeastern Arabia, in South Yemen (see *Aden*). It is also the language they speak there.

Maia *(MAH-yah)* Two distinct characters from classical mythology, often mistaken for one. The Greek Maia was a mountain nymph of Arcadia, the daughter of Atlas, and thus one of the Pleiades, and the mother, by Zeus (q.v.), of Hermes. The Roman goddess Maia, for whom the month of May was named and to whom May Day was originally dedicated, was the consort of

Vulcan and was an earth and fertility deity. A star in the Pleiades constellation and a genus of spider crabs have been named for them. A **maia** is also a silkworm moth.

Maia is on the right.

maja *(MAH-ha)* A Spanish belle of the lower classes. Francisco Goya (q.v.) painted two nearly identical portraits of such a woman, depicting her clothed in one and naked in the other; many have believed that the Duchess of Alba (q.v.) was the model. When Spanish postal authorities issued a stamp representing the more celebrated (naked) one, parents of stamp-collecting children protested the choice.

mako *(MAH-koe)* In New Zealand, a cosmopolitan shark, a tree, and a bird. The shark *(Isurus glaucus),* a rather large (to half a ton) blue creature with a pointed

snout, is sometimes called the blue pointer and is found in both Atlantic and Pacific waters, where it is sought as a gamefish and, recently, as a delicious food fish. The tree *(Aristotelia racemosa)* is also called makomako and wineberry, and yields

A bellbird, or mako.

berries from which a local wine is made. And the bird *(Anthornis melanura)*, whose notes are likened to the sound of a bell, is sometimes called the bellbird. Thus the three are rarely confused.

mala See *malum*.

Malawi See *Nyasa*.

Malay *(MAY-lay)* Among other things, the 700-mile-long peninsula constituting the southernmost extremity of Asia and comprising parts of Burma, Thailand, and Malaysia; the Malay Archipelago, the great islands group between Australia and Asia that was once called the East Indies; a member of the dominant brown race of the region (including parts of Indonesia and the Philippines); the language spoken in these places by these people; and a breed of fighting cock raised there by them.

Mali *(MAH-lee)* Until the old French Sudan became independent and changed its name to Mali in 1960, the word was defined as "an Indian gardener." Now Mali is frequently clued as "where Timbuktu is"; the capital of the country is Bamako, a bit higher up on the Niger River than its more famous sister outpost.

Malta *(MAWL-tah)* A group of three small islands (Malta, Gozo, and Comino) in the Mediterranean southwest of Sicily, conquered and occupied at different times by just about everyone from North Africa to Great Britain, and now an independent nation with Commonwealth membership. The capital is Valletta, the official languages are English and Maltese, plus, unofficially, Italian, and the leading claims to fame are the local breeds of dog, cat, and crusading knight, all called Maltese. Malta can also claim the award to the entire populace of the George Cross for bravery during heavy German bombing in World War II occasioned by the presence of a major British naval base.

malum *(MAH-lum)* Latin for "bad," malum signifies any evil, wrong, or offense against right or law. The legal phrases *malum in se* and *malum prohibitum* cover the two basic types of wrongs: those that are offenses against natural (unwritten) law, and those that break a manmade (written) statute.

Malus *(MAH-luss)* Latin again, this time for "apple." *Malus* designates the genus of all apple trees and many related trees and shrubs, as well as a southern constellation in the shape of a ship's mast.

Paris awarding the apple to Aphrodite, from a painting by Joachim Wtewael.

mamba *(MAHM-bah)* The most dreaded of African snakes, rivaled in the world only by the krait (q.v.). Lightning-fast, aggressive, and highly poisonous bit-ers, mambas, which belong to the cobra family, come in up to 14-foot lengths of black or green slitheriness. Look for the black mamba in the bush, the green mamba in trees. Unlike tarantulas, whose venomous nip reputedly can be remedied by dancing the tarantella, mambas have no dance associated with their bite.

mambo *(MAHM-boh)* A dance, unrelated to the previous entry, adapted from those originally performed in Haiti by voodoo priestesses and eventually, in syncopated 4/4 time, by everyone throughout Latin America. A mambo craze hit the U.S. around 1957, shortly before a major cha-cha craze.

mamo *(MAH-moh)* An extinct Hawaiian bird *(Drepanis pacifica)* whose few tiny golden-yellow feathers relieving otherwise black plumage were used in the cloaks, also called mamos, of now equally extinct Hawaiian royalty. Mamos, along with dodos (q.v.) and moas (q.v.), are the Big Three of extinct birds who have survived in crossword puzzles.

mana *(MAH-nah)* Not to be confused with manas (q.v.) or manna (q.v.), mana is the originally Melanesian metaphysical spirit present in all creation, and responsible for good and evil.

manas *(MAHN-ass)* In Buddhism, the mind of man, which, together with buddhi, the soul or discernment, and atman (q.v.), the life principle, self, or individual essence, constitutes the trinity of elements making up the immortal being of man.

manes *(MAH-nees)* In Roman religion, the spirits of individuals after death. Because they were feared, the Romans placatingly called them the "good gods" *(di manes)*. In time they were considered to be ancestral spirits who were concerned with the family's welfare. Lower-cased, the word is more frequently clued as the plural of lion's or horse's hair.

Manet *(mah-NAY)* Edouard Manet

(1832–1883), the French Impressionist painter, must of course never be confused with Claude Monet *(moh-NAY)* (1840–1926), the French Impressionist painter, or the entry crossing the second letter of the surname will be wrong. Monet generally painted landscapes; Manet, people.

Some sketches of Manet by Edgar Degas.

mango *(MANG-oh)* An oval or pear-shaped tropical fruit with a lovely yellowish-red (sometimes greenish) exterior and ambrosial interior. Eating ripe mangoes in large quantities has been reported by a Harvard pharmacologist to get you "high."

Manito or Manitou *(MAN-ih-toe;*

MAN-ih-too) Among the Algonquian Indians, the power or spirit which pervades all things. The resemblance of Manito to Melanesian mana (q.v.), Buddhist manas (q.v.), and Roman manes (q.v.) is no small coincidence.

Mann *(man; mahn)* The American educator Horace Mann (1796–1859), who improved public schools; Congressman James Robert Mann (1856–1922), author of the Mann Act, which prohibited the transportation of women across state lines for immoral purposes; and German-born novelist Thomas Mann (1875–1955), who won the Nobel Prize in literature in 1929, on the strength of, among other works, *Buddenbrooks* (1901) and *The Magic Mountain* (1924). Thomas's literary brother Heinrich (1871–1950) is better known in Europe than in the U.S.

Thomas Mann.

manna *(MAN-ah)* The divine food which miraculously rained on the Israelites in their journey through the wilderness, when they most needed it. No wonder the word can refer to physical and spiritual food alike. On the physical side, the biblical manna has been conjectured to be the exudate of the tamarix shrub, a kind of lichen, or secretions of insects feeding on plant leaves.

The Israelites gathering manna, from a woodcut by Hans Holbein the Younger.

mantis *(MAN-tiss)* A family (the mantids) of remarkably grotesque insects whose front legs suggest arms folded in prayer. The mantis, whose name is Greek for "prophet," preys upon other insects and so is a great help to man. Their greatest predator is the female praying mantis, who often eats the male alive after mating.

Manu *(MAHN-oo)* One of a series of Hindu authors of human wisdoms, the seventh and most recent of whom lived around the time of Christ and wrote the Laws (or Code) of Manu, which discusses the creation of the world, the state of the soul after death, and everything one needs to know about social and religious duty. It is the "Bible" of Hindu law.

Manx *(manks)* This adjective describes a person or thing that comes from the Isle of Man, an island in the Irish Sea off the northwestern coast of England. The most famous things called by this name are the essentially tailless Manx cats and the form of Goidelic (see *Celt*) that is still spoken by some Manxmen. Man is a dependency of the Crown, but is not subject to British law. It has one of the world's oldest legislative bodies, the Tynwald.

Maori *(MAH-oh-ree; MAHW-ree)* An aborigine of New Zealand, believed to be of Polynesian blood, speaking a language related to several Pacific Island tongues. The Maoris, formerly fearsome cannibals, are still tall, dark, and handsome warrior types. They are skilled at woodcarving, tattooing, and telling their poetic nature myths. They are often clued as "Down-under natives."

Maoris performing in native costume.

marl *(marl)* A type of crumbly soil usually consisting of clay plus limestone or shell, valued as natural top-dressing (or fertilizer) for lime-starved soils. It is also called bog lime. Other and less useful kinds of marl involve mixtures of clay and sand.

maru *(MAH-roo)* A suffix appended to the names of Japanese ships, and sometimes to the names of men and boys. A previous variant spelling was -maro. Thus the gender of Japanese ships, unlike those of most other nations, would appear to be masculine.

Masai *(MAH-sie)* The mixed Hamitic and Negroid people living east of Lake Victoria in Kenya (q.v.) and Tanzania, who are excellent herdsmen, hunters, and warriors, thanks possibly to their staple beverage consisting of equal portions of cow's blood and milk.

A Masai tribesman.

masse *(mah-SAY)* A difficult pool and billiard shot in which the cue stick strokes the cue ball straight downward on one side, causing it to take on so much English as to skip around an obstructing object ball. The massé is the shot that rips up the felt on the pool table. Also in crosswords: "en _____": all together.

Maui *(MAH-oo-ee; MAO-wee)* The chief culture hero of the Polynesian race, Maui is credited with snaring the sun, controlling the winds, bringing fire to man, and fishing up lands from the sea, probably including the 728 square miles of the island that bears his name, the second largest in Hawaii.

maw *(maw)* A generalized body-part word, usually thought of as the stomach alone, but also including at times the throat, the gullet, the craw or crop, and the jaws. The word seems to belong to the paw-jaw-craw-maw family, whose job is the transformation of food. The basic idea behind maw is the receptacle into which food is taken by swallowing; thus, symbolically, the maw is the seat of voracious appetite. Usually in crosswords, maw is simply clued "gullet," or, humorously, "Paw's wife."

Mawsil See *Mosul.*

Mayo *(MAY-oh)* A famous county in northwestern Ireland located in Connaught province and bordering on the Atlantic Ocean. Castlebar is the county seat of this 2,082-square-mile region, which is not where mayonnaise comes from. Also the **Mayo** brothers (Dr. Charles H. Mayo, 1865–1939; Dr. William J. Mayo, 1861–1939) and their famous Mayo clinic in Rochester, Minnesota; actress Virginia Mayo (1922–   ); and, lower-cased the shortened form of mayonnaise, sometimes clued as "short-order word."

Lough Beltra on the coast of County Mayo, Republic of Ireland.

mead *(meed)* A drink of honey fermented with water, yeast, and sometimes other ingredients. Another name for mead is metheglin. Mead is of great antiquity and is frequently mentioned in medieval poetry. Other **Meads**: anthropologist Margaret Mead (1901–1978); Lake Mead, formed by Hoover Dam in the Colorado River; and, lower-cased, the poetic form of meadow.

mease *(meez; maze)* A Scottish-English dialectical unit for counting fish. It usually signifies 500 fish, or the number that can fit in a standard herring box, but there is also a smaller unit for counting fish called the hundred, and since the hundred can vary between 100 and 124 fish, depending on local custom and whim, a mease can at times amount to as many as 620 fish.

Mecca *(MEK-ah)* Non-Muslims are banned from this Saudi Arabian city in the Hejaz (q.v.). Its major shrine is the Kaaba (q.v.), the holiest spot in Islam, to which all

Muslims turn in prayer five times a day and to ' which they attempt a pilgrimage (see *hadji*) at least once in their lifetime. Thus, by logical extension, a mecca is any desirable goal or gathering place. Mohammed was born in Mecca in A.D. 570, and fled in 622 (the Hejira, q.v.), which became the first year of the Muslim era.

mecon *(MEE-kon)* From the Greek word for "poppy," mecon is a poppy-based drug, most probably opium, used and prescribed by Hippocrates, the father of Western medicine. Active components of opium include meconin, meconic acid, and meconinic acid, though doctors are not prescribing it.

An opium poppy.

Mede *(meed)* One of the people of the ancient kingdom of Media (named after Medea [q.v.] and located in what is now western Iran and southern Azerbaijan), which was at the height of its power in the seventh and sixth centuries B.C. The Medes ruled over greater Persia until overthrown in 550 B.C. by Cyrus the Great. Herodotus visited and wrote about these folks, who were later to become a part of Alexander's empire.

A Median nobleman.

Medea *(meh-DEE-ah)* Heroine of tragedies by Euripides and Seneca, Medea was the vengeful enchantress who helped her lover Jason (q.v.) obtain the Golden Fleece. She was also responsible, by various means, for the deaths of her brother, her children by Jason, and her successor in Jason's affections. This accomplished, she made her way to Athens, where she married the king.

Medoc *(may-DOK)* A famous wine district of southwestern France, not far north of Bordeaux. The best red wines of Médoc bear the names of such estates (or châteaux) as Châteaux Lafite, Châteaux Latour, and Châteaux Margaux.

meed *(meed)* A poetic term for a reward, not necessarily in money, bestowed for merit. Originally a meed was a wage, any payment for labor or service. It can also mean a portion, or a share.

Victor McLaglen in The Informer.

Memel *(MAY-mel)* Former name of the Lithuanian Baltic seaport now called Klaypeda or Klaipeda, and located on a large lagoon at the mouth of the Neman or Memel River. An ancient place, it has had many changes of nationality: before World War I and during World War II it was a part, with the rest of Lithuania, of Germany; between the wars an autonomous territory; and afterward a part of the U.S.S.R. The river runs almost 600 miles from near Minsk in the U.S.S.R. and is called the Russ for its last 22 miles. It is the site of a meeting between Napoleon and Tzar Alexander I which resulted in the Treaty of Tilsit (1807). The meeting took place on a raft in the middle of the river.

mene *(MEH-nee)* Mene, as in *"Mene, mene, tekel, upharsin,"* the famous handwriting on the wall appearing miraculously at Belshazzar's feast (Daniel 5:25). Upon consultation, Daniel interpreted these Aramaic words, literally "It has been counted and counted, weighed and divided," to foretell the destruction of Belshazzar and his kingdom. For this information, which was proven correct, Daniel was rewarded with a purple cape and gold necklace.

Mensa *(MEN-sah)* A worldwide organization of people with high IQs, founded in the 1940s with the aim of ending all wars, and now devoted to socializing and game-playing. Other **mensae** (pl.) include the top of the altar in a Roman Catholic church, the grinding surface of a tooth, and a southern constellation also called the Table—which is what *mensa* means.

merle *(murl)* The bluish-gray color that occurs in the coats of certain dogs such as the blue merle collie of Scotland and the Australian cattle dog (or blue heeler). The latter, a cross between the former and a wild dingo (q.v.), has a red face and a two-tone (dark and light blue) speckled body. With or without the final *e*, **merle** is also a blackbird.

mero *(MEY-roh)* The common name, especially in Spanish-speaking lands, for any of several large temperate and tropical groupers in the sea bass family and including the guasa (q.v.), the red grouper, and the rock hind. The largest mero is the black grouper, or giant sea bass, or jewfish, which can weigh up to 700 pounds.

Meroe *(MER-owe-ee)* An ancient Egyptian city on the upper Nile, now located in the Sudan. Meroë was the capital of the Cushite kingdom from the sixth to the fourth century B.C. The city was famous for iron smelting. Today, many ruins remain.

Mersin See *Icel.*

Meru *(MEY-roo)* In Hindu mythology, the fabled mountain where the gods dwell. This is the same idea as the Greek Mount Olympus, except that the latter is an actual geographic place, whereas Meru has not been identified with any place found on a map. There is, however, a Mount Meru, 14,979 feet high, west of Kilimanjaro in Tanzania, which is no relation.

Mesa *(MEY-sah)* A city of south-central Arizona, now virtually a suburb of Phoenix, named for the tablelike rock formations (mesas) throughout the region. A beneficiary of the Sun Belt boom, Mesa more or less doubled in population between 1950–1960 and 1960–1970.

mesne *(meen)* A descriptive for any middleman or intermediary, particularly a medieval lord (mesne lord) who held the land of and was tenant to a superior lord while himself acting as a landlord to his own tenants on the same land. In law, mesne means "middle" or "intervening."

meta *(MEE-tah)* One of the two posts (plural: metae) that marked the turning place or goal in a Roman chariot race. The familiar hippodrome shape of racetracks is an outgrowth of the practice of holding these races on a single long straightaway with wide turning areas at either end and two lanes of traffic flow. **Meta** is also a prefix meaning "beyond," as in the word metaphysics, and is often in crosswords as two words, e.g., "I ____ man with seven wives."

Rounding a meta.

mete *(meet)* To measure or measure out or allot a portion, usually but not necessarily of grain, punishment, or reward. In technical usage, this involves finding the desired quantity, dimensions, or capacity by applying a rule or standard to a specific case.

Meting out a portion.

metic *(MET-ik)* In ancient Greek city-states, any settler or immigrant from another region. The equivalent of a resident alien in the U.S., a metic did not carry a green card and—in Athens, at least—was accorded certain civil privileges, including the right to own land and pay taxes.

metis *(meh-TEES)* This originally French word for "mixed," akin to the Spanish *mestizo,* indicates a person of mixed blood, particularly one with one French and one Indian parent. Metis is masculine, metisse feminine. Exact mixture varies, depending on location, from 50–50 French-English in Canada to 87½–12½ white-black in Louisiana (a situation which occurs when a mostly white person has one black great-grandparent).

Meuse *(muhz; myooz)* An important river of western Europe, flowing from northeastern France to the North Sea via Belgium and the Netherlands. Verdun, Sedan, and Liège are the best-known cities along its 575-mile course. The valley of the Meuse has been a battleground of several wars. The homestretch portion of the Meuse in Holland is known by its Dutch and Flemish name, Maas. There is also a department of France called **Meuse.** It is in Lorraine, bordering on Belgium.

mho *(moh)* A unit of electrical conductance equal to the reciprocal of an ohm (q.v.), which is itself a unit of electrical resistance. The word mho is somewhat unusual in that it was coined by spelling ohm backwards. This actually makes sense because conductance and resistance are the two sides of the electrical coin, conceptually speaking.

mica *(MIE-kah)* Mineralogically speaking, any of a group of crystalline silicates varying widely in composition and color (brown, yellow, violet, green, black, colorless, etc.). Mica is the lustrous, leafy, or sheetlike formation in many igneous and metamorphic rocks. It splits easily into very thin sheets. Its transparent form, also known as isinglass, was once used in lantern covers and window shades.

Micah *(MIE-kah)* A minor Hebrew prophet of the eighth century B.C. who wrote the Old Testament book of Micah, telling of the impending judgment on Israel and Judah, and holding forth hope of the coming of the Messiah. It was Micah who said, "and they shall beat their swords into plowshares, and their spears into pruning hooks" (4:3).

Micah exhorts the Israelites.

Midas *(MIE-dahss)* The mythological king of Phrygia whom the god Dionysus promised to grant any (one) thing he might wish. Midas asked that everything he touched turn to gold. This proved inconvenient around mealtime and in general, so Midas asked Dionysus if he mightn't be released from this folly. Dionysus instructed him to bathe in the River Pactolus, which did the trick and whose sands are golden to this day. An actual Midas reigned in Phrygia in the eighth century B.C.

middy *(MID-ee)* Short for midshipman, the rank just below commissioned officer in the U.S. Navy, comprising all the students of the U.S. Naval Academy at Annapolis as well as graduates doing duty elsewhere but not yet promoted to the grade of ensign. Middies have no prerogatives as officers until they complete their training and are formally commissioned. A **middy** is also a loose overblouse for women and children, with a sailor collar.

A pictographic record of songs used in a midewin ceremony of the Chippewa Indians. These inscriptions are on the lid of a feather box.

mide *(MEE-deh)* Short for midewiwin or midewin, a secret religious society of the Chippewa (Ojibwa) and related Indians. Its purpose was to prolong life by means of herbal substances and magic.

midi *(mee-DEE)* A French word meaning "noon" (viz. "mid-day") and, by logical extension, the south (since that's where the sun is at noon in most French-speaking countries). Thus **Midi,** capitalized, has come to be used as the common word for the South of France.

mil *(mill)* An invariably small measure of a number of disparate things: the thousandth part of an inch (0.0254 mm), when measuring the thickness of wires or sheet plastic; the thousandth part of the radius of a circle, when measuring the chord (straight line connecting the ends) of an arc of that circle; and the thousandth part of an English pound in British-occupied Palestine.

mille *(MILL-eh)* The Latin word for "thousand" and, with *passuum* sometimes added, for "mile." Because Roman legionnaires kept track of distance by counting off in thousands of paces, this word with slight variations has come to mean mile in most European languages. The pace referred to is actually a double step. Since the Romans were generally smaller than the Britons, the Roman mile was about eight percent shorter than the English statute mile used to this day in the U.S. As a proper noun, **Mille** appears in crosswords as "Agnes or Cecil B. de _____."

milo *(MIE-low)* Any of several grain sorghums (also called milo maize) used primarily for stock feed. Milo is closely related to the other cruciverbal sorghum, durra (q.v.), which differs mainly in that it is more palatable to humans. **Milo** or Milos is also a Greek island of the Cyclades group in the Aegean, where the famed statue of Venus was found.

milt *(milt)* The male reproductive secretion of fish or the glands that produce this generally milky fluid. When a male uses his milt to fertilize a female's roe (q.v.), he is for the nonce called a milt fish, the piscine equivalent of a stud animal. The verb for doing this is "to milt."

mime *(mime)* An ancient form of silent drama that still survives, and has been popularized by the talented Marcel Marceau. Its enactors convey motions and emotions by exaggerated, stylized gestures and facial expressions. Mime, which means pantomime and vice versa, has been known in many cultures since dimmest antiquity. It is frequently clued as "copy" or "ape."

Marcel Marceau.

Mimir or **Mimer** *(MEE-mer)* A giant of Norse mythology who lives by the well of wisdom, one of the three springs issuing from the roots of the world tree (Yggdrasill), whose branches and roots embrace the universe. Because he drinks its waters, he knows everything, past, present, and future.

mina *(MY-nah)* or **maneh** *(MAHN-eh)* A biblical, classical, and modern weight and unit of money. The mina was originally one-sixtieth of a talent and was itself divisible into 60 parts called shekels (except when measuring precious metals, in which case 50 shekels was enough to make a mina). In ancient Greece the mina was equivalent to 100 drachmae, and as a modern weight it equals, oddly, not a bit more than 999 grams. Its plural can be minas or minae. **Mina** is also a variant spelling for myna (q.v.).

Ming *(ming)* A dynasty of China from A.D. 1368 to 1644, following the Mongol Yuan dynasty. The Ming period was outstanding for painting, porcelain, and tex-

tiles. It was during this period that the capital of China was moved from Nanking to Peking and foreign settlements at seaports were permitted. The Ming period ended with the Manchu conquest; the Manchu dynasty is of recent memory, having ended in 1912.

An early Ming jardinière.

Minie *(MEE-nee-ay)* Captain Claude Étienne Minié (1814–1879), the French inventor who developed the Minié rifle for delivering his highly effective minié-ball (actually a conical bullet). The ball came to be known familiarly to soldiers as the mini-ball, and it was one of the major reasons for the unexpected bloodshed of the American Civil War.

minim *(MIN-im)* Anything minute, and in general the smallest possible particle of anything. A few specialized uses include the name for the smallest liquid apothecaries' measure (equal, on both sides of the Atlantic, to one-sixtieth of a fluid dram [q.v.]), the smallest downstroke in penmanship, the smallest variety of worker in certain ant-

hills, and—formerly but no longer—the shortest musical note, nowadays equivalent to the not-so-short half note.

Minos *(MIE-nohss)* The eponymous king (or kings) of Crete whose name has been assigned to the wealthy Minoan civilization of Crete and mainland Greece. Famous in mythology is Minos II, the son of Zeus and Europa, the husband of Pasiphaë (who gave birth to the Minotaur after becoming enamored of a bull at Poseidon's instigation). The legendary king was also the father of Ariadne (the eventual wife of Dionysus), and the builder of the labyrinth that sheltered the Minotaur, which was successfully negotiated by Theseus.

Minot *(MIE-not)* A small city in northwestern North Dakota, on the Souris River about 100 miles north of Bismarck. It is the county seat of Ward County.

Minsk *(minsk)* A major city of the Soviet Union, located near the Polish border some 400 miles southwest of Moscow. Minsk is the capital of the White Russian (Belorussian) S.S.R., and with a population of nearly a million is a good deal larger than Pinsk (q.v.), Omsk (q.v.), Lutsk, and Slutsk all rolled into one.

Miro *(mee-ROE)* Joan Miró, the (male) Spanish surrealist painter and sculptor born in 1893. Lower-cased and without the accent (and pronounced *MEE-roe*), either a New Zealand timber tree *(Podocarpus ferruginea)* or the sometimes pure white wood robin living in it.

mise *(meez)* Among numerous other technical-legal senses, the name for two formal declarations concluding hostilities between Henry III and his rebellious barons, one at Amiens in 1264, the other at Lewes (q.v.); each is accordingly so named. As a verb (and pronounced *mize*), it means to do what a miser does. Commonly in crosswords: ''_____ en scene'' (the staging of a play).

miter or **mitre** *(MIE-tur)* The liturgical headdress worn by bishops, abbots, the pope, and others. The conoidal top found on standard chess bishops illustrates this shape. Originally miters were simple round caps but they grew larger and pointier with clerical ambitions through the centuries. As a headdress, a miter is also an ancient Greek women's headband, and

the official headdress of ancient Hebrew high priests. In carpentry it is a tight right-angle joint, four examples of which can be seen in the diagonal corners of most wooden picture frames.

St. Augustine wearing a miter.

mitra *(MIE-tra)* From the Latin word for "miter" (q.v.), this term has been borrowed by science at least twice for designating things that look like a bishop's hat. So it is that the thick, rounded cap of certain mushrooms and a whole genus of East Indian marine snails whose bodies look like miters have the same name.

Mitu *(MIE-too)* or **Mitua** *(MIE-too-ah)* The scientific name for a major genus of the curassow, a large bird of South and Central America sometimes called the guan (q.v.). This bird takes its common name from a spelling-by-ear of the island of Curaçao off the Venezuela coast. It is a large, henlike arboreal creature, easy to tame but hard to breed in captivity.

Mizar *(MIE-zar)* The middle star of the three that make up the handle of the Big Dipper. Mizar actually consists of two stars, one of them invisible to the naked eye, and a third star called Alcor can sometimes be seen in close proximity to it. Their back-to-back relationship is observed in their names: Mizar means "the veil"; Alcor, "the weak one."

mneme *(NEE-mee)* From the Greek word for "memory" and "mind," mneme is the collective effect of the past experience of the individual or of a race persisting or recurring in present and future time. It is the approximate equivalent of what is today called the collective unconscious.

moa *(MOH-ah)* The Maori (q.v.) name of a whole family of large-to-huge (turkey-size to 12 feet tall) flightless birds of New Zealand that have not been seen there or anywhere else in over 500 years. They were frequently hunted for the cooking pot, but the exact cause of their extinction is unknown.

Moab *(MOE-ab)* The land east of the Dead Sea where dwelt the Moabites, an ancient Semitic people closely allied to the Hebrews and mentioned in many books of the Bible. In Moab was found the Moabite Stone, upon which, in Phoenician characters, is a war record confirming certain details of the Scriptures.

Mocha *(MOE-kah)* or **Mukha** *(moo-KAH)* A South Yemeni town on the Red Sea whose name is today familiar mainly in culinary contexts to indicate use of the flavors coffee and chocolate together.

Modoc *(MOE-dok)* The name of a small but determined tribe of Indians originally dwelling in the volcanic region surrounding Mt. Lassen in northern California and in nearby southern Oregon. They were forcibly relocated after the messy

Two Modoc Indians.

Modoc Wars of the 1870s to reservations in Oregon and Oklahoma. They are related to the Klamath Indians with whom they now share a reservation in Oregon.

mogul *(MOE-gull)*   This word indicates a nice variety of things ranging from a small mound on a ski slope best avoided by novices, to a very rich or powerful person, to a playing card of superior make, to a kind of heavy steam locomotive. With a capital *M,* it is a person of the Mongolian race, and particularly and originally, one of the sixteenth-century Muslim conquerors of much of India, where the Mogul (or Moghul) dynasty lasted from 1526 to 1857, when the British took over.

A mogul of the Atchison, Topeka, and Santa Fe Railway.

mohel *(moil)*   The man who circumcises Jewish male infants in the ritual called a briss. The ceremony, which fulfills an ancient covenant with Yahweh, is usually conducted during the first week or two of the child's life.

A mohel holding a child in an 18th-century representation of a briss.

moho *(MOE-ho)*   The name for two groups of birds, one of them extinct. The still-living moho resides in Hawaii, where its yellow breast feathers used to adorn the royal robes (see *mamo*). The has-been was a small flightless rail, also of Hawaii.

mohr *(mohr)*   A North African gazelle with short hooked horns on which are about a dozen prominent rings. In addition, the mohr's alimentary canal can contain a substance (bezoar) which was formerly believed to possess medicinal qualities, especially in the counteraction of poisons.

Mohs *(mohss; mohz)*   The German mineralogist Friedrich Mohs (1773–1839), father of the Ten Scale. Mohs's scale was not concerned with feminine beauty, but rather with the hardness of minerals, as determined by their capacity to scratch one another. Mohs's original number values were as follows: diamond (10—the hardest), sapphire (9), topaz (8), quartz (7), feldspar (6), apatite (5), fluorite (4), calcite (3), gypsum (2), and talc (1—the softest).

Moira *(MOY-rah)*   In early Greek religion, the allotted fate of an individual, and the divine power determining that fate. In later times Moira became the three Moirai (pl.) sisters (better known as the Fates): Clotho the spinner of the thread of life, Lachesis the disposer of lots and determiner of the thread's length, and Atropos the implacable, who cuts the thread at death. In Roman mythology, they were the Parcae: Nona, Decuma, and Morta. Crosswords often mention dancer **Moira Shearer.**

Anton Walbrook, Léonide Massine, and Moira Shearer in The Red Shoes, *1948.*

moire *(mwah-RAY)*   A fabric, especially silk, having a watered, or wavy, pattern. It also means such a pattern in fur (as Persian lamb), or a ripple pattern produced on a stamp as a protection against forgery, or the moiré effect that is produced in printing by intentionally or, more usually, unintentionally, superimposing a repetitive pattern (such as the dot-structure in a halftone engraving) on the same or a different pattern.

molt or **moult** *(mohlt)*   To shed or cast off a (usually superficial) part of the body. Mammals generally shed their hair (once a year); deer and related ruminants shed their horns annually, birds their feathers (up to thrice annually), reptiles their skins, crustaceans their entire exoskeletons and even some interior parts; insect larvae shed their whole outer casement many times en route to adulthood.

Monet See *Manet.*

mono *(MOH-noe)*   The Spanish word for "monkey," mono also refers specifically to a

black howler monkey of Central America *(Alouatta villosa),* any of a group of Shoshonean Indians of inland southern California, and a county and lake of northern California not far east of Yosemite. **Mono** is also a prefix meaning "one," as in monogamy, monologue, etc.

Mono Indian.

Montt *(mohnt)*   Puerto Montt in south-central Chile is the end of the road, the southern terminus of the Pan American Highway and the entire Western Hemisphere road network. It was not until around 1980, when the pesky Darien Gap of Panama was finally bridged for a roadway, that you could finally drive to Puerto Montt nonstop from Circle, Alaska, the northern terminus.

GLAD RAGS

	jupon
aba	*Levi's*
baku	*mamo*
boa	*middy*
chiton	*obi*
chukka	*parka*
coif	*polo shirt*
curch	*purdah*
derby	*sabot*
dhoti	*sari*
dickey	*sark*
Eton	*simar*
jacket	*snood*
fez	*stola*
fichu	*tam*
gamp	*tiara*
gibus	*toga*
gillie	*toque*
grego	*tunic*
haik	*tuque*
ihram	*tutu*

moray *(maw-RAY; MOH-ray)* A voracious and savage eel with strong, knifelike teeth. Morays, often having bright coloration, are commonly found in the crevices of warm-water coral reefs. The moray that occasionally turns up in Continental restaurants under the name of murene is the Mediterranean variety. Others are not eaten. **Moray** is also a Scottish county (shire) on Moray Firth (see also *Firth*).

Moray eels are vicious, and can be dangerous to divers.

morel *(MAW-rehl)* A choice edible mushroom also often found in Continental restaurants, where it occurs in ragouts and sauces. Looking rather like a small sponge, it is so prized and also so rich in flavor that a good commercial ounce of it, dried, goes for several dollars.

Morchella esculenta.

Moro *(MOH-roh)* A member of any of the Muslim tribes who live in the Sulu (q.v.) Archipelago and on Mindanao Island in the extreme southern Philippines (see also *dato*). Their name, which means "Moor" (a North African) both in the Philippines and in Spain, attests to the enormous outreach of Muslim culture. The Moros, who are of mixed Malay (q.v.) and Arab stock, fought a bloody separatist rebellion in recent years, after which they received a few concessions.

Mosul *(moh-SOOL)* or **Mawsil** *(MAW-seel)* If a Kurdish national homeland were ever to be created, this old city across the Tigris from the ruins of Nineveh would likely be its capital. For now, it and its quarter-million inhabitants are residents of northern Iraq. The Kurds (q.v.) come down to Mosul from neighboring Kurdistan, which includes parts of five countries, to sell their famous Mosul rugs.

motet *(moe-TET)* A choral composition based upon both sacred and secular texts, sometimes mingled, and marked by polyphony (melodic independence of the various voices) but sung usually without instrumental accompaniment. The earliest forms, dating from around 1200, have a basis in part on plainsong. This connection is not as evident in later motets, such as those of J.S. Bach.

Mo-Ti *(moh-DEE)* or **Mo-Tzu** *(moh-DZEH)* A Chinese philosopher of the fifth and fourth centuries B.C., famous for his doctrine of love, which is called Moism. After the Burmese diplomat U Nu, Mo Ti is tied with the poet Li Po for second place for the shortest full moniker found in crosswords.

mufti *(MUFF-tee)* An ill-understood title in Muslim lands. A mufti is an official expounder of Muslim law who attends the law courts and assists the judges in their interpretations. In the Ottoman Empire, a mufti was a state official; in recent times the Grand Mufti in Jerusalem had an influential position. In British India **mufti** came to mean the garb of a naval or military officer when not in uniform.

Muir *(myoor)* John Muir (1838–1914), a Scottish-born American naturalist who spent much of his time in the American

West, is easy to remember because of the Muir Woods National Monument, an impressive grove of redwoods to the northwest of San Francisco, established and named for him in 1908.

John Muir.

mulla or **mul-lah** *(MULL-ah)* Not much different from mufti (q.v.), a mulla is a learned teacher and expounder of the law and dogmas of Islam. The best-known mulla is perhaps Mullah Nasrudin, a character of Middle Eastern folk tales who plays both the sage and the fool simultaneously.

A mullah is a teacher or expounder of Sacred Islamic law.

mumbo jumbo *(MUM-boh JUM-boh)* This phrase, now denoting meaningless incantation or activity, or an object of superstitious homage or fear, comes to us from several African peoples, including the Mandingos, for whom it was the village tutelary spirit. When portrayed ritually by a masked shaman, the mumbo jumbo wards off evil and keeps the women in awe and subjection.

mung *(mung)* or **mungo** *(MUNG-oh)* A bean of Asia growing in pods on the slender branches of a bushy annual legume. Mung beans are the chief source of the bean sprouts used in Chinese cookery, and in recent decades they have made their way into American health-food and grocery stores. In Asia the plants are used as livestock feed. **Mungo** is also the waste of milled wool used, with cotton, to make cheap cloth.

Mung beans amid noodles made from these legumes.

Muni *(MOO-nee)* Rio Muni was the minuscule (Maryland-sized) Spanish colony on the Gulf of Guinea surrounded on three sides by French Equatorial Africa. When it attained independence in 1968 and joined up with Bioko (formerly Fernando Po) and a few other offshore islands to become a police state, its name was changed to Republic of Equatorial Guinea despite the fact that the Equator entirely misses all of its land area. A frequent crossword name is that of Paul **Muni** *(MYOO-nee)* the actor.

Citizens of Rio Muni waiting to vote.

Munro *(mun-ROE)* H.H. (Hector Hugh) Munro (1870–1916) was a highly successful British author, mostly of short stories, whose name few people even knew because he wrote under the pseudonym Saki (q.v.). But Saki and Munro are equally famous in crosswords, since one is needed to clue the other.

Hector Hugh Munro, a.k.a. Saki.

Murex *(MYOO-reks)* The scientific as well as common name for at least four types of dual-purpose mollusks whose bodies yield a rich purple dye (the famous Tyrian purple) and whose shells can be used as trumpets. The creatures were especially

prized by the Romans, who required enormous amounts of the dye to do everything in imperial purple.

murre *(muhr)* The common name for three species of large sea birds. The North Atlantic razor-billed auk (q.v.) in black and white has a beak as sharp as it sounds; the North Atlantic group of guillemots includes the foolish, or common, guillemot; and the California murre is the Pacific species.

Mus *(muss)* The genus of the common house mouse *(Mus musculus)*. Its members can be identified by their square-notched incisor teeth, as distinct from the somewhat more beveled look of the related genus *Rattus*. Moreover, mice are rarely more than six inches long, including their tails, whereas rats are much bigger.

A family of common mice.

Musa *(MYOO-zah)* Another genus, this time that of the common banana. A banana grows on a tree, or actually a large herbaceous perennial, that was once native only to tropical Asia but is now found throughout the tropics. The plant has a soft stalk, actually the overlapping bases of the leaves, which are large enough to serve as umbrellas and which yield abaca (q.v.) fiber. The supermarket banana is one of hundreds of different, often bizarre types. *Musa* is also the genus of the plantains, which are cooked as a vegetable.

A banana plant. Clusters of bananas are called hands.

Musca *(MUSS-kah)* And finally—yes, another genus—the common housefly, a scavenger found in all habitable regions of the world. In warm climes, it is the most abundant and familiar creature found in human dwellings, where it is known to transmit such diseases as dysentery and typhoid fever. However, most flies found around the house are not true houseflies; many,

like the fruit fly and the blowfly, belong to other groups. **Musca** is also a constellation supposedly outlining a fly, in the southern heavens near the Southern Cross.

musk *(musk)* The secretion produced in an abdominal sac by a number of different male animals. That of the musk deer of Central Asia probably gets the most attention, for it is from this substance that many perfumes are made. When fresh, musk is chocolate-colored.

myna or **mynah** *(MIE-nah)* A common, shrill-voiced bird of southeastern Asia and most pet shops. Looking something like starlings, to which they are related, but larger and flashier, mynas are dark brown in color with a blackish white-tipped tail and white markings on their wings. They can be educated to speak imitatively; they are excellent mimics.

myrrh *(murr)* A brownish, aromatic, but bitter gum secreted by several African, Asian, and Arabian trees of the *Commiphora* genus, often called incense-trees. It was used in ancient times in incense, perfumes, and medicines. Myrrh was one of the gifts of the Magi (q.v.). It is still used today in dentifrices, tonics, and perfumes.

nabob *(NAY-bob)* A corruption of the Hindu *navab*, the title given provincial governors of the Indian Mogul empire. Their power enabled these officials to become extremely wealthy; hence, the term was later applied to any rich man, such as the hero of Alphonse Daudet's novel *The Nabob (Le Nabab)*, published in 1877.

nacre *(NAH-ker)* The hard, iridescent material found on the insides of the shells of various shellfish, such as the abalone and the pearl oyster. This material is also known as mother of pearl, and is used to create objets d'art, or in the manufacture of jewelry.

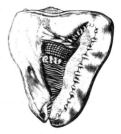

nadir *(NAY-der)* Derived from the Arabic *nazir*, as in *nazir-as-samt*, "opposite to the zenith." The nadir is the point directly under your feet or, by extension, any low point. As a proper noun, there was **Nadir** Shah of Iran (1688–1747), shah from 1736 to 1747, the last great Asian conqueror, who invaded India and sacked Delhi and Lahore, carrying off such treasures as the Koh-i-noor Diamond and the Peacock Throne. During the last of his many campaigns he was assassinated by his guards.

Nafud See *Nefud*.

Naga *(NAH-gah)* Also known as Nagaland, a wild, undeveloped state in northeastern India. A separate state since 1961, the region is mainly inhabited by the Naga, relatively primitive Tibeto-Burman tribesmen who worship rocks and trees, still practice headhunting, and have clashed with Indian troops in attempts to secure their independence.

Nahuath *(NAH-wath)* or **Nahua** *(NAH-wah)* Any member of a group of Mexican and Central American Indian tribes that speak Nahuatl, such as the Aztecs.

That ancient language is still spoken by more than 800,000 people in Mexico, although its Toltec variant is now extinct.

A Nahuath woman photographed c. 1900.

Nahum *(NAY-um)* A minor Hebrew prophet of the seventh century B.C., Nahum gives his name to an Old Testament book which prophesied the destruction of Nineveh, capital of the Assyrian empire. Nineveh did fall in 612 B.C., but scholars aren't sure whether the book was written before or after the event.

naiad *(NAY-ad)* In ancient Greek and Roman belief, any young, beautiful nymph who inhabited a spring, fountain, river, or lake and thus preserved its existence; or, by extension, any woman swimmer. The naiads, like other nymphs, were wont to engage in amorous dalliance with satyrs and gods. They are usually depicted seminude, bedecked with flowers, and bearing water urns. **Naiad** is also the term for the aquatic young of certain fly species, such as the mayfly; a genus *(Naias)* of aquatic plants; a freshwater mussel; and a felicitous homonym of long-distance swimmer Diana Nyad.

An amorous naiad.

Nairn *(nairn)* County seat of Nairnshire, a region of northeastern Scotland located where the Nairn River flows into Moray Firth. Because of its excellent harbor, Nairn has become a fishing center whose charm attracts summer tourists. In 1975, the town was officially designated part of the Highland region.

Nama *(NAH-mah)* The main tribal unit of the Hottentots, a black people native to southern Africa. Nama is also their language. This dialect of Hottentot is distinguished by its use of three vocal tones and nonvoiced clicking sounds.

Namur *(nah-MOOR)* or **Namen** *(nah-MEN)* City in south-central Belgium, located at the junction of the Meuse (q.v.) and Sambre rivers in Namur province. This strategic location was the original site of a Merovingian fortress, and has been fought over throughout history. It was part of the Meuse defense system at the start of World War I.

The citadel looms over the town of Namur in Belgium. The river is the Meuse.

Nana *(NAN-ah)* Either the titular heroine of the famous 1880 novel by Émile Zola (q.v.); the sheepdog who kept an eye on the children in Sir James Barrie's popular fantasy *Peter Pan* (1904); or an Indian leader of the Sepoy (q.v.) Rebellion known as Nana Sahib—adopted son of the last chief of the Mahrattas and instigator of a bloody massacre at the English colony of Cawnpore.

Nanna *(NAH-nah)* In Norse mythology, goddess of the spring flowers and wife of Balder (q.v.), god of light. When he was killed by the blind god Hodur (q.v.), Nanna immolated herself on his funeral pyre. Her name has thus become synonymous with fidelity and loyalty.

naos *(NAY-ahs)* The walled inner area of an ancient Greek temple, usually surrounded by colonnaded porticos. The naos also had a columned porch at its front and was usually where a statue of the temple deity stood. In Roman temples, this area was known as a cella.

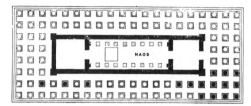

nape *(nape)*   From the Old English for "bowl," an area of the body resembling a small, hollowed-out bowl—the back of the neck just at the base of the skull. The scientific name for this area is *nucha,* a more appropriate word, at least in its derivation, which traces to the Arabic for "spinal marrow."

Nara *(NAH-rah)*   A city in Honshu, Japan. Nara is an ancient cultural and religious center, founded in A.D. 706, and it was the first permanent capital of Japan, 710–784. It is famous for its Todai-ji, a temple housing a 53½-foot-high statue of Buddha, and the Imperial Museum, with art treasures and relics. Nearby Mt. Kasuga is said to be the home of the gods, and its trees are never cut.

nard *(nard)*   Another name for spikenard, a costly aromatic ointment used by the ancients. It is believed to have been made from the dried roots of one of the several plants called spikenard, probably one belonging to the valerian family.

nares *(NAIR-eez)*   A word that has come into English directly from Latin. This is the scientific term for the paired openings of the nasal cavities—the anterior (front) and posterior (back) nares. The term also designates the nostrils. If a doctor wants to refer to one nostril, the correct term is naris.

José Ferrer, in the 1950 film Cyrano de Bergerac, *displays the famous lengthy nares.*

Nast *(nast)*   Thomas Nast (1840–1902), German-born American political cartoonist. Nast is remembered for his work as a staff artist at *Harper's Weekly.* His mordant depictions of Boss Tweed and Tammany as vultures probably played a big role in their fall. He created the elephant and donkey as symbols for the Republican and Democratic parties. Nast was named U.S. Consul to Ecuador in 1902. There is also Condé Nast, (1874–1942), founder of the conglomerate that publishes *Vogue, House & Garden,* and *Mademoiselle* magazines, among others.

A self-portrait of 19th-century cartoonist Thomas Nast.

Natal *(nah-TAHL)* Province of South Africa on the Indian Ocean, acquired by the British from Zulu chiefs in the early nineteenth century. Durban is the largest city. The capital is Pietermaritzburg. Also, a major port city in northeastern Brazil, near the mouth of the Potengi River. Natal is Portuguese for nativity—the Brazilian city was founded on Christmas Day, 1599.

Nauru *(nah-oo-roo)* A Pacific atoll west of the Gilbert Islands, and one of the world's smallest independent states, eight square miles in area. Discovered in 1798 by the British, Nauru was annexed by Germany in 1888, passed into Australian hands after World War I, was occupied by Japan during World War II, and achieved independence in 1968. Phosphate mining is the basis of the economy.

nave *(nave)* The main part of the interior of a church that extends from the entrance to the chancel, and is used exclusively by the laity. Architecturally, however, nave refers to the area between the side aisles and does not include them.

NAVE   NAVE
            ARCADE

Naxos *(NAK-sose)* Largest of the Cyclades Islands of Greece, famous for its olive oil, marble, and wine. In Greek mythology, Náxos is where Theseus deserted Ariadne, who thereupon accepted the consolation of Dionysus and married him. Náxos was originally colonized by Ionia, and has belonged to Persia, the kingdom of Venice, and Turkey. It has been Greek since 1829.

The doorway of the 6th century B.C. Temple of Apollo on the Greek island of Naxos.

neap *(neep)* Either the tongue of a wagon designed to be pulled by a pair of animals; or the tide at the first and third quarters of the moon. During these periods, tides are at their minimum range, so that even high tides seem low. The opposite of **neap** tide is spring tide. Flood (high) tide is the opposite of ebb (low) tide; in any given spot, flood changes to ebb every 6¼ hours.

neb *(neb)* From an Old English word, originally, the beak or bill of a bird. The meaning was eventually extended to include the various proboscises of animals, and then applied in picturesque references to the physiognomy of people, particularly those with long noses.

Nebo *(NEE-boe)* A 2,625-foot mountain in northern Jordan, near the northern end of the Dead Sea. Nebo was actually the summit of Mount Pisgah. In the Old Testament, it was to Mount Nebo that God sent Moses to see the Promised Land before his death (Deut. 32:49, 34:1).

Nefud or **Nafud** *(neh-FOOD)* A desert region about 180 by 140 miles in extent, in the northern Arabian peninsula. The Nefud is known for its red sand, as well as grotesque sandstone outcroppings and 500-foot crescent dunes shaped by sudden strong winds that strike this part of the world. Rain falls only once or twice a year.

Negev *(NEG-ev)* or **Negeb** *(NEG-eb)* Another desert area of the Mideast, this one comprising more than half the total area of Israel. An irrigation project that brings water from the Sea of Galilee has made the Negev arable, and kibbutzim are located there. The Negev saw heavy fighting during the Israeli-Egyptian conflicts. Its principal cities are Beersheba and Arad.

negus *(NEE-gus)* Either the eighteenth-century creation of one Colonel Francis Negus—a libation containing water, wine, lemon juice, sugar, and nutmeg, and served hot; or, as a proper noun, the title traditionally bestowed on the ruler of Ethiopia, from the Amharic meaning "king."

Neman See *Memel*.

Nemo See *Verne*.

nene *(NAY-nay)* From the Hawaiian, this is the name of the famous goose native to the Islands and nearly extinct, except in crossword puzzles. Determined bird watchers interested in going on a wild nene chase can sometimes spot the fowl nibbling berries and vegetation in the arid Hawaiian uplands. It is the official state bird.

neon *(NEE-on)* An inert, colorless, odorless, and tasteless gaseous element discovered in 1898, and named for the Greek word meaning "new." When an electric current is passed through neon in a vacuum tube, it emits an orange-red glow; this is the basis of the neon sign. Other colors are obtained by combining neon with different inert gases.

Nepal *(neh-PAHL)* A kingdom in the Himalayas bordered by India, Sikkim, and Tibet (now part of China). Most Nepalese live in the central section, where the capital, Katmandu, lies in the Valley of Nepal. The south is forested, while in the north are the great mountains, including Mt. Everest, the highest in the world. Nepal is the home of the Gurkhas, renowned as fighting men in Britain's armies.

Nero *(NERE-oh)* Nero Claudius Caesar (A.D. 37–68), the infamous and depraved emperor who may have been responsible for a fire that burned Rome; in any case, he blamed it on the Christians and set about the first persecution of adherents to the new religion. When his legions revolted, some years and many murders later, he committed suicide. Nero is also clued as: _____ Wolfe (Rex Stout detective); pianist Peter; an opera by Handel; and actor Franco _____ .

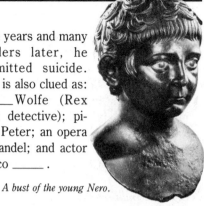

A bust of the young Nero.

ness *(ness)* From the Old English word for "nose," a cape, headland, or promontory. Ness is accordingly part of many Gaelic place names, such as Inverness. Also the name of a Scottish lake, Loch (q.v.) **Ness,** 22 miles long and more than 700 feet deep, which is home to a legendary 50-foot-long "monster," allegedly sighted repeatedly since December 1933. Another **Ness** is TV's Eliot in *The Untouchables*.

Neva *(NEE-vah)* A river of the northwestern U.S.S.R. that originates in Lake Ladoga and flows 46 miles into the Gulf of Finland. The Neva is connected by canals with the Volga River and the White Sea. Leningrad is located on the Neva delta.

neve *(nay-VAY)* A type of snow encountered by skiers, alpinists, and mountain patrols. Névé, which comes from the French, is granular snow, also called firn (q.v.), that accumulates as the snow fields on glaciers, and eventually is compressed into ice under the weight of more snow.

Nevin *(NEH-vin)* Ethelbert Woodbridge Nevin (1862–1901), the American pianist and composer of brief, lyrical works. He is perhaps best known for his song "The Rosary," a big hit in 1898, and that standby in school, "Narcissus."

E. B. Nevin.

newel *(NOO-ehl)* An item strictly associated with staircases. A newel or newel-post is either the vertical post around which a circular staircase is constructed, or the post at either end of a flight of stairs supporting the handrail.

newt *(newt)* Any of several species of semiaquatic salamanders, newts are lizardlike in appearance and rarely longer than six inches. They are brilliantly colored and often secrete irritating substances. Some newts spend their early adult lives on land, and are known as efts (q.v.); thereafter, they live strictly as aquatic creatures.

A pair of Alpine newts.

nexus *(NEK-sus)* From the Latin *nectere*, "to bind," a connection or link between historical events, individual entities in a series, or members of a social, professional, or cultural group. Also, the group or series that has been linked together.

nib *(nib)* Either a synonym for neb (q.v.), the beak of a bird; a sharpened quill used as a pen point and now applied to the business end of any pen including ballpoints; the short, gripping handles located in the snath (shaft) of a scythe; cleaned cocoa beans in the process of chocolate-making; or coffee beans.

Nicaea See *Iznik*.

nidus *(NIE-dus)* From the Latin for "nest," any site where incubation occurs. The term usually refers to the place where the eggs of insects and spiders are deposited, but in medicine it also designates a focus of infection where microorganisms breed.

Niger *(NIE-jer)* The former French colony, now an independent West African republic, bounded by Upper Volta, Mali, Algeria, Libya, Chad, and Dahomey. Niger's capital is Niamey and it is inhabited by nomadic tribes in the northern desert regions, and by agricultural peoples (ninety percent of the population) in the savanna regions. Most of its population, however, lives along the country's 300-mile stretch of the 2,600-mile-long Niger River, one of the longest in Africa.

Nike *(NIE-kee)* In Greek mythology, the goddess of victory and the daughter of Pallas and Styx (q.v.). Nike functioned as a kind of referee, presiding over all contests, including the ultimate contest, war. The best-known representation of Nike is the famous Winged Victory of Samothrace, now in the Louvre.

Niobe *(NIE-oh-bee)* Another mythic figure, the queen of Thebes, who boasted about her 12 children, comparing her fruitfulness to that of Leto (q.v.). For this she saw them all put to death by Artemis and Apollo, children of Leto. The weeping mother was turned by Zeus into a stone image from which tears continued to flow. In Shakespeare's *Hamlet,* the hero compares his mother to "Niobe . . . all tears."

The six sons and six daughters of Niobe being put to death by Artemis and Apollo.

Nisan or **Nissan** *(niss-AHN)* The seventh month of the Hebrew calendar, falling in early spring. A variation results because the Jewish year numbers 354 days, and so, roughly every three years, an extra month of 29 days is inserted just before Nisan. Passover falls on the 15th through 22nd of Nisan.

THE JEWISH ZODIAC

Nisan (Aries)
Iyar (Taurus)
Sivan (Gemini)
Tamuz (Cancer)
Av (Leo)
Elul (Virgo)
Tishri (Libra)
Cheshvan (Scorpio)
Kislev (Sagittarius)
Teveth (Capricorn)
Shvat (Aquarius)
Adar (Pisces)

Nisei See *Kibei*.

nix *(niks)* or **nixie** *(NIK-see)* A supernatural being in Germanic folklore, usually thought of as a water sprite. The nixie was represented as half-human, half-fish, or sometimes as a beautiful siren who lured men to their death. In post-office slang, a **nixie** is an undeliverable letter.

Njord *(nyord)*
A god in the Norse pantheon, he was the father of Frey (q.v.) and his sister Freya (q.v.). Njord ruled over the winds, particularly favoring the north wind, and he also commanded the sea and the waves. He was married to Skadi, goddess of harm.

Njord, looking properly wind-blown.

nock *(nok)* From the Old Norse word *nokke*, meaning "notch," the V-shaped cut at either end of a bow in which the bowstring is secured. Also, a similar notch near the butt end of an arrow into which the string is placed prior to drawing the bow.

noddy *(NAH-dee)* Any of several varieties of tropical, web-footed, long-winged terns with tapering bills. Noddies are comfortable around man, and it is this nodding acquaintance that gives them their name. They are also easily caught. **Noddy** is also applied to people who are considered stupid.

node *(node)* A word of many definitions, including: in anatomy, a bodily protuberance or swelling; in astronomy, the point where a planetary orbit crosses the sun's apparent path; in botany, the part of a stem that produces a leaf; in geometry, the point where a continuous curve intersects itself; or just any knotty complication.

nog *(nahg)* From the Middle English word that gives us "knock," a wooden block built into a masonry wall to accept nails. Also, a kind of British ale and (short for eggnog) a Christmas cup of cheer containing beaten eggs, milk or cream, nutmeg, and brandy.

Noh or **No** *(no)* A form of classic Japanese drama, short plays acted by men and featuring sylized masks, tragic plot lines, extravagant costumes, and the integration of mime (q.v.), music, and dance into the play.

nomad *(NOE-mad)* Any member of a tribe or other social unit without a permanent home, such as the Bedouin desert tribes. The word nomad derives from the Greek term for "living on pasturage," and the reason most nomads wander is to search for food for themselves (in the case of most Australian aborigines or Eskimos) or for their flocks (as in the case of the Bedouins).

A nomadic girl in Iran, with her camels.

Nome *(nome)* A city in Alaska, on the south side of Seward Peninsula. Nome dates back to 1898, when the discovery of gold made it a boom town of 20,000 souls. Today, with about one-tenth of that population, Nome is primarily a supply center for the northwestern part of the state and site of an Air Force base. Nome is known for its Eskimo crafts.

nones *(nones)* From the Latin for "nine," the ninth day before the ides (q.v.) of a month. Also, the fifth of the seven canonical hours, or about 3:00 P.M., the ninth hour of the day counting from sunrise.

nopal *(NOE-pul)* A shortening of the Nahuatl *nopalli*, the prickly pear. The nopal is actually any of several species of cacti, among them the cochineal fig, so named because the plant is used to breed its natural enemy—scale insects from whose crushed bodies cochineal, a red dye, is obtained. Young nopal "pods," the fleshy stems of the leafless plants, are edible.

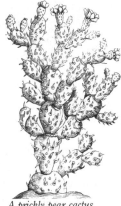

A prickly pear cactus, a.k.a. nopal.

noria *(NOH-ree-uh)* Spanish transliteration of the Arabic *nāʻūrah*, an undershot waterwheel used on the Iberian peninsula and in the Orient to raise water from a stream to a reservoir. This is achieved by paddles that cause rotation, plus buckets on the wheel's circumference that fill and discharge as it turns.

Norn *(norn)* In Norse mythology, one of the three Fates: female deities who spun

and wove the irrevocable fates of men and gods. They were Urth (or Wyrth), the past; Verthandi, the present; and Skuld, the future. The Norns lived at the roots of Yggdrasill, the Tree of the Universe. In Shakespeare's *Macbeth,* the three weird sisters correspond to the Norns.

Norse *(norss)* The name given to the Scandinavian, or North Germanic, group of Indo-European languages. Today, these include Danish, Faeroese, Icelandic, Swedish, and Norwegian. They originated in Old Norse, the language spoken in Scandinavia before A.D. 1000 and written in runes (q.v.), some examples of which trace back to the third century B.C.

Nosu See *Lolo.*

Notus *(NOE-tus)* In Roman legend, the personification of the south wind, born of Eos (q.v.), goddess of the dawn, and Astraeus. Other issue of this union include Boreas, the north wind, and Zephyr, the west wind. Notus was believed to be the bringer of rain and fog.

nous *(nooss)* A Greek word transferred intact into English and used in philosophy. In neoplatonic terms, nous is considered the first principal of God—divine reason. The word is also used to designate understanding or the thinking mind. Often in crosswords, **nous** (pronounced *noo*) is the French "us" or "we," as in "entre-____" (between us; confidentially).

nova *(NOE-vah)* The first part of the Latin term *nova stella,* or "new star," used to refer to a particular phenomenon in stellar evolution. Occasionally, a star's energy will increase slightly, so that it briefly shines several thousand times more brightly, and then fades. Some astronomers think the star of Bethlehem was just such a nova.

Nox *(noks)* In Roman mythology, the goddess of the night, whom the Greeks called Nyx. As the daughter of Chaos

(q.v.), she is one of the most ancient of goddesses. She and her brother Erebus (q.v.), for whom the dark nether region was named, sired two offspring—Aethir (air) and Dies (daylight).

Noyes *(noiz)* Alfred Noyes (1880–1958), the British poet who taught English literature at Princeton University during

Alfred Noyes.

the early 1920s. Noyes is best known for his romantic narrative poems, such as "The Highwayman" and "The Barrel-Organ," with its refrain "Go down to Kew in lilac time..."

Noyon *(nwah-YONE)* A city in northern France. Now an industrial center, Noyon was the site of Charlemagne's coronation in A.D. 768. In 1516, France and Spain signed a treaty in Noyon that temporarily halted the Italian Wars. Noyon sustained heavy damage during both World Wars, but its thirteenth-century cathedral still stands. John Calvin was born in Noyon; his birthplace is now a museum.

nu *(noo)* The thirteenth letter of the Greek alphabet, corresponding to the English letter *N.* Also, U **Nu** (1907–), the Burmese political leader who served as his country's premier for three separate periods. It was he who helped secure Burma's independence from Britain in 1948. His first name (pronounced *oo*) is an honorific.

Nubia *(NOO-bee-ah)* An ancient northeast African country bounded by the Sahara

Desert and the Red Sea. At its height, it extended, north to south, from modern Aswan to modern Khartoum, in the Sudan. It was annexed by the Egyptians in the twentieth century B.C., and many centuries later the Cushites, who were Nubians, conquered Egypt. Nubia collapsed in the fourteenth century after conversion to Christianity (sixth century) and long resistance to Islam. It is now part of Egypt.

nullah *(NULL-ah)*   From the Hindi word *nálá,* meaning "brook" or "ravine," an intermittently dry watercourse.

Numa *(NOO-mah)*   Given name of Numa Pompilius, the legendary king of Rome who was successor to Romulus, founder (c. 750 B.C.) of the city. Numa was revered for his knowledge and piety. Aided by the nymph Egeria, he organized the first college of pontiffs, codified Roman ceremonial law, and initiated various religious practices, including worship of the god Janus (q.v.).

Nurmi *(NOOR-mee)*   Paavo Nurmi (1897–1973), the great Finnish athlete who set 20 world records in track and won nine Olympic gold medals, most of them for distance running. Disqualified in the 1932 Olympics for violations of the amateur athletic code, he went into the sporting-goods business and promptly amassed a fortune. His sobriquet was the Flying Finn.

nux *(nuks)*   Latin for "nut," usually designating the nutmeg, or *Myristica fragrans.* The word also appears in *nux vomica,* a drug extracted from the poisonous seeds of the *nux vomica* tree *(Strychnos nux-vomica)* of Sri Lanka, India, and northern Australia. The seeds contain the alkaloids strychnine and brucine. *Nux vomica* was formerly used medicinally in small doses, as a tonic.

Nyasa *(NYAH-sah)*   A large lake, third in size on the continent, located in the Great Rift Valley of east-central Africa. Also known as Lake Malawi, it is bounded by Tanzania, Mozambique, and Malawi. It

drains into the Zambesi River via the Shiré River. It was discovered by the Portuguese in 1616, and named by missionary Dr. David Livingstone in 1859.

Nydia *(NID-ee-ah)*   One of the main characters in Bulwer-Lytton's classic, *Last Days of Pompeii.* Nydia is the sensitive, blind flower girl who leads Glaucus, the man she secretly loves, and his sweetheart, Ione, out of the doomed city. Afterward, in despair, she drowns herself.

Nym *(nim)*   In Shakespeare's *Merry Wives of Windsor* and *Henry V,* a corporal in the "army" of Captain Sir John Falstaff, which also includes the immortal Pistol and Bardolph. Nym is an unsavory rogue and a thief whose name probably derived from nim, an old word meaning "to steal" or "to filch."

Nym, Bardolph, and Pistol before Mrs. Quickly in Henry V.

nymph *(nimf)*   In Greek mythology, a female nature divinity believed to dwell in a tree, a fountain, or other object. Nymphs are usually represented as young, beautiful, and occasionally amorous. The roll call of nymphs includes, among many, the oceanids and nereids (sea nymphs); naiads (q.v.); oreads and dryads (q.v.).

Nyx   See *Nox.*

Oahu *(oe-AH-hoo)* Third largest, but most important, of the Hawaiian Islands. Oahu is situated between Molokai and Kauai (q.v.). Its most famous sights are the extinct volcano crater called Diamond Head, Waikiki Beach, and the bay that will live in infamy—Pearl Harbor. The state capital, Honolulu, is also located here.

oakum *(OE-kum)* Shortened from a Middle English term that translates literally as "combed out," oakum is the loose fibers of stringy hemp or jute (both q.v.) obtained by separating the strands of old rope and combing them apart. This material is used with pitch to pack the seams of wooden-hulled sailing vessels.

oasis *(oe-AYE-sis)* A fertile area of inde-terminate size in desert regions. Water found in oases (plural) usually comes to the surface from underground springs or from mountains, as in areas of the Sahara where periodic rainfall is trapped in hollows. In Israel, artificial oases have been developed by irrigation of the desert. Oasis has come to denote any place of relief or refreshment.

oast or **ost** *(ohst)* The word is, inter-estingly, derived from the Latin *aestus*, meaning "summer" (a source of heat), which also roughly defines oast. A favor-ite of crossword con-structors because of its two initial vowels, it is a kiln for drying hops, tobacco, or malt.

A grain kiln.

Oates *(otes)* Titus Oates (1649–1705), an English conspirator who fomented the so-called Popish Plot to kill Protestants and burn London. Also Joyce Carol Oates (1938–), prolific American author of realistic novels dealing with violence and love, such as *With Shuddering Fall* (1964), *Expensive People* (1968), the National Book Award–winning novel *Them* (1972), and the

The Fountain of the Sun in the oasis of Siwa in the middle of the Libyan Desert.

best-selling Gothic parody *Bellefleur* (1980); as well as numerous collections of short stories, criticism, and poetry.

Oban *(OE-bun)*   A port and seaside resort on the Firth of Lorne, Argyllshire, Scotland. Oban is the site of the annual Argyllshire Highland Games. Near the ruins of twelfth-century Dunollie Castle, the Gaelic hero Fingal is supposed to have tied his giant dog Bran to a large rock, now called the Dog Stone.

obeah *(OH-bee-ya)*   A West African word designating the witchcraft or magic practiced in certain regions of black Africa, the West Indies, the Guianas, and the southeastern United States. Probably of Ashanti origin, this belief system involves the use of talismans, also called obeahs, and is related to voodoo.

Obeah is practiced in parts of Africa.

obi *(OE-bee)*   A garment accessory exclusive to Japan. Customarily worn with a kimono by women and children, the obi is a wide sash, wrapped around the waist and tied at the back with a large flat, folded bow. In America, it can be seen on waitresses in Japanese restaurants.

obit *(OE-bit)*   Journalistic slang for a newspaper obituary notice, either in an alphabetical listing or as an article that announces the death of someone, with biographical details of his/her life. Detailed obits depend for their length on the importance of the deceased. The word comes from the Latin *obiit,* meaning "he died."

oboe *(OE-boe)*   From the French *hautebois* (high wood), which became, depending on who was mispronouncing, hautboy, or oboe. It is a woodwind and the soprano member of the double-reed family of musical instruments that includes the English horn (alto) and bassoon (bass). Its sound is nasally plaintive, and depends on flawless breath control.

obol *(OE-bul)*   Also called an obolus, this was a coin of ancient Greece equal in value to one-sixth of a drachma. At one time, the name was also applied to several other small coins of various European countries. As a unit of weight, the **obol** was equivalent in the Attic standard to 11¼ grains.

oca *(OE-kah)*   Either of two wood sorrels of the *Oxalis* genus, indigenous to South America and culti-vated for their edible tubers (q.v.). The wood sorrels have leaves divided into three leaflets; some consider them to have been the original shamrocks.

Wood sorrel.

Occam or Ockham *(AH-kum)*   The English scholastic philosopher William of Occam (or Ockham) (c.1285–1349). After becoming involved in a general brouhaha with Pope John XXII, Occam, who had been accused of heresy, fled to the protection of Louis IV. He taught that ideas should be explained with the greatest possible economy, a principle now known as Occam's razor.

ocelot *(AH-seh-lot)*   From *ocelotl*, Na-huatl for "jaguar," a medium-sized mem-ber of the cat family, native to Central and South America but ranging into Texas. Oce-lots are yellow with black spots, stand 16 inches high at the shoulder, and weigh up to 35 pounds. They can be tamed.

ocher or **ochre** *(OH-ker)*   A mixture of clay and iron oxide, used as a paint pigment. If the iron ore is limonite, the ocher is yellow; if hematite, the color is reddish. Ocher is used as a base to make other earth colors, such as sienna and um-ber (q.v.), by adding various chemicals.

Ochoa *(oe-CHOE-ah)*   Severo Ochoa (1905–   ), Spanish-born American bio-chemist, physician, and educator who taught at Heidelberg, Madrid, Oxford, and New York universities. In 1959, he shared the Nobel Prize in physiology and medicine for synthesizing ribonucleic acid (RNA) and deoxyribonucleic acid (DNA), the com-pounds involved with heredity.

ocrea or **ochrea** *(OHK-ree-uh)*   From the Latin for "legging," a bo-tanical term designating the cylindrical sheath that surrounds the stems of certain plants. In zoology, the word is used more generally as the term for any sheathlike structure. When plant or animal tissue in-cludes such a sheath, it is said to be ocreate.

octad *(OK-tad)*   A derivative from the Greek for the number eight, this is any series or grouping of eight entities. In chemistry, an octad is an element or radical with a valence of eight—that is, its ability to combine with eight atoms in a chemical reaction. In crosswords, octad is often de-fined as "eightsome."

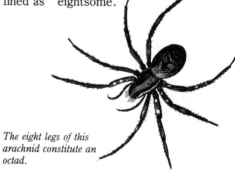

The eight legs of this arachnid constitute an octad.

ode *(ode)*   From the Greek word for "song," a type of elaborate lyric originally designed to be set to music. The Greek odes of Pindar were arranged in stanzas, with a strophe and an antistrophe of identi-cal meter, and an epode (q.v.). Among English poets whose works include odes are Dryden, Coleridge, Milton, Shelley, Wordsworth, and, especially, Keats ("Ode on a Grecian Urn," "Ode to a Nightin-gale").

Küstrin castle on the Oder River in Poland.

Oder *(OE-der)* A 562-mile-long river flowing generally north from Czechoslovakia into Poland, then forming part of the border between East Germany and Poland, and finally emptying into the Baltic Sea at Szczecin (Stettin). The Oder is navigable for most of its course and is connected by canals with the Spree and the Elbe, and via the Warta with the Vistula.

Odessa See *Black*.

odeum *(oh-DEE-um)* From the Greek word *oideion*, which in turn derives from ode (q.v.), a roofed structure where competitions in music and poetry were staged for audiences in ancient Greece and Rome. Today, if the word is used at all, it refers generically to a music hall, or is a proper name often given to movie theaters. Its plural is odea.

Odin *(OE-din)* Supreme deity of the Norse pantheon, also known as Woden, Wotan, or Othin in Germanic myth. Consistent with his exalted status, he presided over art, culture, and war, and

Odin on his horse Sleipnir.

he ruled the dead jointly with Freya (q.v.). The fourth day of the week, sacred to Odin, was named Wednesday, from his German name, in his honor.

odium *(OE-dee-um)* Taken into English directly from the Latin word for "ill will," odium is, simply, hatred or the state of being despised. The term is also used to designate the opprobrium occasioned by despicable actions, such as the traitorous conduct of a Benedict Arnold, Quisling, or Judas (q.v.).

Odium personified by Lon Chaney, Sr., in London After Midnight, *1927.*

Oenone *(ee-NOE-nee)* In Greek legend, a nymph (q.v.), married to Paris (q.v.), who eventually deserted her for the beauteous Helen of Troy. Oenone sent their son to guide the Greeks to Troy and refused to use her healing powers when Paris was wounded, but committed suicide upon learning of his death.

Oeta *(EET-ah)*　A 15-mile-long mountain range, actually the eastern spur of the Pindus Mountains, in central Greece and terminating at Thermopylae on the east. Mt. Oeta, highest point of the range, towers about 7,000 feet. According to legend, Hercules died there on a pyre after being poisoned by the robe of Nessus.

offal *(AW-full)*　Waste products, from the Middle English for "off-fall." More specifically, it is the term used to describe certain parts of a butchered animal. Most often in the U.S. it refers to the entrails, but can also (especially in Britain) designate edible parts like kidneys, sweetbreads, brains, tongue, liver, or tripe, all delicately designated "variety meats."

ogee *(OE-jee)*　Molding with an S-shaped curvature when seen in profile; or, any line or curve approximating the shape of the letter *S*. Archways pointed on top and formed by segments of the letter *S* on each side are also called ogees. This type of arch is popular in Eastern architecture.

Ogier *(OE-jee-uhr)*　Known as Ogier the Dane, this romantic figure was a paladin of Charlemagne. The *Chansons de Geste* relate that he was transported to Avalon by the fairy Morgan le Fay, and after 200 years reappeared to help save France. He is represented as the jack of spades on French playing cards.

Ogpu *(AHG-poo)*　The name for the Soviet secret police organization that succeeded the Cheka in 1922. Ogpu was an acronym: Its letters stood for *Otdelenie Gosudarstvennoi Politcheskoi Upravlenii,* or Special Government Political Administration. In 1934, the Ogpu was renamed the N.K.V.D. *(Narodnyi Kommissariat Vnutrennikh Del).*

ohm *(ome)*　A unit of resistance to the flow of electricity. One ohm equals the

---

CAFE CROSSWORD

DESSERT MENU

NUTS & CHEESE
Areca, betel, cola, pili, tryma.
Brie, Edam, Gouda, Oka, Serac.

COUPE DE FRUITS
Ansu, ber, bleo, gage, guava, haw, kaki, kiwi, mango, rowan, sabra, sloe, titi, whort.

PUDDINGS & PASTRY
Baba au rhum, flan, salep, scone, tansy, torte.

Served with *java* or *pekoe*.
Claros and *coronas* can be purchased in cloakroom.

resistance in a circuit where one volt (q.v.) maintains a current of one ampere. The ohm was named for Georg Simon Ohm (1787–1854), the German physicist and researcher in electricity, acoustics, and crystal interference. Ohm's law was named for him. (See also *mho*.)

Oise *(wahz)* An important river of France rising in southern Belgium in the Ardennes Mountains and flowing south to join the Seine near Pontoise, France. About 185 miles long, it is navigable for most of its length and is a key shipping route.

Oka *(OE-kah)* The name of two rivers of the U.S.S.R.: the 925-mile Oka rising south of Orel and flowing north, east, and northeast to join the Volga at Gorky; and the 600-mile Oka that flows north from the Sayan Mountains of Siberia to the Angara River. **Oka** is also the name of a Canadian village near Montreal where Oka cheese is made at a Trappist monastery.

okapi *(oh-KAH-pee)* A herbivore of the giraffe family, but with a shorter neck. The

okapi sports a reddish-brown coat, black and white striped legs, and blunt horns. Because he grazes by night deep in the jungles of the upper Congo, the okapi was unknown to the rest of the world until 80 years ago.

An okapi, a nocturnal ruminant.

Okie *(OE-kee)* The pejorative name for a Dust Bowl farmer of the 1930s, forced to leave home and seek work elsewhere. Most often, his destination was the fruit orchards of California. Okie is short for Oklahoma, where most of the migrants lived; some of them were referred to as Arkies, for Arkansas. The most famous Okies were the fictional Joads (q.v.) in John Steinbeck's *The Grapes of Wrath,* which won the Pulitzer Prize for fiction in 1940.

Henry Fonda and Jane Darwell as Okies Tom and Ma Joad on their way west in The Grapes of Wrath.

okra See *gumbo.*

Oland *(AW-land)* A narrow island in the Baltic Sea off the southeast coast of Sweden, Öland is known primarily for its fishing and as a summer resort for vacationing Swedes. Its chief town is Borgholm. The island traces its history back to the Stone Age; its location has made it a scene of battle in various Scandinavian wars. **Oland** is also actor Warner Oland, filmdom's most famous Charlie Chan.

oleo *(OE-lee-oh)* Popular term for oleomargarine, a blend of fats, usually oils of vegetable origin, hydrogenated and colored to give the margarine the appearance and consistency of butter. Oleo is sometimes churned with cultured skim milk to enhance its "dairy" character and is usually fortified with vitamin A. Crossword clues: "butterine," "bread spread," "corn-oil product."

olio *(OE-lee-oh)* Linguistically related to the word olla (q.v.), this is a specific term for a mixed stew or ragout of meat and vegetables, usually highly seasoned. The heterogeneous nature of this dish has enlarged the meaning of olio to include any mixture, or assortment of miscellany. Thus, olio can also refer to a medley of music, or a brief bill of theatrical acts.

olla *(AW-lah; OY-ah)* The Spanish, and now English, word for a wide-mouthed earthenware jar used to hold water or to prepare spicy Spanish meat stews. Olla became a synonym for this earthy dish and also gave us olio (q.v.), which, in turn, defines *olla podrida,* an olio whose name in Spanish means "rotten pot."

Omar *(OH-mar)* Given name of Omar Khayyám, the eleventh-century Persian poet and mathematician whose last name is translated as "tentmaker," after his father's occupation. Omar was instrumental in revising the calendar in 1079. But he is best known for his *Rubáiyát,* first translated into English by Edward FitzGerald in 1859. Also General of the Army Omar N. Bradley (1893–1981); actor Omar Sharif (1933–); and Omar (c. 581–644), an early caliph and an adviser to Mohammed.

Omar Sharif.

ombu *(ohm-BOO)* A large, distinctive evergreen in the same genus as pokeweed, and the only tree native to the Argentinian pampas. Ombus have trunks up to 50 feet in girth, grow rapidly, produce soft, spongy wood, and provide needed shade. Their poisonous sap protects them from locusts and grazing animals.

omega *(oh-MAY-gah)* The twenty-fourth and terminal letter of the Greek alphabet. Omega corresponds to the English letter *O,* as pronounced in hope, rather than hop. It is also the symbol for the electrical unit known as the ohm (q.v.). The phrase "from alpha to ____" (from beginning to end) is a frequent crossword clue.

omer *(OE-mur)* An ancient Hebrew unit of volume, used to measure dry materials such as grain or berries. The omer, equal to about 3.7 of today's quarts, survives practically only in dictionaries and crossword puzzles. Not to be confused with the homer.

Omsk *(ohmsk)* A city in western Siberia at the junction of the Irtysh and Om rivers, and an important stop on the Trans-Siberian railroad. This famous fortress (dating from 1716) and thriving metropolis was the headquarters for the anti-Bolshevik forces of Admiral A.V. Kolchak during the civil war following the Revolution of 1917.

Onan *(OE-nan)* In the Bible, the brother of Er, whose widow he was ordered to marry, according to custom (see *levir*), by Judah, his father. For reneging on the union by spilling his seed on the ground, Onan was slain by Jehovah (Gen. 38:10). Often, **onan** is clued as two words, as in "____ even keel."

Onega *(oh-NAY-gah)* A 260-mile-long river in the northwestern U.S.S.R., flowing into the White Sea; and a lake, also in the U.S.S.R., in Karelia. Lake Onega is 150 miles long, the second largest in Europe, and forms an important link in the region's waterway system, despite the fact that it freezes over in November and doesn't thaw until May.

onyx *(AHN-iks)* From the Greek for "nail" or "claw," a semiprecious stone with colors in parallel bands. Onyx is a variety of quartz and related to agate (q.v.). In ancient Rome, vases and other vessels were made of onyx. Black and white specimens are used for cameos.

A 16th-century onyx cameo of Diana.

opah *(OE-pah)* A rare and beautiful species of moonfish, also known as the Jerusa-

An opah.

lem haddock. Silvery or blue-gray, iridescent and brightly spotted, opahs are native to the Atlantic. These are big fish, reaching a length of six feet, and are highly prized as food.

opal *(OE-pul)* From the Sanskrit *upala,* meaning "precious stone," an iridescent semiprecious stone with an irregular arrangement of subtle green, red, and blue coloration. Most of the world's precious opal is mined at the Coober Pedy and Andamooka fields in Australia, but it is also found in Central America and Nevada's Virgin Valley. Opals are often milky or fiery, and are commonly so clued.

Ophir *(OE-fer)* The biblical region from which came the riches of King Solomon (1 Kings 9:28, 10:11, 22:48). Ships arriving from Ophir invariably carried gold, gems, sandalwood, apes, and peacocks. The actual location of Ophir is unknown but most experts place it in the region of southwest Arabia now known as Yemen.

opium *(OE-pee-um)* From *opion,* Greek for "poppy juice," a crude narcotic made from the milky juice exuded through slits in unripe seed pods of the opium poppy. The chief active principle of opium is morphine; it also contains codeine. The drug heroin is synthesized from morphine. Opium has been used as a narcotic since at least 4000 B.C.

orc *(ork)* Another name for the grampus, a small (for its family), black and white, sharp-toothed whale kin to dolphins and known, for its ferocity, as the killer whale. It feeds on other mammals as well as fish and birds, and even hunts in packs. Its scientific name is *Orcinus orca; orca* is Latin for "whale." In Ariosto's *Orlando Furioso,* the **orc** was a great sea monster who de-

voured humans. Angelica was rescued from the orc by Rogero, riding his winged horse, Hippogriff. In the Middle Earth of J.R.R. Tolkien's novels, **orcs** are particularly beastly goblin folk.

ordo *(OR-doe)* As its translation from Latin suggests, this word relates to order. In the Roman Catholic Church, an ordo is a calendar listing the daily offices and feasts for the year. The plural of ordo is ordines, pronounced *or-din-EEZ.*

Orel *(aw-REL)* A city in the central European U.S.S.R., on the Oka River. A rail, trade, and industrial center in a farming region, Orel was founded in 1564 by Ivan IV to protect Muscovy from attack by Crimean Tartars. It was captured by the White Army during the civil war, following the Revolution, and it was virtually leveled during World War II. Orel was the birthplace of the novelist Ivan Turgenev (1818–1883).

oribi or **ourebi** *(OR-eh-bee)* Common name for certain pygmy antelopes native to the African veldt. The oribi's most unusual feature is the tuft of hair that sprouts from each knee. Among his first cousins are the klipspringer, grysbok, steinbok, and dik-dik. Oribi is the Afrikaans version of the Hottentot word for "Arab."

oriel *(OR-ee-el)* Derived from the medieval French for "porch" or "gallery," this is a window projecting from an upper story of a building and supported by brackets, corbels, or a column. Oriels are a standard feature of early Renaissance English buildings. The term is sometimes applied to any large bay window.

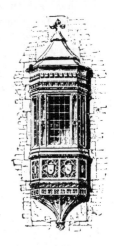

An oriel on a 14th-century English building.

Orion *(oh-RYE-un)* The legendary giant and hunter who cleared the wild animals off Chios Island. For too ardently wooing Merope, Orion was blinded by her father, the King of Chios. But, in one version of the story, he was pardoned by Vulcan, who helped him regain his eyesight. Upon his death, Orion became the heavenly constellation Orion, which includes three stars of the first magnitude—Betelgeuse, Bellatrix, and Rigel—as well as the Orion Nebula.

orle *(orl)* Another of those infernal heraldic terms that keep popping up in crossword puzzles. This one, derived from the Latin *ora,* refers to the inner border of an escutcheon. This border traditionally parallels the edge of a shield. An **orle** can also be a wreath encircling a helmet or, in architecture, a narrow fillet at the top of a column.

Orly *(or-LEE)* A city of Vol-de-Marne in north-central France, and a suburb of Paris, just southeast of the city. Many air travelers to Paris come through the huge international Orly Field.

ormer *(OR-mer)* A term that originated in the French dialect spoken in the Channel Islands, from *or* plus *mer,* meaning "ear of the sea." Ormer can designate any ear-shaped shell, such as that of the abalone, which in most species is perforated near its rim but always lined with nacre (q.v.).

Ormuz *(or-MOOZ)* A small island (also called Hormuz) of Iran, in the Strait of Ormuz, which joins the Persian Gulf with the Gulf of Oman. The town of Ormuz, founded around 1300, was a center of trade with India and China until its capture by the Portuguese in 1514. It was retaken in 1622 by Shah Abbas I and some British men-of-war. The place was then abandoned as a port.

orpine or **orpin** *(OR-pin)* A name for the stonecrops, a family of fleshy, succulent herbs commonly known as hen-and-chickens and sedums. The orpines pre-

White orpine.

fer arid regions and are common garden plants in the southwestern and western United States. Orpine is popular as a planting in cemeteries, where it is known as the live-forever.

orris *(OR-is)* The name applied to certain European species of the iris (q.v.), especially the Florentine iris. The rhizomes of the orris are particularly fragrant, with a violetlike scent. The powdered root is used as a flavoring for toothpaste, a fragrance in perfumery, or a stage makeup hair-whitener.

ort *(ort)* From the Middle English, an ort is a leftover, a morsel of food not eaten during a meal. In good restaurants nowadays, orts are whisked away before dessert is served, sometimes to be returned, in a doggy bag, to the diner.

Good to the last ort.

oryx *(OR-iks)* The name given to several species of small, horselike antelopes of Africa and Arabia. Their most distinctive features are their tufted tails and slender back-pointing horns. The most common oryx species includes the gemsbok of southern Africa and the beisa (q.v.) of Africa. The smallest is the Beatrix (or Arabian) oryx, now almost wiped out by automobile-mounted hunters.

Osage *(OH-saje)* Member of a North American Indian tribe of the Sioux language group, native to the region of the Osage

River in Missouri. The Osage culture, typical of Plains Indians, was geared to war, but their tribes were un-typically divided into Wazhazhe and Tsishu —meat-eaters and vegetarians. The discovery of oil on their barren Oklahoma reservation made the Osage the wealthiest Indians in the U.S.

An Osage mother and child.

osier *(OH-zhur)* A member of the willow genus of the family that includes the poplars, also called cottonwoods, and the aspens. Willows are found throughout the temperate zones of the world, and are valuable for growing farther north than any other woody flowering plant. They grow quickly, are usually the first trees to reforest burned-over woodlands, and are planted to control the erosion of riverbanks. Willow twigs, also called osiers, are used for wickerwork.

A yellow willow, a.k.a. golden osier.

Osler *(OS-ler)* Sir William Osler (1849–1919), the Canadian physician and mentor of physicians, also renowned as a medical historian. Professor of Medicine at McGill, Pennsylvania, Johns Hopkins, and Oxford universities, he wrote the definitive medical text *The Principles and Practice of Medicine* (1892). He was knighted in 1911.

Sir William Osler.

Ossa *(OH-sah)* A mountain in north Thessaly, in Greece. According to legend, giants named Otus and Ephialtes, sons of

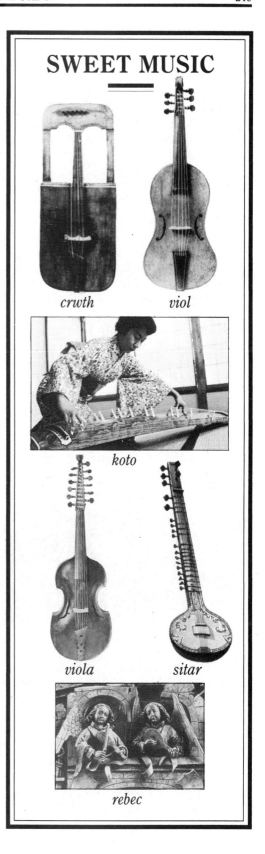

SWEET MUSIC

crwth   *viol*

koto

viola   *sitar*

rebec

Poseidon, attempted to reach the heavens and depose the gods by placing Ossa atop Mt. Olympus, then placing Mt. Pelion atop Ossa. The attempt failed, and the brothers were slain by Apollo. But multiplying futile efforts is still referred to as piling Pelion on Ossa. Lower-cased, **ossa** is also the plural of os, bone.

Osset *(OH-set)*

A native of Ossetia, a region of the central Caucasus, in the southern part of the European U.S.S.R. The Ossets, or Ossatians, are a tall people who may have emigrated from Persia in ancient times. They are assumed to descend from the Alans, who observed a religion containing elements of Islam and Christianity.

Ostia *(OH-stee-ah)*

An ancient city situated at the mouth of the Tiber River in what is now Italy. Ostia was founded in the fourth century B.C. to protect Rome itself from invasion by sea. It became Rome's port but fell into disuse some 700 years later. Its ruins are of important archaeological interest, and are a tourist attraction today.

The ruins at Ostia.

Otho *(OH-thoe)*

The Roman emperor known officially as Marcus Salvius Otho (A.D. 32–69). Some years after his wife, Poppaea Sabina, left him to become the mistress of Nero (q.v.), he joined forces with Galba (q.v.) to overthrow Nero. After Nero's suicide, Galba became emperor. But, consumed with ambition, Otho again conspired successfully, this time against Galba, and took over as emperor himself. He committed suicide after a few months,

when his forces were defeated by those of Vitellias, who had been proclaimed emperor by the army legions in Germany.

Otis *(OH-tis)*

Elisha Graves Otis (1811–1861), the American inventor. Starting with a contraption he had invented to prevent the fall of hoisting machinery, he developed the first passenger elevator in 1857, and launched a giant industrial empire. Otis is credited with making possible the modern skyscraper. Other crossword Otises are Cornelia **Otis** Skinner (1901–   ), actress and author, daughter of eminent actor **Otis** Skinner (1858–1942).

E.G. Otis

Otsu *(OHT-soo)*

A Japanese city, capital of Shiga (q.v.) prefecture, on the island of Honshu. This industrial city is also a tourist center, with excursion steamers operating on Lake Biwa. Once an imperial seat, it was also the site of a seventh-century Buddhist temple. The poet Basho is buried there.

otter *(OT-uhr)*

An aquatic mammal of the weasel family, found on all continents except Australia. Otters have webbed feet and commercially prized thick, brown fur.

They often cavort like children, even playing follow the leader into the pond or, in winter, down snowbanks. The Pacific sea otters, once almost exterminated by fur hunters in California waters, have made a spectacular comeback under international protection.

An otter at attention.

Oudh *(owd)*

A region of northern India, now in Uttar Pradesh state. Once the ancient kingdom of Kosala, Oudh had become part of the Mogul empire, governed from Lucknow, when the British annexed it as a province in 1856, an event that, with other grievances, precipitated the Indian Mutiny the next year. In 1877, Oudh was joined with Agra (q.v.) in the United Provinces (now Uttar Pradesh). Oudh is also the name of the village in Oudh that was the capital of Kosala. It is also called Ajodhya.

Ouida *(WEE-dah)* The pen name of Louise de la Ramée, the English novelist who wrote such romantic, swashbuckling tales as *Moths* and *Under Two Flags*, which was eventually dramatized. She is also known for children's stories, including the classic *Dog of Flanders*.

Ouija *(WEE-jah)* Made up of the French and German words for "yes," the trademark of a device ostensibly employed to receive messages from the spirit world. The Ouija board contains the letters of the alphabet; the fingers of the players rest on a

small, three-legged platform that moves across the board to form words or answer queries.

A Ouija board.

Ouse *(ooz)* The name of two English rivers—the 155-mile-long Great Ouse flowing northeast, past Ely, to the Wash near King's Lynn; and the 60-mile-long Ouse formed in North Yorkshire which flows southeast, past York, to join with the Trent and form the Umber. Navigable to York, this Ouse is a key transportation route.

Outis *(OWT-iss)* In the *Odyssey,* the phony name Ulysses assumed to hoodwink the Cyclops Polyphemus. After Ulysses put the giant's one eye out, his cries of pain brought other giants, demanding the name of Polyphemus's attacker. When told it was Outis, his companions shrugged their shoulders and departed. The name is the Greek word for "nobody."

ouzel or **ousel** *(OO-zul)* A species of bird commonly called the European blackbird, and related to the thrushes. The best-known ouzels are the ring ouzel, a black thrush with white markings; and the water ouzel, a great diver with a predilection for walking on pond bottoms in search of food.

Ovid *(AH-vid)* The name by which we know Publius Ovidius Naso, the Roman poet (43 B.C. –A.D. 18). Ovid's poetry deals with three themes: mythology, as in his hexametric masterpiece *Metamorphoses;* eroticism, e.g., *Ars* (q.v.) *Amatoria* (The Art of Love); and exile. For no reason now known, he was exiled to the Black Sea region in A.D. 8 and died there.

oxbow *(OKS-boe)* As the name suggests, this is the part of a yoke that links oxen together in a span. It passes under and around the neck of each animal and is shaped like the letter *U.* From this shape, oxbow is a name for a looping bend in a river. An oxbow lake forms when a river cuts across the opening of the *U. The Oxbow Incident* was a novel by Walter Van Triburg Clark indicting lynch law. It was made into a film by director William Wyler in 1943, and starred Henry Fonda.

The oxbows go on either side of and under the necks of laboring bullocks.

ozone *(OE-zone)* From the Greek meaning "to smell," a bluish form of oxygen made up of three atoms, with the characteristic fresh odor of the outdoors after a lightning storm. Ozone is formed when an electrical current is passed through oxygen. It is used commercially as a disinfectant and bleaching agent.

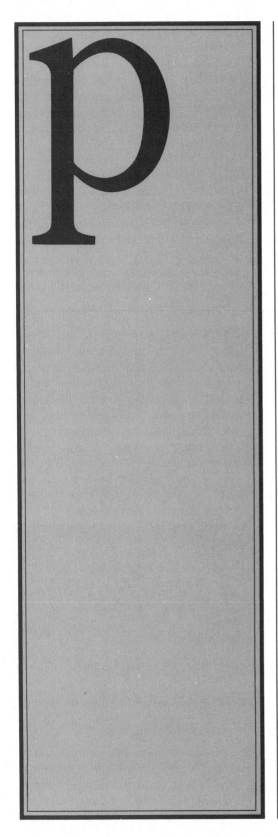

Paarl *(parl)* A town on the Berg River, in Cape Province, South Africa. With an ideal climate for growing grapes, the Paarl region has become the wine center of South Africa. Tobacco is also grown. The city was founded by Dutch farmers in 1687, and there was an influx of French Huguenots in 1690.

paca *(PAH-kah)* Common name for any of several short-tailed or tailless spotted brown rodents of South and Central America, some of them esteemed as food. As a proper noun, the surname of William **Paca** (1740–1799), the American political leader, signer of the Declaration of Independence and governor of Maryland, 1782 to 1785.

paddy *(PAD-ee)* From the Malay word *padi*, this word simply means rice—either growing in a field, or gathered, especially if still in its husk. By extension, paddy has come to mean a field flooded by rain or river water, in which rice is grown. As a proper (nick-) name, **Paddy** is short for Patrick. In slang, a **paddy** wagon is a police van.

Padua *(PAD-yoo-ah)* The northeastern Italian metropolis and industrial center, originally called Patavium by the Romans. Destroyed by the Lombards in A.D. 601, Padua recovered and became one of the great cities of Italy. Its university (founded in 1222), the second oldest in Italy, numbers Galileo among its one-time professors and the likes of Tasso, Petrarch, and Dante (q.v.) among its illustrious alumni.

Aerial view of Padua.

paean *(PEE-an)* From Paian, an epithet for the god Apollo, physician and healer in ancient Greek belief. Thus, a paean was a joyous hymn of praise to Apollo. It can also be any hymn of joy, thanksgiving, tribute, or triumph.

Paez *(PAH-ais)* José Antonio Páez (1790–1873), the Venezuelan patriot who fought against the Spanish and helped Simón Bolívar drive them out of Venezuela after the battle of Carabobo in 1821. Also, the surname of Pedro Paéz (1564–1622), the Spanish missionary who converted the Ethiopian royal family to Catholicism.

pagan *(PAY-gan)* At one time, this term designated any person who was not a Christian. The definition has since been narrowed, so that Jews and Muslims are no longer considered pagans, or heathens. As a proper noun, **Pagan** is a ruined city, archaeological treasure trove, and holy place on the Irrawaddy River in central Burma.

Pakht *(pakt)* An ancient Egyptian goddess, also known as Sekhet. She is portrayed in hieroglyphs with the head of a lioness, and was the wife of Ptah (q.v.). Pakht was the mistress of the sun, using its heat to destroy wicked souls in the Egyptian version of Hell.

Pali *(PAH-lee)* A language of the Indic group of Indo-Iranian languages. Pali was used in the writing of the Buddhist scriptures, or *Tipitaka*. No longer much used in India, it continues to be the liturgical language of Buddhists in Sri Lanka, Burma, and Thailand.

Palos *(PAH-lohss)* The short name for Palos de la Frontera, in Huelva province, southwestern Spain. On August 3, 1492, Columbus embarked from here on the voyage that made him the discoverer of America. In those days, Palos was a seaport, but the harbor has since silted up. **Palos** (Spanish for "woods" or "sticks") is also the

name of the Palos Verdes hills in California, near Los Angeles; the city of Palos Verdes Estates is here.

Palos de la Frontera. On the hill is the 14th-century Church of St. George.

palp *(palp)* Also, palpus. Palpi (plural) are jointed feelerlike structures connected to the mouths of insects and certain crustaceans. The function of the palp is to make contact with food and to test its palatability. **Palp** is part of the verb palpate, meaning to feel or to touch. Commonly it is identified in crosswords as "feeler." Doctors palpate abdomens, etc., regularly.

pam See *loo.*

Pamir *(pah-MEER)* or **Pamirs** *(pah-MEERZ)* A mountain system located mainly in the U.S.S.R., but extending into India, Afghanistan, and China. In 1271, the Terak Pass, one of several across the Pamir, was traveled by Marco Polo on his way to China. Natives of the region call the Pamirs *Bam-i Dun-ya,* "the roof of the world." Many peaks exceed 20,000 feet; Mount Communism (see *Garmo*) is the highest peak, at 24,590 feet, in the range and in the U.S.S.R.

Panay *(pan-AY)* An island in the Visayan group of the Philippines, located between Mindanao and Negros: the sixth largest island of the Philippine archipelago. It is primarily an agricultural region, but horses are bred in the mountains. **Panay** was also the name of an American gunboat sunk by Japanese aircraft in 1937.

panda *(PAN-dah)* A small, reddish-brown nocturnal mammal resembling the raccoon of North America, and native to the Himalayas and the peaks of western China and northern Burma. It is also called the lesser panda and the cat panda. The familiar black and white bearlike animal beloved of children is the giant panda, whose habitat is bamboo forests in the mountains of central China. In 1972, a pair was sent from Peking to the Washington National Zoo in exchange for two musk oxen. Panda is frequently clued as "zoo attraction."

Ailuropus melanoleucus—*a.k.a. panda.*

pandy *(PAN-dee)* From the Latin word *pande*, a command to extend the hand, this is a term often used in Scottish, Irish, and northern English public schools where capital punishment is still administered. A pandy is a blow to the palm by ruler or cane, for committing various proscribed acts.

panne *(pan)* From the Latin word *pinna*, meaning "feather," a textile: panne velvet, a velvet with its lustrous pile flattened in one direction. Panne also describes a heavy silk or rayon satin with a particularly smooth finish.

pansy *(PAN-zee)* A widely cultivated flowering plant of the violet family, related to the smaller violas known as heartsease and Johnny jump-up. Some people profess to see a human face in this flower, which may be why it is associated with remembrance. As a proper noun, **Pansy** was the name of L'il Abner Yokum's mother in Al Capp's famous comic strip.

Panza *(PAN-zah)* Sancho Panza in Cervantes's masterpiece, Don Quixote's peasant squire whose mount was an ass named Dapple. Sancho loved pithy proverbs. He eventually became governor of Barataria and its justice of the peace. A short, fat man, he was probably called Panza because, in Spanish, the word means "paunch."

papaw *(PAH-pah)* A name for the papaya, derived from the Spanish. The papaw, or papaya, is a tropical tree related to the custard apple. It bears large oblong orange-fleshed fruits which are eaten as dessert, crushed for juice, or treated to obtain the enzyme papain, used in commercial meat-tenderizing products and in aids to digestion. Papaw (or pawpaw) is also a tropical-appearing North American tree, *Asimina triloba,* that bears sweet, fragrant fruit. It is not related, except by common name, to the papaya.

Papen *(PAH-pin)* Franz von Papen (1879–1969), the German diplomat who served in the Prussian parliament before becoming chancellor of Germany under Hindenburg in 1932. He formed an alliance with the rising Nazi party and was made vice-chancellor after Hitler came to power as chancellor in 1933. He was thus one of the founders and continued as a shaker of the Third Reich, but was acquitted at the Nuremburg war-crimes trials in 1946.

Papua *(PAP-yoo-ah)* Name for the former territory of Papua, now included in Papua New Guinea, a country comprising the eastern half of the island of New Guinea, plus the Bismarck archipelago, the Trobriand Islands, and Bougainville in the Solomons, plus many lesser islands. Its capital is Port Moresby. Hundreds of languages are spoken by natives, but pidgin

English is widely used. Parts of the country have been in the possession of Great Britain, Australia, and Germany (before World War I). The territories of Papua and New Guinea were administratively united by Australia in 1949; the country became independent in 1975.

Para *(pah-RAH)* A 200-mile-long river of northern Brazil, actually the southeastern estuary of the Amazon. Pará is also a northern Brazilian state, in the Amazon River basin. Belém is the capital. One of the rainiest regions on earth, Pará was settled in the seventeenth century by the Portuguese to keep out the Dutch, English, and French who had established colonies in the Guianas. Belém is sometimes called Pará.

River caravans such as these are common in the Amazon basin.

Paran *(PAY-rahn)* The biblical desert region, or wilderness, in the eastern Sinai peninsula, generally to the south of ancient Palestine. It was here that Ishmael settled after being exiled by Abraham (Gen. 21:21); that David took refuge after the death of Samuel (1 Sam. 25:1); and that the Israelites rested on their way to Canaan.

Pare *(pah-RAY)* Ambroise Paré (1510–1590), the French physician who was surgeon to four kings of France. Paré advocated a more humane practice of medicine than was usual, using ligatures, for example, instead of cauterizing with boiling oil after amputation. Paré was one of the first to provide patients with artificial limbs. As a verb, to **pare** means to trim or peel.

Paris *(PAHR-iss)* According to Greek legend, the son of Hecuba and Priam (q.v.), king of Troy. On a trip to Sparta, Paris,

although already married to Oenone (q.v.), spirited off the beauteous Helen, the wife of his host, King Menelaus, thus setting off the Trojan War. (See also *Eris*.) **Paris** is also the name of the great "City of Light" on the Seine River—the capital of France known in ancient times as Lutetia, and celebrated in song and story.

parka *(PAHR-kah)* An Aleut word for a particular type of cold-weather garment. Parkas are knee-length, heavy coats or jackets, usually lined with fur or pile. An attached hood, with drawstrings to tighten it, keeps the head warm, but unfortunately does nothing for the face. Skiers' parkas are usually shorter, about hip-length.

Parma *(PAR-mah)* A city of northern Italy, capital of Parma province. Originally a Roman colony founded in 183 B.C., Parma is known for its colorful past, having been variously ruled by the Milanese; the French; the descendants of Pope Paul III, beginning in 1545 with Pier Luigi Farnese; the Spanish Bourbons; and the kingdom of Sardinia. Among the famous artists of the Parma school of painting was Correggio (c. 1494–1534). A marketing and industrial center today, it is the home of Parmesan cheese. Parma, in the U.S., is a suburb of Cleveland, Ohio.

The fortress in the northern Italian city of Parma.

Parnu *(PAR-noo)* Estonian seaport on the Gulf of Riga (q.v.), and now, as Pyarnu, part of the U.S.S.R. Founded around 1250 by the Livonian Knights, Parnu, whose German name is Pernau, was a Hanseatic League city. It was fought over in the sixteenth century by the Swedes, Poles, and Russians. In 1918, Parnu became part of the newly independent Estonia.

Paros *(PAH-ros)* One of the Cyclades Islands of southeastern Greece. The chief town is Páros. Settled by Ionia in the seventh century B.C., it was an independent power and sent out colonies of its own until the Athenians captured it in the Persian Wars. The Ottoman Turks held Páros from 1537 to 1832; it joined Greece in 1832. It is the source of Parian marble, first used by sculptors in the sixth century B.C. and still quarried here.

The town of Páros on the Cycladean island of the same name.

Parr *(par)* Surname of various individuals, including Catherine Parr (1512–1548), sixth wife of Henry VIII, who managed to survive him and become queen dowager; and Thomas Parr (c.1483–1635), the allegedly 152-year-old Englishman known as Old Parr, who died after being presented to Charles I and who was buried in Westminster Abbey.

pasan *(PASS-un)* A wild goat, also called the Persian bezoar goat, native to southern Europe and Asia Minor. The pasan is related to the markhor and the ibex (q.v.). It was probably the ancestor of today's domestic goats, all of Old World origin. Goats were first brought to Mexico by Spanish settlers.

Pasha *(PAH-sha)* From the Turkish for "head," a former Islamic title, usually placed after the name. This was the highest honorary, rather than hereditary, title in the Ottoman Empire, and was usually bestowed on ministers, governors, and generals. It is sometimes spelled Bashaw. **Pasha** was also the name of the Yorkshire terrier owned by President Richard Nixon.

Pasht See *Bast.*

Passy *(pah-SEE)* Frédéric Passy (1822–1912), the French lawyer, economist, journalist, and founder in 1867 of the International League for Permanent Peace. Passy was also a member of the chamber of deputies from 1874 to 1889. In 1901, he was one of two recipients of the first Nobel Peace Prize.

Patan *(PAHT-in)* Also known as Lalitpur, a city situated in the Katmandu Valley of central Nepal (q.v.). Patan was founded in the seventh century and is the oldest major city in the country. Legend has it that the four shrines of Patan were built there by the emperor Asoka around 250 B.C.

Pathe *(path-EY)* Charles Pathé (1873–1957), French photographer and father of the movie newsreel. About 1909, he was the first to present a newsreel as a regular attraction at a Paris cinema. Introduced to the United States in 1910, the crowing rooster of the Pathé news title frame became familiar to generations of moviegoers.

Patna *(PAHT-nuh)* A Ganges River city in the state of Bihar, northeastern India. Primarily an agricultural center, it is known for the region's fine rice. Patna, then called Pataliputra, was an imperial city during the Mauryan era (c. 325–185 B.C.) and the Gupta era (A.D. c. 320–545). Archaeologically important ruins stand as a reminder of Patna's past glory.

Patti *(PAH-tee)* Adelina Patti (1843–1919), the celebrated Italian coloratura soprano who became the toast of opera buffs in Paris, Milan, London, and New York.

Adelina Patti.

Adelina set the stage, as it were, for her sisters Carlotta and Amelia, who also sang, and brother Carlo, who conducted. Crossword clues sometimes point to singer **Patti** Page.

pave *(pah-VEY)* From the past participle of a French verb meaning "to pave," pavé is an unusual kind of pavement: a jewelry setting in which the stones are placed in such close proximity that no metal can be seen.

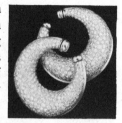

These earrings designed by Paloma Picasso are set with pavé diamonds.

pavis *(PAV-iss)* The word comes from the Italian *pavese,* relating to the city of Pavia, where this item was first made in medieval times. A pavis is a type of shield large enough to protect the entire body. It's doubtful, however, whether any soldier powerful enough to wield a pavis really needed it.

Pavo *(PAY-voe)* The Latin word for "peacock" and name of the genus to which it belongs. **Pavo** is a constellation of 11 stars thought by the ancients to resemble a peacock. It usually appears near the Pole in the Southern Hemisphere. Pavo's neighbors include the constellations of Octans, Telescopium, Indus (q.v.), and the Southern Triangle.

pavor *(PAY-ver)* In psychiatric terminology, a groundless fear or fright, such as *pavor nocturnus,* the night terror sometimes experienced by children.

pawl *(pawl)* In machinery, a device that prevents a cogwheel from turning in reverse. The usual pawl is a hinged metal tab that slides easily over the notches of a cog turning in one direction but would catch in the cog's notches if reversed.

pawn *(pawn)* A small, relatively valueless chessman of which each player has eight; a pawn can be moved only one square at a time after the first move, but can become a queen. By extension, a **pawn** is also or a person who is used without his acquiescence; or something given to assure repayment of a loan, such as the items seen in a pawnshop window.

Pax *(pax)* In Roman religion, goddess of peace and one of the Horae. A temple was finally dedicated to her by the Emperor Vespasian, and she is represented as a beautiful woman bearing a cornucopia and an olive branch. Pax was also the name of a seeing-eye dog in the TV series *Longstreet.* The Latin word for peace, **pax** occurs in the phrase *pax vobiscum* (peace be with you).

pe or **peh** *(pay)* The seventeenth letter of the Hebrew alphabet, comparable to the letter *P* in the English alphabet. Two forms of this character exist—the regular pe, and the one that is used only as the last letter of a word. See also *feh.*

Peary *(PEER-ee)* Robert Edwin Peary (1856–1920), the American explorer who discovered the North Pole. After several unsuccessful tries, Peary reached the Pole, along with a servant and four Eskimos, on April 6, 1909. His achievement was challenged by Dr. Frederick A. Cook, a surgeon who had been with Peary's 1891–1892 expedition, and who claimed to have reached the Pole in 1908. A sensational controversy followed. Peary's wife accompanied him on several expeditions, and gave birth to a daughter in the Arctic.

Josephine Peary.   *Robert Peary.*

peat *(peet)* From the medieval Latin for a lump of sod, humusy material composed of decaying vegetable matter, often sphagnum or mosses, or sedges. Peat is found in swamps and bogs. When dried and cut into blocks, certain types of peat will burn and are used as fuel in Ireland, where coal and wood are at a premium. Peat is a valuable soil conditioner where organic material is required.

peavy or **peavey** *(PEE-vee)* An indispensable item for lumberjacks. It consists of a heavy wooden lever, with a sharp, pointed metal tip and a hinged hook near the end. This arrangement makes it ideal for manipulating floating logs being driven downriver. The device was named for its inventor, Joseph Peavey.

peck *(pek)* Either the motion made by a bird with its beak and, hence, a quick, perfunctory kiss; or a unit of dry volume equal to eight quarts. As a proper noun, it is the surname of George Wilbur **Peck** (1840–1916), American humorist and author of the beloved "Peck's Bad Boy" stories. Also the name of Oscar-winning film actor Gregory Peck (1916–   ).

Pecos *(PEY-koss)* A 926-mile-long river rising in northern New Mexico and flowing generally southeast across the state and into Texas, where it joins the Rio Grande.

There are important reclamation dams on the Pecos that irrigate many thousands of acres. In the early days, "west of the Pecos" referred to the rugged, lawless lands of West Texas, ruled over by the likes of Judge Roy Bean (q.v.). According to American legend, a character called Pecos Bill is supposed to have dug the Rio Grande riverbed.

The bridge in the background carries U.S. 90 high above the Pecos River.

Pecs *(paych)* A city in southwestern Hungary, near the Yugoslavian border, and a coal-mining center. Pécs is one of Hungary's oldest cities, tracing back to a Celtic settlement that became the capital of the Roman province of Lower Pannonia. Under Turkish rule for over 100 years, Pécs is noted for its Turkish minaret, a cathedral, and several churches that were once mosques.

pedal *(PED-uhl)* From the Latin for "foot," a leverlike device operated by the foot. Pedals are used to put certain pieces of equipment into motion, such as sewing machines and bicycles; to make others stop, such as automobiles; or to change the tone of musical instruments like the harp, organ, and piano.

peer *(peer)* Meaning an equal, this word is derived from the Latin *par,* which also refers to equality. In England, however, a peer is a noble. Peers of the Realm include five orders—duke, marquess, earl, viscount, and baron. The 12 illustrious paladins, or knights, of Charlemagne were called peers. The given name **Peer** belongs to the title character of the musical suite *Peer Gynt* (see *Grieg*).

Lord Darnley, Mary Queen of Scots' husband.

Pegu *(peh-GOO)* City in southern Burma, an important river and rail transportation hub, and center of Burmese culture. Pegu's history goes back to A.D. 825, when it was founded by the Mons and became their capital after their king, Binnya U, built his palace there. Among Pegu's many temples, the Shwe Maw Daw Pagoda is outstanding.

Peguy *(paig-EE)* Charles Péguy (1873–1914), French socialist and poet known for long, mystical poems in free verse. A fighter for justice, he was the leading Roman Catholic aligned with Alfred Dreyfus in the Dreyfus Affair. Péguy was killed in action during the Battle of the Marne in World War I.

pekan *(PEK-un)* From an Algonquian word, a large tree-dwelling mammal related to the weasels and the marten and indigenous to the North American continent. The pekan, called the fisher or fisher-cat, is carnivorous and ferocious, often preying on larger animals. Its fur is blackish on top and brown or gray underneath, and is highly valued, ranking with ermine and sable.

pekoe *(PEEK-oh; PEK-oh)* A black tea comprising the smaller leaves that grow at the tips of the plant stems. Pekoe is grown primarily in Sri Lanka and India. Its name, Chinese for "white down," refers to the picking of leaves while in their young, downy state.

Tea leaves being harvested in India.

Pele *(PAY-lay)* In Hawaiian mythology, the deity of volcanoes who lives in Halemaumau, the fire pit of Kilauea volcano. With the second *e* accented, the name by which the world knows Edson Arantes de Nascimento (1940–), the Brazilian soccer star and perhaps the greatest player in the history of the game.

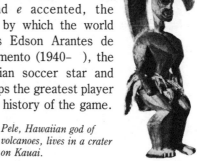

Pele, Hawaiian god of volcanoes, lives in a crater on Kauai.

Pelee *(peh-LAY)* A 4,429-foot-high volcano on Martinique Island in the French West Indies. Pelée last erupted on May 8, 1902, resulting in the deaths of about 40,000 people and burying Saint-Pierre, the city at its base. To this day, the area is a virtual wasteland.

pelf *(pelf)* From the medieval French word *pelfre,* "booty," which also gives us the English word pilfer. Pelf originally referred to booty or assets obtained by extra-legal means. Today the word has become a contemptuous term for mere money, i.e., wealth accumulated for its own sake.

Pelly See *Lewes.*

pelt *(pelt)* Either a term denoting speed, as in "Paul Revere galloped at full pelt," or "pelted along"; or the skin of any furry animal, removed and prepared for tanning. Pelt comes from the Old French word *pele-terie* by way of the Latin *pellis,* for "fur." In France today, a furrier is called a *pelletier.* **Pelt** as a noun means also the dead quarry of a hawk. As a verb it means to strike with missiles.

Groucho Marx examines Harpo's pelt halt while Chico looks on in Go West, *1940.*

Pemba *(PEM-bah)*

A Tanzanian island just off the east coast of Africa, in the Indian Ocean. Originally settled, beginning in the tenth century, by traders from the Persian Gulf, Pemba has been ruled by the Portuguese, Omani Arabs, and British. Pemba is the world's number one supplier of cloves. It became independent in 1963 and part of Tanzania in 1964.

pence *(pence)*

The English plural for penny, which comes from an Old English word related to the root of the German *pfennig.* Pence is abbreviated *d,* the first letter of *denarius,* the Latin for "coin." Until the British adopted the decimal system, 12 pence equaled one shilling. There are now 100 pence to the pound; abbreviated in British speech, penny and pence have become "p."

Penda *(PEN-dah)*

An early monarch (d. A.D. 654) of Anglo-Saxon England. After allying himself with Cadwallon of Wales and defeating Edwin of Northumbria, he ascended the throne of Mercia, an area now generally comprising most of the Midlands, and reigned from c. 632, considerably ex-panding his realm. Mercia was ruled by eight of Penda's descendants, starting with his son, Wulfhere.

pengo *(PEN-goe)*

The Hungarian word for "jingling," which would be the sound made by a pocketful of pengös, originally a coin and then the basic monetary unit of Hungary from 1925 to 1946. The pengö was replaced by the forint (q.v.).

1930 silver 5-pengö piece.

peon *(PEE-ahn)*

In Latin America, formerly anyone forced into involuntary service to pay a debt. Peons could not quit until their creditors were paid, and prices were such that they found themselves always in debt. Nowadays, a peon is simply a member of the working class. Peonage also existed in the American South after the Civil War; a form persists as sharecropping. A **peon** is also a foot soldier or constable in India.

Pepin *(PEP-in)*

The name of three generations of early Frankish nobles, the most famous of whom was Pepin the Short, first Carolingian king of the Franks and father of Charlemagne. Pepin was also spelled Pippin, the title of a successful Broadway musical based very loosely on his life. **Pepin,** no relation, is a lake in the course of the Mississippi near Red Wing, Minnesota.

Pepys *(peeps)*

Samuel Pepys (1633–1703), English official and author of what has been called the greatest diary in the English language. Written in cipher, it presents a vivid overview of life during the early Restoration, covering a period from 1660 to 1669, when failing eyesight caused Pepys to stop working.

Samuel Pepys.

Perak *(PAY-rak)* A Malaysian state in the central Malay Peninsula, on the Strait of Malacca. The capital is Ipok. Perak is noted for its tin mines and output of rubber, copra, and rice. Perak was at various times a subjugated state of the Sultan of Acheh and a British protectorate. In 1896, it became part of the Federated Malay States, and in 1948, a part of the Federation of Malaya.

Perga *(PER-gah)* A city of antiquity situated about ten miles north of what is now Antalya, Turkey. Perga, in ancient Pamphylia, was known as the abode of an Asiatic nature deity, and was the destination of St. Paul on his first journey (Acts 14:25).

Part of the ruins of the ancient city of Perga—not to be confused with Pergamun, also in Turkey.

peri *(PEER-ree)* In Persian mythology, a supernatural being doing penance in order to gain entrance to Paradise, and responsible for such natural phenomena as eclipses and comets. Peris were originally thought to be fallen angels who directed the beneficent to Heaven. According to the Koran (q.v.), they report to Mohammed and Eblis (q.v.).

Perm *(pyerm)* A city on the Kama (q.v.) River in the northeastern U.S.S.R. Founded in 1780, Perm is an important producer of machinery. It is also known for chemical plants, oil refineries, and Gorky University, founded in 1916. From 1940 to 1958, the name of the city was Molotov. As a slang word, **perm** *(perm)* is short for permanent wave, as in the hair.

Peron *(peh-RONE)* Juan Domingo Perón (1895–1974), twice president of Argentina, and proponent of fascism. His totalitarian regime, begun in 1946, faltered with the death of his popular wife, Eva, in 1952. After a period of exile beginning in 1955, he was again elected president in 1973, with his second wife, Maria Estela (Isabel) as vice-president. She became president upon his death, the first woman to head a Western Hemisphere nation. She was overthrown and put under house arrest by a military junta (q.v.) in 1976. The successful Broadway musical *Evita* was based on the life of Eva Perón.

Perth *(perth)* Either of two cities: the capital of Western Australia, founded in 1829, but important only since the Coolgardie gold rush in the 1890s, and now a thriving commercial center; or an historic city on the Tay (q.v.) River in central Scotland, county town of Perthshire. Perth was the capital of Scotland from the eleventh to the fifteenth century. A frequent crossword clue is also "_____ Amboy, New Jersey."

St. Leonard's-in-the-Field Church can be seen across South Inch, a green in Perth, Scotland.

peso *(PEY-soe)* From the Spanish for "weight," by way of the Latin *pensum*, meaning something to be weighed, the peso is a monetary unit of several Latin-American countries where it is usually worth 100 centavos. Peso is abbreviated as P. in the Dominican Republic and as $ in Argentina, Colombia, Cuba, Mexico, and Uruguay. In crosswords, peso is often clued in relation to the countries, as "Mexican wherewithal," "Cuban coin," etc.

Petra *(PEE-tra)* An ancient city called Sela or Selah in the Bible (2 Kings 14:7) and Wadi Musa by modern Jordanians. Occupied variously by Edomites, Nabataeans, Romans (who made it the capital of Arabia Petraea), and Muslims, from the seventh century until its capture by Crusaders, Petra was unknown to the West until 1812. Its ruins were discovered in a high hollow among cliffs reached via a tortuous pass through a gorge. The place is famous for its rock-cut tombs in the surrounding hills and for its Roman ruins.

petrel *(PET-rul)* Any of a number of oceanic birds, including several called Mother Carey's chickens. Some petrels dive, while storm petrels—believed to presage bad weather—fly fast and close to the surface, seeming to walk on water. In fact, the name petrel derives from St. Peter, in allusion to his walking on the Sea of Galilee at Jesus's bidding, following the miracle of the loaves and fishes.

pewee *(PEE-wee)* This is the common name for the phoebe and several other small American flycatchers related to it. There are over 350 different species of flycatchers, distributed from northern Canada to Patagonia. Most pewees are small, shy, and gray-colored, like the Eastern phoebe or water pewee, whose name echoes its call.

Phebe *(FEE-bee)* In Shakespeare's *As You Like It,* a shepherdess who comes upon Rosalind dressed as a man in the forest of Arden, and promptly falls in love with the stranger. When Phebe realizes her error, she is persuaded to return to her original sweetheart, Silvius. Phebe is also an alternate spelling for Phoebe.

phi *(fie)* The twenty-first letter of the Greek alphabet, with a sound comparable to the *f* sound of the letters *ph* in English. Phi is the first letter of Phi Beta Kappa, the oldest Greek-letter society in American academia, founded at William and Mary College on December 5, 1776. It is an honorary society for outstanding scholars. The letters are the initial ones of *Philosophia Biou Kybernetes* (philosophy, the guide of life).

Philo *(FIE-loe)* Alexandrian Jewish philosopher (c. 20 B.C.–A.D. 50) who went to Rome representing Jews who had refused to worship Caligula and wanted their rights restored. As a philosopher, he interpreted biblical doctrines allegorically, in a way that found in them many doctrines of Greek philosophy. Philo is also the first name of S.S. Van Dine's popular fictional detective, Philo Vance.

Phlox *(floks)* From the Greek for "flame," a genus of perennial and annual garden plants with brilliant white, red, pink, purple, and violet flowers. Phlox is also a common name for other plants of the Polemonium family, which includes, besides the *Phlox* genus, wild and garden flowers such as the Jacob's ladder. Phloxes include Sweet William and moss pinks.

A phlox plant.

Phobos *(FOE-bose)* In Greek mythology, the goddess of panic and fear whose name gave us "phobia," meaning an irrational and persistent fear of some object or situation. In astronomy, **Phobos** is the name of the inner and larger of the two moons that orbit the planet Mars.

phot *(fote)* From the Greek word for "light," this is a unit of illumination. Specifically, it is equal to one lumen (q.v.) per square centimeter. If this sounds confusing, think of a phot as the direct illumination produced by a uniform source of one international footcandle upon a surface one centimeter away. Phot, as a prefix, means light or photograph; it is also the abbreviation for photographer or photography.

Piast *(pyahst)*   The first dynasty of Polish monarchs, among them Mieszko I, who reigned from 962 to 992; his son, Boleslaus I, who claimed the crown in 1025; Casimir I, who reigned from 1040 to 1058; and Ladislaus Herman, king from 1079 to 1102. The Piast name derived from the dynasty's legendary founder, a simple peasant.

Piave *(PYAH-vay)*   A 137-mile-long river flowing in a southerly direction from the Carnic Alps of northeastern Italy into the Gulf of Venice. The Piave became famous during World War I when Italian troops held there against heavy Austrian attack until a combined Allied offensive repelled the invaders in October 1918.

pica *(PIE-kah)*   Either 12-point type in printing and its height, used as a measure; or a condition characterized by cravings to ingest such strange things such as hair, sand, or chalk, and caused by nutritional deficiencies. The word is from the Latin for "magpie," a bird of unusual appetites.

pice *(pise)*   An Anglicized version of the Hindi word *paisā,* this is a small Indian coin equal to one-quarter of an anna. In the currency of India, there are 25 annas and 100 pice to the rupee (q.v.).

picot *(PEE-koe)*   From the French meaning "pike" or "point," picot is tatting terminology for any of a series of small, single-thread loops that edge ribbon or lace, or a crocheted edging of small points.

Pict *(pikt)*   Ancient Caledonian inhabitant of Scotland, north of a line between the Clyde and the Forth, from about A.D. 300 to A.D. 850. The Picts harassed both Romans and Britons. Possibly descended from

Bronze Age invaders of Britain, the Picts covered their bodies with woad (q.v.), a plant pigment. Eventually they were amalgamated with other Scots. Their name comes from the Latin word for "paint."

Picus *(PIE-kus)*   In classical mythology, a prophet and soothsayer who was in love with Pomona, goddess of fruit, and who therefore resisted the amorous advances of the siren Circe. In a fit of jealousy, she turned him into a woodpecker, a bird still thought to possess prophetic powers; several types belong to the *Picus* genus.

piet *(PIE-eht)*   Another name for the magpie, a bird related to the jackdaw, crow, jay, raven, and rook (q.v.). Piets tend to congregate in small groups. They destroy other birds' eggs, kill sickly newborn lambs or calves by pecking, eat carrion and harmful insects, emit piercing cries, and will steal and hoard any brightly colored object. Caged, they can be trained to speak imitatively. **Piet** is also the first name of painter Mondrian (1872–1944).

Pieta *(pyay-TAH)*   From the Italian for "pious lady," a representation in painting or sculpture of the Virgin Mary holding the body of Jesus after the Crucifixion. The most famous Pietà is the one by Michelangelo in St. Peter's in Rome. His name is chiseled into the ribbon of Mary's dress. This Pietà suffered damage at the hands of a madman in 1973, but has been restored.

pika *(PIE-kah)*   From the Siberian-Tungusik *piika,* a small, short-eared, gnawing animal native to the mountainous regions of Asia and western North America.

Pikas resemble guinea pigs, but are related to rabbits and hares. They are also known as calling hares, because of the bleating cry they emit to warn each other of danger. Other names are mouse hare and rock rabbit. Some pikas cut, air-dry, and store plants for a winter supply of food.

pilau *(pill-AW)* or pilaf *(pil-AFF)*

Transferred intact into English from the Persian, pilau is a rice dish native to Asia and Asia Minor. Meat or fish is often added, and the pilau is spiced according to national preference. The pilau in Indian restaurants, for example, tends to be much hotter than a Persian or Turkish version.

pili *(PILL-ee)*

Either the name of a tropical tree native to the Philippine Islands, or the edible nut it produces. The pili nut, a one-seeded fruit consisting of a kernel within a hard and woody husk, most resembles an almond. **Pili** is also the plural of pilus, a hair or hairlike structure.

Pilon *(pee-LOHN)*

Germain Pilon (1535–1590), French sculptor under the later Valois kings. Pilon's work appears on the mausoleum of Henry II at Saint-Denis, and his sculptures can also be seen in the Louvre. As controller of the mint under Charles IX, Pilon produced medals and coins that are second to none.

pima *(PEE-mah)*

A strong-fibered cotton developed through selective cultivation of Egyptian cotton plants. Also, a tribe of Nahuatl (q.v.) Indians related to the Aztecs, and the name of their language. In the early 1800s, the Pima and Maricopa tribes were merged. Their descendants, now numbering some 10,000, live on the Gila and Salt River reservations in Arizona.

A Pima Indian.

CROSSWORD CLINIC

AFFLICTIONS

ague	furfur	psora
amok	gout	rale
apnea	grume	sprue
colic	hack	sty
coma	ichor	torus
crick	kibe	tuber
croup	lupus	varix
dolor	pavor	virix
edema	phobia	virus
ennui	pica	wen
fetor	polyp	

CONSULTANTS

Adler	Garth	Pregl
Bevan	Hess	Prout
Binet	Jung	Redi
Coue	Mayo brothers	Reik
Crick		Rous
Doyle	Minot	Roux
Ellis	Ochoa	Spock
Fanon	Osler	Tache
Faure	Pare	Tuke family
Faust	Pinel	
Galen	Pott	Wiley

Pinel *(pee-NELL)* Phillippe Pinel (1745–1826), a French physician and pioneer in psychiatric care, who espoused more humane treatment of the insane. For example, his work *Mental Aberration* advocated the abolition of forcible restraints. Pinel was the first to keep extensive psychiatric case histories for the purpose of research.

pinna *(PIN-ah)* A word with several scientific meanings. In anatomy, it is the part of the ear that stands away from the head; in zoology, a feather, wing, fin, or similar structure; and in botany, one of a group of leaves that resembles a feather. The word *pinna* is Latin for "feather"; the plural is *pinnae*. **Pinna,** from the Greek meaning "a kind of mussel," is also the name of a bivalve mollusk.

An eagle, talons ready, with pinnas spread.

Pinsk *(pinsk)* A city and port at the juncture of the Pina and Pripyat rivers in Belorussia, European U.S.S.R. Today a bustling transport junction, Pinsk once belonged to Lithuania (1320) and twice to Poland (1569 and 1921). During the German occupation of World War II, most of Pinsk's large Jewish population was exterminated.

Pinto *(PEEN-toh)* Fernão Mendes Pinto (c. 1509–1583), a Portuguese adventurer whose book *Peregrinação* is one of the most exciting accounts of world travel ever written. Also, from the Spanish for "painted," the familiar spotted horse of the American West, or the equally familiar spotted **pinto** bean, excellent with chili con carne.

Pippa *(PIP-ah)* The heroine of Robert Browning's dramatic poem "Pippa Passes" (1841). Pippa is an Italian peasant girl who works in a silk factory. On her only holiday, New Year's Day, Pippa appears by chance at crucial moments in the lives of various characters who are unwittingly influenced by her singing.

pique *(peek)* From the French *piquer*, "to sting," a state of displeasure at being stung, slighted, or mistreated. *Pique* is also French for "pike" or "spade"; and *Pique Dame*, as in the title of Tchaikovsky's opera, is a fancy reference to the queen of spades. With an accent, **piqué** *(pee-KAY)* is a firmly woven ribbed cotton fabric.

pirn *(pern)* From the Middle English for "pointed twig," this is an object originally made from a bit of wood—the bobbin, reel, or spool for thread contained within the shuttle used in weaving. To a Scot, a pirn is the reel on his fishing rod.

Pirna *(PEER-nah)* An industrial city on the Elbe River in the Dresden region of East Germany. Pirna can trace its history back to 1233. It has belonged to Bohemia and to Meissen. In 1756, Pirna was the site of the Saxonian surrender to Prussia in the Seven Years War.

Pisa *(PEE-zah)* City in Tuscany, on the Arno in north-central Italy. Once a seaport but now six miles inland, Pisa was formerly a Greek colony and subsequently belonged to the Etruscans, then the Romans. Today it is a thriving industrial center whose 180-foot-high marble tower is famous throughout the world for leaning. It is 16 feet off of the perpendicular. Galileo was born here and later taught at the university. A Renaissance sculptor, Nicola Pisano, took his name from the city.

Though the town has many fine buildings, Pisa is best known for its leaning tower.

Pisco *(PEES-koe)*   A Pacific Ocean port city in southwestern Peru, and a stopping-off place for tourists exploring the nearby Paracaus peninsula and its pre-Inca ruins. Pisco is a cotton-processing center, but is best known as the home of Pisco brandy—a liquor used in the world-famous Pisco Sour.

Piso *(PIE-soe)*   The name of an ancient noble Roman family, including: Lucius Calpurnius Piso Caesoninus, a proconsul who feuded with Cicero and succeeded in having him exiled in 58 B.C.; Calpurnia, his daughter, who married Julius Caesar in 59 B.C.; and Caius Calpurnius Piso, a literary type who plotted against Nero (q.v.) and, when discovered, killed himself.

pitot *(PEE-toe)*   A device that measures the speed at which fluid (and air, in this instance) flows, invented by Henry Pitot (1695–1771). Used in aircraft, it is a tube pointing forward that measures speed by means of a manometer recording the pressure of incoming air. Readings are adjusted for the thinness of air at higher altitudes, and converted to miles per hour or, for supersonic planes, to Mach numbers (one Mach equals the speed of sound). The distance and speed of a ship are measured by application of the same principles.

Pitta *(PITT-ah)*   A single genus within a family of small, brilliantly colored, stubby-tailed, long-legged birds also known as jewel thrushes and ground thrushes. Pittas inhabit tropical forests and move by hopping rather than flying. They do fly when migrating, however. One of the best known is the Australian noisy pitta, who spends his days cracking snail shells open on a rock.

pixie or **pixy** *(PIK-see)*   A word of obscure origin, meaning a small sprite, elf (q.v.), or fairy. Used mostly in the British Isles, pixie designates a happy, somewhat capricious supernatural being given to playing pranks and dancing around mushrooms under a full moon.

plebe *(pleeb)*   Another form of the word pleb or plebeian, any one of the people who made up the main body of Roman citizenry, as compared to patricians, with whom they achieved political equality only after establishment of the tribune of the plebeians (500–450 B.C.). Today, plebes are the "common people" anywhere, or freshmen at West Point and Annapolis.

Pliny *(PLIN-ee)*   Caius Plinius Secundus (A.D. 23–79), known as Pliny the Elder, Roman naturalist who wrote extensively, but often inaccurately, about science, and died in an eruption of Mount Vesuvius. Also, his nephew, Caius Plinius Caecilius Secundus, known as Pliny the Younger (A.D. c. 62–113), the orator and statesman famous for letters giving a detailed picture of Roman life.

Pluto *(PLUE-toe)*   In Greek mythology, son of Cronus and Rhea (q.v.), brother of Zeus (q.v.) and Poseidon, and god of the underworld, who was sometimes called Hades (q.v.) after his realm. Persephone was his consort. The entire cast of characters, renamed (Pluto became Dis—q.v.), were in the Roman pantheon as well. **Pluto** is also the ninth and outermost planet of the solar system discovered in 1930 by Clyde W. Tombaugh. And, of course, the irrepressible dog belonging to Mickey Mouse in Walt Disney cartoons.

Po *(poe)* Stretching over 400 miles, this is the longest river in Italy. The Po rises in the Cottian Alps of northwestern Italy and flows east past Turin, Cremona, and Ferrara to its marshy delta on the Adriatic. Small craft can navigate most of the Po, and its valley is the most important agricultural and industrial region of Italy. Also, in Maon and Polynesian mythology, **Po** is the equivalent of Hades (q.v.).

Poe *(poe)* Edgar Allan Poe (1809–1849), morbid and erratic but brilliant American poet, critic, and short-story writer. Poe is

Edgar Allan Poe.

famous for such Gothic tales of horror as *The Pit and the Pendulum* and *The Black Cat,* and is considered the father of modern detective fiction. The mystery writers' equivalent of the Oscar award is the Edgar, named in his honor.

pogy *(POE-gee)* From the Algonquian word *pauhaugen,* the menhaden, a fish related to the herring and found along the Atlantic Coast from New England to the Carolinas. Too oily to be particularly edible, the menhaden is used for bait and as a source of oil and fish meal for fertilizer.

poi *(poy; POE-ee)* A word that has entered English from the Hawaiian, poi is a food made by roasting roots of the taro (q.v.), peeling them, grinding or pounding them, and then allowing fermentation to occur. The result is a sticky paste, eaten with meat or fish in the islands of the Pacific.

poilu *(pwah-LOO)* French for "hairy," or "virile," poilu was the somewhat complimentary slang term by which French soldiers were known during World War I. Balzac had used it earlier to denote bravery. The poilu's Allied army counterparts were the English Tommy and the American Yank.

Poins *(poynz)* Edward Poins, an "irregular humorist" in both parts of Shakespeare's *Henry IV.* Poins, along with Bardolph, Pistol, Peto, and Gadshill, was a crony of Captain Sir John Falstaff, soldier, wit, and raffish pal of "Mad-cap Hal." Poins took part in many of Falstaff's outrageous practical jokes.

Pola See *Siren.*

polo *(POE-loe)* Variation of *pulu,* Tibetan for "ball." Polo is a game of Asiatic origin in which two four-player teams on horseback try to hit a wooden ball between each other's goal posts (see *chukka*). Also, the surname of Marco **Polo** (c. 1254–1324), Venetian traveler to the Orient who reached Peking and became Kublai Khan's favorite. The **polo** shirt is a short-sleeved pullover garment with a placket neckline.

A game of polo being played in Great Park, Windsor, England.

polyp *(POL-ip)* Either a type of elongated, flowerlike, aquatic animal such as the sea anemone, with small tentacle-like structures fringing its mouth; or, in medicine, a tumor, usually benign, growing from a mucous membrane. Polyp comes from the Greek for "many-footed."

THE GRAND TOUR

Accra (W. Afr.)
Agra (Ind.)
Aix (Fr.)
Akita (Jap.)
Albi (Fr.)
Amiens (Fr.)
Amman (Jordan)
Anzio (It.)
Arles (Fr.)
Arras (Fr.)
Aswan (Egypt)
Avila (Sp.)
Blois (Fr.)
Brno (Czech.)
Como (It.)
Cuzco (Peru)
Dacca (Bangl.)
Davao (Phil.)
Davos (Switz.)
Dax (Fr.)
Delft (Neth.)
Delhi (Ind.)
Derby (Eng.)
Dijon (Fr.)
Eboli (It.)

Edfu (Egypt)
Eger (Hung.)
Enns (Austr.)
Epsom (Eng.)
Fez (Morocco)
Fulda (W. Ger.)
Gagra (U.S.S.R.)
Gaspe (Que.)
Ghent (Belgium)
Giza (Egypt)
Graz (Austr.)
The Hague (Neth.)
Halle (E. Ger.)
Hilo (Haw.)
Hue (S. Vietnam)
Ica (Peru)
Iona (Hebrides)
Ipin (Ch.)
Ise (Jap.)
Isna (Egypt)
Jaen (Sp.)
Jedda (Saudi Arabia)

Jehol (Ch.)
Jena (E. Ger.)
Jerez (Sp.)
Jinja (Uganda)
Kabul (Afghan.)
Kandy (Sri Lanka)
Kano (Nig.)
Kirov (U.S.S.R.)
Lech (Austr.)
Lhasa (Tibet)
Lido (It.)
Liege (Belg.)
Lille (Fr.)
Lyon (Fr.)
Meroe (Egypt)
Minsk (U.S.S.R.)
Nairn (Scot.)
Nara (Jap.)
Nome (Alaska)
Noyon (Fr.)
Omsk (U.S.S.R.)
Orel (U.S.S.R.)
Ostia (It.)
Otsu (Jap.)

Paarl (S. Afr.)
Padua (It.)
Pagan (Burma)
Palos (Sp.)
Para (Belem; Braz.)
Parma (It.)
Patan (Nepal)
Patna (Ind.)
Pecs (Hung.)
Pegu (Burma)
Perm (U.S.S.R.)
Perth (Austrl.; Scot.)
Petra (Jordan)
Pisa (It.)
Poona (Ind.)
Posen (Pol.)
Praha (Czech.)
Prato (It.)
Pskov (U.S.S.R.)
Pully (Switz.)
Puri (Ind.)

Qina (Egypt)
Quito (Ecuador)
Qum (Iran)
Radom (Pol.)
Ramla (Isr.)
Rasht (Iran)
Reims (Fr.)
Reus (Sp.)
Ripon (Eng.)
Riva (It.)
Rodez (Fr.)
Ronda (Sp.)
Roros (Nor.)
Safi (Morocco)
Sana (N. Yemen)
Sens (Fr.)
Sian (Ch.)
Sibiu (Rom.)
Siena (It.)
Sikar (Ind.)
Simla (Ind.)
Sitka (Alaska)
Skara (Swed.)
Sligo (Ire.)

Sochi (U.S.S.R.)
Soria (Sp.)
Stip (Yugo.)
Tegea (Gr.)
Tepic (Mex.)
Thun (Switz.)
Tikal (Guatemala)
Tigre (Argentina)
Tomar (Port.)
Tula (Mex.)
Turin (It.)
Ulm (W. Ger.)
Uxmal (Mex.)
Vaduz (Liechtenstein)
Vilna (U.S.S.R.)
Vina (Chile)
Wels (Aust.)
Wesel (W. Ger.)
Wien (Aust.)
Wolin (Pol.)
Wusih (Ch.)

pome *(pome)* From the Latin word *pomum,* which designates an apple or fruit in general, pome is botanical terminology for any fleshy fruit encircling a core, usually containing five seeds within a bony or paperlike capsule. Examples of pomes include the apple, pear, and quince. A **pome** was also a medieval small ball or globe.

Pomo *(POE-moe)* A tribe of northern California coastal Indians, who lived just to the north of the zone of influence of Franciscan missionaries in the eighteenth and nineteenth centuries. The Pomo are renowned

for their baskets and other craft objects, many of which are now in art museums and private collections. At this writing, only about 1,000 Pomo survive.

A Pomo woman.

Ponca *(PONK-ah)* North American Indians of the Siouan linguistic group, originally inhabiting the Ohio valley. Subsequently, the Ponca lived in what is now Minnesota, South Dakota, and Nebraska, where they were encountered by the Lewis and Clark expedition. A commission appointed by President Hayes in 1880 gave the Ponca land in Nebraska and Oklahoma, where most of them now live.

A Ponca tribesman.

Ponce *(PONE-say)* A large port city on the Caribbean, in southern Puerto Rico. Founded early in the sixteenth century, Ponce is one of the oldest cities in the Western Hemisphere. It is also a given name of Juan **Ponce** de León (c. 1460–1521), Spanish explorer and seeker of the Fountain of Youth who discovered Florida during his search.

pone *(pone)* From the Algonquian Indian word for "bread," a loaf or cake made from cornmeal, highly favored in the southern United States. Also, from the Latin word *ponere,* "to place," the **pone** in certain card games is the player to the dealer's right; also, a writ in old English law.

pons *(pohnz)* In anatomy, tissue connecting two parts of an organ, such as the *pons varolii,* a band of fibers linking the cerebrum and cerebellum of the brain. *Pons* is Latin for "bridge." As a proper noun, it's the surname of Lily **Pons** (1904–), the French coloratura soprano who won America's heart in the 1930s.

pood, paud, or **pud** *(pood)* In Russia, a unit of weight equal to about 36.113 pounds avoirdupois. The Russian word *pud,* which derives from the Old Norse *pund,* eventually transmuted into the English pound.

pooka *(POO-kah)* In Irish folklore, a malign spirit or hobgoblin who ushers mortals to their destruction. Pookas may take the form of a horse (most common) or eagle. In Mary Chase's Pulitzer Prize–winning play *Harvey,* the hero's pooka friend was an invisible rabbit of gentler disposition.

Poona *(POO-nah)* A city of west-central India in the state of Maharashtra. In the seventeenth and eighteenth centuries, Poona was the capital of the powerful Mahratta confederation; under the British, it became a regional military headquarters. Today, it is a commercial center specializing in metalworks, and the home of a major university, a meteorological observatory, and a national-defense academy.

poop *(poop)* From the Italian *poppa,* the stern of a ship, this is the raised stern deck, occasionally forming the roof of a cabin below, in a sailing ship. In slang, **poop** is synonymous with inside information or, more often, rumor. In general parlance, to be **pooped** is to be exhausted.

Poopo *(POE-oh-poe)* A salt lake located more than 11,000 feet above sea level on the high plateau of western Bolivia. Large but shallow (average: 10 feet deep), Poopó drains west to the Salar de Coipasa, a salt flat, at times of flood.

porgy *(PORE-gee)* Several spiny-finned food fish native to coastal Atlantic and Mediterranean waters, with a family relationship to the scups and sheepsheads. As a proper noun, **Porgy** is the hero of DuBose and Dorothy Heyward's story, *Porgy,* which became the black folk opera *Porgy and Bess* (1935), with a memorable score by George Gershwin.

poros *(POE-ros)* From the Greek for "chalkstone" or "bladderstone," a coarse limestone found in southern Greece, particularly the Peloponnesus. The ancient Spartans maintained quarries there, using the stone as a building material.

Porte *(port)* The name used, for short, for the Ottoman Turkish Government; sometimes, the Sublime Porte. Porte derives from a translation of the Turkish *Bab-i-humajun,* meaning "high gateway," such as that of the Constantinople palace from which official edicts were issued. In crosswords, porte is often clued as "door: Fr." or as "_____ -cochere," (carriage porch).

Posen *(POE-zen)* The German name for Poznán, a large city on the Warta River in western Poland. Posen's history goes back to the tenth century A.D. Since then, it has bounced back and forth between Germany and Poland, reflecting the tides of war. The city was heavily bombed in World War II.

The city hall, Posen.

posse *(PAH-see)* An abbreviated form of the medieval Latin term *posse comitatus,* meaning "when a county holds power." Posse now designates a force of inhabitants of a place, usually armed, given legal power by a sheriff to perform a particular peace-keeping job, such as going after the bank robbers in the old horse operas of early Hollywood.

Poti *(POHT-yee)* Georgian city of the U.S.S.R., at the mouth of the Rion River on the Black Sea. Manganese, corn, and lumber are some of the products shipped from this port, which was known as Phasis in the fifth century B.C. when it belonged to Greece. Subsequently under Turkish rule, Poti was taken by Russia in 1828.

Pott *(pot)* Percival Pott (1714–1788), the famous English surgeon who in 1779 described a deformity of the spine due to tuberculosis that is still known as Pott's disease. He also described a specific type of ankle fracture.

potto See *loris.*

pouf or **pouffe** *(poof)* From the same French word that gave puff to the English language, an elaborate puffed-up woman's hairstyle made popular in the eighteenth century. Also, any other puffy item such as a billowy gather or puffed sleeves on a dress.

Both Lucille Ball and Red Skelton do "pouffed" wig balancing acts in Dubarry Was a Lady, *1943.*

poult *(polt)* From the Middle English *pulte*, poult nowadays means a very young turkey, but is sometimes used for the chicks of pheasants, grouse, and other fowl.

Powys *(POE-iss)* Either a metropolitan county in central Wales; or the surname of John Cowper Powys (1872–1963), the English critic and novelist whose works reveal an abiding and mystical love for nature. Among his best-known works are *Wolf Solent* (1929), *Maiden Castle* (1936), and *Owen Glendower* (1940). He was one of a literary family; other writing Powyses were his novelist brother Theodore Francis Powys (1875–1953) and another brother, Llewellyn Powys (1884–1939).

Prado *(PRAH-doe)* The world-renowned national Spanish museum of painting and sculpture in Madrid. Commissioned by Charles III, it was begun in 1785 and completed under Ferdinand VII in 1819. The building is located on the Paseo del Prado, a fashionable promenade. In Spanish, *prado* means "meadow."

A gallery in Madrid's great Prado.

Praha *(PRAH-ha)* Prague, to Czechoslovakians. The country's capital and one of Europe's major cities. Dating from the tenth century, Prague has been home to astronomers Johannes Kepler and Tycho Brahe (q.v.); writers Rainer Maria Rilke and Franz Kafka (both, q.v.); and composers Bedrich Smetana and Antonin Dvorák. Prague was where some Czech nobles threw two royal councilors through a window and started, by the Defenestration of Prague, the Thirty Years War.

Praia *(PRIE-ah)* Capital of the Cape Verde Islands, an archipelago of volcanic origin off the coast of Africa, about 300 miles west of Dakar. The islands are an overseas province of Portugal. Praia is located on São Tiago, largest of the mountainous islands and islets discovered in 1456 by Luigi da Cadamosto, a Venetian navigator sailing under the flag of Prince Henry of Portugal.

pram *(pram)* Used mostly in the British Isles, this is a contraction of the word perambulator, that conveyance which English nannies can be seen propelling through London's Regent's Park, and which Americans usually refer to as a baby carriage. To yachtsmen especially, a **pram** is a small, flat-ended boat that is carried aboard, or towed, for use as a tender.

prase *(praze)* Derived from the Greek word *prason*, meaning "a leek," prase is a translucent quartz, a type of chalcedony, with a greenish color resembling that of a leek.

Prato *(PRAH-toe)* A Tuscan city in central Italy known for its textiles and leather. Originally an Etruscan settlement, Prato was absorbed by Florence in the fourteenth century. Tourists come to see its medieval town hall and fortress and its cathedral, which is decorated with art by Filippo Lippi, Giovanni Pisano, and Andrea della Robbia.

The cathedral of Prato, Italy.

Pratt *(prat)* Surname of various luminaries, including: Charles Pratt (1714–1794), English jurist opposed to Britain's policy toward the American colonies; Parley Parker Pratt (1807–1857), Mormon apostle and framer of the constitution for Deseret; and Edwin John Pratt (1883–1964), Canadian poet whose "Dunkirk" is considered one of the best poems of World War II. **Pratt** is also the name of a noted institute of design which was the site of the first public library in Brooklyn (1896).

Parley P. Pratt.

prawn *(prawn)* Any of a number of crustaceans having five appendages, including one pincerlike structure on either side of its body. Close cousins of the shrimp but with anatomical differences, prawns make good eating; the prawns of Dublin Bay and of Venice are notable. In restaurants, shrimp are often billed as the scarcer and costlier prawns.

Pregl *(PRAY-gul)* Fritz Pregl (1869–1930), the Austrian physiologist and chemist who developed a test for measuring the solid substances excreted in urine as an index of kidney function. Pregl won the 1923 Nobel Prize in chemistry for his work on quantitative organic microanalysis.

presa *(PREH-sah)* Italian for "take up," "grasp," or "seize." This is a type of musical symbol indicating where each successive voice is supposed to take up the melody. Prese (plural) are usually encountered in music where passages are repeated exactly in the same or related keys, as a round or canon (q.v.).

prexy *(PREK-see)* A semihumorous slangy affectation of university students and sportswriters, who use this word as a substitute for president. The word apparently came into existence as a fanciful contraction of president. At some colleges, it is even truncated to prex.

Priam *(PRIE-um)* In Greek legend, the king of Troy when it was sacked during the Trojan War. Priam was slain when the Greeks, hidden in the wooden horse admitted as a gift from the Greeks, threw open the gates of Troy to their comrades. He was survived by his chief wife, Hecuba, and some of his approximately 50 children, who included Paris (q.v.), Troilus, Cassandra, and Polydorus.

prig *(prig)* Of obscure origin, this was originally sixteenth-century slang for an odious person. It now means any smug moralist. In current English slang, a **prig** is a thief or pickpocket. It's also the surname of Betsy **Prig,** in Dickens's *Martin Chuzzlewit,* crony of Mrs. Gamp (q.v.).

A decidedly priggish Antonio Moreno upbraids his bride, Pauline Starke, in Love's Blindness, *1926.*

prism *(PRIZ-um)* From the Greek word for "something sawed," this is a piece of crystal cut so that its ends are equal and parallel triangles, and its three sides are parallelograms. Light shining through such a body is refracted and broken into the spectrum—bands of colors shading continuously from red to violet. **Prism** is also the name of a solid figure in geometry.

privy *(PRIV-ee)* From the Latin word for "private," in law, any party to a contract involving private mutual interests, such as either a lessor or lessee. Privacy is also inherent in other meanings of privy, as in privy council and privy seal; to be privy to (or in on) a secret; and, finally, the privy as a small structure containing a toilet, usually without means of automatic discharge.

proa *(PROE-ah)* In Malaysia, a prau, a canoelike craft fitted with a lateen sail and an outrigger to prevent tipping in high seas or at high speed. The proa is a model of maneuverability and speed.

proem *(PROE-em)* This word derives from the Greek *pro,* a prefix meaning "before," and *oime,* meaning "song." A proem is therefore any kind of brief introduction, such as the preface to a literary work; a preamble to a long poetical work; or comments before a formal speech.

prong *(prong)* Probably from the Middle Low German *prange,* a pincerlike instrument, this is either the tine of a fork or, formerly, the fork itself; or the end of any projection with a point, such as an antler or horn of an animal—the pronghorn, for example, is an antelope with pointed, branched horns. Gem settings have prongs to hold the jewel in place.

An elephant's prongs.

Pross *(pross)* Solomon Pross, a.k.a. John Barsad, a character in Dickens's *A Tale of Two Cities.* This unsavory individual works in revolutionary Paris as a spy and informer. He even robs his own sister, Miss Pross, who aids the fleeing Manettes and is instrumental in the death of their implacable foe, Mme. Defarge.

Prout *(prowt)* Surname of both William Prout (1785–1850), the English chemist and physician who became famous for proving the presence of hydrochloric acid in the stomach; and Father Prout, the pen name of Francis Mahoney (1805–1866), the Irish writer, himself a priest, who created a series of hilarious stories of parish life.

Provo *(PROE-voe)* City on the Provo River in north-central Utah. This shipping center for the region's fruit, vegetables, and minerals was settled by the Mormons in 1849. In the 1860s, Provo defended itself in the Indian wars of the period. It is the home of the Brigham Young University.

prow *(prow)* From either the French word *proue,* the Provençal *proa,* the Latin *prora,* or the Greek *proira,* all of which mean the same thing—the bow or stem of a ship. Also, by extension, the front of any other type of craft, such as the prow of a dirigible.

A Roman vessel with a curved prow.

proxy *(PROK-see)* A contraction of the Latin for "procuracy"—the function of a procurator. This was originally a Roman official responsible for provincial finances, and eventually became anyone who manages another's affairs. A proxy is thus either an agent, or a document which legally empowers that agent to act in your behalf.

Prut or **Pruth** *(proot)* A 530-mile-long river flowing southeast from the Carpathian Mountains in the Ukraine and joining the Danube at Reni. It forms part of the border between Romania and the U.S.S.R. In 1711, during the interminable Russo-Turkish wars, Azov (q.v.) was restored to the Turks by the Peace of the Pruth.

psi *(sie)* Twenty-third letter of the Greek alphabet, equivalent to the English sound *ps,* as in tops. When the letter appears in English derivatives, it's given a simple *S* sound, as in psychiatry. As it is the next-to-last Greek letter, it is often clued in crosswords as "penultimate Greek letter." The word **psi** is sometimes used as an acronym for "pounds per square inch" in measurements of pressure.

Pskov *(pskahv)* A major rail and industrial center on the Velikaya River in the northwestern European U.S.S.R. Pskov's history traces back to antiquity. In the Middle Ages, it was an independent city-state, and in 1510 was annexed by Moscow. In 1917, Tzar Nicholas II abdicated in the Pskov railroad station.

psora *(SOR-ah)* An annoying chronic skin disorder much publicized as "the heartbreak of" psoriasis in advertisements for palliatives. Transported into English directly from the Greek, the word *psora* means "itching."

Ptah *(ptah)* In Egyptian mythology, the major deity of Memphis, architect of the universe and sire of gods and mortals. He was also a craftsman and therefore the patron of artisans and metalworkers. Identified by the Greeks with Hephaestus, Ptah is usually represented bearing the scepter of life, power, and force. His wife was Pakht (q.v.).

Puah *(PYOO-ah)* Either of two biblical characters: the father of the judge Tola (Judges 10:1) or a midwife who earned a footnote in Hebrew lore—and immortality in crossword puzzles—when she disobeyed the order of Pharaoh to kill all Jewish male infants at birth (Ex. 1:15-17).

puce *(pyuce)* Technically a shade of red, puce can best be described as the color of a purple eggplant after it has become too ripe. The word *puce* is French for "flea," and our flea market comes directly from the French for same: *marché aux puces.*

pug *(pug)* Formerly a term of endearment, as for a sweetheart, pug now designates a short, snub-nosed dog of China brought to England, where it became extremely popular with the nobility; also, the footprint of an animal; or slang for a mediocre prizefighter, from the pushed-in appearance of his nose; or a blunt, turned-up human nose.

puku *(POO-koo)* A small, reddish, gregarious antelope dwelling in marshlands of equatorial Africa. It is related to the waterbucks, kobs, and lechwes. The puku is distinguished by his horns, which curve back, up, and forward; females are hornless. Excellent swimmers, pukus will readily take to the water when attacked.

Pul *(pull)* An ancient region of Africa that may have been the region also known as Punt, probably somewhere along the present Somali coast. The Egyptians, during the reign of Hatshepsut, raided this land for slaves, gold, and incense. **Pul** was also the name of the biblical Assyrian king, a.k.a. Tiglath-Pileser III, who invaded Israel (2 Kings 15:19).

Pula or **Pola** *(POO-lah)* A Yugoslavian city on the Adriatic, at the southern end of the Istrian peninsula. Now a major seaport and industrial hub, it has been ruled by ancient Rome and, subsequently, Venice, Austria, and Italy. It has many Roman ruins. While under Austrian control, Pula was the key naval base of the Hapsburg empire. It was ceded to Yugoslavia after World War II.

An ancient arena in Pula.

puli *(PYOO-lee)* A breed of working dog developed in Hungary almost 1,000 years ago. Lean, sinewy, and about 16 inches high at the shoulder, the puli was originally raised to help Magyar shepherds. Today, it is popular on both sides of the Atlantic.

Pully *(puh-LEE)* Town on Lake Geneva in the canton of Vaud, western Switzerland. Pully is not only a residential community for people who work in nearby Lausanne, but also a tourist center. It features a fifteenth-century church, plus a museum honoring the famous local, Charles Ferdinand Ramuz, a nineteenth-century novelist.

puma *(PYOO-mah)* Tawny, slenderly built, carnivorous animal belonging to the cat family, and also called cougar, mountain lion, panther, and catamount. Pumas range from southwestern Canada to southern South America, with the larger species usually found in cooler regions. They sport 30-inch tails and, unlike their cousin the jaguar, are spotless.

puna *(POO-nah)* Taken directly from the Quechua word, puna designates the cold, dry, mineral-rich plateau region 12,000 to 15,000 feet above sea level between ridges of the Andes in Bolivia and Peru. Despite the inhospitable environment and icy winds, also called puna, this region is home to descendants of the Incas (q.v.).

pung *(pung)* In the backwoods of New England, a box-shaped sleigh, usually drawn by one horse. The word is a contraction of the Algonquian *tow pong,* which is related to the Micmac term *tobâgun*—just a few letters removed from the spelling of its derivative, that familiar snow vehicle, the toboggan.

Punt See *Pul.*

pupa *(PYEW-pah)* A stage in the metamorphosis of insects. Before the pupal phase, insects are known as larvae and are wormlike creatures that eat voraciously. As a pupa, the insect rests inside a shell-like structure until ready to emerge as an adult. The cocoon, for example, shelters the pupa of the moth.

Pupin *(pyoo-PEEN)* Michael Idvorsky Pupin (1858–1935), the Hungarian-born physicist and inventor who for 30 years was professor of electromechanics at Columbia University, where a building is named for him. Among Pupin's achievements were many electrical devices used in telegraphy. His autobiography, *From Immigrant to Inventor,* was awarded the 1924 Pulitzer Prize.

Michael Idvorsky Pupin.

purdah *(PUR-dah)* From the Hindi word *parda,* "screen," this is a curtain or screen used in Hindu homes in India to isolate a section of the house where women are secluded. Purdah also designates the clothing, especially veils, that shields women from public observation.

Puri *(POO-ree)* Town on the Bay of Bengal in Orissa state in east-central India. Puri is the center of the cult of Juggernaut, or Jaganath, a form taken by the Hindu god Krishna. Every summer Juggernaut's image is placed on a massive cart and dragged by hundreds of pilgrims through the streets of this otherwise unremarkable community. Contrary to popular belief, the instances of worshipers casting themselves under the wheels have no relation to the ceremony.

Purim *(POO-rim)* Jewish festival celebrating Esther's deliverance of the Jews from a prospective massacre by Haman (q.v.), as described in Esther 9:15–32. Pu-

Esther confronting Haman; thanks to her intercession the Jews of Persia were saved.

rim derives from the Hebrew word for "lots," cast by Haman to determine the order of execution. Occurring in early spring, Purim is the time to eat hamantashen—prune-stuffed pastries shaped like Haman's headgear—and to make merry.

Purus *(poo-ROOSE)*   A major river of South America rising in the Andes of eastern Peru and flowing more than 2,000 miles generally northeast to the Amazon in northwestern Brazil. The Purus is generally navigable, and serves as a route for transporting crude rubber to the port of Belém.

Pusan *(POO-san)*   Second largest city in South Korea, a port on the Korea Strait at the seaward end of the Naktong River basin. This major industrial and commercial center was Chinese until its occupation by Japan in the 1590s. It has been culturally and economically involved with Japan ever since. (Its Japanese name is Fusan.)

putty *(PUTT-ee)*   A soft, pliable mixture of calcium carbonate and boiled linseed oil used to fasten panes of glass into frames. Oxygen drawn from the air by the oil causes the mixture to harden, forming a solid, plasterlike seal. Putty is being replaced by silicones, which are more expensive but last longer.

Pwyll *(pwill)*   The Prince of Dyfed and a hero of the *Mabinogion,* an eleventh-century Welsh version of the Arthurian legends. According to one tale, Prince Pwyll materialized a bag into which could be placed all the food of the world without its ever becoming full.

Pydna *(PIDD-nuh)*   An ancient city of Pieria in Macedonia, northern Greece, near the Gulf of Salonica. Near Pydna was the field of a battle in 168 B.C. in which the Roman general Aemilius Paullus vanquished Perseus, thus writing finis to the kingdom of Macedonia and making the land a Roman dominion.

Pye *(pie)*   Either the surname of John Pye (1782–1874), English engraver and father of modern landscape engraving; or of Henry

James Pye (1745–1813), English poet laureate in 1790 and writer of patriotic verse. Pronounced PIE-*ay*, it's an important Irrawaddy River port city in Burma, founded in the eighth century A.D. by the

John Pye.

Pyus.

Pygmy or **Pigmy** *(PIG-mee)*   From the word *pygmaios,* "length of the forearm," used in Greek legends for a race of dwarfs. It has come to mean any people whose adult males stand under five feet tall, e.g., the Batwas of the Congo valley and the Akkas of the upper Nile, who were known to the ancient Egyptians. Other Pygmies include the Aetas of the Philippines. Low birth rates and high mortality now threaten Pygmy tribes with extinction.

An ancient frieze depicts a group of pygmy hunters.

Pyle *(pile)*   Surname of either Ernest "Ernie" Taylor Pyle (1900–1945), American World War II correspondent and 1944 Pulitzer Prize winner who was killed by Japanese machine-gun fire on a Pacific island; or Howard Pyle (1853–1911), American artist who illustrated adventure books for young people, notably *The Merry Adventures of Robin Hood* and *The Garden Behind the Moon.* Often clued in crosswords is the Jim Nabors role as Gomer Pyle on TV.

Ernie Pyle.

pylon *(PILE-ohn)* Directly from the Greek for "gateway," this was originally a roughly pyramidal structure indicating the entrance to an Egyptian tomb. Today the term usually designates the tall, slender towers that mark the course of an airplane race or support high-tension power lines.

Pylos *(PILE-ose)* An ancient town in southwestern Greece, on the Bay of Pylos, site of a great naval battle between Athens and Sparta in 425 B.C. The region is rich in archaeological finds, including a Mycenaean palace of the thirteenth century B.C. and 600 clay tablets that provided clues to deciphering the late Minoan script. The nearby modern town of Pilos was formerly called Navarino. The bay was again a naval battlefield in 1827, with the battle of Navarino during the Greek War of Independence.

The main harbor of the Greek town of Pilos.

Pym *(pim)* Surname of John Pym (c. 1853–1643), English statesman who opposed Charles I, supported colonization of the West Indies, and orchestrated the impeachment of George Villiers, First Duke of Buckingham, in 1626. During the civil war of 1642, he arranged an alliance with Scotland based on English acceptance of the Presbyterian religion. Pym is also a servant in George Eliot's *Adam Bede,* and the narrator and hero of Edgar Allan Poe's (q.v.) *The Narrative of Arthur Gordon Pym.*

John Pym.

pyre *(pire)* From the Greek *pyra,* pyre rhymes with fire, a key word in its definition. Pyres have been used since remote antiquity to cremate the dead, as is still done in India. A pyre is a large heap of wood or any other combustible material. Oil is often added to hasten burning.

Pyrus *(PIE-ris)* The genus of trees frequented by partridges at Christmas—the pear tree. Related to the rose, the pear tree produces hard, shiny leaves framing the familiar fruit with the narrow top, wide bottom, and gritty feel on the tongue. *Pyrus* is a variant spelling of the Latin word for pear tree.

pyx *(piks)* From the Greek word for "box," either a small vessel or tabernacle used to hold the consecrated wafer of the Holy Communion in many Christian denominations, or a container in which specimen coins are kept while awaiting annual assays for purity and weight at the British mint.

The Mass of St. Martin of Tours, *by the Franco-Rhenish master, c. 1440.*

pyxie *(PIK-see)* A contraction of *Pyxidanthera barbulata,* several species of creeping mosslike evergreen shrublets related to the galax (q.v.). The pyxie has tiny leaves, white star-shaped blossoms, and a predilection for the soil that produces the pine barrens of North Carolina and New Jersey. It is also called flowering moss and pine barren beauty.

pyxis *(PIK-sis)* Either an ancient Roman or Greek vase with a cover or, in botany, a seed case—also known as a pyxidium—composed of two parts, with the upper acting as a lid. The plural is pyxides. Also, a section of the Southern Hemisphere constellation Argo (q.v.), situated roughly between Canis Major and the Southern Cross.

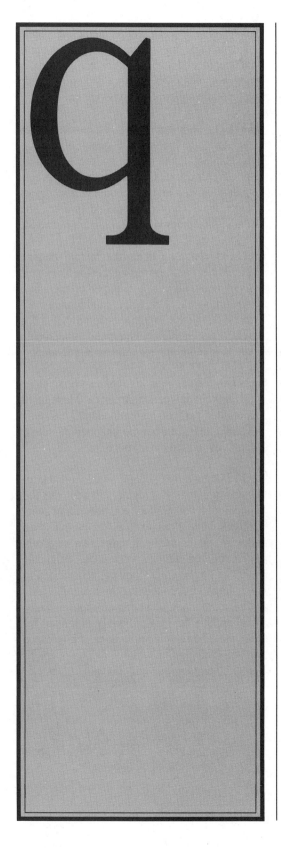

Qatar or Katar *(KAH-tahr)*

A sheikdom on the east coast of Arabia, on a peninsula extending into the Persian Gulf. The capital is Doha. Barren and inhabited mostly by Arabs of the Wahabi sect of Islam, Qatar had an economy based mostly on fishing until oil was discovered in the 1940s. Commercial production began in 1949, and the rest is history.

Qina or Keneh *(KIN-ah)*

A town on the Nile in east-central Egypt, Qina is known for its pottery and ruins. It was built on the site of the ancient city of Caene. During World War II, Qina assumed importance as a road terminus on the route through the mountains to the Red Sea.

Qabis See *Gabès.*

quail *(kwale)*

Any of a variety of small game birds related to the partridge, pheasant, and grouse, common throughout the world. Quails usually don't wander very far afield, except for the Eurasian quail, which migrates over tremendous distances. The American quail is the familiar bobwhite, whose call tells the listener his name. To **quail,** as a verb, means to lose courage, or to cower.

A quail hen with two chicks.

quay *(kee)*

From the French, quay designates any sturdily constructed wharf, nowadays usually with cranes for unloading ships. As a proper noun, pronounced *kway,* it is the surname of Matthew Stanley **Quay** (1833–1905), American senator who helped elect Benjamin Harrison President, and then became involved in a graft scandal.

Matthew S. Quay.

quern *(kwern)* An ancient device for grinding grain, consisting of two stones between which the grain is placed; the upper stone is turned by hand. Some modern hand mills for grain, popular with at-home breadmakers, are actually querns.

queue *(kyew)* A word that passed into English from the Latin *cauda* and the Old

French *coue*, both meaning "tail," a queue is a plaited strand of hair, or pigtail, at one time affected by Chinese men. Also, **queue** designates the line of people waiting for a bus in England; the tail of a beast, in heraldry; and the tailpiece of a violin, in music.

A braided queue.

quica *(KEE-kah)* From the Portuguese *cuica* by way of the Tupi Indians, any of several small South American tree-dwelling mammals that hunt at night and carry their young in a pouch. Because of a patch of light hair above each eye, quicas are also known as four-eyed opossums.

quila *(KEE-lah)* A coarse grass native to the southern regions of South America and Patagonia. Quila resembles bamboo, contains a fiber used in papermaking, and is used as forage for cattle. The word derives from the Araucan Indian *cula*.

Quilp *(kwilp)* One of the most odious characters in fiction. In Charles Dickens's *The Old Curiosity Shop*, Daniel Quilp is a hideous, malicious dwarf. Scheming, sadistic, and just plain mean, Quilp ate hard-cooked eggs, shell and all, for his breakfast, and devoured prawns with their heads on.

quipu *(KEE-poo)* From the Quechuan word for "knot," the quipu was a device used by the Incas for keeping accounts,

doing simple math, and sending messages. It was made up of groups of colored cords arranged and knotted in ways to convey specific meanings. Quipus had to be made up and deciphered by experts.

quira *(KEE-rah)* Any of several trees belonging to a particular genus of leguminous plants, and native to the tropics of South America. Quiras produce a pretty yellow flower and an economically important, heavy, brownish-colored timber. The tree is also known as the Panama redwood.

quire *(kwire)* From the Middle English *quair*, a book of loose pages, this term now designates any stack of paper of the same size or stock. The quire traditionally contains 25 sheets and represents $1/20$ of a ream. Its classic translation is reflected in the term "in quires," meaning unbound.

quirt *(kwirt)* From Mexican Spanish, a riding whip of western America. Made up of a braided rawhide lash attached to a stubby handle, the quirt can be snapped to sound like a pistol-shot by experts.

Quito *(KEE-toe)* Capital and second largest city of Ecuador, lying just south of the equator. Its 9,350-foot elevation, however, makes Quito pleasant to live in except when hit by earthquakes; it has been severely damaged on several occasions. Originally settled by the Quito Indians, it belonged to the Incas until conquered by Spain in 1534. There are many surviving examples of colonial architecture, and the city is known for its beautiful setting at the base of a volcano.

A group on their way to a rally in Quito, Ecuador.

Qum, Qom, or Kum *(kawm)*

Holy city in Tehran province, west-central Iran, with large petroleum deposits nearby. The home base of Ayatollah Khomeini, Qum is a religious center for Shiite Muslims and the burial place of Fatima al-Masuma, a revered figure. The shrine above the tomb was rebuilt after Qum was pillaged by the Afghans in 1722.

quoin *(koin)*

Either the cornerstone of a building, made of a contrasting stone; the wedge-shaped segment, or keystone, of an arch; or any wedge-shaped object that keeps such things from moving. Accordingly, other quoins control such movables as the type bars arranged in a tray (galley); casks that tend to roll in wineries; or rolls of newsprint on the back of a truck.

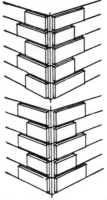

Quoins interlock at the corner of the building to provide strength.

quoit *(kwoit)*

From the Old French word for "cushion," this is a ring, usually made of heavy rope, used in a game similar to horseshoe pitching. The rings are thrown at a stake driven into the ground, with points awarded for encircling the post or getting close to it.

Qutb *(KAW-tub)*

Islamic saint responsible for the invisible government of the world, and commemorated by the Qutb (or Kutb) Minar, a minaret near New Delhi, India. This monument was built in 1230 by Iltutmish of the Delhi Sultanate. It stands almost 250 feet high and has elaborate carvings along its entire length.

The Qutb Minar in New Delhi.

THE DRAFTING BOARD

cant

conge
corbel
corona
cowl

cyma
dado
dais
ell
flue
foyer
glyph
gula

herse
joist

lanai
lath
lobby
newel
ogee

oriel
orle

ovum
putty

quoin
stile
stoa
truss

Rab *(rahb)* One of the Dalmatian Islands, now a seaside resort in the Adriatic, off Croatia, Yugoslavia. Rab was ruled by the Venetians until the late eighteenth century. Also, in John Brown's novel *Rab and His Friends,* **Rab** is the faithful dog who was so distraught at his master's death that he had to be destroyed.

The Yugoslavian resort town of Rab.

Raba *(RAH-bah)* A 160-mile-long river rising in the mountains of southeastern Austria and flowing southeast, then northeast through Hungary, to the Danube River. The Rába valley is a farm region.

rabbi *(RAB-eye)* Originally meaning "teacher" or "scholar," the word has come to mean also a Jewish spiritual leader of a congregation or temple. In Israel, there is one chief rabbi for the Ashkenazic Jews and a second for the Sephardic community.

Rabi *(RAHB-ee)* Isidor Isaac Rabi (1898–), Austrian-born American physicist who received the 1944 Nobel Prize in physics for his work with atomic nuclei. Also, either **Rabi I** or **II,** the third and fourth months of the Islamic calendar.

Rabin *(rah-BEEN)* Israeli military man and diplomat Yitzhak Rabin (1922–), former prime minister of Israel, succeeding Golda Meir. A member of the Jewish military group called the Haganah in 1940, he later fought in the

Yitzhak Rabin.

British army. He was Israeli chief of staff during the Six Day War in 1967, receiving acclaim for his role in Israel's victory.

radix *(RAY-diks)* From the Latin word meaning "root," the term denoting the underground part of a plant that anchors it in position and draws nutrients from the soil. Also, radices are either numbers that form the bases of logarithms, or the parts of cranial and spinal nerves that hold them in place; or, in linguistics, the roots of words.

Radom *(RAH-dom)* A southeastern Polish city dating back to 1187. Beginning with Casimir the Great in 1364, it was the seat of Polish diets and other government bodies for several centuries. Radom belonged variously to Austria (1795) and Russia (1815), and was returned to Poland after World War I. Today, it is an important industrial center.

Rafa or **Rafah** *(RAH-fah)* This is a border town in the Gaza Strip which was called Raphia in ancient Egypt. It was the scene of a battle in 217 B.C. in which the invader, the Syrian king Antiochus III, was defeated by Ptolemy IV of Egypt.

raff *(raff)* Short for riffraff in British slang. As a proper noun (and pronounced *rahf*), it's the surname of composer Joseph Joachim **Raff** (1822–1882), whose opera *King Alfred* was produced by the music director at Weimar, Franz Lizst.

Joachim Raff.

raggi or **raggee** *(RAG-ee)* From the Sanskrit word *rágin,* meaning "red," a cereal grass native to the islands of Indonesia. Related to the millet and sometimes called the finger millet or korakan, raggi produces seeds which are ground into a flour that's a dietary staple.

Rahab or **Rachab** *(RAY-hab)* In the Bible (Josh. 2), the woman of Jericho whose protection of the Israelite spies led to her and her family's salvation when the rest of Jericho was destroyed by Joshua. (The walls of Jericho "came tumbling down" after Joshua sounded his trumpet seven times.) Also, the name of a monster mentioned in several books of the Bible.

Rahu *(RAH-hoo)* From the Hindu word meaning "void" and, by extension, darkness, the demon who drank of immortal nectar. The sun and moon caught Rahu in the act and told the god Vishnu (q.v.), who decapitated him. The head, however, being immortal, is said to take revenge by causing solar and lunar eclipses.

raia or **rayah** *(RAH-yah)* From the Arabic and Turkish word *ra-āya,* meaning "herd" or "flock," the designation for any non-Muslim inhabitant of a Muslim country. The term has some pejorative overtones, seemingly comparable to the word gringo in Latin-American countries.

rajah or **raja** *(RAH-zhuh)* From the Sanskrit *rājan,* meaning "king," cognate of the Latin *rex,* a Hindu title for a ruler or chief. Also, a title for royalty, such as an Indian prince. During British rule of India, the colonial government apparatus was known collectively as the Raj, or the British Raj. **Rajah** is also the nickname of Rogers Hornsby, a Hall of Fame baseball player.

A properly regal-looking rajah.

raki or **rakee** *(rah-KEE)* In the Near East and such areas of southern Europe as Greece, raki is a pungent alcoholic beverage made by fermenting fruit. It is related in both name and composition to the strong, intoxicating liquor of the Orient, arrack, from the Arabic *'araq,* meaning "sweat."

rale *(rahl)* Anglicized version of the French *râler,* meaning "to rattle." In medicine, rales are abnormal bubbling or rustling sounds superimposed on natural breathing sounds, and heard with the aid of a stethoscope. Indicative of disease in the respiratory tract, rales are classified, running the gamut from clicking to tinkling to sonorous.

Rama *(RAH-mah)* The seventh avatar (q.v.), or incarnation, of the Hindu god Vishnu (q.v.), and the hero of the *Ramayana,* one of the two classic Indian epics. In this legend, Rama enlisted the aid of Sugriva, monarch of the monkeys, when his wife, Sita (q.v.), was abducted by a demon. Rama is also the name of several kings of Thailand, including Rama Kamheng, who gave the Thais their alphabet in the thirteenth or fourteenth century; and Rama IV, or King Mongkut (1804–1868), whose reign was touched on in the popular musical *The King and I,* which was based on Margaret Landon's *Anna and the King of Siam.*

ramie *(RAY-mee)* A plant with heart-shaped flowers belonging to the nettle family. Native to Southeast Asia, ramie yields a strong, silky, hard-to-extract fiber that makes superior paper and cloth. The plant is therefore being cultivated in other parts of the world. Ramie is also known as China grass.

Ramla or **Ramleh** *(RAHM-leh)* The Arabic word for "sand," but now the name of a town in central Israel. Founded around A.D. 700 by the Arabs, it was once the capital of Palestine and survived the Crusades. It became part of Israel during the 1948 war. Ramla's previous tenants built the Great Mosque, once a Crusades church.

ramus *(RAY-mus)* Latin for "branch," a biology term used to indicate a branchlike process or projecting part. In anatomy, for example, rami (plural) usually refer to the treelike branches of veins, arteries, or nerves, such as the ramus cardiacus, the branch of the vagus (q.v.) nerve that goes to the heart.

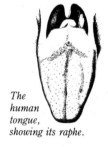

rand *(rand)* Either the basic monetary unit of South Africa, named after the Witwatersrand, the site of rich gold fields; any unploughed strip surrounding a field; or, in shoemaking, a leather strip applied under the heel. As a proper noun, it is the surname of Ayn **Rand** (1905–1982), Russian-American novelist and philosopher who wrote *The Fountainhead,* among other works; of one-half of the map-publishing partnership of Rand McNally; name of fan dancer Sally Rand, hit of the 1933 World's Fair, in Chicago.

Rao *(rau)* Rajo Rao (1911–), Indian novelist and intellectual who in 1965 was appointed a professor of philosophy at the University of Texas. His belief in nonviolence as advocated by Gandhi is reflected in his books.

raphe *(RAY-fee)* From the Greek meaning "seam" or something stitched together, this is an anatomical term for the juncture line between two symmetrical halves of a structure, such as the palate or pharynx. In botany, it is a band of tissue that forms a seam along the sides of certain ovules.

The human tongue, showing its raphe.

Rashi *(RAH-shee)* An abbreviation of Rabbi Solomon bar Isaac, the name of the famous Jewish scholar born in 1040 in

Troyes, France, where his family owned a vineyard. Rashi's exegesis of the Pentateuch, printed in 1475, was the first dated book ever printed in Hebrew, and is said to have influenced the thinking of Martin Luther. The script he employed in writing his commentaries is called the Rashi script.

Rasht *(rasht)* or **Resht** *(resht)* City in northwestern Iran, near the Caspian Sea. Rasht is known for its silks and is also a shipping center for the cotton, rice, and peanuts produced nearby. It was here that Shah Abbas I had his eldest son, Safi Mirza, assassinated. In 1631, the town was pillaged by a band of Cossack marauders under Stenka Razin (q.v.). In World War I fighting, Rasht suffered heavy damage.

Raspe *(RAH-spuh)* Rudolf Erich Raspe (1737–1794), German archaeologist and author of a work detailing the adventures of Baron Münchhausen, the Teutonic huntsman and soldier whose name, often spelled Munchausen, has become synonymous with tall tales. During Raspe's checkered career, he perpetrated a swindle by pretending to find gold on an Englishman's estate.

ratel *(RAY-tul)* A small nocturnal animal of India and southern Africa. This carnivore, called the honey badger, is related to such important fur-bearing animals as the mink and otter, as well as the weasel and polecat. Ratels love honey and are said to be led to honey sources by a bird called the honey guide.

rath *(rahth)* From the Gaelic, a circular fortification sitting atop a hill and surrounded by earthworks. These were often the strongholds of early Irish chiefs, and served as refuges for tribesmen under attack. Many raths can still be seen throughout Ireland, especially at Tara (q.v.), ancient seat of Irish kings.

Rauch *(rowkh)* Christian Daniel Rauch (1777–1857), German sculptor who became famous for such tombs and monuments as those erected in honor of Emperor Alexander and Queen Louise of Germany. Rauch's best-known work is a huge bronze statue of Frederick the Great on horseback, with bas-reliefs of his generals on the pedestal.

Rauma *(ROW-mah)* City in southwestern Finland, on the Gulf of Bothnia. Chartered around 1445, Rauma became a major medieval trade center, and today is Finland's chief western port. It is also a center for the chemical, paper, and textile industries. Its Swedish name is Raumo.

ravel *(RAV-uhl)* A loose thread working its way out of a piece of material, or tangled

into a whorl. As a proper noun (pronounced *rav-ELL*), it is the surname of Maurice Joseph **Ravel** (1875–1937), the French pianist and Impressionist composer who is perhaps best known for the exotic *Bolero*.

Maurice Ravel.

raven *(RAY-ven)* A large, black, long-lived bird with shiny feathers. This cousin of the crow and largest member of the family inhabits all temperate regions of the Northern Hemisphere, is associated with superstition and legend, and can evidently be taught like a parrot to speak—at least the word nevermore, according to the famous poem by Edgar Allan Poe (q.v.). There are ravens at the Tower of London who are carefully encouraged to stay because of a legend that as long as they remain, Britain will retain its power.

Ravi *(RAH-vee)* A 475-mile-long river, one of the five great rivers of the Punjab region of the Indian subcontinent. The Ravi rises in northwestern India in the Himalayas, and flows west to join the Chenab

River in northeastern Pakistan. Use of its waters for irrigation was disputed until India and Pakistan signed an agreement in 1960. In crosswords, **Ravi** is often the first name of Indian sitarist Shankar.

Razak *(RAH-zahk)* Abdul Razak (1922–), the Malaysian statesman who held various elective offices and cabinet posts before becoming prime minister in 1970. He succeeded Tunku Abdul Rahman, and after his election also held the titles of foreign minister and defense minister.

Razin *(RAH-zeen)* The redoubtable Stenka Razin (d. 1671), Cossack hero and leader of a revolt against the tzar in 1670. His band of some 7,000 serfs and peasants took several cities, but Razin was eventually captured and executed in Moscow. His fame and exploits are celebrated in legends, literature, and music.

rebec *(REE-bek)* A medieval musical instrument whose strident tone was produced by drawing a bow over its three to five strings, as if playing a violin. It differs from its progenitor, the rebab, in its form, which is pear-shaped, and its neck, which is more slender than that of the lutelike rebab. It is often clued as "violin's ancestor."

The figure on the left is playing a rebec.

rebus *(REE-bus)* The Latin word that means "by things," and a type of puzzle in which messages are conveyed by objects rather than words. In a rebus, the sounds of the items pictured suggest words. Drawings of an automobile and a 2,000-pound

weight, for example, would be a rebus for carton. **Rebus** is also any device used in heraldry which conveys an allusion to the family name, as a castle for the Castletons.

Redi *(RAY-dee)* Francesco Redi (c. 1621–1698), an Italian who wrote dithyrambic odes and attended to the health of the Tuscan dukes as court physician. In a celebrated scientific experiment, Redi proved that maggots do not appear spontaneously in rotting meat, but are generated from flies' eggs in the natural process of reproduction.

Francesco Redi.

Redon *(ruh-DONH)* Odilon Redon (1840–1916), the French painter and engraver. Redon's works have a mystical, dreamlike quality and are rich in symbols. He was considered a member of the post-Impressionist school, and his influence on the Surrealists' work is evident. Redon's best-known paintings are of flowers.

A Redon.

reef *(reef)* From the Old Norse for "rib," either a riblike ridge of rock, coral, or sand that lies close to the surface of the ocean and constitutes a hazard to shipping; or a section of sail that can be folded away, reducing sail area and, therefore, the propulsion supplied by the wind. **Reef** is also a bed of ore in mining, and the name of a kind of sponge.

reeve *(reev)* A derivative of the Old English *gerefa,* from which we also get the word sheriff. Reeves survive as the chief officers, or officials with specific lesser responsibilities, of certain English, Canadian, and U.S. communities. The word is also applied to the females of a certain sandpiper species, the male of which is called a ruff (q.v.). As a verb, **reeve** means to pass a line or rope through a block or other device. As a proper noun, **Reeve** is the surname of Christopher, star of the movie *Superman*.

Regan *(REE-gan)*

In Shakespeare's tragedy *King Lear,* the second of Lear's two evil daughters, the wife of the Duke of Cornwall. With her sister Goneril, she schemes to cheat the youngest sister, Cordelia, out of her inheritance, and drives her father mad. Small wonder she is described in the play as "most barbarous, most degenerate."

Reger *(RAY-gur)*

Max Reger (1873–1916), the German composer and pianist best known for organ works of unusual complexity. Included in his prodigious output were the *Fantasy and Fugue in C Minor* for organ, and the *Symphonic Prologue to a Tragedy* for orchestra plus more than 300 songs.

Max Reger.

Reik *(rike)*

Theodor Reik (1888–1969), pupil of Freud and a giant on the American psychoanalytical scene. He founded the National Psychological Association for Psychoanalysis in 1948 and wrote extensively. Reik is perhaps best known to laymen for his book *Of Love and Lust.*

Reims or Rheims *(reems; rhehm)*

A thriving city situated among the important vineyards of northeastern France, Reims is the center of the Champagne industry. Originally part of Roman Gaul, it was where all kings of France after Louis VII were crowned. In the cathedral here Joan of Arc stood up with Charles VII in 1429 when he was crowned. On May 7, 1945, the unconditional surrender of Germany was signed here, officially ending World War II.

The cathedral at Reims is one of France's most spectacular structures.

reis *(rase)*

The plural of real, at one time a unit of currency in Portugal and Brazil. Reis were worth only small fractions of the American cent, and thus became victims of worldwide inflation. They were replaced by the centavo, which represents $1/100$ of the Portuguese escudo or of the Brazilian cruzero. **Reis** is also a Muslim title of authority, especially for a ship's captain.

Remus *(REE-mus)*

Twin brother of Romulus. According to legend, the boys, sons of Mars, were suckled by a wolf when their mother, Rhea Silvia, was killed. An omen (q.v.) indicated that Romulus was to be the one to found Rome, and in the ensuing strife Remus was killed. Remus is also the lovable plantation slave and storyteller created by Joel Chandler Harris in his "Uncle Remus" stories.

Renan *(ruh-NANH)*

Ernest Renan (1823–1892), the French scholar, author, critic, and seminary dropout who approached religion from a historical, rather than theological, orientation. His best-known book, *The Life of Jesus* (1863), portrayed Christ as a man. Renan was named director of the Collège de France in 1883.

renin *(REE-nin)* From the Latin *ren,* meaning "kidney," a protein excreted by the kidney and assumed to cause the liberation of angiotensin. This substance produces high blood pressure in man and experimental animals. Renin is excreted when a loss of body fluid, as in bleeding, causes blood pressure to drop.

rente *(rahnt)* A term that has taken the jump directly from French into English and also given us the word rent. Rente is an annual income, or annuity. In France, rente refers to the yearly interest paid by the government on the consolidated debt, represented by stocks, bonds, and other securities. It does not have the meaning of tenant's payment—there is another word, *loyer,* for that.

Reo *(REE-oh)* An automobile that rumbled across the American landscape between 1904 and 1936, and then went the way of the Stanley and Stutz and, later, the DeSoto, Packard, and Nash. The name Reo comes from the initials of Ransom Eli Olds, the automotive pioneer who is the only person for whom two cars are named.

resh *(raysh)* This is the Hebrew for "head," and also the twentieth letter of the Hebrew alphabet, corresponding to the English *r* and the Greek rho (q.v.). Resh is also the designation of the letter *"R"* in the Phoenician and other Semitic alphabets.

resin *(REZ-in)* Derived from the Latin *resina,* a solid or semisolid substance, usually yellowish-brown, obtained from various plants or trees, and also produced synthetically. Resins will dissolve in alcohol or ether, and are used in medicines, printing inks, plastics, shellacs, and incenses. The best-known resin is probably amber (q.v.).

rete *(REE-tee)* Latin for "net," rete now designates any type of mesh, and is also the root of the word retina. The plural is retia.

In astronomy, a **rete** is a kind of plate with apertures, used to indicate the positions of stars; in anatomy, it is a network of such structures as blood vessels and nerve fibers.

retem *(REE-tum)* From the Arabic *ratam,* this is a shrub that thrives in arid soil and is common in desert regions, especially in Asia and Asia Minor. A member of the bean family, it produces an abundance of tiny white flowers. Retem is probably the "juniper" referred to in the Old Testament.

Reus *(REH-oos)* A city on the Mediterranean Sea, in the Catalan region of northeastern Spain. Reus was a quiet little fishing town of Tarragona province until English businessmen started a cotton-spinning industry here in the eighteenth century. It has since become a major commercial and industrial center.

Reyer *(ray-AYE)* Ernest Reyer, originally Louis Étienne Ernest Rey (1823–1909), the self-taught French composer. Reyer was not only influenced by Berlioz, he succeeded him as critic of the *Journal des Débats.* Among Reyer's works are the operas *Sigurd* and *Salammbô,* the latter based on a Flaubert novel.

Reza *(REE-zah)* Part of the royal signature of Reza Shah Pahlevi (1877–1944), shah of Iran. Starting his career as an army officer named Reza Khan, he engineered a series of coups that brought him to the throne in 1925. Among a mixed bag of achievements, he officially changed the name of Persia to Iran in 1935. Reza Shah abdicated in favor of his son, Muhammed Reza Shah, whose exile in 1979 under pressure from the Ayatollah Khomeini was followed by his death the next year.

rhea *(REE-ah)* Common name for a large South American bird that resembles an ostrich and produces two-pound eggs incubated by the males. As a proper noun, **Rhea** was an ancient Greek deity, one of the Titans, wife and sister of Cronus, and

TAKE A BOAT, TAKE A TRAIN

OVERLAND

araba
biga
coupe
dinky
Edsel
Fiat
gig
hack
howdah
jeep

kago
mogul
paddy
pram
pung
Reo
sado
tonga
tram

NAUTICAL

bidar
coble
cog
dhow
dinghy
dory
gig
hoy
kayak

ketch
oram
prau
scull
skiff
umiak
xebec
yawl

mother of the principal gods. Her worship included fertility rites. Named for her is one of Saturn's 10 known moons. See also *Hera* and *Pluto*.

Rhine *(rine)* Celebrated in song and legend, this is the principal river of Europe, rising in the Swiss Alps and flowing north 820 miles through Switzerland, Liechtenstein, Austria, West Germany, France, and the Netherlands before emptying into the North Sea through an intricately channeled delta. The Rhine carries more traffic than any other river in the world, and it is linked through tributaries and canals with a huge system of waterways. Most famous of the points of interest along the river is the rock in a narrow section near Bingen, the legendary home of the Lorelei, a fairy who lured sailors to their death. The Lorelei was immortalized by Heine's poem.

The Rhine flows through the Swiss city of Basel.

rho *(roe)* The seventh letter of the Greek alphabet which, despite the fact that it is written as *p*, corresponds to the letter *r* in the English alphabet.

Rhone *(rone)*   Another major river of Europe. About 500 miles long, the Rhone originates in Valais, Switzerland, and flows generally south, with local aberrations, through Lake Geneva and then France before reaching the Mediterranean near Marseilles. It generates hydroelectric power at plants near Geneva and Sion, and has the greatest water flow of any French river.

rhumb *(rum)*   From the Latin *rhombus*, this term refers to any of the 32 points on a marine navigational compass. Also, a line on a map, chart, or globe that crosses all meridians at the same angle. Called a loxodromic curve, or a rhumb line, this is a course that follows a constant compass direction.

Rhys *(rees)*   Ernest Rhys (1859–1946), the Welsh coal miner and poet who was named editor of the Everyman's Library Collection; Jean Rhys (1894–1979), English writer whose intense, sparely written feminist novels of the 1930s were rediscovered in the 1970s; and the given name of Rhys ap Gruffydd (c. 1132–1197), an early ruler of South Wales.

riata *(ree-AH-tah)*   From the Spanish word *atar* and the prefix re-, meaning "to tie again," this is another word for a cattle herder's lariat, usually a rope for tethering horses. Fitted with a sliding noose at one end, the riata becomes a lasso, which is thrown to capture animals on the run. The riata is often clued as "gaucho's gear."

Riau *(REE-ow)*   An Indonesian archipelago lying opposite the entrance to the Strait of Malacca. The group is separated from Malaysia by the Strait of Singapore. Bintan, largest of the islands, is known for its rich mineral deposits and ships bauxite and tin from Tanjung Penang, main city of the archipelago.

ricin *(RIE-sin)*   From the Latin *ricinus*, for the castor-oil plant (genus *Ricinus*), ricin is a poisonous substance found in the castor bean. After the oil is expressed from the seeds, ricin is removed and the residue is used for fertilizer and cattle feed.

Riel *(ree-ELL)*   Louis Riel (1844–1885), Canadian firebrand who led bands of Indians and half-breeds, convinced they were being cheated out of their land, against the government in the Red River Rebellion of 1869. In 1885, Riel led another rebellion in Saskatchewan. He was captured, tried for treason, and hanged.

Riesa *(REE-zah)*   Town on the Elbe River in the Dresden district of East Germany. This center of industry is noted for furniture, steel products, and rubber goods, and it has extensive river shipping facilities. Riesa's best-known landmark is the ruin of a twelfth-century Benedictine monastery, around which the city grew.

Riff *(rif)*   A member of the Berber tribe of Muslims who are native to the Rif range (Rif Atlas) of the Atlas Mountains in northeastern Morocco. As a common noun, **riff** is jazz slang for a melodic passage that recurs throughout a musical number as background, and then brings it to a conclusion.

Riga *(REE-gah)*   A major Baltic seaport and capital of Latvia, Riga is one of the leading centers of culture and industry in the U.S.S.R. It dates back to the eleventh century, saw the founding of the Livonian Knights within its precincts, was a Hanseatic town in medieval times, was ruled previously by Germany and Sweden, and experienced fighting in both world wars. Latvia became a Soviet republic in 1940, with Riga continuing as its capital.

Rigel *(RIE-jel)*   From the Arabic word for "foot," a first-magnitude star near the hunter's foot in the constellation Orion. Rigel burns with about 40,000 times the luminosity of the sun, which makes it the seventh-brightest star in the sky. It is roughly 1,000 light-years distant from the earth.

Riggs *(rigs)* Surname of several people, including: Elias Riggs (1810–1901), American missionary who translated the Scriptures into Armenian; Lynn Riggs (1899–), playwright, whose *Green Grow the Lilacs* was transformed into the musical *Oklahoma!;* and the redoubtable Bobby Riggs (1918–), former tennis champion and male chauvinist who was defeated by Billie Jean King in a memorable challenge match before 30,000 spectators in 1973.

A scene from Lynn Riggs' play Green Grow the Lilacs *of 1931.*

Rigi *(REE-gee)* Peak of the Swiss Alps rising above the lakes of Lucerne, Zug, and Lauerz. Its highest point is the Kulm, 5,908 feet above sea level, reached by a rack-and-pinion railway built in the 1870s. The spectacular 180-mile panoramic view from the top is one of the world's most famous.

A cog railway serves the Rigi, a popular recreation area in the Swiss Alps.

Riis *(rees)* Jacob August Riis (1849–1914), Danish-born American journalist and social reformer whose exposés of living conditions in New York slums won him the backing of Theodore Roosevelt. Resultant attempts to improve matters produced a pioneer settlement house and Jacob Riis Park—the familiar watering spot sometimes facetiously referred to as the New York Riviera. Riis wrote *How the Other Half Lives* and the famous autobiography *The Making of an American.*

Jacob Riis.

Rijeka See *Fiume.*

Rilke *(RILL-kuh)* The foremost modern German lyric poet, Rainer Maria Rilke (1875–1926). Once secretary to the sculptor Rodin (q.v.), Rilke penned works of profound beauty. He fought for Germany in World War I and then retired in 1917 to Valais, Switzerland, where he died of blood poisoning from a rose-thorn prick.

Rainer Maria Rilke.

rill *(rill)* From the Dutch or Low German, this is the term for a small stream, brook, or rivulet. In astronomy, **rill** is also spelled rille, and has a somewhat different meaning. Based on the Greek for ''groove,'' in this meaning rill refers to the long, narrow, trenchlike valleys seen on the surface of the moon.

Rima *(REE-mah)* Heroine of W.H. Hudson's romantic tale of the South American jungle, *Green Mansions* (1916). This story revolves around the hero's tragic love for Rima, the ''bird girl'' who lives in the forest and speaks the language of its avifauna.

Rimac *(REE-mahk)* An 80-mile-long river rising high in the Andes of western Peru, then coursing precipitously westward through a scenic valley and the city of Lima before flowing into the Pacific near Callao. The Rimac supplies water for irrigation, and its valley is a major communications route through the region.

rime *(rime)* From the Old Norse word *hrim,* "to touch lightly," by way of Old English. This light, white icing of frost dusts grass and trees, creating a Christmas-card landscape under atmospheric conditions in which humidity is high and temperature hovers around the freezing mark. Rime is frequently defined as "hoarfrost." **Rime** is also a spelling for rhyme and may mean "poem" or "ballad," as in Coleridge's "Rime of the Ancient Mariner."

Rinde *(RIN-duh)* In Norse mythology, one of the wives of Odin (q.v.) and the mother of Vali (q.v.), despite the frigidity associated with her name, for Rinde was supposed to have presided over the frozen surfaces of the earth in winter.

Riom *(ree-OMH)* A town in south-central France, Riom traces its history to the eleventh century. It was the capital of the dukes of Auvergne. The town, though small, supports such industries as distilleries and appliance plants. In 1942, certain French leaders were tried inconclusively here by the Vichy government for involving France in World War II.

Ripon *(RIP-un)* A municipal borough on the Ure River in the West Riding of Yorkshire, England, on the site of a seventh-century monastery. Although Ripon has factories and breweries, it is noted for its old buildings and churches. In the present cathedral (begun in the 1100s), a narrow passage called St. Wilfrid's Needle allegedly permits only virtuous women to squeeze through it. Ripon is also the title borne by: Frederick John Robinson, first Earl of Ripon (1782–1859), better known as Viscount Go-

derish, a statesman who was prime minister in 1827–1828; and his son, George Frederick Samuel Robinson, first Marquess of Ripon (1827–1909), whose many government positions included Viceroy of India from 1880–1884. **Ripon** is also a town in Wisconsin.

Rishi *(REE-shee)* In the Hindu faith, one of seven poets associated with sacred songs, who were born from the mind of Brahma. These seven holy men, seers, and soothsayers were so venerated that, as the legend goes, they were carried to the heavens after death to become the Big Dipper.

Riva *(REE-vah)* Also known as Riva di Trento, a picturesque village sitting at the northern end of Lake Garda in Trentino-Alto Adige, northern Italy. With great natural beauty, Riva has become a world-famous resort and tourist center. It was originally Austrian, but came under Italian rule following World War I. **Riva** Ridge is also a famous racehorse that won the Kentucky Derby and the Belmont Stakes in 1972.

The old port section of Riva, the Italian resort town.

Rizal *(ree-ZAHL)* José Rizal (1861–1896), Philippine author, physician, national hero, and, eventually, martyr. In his novel *Noli Me Tangere,* Rizal railed against Spain's repressive policies and was sent into exile. He lived in various countries, but upon returning to Manila, he was arrested, tried as a revolutionary, and executed.

roan *(rone)* From the Spanish word meaning a color mixture, the term applied to horses whose basic coat color is sprinkled with white and gray; hence such descriptives as blue roan, strawberry roan. Unless otherwise specified, a roan horse is brownish. **Roan** is also a flexible sheepskin used in bookbinding to replace Morocco leather; in this case, it derives from a distortion of Rouen (q.v.), the French city where this material is produced.

roble *(ROE-blay)* From the Spanish for "oak," any of several trees yielding hard wood, such as the California white oak and the live oak of the West.

A common oak.

roc *(rok)* One of the fabulous beasts of all time, a bird of *The Arabian Nights*. In the tale spun by Scheherazade, the roc was the huge white bird encountered by Sinbad the Sailor. It was powerful enough to pick up an elephant in its talons, carry the pachyderm off, and devour it at one sitting.

Roca *(ROE-kah)* A cape, Cabo da Roca, on the Atlantic coast of Portugal, near Lisbon. It is the westernmost point on the European continent. **Roca** is also the surname of Julio Argentino Roca (1843–1914), general and statesman who served two terms as president of Argentina.

Roch *(rok)* Patron saint of pestilence victims. Roch was himself afflicted, and is usually represented in a pilgrim's garment, lifting his skirts to show a plague bubo. He is always accompanied by his faithful dog.

Rodez *(roe-DAY)* Capital city of Aveyron, in the South of France. Today a thriving little community where gloves and plastics are manufactured, Rodez is also a center for farm products grown in the region. It has been in existence since the fourth century A.D., and boasts an impressive Gothic cathedral.

Rodin *(roe-DANH)* Auguste Rodin (1840–1917), French sculptor, whose realistic yet romantic art is considered among the great sculpture of the world. Among his works in museums throughout the world, including those named for him in Paris and Philadelphia, are the famous *Thinker, The Burghers of Calais,* and *The Kiss.* Rodin is credited with creating emotion out of marble.

August Rodin in his studio.

roe *(roe)* From the Greek for "red," roe refers to fish eggs, especially when still within their enclosing membrane. Caviar, the lightly salted eggs of sturgeon, makes the roe of the various sturgeon species the most coveted of all. **Roe** is also a small European and Asiatic deer and the term for the female red deer. Richard **Roe,** in legal proceedings, is the counterpart of John Doe (q.v.). In baseball, pitcher "Preacher" Roe was famous.

Roehm *(rerhm)* Ernst Roehm (1887–1934), an architect of Germany's

National Socialist Party. Among Roehm's dubious achievements was the organization of the SA, the brown-shirted *Sturmabteilung,* or Nazi storm troops. Roehm made the mistake of challenging Hitler for party leadership. In June of 1934, he was brutally murdered.

Rolfe *(rahlf)* Colonist John Rolfe (1582–1622), the Englishman who foresaw that Virginia would be suitable for the cigarette industry, and introduced regular cultivation of the tobacco being grown by the Indians. He is perhaps best known as the husband of Indian chief Powhatan's daughter Pocahontas, who, according to the legend, saved him from being killed by her tribesmen. It is not known why they were after him.

Rollo *(RAHL-oh)* A Norman pirate, also known as Hrolf, who lived between A.D. 860 and 930. As part of the treaty of Saint-Clair-sur-Epte in 911, Charles III ceded him the region which thereupon became the duchy of Normandy. Rollo's part of the deal was to accept Christianity; upon baptism, he became Robert, first Duke of Normandy. Among his descendants was William the Conqueror. Rollo was also the boyish hero of the Rollo books, a series of juveniles by Jacob Abbott.

Romer *(ROH-mehr)* Olaus Romer (1644–1710), the Danish astronomer who discovered that light is not transmitted instantaneously, but travels at a fixed velocity. He estimated the speed of light by observing variations in the eclipse time of Jupiter's moons. Also, the German scientist Ferdinand Romer (1818–1891), an expert on the geology of Texas.

Romo *(ROME-ih)* One of the North Frisian Islands of southwestern Denmark, in the North Sea. In the eighteenth century, Rømø served as a whaling base. It was ruled by Germany from 1864 to 1920, when it became Danish. Today this sparsely settled island is a bathing resort.

Ronda *(ROHN-dah)* Picturesque town situated in high mountainous country of the Sierra de Ronda, in Andalusia, southern Spain. Ronda is actually two towns—the old Moorish village and the new town, separated by the deep gorge of the Guadelevin River. The area is popular in the summer.

A scene in the Sierra de Ronda mountains of Andalusia.

rondo *(ROHN-doe)* From the French word *rondeau,* for "round," a musical composition—usually the last movement of a sonata—within which the main theme is repeated three times in the same key. Also, a gambling game involving the movement of billiard balls on a pool table, whose issue is determined by whether the remaining balls are odd- or even-numbered.

ronin *(ROE-nin)* Originally, Japanese Samurai (knights) whose lords had fallen upon bad times and had to turn them loose. Leaderless and thus displaced in feudal life, the ronin became farmers, monks, soldiers of fortune, or bandits. Today, this term often refers to Japanese high school graduates who have not yet passed college entrance examinations.

rood *(rood)* From the Middle English that also gives us the word rod, this is the word for the cross on which Christ was crucified. Today it means any representation of the cross or crucifix, usually the large one at the entrance to the chancel or choir in a fifteenth- or sixteenth-century European church. (See *jube*.) The term **rood** also refers to a measure of length in England, and a varying measure of area.

rook *(ruhk)* Either a species of European crow that loves company and builds its nest in trees near human habitations (see also *piet*); or a powerful chess piece also called a castle. The **rooks** initially occupy all corners of the chessboard, and can move on either ranks or files over any number of unoccupied squares. They are shaped like fortress battlements and can be instrumental in the protection of the king via a coordinated maneuver known as castling.

roque *(roke)* Outdoor game derived from and resembling croquet, in which balls are driven through hoops. Roque is played on a hard court rather than grass, with considerably heavier mallets than those used in croquet. The edge of the court is raised as a cushion for bank shots, giving roque a special complexity and challenge.

Roros *(REHR-ess)* A small town on Sør-Trøndelag, Norway, near the Swedish border. Røros traces its history back to 1644 when its copper mines, which remained for many years the most important in Norway, were first opened. Today the town is known primarily as a tourist center and mecca for winter sports enthusiasts.

Røros in the snow. The church was built in 1780.

THE UNDESIRABLES

carl	hack
chit	harpy
chuff	hulk
churl	jade
crock	loon
crone	noddy
cur	pawn
dodo	prig
dolt	raff
doxy	roue
fakir	rube
felon	scrag
fink	shill
fop	shrew
frump	spiv
gimp	tyke
goon	tyro
grub	vixen

Rota *(ROE-tah)* Island in the southern part of the Marianas chain in the western Pacific. Rota was a Japanese base during World War II and served as jumping-off point for the attack on Guam on December 11, 1941. Subsequently bombed by American planes, Rota was not occupied until the war ended. In Spain, Rota (near Cádiz) is the site of a U.S. air base. Lower-cased, a **rota** is also a Roman Catholic tribunal; a British political club; and, most commonly, a duty list or roster.

rotor *(ROE-ter)* A contraction of rotator, this is any part of a motor or turbine that moves in a circle, as opposed to stators, which are stationary. In aerodynamics, the term refers to a system of rotating airfoils that supply lift to such wingless aircraft as the helicopter.

A helicopter's large rotor supplies lift; the small one at the rear keeps the craft stable.

roue *(roo-WAY)* The past participle of *rouer,* French verb meaning "to break on the wheel," roué designates a dissolute pursuer of sensual pleasures. Originally, roué was the nickname for friends of the Duc d'Orléans, whose debauches in the fleshpots of Paris left them feeling as if they had been broken on the wheel.

Rouen *(roo-ANH)* A major city in northern France, located on the Seine River near its mouth on the English Channel, about 70 miles from Paris. This commercial and manufacturing center is the port for Paris and is known for its ancient market buildings, its medieval Gothic cathedral, and the famous fourteenth-century abbey of Saint Ouen. Joan of Arc was tried and burned in Rouen in 1431. Writers Pierre Corneille and Gustave Flaubert were born there.

Street scene in the French city of Rouen.

roup *(roop)* From the Middle English word *roupen,* "to cry aloud," this is bad news for Frank Perdue and other poultry farmers. Roup is an infectious disease of fowls characterized by such symptoms as sinusitis, inflammation of the upper air passages, catarrhal discharge from the eyes, and a hoarse cry. More cheerfully, **roup** is also a public auction in Scotland.

Rous *(roos)* Francis Peyton Rous (1879–1970), the American physician whose research on liver physiology and blood led to the development of blood banks. Rous was a winner of the 1966 Nobel Prize in physiology and medicine for his landmark discovery of certain viruses that can cause cancer.

roux *(roo)* In cooking, a paste of flour and butter used to thicken sauces or gravies. A roux can be white or, as its French name suggests, brown, depending on the heat applied. In medicine, **Roux** is the surname of Wilhelm Roux (1850–1924), German anatomist and so-called father of embryology; and Pierre Paul Émile Roux (1853–1933), French bacteriologist, and pioneer in developing antitoxins.

Pierre Paul Emile Roux. *Wilhelm Roux.*

Rovno *(ROHV-nuh)* City on the Ustye River in the Ukraine region of the U.S.S.R. Today, it is a center of the high-voltage equipment and reinforced concrete industries. Rovno dates back to medieval times, when it was a simple Ukrainian settlement. The city came under the rule of Poland briefly from 1921 to 1939. In Polish, it is Równe; in Ukrainian, Rivne.

rowan *(ROW-an)* Another name for the European or American mountain ash, a tree bearing white blossoms and ornamental red

berries long used in folk medicine and to make a tart jelly. As a proper noun, it is the surname of Andrew Summers **Rowan** (1857–1943), American army officer sent on a diplomatic mission to Cuba, and bearer of the famous "Message to Garcia." Also comedian Dan Rowan, of TV's "Laugh-In."

Andrew Summers Rowan.

rowel *(ROW-ell)* From the Old French *rouelle,* which also gave us the word roulette, this is a small

wheel with points or teeth around its perimeter. Rowels are fastened at the ends of spurs, where they can galvanize a horse into motion, or, when a cowboy is afoot, supply sound effects for his stride.

rowen *(ROW-uhn)* This term is derived from the Old Norman French *rewain,* etymon of the English word regain. Rowen refers to the second crop of grass a farmer obtains from his fields in a single growing season, when atmospheric and soil conditions permit, and also to a field left unplowed so cattle can graze on it. By extension, rowen now denotes any kind of aftermath.

Roxas *(ROE-hahs)* Manuel Roxas (1894–1948), Philippine political figure who was captured by Japanese invasion forces in 1942, and ostensibly served in their puppet government. After the war, it was revealed that Roxas was actually an intelligence agent for the Philippine underground. He was elected first president of the Philippine Republic in 1946.

Manuel Roxas.

Ruach *(roo-AHSH)* The so-called Isle of Winds visited by Pantagruel and his cohorts while on their way to commune with the oracle of the Holy Bottle in Rabelais' *Gargantua and Pantagruel.* In the tale, the people of Ruach live on nothing but hot air in the form of flattery and promises.

rube *(roob)* Somewhat pejorative term derived from Reuben, a name conceived by certain rough urban types to belong exclusively to farmers. It is circus and traveling-salesman slang for a rustic, or any individual living in a rural area and supposedly lacking sophistication or the social graces. In cartooning, it is the immortal **Rube** Goldberg, whose name is synonymous with outlandishly complex contraptions for achieving minimal results.

ruble or **rouble** (ROO-*bul*)   From the Old Russian *rubli*, meaning "block of wood," this is the basic unit of currency in the U.S.S.R. The ruble is equivalent to 100 kopeks, and by agreement with the International Monetary Fund (January 1961), its value was pegged at 0.987412 grams of fine gold. As we went to press it was worth about $1.35.

ruche or **rouche** (*roosh*)   This is the French word for "beehive," to which this item bears something of a resemblance. A ruche is a mass of frills or pleats, arranged in rows, used as trimming on women's dresses. It can be made of lace, ribbon, muslin, net, or other sheer or lacy material.

These 19th-century French ladies wear ruches at their necks.

rudd (*rud*)   A freshwater fish also known as the red-eye. Rudds live in streams in the forests and fields of northern Europe, are related to the carp, American sunfish,  golden shiner, and roach, and are close cousins to the goldfish.

Rudge (*rudge*)   Half-witted hero of Dickens's semihistorical novel *Barnaby Rudge*. This gangling, unkempt youth kept a pet raven, Grip, who continually croaked, "Polly put the kettle on." After allowing himself to be talked into participating in a riot, Barnaby was arrested and sentenced to die, but was saved through the intervention of a kindly locksmith. The period of the story is that of the "No Popery" riots of 1780.

Rudra (ROOD-*rah*)   In the Hindu Vedas, Rudra is master of the Maruts, the deities of tempests. He can also cause or cure diseases. Sanskrit for "weep" and "run," the name Rudra was bestowed by Brahma, who took pity on the young god, always running about in tears because he was nameless. Later on, he was identified with the god Shiva (q.v.).

rue (*roo*)   A huge family of plants, the herbs among them being most often represented in gardens by the common rue, a strong-smelling woody herb with yellowish blossoms and bluish-green leaves resembling maidenhair fern. Rue yields an oily substance once used as an irritant in skin medications and still used in flavorings. Traditionally, rue has been a symbol of sorrow, regret, or grief, and also of repentance and memory; hence the definition of the verb **rue,** meaning to regret. In French, *rue* is "street"; hence crossword clues like "____ de la Paix."

Rue.

ruff (*ruf*)   Either a densely pleated, flaring circular collar of silk or starched muslin, worn by sixteenth-century gentry; a "collar" of feathers on a bird; a freshwater fish of the perch family; a type of sandpiper, the female of which is called a reeve (q.v.); or an old card game similar to whist. As a verb, **ruff** means to trump (as in bridge), to hit without trussing (in falconry), and to separate flax.

Rugby (RUG-*bee*)   Either the important railroad junction and engineering center in the Midlands of central England; the famous public school founded there in 1567 by a wealthy native son; or, lower-cased, a type of football game originated at the school in 1823 and described in the classic *Tom Brown's School Days*. The school became famous under the headmastership of the father of the poet Matthew Arnold.

Ruhr *(roor)* Region along the Ruhr River in West Germany, which has been one of the world's largest industrial regions since the nineteenth century, when giant steel and coal industries were launched by the Krupps and Thyssens. Its industrial concentration made the Ruhr a perfect target for Allied bombs during World War II. Essen is its best-known city.

Ruml *(RUM-uhl)* Beardsley Ruml (1894–1960), American economist and guiding force behind both a department store and the Federal Reserve Bank of New York. Ruml's most important achievement was his "pay-as-you-go" plan, the withholding tax adopted by Congress in 1943 and still plaguing American wage-earners.

rune *(roon)* Any character in an alphabet used in inscriptions of Teutonic, Anglo-Saxon, and Scandinavian origin which first appeared around A.D. 300. Runes were mostly perpendicular, angular lines, ideal for carving into wood or stone, and were used until they became associated with paganism or un-Christian practices. They persisted longest in Scandinavia. The word rune comes from Old English for "secret."

rupee *(ROO-pee)* Derived from the Hindi *rupiyah*, meaning "wrought silver," the standard monetary unit of India, Pakistan, and Sri Lanka, equal respectively to 100 naye paise, 100 pice, or 100 cents. Give or take fluctuations, there are about 11 rupees to the dollar.

R.U.R. See *Čapek*.

Rurik *(ROO-rik)* Legendary Scandinavian warrior who founded the royal dynasty of Russia in the Middle Ages. He and his brothers captured Novgorod in A.D. 862, his successors founded the state of Kiev, and his house came to rule the grand duchy of Moscow plus all of Russia until Feodor I died in 1598.

Rutli or **Grutli** *(ROOT-lee)* A large meadow area near Lake Lucerne in Uri canton, central Switzerland. It was here, according to the legend of William Tell, that representatives of the cantons of Uri, Schwyz, and Unterwalden met in 1307 and took the Rütli Oath, which gave rise to Swiss freedom. Although not authenticated, the meadow and a nearby chalet have been made national monuments.

The Rütli meadow on Lake Lucerne.

rynd or **rind** *(rind)* From a Middle Dutch word used and understood widely by millers, this is an iron fitting that traverses the grinding surface of the upper millstone in a gristmill. Usually cross-shaped with flared ends, the rynd is fixed across the hole in the stone and supports it on the spindle.

Rzhev *(rzhef)* City of the U.S.S.R. dating from the eleventh century, straddling the upper Volga River about 125 miles southwest of Moscow. Rzhev was held by the German army during World War II, and served as a base for attacks on Moscow. It was recaptured in early 1943.

Saale *(ZAHL-uh)* Two rivers of Germany: one, also called the Thüringer Saale, is a 225-mile-long river in northeastern Bavaria, flowing generally north through East Germany to the Elbe River near Magdeburg. The Saale's course reflects the old and the new, from the dramatic castles of the Middle Ages to the present-day agriculture of the sugar-beet fields. The Franconian (Fränkische) Saale is about 85 miles long. It flows from the Thüringian Forest across central West Germany to its junction with the Main.

Saar *(zahr)* Another river, about 150 miles long, flowing generally north and northwest from France's Vosges Mountains to the Moselle near Trier, in West Germany. Saar is also a state in West Germany, at times under French control, formerly called the Saar or the Saar Territory, now called Saarland. This is a heavily industrialized area with many coal fields, which account for much iron and steel production. The capital and industrial center is Saarbrücken.

Saba *(SAH-bah)* A picturesque and rugged island of the Leeward group in the Netherlands Antilles whose capital, The Bottom, is most appropriately located in the crater of an extinct volcano. Also, the sometime name of the biblical land Sheba (q.v.).

sable *(SAY-bul)* A carnivorous mammal, *Martes zibellina,* of the weasel family, this is a close relative of the marten. Sable are indigenous to the northern areas of the U.S.S.R. and Finland, but are found as far east as Japan. Their dark brown to black fur

The sable is a protected species in parts of the U.S.S.R.

is highly prized, but the silver-tipped, bluish-black type makes the most expensive coats. The animals, now scarce in the wild, are also reared in captivity. **Sable** is also a cape in Florida and an island off Nova Scotia.

sabot *(SAB-oh)* The wooden shoe stereotypically pictured on the feet of little Dutch

boys and girls, but, in fact, worn as well in other European countries. From the French word *sabot* comes the word sabotage, which literally means the destruction of machinery, either by wooden shoes (usually thrown) or, perhaps, by the wearers of wooden shoes; by extension, all methods of subversion.

Sabots are worn by the Dutchman on the left.

sabra *(SAHB-rah)* This name for the fruits of a tough, hardy cactus growing in the deserts of Palestine has, by its attributes, lent its name to the native-born people of Israel. In old ballads, **Sabra** is a princess saved from a dragon's clutches by St. George.

A group of sabras enjoying a meal break.

Sacco *(SAHK-oh)* Nicola Sacco (1891–1927), who, along with Bartolomeo Vanzetti (1888–1927), was accused, tried, and electrocuted for shooting a paymaster and his guard and stealing $15,000 in Massachusetts in 1920. The two were Italian-born anarchists, and the widespread belief that the trial had been unfair in a time of antiradical feeling inspired protests.

Nicola Sacco.   *Bartolomeo Vanzetti.*

sadhe *(SAHD-uh)* Another letter of the Hebrew alphabet, this one the eighteenth. It has no equivalent in English, but sounds like the *ts* in toots. The letter is also called tsadi *(TSAH-dee)*, and comes in two varieties, with the one resembling a *y* used only as the last letter of a word.

Sadi or **Saadi** *(SAH-dee)* Born Muslih-ud-Din (1184–1291) in Shiraz, in what is now southwestern Iran, he was one of Persia's greatest poets and a fervent Muslim. Sadi's *Gulistan* (1258), meaning "rose garden," is considered his best work. His tomb, in a garden in Shiraz, is treated as a shrine.

Sado *(SAH-doe)* An island off Honshu, Japan, in the Sea of Japan, whose main industries are agriculture and fishing, Sado is known, too, for gold and silver mines. Lower-cased, **sado** is a Malaysian modification of *dos-à-dos,* French for "back to back." This is a four-wheeled Javanese carriage in which the occupants sit with their backs to each other.

Safa *(SAH-fah)* In Islamic legend, an Arabian peak on which Adam and Eve were reunited after a 200-year separation. During this time, they were supposed to have roamed the world after their banishment from the Garden of Eden.

Safaqis See *Sfax.*

Safi or **Saffi** *(SAH-fee)* Western Moroccan city and port, and an important fishing center. Allied forces landed there in the African campaign of 1942. **Safi** was also the baby monkey who, in 1970, sailed with Norwegian explorer Thor Heyerdahl, on Ra I from Morocco to Barbados (the voyage was completed on Ra II).

Sais *(SAY-iss)* An ancient Egyptian city situated roughly in the center of the Nile delta. From 663 to 525 B.C., Saïs was the royal residence of the twenty-sixth dynasty. It also played host to many visitors as a shrine of Neith and Osiris.

saki *(SAH-kee)* A squirrel-sized, curly-haired, bushy-tailed monkey native to the rain forests of South America. As a proper noun, **Saki** is also the pen name of H.H. (Hector Hugo) Munro (1870–1916), Burma-born English newspaper reporter and author who wrote strangely disquieting short fiction and novels. Munro (q.v.) was killed in action during World War I.

salep *(SAL-ip)* or **saleb** *(SAL-eb)* A rather exotic food similar to tapioca, made from the starchy, mucilaginous tubers of certain European and East Indian orchids. Salep is also used in medicine as a demulcent, and was formerly a diet drink of the working classes of London.

Salii *(SAL-ee-eye)* In Roman religion, the so-called leaping priests of Mars, the god of war, who at the god's festivals danced before his altar clad in armor and beating on sacred shields. They included in the proceedings animal sacrifices, chariot races, and banquets.

salmi *(SAL-mee)* Probably a contraction of the French *salmigondis,* whence also comes salmagundi, a dish made of highly seasoned chopped meat. Salmi is a favorite Victorian dish, also well seasoned, but consisting mainly of roasted game or fowl sautéed with mushrooms and wine.

Salop *(SAL-up)* Another name for Shropshire, a county in western England drained by the Severn River. An agricultural and coal-mining region, Salop originally belonged to the kingdom of Mercia. It is dotted with the ruins of castles dating back to the Norman conquest. Its countryside is vividly recalled in poet A.E. Housman's classic *A Shropshire Lad.*

Lowtown and the Severn River in Shropshire (Salop).

salpa *(SAL-pah)* A lower form of marine life closely related to the sea squirt. The salpa is shaped like a barrel open at both ends, and is enclosed in a kind of tunic made up of muscular tissue. Salpae reproduce either asexually by budding or, in hermaphroditic forms, by fertilization of eggs. The larvae of the latter are called tadpoles.

Salus *(SAY-lus)* In Roman religion, Salus was the deity of health and prosperity. (The word *salus* in Latin means "health.") Her name is evident in such health-

British men-of-war fire heavy salvos at an enemy fleet.

associated words as salubrious. Identified with Hygeia by the Greeks, she is represented with a globe at her feet, pouring fluid onto an altar.

salvo *(SAL-voe)*   The firing in unison or succession of artillery pieces, as in a broadside during naval engagements. Among writers of colorful prose, a barrage of applause or cheers is also called a salvo. In law, the word designates an escape clause, and derives from the Latin *salvere,* "to be safe."

Samoa *(sah-MOE-ah)*   A 350-mile-long chain of islands, formerly called the Navigators, lying about halfway between Hawaii and Australia. Discovered by the Dutch in 1722, and divided between the United States and Germany in 1899, Samoa now encompasses American Samoa, with its capital at Pago Pago, and the independent state of Western Samoa, with Apia as the capital.

Samos *(SAH-mos)*   A Greek island of the Sporades archipelago in the Aegean Sea off the coast of Turkey. Samos was colonized in the eleventh century by the Ionians, and today is noted for its wine, tobacco, fruit, and picturesque mountains. Among locals who left their mark were Anacreon, Aesop (q.v.), and Pythagoras.

samp *(samp)*   From the Algonquian word *saump,* this is an American Indian word for "porridge." Among the Narragansett Indians, who called it *nasaump,* it also designated a kind of hominy mush. Samp, from early colonial days to the present, has also been a name for coarsely cracked dried corn, or hominy.

Sana *(suh-NAH)*   Capital of North Yemen and its largest city, situated high on an inland plateau. Dating from the pre-Islamic era, Sana was ruled by Ethiopia in the sixth century A.D., and by Turkey twice, until Yemen achieved independence in 1918. The city, with its Muslim university, is an important center of Arabic culture.

Sansei   See *Kibei.*

Saone *(sohne)*   An approximately 270-mile-long river that originates in the Vosges

The Saône flows under the Bonaparte bridge at Lyons.

Mountains of eastern France and flows southwesterly until it reaches the Rhone at Lyons. The Saône's smooth, gentle flow makes it more conducive to shipping than the Rhone, and it is linked by canals to other important waterways.

sard *(sard)* A deep-orange semiprecious variety of chalcedony, used in jewelry since antiquity. The word originates from Sardis, ancient capital of Lydia, where the stones were mined. A sard may have been the sardius, one of the 12 precious stones worn in the breastplates of Jewish high priests in biblical times (Ex. 28:17).

sari *(SAH-ree)* A Hindi word that has come into English intact, this is the main

article of outer attire worn by Hindu women. The sari usually consists of one long section of patterned or plain cloth that is wrapped skillfully about the body and fastened strategically to eliminate gapping. The finer the material, the richer the woman or her family. Saris often have elaborately ornamented borders.

The sari is the traditional garment of Hindu women.

sark *(sark)* An archaic Scottish word still used poetically for verbal color, this is simply an undergarment worn by women, and resembling either a short slip or a long T-shirt. As a proper noun, **Sark** is one of the Channel Islands of Britain. It belongs to the Guernsey district, and still has a local government on the feudal pattern.

Sarsi or **Sarcee** *(SAR-see)* Tribe of American Indians who lived on the upper reaches of Canada's Saskatchewan River during the nineteenth century. When the Cree invaded their hunting grounds, the

peaceful Sarsi allied themselves with the Blackfoot, eventually ceded their lands to the Canadian government, and in 1880 moved to a reservation in Calgary.

Members of the Sarsi tribe pose before a tepee.

sasin *(SAY-sin)* From the native term, the Indian antelope or black buck. Of medium size, these extremely fast animals can easily outrun a greyhound and clear high fences without a running start. Males have long, spiral horns, white underbellies, and a distinctive white eye patch.

Satie *(sah-TEE)* Erik Satie (1865–1925), French composer and pianist. In his most famous works, the *Sarabandes* and *Gymnopédies,* Satie exhibited a sensitive, delicate style that probably influenced Debussy and Ravel. After World War I, he led a group of ultramodern French composers known as Les Six.

Erik Satie.

satyr *(SAT-uhr)* In Greek mythology, a horned creature, part man (top half) and part goat (bottom half), attendants of Bacchus much given to lecherous pursuits and riotous partying. The Romans called them fauns. By extension, the word satyr has come to designate anyone inordinately involved in the pleasures of the flesh. **Satyr** is also the name of a pretty gray-and-brown spotted butterfly.

Sauk *(sawk)* Also known as the Sac, any member of the Algonquian American Indian people originally inhabiting the region encompassed by Illinois, Michigan, and Wisconsin. In 1804, a dishonest treaty pushed the Sauk west of the Mississippi and precipitated the Black Hawk War. Today, they live on reservations in Oklahoma and Kansas. Sinclair Lewis was born in the town of **Sauk** Centre, Minnesota.

A Sauk tribesman.

saury *(SORE-ee)* From the Greek *saura,* meaning "lizard," this is an Atlantic fish with a long, pipelike body and a pointed snout. Native to temperate waters, the saury is related to the needlefish and has jawfuls of sharp teeth, which it puts to good use in satisfying its voracious appetite. The Greek root *saura* also appears as a suffix in such terms as dinosaur.

Sava *(SAH-vah)* Yugoslavia's longest river, originating in the Julian Alps near the Italian border and flowing about 580 miles in a southeasterly direction before joining the Danube at Belgrade. Navigable for much of its length, the Sava is a major transportation route and an important shipping conduit for its valley's agricultural products.

Savoy *(sah-VOY)* Either a one-time duchy of Sardinia; a European ruling house in existence from the eleventh century until the twentieth; an Alpine region of eastern France, with its historical capital at Chambéry; or a type of crinkly-leaved, compactheaded cabbage. In London, the **Savoy** was a parish, for which was named the Savoy Theatre and the historic Savoy Chapel, built by Richard D'Oyly Carte (q.v.) as the home of his Gilbert and Sullivan opera produc-

tions. Aficionados of these productions are still called Savoyards.

Savoy might also be clued in crosswords as "great London Hotel."

Saxon *(SAK-son)* A people living in northern Germany around the second century A.D., according to the historian Ptolemy. In the fifth and sixth centuries, the warlike Saxons and their allies, the Angles, invaded and conquered areas of eastern England, founding the Anglo-Saxon kingdoms. The Saxons on the Continent were eventually absorbed into the empire of Charlemagne. English place-names ending in -sex take these names from the Saxons, e.g., Wessex, which was the kingdom of the West Saxons, and Essex, Sussex, etc.

A band of Saxons readying themselves for battle.

Scala *(SKAH-lah)* Its full name is Teatro alla Scala, often abbreviated as La Scala, Italian for "stairs." This is the premier opera house of the world, located in Milan. Designed by Giuseppe Piermarini, La Scala was built on the site of a church and opened in 1778. It was bombed during World War II and restored in 1946. Many great operas premiered here: Verdi's *Otello* and *Falstaff;* Puccini's *Turandot* and *Madama Butterfly;* and Bellini's *Norma.*

Milan's La Scala, one of the great opera houses.

scarp *(skarp)* From the Italian *scarpa,* meaning "slope," this is a sudden, steep incline along the side of a gentle, sloping hill or a clifflike face created by erosion where faulting has brought hard and soft rock together. Fortification builders often incorporated the scarp on the inner side of a ditch leading up to a rampart, thus assuring an uphill battle for would-be invaders.

scaup *(skawp)* Any of a genus of northern wild ducks of the pochard group. Scaups, both greater and lesser, are the so-called diving or bay ducks, with compact bodies that make it easier to knife into the water. Best known of the scaups' relatives are the brown, black, and white canvasbacks of North America and the handsome, solitary redhead.

scone *(skone; skoon)* Scotch contraction of the Middle Dutch word *schoonbrot,* meaning "beautiful bread," this is a biscuit, formerly always baked on a griddle, served in the British Isles with tea. Also, the name of a village in Perthshire, Scotland, where originally rested the Stone of **Scone,** the Coronation Stone upon which all Scottish kings from the ninth century to 1296 were crowned. In the nineteenth century, a palace was built on the site of the twelfth-century abbey that was torn down by the Protestants four centuries later.

scrag *(skrag)* From the Norwegian epithet *skragg,* "a feeble cripple," this word has come to mean any skinny, scrawny person or animal. By extension, it also designates a weak, stunted tree. And, in recognition of its unmeatiness, **scrag** also refers to the neck of mutton.

A scraggy messenger receives a note in this print by Honoré Daumier.

scree *(skree)* This word derives from the Old Norse *skritha,* meaning a landslide. Scree designates an area of small pebbles or stones, especially in rock gardens, in conversational British and general gardening English. It is also the term for an accumulation of such stones usually seen at the foot of a cliff bearing the sign "Fallen Rock Zone."

scrim *(skrim)* Probably an anglicization of the German *schirm,* which gives us the English word screen. A scrim is a loosely woven cotton curtain used for various effects on the stage; it is transparent to the audience when lit from behind, but opaque when light is played on its front side.

scrip *(skrip)* A shortening of script, this word has various meanings related to writing. Scrip can be a scrap paper with writing on it; a certificate in lieu of an actual object;

such as shares of stock; or temporary paper coupons used as money by department-store shoppers or invading armies (see also *chit*). In tales of yore, a **scrip** was a pilgrim's wallet. In crosswords, scrip is often defined as "emergency currency" or "redeemable certificate."

scrod *(skrahd)* A popular New England name, also spelled "schrod" in fancy seafood restaurants, for fillets of young codfish. It is sometimes used for such other fish as haddock. The word originates from the Middle Dutch *schrode,* a cut-off piece or strip.

scuba *(SKOO-ba)* Acronym for *s*elf-*c*ontained *u*nderwater *b*reathing *a*pparatus. Scuba gear is slung on the back of a diver, and includes a small oxygen or air tank, various valves, lengths of tubing, and a mouthpiece. It was developed during the first half of the century by Émil Gagnan and Jacques Yves Cousteau.

scull or **skull** *(skull)* From the Middle English *skulle,* either a light, concave oar or a sleek racing boat for one to four oarsmen; or, as a verb, to move a boat by a single stern oar worked in a sweeping side-to-side motion.

scute *(skoot)* In zoology, the external "armor plate" seen on certain snakes and other reptiles, or the scales on fish. In anatomy, a common term for the tegmen tympany, the roof of a cavity containing one's ear drum. The definition of this word is evident from its Latin root *scutum,* meaning "shield."

A fish's scales provide it with a scute.

Sebek *(SEB-ek)* Another of the many deities who walk through the hieroglyphics of Egyptian myth, Sebek was an evil god whose chief responsibility was tending to the welfare of crocodiles. He could, however, also wield the sun's destructive power. Sebek is immediately recognizable by his crocodile head.

sebum *(SEE-buhm)* From the Latin word for "tallow," this is the body's natural grease, a viscid fluid secreted by the sebaceous glands of the skin, combined with the debris of fat-producing cells which have been replaced. Sebum is a valuable skin and hair lubricant, but, if oversupplied, skin problems may develop.

Seder *(SAY-der)* The traditional Jewish feast that commemorates the Exodus from Egypt, held on the first and second days of Passover, the most important Jewish festival. During the dinner, the eldest male retells the story of Jewish bondage and liberation, dwelling at length on what makes the Seder night "different from all other nights;" there is general thanksgiving and rejoicing, and symbolic foods are served. The Last Supper of Jesus was a Seder.

A Jewish family enjoying a traditional Passover Seder.

sedge *(sedj)* From the Middle English *segge,* meaning "cut," sedge is a coarse grasslike marsh plant cut for matting. Unlike grasses, sedges have solid, usually triangular stems; some are also called bulrushes. Those that hid the infant Moses were probably the sedge the Egyptians used to make papyrus.

Bulrushes—or sedge.

sedum *(SEE-dum)* This is the Latin word for the plant commonly called house-leek, but in general use it designates any species in a large ge-nus. Sedum, as a common name, is in-terchangeable with orpine, stonecrop, and hens-and-chick-ens. Often found growing in rock gar-dens these plants have fleshy leaves and white, yellow, pink, or purple flowers.

A variety of sedum, a hardy perennial.

Segni *(SEN-yee)* Antonio Segni (1891–1972), the Italian political leader who started his career as a university professor and founded the forerunner of the Christian Democratic Party. Segni was elected presi-dent of Italy in 1962, and resigned after suffering a stroke in 1964. Lower-cased, **segni** is also the plural of the Italian word *segno* (sign), a mark used in music to indicate repetition. It looks like this—:S:.

Antonio Segni, president of Italy in the 1960s.

sego *(SEE-goe)* From the Shoshonean word *sígo,* this is a bulb-producing plant also known as the sego lily and native to western North America. It produces a showy, tulip-like white flower with purple, lilac, or yel-low markings. The sego lily is the state flower of Utah and is used in Mormon church ceremonies. In parts of the West it is best known as mariposa lily.

Seir *(SEE-ur)* A rugged, mountainous area south of the Dead Sea in Jordan and Israel. Its highest point is Mt. Hor. In the Bible, the region is identified with Edom (q.v.) (Gen. 36:20; 1 Chron. 1:38). In the book of Joshua (15:10), Seir is also the name of a mountain placed at the border of Judah.

Sekhet See *Pakht.*

Sela or **Selah** *(SEE-lah)* Hebrew for "rock," this was a town somewhere in the rocky, mountainous region of the Holy Land south of the Dead Sea. Selah was renamed Joktheel by its conqueror, Amaziah (2 Kings 14:7). It is often identified with Petra (q.v.). The word **selah** appears often in the Psalms, and three times in the third chapter of Habakkuk in the Bible. It is perhaps a musical or liturgical indication, or it may signify a pause; its exact meaning is un-known. It is frequently clued as a "biblical mystery word."

Selim *(sel-IM)* The name of three Otto-man sultans: Selim I, known as Selim the Grim, who ruled from 1512 to 1520; Selim II, who rejoiced in the name Selim the Drunkard and ruled from 1566 to 1574; and Selim III, sultan from 1789 to 1807, upon whom the Otto-man Empire col-lapsed.

Selim III, the last Selim.

Selma *(SEL-mah)* A city in Alabama, and an agricultural and industrial center. During the Civil War, Selma was the site of a Confederate armory and was almost de-stroyed in 1865. The town is famous, how-ever, as a focal point of the black civil-rights movement led by Dr. Martin Luther King in the 1960s. Also, **Selma** Lagerhöf (1858–1940), the Swedish novelist who was awarded the 1909 Nobel Prize in literature.

sen *(sen)* From the Chinese word *ch'ien,* meaning "coin," this is a small unit of currency in various Asian countries, usually a copper or bronze coin. In Japan, it is equal to $^1/_{100}$ of a yen; in Cambodia, to $^1/_{100}$ of a riel; and in Indonesia, to $^1/_{100}$ of a rupiah. It is often clued as "Ginza (q.v.)change."

senna *(SEN-ah)* Any of several plants belonging to the pulse family. Senna species with medicinal uses produce yellow or pinkish flowers; their leaves, when dried, are used as a cathartic. Also, from the name of an Iranian town, **senna** (or sehna) designates a small rug with a very fine weave.

Sens *(sanh)* Town on the Yvonne River in north-central France, dating from the period of Caesar's Gallic Wars, when it was known as Agendicum. Sens is known for its Gothic cathedral (begun 1140), for the council held here in 1121 that condemned the teachings of Abelard, and for an infamous massacre of Huguenots that took place here in 1562.

sepal *(SEE-puhl)* A leaf or any part of the calyx (q.v.), the outermost part of a flower. The term was coined from the Latin words for "separate" and "petal" by botanist H.J. de Necker in 1790.

Sepia *(SEE-pee-yah)* From the Greek *sepia,* for "cuttlefish," any of a genus of cuttlefish, squidlike marine cephalopods having arms with suckers attached, a hard internal shell, and an ink sac that ejects a black, inklike fluid to confuse pursuers. **Sepia** also refers to the dark, reddish-brown pigment made from the fluid, and to photographs printed in a similar shade, often found in old albums.

sepoy *(SEE-poi)* From the Hindi word for "army," the term applied to a native Indian who served in the Bengal army of the British East India Company during the time of the Raj (see *rajah*). In 1857, the great

Indian Mutiny began when the sepoys' concerns were disregarded. Among some concerns were the loss of caste when they crossed the sea (as some had to do) and the issuance of cartridges of a type that had to be bitten before use, said to be greased with tallow (from an animal sacred to Hindus and abhorred by Muslims). A general cause of unrest in India was the policy of "John Company," amounting to heedless expansionism, including the 1856 annexation of Oudh (q.v.), homeland of many sepoys. Also called the Sepoy Rebellion, the uprising was quelled at great cost in lives, with atrocities on both sides.

seps *(seps)* The "poisonous" reptile of classical literature, then thought to be a snake but actually a lizard of the skink (q.v.) family, with a snakelike body, tiny legs, and overlapping scales. Seps is derived from a Greek root related to that for "decay," possibly referring to the effects of the creature's bite.

The seps is often mistaken for a snake.

ser *(seer)* Translated from a Hindi word, this is a unit of dry weight used in certain retail establishments on the Indian subcontinent. The ser is equal to slightly over two pounds, or about one kilogram. Metrologists also fix the weight of the ser at $^1/_{40}$ of a maund. Often in crosswords, **ser** is used as the abbreviation for sermon and is clued as "Sunday discourse: abbr."

serac *(SAY-rak)* Originally a type of white cheese in Switzerland and France, sérac refers to a natural phenomenon that resembles a wedge of it—a jagged or pointed block of ice standing in a crevasse of a glacier. Because these sometimes resemble kneeling figures, the Spanish call them *nieve penitente* (penitent snow.)

serai *(seh-RAH-ih)* A type of Middle Eastern motel, with facilities for camels. Because these inns were usually scattered along the route of caravans, they are also known as caravanseries. Serai is transliterated from the Persian word for "palace," which is also the root of seraglio, a mansion for concubines.

Serb *(serb)* A Slav native to Serbia, the largest of the republics of Yugoslavia. Serbs differ from their Croat and Slovene neighbors by belonging to the Orthodox Eastern Church and using the Cyrillic rather than the Roman alphabet. It was a Serb who assassinated Archduke Ferdinand of Austria in 1914, precipitating World War I.

This Serbian costume shows a Byzantine influence.

serf *(serf)* From the Latin word *servus*, meaning "slave," a peasant farmer under the feudal system. The serf was considered to be attached to the land on which he labored and often passed with it to a new owner. Today the term can refer to any menial, low-paid worker trapped in his job.

serge *(serj)* From medieval French by way of Middle English, serge is a twilled, hard-surfaced fabric with fine diagonal ribbing, made of either long-staple wool or silk. Wool serge suits are notorious for taking on a shine after being worn for a while. Also **Serge** Koussevitzky (1874–1951), Russian-born conductor of the Boston Symphony (1924–1947) and proponent of modern symphonic music.

serif *(SER-if)* Term used by printers, type designers, and art directors to designate the fine horizontal lines projecting from vertical strokes of letters in certain styles of type. Type devoid of this feature is described as sans serif (*sans,* in French, means "without").

serin *(SER-in)* A small bird of the finch family, indigenous to Europe. The serin sports yellowish-green feathers and is related to the American siskin, which it closely resembles, except for its darker crown. The canary evolved from serins who migrated to the Atlantic islands eventually named for their descendants.

serow *(SEH-roe)* Transliteration of the Tibetan or Sikkimese name for any member of a group of goat antelopes widely found in Asia, and especially common in the Himalayas. In the genus *Capricornus,* they are as adept as goats at climbing.

Sert *(surt)* José María Sert (1876–1945), Barcelona-born Spanish muralist who decorated walls in the Council Chamber of the League of Nations, the RCA building in New York City, and the old Sert Room at New York's Waldorf-Astoria Hotel.

serum *(SEAR-um)* From the Latin for "whey," this is the thin, watery, yellowish fluid that separates from the clot as blood coagulates. The plural is sera. Serum (or blood serum) is often taken from animals made immune to a given disease by inoculation, then purified and injected into humans to help prevent that disease.

seta *(SEE-tah)* Taken into English directly from the Latin, seta is the botanical and zoological term for a bristle or bristle-like part. Among veterinarians, this is also called a vibrissa—from the Latin for "nose hair"—and refers to the long, stiff hair on the faces or bodies of certain animals.

Sete *(set)* A port on the Mediterranean in southern France, Sète is a major fishing and shipping center for a region producing wines and chemicals. The old harbor designed by Colbert and built by Vauban dates back to 1666. Among Sète's famous sons was Paul Valéry, the philosopher-poet who lies buried there. The town was formerly called Cette.

Seti *(SAY-tee)* The name of two ancient Egyptian kings. Seti I of the XIX dynasty followed his father, Ramses I, to the throne c. 1302 B.C. and ruled for about 12 years. Seti II, also of the XIX dynasty, succeeded Merneptah around 1209 B.C. and died four years later. His reign was followed by anarchy until Ramses III took the throne.

Seti I (right) before Osiris.

seton *(SEE-tun)* Obsolete medical term for a horsehair inserted under the skin to cause or maintain a discharge. As a proper noun, it's the family name of Ernest Thompson **Seton** (1860–1946), American writer-illustrator of nature books and founder in 1902 of the Woodcraft Indians, an organization that probably spawned the Boy Scouts. Also, author Anya Seton; and Mother Seton (Elizabeth Ann Seton),

Ernest Thompson Seton's name was originally Ernest Seton Thompson.

founder of the first U.S. congregation of the Sisters of Charity, who was canonized in 1974, making her the first native-born American saint. **Seton** Hall University is in South Orange, New Jersey.

Sfax *(sfaks)* Also known as Safaqis, a Mediterranean seaport of Tunisia on the Gulf of Gabès (q.v.). Sfax is the second largest city in Tunisia, and exports olive oil and sponges. In antiquity, it was ruled by Phoenicia and Rome, later by Sicily and Spain. The dreaded Barbary pirates once lurked here.

Sfax (circled) is a city of about 71,000 people.

Shaba *(SHAH-bah)* The former province of Katanga in Zaire, Shaba encompasses one of the world's richest mining areas, especially for copper and cobalt. It was once part of the Belgian Congo. Declaring its short-lived independence in 1960, under Moise Tshombe, Shaba saw much violence, including the assassination of Premier Patrice Lumumba.

shad *(shad)* Saltwater fish native to the Atlantic but recently introduced on the Pacific coast. One of the largest of the herrings, it makes excellent eating and its roe (q.v.) is prized as a seasonal delicacy. Because shad spawn in rivers, their population has been drastically reduced by water pollution.

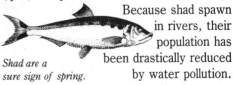
Shad are a sure sign of spring.

shag *(shag)* Either any tangled, knotted mass; heavy, rough nap, as on some wools, especially rugs; coarsely shredded tobacco; a cormorant or small marine bird distinguished by its matted crest during the mating season; or a dance step of the 1930s in which participants hopped on one foot, and then on the other. **Shag** is a slang verb in baseball that means to chase after fly balls.

Shahn *(shahn)*

Ben Shahn (1898–1969), the Lithuanian-born American artist and social commentator whose paintings of the Sacco (q.v.)–Vanzetti trial first brought him to public attention. Among his works are a series of murals at the Bronx Central Annex Post Office in New York City and many paintings in leading museums.

shako *(SHAK-oh)*

From the Hungarian *csákó*, meaning "peak," this is a high military dress hat shaped like a cylinder, with a flat top and a plume attached for decoration. Shakos are traditionally worn by the West Point Cadet Corps, and furry versions adorn the heads of British Foot Guards.

Bavarian gendarmes in plumed shakos.

shale *(shale)*

Derived from various Anglo-Saxon, Middle English, and Old German words meaning "shell," the word refers to fine-textured sedimentary rock formed when mud or clay hardens. It splits easily between layers. About half of the sedimentary rock on earth is shale and much interest today is centered on oil shales as a future energy source.

sham *(sham)*

Probably a dialect variation of shame, this word at one time specifically designated a trick or fraud. Today, the meaning has been broadened to include imitations, whether animate or inanimate, intended to deceive, e.g., everything from counterfeit money to ornamental plastic brick to political discourse. A pillow **sham** is a decorative covering for a bed pillow.

Shan *(shan)*

The name given to any member of certain Mongoloid tribes native to parts of Indochina. These peoples speak a Thai language also known as Shan. The Tien **Shan** is a great mountain system with peaks over 24,000 feet high, stretching for 1,500 miles in central Asia. **Shan** was also the name of former President Gerald Ford's pet Siamese cat.

shank *(shank)*

From the German for "thigh" and Middle English for "bone," the part of the leg between the ankle and knee. Also, analogous objects such as the stem between an instrument's handle and working end; the narrow area of a shoe sole; a cut of beef, veal, or lamb; or the end of anything.

shard *(shard)*

This word is derived from the Middle English for "shear" or "break off." Shard designates a fragment or chunk chipped from an object, usually pottery. In archaeologic circles, such pieces are known as potsherds. A **shard** is also the shell-like covering on a beetle's wing.

Shari or Chari *(SHAH-ree)*

A 650-mile-long African river flowing northwest from the Central African Republic upland across Chad (q.v.) and fanning out into a broad delta before entering Lake Chad. The Logone River joins the Shari at Ndjamena (formerly Fort Lamy), site of an important Allied base during World War II. **Shari** is also TV puppeteer Shari Lewis.

shawm *(shawm)*

Taken from a diminutive form of the Latin for "reed," this is an obsolete wind musical instrument fitted with a double reed. The shawms eventually gave way to the modern oboe (q.v.), which is similar in appearance and tone. The bass member of the shawm family was called a bombardon.

Sixteenth-century dragon shawms.

NATIVE AMERICANS

Caddo

Acoma

Pomo

Zuni

Haida

Sauk

Hupa

Sioux

Erie

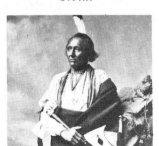

Ponca

Mono

Sheba *(SHEE-bah)*   Biblical region of the southern Arabian peninsula, including the present North and South Yemen. An ancient culture flourished there, and the people, the Sabaeans, were said to be very wealthy. Sheba's best-known citizen was its fabled queen, who consorted with King Solomon, presumably to verify his wisdom and glory at first hand (1 Kings 10:1-13).

The queen of Sheba being received by Solomon.

Shem *(shem)*   In the Old Testament (Gen. 5:32, 7:13), eldest of Noah's three sons, who sired the post-flood offspring called Semites in his honor. Shem is supposed to have lived 602 years, possibly accounting for the large number of descendants. He was literarily reincarnated as Jerry Earwicker in James Joyce's *Finnegans Wake*.

sheng *(sheng)*   Chinese musical instrument made of pipes of varying length inserted into a gourd. It is played by blowing through a mouthpiece and closing finger holes in the pipes. The sheng, first seen in the West in the eighteenth century, probably was an ancestor of such instruments as the accordion, concertina, and organ. **Sheng** is also a Chinese unit of liquid capacity equal to a bit more than a quart.

Sheol *(SHEE-ole)*   In ancient Jewish belief, the place to which the dead repair in the nether world. Sheol was thought of as a land far removed from the upper world, but without either joy or sorrow.

Shiah or **Shi'a** *(SHEE-ah)*   Alternate name for a Shiite, from the Arabic *shi'i*, "follower." Shiahs follow one of the two mainstreams of Muslim thought—namely, that Ali, fourth of the caliphs and son-in-law of Mohammed, is the Prophet's rightful successor, an idea rejected by the Sunni. Shiism is the religion of Iran.

Shiel *(sheel)*   A 17-mile-long lake, or loch (q.v.), as such bodies are known in Scotland, situated between Argyllshire and Inverness-shire. Loch Shiel drains into Loch Moidart. In 1745, Prince Edward Charles Stuart (Bonnie Prince Charlie) led an uprising on behalf of his claim to the English throne from Glenfinnan, a town on Loch Shiel.

Shiga *(SHEE-gah)*   A prefecture (or municipality) of southern Japan. Primarily a rice-producing and textile-manufacturing region, Shiga includes the cities of Hikone and Otsu, its capital (and a popular crossword town).

shill *(shill)*   A shortening of shillaber, originally a circus employee who mingled with the crowds and made a show of buying tickets in order to influence others. The word has become slang in general for a gambler's or charlatan's confederate who pretends to participate in order to lure spectators into the proceedings.

shim *(shim)*   A shim is one of those useful objects you see every day but never know the name of. This is a wedge-shaped piece of wood or metal used to level something—a shim is pushed as a space-filler under a piece of furniture, for example, to keep it from tilting on an uneven floor. A tool used to weed or cultivate between rows is called a **shim** plow. Sculptor's shims are thin strips of brass used to separate sections when making a mold in several pieces.

Shinn *(shin)* Everett Shinn (1876–1953), American artist first noticed for murals done for the famous New York architect Stanford White. Shinn's best-known works depict theater life; his *London Music Hall* hangs in New York's Metropolitan Museum of Art. Shinn also wrote a play, *Hazel Weston,* that ran for 25 years.

shire *(shire)* From *scire,* the Old English word that also (with reeve—q.v.) spawned sheriff and means "official charge," this is the generic term for a British county, or a specific county ending with -shire, as Yorkshire. The **Shire** horse is an English breed that went from carrying knights in armor to pulling wagons. Pronounced SHEE-*ray,* is a 250-mile-long river in Malauri, southeastern Africa. It flows from Lake Nyasa to the Zambezi River.

Shiva *(SHEE-vah)* or **Siva** *(SEE-vah)* The Hindu deity of death called the Destroyer, one member of the supreme trinity that also includes Vishnu (q.v.) and

Brahma. His consort is Kali (q.v.). Shiva is invoked in the epic verses called Puranas. His image is the *lingam,* or symbolic phallus, and his mount is a bull named Nandi. Like other Hindu gods, he has several aspects, each with its own name.

shive *(shive)* An anglicized version of the German *scheibe,* a flat, round object, and the Middle English *schive,* meaning "disc." Shives are splinters, or fragments broken from a larger mass. Also, the stiff chunks of husk from flax; a splinter remaining in scoured wool; or a thin, shallow cork used to stop up a wide-mouthed bottle.

shoal *(shole)* Derived from the Old English *sceald,* which gave way to the English shallow, this is a place where the bottom rises very close to the surface, as in a sandbar, creating navigation hazards. **Shoal** is also a collective noun for a group of fish, such as a shoal of herring.

shott See *chott.*

shrew *(shroo)* A small, long-snouted rodent related to the mole. The shrew's soft brown fur and cuteness belie its voracious appetite for worms, insects, and even mice larger than itself. Among the smallest of the mammals, the shrew is also known for its unpleasant disposition. Certain similarities have broadened the word **shrew** to mean a scolding, ill-tempered woman, like Kate in Shakespeare's *The Taming of the Shrew.*

Shrews starve to death if deprived of food for even half a day.

Shri *(shree)* The Hindu goddess of good fortune, love, and beauty, also worshiped as Loka Mata and Lakshmi. She is the consort of Vishnu (q.v.). Reportedly conceived in an ocean of milk wrung from ambrosia, Shri is represented as a golden maiden sitting on a lotus. **Shri** is also a variation of Sri, which is a title of respect like our "sir" in India. Sri is a frequent crossword repeater and is often clued as the country "_____ Lanka."

Shushan See *Susa.*

Sian or **Hsi-an** *(SEE-ahn)* A thriving commercial city called home by a million and a half Chinese, this is the capital of Shensi province. On the Lung-hai Railroad, Sian is an industrial and commercial center. Under various names, it traces back to the years before the Ch'in dynasty, itself beginning more than 200 years before Christ. Sian was once a capital of the T'ang dynasty, a period during which it was also home to an ancient enclave of Nestorian Christians. In 1936, Chiang Kai-shek was imprisoned here by an insurgent associate. A major archaeological discovery was made in Sian recently with the excavation of thousands of life-size stone soldiers in perfect repair, with different faces and clothing.

sib *(sib)* From the Middle English for "kinship," the term for a blood relative. In anthropology, it designates a group descended from one common ancestor, often—as is the case among Indians—with one common totem. (By contrast, clans and septs are based on descent in both male and female lines.) The term sibling refers to either one's brother or sister.

Cain and Abel, an early case of sibling rivalry.

Sibiu *(see-BYEW)* Busy industrial and cultural center of Transylvania, in the heartland of Romania. Known today for chemicals, textiles, and machinery, Sibiu dates from the twelfth century, when it was founded by German colonists. The city retains much of its medieval Teutonic character, and is still known by its German name, Hermannstadt.

Sibyl *(SIB-uhl)* One of the 10 or so major and minor prophetesses scattered through classical mythology. The Cumaean Sibyl (see *Cumae*), according to Vergil's *Aeneid*, offered a set of books containing her predictions to Tarquin. When he hesitated, she destroyed several books and repeated the offer. This continued until he finally purchased the last three, still at the original high price. These Sibylline books, reportedly kept in Rome and consulted during emergencies, burned in the fire of 83 B.C. Sibyl has come to mean fortuneteller.

Siena *(see-EN-ah)* City of Tuscany, in central Italy, one of the country's most famous art centers. Founded by Senus, son of Remus, Siena was once an independent republic, much fought over during the Middle Ages. A popular tourist center, Siena is known for its marble as well as its architecture and art treasures. A horse race, the Palio festival, first held in 1656, is run there twice each summer.

Siena's historic Mangia tower.

Sif *(sif)* In Scandinavian mythology, Thor's (q.v.) consort, personification of Mother Earth, and mistress of marriage and families. Sif's crowning glory was her long blond hair, which the mischievous Loki (q.v.) sheared while she slept. Through Thor's good offices, she was given a new golden fall—symbolizing the reappearance of foliage on earth in springtime.

sigil *(SIDJ-uhl)* From the Latin *sigillum,* a diminutive of *signum,* meaning "sign," sigil denotes a seal or signet. It also refers to the items that made up the stock-in-trade of astrologers, magicians, and sorcerers of

old—signs, words, or other occult formulas said to possess mysterious powers, usually in direct proportion to the contents of a client's purse.

Martin Luther's sigil.

sigma *(SIG-mah)* The eighteenth letter of the Greek alphabet, corresponding to the letter *s* in English. Objects shaped with a double curve like this letter are usually described as sigmoid; an example is the ogee (q.v.), an S-shaped molding.

Sikar *(SEE-kar)* A walled town sitting on a high plateau in the state of Rajasthan, northwestern India. Main shipping point for the region's grain and tobacco, and an administrative center, Sikar is the site of the Harasmuth temple, built around 1000 B.C.

Sikes *(sikes)* The infamous Bill Sikes, the low-class brute and ruffian, accomplice of Fagin (q.v.), in Charles Dickens's classic *Oliver Twist.* In one of the most dramatic Dickensian episodes, Sikes kills his sweetheart, Nancy, with the butt of a pistol, when he suspects that she has betrayed him.

Sikh *(seek)* Hindi for "disciple," this term designates a believer in the tenets of a 500-year-old offshoot of Hinduism which rejects polytheism and the caste system. Sikhs hold the pious warrior in respect and themselves developed military skills that led to their conquest of the Punjab, where they once established a Sikh state. Their sacred city is Amritsar, site of the Golden Temple. All Sikhs are named Singh (lion), and all wear turbans, carry a concealed dagger, and never cut their hair or beards. They traditionally served in the British armies in India.

silo *(SILE-oh)* Farm structure for airtight storage of fresh fodder, or ensilage (silage). Silos are a standard on the rural scene. They may be as simple as the pit silos of ancient Rome or costly glass-lined towers. Today, silo also designates a storage and launching site for nuclear missiles.

silva or **sylva** *(SILL-vah)* What fauna (q.v.) is to animals, silva is to trees—the arboreal population of a geographical region. As a proper noun, **Silva** is the surname of Antonio José da Silva (1705–1739), Brazilian-born Portuguese lawyer/playwright who was, with his family, brought before the Inquisition in 1737. They were convicted of practicing Judaism, strangled, and burned at the stake.

simar *(sih-MAR)* A style of loose-fitting coat-dress for women. The etymology of simar traces back from the *haute couture* of Paris, where it was called a *simarre,* to fashion-conscious ancient Rome, where it was a *cimarra.* In Arabic, *sammūr* is a weasel comparable to a marten.

Simi or **Syme** *(SEE-meh)* A Greek island of the Dodecanese group in the Ae-

The harbor of the town Simi, on the island of Simi.

gean, and its principal city. Simi is also a city whose full name is Simi Valley, in Ventura County, Southern California. Incorporated in 1969, it is noted for campers, toothpaste tubes, plastic ware, sewage units, and liquid oxygen.

Simla *(SIM-lah)* Town in the state of Himachal Pradesh, northwestern India, in the Himalayan foothills. Simla's salubrious climate makes it a popular resort; it is also headquarters for the Indian army. Simla was one of the most famous British "hill stations" during their rule. The hill stations were places where all the British who could be spared from their regular posts spent the hot-weather months.

Sinan *(SEE-nahn)* Perhaps the greatest Islamic architect (c. 1489–1578) of all time. At his most productive during the reigns of the Ottoman sultans Selim I and II (q.v.) and Sulayman I, Sinan designed and built such masterpieces as the mosque of Sha Zade in Istanbul, the mosque of Selim II at Adrianople, and roughly 300 other spectacular buildings.

Sind *(sind)* Populous province of Pakistan, in the lower Indus River valley. Its capital and major city is the seaport of Karachi. Hot and arid, Sind is believed to have supported the Indian subcontinent's first civilization. It was ruled by Muslim emirs until captured by the British in 1843, and has been independent since 1947.

sinew *(SIN-yew)* From a Middle English term conveying the sense of binding or connection, this is a synonym for tendon—a band of dense tissue that connects muscle to bone. The word, however, has been broadened to mean any source of strength or power, and is sometimes used interchangeably with muscle.

Sinis *(SINE-us)* Legendary Corinthian bandit called the Pine-Bender. Sinis dealt with his victims rather harshly. He would tie them to the tops of two pine trees bent earthward, and then let them be torn apart when the trees were released. Captured by Theseus, he suffered the same fate—thus more or less hoist by his own petard.

Sinon *(SINE-on)* A classic deceiver, Sinon let himself be captured by the Trojans just to persuade them to accept a soldier-laden wooden horse left by the Greeks as tribute on their apparent departure. The advice of Cassandra to refuse the gift was ignored, the hidden Greeks emerged and opened the gates to their comrades, and Troy fell. In his *Inferno,* Dante (q.v.) consigns Sinon to the tenth Malebolge, with such paragons of infamy as Potiphar's wife and Nimrod.

Sioux *(soo)* Confederation of North American Indian tribes, also called the Dakotas. After receiving land in the Black Hills, the Sioux were dispossessed when gold was discovered there. A revolt, led by such chiefs as Sitting Bull and Crazy Horse, led to Custer's famous last stand and the so-called Battle of Wounded Knee in 1890 at which some 200 Sioux were massacred. In recent years, Sioux have been prominent in the American Indian Movement for redress of wrongs.

Today most Sioux live on reservations in the western and middlewestern U.S.

Siren *(SIE-ren)* A sea nymph, part woman and part bird, who, according to Greek and Roman mythology, sang seductive music on rocky Mediterranean coasts, thus luring sailors to their death. Lower-cased, the word has come to mean any enticing woman, as when silent-movie star Pola Negri is clued in crosswords as "siren

of the silents.'' Also a mermaid, an emergency warning device, and a small lizard with no hind legs.

The legendary sirens often lured sailors to their deaths.

sisal See *hemp.*

Sita *(SEE-tah)* In Hindu mythology, the wife of Rama (q.v.). Sita was abducted by a demon named Ravana, and achieved heroine status in the Indian epic the *Ramayana,* which details her fidelity under stress and her rescue by Rama with the aid of the king of the monkeys, Sugriva, and his monkey general Hanuman. Legend has it that Sita was born in an unusual manner: springing from a furrow which her father, Janoka, was plowing.

Sita being abducted by Ravana.

sitar *(sih-TAHR)* Lutelike Indian instrument with a long neck, rounded body, anywhere from three to seven gut strings, and a set of wire strings that vibrate when the gut ones are plucked. It was popularized in the West by Ravi (q.v.) Shankar.

Sitar music has a hypnotic, exotic quality.

Sitka *(SIT-kah)* Principal town of Baranof Island in the Alexander archipelago off southeastern Alaska. Primarily a fishing center, but with several industries, Sitka was founded in 1799 by the Russians, who made it the region's capital. In 1867, Alaska became an American territory by a treaty signed in Sitka, which was the territorial capital until 1900. This event is celebrated every October during the Alaska Day Festival.

Siva See *Shiva.*

Sivan *(see-VAN)* Ninth month of the Hebrew calendar. Sivan has 30 days and falls during the late spring or early summer. On the sixth and seventh days of Sivan, Jews celebrate Shabuoth, the Feast of Weeks, or Pentecost, originally commemorating the spring harvest but now associated with the revelation of the Ten Commandments.

Sivas *(sih-VAHSS)* City in central Turkey, on the Kizil Irmak, longest river of the country. Sivas dates from ancient times, when it was known as Sebaste, or Cabira, and has been ruled by the Romans, Byzantines, and Seljuk Turks. Later it was taken over by the Ottoman Turks. In 1919, it was the site of a nationalist meeting held by Kemal (q.v.) Ataturk.

Seljuk minarets in Sivas.

Siwah or Siwa *(SEE-wah)* Important date-producing oasis (q.v.), much of which lies below sea level, in the Libyan (Western) Desert of northwestern Egypt. In antiquity, Siwah was the site of a temple honoring Zeus Amon, an oracle illustrious enough to be consulted by Alexander the Great.

sizar *(SIZE-uhr)* From the word size, which, at some English schools such as

Cambridge, signifies a stipend, sizars are students who receive a scholarship allowance from the school. At one time, holders of sizarships were expected to do the menial jobs of servants.

Skadi See *Vanir.*

skald or **scald** *(skawld)* Derived from the same Old Norse word that gives us scold (which originally meant to regale with verse, sometimes scurrilous), the skalds were poet-historians of ancient Scandinavia, usually in the employ of chieftains and monarchs. They sang of gods, kings, and heroes, recited eulogies, and also served as hostages because their persons were considered sacred.

Skara *(skah-RAH)* City in a rich agricultural region of southern Sweden. Skara enjoys the distinction of being one of Sweden's oldest cities, dating from at least the ninth century A.D. It is best known for its medieval cathedral and for its institutions of higher learning. The first universities in Sweden were founded here. Also Skara Brae, famous Stone Age village on Mainland, largest of the Orkney Islands of Britain. Dating from c. 2000 B.C., it was long preserved under a sand dune.

skat *(skat)* From the Italian *scartare,* meaning "to discard," this is a card game for three, using a deck from which 20 cards have been removed. Players bid in an attempt to make contracts. Points are accumulated on the basis of contracts played, trump suits, points taken, and number of matadors, meaning the jack of clubs and each other trump held in sequence with it.

skeet *(skeet)* A type of trapshooting in which guns are fired at clay discs called pigeons that are catapulted into the air from traps. In skeet, the shooter fires from eight different angles. Also, a poker hand containing five low cards but no pairs; in some circumstances, it beats three of a kind but not a straight.

skeg or **skag** *(skeg)* From the Old Norse for "beard," or, more generally, "projection," this is nautical terminology for that part of a ship's keel closest to the stern. Skeg also designates an extension of the keel to which the rudder is connected or the protective part under an outboard motor's propeller.

skep *(skep)* Related to the Old Norse *skeppa,* meaning "bushel basket," this is a type of round basket made of wicker or wood. By extension, a skep comprises the amount such a basket will hold, and also designates a domed, woven-straw beehive.

skete *(skeet)* The word comes from *Sketis,* the Greek name for a desert in lower Egypt, formerly dotted with hermitages. In the Greek Orthodox Church, **skete** designates a community of monks living solitary lives in satellite dwellings around a church or parent monastery.

skink *(skink)* Any of a large family of snakelike lizards with shiny bodies, small scales, and stubby legs. (See *adda.*) Numbering more than 600 species, skinks live in dry, sandy places, usually with just their heads showing. **Skink,** from the Gaelic, is also Scottish and Irish for a soup-stew made from meat and vegetables. Cullen skink is made with smoked haddock, potatoes, and onions.

One of many skinks.

skua *(SKEW-ah)* Predatory sea bird whose name has roots in the Faroese *skugver.* Related to the gulls and also called skua gulls and jaegers, skuas are darker and heavier. They range the open seas from the North Atlantic to the Antarctic and are known as bullies who force weaker birds to surrender their food. Skuas also raid the nests of penguins and other sea birds.

Skye *(skie)* An island of the Inner Hebrides of Scotland, off the northwest coast. A part of Inverness-shire, Skye is known for the sheep and cattle raised among its lochs (q.v.), and shipped from its principal city of Portree. The island has also given its name to the shaggy Skye terrier.

The island of Skye is arable with a mild climate.

Sligo *(SLIE-goe)* The "auld sod" to countless Irish-Americans, both a county and its main city in the Republic of Ireland. Sligo is known for its rugged coastline, mountainous interior, and fine cattle. Before the potato famine of the nineteenth century, Sligo's population was about triple what it is today. W.B. Yeats was born in Sligo.

sloe *(slow)* This is the small, bluish-black fruit of the blackthorn, a wild plum. The shrub also yields hard wood and bears white flowers. Sloe gin is flavored with this fruit. The name is sometimes applied to other small wild plums, and appears in the term sloe-eyed (having large, dark eyes).

A blackthorn (sloe) branch.

sloth *(slawth)* A family of arboreal mammals, many of them native to Central and South America. Sloths, known for slowness and apparent lack of drive, have given their name to the quality described as a disinclination to work or to exert oneself. They are usually found hanging head down from the branches by two- or three-toed feet. The sloths of the West Indies have two toes; those of South America, with three digits, include the ais (q.v.).

Sloth is also defined as "one of the Deadly Sins"—in this sense it means spiritual sluggishness.

A sloth in an unusual all-fours pose.

Smee *(smee)* In Barrie's classic children's story, *Peter Pan,* Smee is the right-hand man of the one-armed pirate Captain Hook, Peter's sworn enemy. The story has been made into a perennially popular play, a musical, and a memorable Walt Disney film. A **smee** is also the name of a pochard (diving duck), as well as a widgeon or baldpate, another wild duck.

smelt *(smelt)* From Anglo-Saxon, the common name for a group of small, silvery food fish resembling trout but related to the salmon. Most smelt live in the sea and ascend streams to spawn, but some live in landlocked lakes. One smelt found off Alaska is so fatty that Indians often dried it, strung it on a wick, and burned it as a candle. Appropriately enough, it is called candlefish. **Smelt** is also a verb, meaning "to melt or fuse," as when smelting ore, or to refine or extract metal in this way. Also, in Britain, a **smelt** is a half-guinea, and it is, to all speakers of English, the alternative to smelled as the past participle of smell.

Smike *(smike)* In Charles Dickens's *Nicholas Nickleby,* an inmate of Dotheboys

A typical chaotic scene at Dotheboys Hall.

Hall, an infamous "school" for boys. Smike, an autistic, half-starved creature, is befriended by Nicholas and accompanies him on a series of adventures that includes a stint as Friar Lawrence in a country theatrical company version of *Romeo and Juliet*.

smolt *(smolt)*   A young salmon when it leaves the fresh water where it was spawned and swims downstream to the sea a year or two after hatching. Smolts turn silvery at this time, which is why they bear a name similar to smelt (q.v.).

Smuts *(smuts)*   Jan Christiaan Smuts (1870–1950), South African soldier-statesman and twice prime minister. Born a British subject and educated at Cambridge, he gave up his British citizenship and became a partisan of the South African Republic. He was a general in the Boer War, helped to form the Union of South Africa, and organized its army in World War I. He also served with distinction as a field marshal in World War II. His advocacy of cooperation with Britain, along with his rejection of apartheid, cost him his popularity in later life.

Jan Christiaan Smuts.

Smyrna See *Izmir*.

snark *(snark)*   This fabulous animal was created by Lewis Carroll in his quasi-heroic poem "The Hunting of the Snark." When trapped, this elusive creature would confound hunters by turning into a boojum. **Snark** was also the name of author Jack London's yacht, on which he lived and sailed from 1906 to 1908.

Snead *(sneed)*   Known to his friends as "Slammin' Sammy," the legendary Samuel Jackson Snead (1912–), American golfer par excellence. He won every important professional golf title, and is still one of the highest money winners of all time. In 1961, Snead teamed with Jimmy Demaret to help win the coveted Canada Cup. Another golfing Snead is J.C. Snead (nephew of Sammy), also a top money winner.

snipe *(snipe)*   From Old Norse and Middle English, a common name for certain wading birds related to the sandpiper and the woodcock and distinguished by their long, flexible beaks, which are ideal for dislodging worms. Snipes are usually found in bogs or marshes and are known for their weird mating gyrations. **Snipe** as a verb means to shoot from a hidden position. Critical comments, especially if unattributed, are called "sniping" by their targets.

snood *(snood)*   From the Anglo-Saxon *snod,* a string or cord, this is that indispensable item of *haute couture* in the 1940s, a revival from earlier eras of the netlike sack worn at the nape to hold a woman's hair. Originally, snoods were just hair ribbons, usually affected by young unmarried Scottish women.

Sochi *(SOE-chee)*   A resort city hugging the eastern shore of the Black (q.v.) Sea in Krasnodar Kray, the U.S.S.R. Framed by the Caucasus Mountains, this populous, picturesque city and port enjoys a subtropical climate. Sochi was established as a health resort in 1910, and about 300,000 people use its facilities each year.

Soddy *(SAH-dee)*   Frederick Soddy (1877–1956), the English physical chemist whose research in radioactivity led to a theory of isotopes that won him the Nobel Prize in chemistry

Frederick Soddy.

in 1921. Also something of a pundit in politics and economics, he was an early proponent of technocracy and the social credit movement. As an adjective, **soddy** means "abounding in turf."

Sodom *(SAH-dum)* In the Bible, a wicked, wide-open place, foremost of the Cities of the Plains. Sodom, with its neighbor in sin, Gomorrah, was destroyed by Jehovah in a rain of fire after Abraham failed to locate 10 honest citizens. Lot and his wife were permitted to leave, but on looking back she was transformed into a pillar of salt. Historically, Sodom was one of Syria's most ancient cities, probably lying to the south of the Dead Sea.

sofar *(SOE-far)* A detection system similar to sonar (q.v.) for determining the location of underwater sounds at great distances. With sofar, such sounds can be picked up from as far away as 2,000 miles, a tremendous help in rescue operations following sea disasters. Sofar is an acronym for *sound fixing and ranging*. Also, as **"So Far,"** the title of a song by Rodgers and Hammerstein, written for the musical *Allegro* (1947).

Soho *(SOE-hoe)* The name of two metropolitan areas. In London, Soho is a section of the West End known for its theaters and

A street in London's Soho section, an area famous for theatres and restaurants.

ethnic restaurants. In New York, where its name is derived from its location *so*uth of *Ho*uston Street, SoHo is a partially converted commercial area, with artists' studios, residential lofts, art galleries, boutiques, and restaurants.

sol See *gel*.

soldo *(SOHL-doe)* From the Latin *solidus,* meaning "firm," this was a small copper coin of Italy, equal to roughly $1/20$ of a lira. With inflation, the lira so decreased in value that the soldo became practically worthless and was eventually relegated to the status of a numismatic curiosity.

Solon *(SOLE-on)* The celebrated Athenian lawyer and early champion of freedom (c. 639–559 B.C.). As chief archon, he enacted laws protecting the land of Attic peasants, made it possible for all freemen to enter the assembly, replaced the severe law code of Draco (q.v.), and gave new powers to the Areopagus— the prime council of Athens. In his spare time, he wrote poetry.

Solon.

soma *(SOE-mah)* The Greek for "body," brought intact into English and designating any complete animal or plant entity. Also, a leafless vine of India or a psychotropic plant of unknown identity whose juice was used in ancient India by Vedic worshipers. It has been recently identified with a mushroom, the fly agaric.

Somme *(sum)* Both a department in Picardy, northern France, with Amiens (q.v.) as its capital, and a 159-mile-long river emptying into the English Channel. The Somme valley has been a frequent battleground. In 1916, the British launched an offensive there; and in June of 1940, the valley was captured by the Wehrmacht and held until 1944.

sonar *(SOE-nahr)* An acronym for *s*ound *n*avigation *a*nd *r*anging, this is a device that sends high-frequency sound waves through water and records the vibrations reflected back from any objects intercepted. First used in World War II to detect enemy submarines, sonar has been converted to peacetime application, especially for locating schools of fish.

sora *(SOE-rah)* A small North American wading bird, also called the sora rail, with a stubby beak and long toes that help it run on soft mud. During migrations, soras are especially common in marshlands of the Atlantic seaboard.

sorb *(sorb)* From the Latin *sorbum,* the service tree, a European family of trees related to the apple and pear; its small fruits are called sorb apples. As a proper noun, **Sorbs** are Slavs living in the Lusatian region of East Germany. In the Middle Ages, the name applied by Germans to these people was Wends (q.v.).

Sorel *(sawr-ELL)* Albert Sorel (1842–1906), French historian who wrote the monumental *Europe et La Révolution Française;* Georges Sorel (1847–1922), French social philosopher and advocate of syndicalism; Agnès Sorel (c. 1422–1450), mistress of Charles VII of France; and Julien Sorel, protagonist of Stendhal's great novel *The Red and the Black* (see *Beyle*). **Sorel** is also a Canadian industrial town in Quebec, situated on the site of Fort Richelieu, built in 1665.

Soria *(SAWR-yah)* Capital of Soria province on the Douro River in Old Castile, north-central Spain. Soria is known for its old palace of the counts of Gomara and the nearby ruins of Numantia, the last settlement conquered by Rome (133 B.C.) in its annexation of Spain.

A view of the Spanish town of Soria.

Sosia *(SOE-shah)* In Plautus's comedy *Amphitryon,* a servant victimized by the god Mercury, who takes the guise of Sosia's double. The name has been broadened to mean any living double of another, such as the brothers in Shakespeare's *Comedy of Errors. Amphitryon* was adapted by both Dryden and Molière.

sotol *(SOE-tole)* From the Spanish *zotol,* by way of the Nahuatl *tzotolli,* any member of a family of treelike desert plants resembling the yucca (q.v.), to which they are related. Sotols characteristically bear dense clusters of whitish flowers suggestive of the lily. They are common in desertscapes of the southwestern United States and Mexico. Sotol is also a Mexican distilled liquor made from the trunks of these plants.

Soule *(soo-LAY)* Pierre Soulé (1801–1870), the French-born American statesman who served as senator from Louisiana and minister to Spain. In 1854, Soulé helped draft the Ostend Manifesto, in which

Pierre Soulé.

the U.S. attempted to coerce Spain into selling Cuba under threat of having it taken by force. Also, without the accent mark (pronounced *sool*), an ancient Basque province that is now part of France.

Sousa *(soo-zah)* The family name of two famous men: Martim Afonso de Sousa (c. 1500–1564), Portuguese administrator

John Philip Sousa.

and founding father of Brazil; and John Philip Sousa (1854–1932), renowned "March King," leader of the U.S. Marine Band from 1880 to 1892, and composer of more than 100 marches, including "The Stars and Stripes Forever."

sowar *(SOE-war)* From the Persian word *sūwar,* meaning "horseman" or "rider," sowar was the term for an Indian member of the crack Bengal Lancers and other light-cavalry units of the British forces during the time of the Raj (see *rajah*). The term also designates a mounted policeman; a troop of them is known as a sowarry.

Spaak *(spahk)* Paul Henri Spaak (1899–1972), Belgian statesman who steered his country's foreign policy in the years before and during World War II. Spaak advocated political and economic unification of western Europe. He was the first

Paul Henri Spaak (right) at the U.N.

president of the UN General Assembly, and served as secretary-general of NATO from 1957 to 1961.

spad *(spad)* A special type of nail about one to two inches long, with a hook or eye in the head. These are used for marking locations during the surveying of mine passages. Upper-cased, **Spad** also designates a legendary French fighter plane that flew to glory in World War I.

Spee *(shpay)* Graf Maximilian von Spee (1861–1914), celebrated German admiral of World War I. In 1914, British vessels sent him down with his ship near the Falkland Islands. A German battleship named for Spee was scuttled under British attack 1,000 miles north, in Montevideo harbor, during World War II. See *Graf.*

Speke *(speek)* The great English explorer John Hanning Speke (1827–1864),

John Hanning Speke.

whose treks through Africa with Sir Richard Burton led to the discovery of Lake Tanganyika in 1858. Speke subsequently discovered Lake Victoria Nyanza, primary source of the White Nile and second largest freshwater lake in the world, after Lake Superior.

spelt *(spelt)* From the Anglo-Saxon *spelta,* this is a type of tough-grained wheat, or any of its varieties. It is no longer much grown. The spikelets are usually loose and contain two reddish kernels. **Spelt** is also used for the past tense of spell in England.

Spelt, a kind of wheat.

Spens *(spenz)* Sir Patrick Spens, legendary hero of Scotland, and subject of a famous ballad. Sent on a mission to Norway during winter's height, he, his crew, and his ships went down near the Papa Strongsay, off one of the Orkney Islands. Inhabitants of the island claim that Spens is buried there.

Spes *(spez)* In Roman mythology, goddess of hope, also worshiped by the Greeks as Elpis. In light of her specialty, the Romans dedicated many fine temples to her. She is represented as a maiden holding a flower and lifting her skirt to spot obstacles in her path.

spica *(SPIKE-ah)* From the Latin for "ear of grain," a spikelet, as on a wheat stalk. In astronomy, **Spica** is one of the 20 brightest stars in the sky. It is about 200 light-years distant and can be seen in the southern constellation Virgo—the virgin who holds an ear of grain. A **spica** is also a surgical bandage.

spiel *(speel)* Derived from the German for "game," or "play," spiel is slang for a talk or speech whose object is to trick listeners into specific actions. Spiels are usually delivered by carnival barkers, stand-up comedians, politicians, and other fast-talking salesmen.

spiv *(spiv)* British slang for a person of questionable social value, who lives by

A group of spivs—or overdressed layabouts.

cheating others and is given to overstated attire. Spiv is probably a variation of the nineteenth-century slang word spiff, for flashy (or spiffy) dresser, but it may also be a police acronym for *s*uspected *p*ersons and *i*tinerant *v*agrants.

Spock *(spok)* Benjamin McLane Spock (1903–), American pediatrician whose best-selling books on child rearing made him famous, and whose campaign against the Vietnam War made him controversial. **Spock** was also the name of the Vulcan First Officer in the TV series "Star Trek." He was played by Leonard Nimoy.

Benjamin Spock.

Spode *(spode)* Josiah Spode (1733–1797), the English pottery maker who established his works in Stoke-on-Trent, Staffordshire in 1770. Spode originated fine chinaware that still bears his name. Among his innovations was a method of transfer printing on ware with his characteristic blue underglaze.

Spohr *(shpawr)* Ludwig (or Louis) Spohr (1784–1859), German violinist and composer of operas, symphonies, and chamber pieces for violin and piano. Among his operas are *Jessonda* and *Faust*. Spohr is one of several composers to have written an opera based on the Faust legend.

spoor *(spoor)* From Medieval Dutch via Afrikaans, this is the trail of a wild animal. Spoor can consist of footprints, fur snagged on a tree, characteristic odors, sounds in the brush, or even an animal's dung. Experienced hunters can reckon the distance from a beast by the temperature of its droppings.

spore *(spore)* From the Greek *speirein*, meaning "to sow," a biological term designating the small bodies by which such organisms as mosses, ferns, and mush-

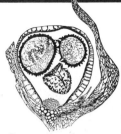

Cross-section of a moss spore.

rooms reproduce. Spores come in two varieties—sexual and asexual. They are resistant to injury, consistent with their function of producing complete new individuals.

sprit *(sprit)* From the Anglo-Saxon *spreot,* for "something that sprouts," this is a pole or spar that sprouts branchlike from a mast aboard a fore-and-aft-rigged sailing vessel. Sprits extend upward at about a 45° angle from near the base of the mast to the uppermost corner of a spritsail, which supports it.

sprue *(sprew)* In foundries, either an opening for the passage of molten metal into a mold; or the chunk of waste material cast in this opening. In medicine, **sprue** is a chronic illness, with tropical and nontropical forms. Symptoms include severe cramps and other digestive disorders, sore throat, anemia and *psilosis*—the term doctors use when they mean falling hair.

spud *(spud)* From the Old Norse *spyd,* a "spear," this is a lancelike tool with a chisel point originally used to strip the bark from trees, and later modified for rooting out weeds. Spuds were also used to dig potatoes. The word eventually became a colloquial synonym for the humble tuber (q.v.).

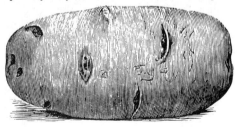

spume *(spyewm)* From the Latin word *spuma,* any type of foam, especially that produced by the action of ocean waves breaking against a rock. Also, less commonly, the froth raised when liquids are stirred; or the scum that collects on the surface of simmering liquid.

Spyri *(SHPEE-ree)* Johanna Spyri (1827–1901), the Swiss author of children's stories about life in Switzerland. Spyri was best known for her ability to capture the emotions of children. Her classic work—the story of a young orphan girl who lives with her grandfather in the Alps—is *Heidi* (q.v.), written in 1880.

Stagg *(stag)* Amos Alonzo Stagg (1862–1965), legendary football coach who became athletic director at the University of Chicago in 1892. Stagg's Chicago teams finished five seasons undefeated. He was forced to leave Chicago after 41 years because of age, but coached for 13 more seasons at the College of the Pacific. A clue reading "the grand old man of football" refers to Stagg.

Amos Alonzo Stagg.

stave *(stave)* Either one of the curved, fitted slats of wood forming a barrel wall; a pole or stick; any rung of a stepladder; or a set of verses. **Stave** also refers to the five horizontal lines and four spaces used for writing music, and sometimes called a staff. As a verb, to **stave** off means to ward off.

Steen *(steen)* Jan Steen (1626–1679), the prolific Dutch artist who painted almost 900 canvases depicting "slices of life," especially banquets and festivities. Steen's works, marked by an almost photographic realism, include the renowned *Feast of St. Nicholas* and *The Prince's Birthday,* both in Amsterdam's Rijksmuseum.

Jan Steen.

stele *(steel)* or **stela** *(STEEL-ah)*
From Greek and Latin words meaning a post or slab, this is an upright stone pillar, usually inscribed, placed to commemorate an occasion or mark a grave, especially in ancient Egypt and Greece. Some surviving funerary stelae (plural) are famous as classical art. In botany, a **stela** is a central tube of tissue.

Sten *(sten)* A type of British machine gun, light enough to be held in the hands while being fired. Widely used in World War II, the Sten gun weighs under eight pounds and can shoot about 550 rounds a minute. Sten, an acronym, was named after its inventors, *S*heppard and *T*urpin, plus *Eng*land. Also actress Anna **Sten,** who played Nana (q.v.) in 1934.

stere *(steer)* From the Greek word *stereos*, which means "solid" and gave us the word stereo, this is a unit of volume equal to one cubic meter—equivalent to a cube measuring 39.37 inches to a side. This is one-tenth the volume of a decastere, and ten times that of a decistere.

stile *(stile)* From the Dutch for "doorpost," a vertical section of a door or window frame. Also, from the Old English *stigan*, to climb, a set of steps used to cross a fence or wall. In a nursery rhyme, a crooked stile was negotiated by a crooked man given to circuitous strolls.

Stip *(shteep)* Town in the Macedonian region of southeastern Yugoslavia. In medieval times, Stip was the seat of Serbian and Bulgarian empires. It is known for the mineral springs that draw visitors to its spas; for well-preserved medieval ruins; and for its chief industry—processing opium poppies.

stipe *(stipe)* From the Latin *stipes*, translated as "log" or "tree trunk," stipe is a botanical term designating the stalk of a plant or, the small structure that holds up the pistil of a flower.

stoa *(STOE-ah)* English directly from Greek, this is a standard feature of Hellenistic architecture. Stoa designates a sheltered arcade or promenade, with columns on one side for support and a building wall on the other. It was designed to provide shade for strollers during hot Mediterranean summers.

stoat *(stote)* A small mammal closely related to the common weasel but a few inches longer; in North America its name is short-tailed weasel. Tawny brown in the summer, stoats usually turn white in winter, but not necessarily in Great Britain. (In Scotland, their fur turns off-white.) They are known as ermines in their white phase, and their fur in this stage is highly prized.

Stoic *(STOE-ik)* A wise and virtuous person seemingly indifferent to pleasure or grief, accepting both with unflinching calmness. This describes the ideal character defined by the classic Stoics, adherents of a Greek school of philosophy founded by Zeno (q.v.), c. 300 B.C., and so named because he taught in a stoa (q.v.) in Athens. Stoicism was embraced and developed by later Greek and Roman thinkers, including Seneca and Epictetus.

A bust of Zeno, the father of Stoicism.

stol *(stole)* Acronym for *s*hort *t*ake-*o*ff and *l*anding aircraft—specifically, craft needing 1,000 feet or less of runway to rise from or descend to the ground, clearing a 50-foot obstacle at the end of the strip en route. This capability results from such aerodynamic features as special wings, flaps, and spoilers.

stola *(STOE-lah)* Latin word, now English, that designated the long, robelike outer garment, an adaptation of the Greek chiton, affected by ancient Roman matrons. The word has been modified to stole, for the decorated cloth strip worn like a scarf by clergymen during services; and for a woman's cloth shawl or fur shoulder piece.

stoma *(STOE-mah)* From the Greek for "mouth," this is any opening through which respiration occurs in a living organism. In botany, stomata are the often microscopic breathing pores in various plant surfaces; in animals, they are any mouthlike part. The word is evident in stomatitis, medicalese for a mouth inflammation.

Stoss *(shtawss)* Veit Stoss (c. 1445–1533), renowned Nuremberg sculptor. His Gothic pieces reflect an idealized realism particularly appropriate for the religious subjects he carved. Among Stoss's best-known works are *The Annunciation*, a huge wooden altar in St. Mary's Church in Kraków; and his stone tomb for Polish King Casimir IV. Lower-cased, **stoss** is also an adjective meaning "facing a glacier."

stoup *(stoop)* From the Middle English *stowpe*, meaning a "bucket," this is a basin for holy water in a church; or simply the colloquial term for bucket in Scotland. In England the word designates a tankard, drinking vessel, or flagon. A stoup is mentioned in Robert Burns's "Auld Lang Syne."

Stowe *(stoe)* Harriet Beecher Stowe (1811–1896), American author whose novel *Uncle Tom's Cabin* (1852) affected American history by awakening many to the evils of slavery. The book sold over 300,000 copies in its first year—unlike her second slavery novel, *Dred*, or her books on temperance and women's rights. **Stowe** is also a noted ski resort near Mt. Mansfield, in north-central Vermont.

Harriet Beecher Stowe's oeuvre fills 16 volumes.

Strad *(strad)* Familiar name for that superb example of the violin-maker's art, the Stradivarius. This instrument was named for Antonio Stradivari (1644–1737) of Cremona. He is said to have produced over 1,100 instruments, including at least 540 violins, 12 violas, and 50 cellos, as well as viols, mandolins, and guitars. His best instruments were produced after 1700.

Three views of the high-quality Stradivarius.

Stuka *(STEW-kah)* The dreaded German dive bomber of World War II. Aside from its use as a tactical weapon, the Stuka was an instrument of psychological warfare, fitted with a howling siren that signaled the prospect of death for all within earshot. The name is an acronym for *Sturzka*mpfflugsteug—"diving battle plane."

stull *(stul)* From the German word *stollen*, meaning a "support" or "prop," this is the generic name for any of a variety of structures designed to support platforms and prevent cave-ins in mine passages or chambers. Stulls are usually assembled from sectional metal tubes, unlike another type of mine support—the sprag.

stum *(stum)* From the Dutch word meaning "mute," this is a vintner's term for grape juice that has not yet fermented, or juice in which fermentation has been artificially arrested. Stum is also known as must. When wine has gone flat, fermentation can be revived by adding stum.

stupa *(STOO-pah)* A Sanskrit term taken directly into English, stupa designates a Buddhist tumulus, or domelike mound, containing relics. Stupas are also known as dagobas and topes. They probably originated as burial mounds in pre-Buddhist times, and are found wherever Buddhism flourished—for example, the Borobudur in Java and the Mingalazedi stupa in Burma.

stupe *(stoop)* A therapeutic measure ordered more often by physicians in the days before effective analgesics became available. A stupe is a soft cloth dipped in hot water, wrung dry, sometimes sprinkled with a counterirritant such as turpentine, and applied to the skin to relieve pain or aid circulation.

Sturt *(stert)* Charles Sturt (1795–1869), English explorer of Australia. In 1828, he discovered the Darling River, and a year later found the junction of the Murrumbidgee and the Murray, which he traced to Lake Alexandrina. The John Speke (q.v.) of Down Under, he was the first white man to follow Australian rivers to the continent's center.

sty *(stie)* From the Old English word *stig*, meaning "enclosure," a sty is a pigpen, and therefore any dirty, repulsive place. It is

sometimes clued as "a pig's digs." Also, from the related noun *stigend*, a rising, **sty** designates an inflamed and swollen sebaceous gland on the edge of the eyelid. Doctors refer to this as a hordeolum.

Children paying a visit to a pig in its sty.

Styr *(stir)* A river approximately 300 miles long, rising in the northwestern Ukraine, European U.S.S.R., and flowing generally northwest before emptying into the Pripyat River near the Polish border. The Styr actually ends up in the Pripyat marshes, a 38,000-square-mile swamp and forest region along the river.

Styx *(stiks)* In classical mythology, the river separating the world of the living from the infernal regions. The Styx had to be crossed by the newly dead en route to Hades (q.v.); the ferryman, Charon, exacted a fee from each passenger. Other

Charon ferrying Psyche across the Styx.

rivers of Hell, include the Acheron, Cocytus, Phlegethon, and Lethe (q.v.); the dead drank of Lethe, the river of forgetfulness.

Suben *(soo-bin)*

In ancient Egyptian religion, the deity of maternity and protectress of women, invoked during the pain of labor and childbirth. The Romans identified her with the goddess Lucina. Worshiped particularly in southern Egypt, Suben was usually represented in art with her somewhat inappropriate symbol—a vulture.

Sudak *(soo-DAHK)*

Black (q.v.) Sea port and resort area of the U.S.S.R., famous for wines and rose oil. Founded by Greeks in the third century A.D., this city on the Crimean peninsula was ruled at times by Greece, Genoa, and the Crimean Tartars before the Crimea was acquired by Russia in 1783.

Sudra *(soo-drah)*

Lowest of the four major castes (q.v.) of Hinduism, considered to have sprung from the feet of Brahma. Sudras were believed to be racially inferior, and were therefore required to serve the higher castes (Brahmans, Kshatriyas, and Vaisyas) as laborers, mechanics, petty tradesmen, or farmers. Some became writers, however, and others even grew rich.

Sufi *(soo-fee)*

From the Arabic word for "man of wool," or "ascetic," someone belonging to a sect of Muslim mystics. Sufism is practiced primarily in Iran, and has generated its own literature of poetic symbolism. The name appears in writings of Omar Khayyám, who himself was a Sufi.

Omar Khayyám, a Sufi, working out the calendar.

Sulla *(SULL-ah)*

Lucius Cornelius Sulla (138–78 B.C.), the Roman general who fought Mithradates VI and ravaged Athens in 86 B.C. Returning to Rome, he embroiled himself in civil war. Sulla massacred more than 8,000 prisoners during this struggle, and then declared himself dictator of Rome. His subsequent rule was notoriously bloody and grasping.

Sulu *(soo-loo)*

Either a large sea within the Philippines; or a major archipelago of the Philippines, southwest of Mindanao. Also, a Moro (q.v.) tribesman native to the Sulu Archipelago; or the tongue he speaks. In the TV series *Star Trek,* Lieutenant **Sulu,** played by George Takei, was helmsman, one of the 430 crew members aboard the starship *Enterprise.*

sumac *(soo-mak)*

Common name for several members of a widely distributed family of trees and shrubs that includes poison ivy. In the autumn, the large, featherlike leaves of the eastern staghorn sumac, which bears stout fruiting spikes of fruit usable for tea, turn a brilliant red, dressing up the sometimes drab stretches along major highways. A notorious relative in the same genus is poison sumac, with drooping rather than upright fruit clusters. This troublemaker grows in swampy areas and produces an itching rash on contact. **Sumac** is also Yma Sumac, the singer.

A Navaho woman boils sumac to make dye.

Sumba *(SOOM-bah)*

Indian Ocean island in the Lesser Sunda (q.v.) archipelago of Indonesia, a few hundred miles west of Timor (q.v.). Sumba was famous for its sandalwood trees, and still is known by its English name, Sandalwood Island. It has been ruled by the Dutch and the Japanese, and bears traces of prehistoric inhabitants.

Sumer *(SOO-mer)* A region of antiquity in the southern part of Mesopotamia. One of the cradles of civilization, Sumer dates back at least to 4000 B.C. Its non-Semitic people were farmers, canal builders, metalsmiths, artists, and scholars. Sumerians are also given credit for originating the cuneiform system of writing.

A Sumerian votive plaque from the 3rd millenium .

Sunda *(SUN-dah)* A group of Indonesian islands making up the western part of the Malay Archipelago, between the Indian Ocean and the South China Sea. Included in this chain are the Greater Sunda islands of Borneo, Sumatra, and Java (q.v.); and such Lesser Sundas as Timor, Sumba, and Bali (all, q.v.). The Lesser Sundas were renamed Nusatenggara in 1954.

sunn *(sun)* From the Sanskrit word *sana,* meaning "hempen," this is a species of plant native to the East Indies. The stem fiber, known as sunn hemp, is unusually strong and is used for sail canvas and rope. Recognizable by its silvery, lance-shaped leaves, sunn also produces a handsome yellow blossom.

Suppe *(ZOO-pey)* Franz von Suppé (1819–1895), Dalmatian-born composer who lived in Austria. Suppé was prolific, writing ballets, symphonies, and Masses. He is best known, however, for lighter music, such as operettas. His "Poet and Peasant" and "Light Cavalry" overtures are revered warhorses of the orchestral repertoire.

Franz von Suppé.

sura *(SOOR-ah)* From the Arabic word *surah,* meaning "degree" or "step," this designates any of the major divisions or chapters of the Koran (q.v.). Sura is also a transliteration of the Sanskrit for "wine" or "spirits," and in the East Indies identifies fermented juice of the palmyra palm.

surah *(SOOR-ah)* Originating in India, a soft, shiny fabric of silk (or nowadays a combination of silk and rayon) with a twill weave. Surah is prized as a textile for saris, dresses, ties, and scarves. The name surah probably derives from its place of origin— the city of Surat (q.v.).

Surat *(soo-RAT)* Seaport on the Gulf of Cambay near the mouth of the Tapti River, north of Bombay on India's west coast. Surat was the first British settlement in India and also had early Dutch traders. It is known for carpets, inlaid work, and silk brocade.

surd *(serd)* From the Latin *surdus,* meaning "mute" or "without reason" and the root of the word absurd, this is a mathematician's term for any quantity that cannot be expressed as a rational number, e.g., the square root of $2/5$. In phonetics, it is an unvoiced speech sound, like the *gh* in through—and the opposite of a sonant.

Surma *(SOOR-mah)* A 320-mile-long river of northeastern India and Bangladesh. Rising in the Manipur hills, it flows generally southwesterly through Assam and past Sylhet, a former district of the Surma Valley and Hill Division. The Surma then divides into two branches that reunite to form the Meghna in northeast Bangladesh.

Surya *(SOOR-yuh)* In Hindu mythology, the deity of the sun and lord of the sky gods. Surya was therefore an equal of Agni (q.v.), who presided over the gods of the earth; and of Indra (q.v.), to whom the gods of the air reported. Surya is usually represented driving a horse-drawn chariot.

The solar wheel of Surya, Konarak, India.

Susa *(soo-sah)* An ancient city—the capital of Elam, also called Shushan in the Bible. Located near what is now modern Dizful, Iran, Susa was where Darius built his winter palace and where the code of Hammurabi was uncovered.

Susak *(soo-zak)* Suburb of Fiume (q.v.), northwestern Yugoslavia. This Adriatic seaport served as main base of the Hungarian navy before World War I. Contested by Italy and Yugoslavia, Fiume was divided, with Susak going to Yugoslavia. After World War II, they reunited to constitute the largest seaport in Yugoslavia.

sutra *(soo-trah)* Transliteration of the Sanskrit for "thread" or "string." The sense of tying things together is evident in its meaning: an axiom or precept of Brahmanism. Sutras cover everything from instruction on religious rituals to the rules of grammar; the *Kama Sutra,* whose subject is love, is widely known in the West. In Buddhism, sutras present all the world's wisdom as dialogues of the Buddha.

Suva *(soo-vah)* Capital city of Fiji (q.v.) on the southeastern coast of Viti Levu island. This thriving shipping and commercial hub is one of the largest in the South Pacific. Its most important products include coconut oil, copra, sugar, and gold. During World War II, Suva was a key Allied air base.

Svir *(sveer)* A river in the northwestern U.S.S.R., near the Finnish border. This 140-mile-long stream flows west from Lake Onega to Lake Ladoga, with hydroelectric power stations at Svirstroy and Podporozhye. The Svir is an important link in the Volga-Baltic canal and river system linking Moscow and Leningrad.

swage *(swaje)* Derived from the Old French *souage,* this is a machinist's device used to bend metal parts into specific shapes or to hold metal rods while they are being worked or stamped. In surgery, this term is used to identify the end of a needle to which the suture is attached.

swale *(swale)* Homeowners will recognize this as the shallow depression builders work into a lot when grading it to channel the runoff of water after a rain. Natural swales are those created by water drainage in marshy or wet ground. The word is probably derived from the Old Norse *svalr,* meaning "cool."

swami *(SWAH-mee)* Anglicized version of the Hindi word *svami,* a "lord." In India, swami is another name for a pandit—the title of respect usually accorded a wise elder, an ascetic, or a revered Hindu teacher. It is often clued in relation to the word yogi. The term has been preempted by American carnival types who bestow it on any performer wearing a turban.

sward *(swahrd)* The etymon of this somewhat poetic word is the Old English *sweard,* meaning "skin" or "hide." Sward is simply grassy turf, sometimes referred to redundantly as greensward.

Swazi *(SWAH-zee)* A Bantu (q.v.) native of Swaziland, the small, mountainous kingdom surrounded on three sides by the Republic of South Africa. The capital is Mbabane, and the country became independent of Britain in 1968. The Swazi probably moved here from the north in the sixteenth century to escape Zulu attacks. Most Swazis are employed in local mines, a number of industries, and fruit plantations, and all adult males serve on the National Council. In recent years, casinos and recreational facilities have attracted hordes of tourists from neighboring South Africa.

Sweyn *(swain)* Famous Dane (c. 960–1014), king of Denmark and son of the unappealingly named Harold Bluetooth. In Sweyn's checkered reign, he defeated Olaf I of Norway in alliance with Sweden, and invaded England twice; the second time, he was accepted as king. Sweyn's younger son was Canute (or Knut), the English king who, according to flimsy legend, whipped the sea in an effort to make it obey him.

syce *(sise)* From the Arabic word *sa'is,* meaning "to tend a horse," this is a groom or stable hand in India. In the extensive stables belonging to the Indian nobility, syces enjoyed considerable status, often attending to their duties on horseback. They also served the British and were excellent polo players.

sycee *(sie-SEE)* At one time, a form of money in China. Sycees were stamped silver ingots, measured by weight.

sylph *(silf)* Term possibly coined by Paracelsus from the first syllable of *sylvestris,* "forest," and the last letters of *nympha,* "nymph." In any case, a sylph was originally a mortal, but soulless, creature of the air. The term now designates females with slim figures; and South American hummingbirds with long forked tails.

Synge *(sing)* John Millington Synge (1871–1901), Irish poet, playwright, friend of W.B. Yeats, and founder of the Abbey Theatre. He is best known for the dramas *Playboy of the Western World* and *Riders to the Sea.* Also, the British biochemist Richard L.M. Synge, winner of the 1952 Nobel Prize in chemistry for discovering partition chromatography, a method of separating and identifying chemical substances.

John Millington Synge.

synod *(SIN-od)* From the Middle English by way of Latin and Greek terms conveying the sense of coming together, this is an assembly of churches or council of religious officials. In recent years, the term has lost some of its ecclesiastical flavor and now can refer to any gathering of VIPs.

A turbaned syce at a racetrack in India during the days of the British Raj.

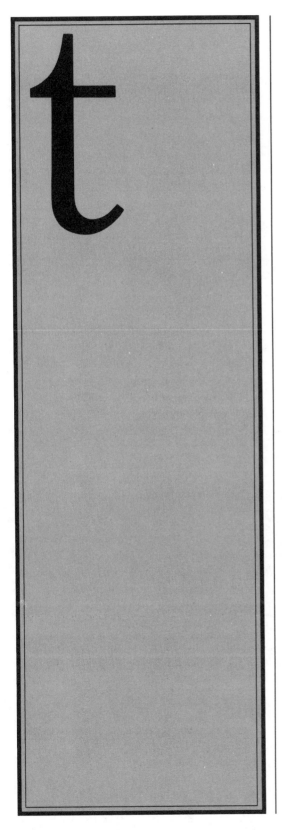

Taal *(tahl)* From the Dutch word for "language" or "speech," another name for Afrikaans, the dialect spoken by descendants of the original Dutch settlers in South Africa. Also, a lake in Luzon, the Philippines, south of Manila. Lake **Taal** is the site of Volcano Island, with an active crater, Mount Taal, that last erupted in 1968.

taboo or **tabu** *(tah-BOO)* Transliteration of the Polynesian word for a primitive prohibition on things, people, or actions that makes them forbidden or untouchable. These restrictions, often declared to commemorate births or deaths, are placed on a tribe's symbolic guardian, or totem (q.v.). Breaking taboos requires ceremonial purification, and is sometimes punishable by death.

tabor *(TAY-buhr)* A small drum, usually played to accompany a fife. As a proper noun, the name of a 2,000-foot mountain in northern Israel; an industrial city in western Czechoslovakia that was the headquarters of the Taborites, a wing of the Hussites (John Huss had lived here after 1412); and the surname of Horace Austin Warner Tabor (1830–1899), fabulously wealthy Colorado silver miner whose second wife inspired the opera *The Ballad of Baby Doe.*

H.A.W. Tabor.   *Elizabeth (Doe) Tabor.*

tabun *(TAH-bun)* Colorless to brownish liquid compound that induces nerve paralysis when absorbed through the skin. Its vapor, which is not absorbed, suggests the odor of bitter almonds. Tabun can be destroyed with bleaching powder, but then gives off a poison gas. Chemists refer to tabun as cyanodimethylaminoethoxphosphene oxide. The **Tabun** man was a Neanderthalic strain of Palestine man whose remains were found in a cave of Mount Carmel called Tabun.

taco *(TAH-koe)*   Originally a south-of-the-border sandwich made from a fried tortilla surrounding such fillings as meat or chicken with lettuce, tomatoes, and onions, with or without a spicy sauce. This Latin-American nosh has since penetrated the United States as a staple at Tex-Mex fast-food eateries.

tael *(tale)*   Portuguese version of the Malay word *tahil*, "a weight." In the Orient, it designates various units of weight, but more specifically, the Chinese liang, equal to about 1½ ounces avoirdupois, or ¹/₁₆ of a catty.

tafia *(TAF-ee-ah)*   An anglicized West Indian Creole word which is a truncated version of the Jamaican *ratafia*. It designates a crude and cheap West Indian rum distilled from the waste products of sugar refining and is notorious for its harshness.

tagua *(TAH-gwah)*   Also called coroza, this is the fruit of the ivory-nut palm, native to northern South America. Each pod holds up to 40 hard, white seeds used in place of ivory for the manufacture of buttons. Tagua (or vegetable ivory) buttons are easily mistaken for ivory, but the material turns red when treated with sulfuric acid.

Tagus *(TAY-gus)*   English form of the Spanish *Tajo* and the Portuguese *Tejo,* Tagus is the name of a river originating in the Iberian Mountains of central Spain and flowing generally westward, past Toledo and across Portugal, before reaching the Atlantic near Lisbon. The 12-mile-long Tagus estuary is one of Europe's finest harbors. At about 600 miles, the Tagus is one of the longest rivers of the Iberian peninsula.

Taiga *(TIE-gah)*   Transliterated from the Russian, this is a familiar term to ecologists,

earth scientists, and lumber interests. It designates the belts of coniferous forest that gird northern regions of the North American and Eurasian continents. In Russia, the Taiga lies between where the tundra ends and the steppes begin.

Taj See *Agra.*

takin *(tah-KEEN)*   A large, oxlike goat antelope related to musk oxen and native to the forested highlands of western China and the Himalayas. Dangerous when cornered, takins have large, broad heads and high, outward-curving horns. They are surefooted on rocks. Takins range in color from brownish to ocher, except in Shensi province, where they are a stunning metallic gold.

talon *(TAL-un)*   From the Latin word for "ankle," this is a sharp claw used for grasping and tearing by predatory animals and birds. **Talon** also designates part of the bolt in a lock; a type of ogee (q.v.) molding in architecture; in certain card games, the stock, or cards remaining after a hand is dealt; and a kind of bond certificate.

Talos *(TAY-los)*   To students of Greek mythology, either an inventor slain by his uncle Daedalus in a fit of jealousy; or the bronze image presented as a sentinel to Minos, ruler of Crete, by Zeus. **Talos** is also the name of a long-range guided missile in the arsenal of the United States.

talus *(TAY-lus)*   In anatomy, the astragalus, or ankle bone, connecting with the bones of the leg. In geology, **talus** refers to rock fragments piled up at the base of a cliff or steep slope.

As they weather, tali break up into smaller chunks and migrate downslope, pushed imperceptibly by new rocks coming down.

tam *(tam)* Short for tam-o'-shanter, the familiar round Scottish headgear, a floppy woolen cap with flat top and center pom-pom. It was named for the hero of Robert Burns's narrative poem, "Tam O'Shanter," who presumably wore one while fleeing from bogies unable to pass the middle of a running stream. In crosswords it is often clued as "Highland headgear."

Tamar *(TAH-mahr)* In the Bible, the childless widow of Er and subsequently wife of his brother Onan (q.v.). After that union failed, Tamar masqueraded as a harlot and deceived Judah, her father-in-law. She bore him two sons, and he could not reproach her since by custom (see *levir*) she should have wed Shelah, the youngest brother.

Tamil *(TAM-ahl)* Any person belonging to the Dravidian language group of southern India and northern Sri Lanka. Tamil—along with Malayalam, Kanarese, Kurukh, and Telugu—is also a language of this group. Tamil Nadu, formerly Madras, is a major state of India on the Bay of Bengal.

Tanit or **Tanith** *(TAN-it)* A Phoenician goddess, patroness of Carthage. Tanit is sometimes identified with Astarte, the goddess of fertility. She is considered the counterpart of Aphrodite. Characterized as the virgin queen of the moon and heavens, Tanit is symbolized by the solar disc and a crescent.

tansy *(TAN-zee)* Generic name for a group of pungent perennial herbs with small yellow flowers, native to temperate climates. Tansy leaves were formerly used to flavor puddings, custards, and cakes eaten around Easter. As a tea, tansy can drive out worms, and tansy oil has been used as a liniment for bruises.

Tao *(daow; taow)* Chinese word for "the Way," this is an Eastern religious system and way of life based on teachings of Lao-tze, a philosopher who lived in the sixth century B.C. Taoists reject all striving, and escape desire through mystical contemplation. Taoism is the basis of some Chinese secret societies.

tapa *(TAH-pah)* Polynesian name for unwoven cloth made from the pounded inner bark of certain tropical and subtropical trees, particularly the paper mulberry and breadfruit. Tapa has been made virtually everywhere the raw material is available. In the Pacific it is usually decorated with geometric figures. Formerly a staple textile, it is now mostly sold to tourists.

tapir *(TAY-per)* Hooved, nocturnal herbivore indigenous to the jungles of Central and South America and southeast Asia. Related to the horse and rhinoceros, the tapir stands about three feet high at the shoulder and resembles a hog. Its most unusual features are its feet—the front ones have four horned toes, the rear ones have five. A flexible snout gives the tapir a somewhat disdainful appearance. An endangered species, the Central American tapir stands as tall as a donkey.

An Asian tapir.

Tara *(TAH-rah)* Village in County Meath, eastern Ireland, where sat the Hill of Tara—until the sixth century, the place where Irish monarchs were crowned and set up shop. St. Patrick is said to have preached there. In the book and film *Gone with the Wind*, **Tara** was the name of the O'Hara plantation.

tare *(tare)* From the Arabic meaning "to reject," this is the weight of a container deducted from the total weight of container plus contents. The term is used in shipping commodities (see also *tret*). Also, from the Middle Dutch word for "wheat," a small climbing or trailing vetch (q.v.) used as fodder; or the noxious weed of the Bible, probably darnel rye grass.

tarn *(tahrn)* From the Middle English for "waterhole," this is a small, steep-banked mountain lake, often one scooped out by the action of an ancient glacier. As a proper noun, **Tarn** is a department and 235-mile-long river in southern France, flowing into the Garonne.

taro *(TAH-roe)* Common name for certain large-leaved perennial herbs of the arum (q.v.) family. The taro has starchy rootstocks used as food on some Pacific islands, and is prepared by baking, boiling, or pounding, as in making poi (q.v.).

tarot *(TAHR-oh)* Playing cards used in telling fortunes, and thought to have been

brought to Europe by gypsies during the fifteenth century. In each pack of 78 cards are 56 minor arcana, similar in appearance to a modern deck, and 22 numbered cards called the major arcana. Pictures on the cards represent the vices and virtues of men.

A 19th-century Italian tarot card.

Tass *(tahss)* The national agency responsible for gathering and disseminating news in the U.S.S.R. The name is an acronym for *Telegraphnoye Agentsvo Sovyetskova Soyuza*, which in English is Telegraph Agency of the Soviet Union. As a common noun, **tass** is Scottish dialect for a small drinking cup or goblet.

tasse *(tass)* From the Old French for "purse," a tasse is any of a set of metal plates fitted with overlapping joints. Together these form the shirtlike portion on a suit of armor, just above the cuisses, or thigh guards. Tasses protect the lower torso of the wearer. **Tasse** is also French for "cup," most familiar in demitasse, the diminutive cup for after-dinner coffee.

Tatar *(TAH-tar)* or **Tartar** *(TAHR-tar)* General name for any member of the Mongolian or Turkic tribes that overran western Asia, Russia, and Europe in the thirteenth century. Originally nomads, they were called the Golden Horde because of their beautiful tents. With the rise of Western civilization, the Tatars drifted eastward, continuing to dominate Russia and Siberia. They adopted Islam as their religion in the fourteenth century. In the fifteenth century, Tamerlane's invasion and the arrival of Ottoman Turks disintegrated their powerful empire. Today, roughly five million Tatars, most of them Sunni Muslims, still live in the U.S.S.R., many in the Tatar Autonomous S.S.R. and the Bashkir Autonomous S.S.R.

Tatars from the Crimea.

Tatra or **Tatras** *(TAH-truh)* Highest mountain range of the Carpathian Mountains of east-central Europe, roughly following the border between Poland and Czechoslovakia; the highest peaks are under 9,000 feet. The region is known for its scenery, its national park, and its winter sports resorts, such as Zakopane, in Poland.

tau *(taw)* Nineteenth letter of the Greek alphabet, corresponding to the English letter *t* and represented by the same character in the upper case. A tau cross is one shaped

like a T and also known as St. Anthony's cross. Crosses of this shape were used to execute criminals by crucifixion in pre-Christian times and are seen in heraldic devices.

Taupo *(TAO-poe)* A sport-fishing mecca in New Zealand. Rainbow trout abound in this lake, largest in New Zealand, situated in the Hot Springs district of North Island. In certain sections, Taupo is over 500 feet deep. More than 20 streams feed the lake, and it is picturesquely ringed with volcanos.

Tauri *(TAW-ree)* Legendary tribe of savage cave-dwellers who lived in the Caucasus Mountains in ancient Sarmatia, now the southern U.S.S.R. Woe to the traveler passing through, since all strangers were sacrificed forthwith. In *Iphigenia Among the Taurians,* Euripedes recounts how the heroine saved her brother from these inhospitable folk.

tav *(tahv)* Twenty-third letter of the Hebrew alphabet, comparable in sound to the Greek tau (q.v.) or the English letter *t.* A variant of this letter, *thau,* written without the dot in the middle, is used like the English sound *th,* but is not counted as a letter in the Hebrew alphabet.

taw *(taw)* Probably derived from the Greek letter tau (q.v.) and signifying a T-shaped mark from which marble players shoot. By extension, taw evolved first into the name of a type of marble game, and eventually into the name of the big, fancy, and colorful marbles so dear to the hearts of American boys. As a noun, it's also a square-dance partner; the starting line in any sport or race; and a sum of money invested. **Taw,** as a verb, means to prepare a natural product for use.

Tay *(tay)* River rising in the Grampian Mountains of eastern Scotland, flowing northeast through locks and emptying into the North Sea through the Firth of Tay. At about 120 miles, it is the longest river in Scotland; for part of its course it is called the Fillan and the Dochart. A bridge crossing the Firth of Tay at Dundee collapsed in a storm in December 1879, with the loss of 90 lives. Also Loch **Tay,** about 14 miles long, which the river enters as the Dochart and leaves as the Tay.

The Tay passes the town of Perth in central Scotland.

Tebet, Tebeth, or Tevet

(TAY-viss) Fourth month of the Hebrew calendar. Tebet is 29 days long and usually falls around the time of the winter solstice. It is ushered in by the last day of Hanukkah, the Jewish Festival of Lights. The holiday is observed by the lighting of candles on eight successive nights and celebrates the new altar installed in the Temple of Jerusalem.

Tegea *(TEE-jee-ah)* An ancient city in the Peloponnesus of Greece. Tegea was ruled by Sparta from the sixth century to the fourth century B.C. Today, tourists come to visit its ruins of the temple of Athena Alea, designed and ornamented by the celebrated sculptor Scopas.

teil *(teel)* From the Latin *tilia* (meaning "lime"), the botanical name of the European linden or lime tree, this is another name for that tree. Lindens are handsome shade trees that produce blossoms dried and used as a tea. A highly prized honey is made by bees who visit the flowers.

Tempe *(TEM-pee)*   City, health resort, and site of Indian ruins, in the Salt River valley of southern Arizona. Also, a valley between mounts Olympus and Ossa (q.v.) in Greece. Famous for its natural beauty, the Vale of Tempe served as a retreat for Apollo and the Muses, and was immortalized in Vergil's *Georgics*.

Grady Gammage Auditorium at Arizona State University, Tempe.

tempo *(TEHM-poe)*   Italian for "time," this general musical term designates the rate of speed at which a composition is played. Major tempi (plural) are indicated by such Italian terms as *largo* (very slowly); *lento* (a trifle faster than *largo*); *adagio* (slowly); *andante* (like walking); *moderato* (moderately); *allegro* (quickly); *vivace* (lively); and *presto* (very quickly). **Tempo** also means any rate of speed; a turn at chess; and an old Japanese coin of the nineteenth century.

Tenes *(TEN-iss)*   Son of Cycnus, monarch of Colonae in the Troad (q.v.). When Tenes resisted his stepmother Philonome's advances, she accused him of rape. Cycnus forthwith cast him into the sea in a chest, which floated to the island of Leucophrys. Believing him divine, the natives named Tenes their king.

tenet *(TEN-et)*   Third-person singular form of the Latin verb *tenere*, "to hold." A tenet is part of a system of beliefs—a doctrine or principle considered to represent absolute truth. Tenets are usually held in common by social, philosophical, professional, fraternal, or patriotic groups.

tenon *(TEN-en)*   From the Latin *tenere*, "to hold," via the Middle English word *tenown*. This carpentry term designates a projection on a length of wood shaped to fit into an opening (called a mortise) on another length to hold the two together. Making these joints is considered an art among cabinetmakers. The tenon is often clued as "mortise's counterpart."

Tepic *(tay-PEEK)*   Capital city of the state of Nayarit, on the Tepic River in western Mexico. As the hub of a region that raises cattle, corn, and sugar cane, Tepic is an important stop on the Mexican National Railway coastal line. Most tourists, however, come for the colonial charm and wild mountain vistas.

Terah *(TEHR-ah)*   Old Testament patriarch and father of Abraham. While traveling with Abraham and his other descendants from Ur to Haran in Canaan, he reached the ripe old age of 205 years (Gen. 11:31–32). The secret of his longevity may have been idol worship (Joshua 24:2).

Terek *(TYEH-rik)*   A 370-mile-long river formed by streams born of glaciers near Mount Kazbek in the Caucasus region of Georgia, the U.S.S.R. The Terek flows in a generally northeasterly direction, past Ordzhonikidze and Grozny, before emptying into the Caspian Sea. In its lower reaches, the Terek is used for irrigation.

tern *(tern)*   Sea bird related to the gull, but considerably smaller, with a forked tail and long, pointed wings that help it dive to catch fish while in flight. Sometimes called sea swallows, terns are known for migrating great distances. Arctic terns, for example, spend the summer near the Arctic Circle and then fly more than 10,000 miles south to summer in the Antarctic. *Sooty tern.*

Tesla *(TESS-lah)* Nikola Tesla (1856–1943), Croatian-born American inventor who worked briefly for Edison and was responsible for numerous inventions

in the field of electricity. Among Tesla's achievements was the design of the mammoth power system at Niagara Falls. He is celebrated in Robert Johnson's poem "In Tesla's Laboratory."

Nikola Tesla.

Tet See *Hue.*

teth *(teth)* Ninth letter of the Hebrew alphabet, with a sound corresponding to that given the letter *t* in English. This is the second of two *t* sounds in the Hebrew alphabet, and it is used alternatively with the letter tav (q.v.).

Teton *(TEE-tahn)* Either of two rivers—the 143-mile-long Teton rising in northwestern Montana and flowing east to the Marias River; or the 60-mile-long Teton formed in western Wyoming and joining Henrys Fork to the northwest, in Idaho. Also, the name of a spectacular range of the Rockies in Wyoming and Idaho. Grand Teton, 13,747 feet, the highest peak, draws thousands of tourists annually to Grand Teton National Park.

Thais *(THAY-iss)* The given name of two scarlet women: the Athenian courtesan who accompanied Alexander the Great during his Asiatic campaigns in the fourth century B.C. and who married Ptolemy Lagos of Egypt after Alexander's death; and the legendary Alexandrian courtesan of the

Geraldine Farrar as Thaïs.

fourth century A.D., who was converted to Christianity by St. Paphnutius, according to the book and the opera that Anatole France and Jules Massenet, respectively, wrote about her, both titled *Thaïs.*

thane *(thane)* Early Scottish noble, usually the head of a clan and custodian of royal real estate, whose rank was equivalent to a baron. Macbeth was Thane of Glamis, and later Thane of Cawdor.

theca *(THEE-kah)* From the Greek *theke,* meaning a "case," this is a spore (q.v.) capsule or sac containing the reproductive cells of certain plants, such as ferns and mosses. In zoology and anatomy, thecae (plural) are any containers that enclose an entire organism, e.g., the cocoon of a silkworm.

Theia *(THEE-yah)* In Greek mythology, a Titaness belonging to the legendary race of giant gods later overthrown by Zeus and other Olympians (see *Titan*). Theia's parents were Uranus and Gaea, deities, respectively, of heaven and earth. As the mother of Helios, Eos, and Selene, deities of the sun, dawn, and moon, she came to be considered the goddess of light.

therm *(therm)* From the Greek *therme* (heat), this is generally a unit of heat quantity, such as the small calorie or great calorie (the amounts of heat needed to raise one gram or one kilogram of water one degree Centigrade). Therm also designates a unit of heat equal to 1,000 great calories, or 100,000 British thermal units (BTUs).

theta *(THAY-tah)* The eighth letter of the Greek alphabet. Theta is without any comparable English symbol. It supplies the sound *th*—either voiced, as in the word "there," or as in the surd (q.v.) in "with." As the initial letter of thanatopsis (Greek for "death"), theta has been used as a kind of shorthand for death.

WATER WORLD

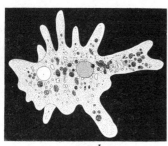

amoeba

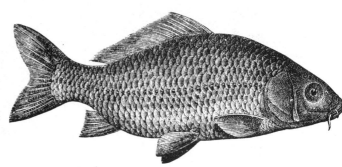

carp

dab

grebe

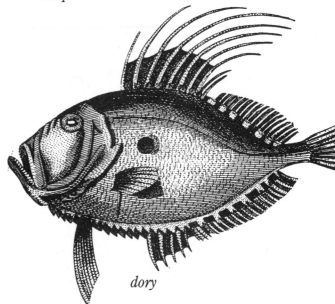

dory

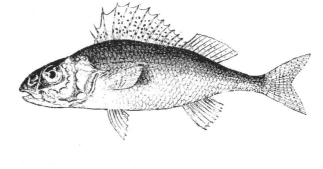

opah   ruff

chub

cod

fucus

fluke

gar

loach

rudd

whelk

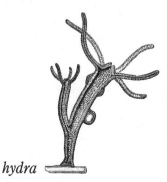
hydra

NOT APPEARING HERE

FISH

aboma	boga	mero
acara	cisco	orc
atka	cobia	pogy
awa	cuddy	porgy
ayu	dace	saury
bagre	gadid	scrod
baleo	goby	shad
blay	hake	smelt
bobo	lant	umber
boce	ling	

SHELLFISH

awabi	conch	pinna
ayuyu	naiad	prawn

TURTLES

arrau

WATER CREATURES

Ascon	moray	salpa
Galba	Murex	sepia
mitra	polyp	

WATER PLANTS

alga	hydra	lotus

WATER BIRDS

arrie	erne	petrel
auk	grebe	shag
brant	heron	skua
cobb	ibis	snipe
coot	loon	sora
crake	murre	tern
crane	noddy	titi
egret	ouzel	

Thira or **Thera** *(THEER-uh)* One of the Cyclades Islands in the Aegean Sea off southeastern Greece. Of volcanic origin, its chief products are pumice, tufa (q.v.), and wine. The island was initially settled by the Phoenicians, and later sent out colonists to Africa. Thira is also referred to as Santorin, a name used since the Middle Ages and derived from the name of its protectress, St. Irene.

The harbor of Thira.

Thor *(thor)* In Scandinavian mythology, the god of thunder, son of Odin (q.v.), and second most important deity in the Norse pantheon. He is associated with the Roman Jupiter. Legend gives Thor prodigious strength, and he owned a magic hammer which returned to him when he threw it, like a boomerang. He tried and failed, however, to lift the Midgard serpent off the earth, conquer old age, and empty a drinking horn connected to the sea. Thursday is named for Thor (Thor's day). See also *Donav.*

thorp, or **thorpe** *(thorp)* From the German word *dorf,* for "village," by way of Middle English, this was originally a small cluster of houses, or hamlet, in a rural setting. Thorp has since come to designate any settlement and often appears as part of a village or personal name.

Thoth *(thahth)* Egyptian god of wisdom and the arts who invented astronomy, writing, and mathematics. Also serving as messenger and scribe for the gods, he was identified by the Greeks with Hermes. In art, Thoth is represented as an ibis-headed man or as a baboon.

thrum *(thrum)* From the German *trumm,* this is a weaver's term designating the row of warp thread ends remaining on a loom after the web is cut away. Among nautical types, to thrum means to insert short lengths of rope yarn (thrums) into canvas used to wrap rigging and keep it from chafing; also to fringe, or furnish with thrums, and to play idly or strum on a musical instrument.

Thrym *(thrim)* According to Norse mythology, Thrym was a giant enamored of Freya (q.v.). To impress her, he stole Mjoelnir, Thor's favorite boomerang. Thor (q.v.) discovered the theft, disguised himself as Freya, and was given the boomerang as a wedding present from Thrym. In retaliation, Thor killed not only Thrym, but all his fellow giants as well.

Thule *(THOO-lee)* The name given by the ancients to the northernmost land reached, probably around 310 B.C., by Pytheas, and variously placed today in Scandinavia, Iceland, or the Shetlands. The word is part of Ultima Thule, a phrase figuratively denoting the limit of human imagination and endeavor. **Thule** is also a settlement in Greenland used as a major U.S. air base.

Thun *(toon)* A city located where the Aare River leaves Lake Thun in the canton of Bern, central Switzerland. Set against the picturesque Bernese Oberland, the city is famous for watches and medieval buildings. **Thun** was also king of the Lion Men on Mongo in the old "Flash Gordon" movie serials.

A street in Thun, Switzerland.

Thyia *(THIE-ya)* In Greek mythology, the daughter of Castalius, paramour of Apollo, and worshiper of Dionysus, whom she honored by organizing and conducting orgies on Mount Parnassus. Athenian women attending the proceedings became known as Thyiads, a name still used by scholars when referring to female cele-brants at a wild party. Thyia derives from the Greek word meaning "to rage" or "to seethe."

thyme *(time)* From the Greek *thymos*, a genus of culinary herbs belonging to the mint family. Garden thymes produce white, pink, or violet flowers and aromatic leaves

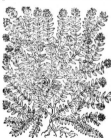

containing thymol, extracted for medicinal use. The leaves, fresh and dried, are a much-used seasoning in many cuisines. Wild thyme is mentioned in *A Midsummer Night's Dream*.

tiara *(tee-AH-rah)* Transliterated from the Greek but probably of Oriental origin, this word originally denoted a headpiece worn in ancient Persia. Later it designated the Pope's crown and, by extension, symbolized his authority. Today, it refers to any crownlike headdress, usually jewel-encrusted, affected by women of rank.

Tiber *(VIE-bur)* Historic river 250 miles long, flowing southward from the Tuscan Apennines through central Italy and winding through Rome before emptying into the

Tyrrhenian Sea at Ostia (q.v.). Known as the Tevere *(TAY-veh-reh)* locally, and the Tawny Timber by poets, it separates the historical center of Rome into two sections.

The Tiber flows serenely through central Italy on its way to Rome and the sea.

tibia *(TIB-ee-ah)* The shinbone, the large inner bone of the human leg between the ankle and knee. Any corresponding bone in other vertebrates is also called the tibia, and it is the fourth segment of an insect's leg counting from the base. In ancient times, animal tibiae (plural) were used to make primitive flutes.

tical or **tikal** *(tik-AHL)* Either a Thai unit of weight equal to roughly one-half ounce; or a former monetary unit of Thailand that is now known as the baht (q.v.) and contains 100 satangs. Spelled with a *k* and pronounced *tee-KAHL*, **Tikal** is also the largest and perhaps oldest of the ruined Maya cities in northern Guatemala. Tikal is famous for its courts and plazas built among lakes and linked by bridges and causeways. In the plazas are the ruins of palaces and temples, including one 229 feet high.

Tigre *(TEE-gray)* Populous city of Buenos Aires province in eastern Argentina. Tigre is a rail terminus serving shippers of fruit grown in the area. With the second syllable accented *(tee-GRAY)*, this is a province in Ethiopia. Once an East African kingdom, Tigre was conquered by Lij Kasa in 1855 and incorporated into Ethiopia when he became Negus the same year. The word in French, pronounced *TEE-gruh*, means "tiger."

Tijou *(tee-ZHEW)* Jean Tijou (1689–1711), French designer of iron grillework who became famous in England. Tijou's ornate rosette-and-leaf-patterned gates and railings can be seen on the grounds of Hampton Court Palace. He also designed screens and grilles for St. Paul's Cathedral in London under Sir Christopher Wren.

Tiki *(TEE-kee)* In the religion of Polynesia, the first man and superhuman progenitor of mankind. A **tiki** is also a stone or wooden image in which gods temporarily take up residence, and a Maori image rep-

resenting an ancestor. *Kon-Tiki* was the name of Thor Heyerdahl's raft, and the title of his book describing his Pacific crossing on a counterpart of an ancient Polynesian craft. Doubling the word yields **tikitiki**—an extract made from rice polishings. Tikitiki is widely used in the treatment of beriberi.

The Polynesian god Tiki.

til or **teel** *(teel)* From the Sanskrit *tila*, a plant native to the Indian subcontinent and known in the West as the sesame. This herb has long been cultivated for its seeds, which are used in breads, pastries, and confections in much of the world. The seeds, called benne (q.v.) seeds, yield an oil used especially in Chinese cookery.

Tilak *(TEE-lak)* Bal Gangadhar Tilak (1856–1920), journalist and nationalist leader of India, who sought complete independence for India from Britain, or *swaraj*. He led an extreme wing of the Indian National Congress, and advocated passive as opposed to moderate resistance. As a common noun, **tilak** *(TIL-lak)* designates the ornamental spot worn as a sectarian mark on the foreheads of Hindus.

tilde *(TILL-dah)* From the Latin *titulus*, meaning "sign," a mark added to certain letters to indicate pronunciation. In Spanish, for example, the tilde over an *n* gives it a sound approximating *nya,* as in señor. This diacritical mark is also used to nasalize first vowels in Portuguese diphthongs, as in São (pronounced *sowm*) Paulo.

Tilly *(TILL-ee)* Johan Tserclaes, Count of Tilly (1559–1632), Flemish field marshal appointed in 1610 to reorganize the armies of Duke Maximilian I of Bavaria. Among his victories during the Thirty Years War were those at White Mountain (1620), Lutter am Barenberge (1626), and Magdeburg (1631), where history records his armies massacred the residents and sacked the town.

Timon *(TIE-mon)* The name of two Greeks: Timon of Athens, a bitter misanthrope and supporter of the statesman-soldier Alcibiades in the war against Sparta, who was the leading character in Shakespeare's *Timon of Athens;* also Timon of Phlius, the philosopher/sillographer whose satirical poems lampooned dogmatic philosophers of his time and preserved the doctrines of his fellow Skeptics.

Timor *(TEE-more)* Largest and most easterly island in the Lesser Sundas (q.v.) of Indonesia. This long, mountainous island, famous for sandalwood, was originally divided between Portuguese Timor, the eastern half of the island, and Dutch Timor, the western half. When Indonesia was created in 1949, Dutch Timor was ceded to the new state. It is now the province of Loro Sae, with its capital at Dili.

Tinos or **Tenos** *(TEE-nohs)* One of the Cyclades Islands of Greece, in the Aegean Sea. This one is known for silk, figs, wine, and an unusual greenish marble. A Venetian colony until 1715, Tinos was also held by the Ottoman Turks. Pilgrims come to a church here to venerate a special icon of the Virgin Mary.

Tinos was a colony of Venice for 300 years until it was captured by the Ottoman Turks.

Titan *(TIE-tan)* In Greek mythology, a member of a family of giants, led by Cronos and including Coeus, Creus, Hyperion, Iapetus, Mnemosyne, Oceanus, Phoebe, Rhea (q.v.), Tethys, Theia (q.v.), and Themis, as well as some of their descendants (Prometheus, Atlas, and others). They were overthrown by the Olympians, led by Zeus (q.v.), who thereafter reigned over the Greek pantheon.

tithe *(tithe)* The etymon of this word is the Old English *teotha,* meaning "one-tenth." Originally, the tithe was a kind of tax amounting to 10 percent of an individual's yearly crop, or its cash equivalent, levied to support the clergy and the church. Payment in grain or firewood was known as a praedial tithe.

titi *(TIE-tie)* A low evergreen shrub native to swampy regions of the southern United States. Known also as buckwheat tree or sourwood, titis produce fragrant white blossoms and a one-seeded fruit. Pronounced *TEE-tee,* it's either a small South American monkey or a blue-footed petrel, also known as the sooty shearwater.

Tito *(TEE-toe)* Name taken by Josip Broz (1892–1980), Communist dictator of Yugoslavia. A blacksmith's son, he fought with the Austro-Hungarian army in World War I, became a union organizer, and, in 1937, reorganized the Communist Party in Yugoslavia. During World War II he led partisans against the occupying Axis powers. After the war he came to power at the head of the National Liberation Front and deposed King Peter II. Under his leadership, Yugoslavia became the most liberal of the European Communist countries.

Tiw or **Tiu** *(TEE-oo)* Teutonic deity known as Tyr *(tuhr)* in Scandinavia. One-handed after putting his arm in the mouth of the wolf Fenris, Tiw presided over sports events and war. He was therefore identified with Mars, and among Germanic folk, Mars's day, the second day of the week, became Tiw's day.

A 6th-century A.D. die depicts the god Tyr.

Tiy *(tee)* Queen of Egypt during the XVIII dynasty, and wife of Amenhotep III. Sagacious despite her humble origins, she achieved recognition unheard of in those ancient, male-dominated times. She was the mother of Ikhnaton. Another Tiy was the wife of Ramses III in the XX dynasty. This Tiy led an unsuccessful conspiracy against her spouse.

Tobit *(TOE-bit)* or **Tobias** *(toe-BIE-ahs)* In the Apocrypha, a devout Israelite carried captive to Assyria; his name was given to the Book of Tobit. Blinded, he asked God for death; on the same day a woman named Sara, who had killed seven would-be husbands on their wedding days, also prayed to God for her death. God dispatched the archangel Raphael to set matters right: in disguise, he lead Tobias, Jr., to Sara; they married safely, exorcised her demon, and returned to Tobias's home, where he cured his father of blindness.

Tobol *(toh-BAWL)* Siberian river over 1,000 miles long, flowing from the Mugodzhar Hills in Kazakstan past Kustanay and Kurgan, before joining the Irtysh at Tobolsk, administrative center of this region until replaced by Omsk in 1824. It is navigable at its lower end and is an important transportation link of western Siberia.

tod *(tahd)*   From the Middle English word *todde,* meaning a bundle, pack, or load, this was formerly a British unit of weight used exclusively for wool. It was equal to about 28 pounds. **Tod** also designates a bushy clump of vegetation; and—because its tail is bushy—a fox, in Scotland.

toddy *(TAH-dee)*   An alcoholic concoction usually served hot. Derived from the Hindi word *tari,* the fresh or fermented sap of certain palm tree buds, a toddy contains liquor plus sugar, water, cloves, and other spices. The palmyra and other East Indian palm trees are also known as toddy palms.

tody *(TOE-dee)*   General name for several species of small, insect-eating birds related to the kingfisher and native to the West Indies, from the Latin *todus,* a small bird. These bright green forest birds with red throats are called robins in Jamaica, although they are not related to those red-breasted creatures of North America. In Haiti, tody eggs are considered a delicacy.

toga *(TOE-gah)*   Loose-fitting, one-piece outer garment worn only by the citizens of ancient Rome, known as the *gens togata* (toga-wearing people). This item, usually made of undyed wool and often sporting an ornamental border, was worn draped to cover the left arm. The *toga virilis* (toga of manhood) was assumed by boys approaching the age of fifteen.

A Roman in his toga.

Togo *(TOE-goe)*   Either the surname of Count Heihachiro Togo (1847–1934), the Japanese admiral and naval hero of the Russo-Japanese War; or a republic on the Gulf of Guinea in West Africa. Known for its

THE APOTHECARY

adad

aloe
asak
badam
baobab
bija
cacao
cade

clary
cubeb
elemi
ergo

flax

fungi

guaco
ipecac

jalap
kava
myrrh
nard
nux
orris
resin

rowan
rue
senna

tansy
thyme
til
wahoo
woad

coffee, cacao, cotton, and copra, it was part of French Togoland before achieving independence in 1960. The historic region called Togoland has been divided between Ghana and the Republic of Togo; it is also referred to as Togo.

Tojo *(TOE-joe)* The archvillain of World War II, Hideki Tojo (1884–1948), Japanese general and statesman who favored war with the Allies and served as premier from 1941 to 1944. He was the most powerful leader of the Japanese government in that period and was responsible for the attack on Pearl Harbor. Japan's loss of Saipan in 1944 caused him to lose face, and he resigned. After a botched attempt at suicide, he was executed as a war criminal.

Tokay *(toe-KAY)* Golden dessert wine, made near Tokaj on the Tisza River in northeast Hungary. The rarest Tokay is made from juice that oozes, without squeezing, from overripe Tokay grapes.

tola *(TOE-lah)* A derivative of the Sanskrit *tula,* for "balance" or "scale." In India, a tola is a unit of weight equivalent to 180 grains, originally the weight of a silver rupee. As a proper noun, there are two biblical **Tolas:** the son of Issachar (Gen. 46:13) and a judge of Israel (Judges 10:1–2).

tole *(tole)* This word comes to us via the French *tôle,* meaning "sheet iron." Tole refers to a type of lacquered or enameled houseware popular among the gentry in the eighteenth century. Today, it usually takes the form of black metal trays decorated with gilt and fancifully colored flowers.

Tomar *(toh-MAHR)* A town in Ribatejo, central Portugal. It is most famous as the headquarters of the Knights Templars, a medieval religious military force which in 1190 successfully turned away an assault by the Moors. In 1581, Philip II of Spain selected Tomar as the site to proclaim his rule over Portugal.

Tonga *(TOHNG-ah)* A nation of the South Pacific, lying about 2,000 miles northeast of Sydney, Australia. The only kingdom still extant in the region, Tonga comprises more than 150 islands, mostly volcanic in origin. Tonga was discovered by the Dutch and later visited by Captain Cook, who named the group the Friendly Islands. It achieved its independence from Great Britain in 1970, and is presently ruled by King Taufaahau Tupou IV, son of the famous Queen Salote Tupou III. **Tonga** is also a people of Africa; and as a common noun, it is a two-wheeled vehicle of India, a creeping plant of Malaysia, and a drug extracted from the plant.

tonka *(TOHNK-ah)* An almond-shaped seed produced by certain tropical South American trees of the pulse family. The tonka (or tonqua) bean contains a substance called coumarin, used as a vanilla substitute. The chemical, today mostly synthetic, is used for flavoring or fragrance in perfumes, soap, tobacco, and food products.

Tonto *(TOHN-toe)* A basin south of the Mogollen Mesa in central Arizona; a creek flowing south from the basin; and a national monument protecting fourteenth-century cliff houses built by the Salado Indians. A descendant of these native Americans might well have been the prototype of **Tonto,** the legendary faithful Indian companion of the Lone Ranger.

toque *(toke)* From Old Spanish, a small, round hat, with or without a brim, worn by chic women. In the Middle Ages, toques sported plumes and were unisex. Today the word is most familiar in the Anglicized French term toque blanche—the tall, white headgear affected by chefs. **Toque** is also an Asian monkey.

Torah *(TOH-rah)* Transliteration from the Hebrew for "law," this is a parchment scroll containing the Pentateuch—the first five books of the Bible, also known as the Books of Moses, believed to have been given to him on Mount Sinai. Torahs can be found in every synagogue, placed for safekeeping in richly decorated arks. In an extended sense, Torah also means the whole body of Jewish religious literature, including the Scriptures and the Talmud.

torii *(TOE-ree-yee)* A structure associated with Japanese culture and seen at the entrance to a Shinto temple. Torii are gateways consisting of two uprights supporting a curved crosspiece with a straight one directly beneath it. Similar gateways of other Eastern cultures include the pailau of China and the toran of Indian Buddhist temples.

A torii at the Miyajima shrine in Japan.

torte *(tort)* Type of rich, flat cake or pastry made with eggs, butter, chopped nuts, and either bread crumbs or a small quantity of flour. Originally, the word was known only to German-speaking people, but it has become universal wherever gourmets congregate. Best known are the rich chocolate Sacher torte, invented at Vienna's Sacher Hotel, and the Linzer torte, made of pastry topped with raspberry jam.

torus *(TAWR-us)* From the Latin meaning "bulge" or "protuberance," this is the large convex molding seen just above the plinth at the base of a column. In botany, **torus** designates the cuplike part of a flower, or receptacle, from which floral leaves grow. And, in anatomy, it is any swelling.

Tory *(TOR-ee)* Derived from the Irish *toruidhe,* for "robber," this was a dispossessed Irishman who preyed on the English in the seventeenth century. **Tory** has also designated either a supporter of England in the American Revolution; a member of the English political party now known as Conservative; or any extreme right-wing politician. It is often clued as "Whig's opponent." See *Whig.*

Tosca *(TOHSS-ka)* One of Puccini's best-known operas, based on a Sardoux play. It tells of a beautiful singer; her revolutionist lover, Cavarodossi; and Scarpia, the double-dealing police chief. Scarpia promises freedom for Cavarodossi in return for Tosca's favors, which she denies by stabbing him. Eventually, Cavarodossi is executed and Tosca commits suicide.

Emma Carelli, early 20-century Italian soprano, in Tosca.

totem *(TOE-tum)* North American Indian word for "animal image" taken as the identifying symbol of a primitive clan or family. These images were often carved into poles placed before dwellings, particularly in the Pacific Northwest and southern Alaska. Among other things, totems served to prevent intermarriage. The punishment for congress between couples of the same totem was often death. By extension, totem means something that serves as an emblem.

Totem poles of the Tlingit Indians in Alaska.

Toto *(TOE-toe)* Either the mate of the much-publicized gorilla Gargantua; or the little pet dog who accompanied Dorothy to the Land of Oz. This was the setting for the children's story *The Wonderful Wizard of Oz,* written by L. Frank Baum in 1900 and made into a movie starring Judy Garland.

Toto watches expectantly as Ray Bolger, Judy Garland, and Jack Haley point the way down the Yellow Brick Road in The Wizard of Oz.

toxin *(TOK-sin)* From the Latin *toxicum,* meaning "poison," a harmful protein produced by either plants, animals, or disease-causing bacteria. Unlike chemical poisons, these compounds are toxic only to species other than those that manufacture them. Certain toxins are weakened and administered to immunize individuals by causing them to develop antibodies (or antitoxins).

tram *(tram)* Either a British streetcar; an open rail car used to transport ore in mines; a passenger conveyance that runs on a cable; a device for lining up or adjusting certain parts of a machine; or a silk thread used as a weft (q.v.) in expensive silks or velvets.

trawl *(trawl)* From the Dutch *tragel,* meaning "dragnet," a large, dunce–cap shaped net with a circular mouth kept open by a metal ring. This item is dragged by a trawler across the ocean floor to catch fish or other marine life not smart enough to escape through the open end.

trek *(trek)* From the Afrikaans word *trecken,* "to pull," as a wagon. This term was applied to migrations, such as the Great Trek of Boer farmers who hitched up their wagons and left the Cape of Good Hope in 1835 to escape British dominion. Today it denotes any extended journey.

tress *(tress)* From the Middle English *tresse,* meaning much the same, this was originally a braid of hair. It has come to mean locks of long hair. Among owners of noteworthy tresses were Rapunzel, the fairy-tale heroine whose boyfriend used her hair as a rope ladder; and Lady Godiva, the nude equestrienne. A crossword clue is "barbershop sweep-up."

Veronica Lake, one of Hollywood's best-tressed actresses of the 1940s.

tret *(tret)* From the Latin *trahere,* "to draw," a term that finds its way into crossword puzzles with unsettling frequency. This was once an allowance given to buyers of certain merchandise that could be expected to lose value in transit through damage or deterioration. The tret was usually 4 pounds for every 104 pounds of weight, or the weight of the commodity after the tare (q.v.), or weight of its container, had been deducted.

triad *(TRIE-ad)* The sense of this word is inherent in its prefix—generally, any group of three entities. In music, it refers to a chord containing three tones, usually the

root plus its third and fifth. In poetry, it refers to the three strophes of a classical ode. In chemistry, it means a trivalent atom.

trill *(trill)* Any rapid change from one musical note to another that is close in pitch. This is sometimes called a vibrato, or, in singing, a tremolo. The term is also applied to a rapid vibration of the tongue or uvula to produce the rolling *r* affected by Shakespearean and ham actors. It can also mean a warble or bird call.

tripe *(tripe)*
Depending on one's taste in food, this is either delectable or detestable. Tripe comprises the stomach lining of oxen, sheep, or other animals, and is relished by some, particularly the French of Normandy, who simmer it for hours in Calvados. **Tripe,** however, is also synonymous with trash, garbage, and bad writing.

Troad *(TROE-ud)* or Troas *(TROE-us)*
The region on the Hellespont in the vicinity of ancient Troy, locale of Homer's *Iliad* (see *Ilium*), the Troad saw many struggles for the control of the Dardanelles straits. In biblical times, another Troas was a Greek seaport, also known as Mysia, in northwestern Asia Minor (Acts 16:8, 11; 20:5–6).

troll *(trole)*
In Scandinavian folklore, a creature who lived in caverns or under mountains. Trolls were represented as misshapen dwarfs who stole children and hated noise—a throwback to their efforts to dodge Thor's clangorous hammer. The best-known troll was the Mountain King in Ibsen's and Grieg's *Peer Gynt* (see *Grieg*). As a verb, to **troll** is to sing lustily, as in "troll the ancient Yuletide carol . . ."

A devilish-looking troll.

Troy See *Ilium*.

Truk *(truk)*
A group of roughly 50 volcanic islands surrounded by an atoll (q.v.) reef. It lies in the eastern group of the Carolines in the western Pacific, and is known for copra and dried fish. During World War II, Truk was a Japanese naval base and target of American bombers.

trump *(trump)*
From the French *triomphe* (a victory). In various card games, trump designates any card whose suit rates higher than any other suit for the particular hand being played. A trump card can therefore take cards of all other suits. **Trump** is also the colloquial term for a nice guy.

truss *(truss)*
In engineering, a framework of tie beams, girders, and struts that support a roof or bridge. These members lie in a single plane and usually form triangles, considered to provide the greatest rigidity. In a surgical supply outlet, **truss** refers to an appliance worn to hold a hernia in place. To **truss** a chicken means to tie its legs and wings in place for roasting.

tryma *(TRIE-mah)*
From the Greek *tryme,* meaning "hole," this is any nut whose fibrous epicarp and mesocarp, or outer layers, separate as a fibrous rind from its hard endocarp, or inner layer, when ripe. Among the most popular of nuts, trymas include the hickory and walnut.

tryst *(trist)*
In Scotland, a market or fair. The word, however, is usually recognized as an appointment between lovers at a specific location for the purpose of amorous

Trysts have long been popular movie subjects. The one being anticipated here was in Curses! They Remarked, *1914.*

dalliance. Tryst comes from the Old French for "hunting station," and is a favorite of newspaper headline writers needing a shorter word than rendezvous.

tuba *(TOO-bah)* The Latin word for "trumpet," tuba now refers to any low-pitched brass instrument, such as the helicon and sousaphone,  which wind around the player. The baritone and euphonium are small tubas. Tubas trace back to Berlin in the 1820s, when they began replacing serpents and ophicleides in bands. This use was popularized by the composer Richard Wagner.

William Bell, a tuba virtuoso of the 1930s.

Tubal *(TOO-buhl)* In the Old Testament, Tubal was the son of Japheth, youngest of Noah's three boys (Gen. 10:2). Also mentioned in Genesis (4:22) is Tubal-cain, son of Lamech, and an early worker in copper and iron. Tubal was also the wealthy Jew and friend of Shylock in Shakespeare's *Merchant of Venice*. As an adjective, it is clued as "relating to a tube or pipe."

tufa *(TOO-fah)* From the Italian word *tufo,* a type of porous stone formed by the deposition of calcium carbonate by streams and springs, in the same way stalactites and stalagmites are built. One form, calcareous tufa, is known variously as Mexican onyx, travertine marble, and Oriental alabaster.

Tuke *(tewk)* Surname of an English philanthropic family interested in better treatment of the insane. The family included William Tuke (1732–1822), merchant and founder of the York retreat for insane persons; his son, Henry Tuke (1755–1814), co-founder of the retreat; and a great-grandson, Daniel Tuke (1827–1895), a physician who studied insanity.

Tula *(TOO-lah)* An ancient central Mexican town in Hidalgo state, believed to be Tollan, legendary capital of the Toltec empire. It has important archaeological sites, some restored. Tula is also the name of a rail and manufacturing center of the U.S.S.R., south of Moscow. Founded in the twelfth century, and a sixteenth-century fortress city, it withstood repeated German attacks during World War II.

Tulle *(tool)* Industrial city in south-central France, southeast of Limoges. Tulle is known nowadays for metal products, including firearms, but it earlier gave its name to a gossamer silk fabric first made there. Founded in the seventh century, it was one of the hardest hit areas during the Black Death epidemic of the Middle Ages.

Tully *(TULL-ee)* Anglicized name of Marcus Tullius Cicero (106–43 B.C.), great Roman orator and statesman who spoke out against the conspirator Catiline. Opposed to Caesar, he was put to death by Antony when Octavian (later Augustus) came to power. Tully is also the surname of Jim Tully (1891–1947), American writer of popular fiction.

tun *(tun)* Huge cask for holding beer or wine. While coopers don't ordinarily build tuns to exact specifications, these containers generally hold about 252 wine gallons. The **tun** was also a period of the Mayan calendar, to which the five-day-long uayeb was added, bringing the year to 365 days.

A monk toasting the contents of a tun.

tunic *(TEW-nik)*   A loose-fitting item of attire resembling a gown, and worn by both men and women of ancient Greece and Rome. Tunic also designates a short jacket sported by members of the British constabulary, in general, it is an overblouse or surcoat. In biology, the word basically covers such life forms as plants, animals, or organs.

Tunja *(TUNE-ha)*   City in central Colombia, a center of commerce and a shipping point on the Pan-American Highway for the region's products and cattle. Tunja is the capital of Boyaca, the department where, on August 7, 1819, Simón Bolívar won the battle that liberated Colombia and Venezuela from Spain.

Tupac *(too-PAHK)*   Peruvian Indian freedom fighter José Gabriel Condorcanqui (c. 1742–1781), who took the name of his Inca ancestor Tupac Amaru. He fought for reforms for his people, which were eventually gained, though he led them unsuccessfully in a revolt in 1780. Captured by the government, he was brutally executed.

tuque *(took)*   From the French *toque* (q.v.), a type of cap, this is specifically a knitted stocking hat, made by folding one closed end of a knitted tube up into the other closed end. Worn in cold weather for warmth, especially in Canada, the tuque has become a familiar piece of attire on ski slopes and at football games.

Turan *(too-RAHN)*   Desert region in western Turkistan, central Asian U.S.S.R., where little rain and few people are found. Turan is divided into three parts by the Amu Darya and Syr Darya rivers, which provide water for limited irrigation. Gold deposits have been found in the central Kyzyl-Kum desert.

Turin *(TUHR-in)*   Major industrial city in northwestern Italy, and an important car-producing capital for Lancias and Fiats. One-time capital of the kingdom Sardinia, it was also ruled variously by the House of Savoy and the French. In 1861 it became capital, for a few years, of the new Italian kingdom. It has a number of notable buildings, including a fifteenth-century cathedral where the principal relic is the Shroud of Turin, a cloth believed by some to have wrapped Christ after the descent from the Cross.

The Palazzo Madama, Turin.

Turku *(TUHR-koo)*   A port in southwestern Finland on the Aurajoki River at its mouth on the Baltic, this is the nation's major harbor, second largest city, and an important industrial center. One of the oldest cities in Finland and its capital until 1812, it is called the cradle of Finnish culture.

tutu *(TOO-too)* From French baby talk connoting "backside," this is the (usually) *très* short, full ballet skirt that stands out from the body for maximum freedom of movement and grace. The tutu is often made of stiff netting, and is generally complemented by a pair of tights and ballet slippers. A **Tutu** is also a group of New Zealand shrubs.

Skating star Sonja Henie often wore a tutu.

Tyana *(TIE-ah-nah)*   Ancient town in Cappadocia, in present-day south-central Turkey, and site of major ruins. As part of the Roman Empire after the third century

A.D., Tyana was a place of military might and thriving commerce. It was called home by Apollonius of Tyana, the Greek philosopher known as a prophet and miracle-worker.

Tyche *(TIE-kee)*   From the Greek meaning "chance," the goddess of luck or fortune. Corresponding to the Roman goddess Fortuna, Tyche was thought to have once been the goddess of fertility. She is usually shown with a cornucopia or a wheel.

Tycho See *Brahe.*

tyke or **tike** *(tike)*   From the Old Norse *tik* (a bitch), by way of Middle English, this means a dog, specifically one of mixed breed. **Tyke**, however, takes on various other meanings, such as an eccentric or boorish individual. Used colloquially, it's an affectionate term for a little child, particularly an animated and playful one.

A determined tyke leads the pack in a London playground.

Typee *(tie-PEE)*   Novel (1846) by Herman Melville, American author known for his adventure stories of the South Seas. In this largely autobiographical work, Melville (as Tom, the hero) abandons a whaling ship upon reaching the Marquessas. Considering that he is captured by the Typees, a cannibal tribe, the subtitle, *A Peek at Polynesian Life,* seems inappropriately idyllic. In real life, Melville's captors treated him kindly until his rescue by a whaling vessel.

Tyr See *Tiw.*

Tyre *(tire)*   An ancient Phoenician city-state, now called Sur, in present-day Lebanon. Tyre, frequently mentioned in the Bible, was famous for the superiority of its sailors and for the purple Tyrian dye obtained from shellfish and favored by the Greeks and Romans. In the ninth century B.C., the city of Carthage was founded by Tyrians. Today, Crusaders' buildings, in ruins, are the principal reminders of Tyre's long history.

tyro or **tiro** *(TIE-roe)*   From the Medieval Latin *tiro,* meaning "young soldier," the term for any novice or beginner. This term applies to one lacking experience, knowledge, or ability in a trade, profession, or life situation. Tyro is often clued as "rookie," or "raw recruit."

Tyrol *(TIH-rahl; tie-ROLE)*   A province in the Alps of western Austria, and a region extending down into northern Italy. A strategically important area historically, it is traversed by the Brenner Pass, connecting the Tyrol capital, Innsbruck, with Bolzano in Italy. The Tyrolean Alps are noted for their magnificence and picture-book settings that make the region a mecca for skiers and tourists.

tzar or **tsar** *(zahr; tsahr)*   Also spelled czar, this is one of the most common crossword puzzle entries. The etymology of tzar is lengthy: it derives from the Russian word *tsar',* a contraction of *tsesari,* via the Gothic *kaisar,* and is related to the Latin *caesar.* Tzar designates an autocratic Russian emperor; or, in newspaper slang, the absolute boss. Because it is such a frequent crossword repeater, many clues have been brought into play, e.g., "Kremlin autocrat," "one of the Romanovs," "Anastasia's father," "Cossack's ruler," etc.

Ivan the Terrible.

Uayeb See *tun*.

Udall *(YOO-dahl)* Surname of various luminaries, including John Udall (c. 1560–1592), English clergyman who denounced the episcopacy, was sentenced to death and died in prison; Nicholas Udall (1505–1556), British dramatist who wrote the first English comedy, *Ralph Roister Doister;* and Stewart Lee Udall (1920–), American politician and secretary of the interior under presidents Kennedy and Johnson.

Stewart L. Udall.

udo *(oo-doe)* Transliteration of the Japanese name for a stout herb of the *Aralia* genus. Its blanched shoots are used as a vegetable and salad ingredient. In the United States, finer Japanese restaurants incorporate it into their sukiyaki, along with the soy sauce.

Ufa *(oo-FAH)* Industrial city and capital of Bashkir in the eastern European U.S.S.R., situated in the Urals at the confluence of the Belaya and Ufa rivers. Ufa was founded in the sixteenth century as a Russian fortress on the trade route to Siberia. In 1919, it was captured by Kolchak's army during the Russian Civil War.

Ugric *(YOO-grick)* or **Ugrian** *(YOO-gree-an)* Among philologists, this word designates a branch of the Finnic-Ugric family of languages. Main entities of this subgroup include: Hungarian, spoken by about 12 million people; Ostyak, the tongue of about 20,000 souls in western Siberia; and Vogul, used by roughly 6,000 other western Siberians.

uhlan *(oo-lahn)* Anglicized version of a Germanicized Polish word derived from the Turkish *oglan,* meaning "a youth." Originally, uhlans (or ulans) were cavalrymen of the Polish army, whose primary weapons were lances. The name, however, was popularized by mounted lancers of the Prussian army in the days before mechanized warfare.

Uigur or Uighur *(WEE-goor)* A

Turkic-speaking Asian people who inhabited western China and who were referred to in ancient Chinese records as *Yue-che.* For almost 100 years (A.D. 744–840) they controlled Mongolia; after being ousted they moved to Tu-lu-fan in the Sinkiang province of China, where they maintained an empire until the Mongol invasions in the thirteenth century. The Uigur eventually became Sunnite Muslims, and today their descendants constitute most of the population of the Sinkiang region.

Uinta *(yew-INN-tah)* Range of the Rocky

Mountains, extending roughly 120 miles from northeastern Utah to southwestern Wyoming. Highest point in the Uintas, and in Utah, is the 13,528-foot Kings Peak. Known for phosphate mining, this is the largest range running in an east-west direction in the United States. It lies almost entirely within national forests.

Ujiji *(oo-JEE-jih)* Former city in Tanza-

nia, now included in the municipality of Kigoma-Ujiji, on Lake Tanganyika. Connected by rail with the seaport of Dar es Salaam, Ujiji and neighboring Kigoma were important depots for slave traders in the nineteenth century. It was here that Henry Stanley, on November 10, 1871, successfully concluded his search for Dr. Livingstone.

ukase *(YEW-kaze)* Transliteration of the

Russian word for "edict." In tzarist Russia, a ukase was any imperial order enforceable under the law. Today, the term has been broadened to mean any rigid decree issued by a person in authority.

ulama or ulema *(oo-luh-mah)* A

Turkish or Arabic word transliterated into

English from the plural of *alim,* meaning "learned." In Muslim countries, the ulema are scholars and respected authorities in the disciplines of philosophy, religion, and, especially, law. By extension, the term has come to be applied to groups of experts in any field.

Ullur *(YEW-ler)* In Scandinavian mythol-

ogy, a stepson of Thor (q.v.) and lord of hand-to-hand combat, archery, and the chase. This macho deity, known for his handsome looks, lived in Ydaler, the valley of rain. As an athlete, however, he was virtually unbeatable at such snow-oriented sports as skiing and snowshoe racing.

Ulm *(oolm)* City on the Danube in

Baden-Württemberg, West Germany. A commercial center since the Middle Ages, Ulm produces metal products, textiles, and beer. But its main claim to fame is as the birthplace of Albert Einstein. More than half the town was destroyed by Allied air attacks during World War II.

The Danube River and the city's huge Gothic minster are prominent in this view of Ulm.

ulna *(ULL-nah)* From the Latin for "el-

bow," this is the larger of the two bones of the forearm, the one on the same side as the pinkie. The ulna is hinged to the carpal joints of the hand, to the radius of the forearm at wrist and elbow, and to the humerus of the upper arm at the elbow.

ulu *(oo-loo)*   Coarse grass native to India, where it serves for forage and pasture. Also, a transliteration of the Inupik Eskimo word for "woman's knife." This device looks like a food chopper, with a crescent-shaped blade that's ideal for making small chunks of blubber out of big ones.

umbel *(UM-bel)*   From the Latin *umbella,* which became the English word umbrella, this is a type of inflorescence, or arrangement of flowers on an axis. Umbels are parasol-shaped floral clusters, the individual flower stalks all of equal length, and originating from roughly the same joint, just like the ribs of an umbrella.

umber *(UM-ber)*   Anglicized version of the Italian *terra d'ombra,* "earth of Umbria," which presumably is brown in color. Used as a pigment, this earth is colored by various metallic oxides that determine the difference between raw umber and burnt umber. **Umber** is also another name for the grayling, a game fish of the salmon family.

umbo *(UM-boe)*   In heraldry, the boss, or projecting stud, at the center of a shield. By extension, certain elevations resembling it, especially those with corresponding depressions on opposite surfaces, are called umbones (plural). These include the prominence on each side of a clam shell near the hinge, and cone scales of some pine trees.

umiak *(oo-mee-ak)*   An eastern Eskimo word transferred intact into English, this designates a type of small, open boat, propelled by paddling, used for fishing and transportation in northern waters. The um-

iak is constructed by stretching skins over a wooden frame, and is known as a woman's boat, in contrast to the more macho hunter's kayak (q.v.).

Una *(YEW-nah)*   In Spenser's *Faërie Queene,* Una was the heroine of the first book. The sweetheart of St. George, the Red Cross Knight and dragon-slayer, she also embodied truth. Una was so beautiful that a lion, coming upon her sleeping, not only spared her but became her protector.

unau *(YOO-noe)*   Native Brazilian, or Tupi, name for the two-toed sloth (q.v.) indigenous to the South American rain forests. As sloths go, this is the most animated of these creatures. The unau is so nimble, that it can even come down the trunk of a tree head first, unlike its slower three-toed cousin, the ai (q.v.).

Uncas *(UNK-ahs)*   In James Fenimore Cooper's novel, the offspring of Chingachook, and last of the Mohican Indians. His courageous, noble character does not seem to jibe with the real Uncas (c. 1588–1683), chief of the Mohegans (or Mohicans), who constantly fought the English and his fellow redmen. He is reportedly buried in the Moravian Missionary Cemetery in Bethlehem, Pennsylvania.

Heather Angel, Philip Reed, and Bruce Cabot in The Last of the Mohicans.

Uniate or **Uniat** *(YEW-nee-at)* From the Latin *unus,* meaning "one," via the Russian *uniya,* "union," Uniate is the term for any of several Eastern-rite Christian groups that recognize the Pope's primacy but retain their own rites, liturgy, and governing patriarchs. Included under this definition are some Copts, some Jacobites, and certain Nestorians, also called Chaldean Catholics.

Unruh *(OON-roo)*   Fritz von Unruh (1885–1970), writer and general's son who hated war and lauded the free soul. It was therefore not surprising that Unruh left Germany in 1928 and did not return until 20 years later. He is best known for the anti-Nazi novel *The End Is Not Yet.*

upas *(YEW-pas)*   Truncated form of *pohon upas,* Malay for "poison tree." Related to the mulberry, this is a tall, pale-barked tree found in Java (q.v.) and other tropical regions. Its bast fiber is used to make paper; its latex, as an arrow poison. Another tree known as upas is of the Logania family and yields strychnine, similarly used as arrow poison.

Upolu *(oo-POE-loo)*   A volcanic island in Western Samoa (q.v.), Upolu is dotted with rolling mountains, the highest of which is 3,600-foot Vaaifetu. The copra (q.v.), bananas, rubber, and cacao (q.v.) from Upolu's fertile valleys is shipped out of its chief port, Apia, capital of Western Samoa. Elsewhere, a cape on the northern shore of Hawaii Island is called **Upolu** Point.

Ural *(YOO-ral)*   Both a river and mountain range of the U.S.S.R. The 1,500-mile-long Ural River parallels the mountain range and empties into the Caspian Sea. The mineral-rich Ural Mountains form the traditional border between Europe and Asia, and Asia is often clued as "east of the Urals." During World War II, industries were moved here to keep them out of German hands.

Urdu *(OOR-doo)*   The language used by about 20 million Muslims in Pakistan and India. One of 15 official Indian tongues, Urdu is both the official and literary language of Pakistan. It is written in modified Arabic characters and stems from Hindu-stani, which linguists place in the Indo-Iranian subfamily of Indo-European languages. The word Urdu comes from the Hindi *zaban-i-urdu,* meaning "camp language."

urea *(yew-REE-ah)*   From the Greek word *ouron,* meaning "urine," this is a highly soluble organic compound, the end product of nitrogen metabolism that is found in the urine of mammals. In 1828 urea became the first natural compound to be made synthetically in the laboratory. It is used in the manufacture of adhesives and plastics.

The alchemists' sign for urine.

Urey *(YOOR-ee)*   Harold Clayton Urey (1893–), American chemist, who in 1934 won the Nobel Prize for chemistry for his work with deuterium, or heavy hydrogen. He later isolated other "heavy" isotopes. During World War II, Urey's research helped pave the way for production of the first atomic bomb.

Uri *(oo-ree)*   One of the Four Forest cantons of central Switzerland, known for its Alpine glaciers and picturesque upland pastures. The capital is Altdorf. It was in Uri that William Tell accurately aimed and let fly his legendary arrow. Eventually Uri joined with Unterwalden and Schwyz to form the league that ultimately became the Swiss nation.

Sir William Tell

A turn-of-the-century photograph of a Ute Indian couple in Colorado.

Uriah *(yoo-RIE-ah)* Hebrew for "light of Jehovah," and the name of a Hittite captain in David's army, according to the Old Testament. After Uriah's wife, Bath-sheba, had been seduced by David, the king arranged for the Hittite to be killed in battle, and married the beautiful widow (2 Sam.). Their first child died of a sickness inflicted by God as punishment for the death of Uriah; their second child, also a son, was Solomon. Dickens created **Uriah** Heep, in *David Copperfield,* as a character whose unbounded " 'umbleness" has made his name synonymous with repellently obsequious behavior.

Ursa *(UR-sah)* Latin for "she-bear," Ursa appears in the names of two constellations of the northern skies: Ursa Major, the Big Bear, consisting of 53 visible stars of which seven make up the Big Dipper; and Ursa Minor, called the Little Dipper, with 23 stars—including Polaris, the North Star, used for navigation because it is always due north from the observer.

Ute *(yute)* Member of a fierce tribe of Shoshonean Indians who once lived in parts of Utah, Arizona, New Mexico, and Colorado, and now live near the point where these four states meet. In crosswords, it is sometimes clued as "Chief Ouray's people," or "Salt Lake City team (or player),"

since a **Ute** is the nickname for a member of the University of Utah team. Pronounced *oo-tuh,* this is the name of a Burgundian queen, and mother of Kriemhild and Gunther—heroine and villain, respectively, of the *Nibelungenlied.*

uvula *(YEW-vyoo-lah)* Diminutive form of *uva,* Latin for "grape," to which this anatomical structure bears a resemblance. The uvula is that fleshy appendage hanging from the middle of the soft palate above the back of the tongue. Doctors often ask patients to say "Ahhh" to lift the uvula out of the way.

Uxmal *(oosh-MAHL)* Ruined Mayan city nestling in the Puuc hills of the Yucatán peninsula, Mexico. At its prime between A.D. 600 and 900, Uxmal is an archaeologists's dream come true. It is famous for structures like the Pyramid of the Magician and the Governor's Palace, which has 20,000 carvings on its façade.

Uzbek *(ooz-bek)* A Soviet Socialist Republic in the central Asian region of the U.S.S.R., to the north of Afghanistan. It is also known as Uzbekistan. Major Uzbek cities are the fabled Tashkent, the capital, and Samarkand, along the old caravan routes. Uzbek additionally means an inhabitant of this region and his Turkic language.

Vaal *(vahl)*   A 750-mile-long river rising in the Transvaal in the Republic of South Africa, and flowing west to the Orange River in the Orange Free State. An important hydroelectric source for the region's industries, the Vaal is punctuated by major dams along its route.

Vaasa *(VAH-sah)*   City and provincial capital on the Gulf of Bothnia in Vaasa province, western Finland. This busy port was founded in 1606, destroyed by fire in 1852, rebuilt at its present site in 1855, and renamed Nikolainkaupunki after Tzar Nicholas. Vaasa's present name dates from the civil war of 1918 when it was White Finland's capital. Both Swedish and Finnish are spoken; the city's Swedish name is Vasa.

Vach *(vahsh)*   In early Hindu mythology, Vach was the goddess of speech and communication, through whom the wisdom of the gods was transmitted to mankind. Later, as Brahma's consort under the name Saraswati, she presided over the arts.

Vaduz *(vah-DOOTS)*   Capital of Liechtenstein, the tiny principality with no army and few police, located along the Rhine River between Austria and Switzerland. Vaduz is popular with tourists, who come to see its splendid medieval castle. Because of low taxes, many international companies choose Vaduz as a location for their headquarters.

The Government House in tranquil Vaduz, Liechtenstein.

vagus *(VAY-gus)*   Taken directly from the Latin, this literally means "wandering." Vagus designates either of the tenth pair of cranial nerves in the peripheral nervous system that control activity in the larynx, lungs, heart, esophagus, and most of the abdominal organs.

Vah *(vahk)* A 245-mile-long river in eastern Czechoslovakia. It originates at the junction of the Biély Váh, flowing from the High Tatra, and the Cierny Váh, which rises in the Low Tatra. The Váh empties into the Danube at Komárno on the Czech-Hungarian border.

vair *(vare)* Derived from the Latin *varius,* meaning "variegated," this is a type of fur obtained from gray and white squirrels, and used by medieval furriers as a lining and trimming. In heraldic design, this fur was represented by a design in which rows of upright bells alternated with overturned bells.

Vala *(VAH-lah)* The Norse prophetess whose song, the "Voluspa," is the oldest of Norse poems. In it, Vala considers the serious concerns of life, from the creation of man and the universe to the inevitability of death, for gods as well as for men.

Vali *(VAH-lee)* In ancient Scandinavian mythology, Vali was the second son of Odin (q.v.) and the silent god of justice. In this role, he executed Hodur (q.v.), who had slain Balder (q.v.) during a fight for the hand of the fair Nanna. Vali survived the Twilight of the Gods, assuring that justice would prevail on earth.

Valmy *(vahl-MEE)* Small village in the department of Marne in northeastern France. The first skirmish of the French Revolutionary Wars took place here on September 20, 1792. Called the "cannonade of Valmy," the French artillery barrage repelled Austrian and Prussian invaders bent on reaching Paris to restore the monarchy.

vamp *(vamp)* Any of several meanings, including: the front part of a shoe, covering the toes and arch of the foot; a simple

accompaniment improvised to fit a song, or introductory music played, sometimes repeatedly, before a soloist begins; an item patched up to appear like new; the slang term for a volunteer fireman; or, as short for vampire, a woman who tempts men by use of feminine wiles. A frequent crossword clue is Theda Bara, a famous **vamp** of silent movies.

Theda Bara, the ultimate vamp, in a typical posture.

Vane *(vane)* Sir Henry Vane (1613–1662), English statesman, Puritan leader, and governor of Massachusetts at the time of the founding of Harvard College. As a common noun, a **vane** is a device made of metal, wood, or cloth, often found atop a structure, that indicates the direction of the wind.

Sir Henry Vane.

Vanir *(VAH-ner)* A race of Norse gods who presided over nature, ruling the land, seas, and air. The chief god was Niörd, the water god; his wife was Skadi and his son and daughter were Frey and Freya (both q.v.). The Vanir preceded the Aesir (q.v.), another race of Scandinavian gods which included Odin (q.v.) and Thor (q.v.). The two groups often found themselves at war; the Vanir were finally defeated by and incorporated into the Aesir.

Vanoc *(VAN-ahk)* The son of Merlin, magician and counselor of King Arthur's court. So shrouded in mystery are the real Merlin, a fifth-century Welsh bard, and the legendary Merlin, that little is known about Vanoc—except his penchant for turning up in crossword puzzles.

vara *(VAH-rah)* From the Spanish or Portuguese meaning "stick" or "pole," this is an Iberian and Latin-American unit of linear measure, equivalent to anywhere from 32 to 43 inches, depending on where the measurement is taking place.

Vardo *(VAHR-doe)* Port and fishing village on an island, Vardoye, at the entrance of the Varangerfjord in northeastern Norway. Although lapped by the Arctic Ocean, the harbor of Vardo is ice-free. In 1307 a fortress, most northerly in the world, was built here. In 1893–1896, Fridtjof Nansen used Vardo as a base for Arctic exploration.

varix *(VAR-iks)* From the Latin meaning "enlarged vein," varix is the word physicians use to designate a severely and chronically swollen blood or lymph vessel. Varices (plural) chiefly refer to dilated veins called varicose veins, most often occurring in the lower part of the legs or the thighs. The condition results from weakness of the vein's valves.

Varna *(VAHR-nah)* Known by the name Stalin from 1949 to 1956, Varna is a major seaport in northeastern Bulgaria, on the Black (q.v.) Sea. It is a popular summer resort and has shipyards and the country's largest cotton-textile industry. Ruled for centuries by the Turks, Varna was ceded to Bulgaria in 1878. It was the chief naval base of the British and French in the Crimean War.

Varro *(VARE-owe)* Marcus Terentius Varro (116–27 B.C.), Roman scholar, prolific writer, and reputedly the most learned of the Romans. Julius Caesar made him superintendent of a proposed public library.

Knowledgeable in all fields of learning of his time, Varro wrote more than 600 books; only one—a work on farming—survives intact. Still extant are portions of another, on the Latin language.

Marcus Terentius Varro.

Varus *(VARE-us)* Publius Quintillius Varus, Roman general, and governor of Germany from A.D. 7 to 9. In a battle east of the Rhine against the troops of Arminius (or Hermann), the German leader, Varus's entire force was destroyed. Disgraced, he committed suicide. Legend has it that these events caused the Roman emperor, Augustus, to wake from sleep crying, "Varus, Varus, give me back my legions!"

varve *(vahrv)* From the Swedish word for "layer," this is geological terminology for a pair of bands of sediment deposited each year in still water, such as glacial lakes. Varves are useful for interpreting the length of time involved in forming sedimentary rock.

Vasa *(VAH-zah)* Royal dynasty of Sweden (1523–1654) and Poland (1587–1668), founded by Gustavus I. His grandson, Sigismund III, became king of Poland and later king of Sweden as well. When a religious split developed—Catholicism in Poland and Protestantism in Sweden—the house divided, and the two fought incessantly.

Vatel *(vah-TELL)* François Vatel, seventeenth-century major-domo or steward of the Prince de Condé. A possibly apocryphal story, but one current at the time, tells of Vatel's demise by his own hand because of complications involved in a series of banquets given by the prince for King Louis XIV. When Vatel mistakenly believed that a small shipment of fish had to suffice, he threw himself on his sword. The rest of the fish arrived later.

Vaud *(voe)* A French-speaking canton of western Switzerland, on Lake Geneva. Its towns produce wine, watches, tobacco products, and cereals, and many popular resorts dot the area. Vaud's capital is Lausanne, a trade and commercial center, the site of the University of Lausanne, and the eighteenth-century home of Rousseau and Voltaire.

A medieval castle surrounded by a vineyard in the Swiss canton of Vaud.

Vazov *(VAH-zawf)* Ivan Vazov (1850–1921), celebrated man of letters, and apparently the first of his kind in Bulgaria. His poems, novels, and plays deal with the trials of his people under Turkish domination, a subject that several times forced him into exile. Vazof is best known for his novel *Under the Yoke* (1893) and the play *Vagabonds* (1894).

Ivan Vazov.

Veck *(vek)* Toby "Trotty" Veck, a character in Dickens's Christmas story *The Chimes* (1844). After eating a New Year's Eve dinner of tripe (q.v.), Trotty, a London ticket-porter and messenger, has a nightmare, in which goblins emanate from Christmas bells, symbolizing his dreams and fears.

Veda *(VEY-dah)* From the Sanskrit meaning "knowledge," the most ancient Hindu religious writings. The four books—the *Rig-Veda, Yajur-Veda, Sama-Veda,* and *Atharva-Veda*—contain collections of hymns, prayers, chants, and spells which accompanied the fire sacrifices and offerings made to the Vedic gods of earth, air, and sky in the period ending about the sixth century B.C. Many of the Vedic teachings are recognized as basic to Hinduism.

Vega *(VEY-gah)* Name of several luminaries, including: Garcilaso de la Vega (1539–1616), Peruvian historian called El Inca, who wrote of the conquest of Peru and of Incan history; and Lope de Vega Carpio (1562–1635), dramatist and founder of the Spanish national drama. **Vega** is also a first-magnitude star, brightest of the constellation Lyra, or the Lyre.

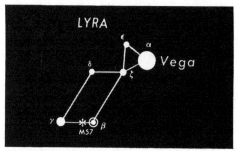

Vega's constellation Lyra has been depicted as both a bird and a tortoise.

Veii *(VEE-yie)* Ancient city of Etruria, now called Veio, just northwest of Rome. Veii was a principal center of art, especially statuary, of the Etruscan civilization. A member of the Etruscan League, which was frequently at war with Rome, it was the first Etruscan city to fall to the Romans, c. 396 B.C., after 10 years of fighting.

Velay *(vuh-LAY)* Region of France's heartland in the mountains of the Massif Central in northeastern France. Velay's major city, and its ancient capital, is Le Puy, capital of the department of Haut-Loire, and a must for tourists interested in buying fine lace. Velay was ruled variously throughout its early centuries by the suzerains of Toulouse and the English rulers of Aquitaine. It was acquired by Louis VIII of France in the twelfth century.

velum *(VEE-lum)* From the Latin meaning "curtain" or "veil," vela are membranous, veillike parts or coverings, such as the soft palate in the back portion of the mouth. This structure is composed of muscular tissue that forms a partition between the mouth and throat.

Verde *(VEHR-dee)* From the Spanish and Portuguese for "green," Verde is a 190-mile-long river in Arizona, punctuated with dams and Indian ruins in its valley. Cape **Verde** (pronounced *verd*), the westernmost extremity of Africa and site of Dakar (q.v.), French West Africa. The Cape Verde Islands of Portugal are located 350 miles to the west.

Horseshoe Dam on the Verde River in Arizona.

Verdi *(VAIR-dee)* Giuseppe Verdi (1813–1901), Italian operatic composer. An innkeeper's son, he wanted to become a professional organist. Instead, he began writing operas at age 28. He penned his last work, *Falstaff,* when he was 80. In between, he created some of the best-loved operas of all time, including *Aïda, Rigoletto, Otello,* and *La Traviata.* He was offered two political positions, which he graciously declined.

Giuseppe Verdi.

Verne *(vern)* The French novelist Jules Verne (1828–1905), considered the father of modern science fiction. Originally a lawyer, he used an interest in science and a fertile imagination to predict many scientific advances of the twentieth century. Included in his more than 50 works are *A Journey to the Center of the Earth* (1864) and *Twenty Thousand Leagues Under the Sea* (1870). Captain Nemo, of the submarine *Nautilus* in the latter is a frequent crossword entry.

Jules Verne.

verso *(VER-soe)* In bookbinding, any left-hand page, and therefore the back of a page, as opposed to the front, or recto. The verso is usually an even-numbered page, as in this book. In numismatics, the **verso** side of a coin is the reverse side, usually the one designated tails.

vert *(vert)* From the Latin *viridis,* for "green," by way of French, this is British forestry legalese for the growth that serves as cover for deer, or for the right to cut down trees. **Vert** is also the heraldic term for green, which is indicated in black-and-white printing by diagonal lines from dexter (right) to sinister (left).

verve *(verv)* One of those etymologically obscure words whose current meaning bears little resemblance to the term from which it is derived, in this case the Latin *verbum,* meaning "word." Verve, on the other hand, is vigor or energy, especially in style or thinking. Actors usually recite their lines with verve.

Verve à la diva Geraldine Farrar.

Vesta *(VEST-ah)* In Roman mythology, goddess of the hearth and home, known in Greece as Hestia. Because her favor meant domestic tranquillity, her worship was a household custom. In the sacred buildings dedicated to her at Rome, Vesta's priestesses, the Vestal Virgins, tended a communal fire which was never extinguished. If any Vestal Virgin broke the vow of chastity, taken for 30 years, she was entombed alive.

The goddess Vesta.

vetch *(vetch)* A weak-stemmed, widely distributed plant of the pulse family, used as animal fodder and as a cover crop because of its ability to restore the nitrogen content of soil. The many species include Russian, Siberian, and winter vetch. In Europe, a widely cultivated vetch is the broad bean, or fava (q.v.), the only edible bean native to the Old World. The bitter vetch plant is the ers, a frequent crossword repeater.

veto *(VEE-toe)* Latin for "I forbid," this is any order of prohibition by an authority. Thus, the President of the United States can veto a law passed by Congress, which in turn can override his veto by a prescribed preponderance of its membership. Failure to sign a law before Congress adjourns is known as a pocket veto.

vial *(VIE-ahl)* From the Greek *phiale,* meaning "shallow cup," this is a small glass

container used to store or transport liquid medicines or other fluids; it is often clued as "lab receptacle." In the palaces of medieval Europe, vials were widely used for carrying around the poisons with which to dispatch one's enemies.

HIGHLY IMPOSSIBLE TREES

aali	*bobo*	*ombu*
abele	*cacao*	*osier*
Abies	*cade*	*papaw*
Acer	*Ceiba*	*pili*
Aegle	*cycad*	*Pyrus*
arar	*deodar*	*quira*
areca	*guava*	*roble*
asak	*henna*	*rowan*
atap	*huon*	*sorb*
bago	*ilex*	*teil*
bahan	*loa*	*toddy*
balao	*lotus*	*upas*
bija	*Maba*	*wahoo*
bixa	*Malus*	*Zamia*

vicar *(VIK-er)* From the same Latin root that gives us vicarious, vicar is a substitute—for example, a religious deputy, such as a church minister who is not the titular head of the parish, but reports to another (such as a bishop) who *is* in charge. The Pope is called the Vicar of Christ.

Vichy *(VEE-shee)* Famed spa in the Allier department, central France, noted for its hot mineral springs and bottled water. Vichy has also lent its name to the cold potato soup vichysoisse (actually devised by French chef Louis Diat while in the U.S.), and was capital of unoccupied France from 1940 to 1944. The Vichy government, headed by Marshal Henri Pétain, was never recognized by the Allies, who cited the record of Nazi collaboration by such officials as Laval and Darlan.

Vidar *(VID-ahr)* Son of Odin (q.v.) and Freya (q.v.), and the god of science and wisdom, whose gaze penetrated so deeply that he could read minds. At Ragnarok, doomsday of the world in Norse mythology, Vidar killed the giant wolf-demon Fenris, who had swallowed up his father. He and his brother were assigned the job of rebuilding the universe.

Vidin *(VEE-din)* An ancient Roman fortress city originally called Bononia, Vidin is a Danube River port in northwestern Bulgaria. It is known for metal goods, ceramics, and medieval ruins. Reflecting the varied composition of its populace through the years, the city is dotted with old synagogues, churches, and mosques.

Vigo *(VEE-goe)* Busy seaport and naval base on Vigo Bay in Galicia, northwestern Spain, a center of tuna and sardine fishing, shipyards, and canneries. Pronounced *vee-GOE*, it's the surname of Francis **Vigo** (1747–1836), Italian-born American frontiersman, fur trader, and patriot. Vigo furnished money and supplies to General George Rogers Clark, who recaptured Vincennes in 1783.

A quayside scene in the Spanish seaport of Vigo.

Vili *(VILL-ee)* Brother of Odin (q.v.) and Ve in Scandinavian mythology. All three took part in the Creation by slaying the giant Ymir (q.v.), fashioning the world from his body, and making man and woman from trees. Vili gave mankind motion and reason, Ve contributed speech and sensation, and Odin provided life and soul.

Vilna *(VILL-nah)* Name of the formerly Polish city now called Vilnius, and the capital of the Lithuanian Soviet Socialist Republic. An important industrial and commercial city, Vilna is the site of one of Europe's oldest universities. During the German occupation of World War II, the city suffered considerable damage, and its sizable Jewish population, largely responsible for making Vilna an Eastern European center of culture and education, was wiped out.

Vimy *(VEE-mee)* Town in the department of Pas-de-Calais, on the Strait of Dover, in northern France. During World War I, a battle took place at nearby Vimy Ridge, a German stronghold, which was captured by British and Canadian troops.

vina *(VEE-nah)* From the Sanskrit and Hindi, this is a stringed Indian musical instrument of the zither family, with a long, fretted fingerboard, usually made of bamboo, and gourds at both ends for resonance. As the capitalized and accented **Viña** *(VEE-nyah)*, it's a popular name for the elegant Chilean seaside resort Viña del Mar.

viol *(VIE-ohl)* Stringed, bowed musical instrument, popular from the fifteenth to the seventeenth century, the viol usually

has six strings, a fretted board, and a flat back. Types of viols include the viola da bracchio, or arm viol, a forerunner of the violin, and the viola da gamba, or knee viol. The double-bass viol is a standard instrument in today's orchestras.

Two views of a bass viol made in 1701.

viola *(vee-OH-lah)* Member of the violin family, but larger than a violin and tuned lower; also, a relative of the violet and the pansy (q.v.), bearing white, yellow, or purple flowers. As a proper noun, **Viola** is the Shakespearean heroine who disguises herself as a boy while searching for her twin brother, Sebastian, in *Twelfth Night*.

viper *(VIE-per)* Any venomous fanged snake of the Viperidae, or viper family. The true vipers slither through Europe, Asia, and Africa, and include the puff adder, the asp (q.v.), and the common European viper. Rattlesnakes, water moccasins, and copperheads belong to the Crotalidae family. On the sides of their heads are heatsensory pits which alert them to approaching prey; they are sometimes called pit vipers for this reason. By extension, a viper is a malicious or spiteful person.

vireo *(VIH-ree-oe)* Any of 45 known species of the New World family Vireonidae, vireos are small migratory and insectivorous tropical American and North American songbirds, with greenish plumage and, occasionally, rings around their eyes. They are especially notorious for their noisy and raucous calls. American species include the self-descriptive blue-headed, yellow-throated, and white-eyed vireos.

Virgo *(VIR-goe)* From the Latin meaning "virgin," a constellation consisting of 39 stars, the brightest of which is the bluish-white Spica. Virgo supposedly resembles a woman bearing grain, and represents the harvest in mythology. Astrologically, **Virgo** is the sixth sign of the zodiac, spanning the period from August 22 to September 23.

virtu or **vertu** *(ver-TOO)* From the Latin meaning "strength," via the Italian for "excellence," this is a love of objets d'art, particularly antiques and curios. The word often refers to the objects themselves.

virus *(VIE-rus)* Any of many organisms causing infections in plants, animals (including man), and bacteria. Viruses grow and multiply in living cells, making use of the host's energy and functions in order to reproduce. These organisms, composed mostly of nucleic acid, can be seen only with an electron microscope. Among diseases caused by viruses in man are smallpox, measles, yellow fever, and influenza. By extension, virus can also mean the venom of a snake, or any evil or harmful influence.

visa *(VEE-zah)* Feminine form of the Latin *visus*, the past participle of *videre*, meaning "to see." This is a certification, usually in the form of a very official-looking seal, that one's passport has been seen by authorities of a country and permission to enter has been granted. Traditionally, visas are stamped with much panache.

Visby *(VEEZ-buh)* or **Wisby** *(WIZ-bee)* Swedish seaport on Gotland Island in the Baltic Sea, capital of Gotland County. Now a resort area, where cement and sugar are coincidentally produced, Visby first achieved importance as an ancient industrial and trade center. As an independent republic, it became a member of the Hanseatic League in the eleventh century.

The 13th century city wall of Visby is one of the best preserved in Europe.

Vishnu *(VISH-noo)* In the Hindu pantheon, second member of the Trimurti, or sacred trinity of Brahma, Vishnu, and Siva (q.v.). Referred to as The Preserver, Vishnu is believed to have enjoyed nine avatars (q.v.), or incarnations, in which he took mortal form. In the tenth, he is supposed to return astride a white horse, carrying a fiery sword to punish the wicked. Among the prior incarnations of Vishnu are Buddha, Juggernaut, and Krishna.

vitta *(VIT-ah)* From the Latin for "fillet" or "headband," in ancient Rome this was a ribbonlike article worn about the forehead in much the same way, and for perhaps the same reason, as a tennis sweatband; it was sometimes a garland. In botany, the word refers to an oil duct in certain plants, or any streak of color.

Vitu *(VEE-too)* Group of small volcanic islands in the Bismarck Archipelago north of New Britain, and part of Papua (q.v.) New Guinea. The largest islands are Garove and Unea. Formerly called the French Islands, they comprise the main copra (q.v.) region of Papua New Guinea.

Vitus *(VIE-tus)* Patron saint of actors and dancers. In sixteenth-century Germany, people danced before St. Vitus's statue on his feast day, June 15, to ensure good health for a year. This maniacal dancing resembled the twitching of chorea, a disorder subsequently called St. Vitus's dance, in the belief that he could cure it. **Vitus** is also the first name of the explorer Vitus Bering, for whom the Bering Strait, Island, and Sea are named.

vixen *(VIK-sen)* From Old English by way of Middle English, this term originally designated a female fox, and still does, especially in hunt country. Supposed character traits of the female fox gave rise to vixen as a synonym for any ill-tempered, shrewish woman.

A gray fox on the alert.

vodka *(VOHD-kuh)* Diminutive form of the Russian *voda*, meaning "water," so named because of its clarity. This alcoholic beverage—distilled from such humble sources as wheat and potatoes—is widely consumed in Bloody Marys (with tomato juice), and Screwdrivers (with orange juice), and in place of gin in martinis. It is a barside folk-belief that vodka leaves no telltale odor on the breath. Traditionally a favorite in Russia, vodka has also become the most popular liquor in America.

vole *(vole)* A stocky, short-tailed rodent related to muskrats and lemmings. Like

In the U.S., voles are known as field mice.

lemmings, voles—including the North American meadow mouse and field mouse—undergo sudden population explosions, during which periods they can inflict substantial damage on vegetation. In certain card games, a **vole** is a grand slam, with all tricks taken. **Volé** *(voe-LAY)*, said of a step in ballet, indicates that it has been executed with the greatest possible elevation.

Volga *(VOHL-gah)* Longest river in Europe and the major waterway of the U.S.S.R., this 2,300-mile-long stream rises in the Valday Hills and flows east and south to the Caspian Sea. The Volga is almost entirely navigable. It is linked by waterways and canals with the Baltic, Azov (q.v.), and Black (q.v.) seas, and is plied by boatmen with deep voices.

volt *(volt)* A unit of measurement in electricity. One volt equals the force that drives a 1-ampere current along a conductor having a 1-ohm (q.v.) resistance. A **volt** is also a turn around a central point by a horse moving sideways; or, in fencing, a leaping movement to keep an opponent from hitting his mark.

Volta *(VOHL-tah)* The 290-mile-long river formed by the meeting of the 850-mile-long Black Volta and the 450-mile long White Volta in central Ghana, West Africa. Akosombo Dam on the Volta impounds Lake Volta (280 miles long), the world's largest artificial lake. **Volta** is also Count Alessandro Volta (1745–1827), Italian physicist and pioneer in electricity, who invented the voltaic cell and Volta's pile, and whose name was immortalized as an electrical unit, the volt (q.v.).

Vor *(vawr)* In Scandinavian mythology, the Norse goddess who presided over betrothals and marriage. Vor took her responsibilities seriously, and wreaked severe retribution, stoked by vindictiveness, upon those who deviated from their commitments and vows.

Vouet *(voo-WAY)* Simon Vouet (1590–1649), French artist and court painter to Louis XIII. Vouet experimented with illusionism, introduced the Italian baroque style into France, and laid the groundwork for the seventeenth-century French school of art whose adherents included Pierre Mignard and Charles le Brun. Aficionados can see examples of Vouet's work in the Louvre.

Vries *(vreez)* Either David Pietersen de Vries (born c. 1593), Dutch merchant skipper who founded settlements on Delaware Bay (1631) and Staten Island (1639) which were later destroyed by the Indians; or Hugo de Vries (1848–1935), Dutch botanist who studied evolution and developed the theory of mutation as the means by which new species evolve; or Adriaen de Vries (c. 1560–1626), Dutch sculptor whose work is in the Louvre; or, perhaps most familiar, contemporary American novelist Peter de Vries (1910–   ).

David P. de Vries.

vug, vugg, or **vugh** *(vuhg)* From *fovea* (q.v.), the Latin for "a minute pit," via the Cornish *vooga*, meaning "cave" or "underground chamber," this is a mining term that refers to any small, often crystalline, unfilled cavity or hollow in a rock, such as a geode or lode (both q.v.).

Vye *(vie)* Eustacia Vye, the independent-minded heroine of Thomas Hardy's *The Return of the Native* (1878). She marries Clem Yeobright, a schoolmaster, but, bored with country life, takes up with another man. When her lover deserts her, Eustacia, now separated from her broken husband, drowns herself. Throughout the book, Hardy's use of atmosphere dramatically highlights the turmoil of her moral dilemmas.

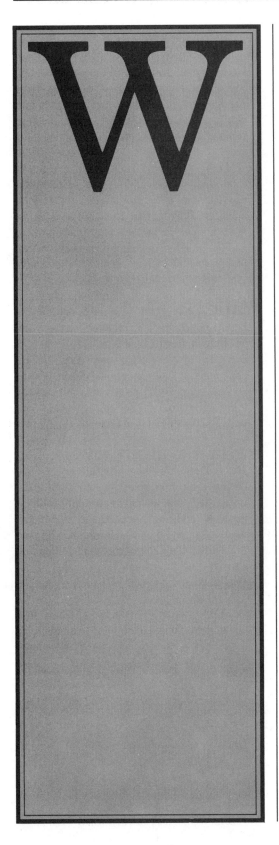

Waag See *Vah*.

Waal *(vahl)* A major distributary of the Rhine, branching off from the main river near the West Germany–Netherlands border, then flowing 52 miles west through the Dutch town of Nijmegen, just across the border. The Waal joins the Maas (or Meuse, as it is known in France) near Gorinchen, where the two streams become the upper Merwede.

Waals *(vahls)* Johannes Diderik van der Waals (1837–1923), Dutch physicist who shed light on the properties of gases. Van der Waals developed an equation bearing his name and containing factors that recognize the weak forces of attraction between molecules. In 1910, he received the Nobel Prize in physics.

Wace *(wase)* Norman French poet (c. 1100–1174), sometimes erroneously called Robert Wace. He is best known for two verse stories in Norman French: the *Roman de Brut,* which played a role in the development of the Arthurian legend; and the *Roman de Rou,* with its vivid account of the Battle of Hastings.

Waco *(WAKE-oh)* City on the Brazos River in east-central Texas. The town got its name from the Hueco Indians, who once called the area home. Among Waco's tourist attractions are a suspension bridge constructed in 1870, a rebuilt Texas Rangers fort dating from 1837, Baylor University, and the annual Wild West rodeo.

The Brazos Queen, a replica of a 19th-century sternwheeler, cruises through Waco, Texas.

Wadai *(wah-DIE)* A former sultanate just east of Lake Chad, in Chad (q.v.). Wadai dates from the sixteenth century. Since then, it has come under the loose control of Darfur, a former Sudanese sultanate; the Muslim brotherhood known as the Sanusi; and, at the start of the twentieth century, the French.

wadi *(WAH-dee)* Transliteration of the Arabic word meaning "channel of a river." Wadi designates the head of a river with seasonal flow, a ravine through which water flows intermittently, or an oasis (q.v.). **Wadi** is also used as a place-name, most notably in Wadi Halfa, Kitchener's headquarters during a 13-year campaign to recapture the Sudan.

Wafd *(wahft)* An Egyptian political party whose name derives from the Arabic word for "delegation." Formed in 1919 to promote independence from Great Britain, the Wafd also urged extensive social reforms. The party repeatedly won seats in parliament and even controlled the government, but charges of corruption and the British support it received during World War II gave King Farouk a pretext to disband it during a series of riots in Cairo.

wahoo *(wah-HOO)* Any one of several trees. From the Dakota Indian word *wahu,* meaning "arrowwood," a large shrub or small tree also known as burning bush; and a related member of the *Euonymus* genus that is also called strawberry tree. Wahoo also designates two American elms, plus the cascara buckthorn which yields a legendary laxative, whence may come **wahoo**'s ultimate form—a cry used to express exuberance.

waif *(wafe)* From the Old Norse *veif,* meaning "something flapping loosely," waif originally described something found by happenstance and belonging to nobody. It has become specific and now refers to a homeless child; a stray animal; and a flag marking the position of a harpooned whale.

wale *(wale)* From the Middle English *wale* (weal), Anglo-Saxon *walu* (ridge), and Gothic *walus* (rod or staff), a welt raised on the skin by a blow from a rod or whip. Other meanings include: a rib or ridge woven into cloth such as corduroy; or, in shipbuilding, reinforcing planks fastened to the hull.

Waley *(WAY-lee)* Adopted name of Arthur Waley (1889–1966), English academician and one of the world's leading Oriental scholars. Born Arthur David Schloss, he is best known for excellent translations of Chinese and Japanese poetry and of the Noh (q.v.) plays of Japan. Despite his specialty, Waley never traveled to the Orient.

Walid *(wah-LEED)* Either of two caliphs belonging to a dynasty which ruled the Muslim Empire from A.D. 661 to 750. Walid I (c. 675–715) enjoyed a glorious reign, making conquests in Asia, India, and Spain, where he built schools, hospitals, and mosques. A less illustrious descendant, Walid II, reigned from 743 to 744.

walla or **wallah** *(WAH-lah)* In India, someone associated with a specific job or a person who holds an important position, such as a "government walla." Squared and upper-cased, it yields the name of a city in southeastern Washington State near the Oregon border, set on the site of the fur-trading post called Fort **Walla Walla**.

Walpi *(WAHL-pee)* Pueblo situated on a mesa near Flagstaff in northeastern Ar-

Walpi has changed little since its founding centuries ago.

izona, in an area inhabited by Hopi-speaking Pueblo Indians. Many of them earn their living by carrying on activities that attract hordes of tourists to the pueblo. In even-numbered years, they hold the antelope ceremony; in August of odd years, the Hopi (q.v.) snake dance.

Wamba *(WAHM-bah)* A character in Sir Walter Scott's romantic novel *Ivanhoe.* Wamba is a serf who ministers to the hero's father, Cedric the Saxon, whom he entertains in the capacity of zany and jester. A brave fellow nonetheless, Wamba risks his life to save his master. In the book, he is known affectionately as "son of Witless."

Warri *(WAR-ee)* Busy Nigerian city and transshipment point on the Warri River, where rubber, cacao, nuts, and hides are transferred from Niger River boats onto oceangoing steamers. Founded in the fifteenth century, Warri grew rich trading in palm oil, before coming under British protection in 1884.

Warta *(VAHR-tah)* River of Poland, about 475 miles long. Rising in the Kraków region, the Warta courses through Czestochowa and Poznan (see Posen) before joining the Oder near Kostrzyn. It is navigable for about half its length. A section of the Warta, which once flowed through Germany, became Polish after World War II.

Washo *(WASH-oe)* American Indian tribe originally living in the Lake Tahoe and Washo Lake region of western Nevada and eastern California. Before white settlers arrived, the Washo were repeatedly attacked and finally beaten by their traditional enemies, the Paiute. The Washo now live on reservations and number fewer than 1,000 souls.

Washo basketmaker.

watt *(waht)* Unit of electric power equal to one joule (q.v.) per second, one ampere of current under one volt (q.v.) of pressure, or $1/746$ of one horsepower. It was named after James Watt (1736–1819), Scottish inventor who developed early steam and rotary engines. He also coined the term horsepower. Watt is frequently clued as "word on a bulb."

Waugh *(wau)* Family name of two English writers: Evelyn Waugh (1903–1966), satirist and author of such popular works as *The Loved One* and *Brideshead Revisited,* the latter made into a successful television series; and his brother, Alec Waugh (1898–1981), author of novels and travel books such as *Island in the Sun* and *The Loom of Youth.*

Alec Waugh.

weal *(weel)* From the Old English word *wela,* meaning "wealth" or "well-being," this is a term for a state of economic soundness and contentment in society. Used rarely today, references to the common weal as a synonym for general welfare continue to pop up in the speeches of politicians. It is also a synonym for wale (q.v.).

weber *(VAY-ber)* A unit used to measure magnetism. As a proper noun, it's the

The comedy team of Weber (right) and Fields.

surname of Wilhelm Eduard **Weber** (1804–1891), German physicist for whom the weber was named; and Carl Maria von Weber (1786–1826), famed German composer and father of German romantic opera, known for *Der Freischutz* and *Oberon*. Pronounced WEB-*ur*, it identifies the American painter Max Weber (1881–1961); and Joe Weber (1867–1942), half of the American vaudeville team of Weber and Fields. The **Weber** is also a river in Utah.

Weems *(weems)*

Mason Locke Weems (1759–1825), American clergyman and author known as Parson Weems. Salesman for

a publisher for 30 years, Weems is responsible for the famous George Washington cherry tree story, which he invented to hype sales for his book about the father of our country.

Mason Locke Weems.

weft *(weft)*

From the Old English word *wefan*, meaning "to weave," this term designates the threads wound on the bobbin of the shuttle in a loom. In weaving, the shuttle passes back and forth between the warp threads, interlacing them with the weft, also known as the woof or the filling threads.

Wegg *(weg)*

One-legged rascal, fruit-stand entrepreneur, and inept blackmailer in Dickens's *Our Mutual Friend*. Hired to read *The Decline and Fall of the Roman Empire* to the ignorant Boffin, Silas Wegg finds sections of the text beyond his reading ability and freely substitutes familiar words without his benefactor being the wiser.

Weill *(vile)*

Kurt Weill (1900–1950), German composer who settled in America in 1935 and proceeded to write such musical comedies as *Knickerbocker Holiday* and *Lady in the Dark*. He wrote *The Threepenny Opera* with Bertolt Brecht, which has become a musical classic. From these have come a spate of popular numbers, including "September Song," "Speak Low," and "Ballad of Mack the Knife."

Kurt Weill.

weir *(weer)*

From the Anglo-Saxon *werian*, meaning "to defend" or "to hinder," this is a kind of low dam built to divert running water for use as a power source, or in order to measure its rate of flow. Also, a kind of picket fence placed in a stream to catch fish.

weka *(WAKE-ah)*

Maori word designating any of several flightless birds native to New Zealand. Related to the rails and also known as Maori hens, they display short wings, belligerent dispositions, and a tendency to steal from fellow avifauna. The name weka comes from the sound of the bird's cry.

Wels *(vels)*

City on the Traun River in western Austria. This industrial center, whose products include machinery, textiles, and paper, traces to the Roman era. It subsequently became a redoubt against marauding Avars and Magyars. The city's most popular tourist attraction is the castle where Emperor Maximilian I died in 1519.

Welty *(WELL-tee)*

Eudora Welty (1909–), the American author who has won worldwide acclaim for her stories of rural Mississippi and her odd, but delightful characters. Her novelette *The Robber Bridegroom* (1942) was made into a Broadway musical; *The Ponder Heart* (1954) was dramatized; and in 1972 she won the Pulitzer Prize for *The Optimist's Daughter*.

wen *(wen)*

Either an ancient rune having the sound of *w* and replaced in the English alphabet by that letter in the thirteenth century; or a benign, painless cyst on the skin formed by obstruction of a sebaceous gland duct.

Wend *(wend)* Any member of a Slavic ethnic group, also known as Sorbs (q.v.), living in eastern Germany and speaking Lusatian. Germanic conquest of the region was completed in the eighth century by Charlemagne, but crusades led by Henry the Lion of Saxony and Albert the Bear of Brandenburg took place against the pagan Wends in the twelfth century. The area has been German and Christian ever since.

Wesel *(VAY-zuhl)* City on the Rhine River near the mouth of the Lippe, in the Ruhr district of West Germany. This industrial center, known for precision instruments and processed food, was founded in the eighth century, and became a Hanseatic League city in 1407. It was at Wesel that the Allies crossed the Rhine in 1945, almost totally destroying the city.

Weser *(VAY-zah)* A West German river formed by the confluence of the Fulda (q.v.) and Werra rivers near Münden. The Weser flows north about 300 miles before emptying into the North Sea near Bremen. It is navigable to Kassel, on the Fulda, and is linked via the Midland canal system to the Ems, Elbe (q.v.), and Rhine (q.v.) rivers.

whelk *(welk)* From the Old English *wioluc,* meaning "turns," whelk designates any of several spiral-shelled marine snails related to the conchs and oyster drills. Many are gathered as food.

whelp *(welp)* From the Anglo-Saxon *hwelp,* this word refers specifically to a puppy or generally to the young of other doglike carnivorous animals. A **whelp** is also any obstreperous young child; a tooth on a sprocket wheel; or, aboard ship, a projection on a capstan drum.

PHYS. ED.

alba	gall	psoas
caul	genu	pubis
cecum	Gula	radix
chyle	hilum	ramus
chyme	ilium	raphe
cilia	incus	rete
cleft	inion	reuin
colon	intima	ruga
costa	iris	scute
coxa	lymph	sebum
crus	maw	serum
derma	nape	shank
digit	nares	sinew
dorsa	node	stoma
duct	ocrea	talus
femur	ovum	tibia
filum	pili	torso
fovea	pinna	ulna
	pons	urea
		uvula
		vagus
		velum

Whig *(wig)*   Former name of two political parties. In England, it was the forerunner of the current Liberal party and the traditional opponent of the Tory (q.v.) party. In America, it designated a supporter of the American Revolution and, later, a party opposing the Democrats. Whig was derived from whiggamore, a pejorative term meaning "cattle driver," used for Scottish Presbyterians in the seventeenth century. That word came from *whiggamaire,* a cry to mobilize horses.

whin *(win)*   A name applied generally to coarse, weedlike grass and specifically to gorse (q.v.), a squat, thorny evergreen shrub known for its ability to thrive in poor soil. Whin is also the name of certain yellow-flowered brooms, especially tyer's broom. In geological circles, **whin** (or whinstone) refers to various hard varieties of basaltic rock, also known as greenstone and trap.

whort *(wert)* or **whortle** *(WERT-uhl)*   In Britain, short for the whortleberry (or hurtleberry), a blueberry native to Europe. It bears pink blossoms and dark, sweet fruit. A dialect name for the fruit is "hurts."

Wien *(veen)*   Vienna, to the Viennese; the fabled Danube city of wine, women, and song. Capital of Austria, it dates from 1365 and has been called home by Beethoven, Mozart, Brahms, and Freud. **Wien** is also the surname of Wilhelm Wien (1864–1928), German physicist and winner of the 1911 Nobel Prize for physics, noted for his work with X-rays.

Wigan *(WIG-an)*   City on the Douglas River in Lancashire, in the metropolitan district surrounding Manchester, England. At one time noted for bell-founding, Wigan is now known primarily for its coal mines and manufacture of machinery and cotton goods—including lower-case **wigan,** a canvaslike material used as interlining, e.g.,for stiffening the lapels of gentlemen's jackets.

Wiggs *(wigs)*   The indomitable widow and heroine of *Mrs. Wiggs of the Cabbage Patch,* a semihumorous novel by Alice Hegan Rice. In addition to raising her children—Australia, Europena, Asia, and Jimmy—Mrs. Wiggs dispenses advice to neighbors in the Kentucky shantytown where they live in the lap of poverty.

Pauline Lord (left) and ZaSu Pitts comfort Virginia Weidler in Mrs. Wiggs of the Cabbage Patch, *1942.*

Wight *(wite)*   Small island off the coast of Hampshire in southern England, called the Isle of Wight. This picturesque resort, whose occupation dates from the Roman conquest in A.D. 43, boasts Queen Victoria's seashore estate and was also called home by poet Alfred, Lord Tennyson. The town of Cowes is a famous yachting center. With a lower-case *w,* **wight** is the archaic term for either a human being or an unearthly creature.

The Isle of Wight has many pleasant villages.

Wiley *(WIE-lee)*   Harvey Wiley (1844–1930), American chemist whose crusade against food adulteration led to enactment in 1906 of the Food and Drug Act, which he subsequently administered. From 1912 until his death, Wiley wrote books on food adulteration and headed a department concerned with food and health for *Good Housekeeping* magazine. Also, Wiley Post (1899–1935), noted aviator killed, together with Will Rogers, in a crash in Alaska.

Harvey Washington Wiley.

Wilts *(wilts)*

County also known as Wiltshire, in south-central England. Its county town (capital) is Salisbury. This predominantly agricultural and dairying region is occupied by chalklands, including Salisbury Plain, site of Stonehenge, the prehistoric structure dating back four millennia to Britain's earliest history. The county is rich in other prehistoric and historical sites. Among distinguished native sons of Wilts are John Gay, John Dryden, and Christopher Wren (q.v.).

Despite much study, the purpose of Stonehenge, Wilts, is still disputed.

winch *(winch)*

From the Anglo-Saxon *wince,* meaning "curved," a mechanical device for lifting or pulling. It consists of a crank that turns a drum, on which can be wound a rope or chain connected to a load.

winze *(winz)*

This is mining argot for a shaft or steep passage that connects any work area in a mine with a lower one. Also, from the Flemish *wensch* (a wish), **winze** in Scotland denotes an ill wish or curse.

Wirtz *(werts)*

William Willard Wirtz (1912–), American academician who served in various U.S. government posts. He was chairman of the National Wage Stabilization Board after World War II, and, as secretary of labor under presidents Kennedy and Johnson, became known for decisive action during a rash of strikes in the 1960s.

witan *(WIT-ahn)*

From the Old English for "wise man," the witan were counselors to Anglo-Saxon kings and members of the witenagemot, the royal advisory council. They included nobles, high-ranking ecclesiastics, and other influential types appointed by the king.

Witla *(WIT-lah)*

The protagonist, Eugene Witla, in Dreiser's *The Genius* (1915). This novel—banned by the courts for such "objectionable" themes as lust for women and power—chronicles the love life of Witla through many a dalliance as he aggressively pursues his career as artist and illustrator.

Witte *(VIT-eh)*

Count Sergei Yulievich Witte (1849–1915), Russian statesman who was variously minister of finance, commerce, industry, and communications. He developed Russian industry, brought in the gold standard, and made Siberia more accessible by rail. Under Tzar Nicholas II, Witte was the first constitutional premier of Russia.

woad *(wode)*

A European herb of the mustard, or Cruciferae, family, whose small leaves yield a blue dye after fermentation and oxidation of their indican content. Woad-growing lined the coffers of the early Germans before the dye was replaced in the

A woad plant.

seventeenth century by the truer-blue vegetable dyes obtained from indigo. The "blue-painted Britons" noted by the ancients got that way by using woad.

Woden See *Odin*.

wold *(wold)* A high, rolling plain, especially in Britain, barren of trees and woods;

or a European flower, dyer's rocket, also known as weld, woald, or would. The plant has wedge-shaped leaves that yield a yellow dye. In Scotland, tartans were colored with such vegetable dyes, fixed with a mordant of urine.

Wolin or Wollin *(VAW-leen)*
Polish island in the Baltic Sea, in Szczecin province, formerly part of Pomerania. Cattle raising and fishing are the main businesses, and there are several resort areas. Variously ruled by Sweden and Prussia, Wolin has belonged to Poland since the 1945 Potsdam Conference.

Wolof *(WOLE-uhf)* A black ethnic group
of West Africa, inhabiting the coastal areas of Senegal and Gambia. Its traditional society was organized on a strict class system. Below the chieftains were, in descending order, the nobles; farmers and merchants; skilled tradesmen; craftsmen; and entertainers, with slaves in their traditional place at the lowest level. The Wolof have been Muslims since the eighteenth century.

Wolpe *(VOHL-peh)* German composer of
operas, cantatas, and chamber music, Stefan Wolpe (1902–1972). His Jewish heritage may have led him to emigrate to Palestine in 1933, but he left that promised land for the United States in 1938. Among Wolpe's works are the opera *Zeus and Elida* and a cantata, *On the Education of Man*.

Woolf *(woolf)* English novelist, essayist, and critic Virginia Woolf (1882–1941),
noted for her innovations in the form of the novel and her use of the stream-of-consciousness technique, most prominent in *The Waves* (1931). A literary coterie that gathered at her home was known as the Bloomsbury group, and included Lytton Strachey, E.M. Forster, and John Maynard Keynes. Her importance on the literary scene is obliquely reflected in the title of Edward Albee's hit play *Who's Afraid of Virginia Woolf* (1962), subsequently made into a movie starring Elizabeth Taylor and Richard Burton.

wort *(wert)* An infusion of malted grain,
used in making beer and ale. Also, from the Old English *wyrt,* meaning "root," a plant, especially an herbaceous one.

Wouk *(woke)* The contemporary American novelist Herman Wouk (1915–),
whose best-sellers include *Marjorie Morningstar, The Caine Mutiny,* and *The Winds of War.*

Wouk's forte is strong plotting and characters every reader seems to know. Wouk cut his writing teeth as a deviser of comedy material for radio comedian Fred Allen.

Herman Wouk.

Wray *(ray)* Surname of such worthies
as John Wray or Ray (1627–1705), English

Distressed Fay Wray and John Cabot in King Kong, *1933.*

naturalist and classifier of the vegetable kingdom in his *Historia plantarum;* Enoch Wray, the revered 100-year-old title character in George Crabbe's poem "The Village Patriarch"; and Fay Wray (1907–), film actress of the 1930s whom King Kong held in the palm of his hand.

Wren *(ren)*

Family name of two Britons: Percival Christopher Wren (1885–1941), French Foreign Legion adventurer and author of *Beau Geste* (q.v.); and Sir Christopher Wren (1632–1723), great architect of St. Paul's Cathedral, where he is buried. As a common noun, **wren** is any of dozens of species of small songbirds of the family Troglodytidae.

writ *(rit)*

Popular as a crossword puzzle entry, this is a legal order that commands or prohibits an action. Best known is the writ of habeas corpus, which functions as a safeguard against illegal imprisonment. Used archaically, **writ** simply meant something written; thus, the Bible is referred to as the Holy Writ.

Wuhan or Wu-han *(woo-HAHN)*

Major transportation, commercial, and educational hub in central China, at the confluence of the Han (q.v.) and Yangtze rivers. This metropolis of several million comprises the former Chinese cities of Han-k'ou (Hankow), Hanyang, and Wu-ch'ang (Wuchang), which were also called the Han Cities. Wuhan is now the capital of Hupei province. Its port serves oceangoing vessels, and it boasts some of China's most important industries as well as two universities.

Wusih or Wu-hsi *(woo-shee)*

Populous Chinese industrial city on the Grand Canal and Lake T'ai, in Kiangsu province. Important products include silk, cars, and tools. Wusih is also noted for the statuettes of dramatic and operatic personages that have been made here for years. Wusih means "without tin," a reference to its exhausted mines.

Wuyck *(VITCH-ik)*

Jacob Wuyck, a Jesuit who in 1599 translated the Bible into Polish—a labor of love known as Wuyck's Bible. Conditions for completing this monumental work were especially favorable under Catholic King Sigismund III and in the afterglow of the Catholic Reformation of Poland by the Jesuits in 1565.

Wyatt *(WIE-at)*

The surname of various British luminaries, including: Sir Francis Wyatt (1588–1644), colonial governor of Virginia; architect James Wyatt (1746–1813), builder and restorer of cathedrals; and Sir Thomas Wyatt (1503–1542), statesman and lyric poet who wrote the first sonnets in English, modeled on those of Petrarch. He served under Henry VIII, and was suspected of being Anne Boleyn's lover before her marriage to Henry. A more modern Wyatt is marshal Wyatt Berry Stapp Earp (1848–1929), famous gunfighter and law officer of the West. His most publicized scuffle took place in Tombstone, Arizona, and no firm decision was ever reached about whether Earp and his cohorts killed some criminals, or were criminals themselves.

Wyss *(vees)*

Johann David Wyss (1743–1818), Swiss author of *Swiss Family Robinson* (1813), the children's adventure story about a man, his wife, and four sons, shipwrecked on a desert island. It was based on the story of Robinson Crusoe. Also, the name of his son, Johann R. Wyss (1781–1830), a professor of philosophy whose claim to fame was composing the Swiss national anthem.

Wythe *(with)*

The Virginia lawyer and judge George Wythe (1726–1806), who served as a delegate to the Continental Congress and signed the Declaration of Independence. An outstanding teacher, Wythe was professor of law at the College of William and Mary, and influenced the likes of Thomas Jefferson and James Monroe.

xebec *(ZEE-bek)*   From the Arabic *shab-bak,* a small, fast, and highly maneuverable sailing vessel with rakish lines and long, overhanging bow and stern. These craft sported both square and triangular lateen fore-and-aft sails, usually rigged on three masts. They were used by the dreaded Barbary pirates who plied the Mediterranean in search of booty until their suppression by international action in the 1830s.

Xenia *(ZEE-nee-yah)*   Farm-country town in southwestern Ohio, also noted for industry—specifically, the manufacture of furniture, plastics, and hemp products. In 1974, a tornado devastated a large part of the town. In botany, **xenia** designates the formation of a hybrid growth as a result of cross-pollination between two different strains of plants.

xenon *(ZEE-nohn)*   Heavy, colorless, odorless, tasteless rare element, discovered in 1898 by William Ramsay and M.W. Travers. It is called an inert gas—along with helium, neon, argon, krypton, and radon—because it reacts chemically only with a great deal of coaxing. Xenon is used for radiation detection and in high-intensity lamps. Its name comes from the Greek for "stranger."

Xingu *(zing-OO)*   Pronounced *sheen-GOO* in Portuguese, this 1,230-mile-long river of central Brazil rises on the plateau in the interior of Mato Grosso state and snakes north through unexplored wilds to the Amazon River. Its countless areas of rapids and waterfalls render most of the Xingú unnavigable.

xylem *(ZIE-lum)*   From the Greek *xylon,* meaning "wood," the inside layers of woody tissue in the stem of a plant. The xylem has three main functions: support of the plant stem; storage of food; and conduction of sap upward, from the roots to the leaves, in contrast to downward conduction by the phloem. What we think of as wood in a plant is xylem.

Yahoo *(YAH-hoo)* Any of a group of fictitious characters (along with Lilliputians, Brobdingnagians, Laputans, and Houhynhnms) encountered by Lemuel Gulliver during his travels, as detailed in the book by Jonathan Swift. The Yahoos were crude boors with unpleasant dispositions and all the vices extant. By extension, the name is now applied to any ill-mannered, altogether offensive person.

Yama *(YUM-uh)* In Hindu mythology, the first human to die, deified into a kind of Hindu Pluto (q.v.). Yama is both fierce and awesome as the judge and punisher of souls. In artistic representations, he is usually green, with inflamed eyes and four arms, sitting astride a buffalo.

A 19th-century rendition of Yama, lord of death and hell, astride a buffalo.

Yapok *(yah-PAHK)* Named after the Opyapok River of French Guiana, this is a small bare-tailed, web-footed water opossum resembling the otter, and ranging from Brazil to Guatemala. Like other marsupials, it carries its young in a pouch. The yapok, however, can close hers while diving in the course of a semiaquatic existence.

yawl *(yawl)* From the Middle Low Dutch word *jolle,* pronounced approximately like yawl, and precursor of the synonymous term jolly boat. A yawl is a small, ship's sailboat with a mainmast, and a short mizzenmast astern of the rudder post. This vessel is similar to a ketch (q.v.) except that the latter has a tall mizzenmast.

yen *(yen)* Basic monetary unit of Japanese currency—one of the strongest in the world today. Abbreviated as ¥ or Y, the yen is equal to 100 sen. Yen is also defined as a strong urge or desire. The two definitions can sometimes be used interchangeably, as in: "I've got a yen for some Japanese food."

Ymir *(EE-mer)* In Norse mythology, the father of a race of giants from whose dead body the world was made by Odin (q.v.) and his brothers, Ve and Vili (q.v.). The blood of Ymir became the sea, his skull the heavens, his flesh the earth, and his bones the mountains.

yoga *(YOE-gah)* From the Sanskrit word meaning "union," this is the general term

An 18th-century miniature of yoga disciples.

for an Indian philosophy of meditation and concentration, usually upon the deity, to achieve communion. Practitioners also follow mystical disciplines involving postures and breathing that enable them to project their minds beyond their bodies, and even become immune to pain.

yo-yo *(YOE-yoe)* Originally a Philippine toy, the yo-yo consists of two connected discs to whose center spindle a string is fastened. Through hand manipulation, yo-yos can be made to fall and rise by the unwinding and rewinding of the string.

Yser *(ee-ZAIR)* A 50-mile-long river flowing through northwestern Belgium and countless crossword puzzles. The rises in northern France, crosses the gian border into Flanders, becomes an extensive canal system, and empt the North Sea near Niewport, after a generally northeasterly course. Heavy and bloody fighting took place near the Yser during World War I.

yuan *(yew-WAHN)* A former mainland Chinese monetary unit abbreviated as $. It was replaced in 1949 by the People's Dollar, or yuan dollar, equal to 100 fen. On Taiwan, the yuan is abbreviated as NT$ and is worth 100 chiao (q.v.).

yucca *(YUK-ah)* From the Spanish, yucca is both the common and botanical name for this treelike plant of the huge lily family. Yuccas grow wild in the American Southwest, Mexico and Central America, and include the many-armed Joshua tree. They sprout stiff, sword-shaped leaves, and tall spires of fragrant white bell-shaped blossoms. The yucca is the state flower of New Mexico. Some yuccas yield useful fibers and a soap substitute. **Yucca** is also a variation of yuca, which is cassava.

A yucca plant in bloom.

Yuga *(YOO-gah)* From the Sanskrit meaning "to age," yuga designates any of four eras in the world's development. According to Hindu teachings, they are the ˙a Yuga, or golden age, 1,728,000 years the Treta Yuga of 1,296,000 years; ˌapara Yuga of 864,000 years; and the nt age, or Kali Yuga, of 432,000

ˌ *(ZAY-mah)* An ancient Numidian f Africa on the northern coast of ˌt-day Tunisia. There may have been han one Zama, but according to histoˌhis was probably the site of a pivotal ˌof the Second Punic War, in which

Hannibal was defeated by Scipio Africanus Major in 202 B.C.

Zamia *(ZAY-mee-ah)* Genus of tropical American trees belonging to the cycads, an order of primitive seed-bearing plants superficially resembling palms. Zamias are recognizable by their thick, woody bases, oblong cones, and crowns of feather-shaped leaves.

zarf *(zarf)* From the Arabic for "sheath," one of those commonplace items with an arcane name. Originally, it was a small, metal cup-stand used in the Near East for holding hot coffee cups. Most people, however, will recognize the zarf as the holder for the glass in which an old-fashioned ice-cream soda was served.

zayin *(ZAH-yin)* The seventh letter of the Hebrew alphabet, used to produce the *z* sound in English. In terms of placement in the alphabet, zayin is more consistent with the Greek *zeta* (sixth letter); the Arabic *ze* (eleventh letter); and the Russian *z* (eighth letter).

zebu *(ZEE-boo)* From the French *zébu*, which imitates the Tibetan word for this bovine domestic animal indigenous to Asia and certain regions of Africa. Known as Brahmans in the United States, they are distinguished from other cattle by their fatty humps, long legs and long horns, and dewlaps. Zebus tolerate heat well and have

often been crossed with ordinary cattle to produce offspring that thrive in hot climates and supply better meat than the zebu affords.

zend *(zend)* From the Persian, in which it is part of *Zend-Avesta*, the title of the Zoroastrian scriptures, zend means "commentary" or "interpretation." Zoroastrianism (named for its great prophet Zoroaster, or Zarathustra) was practiced in Persia from the sixth century B.C. to the seventh century A.D., but its adherents today are few because of the prevalence of Islam.

Zeno *(ZEE-no)* The name in which two Greeks and a Roman rejoiced. The Greeks were: Zeno the philosopher, who lived in the fifth century B.C. and belonged to the Eleatic school along with Parmenides; and Zeno of Citium (c. 336–264 B.C.), another philosopher and founder of the school of Stoicism (see *stoic*). The Roman Zeno was Emperor of the East, a master politician who saved his domain from Ostrogoth raids by convincing Theodoric the Great to attack elsewhere.

Zeus *(zoose)* Most important god of the ancient Greek pantheon, and equated with the Roman deity Jupiter. The son of Cronus and Rhea (q.v.), Zeus revolted against his father (see *Vanir*) and with his brothers divided up the universe: Poseidon took the oceans; Hades, the underworld; Zeus, the earth and sky (his name means sky). Among the children Zeus bore with his wife Hera (q.v.) and others were Apollo, Hermes, and Aphrodite.

Zeus conquering the Titans.

Zola *(zoe-LAH)* Émile Zola (1840–1902), French novelist and journalist known for his use of naturalism in such works as *Nana* (1880) and *Germinal* (1885). He ruffled official feathers with his famous article "J'accuse," addressed to the president of France in defense of Alfred Dreyfus, the Jewish army officer falsely accused of espionage in the notorious Dreyfus Affair. Zola escaped imprisonment for libel by fleeing to England. He died of accidental asphyxiation not long after his return home under an amnesty.

Émile Zola.

zoril *(ZORE-el)* or **zorilla** *(zoh-RIL-ah)* From the Spanish word *zorillo*, the diminutive form of *zorro*, meaning "fox," the zoril is a small carnivore of the weasel family inhabiting rocky terrain throughout Africa. Zorils burrow and hunt small mammals at night. They resemble the related skunk both in appearance and in possessing glands ejecting an obnoxious odor for self-protection. Zorils are sometimes called striped polecats.

Zuni *(ZOO-nyee)* Tribe of pueblo-dwelling North American Indians of western New Mexico. These placid farmers, jewelry makers, ceremonial dancers, and basket weavers lived in the region thought by the Spaniards to include the legendary gold-laden Seven Cities of Cibola. Naturally, the Spanish conquistador Coronado killed many Zuñi in attempts to locate their nonexistent treasure cities. Today, Zuñi inhabit Zuñi Pueblo, which dates from the seventeenth century and lies within the Zuñi Reservation.

Kistoa, a Zuñi trib

PICTURE SOURCES

Photographers and Picture Agencies

Culver Pictures, Inc.: Asch; Barre; Capek; conga; Dali; dhow; Ezra; frat; Friml; kayak; lyre; mulla; pelt; Savoy; Selim; sty; styx; Sufi; syce./Kenn Duncan (Alvin Ailey American Dance Theater): Ailey./Wilton H. Green (*Marcel Marceau Alphabet Book*, © 1970 by Doubleday and Co., Inc. Reproduced by permission of the publisher): mime./Paul Kellogg (Hartford Whalers Hockey Club): Howe (Gordie)./Helen Levitt: Agee./Helen Marcus (G.P. Putnam's Sons): Barth./Suzanne Rafer: hogan./Sovfoto: Baku./Leslie Tseng-Tseng Yu: Hopeh./Alfredo Valente: Kern.

Tourist Agencies and Consulates

Arizona Office of Tourism: crag; Walpi./Australian Information Service: baobab; bilbi; dingo; emu; koala./ Austrian National Tourist Office: Enns; Graz; Ister./Belgium National Tourist Office: Liège; Namur./Brazilian Tourism Authority: Bahia./British Tourist Authority: Avon; Celt; chiel; chine; Dover; Epsom; Eton; firth; Perth; polo; Skye; Soho; Tay; Wight; Wilts./ Colombia Information Service: llano./Czechoslavakia Travel Bureau: Brno./ Egyptian State Tourist Administration: Aswan; Giza; Khufu./Finland National Tourist Office: Hanko./French Embassy: Camus./French Government Tourist Office: Albi; Amiens; Anjou; arena; Arles; Blois; Brest; Côte; Isère; Reims; Rouen; Saône; Vaud./German Information Center: Fulda; Ulm./ Ghana Information Service: Accra./Greek National Tourist Organization: Athos; Crete; Naxos; Paros; Pylos; Simi; Thira; Tinos./Haitian Tourist Office: istle./Hawaii Visitors Bureau: Hilo; Kauai./Hungarian Travel Bureau: Eger./Government of India Tourist Office: Agra; baloo; Delhi; ghat; Jumna; pekoe; Qutb./Consulate General of Israel in New York: Abba; Rabin./Israel Government Tourism Administration: Ab; Elath; Haifa; Jaffa; luff; sabra./ Italian Government Travel Office: Arno; Bari; Capri; Como; doge; Lido; Ostia; Padua; Parma; Pisa; Prato; Riva; Scala; Siena; Tiber; Turin./Consulate General of Japan: Fuji; Ginza; Ikeda; judo; koto; lade; torii./LASCA Airlines: Irazú./Liechtenstein Information Office: Vaduz./Netherlands Consulate General: Gouda; Hague./New Zealand Consulate General: kiwi, Maori./ Norwegian National Tourist Office: fjord; Glama; Rørøs./Romanian National Tourist Office: Iasi./Spanish National Tourist Office: Avila; Cádiz, Ibiza; Jaén; Jerez; Palos; Prado; Ronda; Soria; Vigo./Sri Lanka Tourist Board: Kandy./ Swedish National Tourist Office: holm, Visby./Swiss National Tourist Office: Aar; froth; Jura; Rhine; Rigi; Rütli; Thun./Texas Travel and Information Division: Pecos; Waco./Turkish Tourism and Information Office: Içel; Inönü; Izmir; Kemal; Perga; Sivas./Yugoslav National Tourist Office: Pula; Rab.

Libraries, Museums, and Special Collections

American Museum of Natural History: geode./American Petroleum Institute: duct, dune, rotor./Basketball Hall of Fame: locus./Courtesy of James Camner: Baker; cole; crimp; dale; Deil; diva; Falla; Fauré; genu; Iago; Patti; raff; Ravel; Reger; Suppé; Thais; Tosca; Verdi; verve; Weill./Ching-Sung Yu: canis; Grus; Lupus; Pavo; Vega./F.A.O.: arna; mung./Free Library of Philadelphia: crwth; rebec; shawm; sitar; Strad; tuba; viol./Maps © Hammond Inc., Maplewood, N.J.: Abbai; Adana; Amman; Azov; Black; Chad; Shaba./Cyril M. Harris: ambry; apse; crypt; corbel; font; herse; kiosk; meta; naos; nave; ogee; oriel; quoin./Courtesy, Library of the Jewish Theological Seminary: Jubal; mohel./The Kobal Collection: jabot; tress; tutu./Movie Star News: cog; curch; gaud; geste; Joad; nares; Okie; pouf; Toto./Metropolitan Museum of Art: avatar (John D. Rockefeller III, Gift Fund 1962); bo (John D. Rockefeller III, Gift Fund 1963); Nero (Harris Brisbane Dick Fund, 1966)./Museum of the American Indian, Heye Foundation: Acoma; Caddo; Cree; Erie; Haida; Hupa; mide; Modoc; momo; Nahuath; Osage; pima; Pomo; Ponca; Sarsi; Sauk; Sioux; sumac; totem; umiak; Ute; Washo; Zuñi./Museum of the City of New York, Theater Collection: Riggs./National Baseball Hall of Fame: Banks, Frick./Danny Peary: cleft; croon; crus; derby; Dunne; fray; friz; Garbo; Kato; kepi; kohl; kris; Moira; odium; Omar; vamp; Wray./Picture Collection, New York Public Library: aam; Abie; Aga; Aipi; aloe; Arden; Ariel; assi; Astor; ᴀer; Bean; Beck; Beyle; Binet; Boas; Bragg; Brant; Bruce; Caen; Canby; ᴀe; Chou; Ciano; civet; coulee; Cuzco; dais; Dante; Davy; depot; dickey; Donne; Dore; Doyle; duce; Duse; Ebert; ecu; egret; Eli; Elia; Ellis; Essex; faro; Finn; fop; foy; Gael; gauss; gavotte; genie; Gide; glyph; Gorki; Goya; Greco; Grimm; Guam; Gwyn; haft; Hals; Heine; Hess; st; Inge; ingot; Jonah; Kafka; Kant; Klee; Kurd; lama; limn; Livy; et; manna; Munro; Nast; Noyes; Nym; oasis; Oder; panda; Pratt; Pye; Pym; Pyx; Redi; Redon; Riis; Rilke; Rodin; Roux helm); Roxas; rowan; sable; Sacco; Sadi; Satie; Saxon; Serb; ts; Soddy; Solon; Soulé; Sousa; Speke; Steen; Stoic; Stowe; hor; troll; tzar; Uri; Varro; Vazov; Verne; vole; Vries; Pro Football Hall of Fame: Blanda./United Nations: Amin; bul; Masai; Muni; oxbow; Pará; Quito; Segni; Spaak./

Vilmorin-Andrieux and Cie., 1911, Paris: anil; benne; x; ramie; spud./*Gray's Anatomy*: incus; lymph; raphe. WERE USED BY PERMISSION OF DOVER PUBLICATIONS: er, © 1979: addax; Aix; ameba; arend; auk; beisa; cavy; ab; elver; Fidia; flews; gar; Gila; gnu; Jynx; kudu; llama; moray; Musca; nacre; newt; okapi; opah; oryx; pitta; rhea; viper; whelk; zebu./*The Book of Trades*, by Amman and mbo; croze; felly; forge; hone; lute./*Costumes of the Greeks* Thomas Hope, 1962: Ceres; Clio; Erato; Flora; nymph;

Diana; toga./*Daumier, 120 Great Lithographs*, by Charles F. Ramus, © 1978: churl, scrag./*Decorative Antique Ironwork*, by Henry Rene d'Allemagne, © 1968: etui; faun./*Dictionary of American Portraits*, by Cirker and Cirker, © 1967: ade; Dawes; Debs; Dewey; Dix; Drake; Drew; Cabot; Cooke; eddy; Fargo; Harte; hoar; holt; Howe (Elias, Julia, and Sir William); Ives; Kiska; Lind; Muir; Nevin; Osler; Otis; Peary (Robert and Mrs. Robert); Poe; Pupin; quay; Stagg; Tabor (Baby Doe and Horace); Tesla; Vane; Weems; Wiley./*The Doré Bible Illustrations*, © 1974: bavin; Esau; Gath; Jael; Judas; logia; Magi; Micah; Purim; Sheba; sib./*Early Floral Engravings*, by Emanuel Sweerts, © 1976: agave; aloe; attar; bikh; canna; corm; mecon; nopal; stipe./*Flaxman's Illustrations to Homer*, by Essick and La Belle, © 1977: Argos; Circe; Eris; Gyes; harpy; Irus; Jove; Siren./*Food and Drink*, by Jim Harter, © 1979: cob; creel; crock; cruet; drupe; java; jowl; lager; mete; ort; stum; tun./*Handbook of Early Advertising Art*, by Clarence P. Hornung, © 1956: carny; churn; coupe; digit; ewer; feria; gibus; habit./*Handbook of Plant and Floral Ornament*, by Richard G. Hatton, © 1960: abele; atis; aute; awn; blite; carob; chard; clary; ebon; flax; furze; gorse; heath; Musa; nard; oca; opium; orpine; osier; roble; rue; sedge; sloe; spelt; tansy; thyme; woad; wold; yucca./ *Historic Costume in Pictures*, by Braun and Schneider, © 1975: Amir; aulos; baba; Bibi; caste; emir; eolith; ephod; fichu; Mede; pavis; peer; rajah; ruche; sabot; sari; shako; Tatar./*Montgomery Ward and Company's Catalogue, Spring and Summer 1895*, © 1969: adz, decoy; dice; hame; hasp; hod; Ouija; pedal; pirn; rowel; skep; vial./*North American Mammals*, by James Spero, © 1978: bobac; coon; lobo; lynx; otter; pika; puma; shrew; vixen./*The Nursery "Alice,"* by Lewis Carroll, © 1966: dodo; hookah./*Plant and Floral Woodcuts for Designers and Craftsmen*, by Carolus Clusius, © 1974: Ilex; sedum./ *Symbols, Signs and Signets*, by Ernst Lehner, © 1950: Ashur; Bast; cornu; Dagon; Indra; Luna; lune; Ptah; Shiva; sigil; Thoth; Torah; urea./

Additional Sources

Arizona State University: Tempe./Baccarat, Inc.: carafe./Fiat Motors of North America, Inc.: Fiat./Food and Wines from France: Brie./Ford Motor Company: Edsel./Bob Fosse: Fosse./Holland Cheese Exporters Ass'n.: Edam./*Illustrated London News*: tyke./King Features Syndicate, Inc., reprinted by special permission: Goon; Jeep./Levi Strauss & Co.: Levi./B. Manischewitz Co.: Seder./William Morrow & Co.: Erle./New Line Future Films: cult./Salt River Project, Phoenix, Ariz.: Verde./Sante Fe Railway: dinky; Mogul./Benjamin Spock, M.D.: Spock./Tartan Marine Co.: jib, ketch./Tiffany & Co.: pavé./Herman Wouk: Wouk.

Special thanks to:

S. Alexandride, Museum of the American Indian; Sally Day, British Tourist Authority; Richard Drew, American Petroleum Institute; Mary S. Duffy and Bob Masto, Dover Publications, Inc.; Lila Goldin, F.A.O.; Bob Jackson, Culver Pictures, Inc.; Nadia Kahan, The Jewish Theological Seminary of America; Gloria Meisel, Library, Westchester Community College; Heddy Schulman, Israel Government Tourism Administration; Karen M. Schwartz, The Free Library of Philadelphia; Lynette Shaw, Australian Information Service; Stephen F. Tripp, Arizona Office of Tourism; Chappaqua (N.Y.) Library; The Horticultural Society of New York; Picture Collection, New York Public Library.

BOXES

ASSORTED ADLERS (p. 16): National Library of Medicine, Bethesda, Md.: Alfred./Picture Collection, New York Public Library: Stella./Batten, Barton, Durstine & Osborn, Inc.: Luther./*Dictionary of American Portraits*, by Cirker and Cirker. Felix and Jacob./CROSSWORD CRUISE (p. 30): Austrian National Tourist Office./SETTLING THE SCORE (p. 54): Picture Collection, New York Public Library./BEST OF THE D'ESTES (p. 114): Picture Collection, New York Public Library./"BOZ" AND THE BARD (p. 120): Picture Collection, New York Public Library: Nym./Culver Pictures, Inc.: all other pictures./MEN OF THE CLOTH (p. 128): Picture Collection, New York Public Library./DOWN UNDER (p. 144): Australian Information Service: bilbi, dingo, emu./New Zealand Consulate General: kakapo, kiwi./*Animals*, by Jim Harter: lory./THE EXOTIC EAST (p. 175): Philippine Government Tourist Office./DOWN THE HATCH (p. 183): *Food and Drink*, by Jim Harter./OUR FEATHERED FRIENDS (p. 188): Culver Pictures, Inc.: aerie./*Animals*, by Jim Harter: Aix, arend, auk, crane, eider, heron, jynx, macaw, petrel, quail, raven, rhea, ruff./LAW OF THE LAND (p. 196): *Historic Costume in Pictures*, by Braun and Schneider./WHERE THE DEER AND THE ANTELOPE PLAY (p. 201): *Animals*, by Jim Harter: addax, axis, beisa, gnu, kudu, roe./Culver Pictures, Inc.: oryx./GLAD RAGS (p. 226). Movie Star News./THE JEWISH ZODIAC (p. 236): Barton's Candy Corp./CAFÉ CROSSWORD (p. 244): *Food and Drink*, by Jim Harter./SWEET MUSIC (p. 249): Consulate General of Japan: koto./Free Library of Philadelphia: rebec./Picture Collection, New York Public Library: crwth, viol, viola./CROSSWORD CLINIC (p. 264): Culver Pictures, Inc./THE GRAND TOUR (p. 268): German Information Center./ THE DRAFTING BOARD (p. 281): all Pictures, collection of Cyril M. Harris./TAKE A BOAT, TAKE A TRAIN (p. 289): Museum of the American Indian, Heye Foundation: umiak./Photo courtesy of Sante Fe Railway: dinky./THE UNDESIRABLES (p. 295): *Engravings by Hogarth*, © 1973, Dover Publications, Inc./ NATIVE AMERICANS (p. 313): All photographs, Museum of the American Indian, Heye Foundation./WATER WORLD (p. 342): *Animals*, by Jim Harter: amoeba, carp, chub, cod, dab, fluke, gar, hydra, loach, opah, rudd, whelk./THE APOTHECARY (p. 348): *Early Floral Engravings*, by Emanuel Sweerts: aloe./ *Handbook of Plant and Floral Ornament*, by Richard G. Hatton: clary, fungi, flax, tansy./HIGHLY IMPOSSIBLE TREES (p. 366) *Handbook of Plant and Floral Ornament*, by Richard G. Hatton./PHYS. ED. (p. 375): Picture Collection, New York Public Library./